The cover image, *Excellence*, is the work of Ernie Barnes, an internationally known artist who played professional football with the Denver Broncos and San Diego Chargers from 1960 to 1965. After his appointment as the Official Artist for the 1984 Los Angeles Olympic Games, Mr. Barnes' talent was recognized around the world. His commissions include a painting that hangs permanently in the Carolina Panthers football stadium and a painting to commemorate the 50th Anniversary of the National Basketball Association that is displayed at the Naismith Memorial Basketball Hall of Fame. His images frequently capture people expressing spirit and determination in the face of scarce resources. *Excellence* is one of six paintings in a motivational sports poster series. All six images may be seen at www.erniebarnesart.com. Mr. Barnes' work is represented by The Company of Art, 8613 Sherwood, West Hollywood, CA 90069 (phone 800-858-2941).

Contents

Preface

PURPOSE OF THE TEXT

The eighth edition of *Sports in Society: Issues and Controversies* has a threefold purpose. First, it is designed to show students how sociology can be used to study sports in society. Second, it is written to encourage students to ask questions and think critically about sports as parts of social life. Third, it is organized to facilitate the use of published literature combined with the Internet and the World Wide Web to learn about sports in society.

I organize chapters around curiosity-arousing issues and questions and then discuss them in terms of recent research and theory in the sociology of sport. Although the concepts and source materials are not taken exclusively from sociology, discussions throughout the book are grounded in a sociological approach. Therefore, the emphasis is clearly on sports and sport-related actions as they occur in social and cultural contexts.

FOR WHOM IS IT WRITTEN?

Sports in Society is written for those taking their first look at sports as parts of culture and society. The content of each chapter is presented so it can be understood by beginning college students who have not taken other courses in sociology or sport science. Discussions of issues do not presume in-depth experiences in sports or a detailed knowledge of sport jargon and statistics. My goal is to push students to think more critically about sports and how sports are related to their social lives. I use concepts, theories, and research as tools that enable us to "dig into" sports and see them as more than activities that simply reflect the world in which we live.

Since the book is organized in terms of an issues approach, the content of many chapters is useful for those concerned with sport-related policies and program administration. My emphasis through the book is on making sports more democratic and making sport participation more accessible to all people.

CHANGES IN THE EIGHTH EDITION

This edition updates and adds important material to the previous edition. My goal for this revision is to clarify points and increase the ease of reading. Integrating this edition with the website (www.mhhe.com/coakley8e) enabled me to cut material from the text and transfer it to the website.

All chapters are updated in connection with new research and theoretical developments in the field. There are more than 270 *new* references cited in this edition. Most of them identify materials published since the seventh edition went to press.

A major challenge in doing this revision was determining what references and topics I would not include. The field has expanded to such an extent that this edition of *Sports in Society* is more of an introduction to the field than an overview of it. To view additional materials, readers may want to use the website (www.mhhe.com/coakley8e) to search chapter-by-chapter links on the site.

Revision Themes and New Materials

This edition continues to emphasize socialization themes as well as the increasing organization, commercialization, and globalization of sports. The connection between sports and ideology is also highlighted in this edition.

Chapter 1 provides a new explanation of ideology and how it has been used by sociologists and in the sociology of sport. Chapter 2 contains a new presentation of critical feminist theories—one that corresponds with the presentations of other theories.

The chapter on history (chapter 3) was extensively revised with new sections contrasting differences between contemporary power and performance sports and physical activities and games in different historical time periods. There is new material on "who tells us about the past" and expanded coverage of recent sports history in the United States. A *Social History Time Line, 1920–1990* helps students grasp the tenor of recent social changes in sports.

The chapters on socialization and youth sports (chapters 4 and 5) have many minor revisions and clarifications, and there is a new section on the actions of youth sport parents. Chapter 6, on deviance in sports, contains new information on the use of nutritional supplements. There is also a new section on the World Anti-Doping Agency (WADA), the United States Anti-Doping Agency (USADA), and the pros and cons of drug testing in sports.

The chapter on violence (chapter 7) has new material on violence among youth sport parents, including a discussion of the "hockey dad" killing in Massachusetts. There also is new material on violence and gender ideology and a new section, "Terrorism: Planned Political Violence at Sport Events," in which the sport-event-related implications of 9/11/01 are discussed.

The chapter on gender and gender relations (chapter 8) has an expanded and updated discussion of Title IX. There also are discussions of the all-male membership policy at Augusta National Golf Club, site of The Masters golf tournament; gender equity in alternative sports; and the connection between football and gender equity in college sports.

The chapter on race and ethnicity (chapter 9) contains a clarification of the concept of racial ideology and a discussion of why there are not more black coaches in college and professional football. There is also new material on Asian American athletes.

The chapter on social class and class relations in sports (chapter 10) has a new section on how public money is used to promote private profits, a discussion of class dynamics and health issues, and expanded discussions of opportunities for women and minorities in sports.

The chapter on economics (chapter 11) contains an expanded discussion of corporate influence in sports in the post-Enron era and updated materials on professional wrestling and the dynamics of spectacle in culture. All data on salaries in professional sports have been updated.

In the media chapter (chapter 12), there is new material on the interdependence of sports and the media. There also are new sections on sport video games and the challenges faced by women athletes when they deal with the media.

The chapter on government, globalization, and politics in sports (chapter 13) contains major revisions, including expanded discussions of sport participation and health, Olympism, and global labor issues and the production of sporting goods, as well as a new discussion of the figure skating judging scandal during the 2002 Winter Olympics.

The chapter on education and sports (chapter 14) pulls together new research on college sports and the achievement of educational goals, along with an expanded discussion of African American women in college sports and how Title IX has not benefited them as much as it has white women.

There are new discussions of world religions in the chapter on religions and sports (chapter 15). A new box on Islamic women athletes raises questions about religion, gender, and sports. Finally, in the discussion of the future (chapter 16), there is new material on technology and genetic manipulation for the purpose of performance enhancement in power and performance sports. There also are new comments on how sports may be used to foster social transformations in the world at large.

Suggested Readings and New Website Resources

Each chapter is followed by updated references to relevant and interesting books, as well as websites that are useful sources of information about the topics raised in the chapters.

New Photographs

There are 136 photos in this edition, including 55 new photos. The use of photos, cartoons, figures, and tables has been carefully planned to visually break up the text and make reading more interesting. A new feature of this edition is that all cartoons are referred to in the text. This enhances the reader's ability to identify the particular points illustrated by visual materials and connect them to the issues discussed in the text.

Online Learning Center

The website www.mhhe.com/coakley8e is an important feature associated with the eighth edition of *Sports in Society*. The site contains general information about this edition, along with links to supplemental materials associated with each chapter. Those materials include

- A downloadable PowerPoint® presentation
- Updated URLs for website resources
- Discussion issues and questions
- Group projects
- Materials from past editions that add depth and background to current chapter topics
- Brief editorial comments that call attention to current issues related to sports in society

- True-false self-tests for each chapter
- Learning objective for each chapter
- Supplemental readings and references to news articles
- A message board enabling you to interact with other readers, respond to each other's questions, and provide information about sports as social phenomena in your locales and lives
- A link to PageOut to help you create your own website

ANCILLARIES

Instructor's Manual and Test Bank

An instructor's manual and test bank has been developed to assist those using *Sports in Society* in college courses. It includes the following:

- *Chapter outlines.* These provide a quick, overall view of the topics covered in each chapter. They are useful for organizing lectures, and they can be reproduced and given to students as study guides.
- *Test questions (multiple choice).* These questions have been designed to test students' awareness of the central points made in each chapter. They focus on ideas rather than single, isolated facts. For the instructor with large classes, these questions are useful for chapter quizzes, midterm tests, or final examinations.
- *Discussion/essay questions.* These questions can be used for tests or to generate classroom discussions. They are designed to encourage students to synthesize and apply materials in one or more of the sections in each chapter. None of the questions asks the students simply to list points or give definitions.

Computerized Test Bank

A computerized version of the test bank for the instructor's manual is available for both IBM and

Macintosh to qualified adopters. This software provides a unique combination of user-friendly aids and enables the instructor to select, edit, delete, or add questions and to construct and print tests and answer keys.

Web Resources: McGraw-Hill's Human Performance Website

The human performance website provides a wide variety of information for instructors and students, from text information to the latest technology. It includes professional organization, convention, and career information. Link to the online catalog to find the perfect text or ancillary for your course. Additionally, web links are also provided here for all our course offerings. Visit the website at www.mhhe.com/hhp

Additional features of the website include:

- *This Just In.* This link provides featured articles, related publications, web resources and more.
- *Faculty Support.* This links to PageOut, online supplements, Online Learning Centers, PowerWeb, and much more.
- *Student Success Center.* This helps students locate new study skills, job-hunting tips, and web links to assist in preparing for the job search and career development.
- *Author Arena.* Contact McGraw-Hill authors, visit their websites, and see the featured *Author of the Month* here.

ACKNOWLEDGMENTS

This book has evolved out of ideas coming from many sources. Thanks go to the students in my sociology of sport courses. Every semester they provide constructive critiques of my ideas and open my eyes to new ways of looking at sports as social phenomena. Special thanks go to friends and colleagues who have influenced my thinking, provided valuable source materials, and given me personal support during difficult times. Nancy Coakley, Danielle Hicks, Rebecca Bauder, Bob Hughes, Peter Donnelly, and Bob Pearton deserve special thanks for their help.

My appreciation goes to the publisher's reviewers, whose suggestions were crucial in the planning and writing of this edition. They include the following:

Don Albrecht, Ph.D.
  Texas A & M University
Robert E. Baker, Ed.D.
  Ashland University (Ohio)
Mark Cozin, M.Phil.
  Raritan Valley Community College (New Jersey)
Brian Keller, M.S.
  Nebraska Wesleyan University
Suzanne Laberge, Ph.D.
  University of Montreal (Canada)
James D. LaPoint, Ph.D.
  University of Kansas
Marvin W. Scott, Ed.D.
  University of Maryland
Sandra E. Short, Ph.D.
  University of North Dakota

My thanks also go to Kimberly Gunn, Tini Campbell, Tom Segady, Jackie Beyer, Kristie Ebert, and Mary Bowden for photos, and to Fred Eyers for his cartoons and his willingness to create images with a critical edge.

Jay Coakley
Fort Collins, CO

(Steve Nesius; AP/Wide World Photos)

The Sociology of Sport

What Is It and Why Study It?

SPORT HAS BECOME . . . a major social institution in American society, and indeed, the modern world. Yet our understanding of this major social phenomenon remains limited.

—**Center for Research on Sport in Society, University of Miami (1999)**

 **Online Learning Center Resources**

Visit *Sports in Society*'s Online Learning Center at **www.mhhe.com/coakley8e** for additional information and study material for this chapter, including

- Self-grading quizzes
- Learning objectives
- Related websites
- Additional readings

A complete outline is available online at
www.mhhe.com/coakley8e.

I LOVE WATCHING. I come here every game. If I
had a television I would do nothing but watch
soccer all the time. Now I have lived the worst.
Soccer takes my mind off it.

      —Abdullah Gutak, a former soccer player
        watching a game in partially bombed out Kabul
        Stadium (his wife and son were killed by a
        Soviet bomb and his leg had been amputated
        after he stepped on a land mine)
        (December, 2001)

3

ABOUT THIS BOOK

Most of you reading this book have experienced sports personally, as athletes or spectators or both. You probably are familiar with the physical and emotional experiences of playing sports, and you may have extensive knowledge of the rules and regulations of certain sports. You probably know about the lives, on and off the field, of high-profile athletes in your school, community, or country. Many of you have followed certain sports by watching them in person and on television, reading about them in the print media or on web pages, or even listening to discussions of them on talk radio.

This book is written to take you beyond the scores, statistics, and personalities in sports. The goal is to focus on the "deeper game" associated with sports, the game through which sports become an integral part of the social and cultural worlds in which we live.

Fortunately, we can draw on our personal emotions and experiences as we consider this deeper game. Let's use our experiences with high school sports in North America as an example. When students play varsity basketball in high school, we know that team membership may affect their status in the school and the way teachers and fellow students treat them. We know it may have implications for their prestige in the surrounding community, for their self-images and their self-esteem. We know that it may affect even their future relationships, their opportunities in education and the workforce, and their overall enjoyment of life.

Building on this knowledge enables us to move further into this deeper game associated with sports. For example, we might ask why North Americans place such importance on varsity sports and top athletes. What does that say about our schools, communities, and values? We might study how varsity programs are organized and connected with widespread ideas about masculinity and femininity, achievement and competition, pleasure and pain, winning and fair play, and

other important aspects of our culture. We might ask how varsity sports influence the status structure that exists among students and how student-athletes fit into that structure. We also might ask if the organization of high school sports is influenced by corporate sponsorships and examine student ideas about the corporations whose names and logos are on their uniforms, gym walls, and score boards.

The assumption underlying these questions is that, sports are more than just games, meets, and matches. They are also important parts of our social lives that have meanings and influence that go far beyond scores and performance statistics. Sports have become integral parts of the social and cultural contexts in which we live. They provide the stories and images that many of us use to explain and evaluate these contexts, the events in our lives, and our connections to the world around us.

People who study sports in society are concerned with the deeper meanings and stories associated with sports in particular cultures. They use their research to develop an understanding of (1) the cultures and societies in which sports exist, (2) the social worlds that are created around sports, and (3) the experiences of individuals and groups associated with sports.

Sociology is very helpful when it comes to studying sports as social phenomena. This is because **sociology**[1] is the study of social life, including all forms of social interaction and relationships. The concepts, theories, and research methods that have been developed by sociologists enable us to study and understand sports as they exist in our everyday lives and as they are connected with history and other aspects of culture and society. Sociology helps us examine social life *in context* and to "see" the connections

---

[1]Important concepts used in each chapter are identified in **boldface**. Unless they are accompanied by a footnote that contains a definition, the definition will be given in the text itself. This puts the definition in context rather than separating it in a glossary.

between our lives and the larger social world. In this book, we will use sociology to see sports as a part of social and cultural life and to describe and understand social issues related to sports. As we do this, it is important that we know what the terms *culture* and *society* mean.

Culture

Culture consists of the ways of life people create in a particular group or society. These ways of life are complex. They come into existence and are changed as people struggle over what is important in their lives, how to do things, and how to make sense of their experiences. Culture is not something that is imposed by some people on others; rather, it is a creation of people interacting with one another. It encompasses all the socially invented ways of thinking, feeling, and acting that emerge in particular groups as people try to survive, meet their needs, and achieve a sense of significance in the process. Of course, some people have more power and resources than others have to use in the "culture creation" process, and sociologists study how people use power in the social world.

As parts of cultures, sports have forms and meanings, which vary from one group and society to the next and vary over time as groups and societies change. For example, traditional martial arts and Sumo wrestling in Asia have different meanings, organizations, and purposes than individual sports such as boxing and wrestling in North America. Basketball's meaning, organization, and purpose have changed considerably since 1891, when it was developed at a YMCA in Massachusetts as an indoor exercise activity for men who did not want to play football outside during the winter. Canadian James Naismith, who invented basketball as part of an assignment in a physical education course, would not recognize his game if he were to see Shaquille O'Neal slam dunk during the Olympics while a billion people watch on television and thousands of others pay hundreds of dollars to see the game

in person. It is important to know about these cultural and historical differences when we study sports as parts of social life.

Society

In this book, the term **society** refers to a collection of people living in a defined geographical territory and united through a political system and a shared sense of self-identification that distinguishes them from other people. The United States, China, and the Netherlands are different societies. Each has a different form of social, political, and economic organization. When people study sports in society, they deal with sports as **social constructions**—that is, as aspects of the social world that are created by people as they interact with each other and live their lives in connection with social, political, and economic processes in particular societies.

Studying sports as social constructions leads to research questions such as these: Why are some sports popular in one society but not another? Why are sports organized in different ways from one society to the next? How are sports connected with other parts of society, such as the family, religion, education, government, the economy, and the media? Who sponsors sports and for what reasons? Who plays certain sports and what kinds of rewards are associated with their participation? Who benefits from and who is disadvantaged by the ways that sports are organized in a society? These and other questions will be addressed throughout this book, and they will be answered to the extent that research enables us to do so. Figure 1.1 illustrates that some people may not be comfortable with the implications of studying sports as social constructions.

In summary, sports are important parts of culture, which differ from place to place and time to time. How they are defined, organized, and integrated into social life varies from one society to another. This means that to understand sports we must view them as social constructions

FIGURE 1.1   If sports are social constructions, it means that we create them and that we can change them. The sociology of sport helps people identify things about sports that should be changed; other people, including those associated with sports, may resist this notion because they benefit from sports as they are currently organized.

created in particular cultural and social contexts. Sociology provides us with tools that help us do this as we discuss major issues related to sports in society in this book.

Finally, you will notice that, throughout this book, I generally use the term *sports* rather than *sport*. I do this to emphasize that the forms and meanings of sports vary from place to place and time to time. I want to avoid the inference that "sport" has an essential and timeless quality apart from the contexts in which people invent, define, and play sports in society.

ABOUT THIS CHAPTER

This chapter focuses on four questions:

1. What is the sociology of sport?
2. Why study sports in society?

3. What is the current status of the sociology of sport?
4. What are sports and how are they distinguished from other activities?

The answers to these questions will be guides for understanding the material in chapters 2 through 16.

WHAT IS THE SOCIOLOGY OF SPORT?

This question is best answered at the end of the book instead of the beginning. However, you should have a clear preview of what you will be reading for the next fifteen chapters.

Most people who do the sociology of sport agree that the field is the subdiscipline of sociology that studies sports as parts of social and cultural life. The focus of much research and writing in this field is on what many of us refer to as "organized, competitive sports," although more of us in the field are studying other physical activities as well (Martin and Miller, 1999; Rinehart, 2000). The people who do this research and writing use sociological concepts, theories, and research to answer questions such as the following:

1. Why have certain activities (rather than others) been selected and designated as sports in particular groups?
2. Why have sports in particular groups and societies been created and organized in certain ways?
3. How are sports and sport participation included in our personal and social lives and how do they affect who we are, how we are connected with other people, and how we define those connections?
4. How do sports and sport participation affect our ideas about the following: our bodies, masculinity and femininity, social class, race and ethnicity, work, fun, ability and disability, achievement and competition, pleasure and pain, deviance and conformity, and aggression and violence?
5. How are the meaning, organization, and purpose of sports connected with social relations, material conditions, and the dynamics of power in groups and societies?
6. How are sports related to important spheres of social life, such as family, education, politics, the economy, the media, and religion?
7. How can people use their knowledge about sports and what sports could and should be as a basis for changing them to make social life more fair and democratic?
8. How can people use their knowledge about sports as social phenomena to understand the organization and dynamics of social life and then participate as effective agents of progressive change in today's world?

Differences Between the Sociology of Sport and the Psychology of Sport

One way to understand the sociology of sport is to contrast it with another discipline that studies sports and behavior. Let's use psychology as a comparison discipline.

Psychologists study behavior in terms of attributes and processes that exist *inside* individuals. Psychologists focus on motivation, perception, cognition, self-esteem, self-confidence, attitudes, and personality. Psychologists also deal with interpersonal dynamics, including communication, leadership, and social influence, but they usually discuss these things in terms of how they affect attributes and processes that exist inside individuals. Therefore, they might ask a research question such as this: "How is the motivation of athletes related to personality characteristics and perceptions of physical abilities in their sports?"

Sociologists study behavior in terms of the social conditions and cultural contexts in which people live their lives. Sociologists focus on the reality *outside and around* individuals. Therefore, sociologists deal with how people form relationships with one another and create social arrangements that enable them to survive and exert some control over their lives. Sociologists also ask questions about how behavior, relationships, and social life are related to characteristics that are defined as socially relevant by people in particular groups. This is why they often deal with the social meanings and dynamics associated with age, social class, gender, race, ethnicity, disability, sexuality, and nationality. A sociologist might ask a question such as this: "How do prevailing ideas about masculinity and femininity affect the way sport programs are organized and who participates in sports?"

When it comes to the application of their knowledge, psychologists focus on the personal experiences and problems of particular individuals. Sociologists focus on group experiences and social issues that have an impact on entire categories or groups of people. For example, when studying burnout among young athletes, psychologists would look at factors that exist *inside* the athletes themselves. Because stress has been identified as a key "inside factor" in human beings, psychologists would focus on the existence of stress in the lives of individual athletes and how stress might affect motivation, performance, and burnout (Smith, 1986). They might use strategies to help individual athletes manage stress through goal setting, personal skill development, and the use of relaxation and concentration techniques.

Sociologists, on the other hand, study burnout in connection with how sport programs are organized, the treatment of athletes in sport programs, and athletes' relationships with parents, peers, and coaches. Since burnout often occurs when athletes feel they have lost control over their lives and feel they have no power to make decisions about important things in their lives, sociological intervention would emphasize the need for changes in the organization of sport programs and athletes' relationships (Coakley, 1992). Such changes might emphasize giving athletes more power within sport organizations and more control over important parts of their lives.

Of course, both approaches have potential value (Gould, 1996). However, some people may see the sociological approach as too complex and too disruptive. They may conclude that it is easier to change individual athletes and the ways in which athletes deal with external conditions than to change the external conditions in which athletes live their lives. This is one reason those who have power and control in sport organizations often resist sociological approaches. They are uncomfortable with recommendations calling for changes in how they exercise power and control within their organizations. Parents and coaches also might resist approaches that call for changes

> **The rituals of sport engage more people in a shared experience than any other institution or cultural activity today.**
> —Varda Burstyn, author, *The Rites of Men* (1999)

in their relationships with athletes, especially since they have developed those relationships in ways they feel are best for everyone involved.

Using the Sociology of Sport

The insights developed through sociological analyses are not always used to make changes in favor of the people who lack power in society. Like any science, sociology can be used in various ways. For example, research findings can be used to assist powerful people as they try to control and enhance the efficiency of particular social arrangements and organizational structures. Research findings also can be used to assist people who lack power as they attempt to change social conditions and achieve greater opportunities to make choices about how they live their lives.

This means that sociologists must consider the possible consequences of their work, as well as how they do sociology. Sociologists cannot escape the fact that social life is complex and that the interests of different groups of people in society are not always the same. Like the rest of us, sociologists must recognize that social life is at least partly shaped by who has power and who does not. Therefore, using sociology is not a simple process that always leads to good and wonderful conclusions for all humankind. This is why we must think critically about what we want sociology to do for us when we study sports.

As a result of my own thinking about sports in society, I have written this book to help you use sociology to do the following:

1. Think critically about sports, so you can identify and understand social problems and social issues associated with sports in society
2. Look beyond issues of physical performance and scores to see sports as social constructions that influence how people feel, think, and live their lives

3. Learn things about sports that you can use to make informed choices about your own sport participation and the place of sports in the communities and societies in which you live
4. Think about how sports in your schools and communities might be transformed, so that they do not contribute to ideas or conditions that systematically disadvantage some categories of people while privileging others.

Controversies Created by the Sociology of Sport

As we have noted, the conclusions sociologists reach sometimes create controversy. This occurs because those conclusions may call for changes in the organization of sports and the structure of social relations in society as a whole. These recommendations often threaten certain people, including those in positions of power and control in sport organizations, those who benefit from the current organization of sports, and those who think the current organization of sports is "right and natural," regardless of its consequences. These are the people with the most to lose if changes are made in social relations and social organization. After all, people with power and control in society know that changes in important parts of society could jeopardize their positions and the privilege that comes with them. This leads many of these people to favor approaches to sports that explain problems in terms of the characteristics of individuals, rather than in terms of social conditions and social organization. If theories put the blame for problems on individuals, the solutions will emphasize better ways of controlling people and teaching them how to adjust to society as it is, rather than emphasizing changes in how society is organized (Donnelly, 1999).

The potential for controversy that results from a sociological analysis of sports can be illustrated by looking at some of the research findings on sport participation among women in many countries around the world. Research shows that women, especially women in low-income households, have lower rates of sport participation than do other categories of people. Research also shows that there are many reasons for this. The most obvious is that women are less likely than men to have the resources they need to play sports, and they are less likely to have the time and freedom to play sports on a regular basis. Women don't often control the facilities where sports are played or the programs in those facilities. The demands of women's jobs combined with the demands of homemaking often cause them to have less free time than men have. Women also have less access to transportation and less overall freedom to move around at will and without fear, and they may be expected to take full-time responsibility for the social and emotional needs of family members—a job that is never completed or done perfectly! Furthermore, the sport programs that do exist in societies around the world are grounded primarily in the values, interests, and experiences of men. They are controlled by men and geared to the way men have learned to think about their bodies, their relationships to other people, and the way the world operates. To the extent that this is the case, many men may choose not to support women's participation—by sharing child care at home and in the community, for example. Furthermore, many women may not see sports as appropriate activities for them to take seriously, and the men in their lives may encourage them to continue thinking this way.

It is easy to see the potential for controversy associated with these conclusions. For example, sociologists might use these conclusions to suggest that opportunities to play sports should be increased for women, that resources for women's programs should be increased, that women and men should share control over sports, and that new variations of sports based on the values and experiences of women should be developed. Other suggestions might call for changes in gender relations, family structures, the organization of work, and the distribution of resources in society. They also might call for changes in who takes care of children, for revised and expanded definitions of femininity and masculinity, and for new forms of social organization that are more sensitive to how women live their lives in particular cultures.

When sociologists make recommendations about how to increase sport participation among women or how to achieve gender equity in sport programs, they may not receive positive responses from certain people. In fact, their recommendations may threaten those who benefit from the existing organization of sports and social life. Recommendations also may threaten those who believe that sports and social life were "naturally intended" to be as they are now, regardless of who benefits and who does not. For this reason, some people see the sociology of sport as either too critical or too idealistic.

My response to this is that, when we study sports as social phenomena, we are obligated to take a skeptical and critical look at the social conditions that affect our lives on and off the playing field. This helps us understand more about our world, even if it makes some people think we are too negative. As we study sports with a critical eye, we must be idealistic as we think about and form visions of what sports and society could and should be in the future. Without idealistic visions, what would motivate and guide us as we become active citizens in our communities, societies, and world? Of course, we must be practical and ready to compromise as we deal with complex issues, but being skeptical and idealistic is important if we want to make a difference and change the world for the better.

WHY STUDY SPORTS IN SOCIETY?

Sports Are Part of People's Lives

We study sports in society because they are important parts of everyday social life around the world. As we look around us, we see that the Olympic Games, soccer's World Cup, the Tour de France, the tennis championships at Wimbledon, and American football's Super Bowl are now worldwide events capturing the interest of billions of people. These events are televised in over two hundred countries. Children around the world grow up with vivid images of televised sports and sport figures, they play video games based on these sports, and they are encouraged to participate in sports by parents, teachers, and the elite athletes who often are presented as role models in their lives.

People of all ages connect with sports through the media. Newspapers in most cities devote entire sections of daily editions to the coverage of sports. This is especially true in North America, where space given to sports coverage frequently surpasses space given to the economy, politics, or any other single topic of interest. Radio talk shows about sports capture the attention of millions of listeners every day in certain countries. Satellites and Internet technology now enable millions of people around the world to share their interest in sports and to have interactive experiences while they watch sports. People around the world recognize high-profile sport teams and athletes, and this recognition fuels everything from product consumption to tourism. Team logos are imprinted on hats, shirts, posters, jackets, and other memorabilia and sold around the world. Sales vary with the ebb and flow of popularity among teams and athletes. People schedule not only their vacations but also their weekends and other free time around playing and watching sports. Even when individuals don't have an interest in sports, the people around them may insist on taking them to games and talking with them about sports to such a degree that they are forced to make sports a part of their lives.

Sport images are so pervasive today that many young people are more familiar with the tattoos and body piercings of their favorite sport celebrities than they are with the local politicians who make policies that have a significant impact on their lives. At the same time, there are legal

Sports, in many forms, are a part of everyday life for many people, especially in wealthy countries, where people have the time, energy, and resources to organize and play physical games. Thousands of people go to this park every Saturday morning in the fall to participate in and watch children, most of them young boys, play football. Issues related to gender, social class, race and ethnicity, family, and community are often apparent on these occasions. They are rich sites for studying sports in society. (Jay Coakley)

fights over who owns the right to profit from selling sport images, especially images that represent the identity or persona of a particular athlete. The media coverage and marketing of celebrity-athletes is another way that sports enter our lives. Clearly, the attention given to certain athletes has turned them into celebrities at least, if not cultural icons and heroes.

People around the world increasingly talk about sports—at work, at home, in bars, on dates, at dinner tables, in school, with friends and family members, and even with strangers at bus stops, in airports, and on the street. Comments about sports provide nonthreatening conversation openers with strangers. Relationships often revolve around sports, especially among men, as well as among an increasing number of women. People identify with teams and athletes so closely that what happens in sports influences their moods and overall senses of identity and well-being. In fact, people's identities as athletes and fans may be more important to them than their identities related to education, career, religion, or family.

Overall, sports and sport images have become a pervasive part of our everyday lives, especially for those of us living in countries where resources are relatively plentiful and the media are widespread. For this reason, sports are logical topics for the attention of sociologists and anyone else concerned with social life today.

Sports Are Connected with Important Ideas and Meanings in Social Life

We also study sports in society because they are closely linked with how people think about and see the world. Sociologists try to understand these links by studying connections between sports and ideologies.

Ideologies are sets of interrelated ideas that people use to give meaning to and make sense of the world. Ideologies are important parts of cultures because they embody the principles, orientations, and viewpoints that underlie our feelings, thoughts, and actions. However, ideologies seldom come in neat packages, especially in highly diverse and rapidly changing societies. Different groups of people in any society often develop their own sets of interrelated ideas for giving meaning to and making sense of the world, and they don't always agree with one another. These groups may struggle over whose way of making sense of the world is the best way, the right way, or the moral way.

As various groups use and promote their ideologies in society, sports become socially relevant. Because sports are social constructions, they can be organized to reinforce or challenge ideas about many things. As people create sports, they organize them around sets of interrelated ideas about bodies, relationships, abilities, character, gender, race, social class, and other attributes and characteristics that they define as important in their lives. Usually, the most popular forms of sports in a society reinforce and reproduce the ideologies favored and promoted by the people that have the most power and influence in that society. In the process, those ideologies be-

come dominant and are used by most people to make sense of the world.

Gender ideology   We can use gender ideology to illustrate these points. **Gender ideology** consists of a set of interrelated ideas about masculinity, femininity, and relationships between men and women. People use these ideas to define what it means to be a man or a woman, evaluate and judge people and relationships, and determine what they consider to be natural and moral when it comes to gender. People also use these ideas as they create and play sports and give meaning to what people do in sports.

Dominant gender ideology in most societies has traditionally emphasized that men are naturally superior to women in any activity that involves strength, physical skills, and emotional control. Through most of the twentieth century, these ideas were used by many people to establish a form of "common sense" and a vocabulary that defined female inferiority in sports as "natural." Therefore, when a person threw a ball correctly, many people learned to say that he or she "threw like a boy" or "like a man." When a person threw a ball incorrectly, they learned to say that he or she "threw like a girl." The same was true when people were evaluated in terms of their abilities to run or do other sports-related physical things. If the physical things were done right, they were done the way a boy or man would do them. If they were done wrong, they were done the way a girl or woman would do them.

Consistent with these ideas about gender and the evaluations that they encouraged was the notion that doing sports, especially sports that were physically demanding, would make boys into men. At the same time, when women excelled at these sports, these ideas caused many people to become confused and to say that playing sports was unnatural for "real" women. They assumed that heterosexual femininity and athletic excellence, especially in physically demanding or heavy contact sports, could not go together. This gender ideology even led these people to describe strong, competent women athletes as lesbians. When these descriptions were combined with related ideas about what was natural or moral, they influenced when and under what conditions women had opportunities to play sports.

This form of gender ideology became such a central part of many sports that some coaches of men's teams even used it to motivate players. These coaches criticized male players who made mistakes or did not play aggressively enough by "accusing" them of "playing like a bunch of girls." They assumed that being a female meant being a failure. These ideas about gender clearly served for many years to privilege boys and men in sports and disadvantage girls and women, who were never considered to be equal to males when it came to allocating resources and providing opportunities and encouragement to play sports. Although this gender ideology has been challenged and discredited in recent years, its legacy continues to privilege some boys and men and disadvantage some girls and women.

However, ideology is never established permanently. People constantly question and struggle over it, and they may even organize challenges that produce changes in deeply felt and widely accepted ideas. In the case of gender ideology, sports have occasionally been sites or "social places" for mounting challenges to dominant ideas about what is natural and feminine. The history of these struggles over the meaning and implications of gender in sports is complex, but recent challenges by both women and men who do not accept the ideas used widely in the past have led to important revisions in dominant gender ideology.

Women athletes have illustrated clearly that females can be physically powerful and capable of noteworthy physical achievements surpassing those of the vast majority of men in the world.

> [Sports] are why some people get out of bed. Sports define many of us. Some superstars command as much attention as heads of state and other leaders. Whether you weigh the good or bad of it—it's a fact.
>
> —Bob Davis, vice-president, American Program Bureau (1999)

Furthermore, the accomplishments of women athletes have raised serious questions about what is "natural" when it comes to gender. We will discuss issues related to gender ideology in sports in nearly every chapter, but especially chapter 8.

The box "The Body and the Sociology of Sport," presents issues related to another ideology issue: what do we consider to be natural when it comes to the body?

Racial and class ideology Sports are sites for many important ideological struggles. For example, certain sports in the United States have been sites for either reproducing or challenging dominant ideas about race and related connections between skin color and abilities, both physical and intellectual. **Racial ideology** consists of an interrelated set of ideas that people use to give meaning to skin color and to evaluate people in terms of racial classifications. Racial ideologies vary around the world, but they are powerful forces in the social lives of many people. They are used to place people into racial categories and they influence important social practices and policies that affect people's lives.

The connections between sports and racial ideologies are complex. Sports have been sites where dominant ideas about race have been reproduced on some occasions and challenged on others. Racial ideology may be used when people evaluate athletic potential or explain athletic success. The notion that light-skinned people can't jump and that dark-skinned people are natural athletes are expressions of the dominant racial ideology in certain cultures. We will discuss the connections between sports and racial ideology in chapter 9.

Ideas about socioeconomic differences and social class also are connected with sports. Dominant sports in the United States, for example,

REFLECT ON SPORTS — The Body and the Sociology of Sport

Until recently, most people viewed the body as a fixed, unchanging fact of nature. They saw the body in biological terms rather than social and cultural terms. But many scholars and scientists now recognize that we cannot fully understand the body unless we consider it in social and cultural terms (Blake, 1996; Brownell, 1995; Cole, 2000a; Loy et al., 1993; Shilling, 1994; Turner, 1997). For example, medical historians recently have shown that the body and body parts have been identified and defined in different ways through history and from one culture to another. They also have shown that this is important because it affects medical practice, government policies, social theories, and the everyday experiences of human beings (Fausto-Sterling, 2000; Laqueur, 1990; Lupton, 2000).

Changes in the ways bodies have been socially defined (or "constructed") over the years have had implications for how people think about sex, sex differences, sexuality, ideals of beauty, self-image, body image, fashion, hygiene, health, nutrition, eating, fitness, racial classification systems, disease, drugs and drug testing, violence and power, and many other things that affect our lives. In fact, body-related ideas influence how people view desire, pleasure, pain, and quality of life. For example, nineteenth-century Europeans and North Americans used insensitivity to pain as a physiological indicator of general character defects in a person and saw muscular bodies as indicators of criminal tendencies and lower-class status (Hoberman, 1992). Today, however, partly in connection with how sports have been defined, people in Europe and North America see the ability to ignore pain as an indicator of strong character, instead of a sign of deviance and defective character. They now regard a muscular body as an indicator of self-control and discipline rather than criminality.

When it comes to sports, the physical body is social in many ways. Sociologist John Wilson explains this in the following way:

> [In sport] social identities are superimposed upon physical being. Sport, in giving value to certain physical attributes and accomplishments and denigrating others, affirms certain understandings of how mind and body are related, how the social and natural worlds are connected. The identity of the athlete is not, therefore, a natural outgrowth of physicality but a social construction. . . . Sport absorbs ideas about the respective physical potential of men versus women, whites versus blacks, and middle-class versus working-class people. In doing so, sport serves to reaffirm these distinctions. (1994, pp. 37–38)

In fact, sports science has invented new ways to see bodies as complex performance machines with promote **class ideology** based on the interrelated ideas that success is always the result of hard work and discipline and that failure is always the result of laziness or a lack of discipline. By extension, these ideas lead to positive conclusions about the character and qualifications of those who are wealthy and powerful in a society and negative conclusions about the character and qualifications of those who are poor and powerless. This class ideology leads many people to assume that winners have strong character, whereas losers have weak character. This connects sports positively with a competitive system of economic rewards that advantages some people and disadvantages others. This will be discussed in chapters 8, 9, and 10.

Sports and ideologies: complex connections   As we think about sports and cultural ideology, we must remember that ideology is complex and sometimes inconsistent and that sports come in many forms and have many meanings associated with them. Therefore, sports are connected with ideology in various and sometimes contradictory component parts that can be isolated and transformed to enhance specialized competitive performances. This, in turn, has led to an emphasis on monitoring and controlling bodies. This body monitoring and controlling take forms such as weigh-ins, tests for aerobic capacity, muscle biopsies and tissue analysis, the identification of responses to various stressors, hormone testing, the administration of drugs and other chemical substances, drug testing, blood boosting, blood testing, diet regulation and restriction, vitamin regulation, and the measurement of body fat percentage, muscle size, anaerobic capacities, and on and on. In the future, we are likely to see brain manipulations, hormonal regulation, DNA testing, body part replacements, and genetic engineering. Therefore, the body is cultural in the sense that it is now interpreted and understood in terms of performance outcomes, rather than in terms of how people experience and enjoy their bodies. In many sports today, pain rather than pleasure has become the indicator of the "good body," and limiting the percentage of body fat has become such a compulsion that bodies are starved to be "in good shape."

This new way of thinking about the body in cultural terms has challenged traditional Western ideas about the separation of mind and body. It also has raised new questions and issues in the sociology of sport. Some people in the sociology of sport are now working with colleagues in other disciplines who share interests in the body. In fact, their research is based on the notion that culture is *embodied* and that we can learn about culture by studying bodies. They are asking critical questions such as the following:

1. How do people form ideas about what is natural, ideal, and deviant when it comes to bodies in sports and in the culture as a whole?
2. What are the moral, cultural, and sociological implications of how bodies are protected, probed, monitored, tested, trained, disciplined, evaluated, manipulated, and rehabilitated in sports?
3. How are bodies in sports marked by gender, race, (dis)ability, and age and what are the social consequences of such marking?
4. How are bodies in sports represented in the media and popular culture in general?

These are crucial questions, although they make many people associated with sports uncomfortable because the answers often challenge taken-for-granted ideas about nature, beauty, health, and the organization and purpose of high-performance, competitive sports. But it is important to ask these questions. *What do you think*?

ways. We saw this in the example showing that sports are sites for simultaneously reproducing *and* challenging dominant gender ideology in society. Furthermore, the forms sports come in can have many social meanings associated with them. For example, baseball is played by similar rules in Japan and the United States, but the meanings associated with baseball and with athletes' performances are different in the two cultures because of ideological differences. Team loyalty is highly prized in Japan and emotional displays by players or coaches are frowned upon, whereas in the United States individualism is emphasized and emotional displays are accepted and defined as entertaining. Japanese baseball games may end in ties, whereas games in the United States must have clear winners and losers, even if it means playing overtime and "sudden death" periods. The complex connections between sports and ideologies make it difficult to generalize about the consequences of sports in society. Sports have the social potential to do many things. This is another reason for studying them as social constructions.

Sports Are Connected to Major Spheres of Social Life

Another reason to study sports in society is that they are clearly connected to major spheres of social life, including the family, the economy, the media, politics, education, and religion. We will discuss these connections in various chapters in this book, but it is useful to highlight them at this point.

Sports and the family   Sports are closely related to the family. In North America, for example, millions of children are involved in a variety of organized sport activities. It is primarily their parents who organize leagues, coach teams, attend games, and serve as "taxi drivers" for child athletes. Family schedules are altered to accommodate practices and games. These schedules also may be affected by the patterns of sport involvement among adult family members. The viewing of televised sport events sometimes disrupts family life and at other times provides a collective focus for family attention. In some cases, relationships between family members are nurtured and played out during sport activities

or in conversations about these activities. Two of these situations are represented in figure 1.2.

Sports and the economy   The economies of most countries, especially wealthy postindustrial countries, have been affected by the billions of dollars spent every year for game tickets, sports equipment, participation fees, athletic club membership dues, and bets placed on favorite teams and athletes. The economies of many local communities have been affected by the presence of sport teams. Most countries use public monies (taxes) to subsidize teams and events. In fact, sports and commerce have fused together, so that corporate logos are tied to sport teams and athletes and are displayed prominently in school gyms and other places where sports are played and watched.

Some athletes make impressive sums of money from various combinations of salaries, appearance fees, and endorsements. Corporations have paid up to $4.4 million for a single minute of commercial time during the telecast of the Super Bowl in the United States. They have paid as much as $100 million to be international

FIGURE 1.2   Families and family schedules often are influenced by sport involvement. Sometimes this involvement disrupts family life and interferes with family relationships (left); sometimes it brings family members together in enjoyable ways (right).

Olympic sponsors and have their corporate names associated with the Olympic name and symbol for four years. Sport stadiums, arenas, and teams are now named after corporations instead of people or images that have local cultural or historical relevance. Sponsorships and commercial associations with sports have been so effective that many people around the world now believe that, without Coca-Cola, McDonald's, Nike, General Motors, and other transnational corporations, sports could not exist. This indicates that sports are cultural practices deeply connected with the material and economic conditions in society.

Sports and the media Television networks and cable stations may now pay billions of dollars for the rights to televise major games and events. NBC in the United States, owned by General Electric, paid the International Olympic Committee (IOC) $2.3 billion for the rights to the Summer Games of 2004 and 2008 and the Winter Games of 2006. People in sport organizations that depend on spectators are keenly aware that without the media their lives would be different.

The images and messages presented in the media coverage of sports also emphasize particular ideological themes, and they influence how people see and think about sports and social life. For example, television's use of zoom lenses, special camera angles, filters, isolated coverage of action sequences, slow-motion replays, video diagrams of action, commentary intended to enhance drama and excitement, and "delayed live" coverage all influence how people "see" sports. For those who don't play sports or attend games in person, the mediated versions of sports are the only versions they know.

The media have converted sports into a major form of entertainment in many societies. Satellite technology makes it possible for the images and messages associated with a single competitive event to be witnessed simultaneously by billions of people. In the process, athletes become global entertainer-celebrities, and the corporations that

sponsor media sports imprint their logos in people's minds and promote a lifestyle based on product consumption. This certainly raises issues that are socially important.

Sports and politics People in many societies link sports to feelings of national pride and a sense of national identity. For example, in the aftermath of the terrorist attacks of 9/11(2001), many people in the United States used sport events as sites for reaffirming their collective sense of "we-ness" as Americans. Many events involved expressions of unity and patriotism, combined with memorials of symbols to commemorate those who died in the attacks. Apart from major sport events, it is rare for 40,000 to 100,000 people to come together in one place on a regular basis, and many spectators in the United States found these collective events to be comforting. The events allowed people at the games and watching on television to experience widely shared feelings and to reaffirm their sense of national identity. At the same time, they had opportunities to focus on and cheer for something familiar in their lives.

Despite frequent complaints about mixing sports and politics, most people around the globe have no second thoughts about displaying national flags and playing national anthems at sporting events, and some may quickly reject athletes and other spectators who don't think as they do about the flag and the anthem.

Political leaders at various levels of government promote themselves by associating with sports as both participants and spectators. Former athletes, even professional wrestlers, have been elected to powerful political positions in the United States by using their name recognition and reputations from sports to attract votes.

International sports have become hotbeds of political controversy in recent years, and most countries around the world have used sports actively to enhance their reputations in global political relationships. Furthermore, sports involve political processes associated with issues such as who controls sports and sport events, the terms of eligibility and team selection, rules and rule changes, rule enforcement, and the allocation of rewards and punishments. Sports and sport organizations are political because they involve the exercise of power over people's lives.

Sports and education   Sports have become integral parts of school life for many students around the world. In many countries, sports are taught and played in physical education classes. Schools in a few countries have varsity sport teams, and some of these teams attract more attention among students and community residents than academic programs do, especially in the United States. At the same time, many of these schools have eliminated or are in the process of eliminating physical education for their student bodies as a whole.

Some U.S. universities even use their varsity teams to promote the quality of their academic programs, making or losing large amounts of money in the process. They may even have public relations profiles built on or seriously damaged by the reputations of their sport programs.

The interscholastic sport programs in U.S. schools are unique. The sports sponsored by schools in most other countries take the form of low-profile, club-based teams that emphasize participation and student control—a model quite different from the one used in the United States.

Sports and religion   There is an emerging relationship between sports and religion in certain cultures. For example, local churches and church groups in the United States and Canada are among the most active sponsors of athletic teams and leagues. Parishes and congregations have been known to revise Sunday worship schedules to accommodate members who would not miss an opening kickoff in a professional football game for anything—even their religious services.

Religious rituals are increasingly used in conjunction with sport participation in the United States, and nondenominational religious organizations have been created for the purpose of attracting and converting athletes to Christian beliefs. Other U.S.-based religious organizations have used athletes as spokespersons for their belief systems in the hope of converting people who strongly identify with sports and athlete-celebrities. Meanwhile, athletes in some cultures have become increasingly likely to display religious beliefs as they play sports and even define their participation in religious terms.

In summary, there is no shortage of reasons for studying sports in society: they are part of our everyday lives, and they are connected with ideology and major spheres of social life.

WHAT IS THE CURRENT STATUS OF THE SOCIOLOGY OF SPORT?

Research and interest in the sociology of sport have grown as organized sports have become increasingly visible and popular in many societies around the world. For example, if you go to *www.Amazon.com* on the Internet, you will see more than 700 books listed in the "Sociology of Sport" category. In 2000, there were fewer than half that number of books listed.

Professional Associations and Journals

Much of the growth in the sociology of sport has occurred since 1980, and it has been fueled partly by the formation of professional associations and academic journals devoted to the field. These associations and journals have enabled scholars from various disciplines to meet with each other and to present and publish their ideas and research on sports in society. The journals related to the field are listed in table 1.1. The major organizations are the following:

1. *The International Sociology of Sport Association.* This organization, formed in 1965, meets

Table 1.1   Publication Sources for Sociology of Sport Research

Journals Devoted Primarily to Sociology of Sport Articles	Journals in Related Fields That Sometimes Include Articles on or Related to Sociology of Sport Topics
International Review for the Sociology of Sport (quarterly) *Journal of Sport and Social Issues* (three issues per year) *Sociology of Sport Journal* (quarterly)	*Adolescence* *Aethlon: The Journal of Sport Literature* *The British Journal of Sport History* *Canadian Journal of the History of Sport* *The European Sports History Review* *International Journal of the History of Sport* *International Journal of Sport Psychology* *Journal of Human Movement Studies* *Journal of Leisure Research* *Journal of the Philosophy of Sport* *Journal of Popular Culture* *Journal of Sport and Exercise Psychology* *Journal of Sport History* *Journal of Sports and Economics* *Leisure Sciences* *Leisure Studies* *Olympika: The International Journal of Olympic Studies* *Soccer and Society* *Society and Leisure* *Sport History Review* *The Sport Psychologist* *Sporting Traditions* *The Sports Historian* *Youth & Society*
Sociology Journals That Sometimes Include Articles on or Related to Sports	
American Journal of Sociology *American Sociological Review* *British Journal of Sociology* *Sociology of Education* *Theory, Culture, and Society*	
Interdisciplinary, Sport Science, and Physical Education Journals That Sometimes Include Articles on or Related to Sociology of Sport Topics	
Avante *Canadian Journal of Applied Sport Sciences* *Culture, Sport, Society* *Exercise and Sport Sciences Reviews* *Journal of Physical Education, Recreation, and Dance* *Journal of Sport Behavior* *Journal of Sport Sciences* *Physical Education Review* *Quest* *Research Quarterly for Exercise and Sport* *Sport, Education, and Society* *Sport Science Review* *Women in Sport & Physical Activity Journal*	

annually and attracts scholars from all over the world. Since 1965, it has sponsored publication of the *International Review for the Sociology of Sport*.

2. *The North American Society for the Sociology of Sport*. This organization, formed in 1978, has held annual conferences every year since 1980, and it has sponsored publication of the *Sociology of Sport Journal* since 1984.

3. *The Sport Sociology Academy*. This loosely organized group is one of ten disciplinary academies in the National Association for Sport and Physical Education (NASPE), which is part of the American Alliance for Health, Physical Education, Recreation, and Dance (AAHPERD), headquartered in the United States. It does not sponsor a journal, but it does sponsor sociology of sport research sessions at annual conferences of AAHPERD, and it represents the interests of the field in the programs and policies of NASPE. There are also similar organizations in many other countries (Sage and Young, 2002).

Future growth in the sociology of sport depends largely on whether scholars in the field conduct and publish research that proves useful for understanding social life in ways that help make the world a better place. However, scholars in the sociology of sport do not always agree on what is "better" or on what types of research will accomplish this goal.

Disagreements in the Sociology of Sport

Not everyone who studies sports as social phenomena is interested primarily in learning about human behavior, social relations, culture, and ideology. Some people are concerned more directly with learning about sports. Their involvement in the sociology of sport focuses on understanding how sports are organized and how changes in that organization might influence sport experiences for both athletes and spectators. The goals of these scholars are often to improve sport experiences for current participants and to make sport participation more attractive to and accessible for those who do not currently play sports. They also may want to help athletes improve their performances, help coaches work more effectively with athletes and win more games, and help sport organizations grow and operate more efficiently and profitably.

The scholars who focus on the organization of sports, generally refer to themselves as **sport sociologists.** They tend to see themselves as part of the larger field of **sport sciences.** They are more concerned with sport science issues than with general social issues or with the structure and dynamics of society.

Scholars concerned more directly with social and cultural issues usually refer to themselves as sociologists who study sports or as cultural studies scholars. Their research and teaching on sports in society are often connected with other interests in leisure, everyday life and popular culture, social relations, and social life as a whole.

Not everyone associated with the sociology of sport sees the field in the same way. People differ in what they prefer to study, how they do their research, the types of questions they ask, the theoretical perspectives they use, and the goals they identify for their research (see chapter 2). For example, some people in the field see themselves as **professional experts** who serve as consultants to those who can afford to pay them. Others dislike this approach because it aligns the sociology of sport with people who have the power and money to hire experts—and people with power and money seldom want to ask tough, critical questions about sports and the way sports are organized.

Those who favor the "professional expert" model argue that the future of the sociology of sport depends on scholars in the field establishing reputations as researchers and consultants. They often focus on obtaining research grants, using research money to fund graduate assistants and recruit young scholars into the field, and using the knowledge produced in their research to maintain a professional image that they can market and sell to sport organizations or other groups interested in sports.

Others in the sociology of sport favor what might be called a **critical transformation** model over the professional expert model. They focus primarily on studying social problems and issues for the purpose of improving the human condition and making social life more fair and democratic. They argue that, if research in the sociology of sport only reproduces what already exists in society, then scholars in the field become mere "efficiency experts" who sell their expertise to people with power and resources. These **critical sociologists** also argue that, if scientific research and knowledge serve primarily people with power and wealth, science and scientists may become agents of control and oppression rather than agents of human freedom and social justice. Therefore, they use research primarily to understand and solve problems in the lives of those who lack power and resources.

Still others in the field favor a **knowledge-building** model, which emphasizes research dedicated primarily to accumulating knowledge that will help us understand social life. Transforming social life may be important to these scholars, but they often argue that efforts to bring about changes cannot be undertaken effectively until we have adequate knowledge about the organization and dynamics of society and social life. Therefore, those who favor this approach tend to emphasize "professional detachment" and objectivity rather than concerns with problem solving and/or social transformation when doing their research.

Debates about the focus and applications of science are not unique to the sociology of sport. They occur among professionals in other fields as well. Like other scholars and scientists, all of us in the sociology of sport must make choices about how we will do our work and what we want the consequences of our work to be. Science is not neutral and value free, as we have been led to believe. Science has always been and will always be connected with issues of power and control. Knowledge is a source of power in our complex world, and power has an impact on how knowledge is produced. In other words, doing research to build knowledge in the sociology of sport has political implications, because it influences how people see sports, think about their lives, and make decisions in their lives. Unless people in the sociology of sport think about these things when they do their work, they will limit their understanding of the diverse meanings that people give to sports in their lives and of the impact that sports and sport participation have on individuals, communities, and societies.

WHAT ARE SPORTS?

This question may seem elementary. We certainly have a good enough grasp of the meaning of sports to talk about them with others. However, when we study sports, it helps to have a precise definition of what we're talking about. For example, can we say that two groups of children

playing a sandlot game of baseball in a Kansas town and a pickup game of soccer on a Mexican beach are engaged in sports? Their activities are quite different from what occurs in connection with Major League Baseball games and professional soccer matches. These differences become significant when parents ask if playing sports is good for their children, when community leaders ask if they should fund sports with public money, or when school officials ask if sports contribute to the educational missions of their schools.

Students ask me if jogging and jump roping are sports. How about weight lifting? hunting? scuba diving? darts? automobile racing? ballroom dancing? chess? professional wrestling? skateboarding? the XGames? paintball? a piano competition? Should any or all of these activities be called sports? In the face of such a question, many scholars feel that we should think about the social organization, social dynamics, and social implications of certain activities to determine which ones are similar enough to be grouped together when we do sociological research. For this reason, many people in the sociology of sport have decided that a precise definition of **sports** is needed. Then we can study sports as distinct from other activities, which may have different social dynamics and social implications, and we can share our research with others who have similar interests.

A Traditional Definition of *Sports*

Although definitions of *sports* vary, those who offer definitions tend to emphasize that *sports are institutionalized competitive activities that involve rigorous physical exertion or the use of relatively complex physical skills by participants motivated by internal and external rewards.* Parts of this definition are clear, but other parts need explanations.

First, sports are *physical activities.* Therefore, according to the definition, chess probably is not a sport, since playing chess is more cognitive than physical. Are billiards and pool physical enough to qualify as sports under this definition? Making this determination is arbitrary, since there are no objective rules for how "physical" an activity must be to qualify as a sport. Pairs ice dancing is considered a sport in the Winter Olympics, so why not add ballroom dancing to the Summer Games? This question was asked by members of the International Olympic Committee (IOC) in connection with the 2000 Games in Sydney, and ballroom dancing was included in the Olympics as a demonstration sport.

Second, sports are *competitive activities*, according to this definition. Sociologists realize that competitive activities have different social dynamics from cooperative or individualistic activities. They know that, when two girls kick a soccer ball to each other on the grass outside their home, it is sociologically different from what happens when the U.S. women's soccer team plays China's national team in the World Cup, so it makes sense to separate them for research purposes.

Third, sports are *institutionalized activities*. **Institutionalization** is a sociological term referring to the process through which behaviors and organization become patterned or standardized over time and from one situation to another. Institutionalized activities have formal rules and organizational structures, which people use to frame and guide their actions from one situation to another. When we say that sports are institutionalized activities, we distinguish what happens when two skiers decide to race each other down their favorite ski slope while vacationing in Colorado from what happens when skiers race each other in a World Cup giant slalom event, which has been highly organized according to strict rules laid down by the International Federation of Skiing. When it comes to defining *sports*, many sociologists would say that the process of institutionalization includes the following:

1. *The rules of the activity become standardized.* This means that sports have rules that are not simply produced by a single group getting together on an informal basis. Rules

in a sport are based on more than spontaneous expressions of individual interests and concerns. In sports, the rules of the game define a formal, official set of behavioral and procedural guidelines and restrictions.

2. *Official regulatory agencies take over rule enforcement.* When the physical performances of teams or individuals are compared from one competitive event to another, it is necessary for a regulatory agency to sanction games and meets and to ensure that standardized conditions exist and rules are enforced. Regulatory agencies can include everything from a local rules committee for a children's softball league to the highly organized central office of the National Collegiate Athletic Association (NCAA).

3. *The organizational and technical aspects of the activity become important.* When competition is combined with external rule enforcement, an activity becomes increasingly *rationalized*. This means that players and coaches develop strategies and training schedules to improve their chances for success within the rules. Additionally, equipment and technologies are developed and manufactured to enhance performance and to maximize the range of experiences available through participation.

4. *The learning of game skills becomes formalized.* This occurs for two major reasons. First, as the organization and the rules of the activity become more complex, they must be presented and explained to people in systematic ways. Second, as the stakes associated with competitive success grow, participants at various skill levels begin to seek guidance from experts. Teaching experts or coaches are often supplemented by others, such as trainers, dietitians, sport scientists, managers, and team physicians.

Fourth, according to the definition, sports are *activities played by people for internal and external rewards.* This means that participation in sports involves a combination of two sets of motivations. One is based in the internal satisfactions associated with expression, spontaneity, and the pure joy of participation; the other motivation is based in external satisfactions associated with displaying physical skills in public and receiving approval, status, or material rewards in the process.

When *sports* are defined precisely, we can distinguish them from both play and dramatic spectacle. **Play** involves expressive activity done for its own sake; it may be spontaneous or guided by informal norms. An example of play is three four-year-olds who, during a recess period at preschool, spontaneously run around a playground, yelling joyfully while throwing playground balls in whatever directions they feel like throwing them. Of course, it makes sociological sense to distinguish this type of behavior, motivated almost exclusively by personal enjoyment and expression, from what happens in sports.

Dramatic spectacle, on the other hand, involves performances to entertain an audience. An example of dramatic spectacle is four professional wrestlers paid to entertain spectators by staging a skillful and cleverly choreographed tag-team match in which outcomes are prearranged for audience entertainment. It also makes sociological sense to distinguish this type of physical activity, motivated almost exclusively by a desire to perform for the entertainment of others, from what happens in sports.

Does this mean that sports do not involve elements of play and spectacle? No, it means that sports involve combinations of both intrinsic enjoyment and extrinsic rewards for performance. The challenge faced in some sports is to preserve a relatively even balance between these two factors. People who use a precise definition of *sports* generally do not spend much time studying playlike physical activities or activities that are "staged" for entertainment purposes.

In summary, many sociologists feel it is important to define *sports* in order to distinguish them from other activities that are sociologically dissimilar. This is a practical approach, but it has potentially serious problems associated with it. For example, when we focus our attention only on institutionalized competitive activities, we may overlook physical activities in the lives of many people who have neither the resources to formally organize those activities nor the desire to make their activities competitive. In other words, we may spend all our time considering the physical activities of relatively select groups in society, because those groups have the power to formally organize physical activities and the desire to make those activities competitive. If this happens, we can create the impression that the activities of these select groups are more important parts of culture than the activities of other groups. This, in turn, can contribute to the marginalization of groups who have neither the resources nor the time to play organized sports or who are not attracted to competitive activities.

Ironically, this outcome would reinforce the very ideas and organization that may have disadvantaged these groups in the first place, and we would be doing this in the name of science. But, if we are aware of this potential problem, we can continue to ask critical questions about how sports have become what they are in particular societies and what social purposes they serve. We also can ask questions about how sports are connected to power, privilege, and social relations and about the changes needed to involve more people in the determination of what sports could and should be in society. However, when we ask such questions, we may begin to wonder if there is another way to deal with the definition of *sports*, a way that does not give priority to organized sports. This has led some scholars to seek an alternative approach to defining *sports*.

An Alternative Approach to Defining *Sports*

Instead of using a single definition of *sports*, some scholars ask two definition-type questions about sports in a particular society:

1. What activities are identified as sports by people in a particular group or society?

Many sociologists define *sports* in precise terms, so that they can distinguish sports from other activities, such as informal play and dramatic spectacle. High school and college wrestling are sociologically different from wrestling that might occur in a backyard or in the televised spectacle *Raw Is War*. I used "action figures" to represent dramatic spectacle, partly because pro wrestling organizations exercise restrictive control over the images of their events and "dramatic personalities." (Jay Coakley)

2. Whose sports count the most in a group or society when it comes to obtaining support and resources?

Asking these questions does not limit the analysis of sports in ways that might happen when a precise definition is used. In fact, asking these questions leads researchers to dig into the social and cultural contexts in which ideas are formed about physical activities. The researchers must explain how and why some physical activities come to be defined as sports and then become culturally important activities in the social life of a particular group or society.

Those who use this alternative approach do not describe sports with a single definition. When they are asked, "What is sport?" they say, "Well, that depends on whom you ask, when you ask, and where you ask." They explain that not everyone has the same way of looking at and defining *sports* and that ideas about sports vary over time and from one place to another. For example, they might note that many people who grew up at the end of the nineteenth century in England would be horrified, confused, or astonished by what people in the United States today consider to be sports. Similarly, the people who watch NFL football games today would look at many activities that were considered sports in nineteenth-century England and say they were not "real" sports because participants did not train, compete according to schedules, play in leagues, or strive to set records and win championships. Maybe people in the year 2100 will define activities played in virtual reality as sports and see what we defined as sports today as backward, overorganized, and funless activities geared to the physical abilities of the few rather than the interests and fantasies of everyone.

Those who use this alternative approach to defining *sports* also note numerous cultural differences in how people identify sports and include them in their lives. In cultures that emphasize cooperative relationships, the idea that people should compete with each other for rewards might be defined as disruptive, if not immoral. For people in cultures that emphasize competition, physical activities and games that have no winners may seem pointless. These cultural differences are important to understand. Instead of letting a definition of *sports* shape what should be studied, those who use this alternative approach do research based on what the people in particular cultural settings think is important in their own lives (see Martin and Miller, 1999; Rail, 1998; Rinehart, 2000).

The assumption underlying this approach is that sports themselves are "contested activities." In other words, there is no universal agreement about the meaning, purpose, and organization of sports; there is no universal agreement about who will participate in sports, about the circumstances under which participation will occur, or about who will sponsor sports or the reasons underlying sponsorship. All these things vary over time from group to group and society to society. The most important sociological issue to recognize when we use this approach is that people in particular places at particular times struggle over *whose* ideas about sports will count as *the* ideas in a group or society. A guide for thinking about these issues is in the box titled "Sports as Contested Activities."

Struggles over whose ideas count when it comes to the meaning, organization, and purpose of sports are much more common than you might think. Consider the different ways *sports* might be defined and the different meanings associated with those definitions in connection with decisions related to the following issues:

- Whether children younger than six years old should be allowed to play sports and how sports ought to be organized and what they ought to mean for young children
- Whether money from a local youth sports budget ought to be given to a program in which young girls are taught to jump rope or to a program in which boys and a few girls

REFLECT ON SPORTS — Sports as Contested Activities

When sociologists say that sports are contested activities, they mean that, through history, people have disagreed about what sports could and should be. These disagreements have led to struggles over three major questions about sports and a number of related questions. As you read the following questions, remember that there are many possible answers to each. Sociologists are concerned with how people in different groups and societies arrive at particular answers at various points in time.

1. WHAT IS THE MEANING, PURPOSE, AND ORGANIZATION OF SPORTS?

The struggles related to this question have raised other questions, such as the following:

- What activities will be defined as "official" sports?
- How are sports connected with social values and people's ideas about each other, social relationships, and the social worlds in which they live?
- What will be the relative importance of different types of physical skills in those activities? Will strength, size, and speed, for example, be more important than flexibility, balance, and endurance?
- How will sports experiences be evaluated? Will emotional enjoyment be more important than competitive success? Will fun and physical pleasure be more important than performance outcomes? How will participants define *fun?*
- What types of performance outcomes will be important and how will success be defined, measured, and rewarded? Will external rewards go to the person who completes an event, the one who achieves a personal best, the one who outscores or dominates others in terms of scores

or another measure, or the one who lives through the experience without being seriously injured or killed?
- How will *excellence* be defined—in terms of one's abilities to be tough, to be aggressive, and to dominate others; in terms of all-around abilities to do different things well; or in terms of being able to maximize enjoyment for self and others?

2. WHO WILL PARTICIPATE IN SPORTS AND UNDER WHAT CONDITIONS WILL THIS PARTICIPATION OCCUR?

The struggles related to this question have raised other questions, such as the following:

- Will females and males be involved in the same sports? Will they play at the same time or be segregated by sex? Will some sports be defined as girls' and women's sports, whereas others are defined as boys' and men's sports? On what basis will people make such distinctions? Will rewards for achievement be the same for females and males?
- Will sports participation be open to people regardless of their social class and wealth? Will the rulers and the ruled, the wealthy and the poor, the powerful and the powerless play and watch sports together? Will they be segregated and for what reasons? Will participation opportunities be equal? Will sponsors support participation for some or all?
- Will sports participation be related to skin color or ethnicity? Will people from different racial and ethnic backgrounds be allowed or encouraged to play together? Will they be segregated? Will the meanings given to skin color or ethnicity influence participation patterns or access to participation?

compete in a roller hockey league at a local skating rink
- Whether the state high school activities associations in the United States ought to include cheerleading as an official high school sport

- Whether skateboarding and hacky sack ought to be funded through a university intramural sport program
- Whether tenpin bowling, darts, and men's synchronized swimming ought to be recognized as Olympic sports

- Will age be a factor in whether people are encouraged or discouraged from participating in sports? Will expectations vary for people of different ages? Will older and younger people play sports together or separately? Will people of different ages have the same access to participation opportunities?
- Will people with able bodies and people with various types of disabilities have the same opportunities? Will they play together or be segregated? For what reasons will integration or segregation occur and who will benefit from what is decided? How will people define the accomplishments of athletes with disabilities?
- Will gay men and lesbians be included in sports in the same ways that heterosexual people are? Will homosexual persons be encouraged to participate in all sports?
- Will athletes be in control of the conditions under which they play sports? Will they have the rights and the power to change those conditions to meet their own needs and interests? Will they be paid? Will they be rewarded in noncash terms? How much will players be rewarded and how will this be determined?

3. HOW WILL SPORTS BE SPONSORED AND WHAT WILL BE THE REASONS FOR SPONSORSHIP?

The struggles related to this question have raised other questions, such as the following:

- Will sports be sponsored by public agencies and organizations for the sake of the "public good"?

Who will determine the public good and how is *public good* defined?

- Will sports be sponsored by nonprofit groups and organizations? Will the reasons for their sponsorship be related to organizational philosophies? Will the reasons be related to the interests of all group members or to the interests of some over others?
- Will sports be sponsored by private commercial organizations? To what extent will private sponsorships be designed for the benefit of athletes and communities or for the purpose of maximizing profits and increasing the power of private individuals and corporations in society?
- To what extent will sponsors control the sports and the athletes they support? What will be the legal rights of the sponsors relative to those of the athletes and others involved in sports?

As you can see, sports are indeed contested activities! They take many forms and have varying consequences in society, depending on how these questions are answered. Furthermore, answers to these questions are never permanent. New answers replace old ones as interests change; as power shifts; as the meanings associated with age, skin color, ethnicity, gender, and disability change; and as economic, political, and legal forces take new and different forms.

This means that any definition of *sports* reflects the structure and organization of relationships and social life in a particular society at a particular point in time. Of course, definitions can be helpful, but they should always be used with caution. *What do you think?*

- Whether a permit to use a sport field in a public park ought to be given to a group that wants to throw Frisbees freely for a couple of hours or to a softball team that plays in an organized community league

- Whether synchronized swimming events ought to be covered in the sports section of a city newspaper or in the lifestyle section
- Whether wrestler "Stone Cold" Steve Austin can be nominated for a "sports person of the year" award

What activities are counted as sports in society? Discussions of this question emphasize that sports cannot be understood apart from cultural values and power relations in a society. As ideas about gender have changed over the past three decades, physical activities such as rhythmic gymnastics have come to be considered sports, despite resistance from some who believe that "real" sports must reflect "manly" attributes. Women athletes and spectators have more power in society today than they have had in the past. (*Colorado Springs Gazette*)

How these issues are resolved depends on what activities are counted as sports in certain societies at certain points in time. These issues also raise questions about the usefulness of a single definition of *sports*. For example, if sports are institutionalized competitive physical activities played to achieve internal and external rewards, then why aren't competitive dancing, aerobics, jump roping, and cheerleading counted as sports? They fit the definition. The fact that they are not considered sports when it comes to important issues such as sponsorships, funding, and formal recognition raises two questions: (1) what is identified as a sport in a society and (2) how do people determine what is identified as a sport? Answering these questions requires a careful analysis of the social and cultural context in which decisions are made in everyday life. Critical issues are raised by asking what activities are identified as sports. These issues force us to look at the cultures in which people live their lives and make decisions about what is important.

SUMMARY

WHY STUDY THE SOCIOLOGY OF SPORT?

Sociology is the study of social life, including all forms of social interaction and relationships. Sociologists are concerned with social issues, social organization, and social change. Their goal is to enable people to understand, control, and change their lives, so that human needs are met at both individual and group levels.

Sociologists study sports as parts of culture and society. They look at sports in terms of their importance in people's lives and their connections to ideology and major spheres of social life. Research in the sociology of sport helps us understand sports as social constructions created by people for particular purposes. As social constructions, sports are related to historical, political, and economic factors.

When sociologists study sports in society, they often discover problems based in the structure and organization of either sports or society. When this happens, the recommendations sociologists make may threaten those who want sports and sport programs to remain as they are now. Therefore, sociology sometimes creates controversies.

Continued growth of the sociology of sport depends primarily on whether those in the field do research and publish books and articles that make meaningful contributions to people's lives. Complicating the issue of future growth is the fact that not everyone in the field agrees on how to "do" sociology of sport. Some use a professional expert model to guide their work, some use a critical transformation model, and some use a knowledge-building model. Differences among these three approaches raise important questions about the production and use of scientific knowledge (see chapter 2). Many scholars in the field are currently debating these questions.

Some scholars in the field define *sports* as activities involving (1) the use of physical skill, prowess, or exertion; (2) institutionalized competition; and (3) the combination of intrinsic and extrinsic reasons for participation. Such a definition is problematic if it leads us to ignore or devalue the lives of people who do not have the resources and the desire to develop formally organized and competitive physical activities. For this reason, many scholars now recommend that, instead of using a single definition of *sports*, we should ask what activities are identified as sports in different groups and societies at different points in time. This question forces us to recognize that sports are contested activities. This focuses our attention on the relationship between sports and power and privilege in society and leads more directly to concerns for transforming social life, so that more people have the resources they need to control their lives and make them meaningful.

SUGGESTED READINGS

Andrews, D. L., and S. J. Jackson. 2001. *Sport stars: The cultural politics of sporting celebrity.* London/New York: Routledge (sixteen articles focusing on the cultural, political, economic, and technological factors that together influence sport celebrity around the world and how sport celebrities influence the everyday private lives of people around the world).

Brownell, S. 1995. *Training the body for China: Sports in the moral order of the People's Republic.* Chicago:

University of Chicago Press (participant observation study of the body and sports in Chinese culture; shows clearly through firsthand examples that sports must be studied in historical and cultural contexts to be understood as social constructions).

Burstyn, V. 1999. *The rites of men: Manhood, politics, and the culture of sport.* Toronto: University of Toronto Press (thorough analysis of the institutionalized world of sports and how it is connected with and informed by a combination of masculinism and capitalism; there is a consistent focus on how hypermasculinity in U.S. culture in particular is perpetuated through a web of interlocking organizations, which includes sports, the media, industry, and the government).

Cashmore, E. 2000. *Sports culture: An A–Z guide.* London/New York: Routledge (unique, dictionary/encyclopedia-like book, which covers everything from aggression, to transsexuals).

Coakley, J., and E. Dunning, eds. 2000. *Handbook of sports studies.* London: Sage (forty-two chapters on the ways sports are studied as social phenomena and on the sociology of sport in various countries and regions around the world).

Dyck, N., ed. 2000. *Games, sports and cultures.* New York: New York University press (ten articles written by anthropologists and cultural studies scholars; good material on the meanings associated with sports in various cultures).

Eitzen, D. S. 2003. *Fair and foul: Beyond the myths and paradoxes of sport.* 2d ed. Lanham, MD: Rowman & Littlefield (selective analysis of issues and contradictions in U.S. sports; practical, problem-oriented discussions of issues related to sports and social integration, the use of sport symbols, deviance, health and fitness, interscholastic sports, and professional sports).

Maguire, J., G. Jarvie, L. Mansfield, and J. Bradley. 2002. *Sport worlds: A sociological perspective.* Champaign, IL: Human Kinetics (analysis of how sports are connected to history, society, and global processes; examples are drawn generally from a European context).

Rinehart, R. E. 1998. *Players all: Performances in contemporary sport.* Bloomington: Indiana University Press (analyzes sport experiences among fans, athletes, coaches, broadcasters and producers, sports tourists, and collectors; analyzes the Olympic Games, the World Wrestling Federation, The eXtreme Games, The American Gladiators, paintball, and the Super Bowl).

Yiannakis, A., and M. J. Melnick, eds. 2001. *Contemporary issues in sociology of sport.* Champaign, IL: Human Kinetics (thirty-four articles by scholars in the field; articles present both theory and research on twelve topics central to the sociology of sport).

WEBSITE RESOURCES

Note: Websites often change. The following URLs were current when this book was printed. Please check our website (www.mhhe.com/coakley8e) for updates and additions.

www.mhhe.com/coakley8e Click on chapter 1; information on why sociologists tend to ask critical questions in their research; discussion of roller hockey and jump rope and what is counted as a sport in U.S. culture.

www.ucalgary.ca/library/ssportsite A guide to online "Scholarly Sport Sites"; this is the most useful starting point I have found as I have looked for online information.

www.nasss.org Official site for the North American Society for the Sociology of Sport; contains a list of experts in the field, along with graduate programs specializing in the sociology of sport.

http://u2.u-strasbg.fr/issa The official site of ISSA, the International Sociology of Sport Association; this organization is a subcommittee of ICSSPE, the International Council of Sport Science and Physical Education, and is affiliated with UNESCO, the United Nations Educational, Scientific and Cultural Organization.

www.handilinks.com/Directory/Sports Provides numerous Internet links useful to sport scholars from many disciplines.

www.pscw.uva.nl/sociosite/TOPICS/Leisure.html SPORT This site, located in the Netherlands, provides excellent links to sites related to the sociology of sport, especially to international sites related to women in sports and to the Olympics.

www.sportinsociety.org Center for the Study of Sport in Society; complete information on all the center's programs dedicated to promoting socially responsible changes in and through sports.

www.sportdiscus.com A comprehensive international database of sports and fitness information, containing more than 500,000 references, which can be searched by using subject-related keywords; this site provides direct links to additional websites that contain articles.

http://physed.otago.ac.nz/sosol Sociology of Sport Online: *sosol* is an international electronic forum that publishes articles and book reviews related to the sociological examination of sport, physical education, and coaching; it is hosted by the School of Physical Education at the University of Otago in New Zealand.

(Elise Amendola, AP/Wide World Photos)

Using Social Theories

How Can They Help Us Study Sports in Society?

IN THIS FRAGMENTED AGE, it often seems that only sports can bind together the nation—across its divides of class, race, and gender—in common cause and celebration. [Sports are] a prism through which we view some of our most complex [social] issues.

—**Mark Starr,** *Newsweek* **(1999)**

 Online Learning Center Resources

Visit *Sports in Society*'s Online Learning Center at **www.mhhe.com/coakley8e** for additional information and study material for this chapter, including

• Self-grading quizzes
• Learning objectives
• Related websites
• Additional readings

A complete outline is available online at
www.mhhe.com/coakley8e.

SPORTS ARE A TREMENDOUS force for the status quo. . . . They do distract millions from more serious thoughts—as do . . . all other "escape" entertainments. As mass entertainment, they are definitely antirevolutionary.

—Leonard Koppett, sports reporter and columnist (1994)

Those of us who study sports in society want to understand the social and cultural contexts in which sports exist and how those contexts are influenced by sports. We also want to understand the social worlds that people create in connection with sports and the experiences of individuals and groups associated with those social worlds. We are motivated by various combinations of curiosity, interests in sports, and concerns about social life and social issues. Most of us also want to use what we know about sports in society to promote social justice, expose and challenge the exploitive use of power, and empower people, so that they might resist and transform oppressive social conditions.

As we engage in this project of studying and changing sports, we use social and cultural theories to assist us. These theories help us identify issues and problems to study. They provide frameworks for asking research questions, interpreting information, and uncovering the deeper meanings and stories associated with sports in particular cultures. They also enable us to be more informed citizens as we apply what we learn in our research to the world in which we live. Because those of us who study sports in society come from many different academic backgrounds and because social life is so diverse and complex, we use a wide variety of theories to guide our work.

The three goals of this chapter are to

1. Identify and describe the theories that have been used most widely to study sports in society
2. Explain how various theories assist us in our efforts to understand sports as social phenomena as well as the society and culture in which we live
3. Outline how various theories lead us to see sports in different ways, take different types of action, and support different types of policies about sports in everyday life

WHAT ARE THEORIES AND WHY DO WE NEED THEM?

Whenever we ask why our social world is the way it is and then imagine how it might be changed, we are "theorizing" (hooks, 1992). Theorizing involves a combination of description, reflection, and analysis. When we theorize, we aren't required to use big words and complex sentences. In fact, the best theories are those we understand so clearly that they help us make sense out of the social world.

When we study sports in society, the best theories are the ones that describe and explain aspects of social life in terms that make sense and are logical and consistent with systematic observations of the social world. Theories developed by social scientists are useful because they provide frameworks that we can use to ask good sociological questions and then interpret information about the social world. When it comes to studying sports in society, theories enable us to see sports from new angles and perspectives, to understand more fully the relationship between sports and social life, and to make informed decisions about sports and sport participation in our lives, families, communities, and societies.

Many people think that theories don't have practical applications. This is not true. Most of our decisions and actions are based on our predictions of their possible consequences, and those predictions are based on our theories about social life. Our personal theories may be incomplete, poorly developed, based on limited information, and biased to fit our own needs, but we still use them to guide our behavior. When our theories are accurate, our predictions help us relate more effectively with others and control more directly what happens in our lives. When we make decisions about sports, formulate policies, or decide whether to fund or cut money from sport programs, we usually base decisions on our personal theories about sports and their connections to social life.

None of the theories discussed in this chapter is perfect, but each can be useful as we move beyond our limited personal perspectives and develop a more broadly informed set of ideas about sports in society. Theories about society and social life are based on a combination of systematic research and deductive logic. Ideally, they are presented in published books and articles, so that other people can evaluate, test, use, and revise them. Most theories are the products of more than one person. They may be refined and improved over time as people test them in research, or they may be abandoned as people discover that they are not very useful in their efforts to understand social life.

Theories of all types are very important in our lives. They help us ask questions, seek answers, make decisions, take action, and evaluate what we do. Without theories, we lack the frameworks we need to make sense out of life and to learn from our experiences.

Six major theories have been used to study sports in society:

- Functionalist theory
- Conflict theory
- Interactionist theory
- Critical theories
- Feminist theories
- Figurational theory

Although there are important differences among them, there are many points at which two or more of them converge and overlap. This is because people read and respond to the ideas of others as they do research and develop their own ideas about society and social life. Therefore, even though I will summarize these six theories in separate sections, we should remember that all social theories are fluid, changing sets of ideas about how social worlds work. They are *not* completely separate frameworks that have nothing in common with each other (Calhoun, 1998) but each theory gives us a different perspective for imagining and studying the many complex connections between sports and society.

As each theory is discussed in the chapter, there are sections that cover the following: a brief overview of the theory, examples of the ideas and research that have been inspired by the theory, explanations of how the theory can be used as we take actions and make policies about sports in our everyday lives, and an overview of the major weaknesses of the theory. Table 2.1 provides a summary of each theory and how it helps us understand sports in society. The table contains a large amount of material. It may look confusing at first, but, as you read through the chapter, you will find it to be a useful reference guide to each theory. Most important, it will help you identify and understand similarities and differences among the theories.

FUNCTIONALIST THEORY: WHAT DO SPORTS CONTRIBUTE TO SOCIETY?

Functionalist theory is based on the assumption that it is possible to study society, discover scientific "truths" about how societies operate, and then develop a system of "social laws," which we might use to understand, control, and even change societies for the better. Those using functionalist theory view society as an organized system of interrelated parts held together by shared values and social processes that transcend differences and promote consensus among people.

According to functionalist theory, the driving force underlying all social life is the tendency for any social system to maintain itself in a state of balance, so that it continues to operate efficiently. This balance is achieved "naturally" as people develop consensus, common values, and coordinated organization in the major spheres of social life, such as the family, education, the economy, the media, politics, religion, leisure, and sport.

When sociologists use functionalist theory to explain how a society, community, school, family, sport team, or other social system works, they

Table 2.1   Using social theories to study sports in society: a summary and comparison

Functionalist Theory	Conflict Theory	Interactionist Theory
ASSUMPTIONS ABOUT THE BASIS FOR SOCIAL ORDER IN SOCIETY		
Social order is based on consensus and shared values, which hold the interrelated parts of society together. All social systems tend toward a state of balance.	Social order is based on economic interests and the use of economic power to exploit labor. Social class shapes social structures and relationships.	Social order is created from the bottom up as people interact with each other. Social life is grounded in social relationships.
MAJOR CONCERNS IN THE STUDY OF SOCIETY		
How do individual parts of social systems contribute to the satisfaction of major system needs and the overall operation of the system?	How is economic power distributed and used in society? What are the dynamics of social class relations? Who is privileged and exploited in class relations?	How are meanings, identities, and culture created through social interaction? How do people define the reality of their own lives and the world around them?
MAJOR CONCERNS IN THE STUDY OF SPORT		
How does sport fit into social life and contribute to social stability and efficiency? How does sport participation influence personal and social development?	How does sport reflect class relations? How is sport used to maintain the interests of those with power and wealth in society? How has the profit motive distorted sport?	How do people become involved in sports, become defined as athletes, derive meaning from participation, and make transitions out of sports into the rest of their lives?
MAJOR CONCLUSIONS ABOUT THE SPORT-SOCIETY RELATIONSHIP		
Sport is a valuable social institution, which benefits society as well as individuals in society. Sport is a source of inspiration on both personal and social levels.	Sport is a form of physical activity that is distorted by the needs of capital. Sport is an opiate that distracts attention away from the problems that affect those without economic power.	Sports are forms of culture created through social interaction. Sport participation is grounded in the decisions made by people in connection with their identities and their relationships.
SOCIAL ACTION AND POLICY IMPLICATIONS		
Develop and expand sport programs that promote traditional values, build character, and contribute to order and stability in society.	Raise class consciousness and make people aware of their own alienation and powerlessness. Eliminate profit motives in sports and allow sports to foster expression, creativity, and physical well-being.	Allow individuals to shape sports to fit their definitions of reality. Make sport organizations more open and democratic. Focus on the culture and organization of sports when trying to control deviance in sports.
MAJOR WEAKNESSES		
It does not acknowledge that sports are social constructions. It overstates the positive consequences of sports. It ignores that sports serve the needs of some people more than others.	It ignores that sports can be sites for creative and liberating experiences. It overstates the influence of economic forces in society. It assumes that people who have economic power shape sports to meet their interests.	It fails to explain how meaning, identity, and interaction are related to social structures and material conditions in society. It ignores issues of power and power relations in society.

Critical Theories	Feminist Theories	Figurational Theory
Social order is negotiated through struggles over ideology, representation, and power. Social life is full of diversity, complexities, and contradictions.	Social order is based primarily on the values, experiences, and interests of men with power. Social life is gendered and based on patriarchal ideas.	Social order is based on interdependencies among individuals and groups. Connections between people take the form of social figurations.
How is cultural ideology produced, reproduced, and transformed? What are the conflicts and problems that affect the lives of those who lack power in society?	How is gender ideology produced, reproduced, and transformed? How do dominant forms of gender relations privilege men over women and some men over others?	How do social figurations emerge and change? How do power balances within figurations influence relationships between individuals and groups?
How are power relations reproduced and/or resisted in and through sports? Whose voices are or are not represented in the narratives and images that constitute sports?	How are sports gendered activities and how do they reproduce dominant ideas about gender in society? What are the strategies for resisting and transforming sport forms that privilege men?	How did modern sports emerge and become so important in society? What are the social processes associated with the commercialization of sports, expressions of violence in sports, and forms of global sports?
Sports are social constructions. Sports are sites where culture is produced, reproduced, and transformed. Sports are cultural practices that repress and/or empower people.	Sports are grounded in the values and experiences of powerful men in society. Sports reproduce male power and distorted ideas about masculinity. Sports produce gendered ideas about physicality, sexuality, and the body.	Sports are exciting activities that relieve boredom and control violence and uncivilized behavior. Sports celebrate masculinity and male power. Global sports are complex activities with local and national significance.
Use sports as sites for challenging and transforming forms of exploitation and oppression. Increase the range and diversity of sport participation opportunities. Challenge the voices and perspectives of those with power.	Use sports as sites for challenging and transforming oppressive forms of gender relations. Expose and resist homophobia and misogyny in sports. Transform sports to emphasize partnership over domination.	Develop a fund of valid knowledge, which can be used to enable people to control expressions of violence, exploitation, and the abuse of power. Increase access to sport participation among those who have lacked power through history.
They have no clear guidelines for identifying and assessing forms of resistance and the value of ideas and actions across situations. They have no unified strategies for dealing with problems, conflicts, and injustice.	They have no clear guidelines for identifying and assessing forms of resistance and the value of ideas and actions across situations. They give little attention to connections between gender and some other categories of experience.	It gives too little attention to problems and struggles that affect day-to-day lives. It understates the immediate personal consequences of oppressive power relations. It gives little attention to the experiences of women and to gender inequities.

focus attention on how each part in the system contributes to the system's overall operation. For example, if Canadian society is the system being studied, a person using functionalist theory is concerned with how the Canadian family, economy, government, educational system, media, religion, and sport are related to each other and how they work together in contributing to the smooth operation of the society as a whole. An analysis based on functionalism focuses on how each of these spheres of social life helps keep the larger social system operating efficiently.

According to functionalist theory, social systems operate smoothly when they have efficient, built-in mechanisms for doing four things: (1) socializing people to learn and accept important cultural values, (2) promoting social connections between people, (3) motivating people to achieve cultural goals through accepted methods, and (4) protecting the system from disruptive outside influences. Functionalists assume that, if these four "system needs" are satisfied, social order will be maintained and everyone will benefit. The first column in table 2.1 (pp. 36–37) summarized functionalist theory.

Functionalist Theory and Research on Sport

Functionalist theory usually inspires discussions and research about how sport as a social institution fits into social life and contributes to stability and social progress in organizations, communities, and societies. In fact, people have often used functionalist theory to guide their thinking as they study many of the issues discussed in the following chapters of this book. Examples include the following:

1. Do sports and sport participation influence social and personal development? This issue is discussed in chapters 4 through 7, 14, and 15.
2. Do sports and sport participation foster the development of social bonds and relationships in groups, communities, and

societies? This issue is discussed in chapters 9, 10, 13, and 14.
3. Does playing sports have a positive impact on success in school and work and does it teach people to follow social rules as they strive for success? This issue is discussed in chapters 4, 6, 7, 10, and 14.
4. Do sports contribute to health and wellness and the strength of society as a whole? This issue is discussed in chapters 7 and 13.

Functionalist theory focuses attention on how sports help keep societies, communities, organizations, and groups operating smoothly, as well as how they influence individuals to contribute to the social systems in which they participate. This is why a functionalist approach is often popular among people who have a vested interest in preserving the status quo in society. These people want sociologists to tell them how sport contributes to the smooth operation of the societies, communities, organizations, and groups in which they live. Many people like functionalist theory because it fits with how they have learned to view the social world and because it leads to the conclusion that sport is a source of inspiration for individuals and societies.

Using Functionalist Theory in Everyday Life

Many people around the world use popularized forms of functionalist theory to make decisions about sports and sport programs at national and local levels. A functionalist approach leads people to promote the development and growth of organized youth sports (to build values), to fund varsity sports in high schools and colleges (to promote organizational loyalty and attachments to schools), to develop sport opportunities for girls and women (to increase achievement motivation among girls and women), to include sports in military training (to increase military preparedness and the fitness of soldiers), and to fund and televise the Olympic Games (to build international goodwill and unity).

One assumption underlying functionalist theory is that social order depends on consensus and common values. Functionalists assume that established social institutions, including the institution of sport, contribute to consensus and common values. (USA Volleyball)

Functionalist theory leads people to promote changes in sport that emphasize what they see as traditional values in society. If individualism, competition, and success were important values in society, a person using functionalist theory would call for changes leading to increases in individual achievement, winning records, and overall participation in competitive sports. Since functionalist theory generally leads to the conclusion that sport builds the kind of character valued in the society as a whole, it also leads to policy recommendations for more organized competitive programs, more structured sport experiences, more supervision of athletes, more coaching education programs, more training centers for top-level athletes, and increased surveillance and drug testing to control disruptive

deviance among athletes. In the case of youth sports, for example, functionalist theory would emphasize actions to increase developmental sport programs, coaching certification requirements, and a sport system that promotes success at elite levels of competition. Functionalist theory leads people to look for and do research on how sports contribute to the development of individuals and society as a whole.

Since many people use a "systems model" to understand how the social world works, their view of sports fits with functionalist theory. In other words, they assume that society is held together by shared values, and they see sport as a part of social life that contributes to the order and stability of society. This is the viewpoint that many students have when they take courses in the sociology of sport, and it leads many of them to feel comfortable with questions, ideas, and research based on functionalist theory and to be uncomfortable with questions, ideas, and research based on other theoretical approaches.

People with power and influence in a society also favor functionalist theory because it provides guidance for maintaining society the way it is. People with power and influence like to keep things the way they are, so that their power and influence can be preserved.

Because the functionalist approach is so widely used in popular explanations, everyday discussions, and media coverage of sports in society, it is important for us to know its weaknesses.

Weaknesses of Functionalist Theory

Functionalist theory has three major weaknesses when it is used to study sports in society. First, it does not acknowledge that sports are social constructions that take many forms as they are created and defined by people interacting with each other. Functionalists talk about sport instead of sports. This is because they see sport as a relatively stable social institution that serves specific functions in societies. Such an approach generally leads people to overlook the diversity of sports, the extent to which sports promote the interests of powerful and wealthy people, and the possibility that sports may sometimes produce or reproduce outcomes that upset the smooth functioning of society.

Second, functionalist theory leads to overstatements about the positive effects and understatements about the negative effects of sports in society. For example, functionalist theory would not help us understand that the emphasis on physical power and the domination of opponents that is so common in many sports has worked to the disadvantage of women in society. Nor would it help us understand how varsity sport teams in high schools and colleges may actually undermine social integration and lead some students to feel marginalized in their schools because of status systems that favor varsity athletes.

" YA KNOW, I CAN'T RELATE TO THESE KIDS' MUSIC ANYMORE, BUT AT LEAST I KNOW WE'LL ALWAYS HAVE SPORTS IN COMMON."

FIGURE 2.1 This man is making the functionalist assumption that sport is grounded in common values and unite people in a society. However, this cartoon suggests that many young people view sports as diverse social constructions that do not link them with many older people in society.

Third, functionalist theory is based on the assumption that the needs of all groups within a society are the same as the needs of the society as a whole. This causes us to underestimate the existence of differences and conflicts of interest within a society and to ignore cases in which sports benefit some groups more than others (see figure 2.1). This limits our understanding of difference, conflict, and the dynamics of change in societies. Conflict theory has been used by those who are interested in these issues.

CONFLICT THEORY: ARE SPORTS ALL ABOUT MONEY AND ECONOMIC POWER?

Conflict theory is based on the ideas of Karl Marx. People using conflict theory view society as a system of social structures and relationships, which are shaped ultimately by economic forces. In other words, society is shaped and organized around money, wealth, and economic power.

Conflict theorists assume that social life revolves around economic interests and that people use their economic power to coerce and manipulate others to accept their view of the world as the correct view. This means that those using conflict theory are concerned with **class relations**—that is, social processes that revolve around who has economic power, how that power is used, and who is advantaged or disadvantaged by the economic organization of society. Studies of class relations focus on the consequences of social inequality and the processes of change in society.

The main goal of conflict theory is similar to the main goal of functionalist theory: to develop a general theory about how society operates as a system. Thus, conflict theory is designed to show that economic power in capitalist societies is entrenched so deeply that progressive changes are possible only if people without economic power become aware of the need for change and take action to make major changes in the organization of the economy and society.

Conflict theorists assume that dominant forms of sport in a society ultimately promote the interests of people with money and economic power. Sport in all its forms, they argue, focuses the emotions and attention of the have-nots in society on escapist spectator events, which distract them from the need to change the economy. In fact, sport, especially spectator sport, is organized and sponsored by those with money and economic power in an effort to affirm the capitalist values of competition, production, and consumption. Thus, conflict theorists see sport as an opiate in society, as activities and spectacles that deaden awareness of economic exploitation among those without power while perpetuating the privilege and position of those who control wealth and the economy.

Conflict Theory and Research on Sport

Conflict theory usually inspires discussions and research about how sport perpetuates the power and privilege of elite groups in society, as well as how sport serves as a tool of economic exploitation and oppression. Those using conflict

theory have studied and discussed the following issues:

1. How and when do athletes become alienated from their own bodies? This issue is discussed in chapters 4 through 7.
2. How does sport contribute to the existence of socioeconomic inequality in society? This issue is discussed in many chapters—especially chapters 8 through 11.
3. How do the processes of commercialization change sport and influence social relationships in society? This issue is discussed in chapters 10 through 13.
4. How do people with economic power use sport to further their own interests? This issue is discussed in chapters 10 through 13.

Conflict theory focuses attention on how powerful people use sports to promote attitudes and relationships that enable them to maintain power and privilege. Like functionalist theory, it is based on the assumption that social life is driven and shaped by specific societal needs, although conflict theory emphasizes the "needs of capital" rather than the general "needs of social systems."

Conflict theory also focuses attention on how sports reflect and perpetuate the unequal distribution of power and economic resources in societies. This leads to an emphasis on the negative consequences of sports and the conclusion that radical changes are needed in sports and society as a whole. According to conflict theorists, the goal of these changes is to bring about the development of a humane and creative society, so that sport can become a source of expression, creative energy, and physical well-being.

Most people in countries with capitalist economies are not comfortable with the assumptions and conclusions of conflict theory. They say that the negative tone of conflict theory does not fit with their ideas about sports or society, and they are uneasy with conclusions that threaten the current structure and organization of sports and society. However, conflict theory has been very useful in calling attention to important economic issues in sports and to forms of inequality that create conflict and tensions in society as a whole.

Using Conflict Theory in Everyday Life

Conflict theory focuses attention on economic factors, class inequality, and the need for changes in how society and sports are organized. These changes emphasize making athletes and spectators aware of how they are manipulated and oppressed for the profit and personal gain of the economic elite in society.

Conflict theory often leads to the conclusion that problems exist in sports because those who participate in sports have no effective control over the conditions of their participation. Therefore, those who favor this approach would support policies and programs that regulate or eliminate economic profit motives in sport, and they would promote the idea that athletes should have more control over sports and the conditions of sports participation. They would call for more emphasis on play and less emphasis on business, so that sports participation could become more liberating and empowering for a greater number of people. They would favor players' unions, as well as organizations that represent the interests of fans and people in communities where large amounts of public money are used to subsidize wealthy team owners.

Actions and policies inspired by conflict theory would emphasize the material conditions of those who lack money and power and the need for radical changes in the overall organization of sports. These actions and policies would discourage the development and growth of spectator sports and would promote the idea that physical games should be for the players themselves. Finally, these actions and policies would promote new sports organized at the grassroots level for fun and would promote doing away with sports organized by people with money for economic profit.

> Today, sports has come to pit race against race, men against women, city against city, class against class, and coach against player.
>
> —Frank Deford, sportswriter (1998)

Weaknesses of Conflict Theory

Conflict theory has three major weaknesses. First, it ignores the possibility that sports can be sites for experiences that empower individuals and groups in capitalist societies. Conflict theorists talk about sport as always being organized to maximize the control that wealthy people have over everyone else in capitalist societies. They see sport as a site where people learn to define their bodies as tools of production and then become alienated from their bodies in the process. They do not acknowledge that sport can take forms that might serve the interests of people with little power or wealth in society. Such an approach generally leads people to overlook cases in which sport participation is a personally creative and liberating experience, or a means of challenging the interests of economically powerful groups and transforming social life in progressive ways.

Second, conflict theory assumes that all social life is driven and shaped by economic factors, by the needs of capital in society. It focuses on the relationship between the economic haves and have-nots, and it assumes that the haves always use their power to control and exploit the have-nots. It also assumes that the have-nots live in a state of powerlessness and alienation. These assumptions lead people who use conflict theory to focus exclusively on economic factors when they study sports. However, many sports, especially those emphasizing recreation and mass participation, cannot be explained totally in terms of economic interests or economic power in society.

Third, conflict theory underestimates the importance of gender, race, ethnicity, age, sexual orientation, and other factors when it comes to explaining how people identify themselves, relate to others, and organize social life. Instead, it emphasizes that history and social organization revolve around economic factors. Therefore, those who use conflict theory to study sports often overlook the possibility that inequalities in society are based also in forms of social relations that are not shaped exclusively by struggles revolving around social class and economic differences.

Beyond the Needs of Society

Functionalist theory and conflict theory both focus on societal needs and how sports are related to the satisfaction of those needs. In a sense, they give us a picture of sports in society from the top down. They do not tell us much about sports in everyday life or how people create sports and the overall society in which they live. They ignore a view of society from the bottom up, from the perspectives of people who "do" sports and give meaning to sports as parts of their everyday lives. They also ignore the complexities of everyday social life and the fact that sports and society are social constructions that emerge in connection with multiple struggles over what is important in people's lives. The theories that focus attention on various aspects of these issues are the interactionist, critical, and feminist theories.

INTERACTIONIST THEORY: HOW DO PEOPLE EXPERIENCE SPORTS?

Interactionist theory focuses on issues related to meaning, identity, social relationships, and subcultures in sports. It is based on the idea that human behavior involves choices and that choices are based on the definitions of reality that people form as they interact with others.

According to interactionist theory, we humans do not simply respond in an automatic fashion to the world around us. Instead, we actively make decisions about our behavior based on the consequences that we think our behavior will have on our lives, the people around us, and the social world in which we live. Furthermore, as we interact with others, we create culture and society.

According to interactionist theory, our ability to reflect on and assess our decisions and actions enables us to develop a sense of who we are and how we are connected to the social world. This sense of who we are in the social world is our **identity.** Identities are key factors as people interact with each other and construct their social worlds. In other words, identity is a basis for self-direction and self-control in our lives. Identity is never formed permanently, because it emerges out of our relationships, and our relationships are constantly changing as we meet new people, as people change, and as we face new situations.

Research based on interactionist theory helps us understand how human beings define and give meaning to themselves, their decisions and actions, and the world around them. It also helps us understand how those meanings are connected with identity and social interaction. Therefore, when people use interactionist theory, they study human beings as choice makers and creators of meaning, identity, and relationships; they do research that focuses on "seeing" the world through the eyes of the people they observe, interview, and interact with. They often do studies of particular groups of people or identifiable cultures, and they try to understand them from inside, from the perspectives of the people themselves. In a sense, they view society from the bottom up rather than the top down.

Interactionist Theory and Research on Sports

Interactionist theory usually inspires discussions and research about the experiences of athletes and how the athletes define and make sense out of their participation in sports. A common goal of interactionist research is to reconstruct and describe the reality that exists in the minds of athletes, coaches, spectators, and others involved with sports in society.

Interactionists use research methodologies designed to gather information about how people see their social worlds and their connections

Interactionists study the meanings and identities associated with sports and sport participation. Meanings associated with youth sports vary from one cultural setting to another, as do the lessons players learn in connection with participation. (Jay Coakley)

to those worlds. Therefore, they do studies that involve participant observation and in-depth interviews. These are the best methods for understanding how people define situations and use those definitions to form identities and make choices about their behavior.

Those who use interactionist theory have focused on the following issues:

1. What are the social processes through which people become involved in sports?
2. How do people come to define themselves and be defined by others as athletes?
3. How do people give meaning to and derive meaning from their experiences in sports?
4. What happens when people retire from sports and make the transition into the rest of their lives?
5. What are the characteristics of sport cultures, how are they created by the people involved in sports, and how do they influence identities and actions on and off the field?

One or more of these issues are discussed in all chapters. They are also discussed in various ways

in many other chapters. This is because I feel that interactionist research provides vivid descriptions of sports experiences, which we can use to understand human action and social life.[1]

Using Interactionist Theory in Everyday Life

Interactionist theory focuses on the meanings and interaction associated with sports and sport participation. It emphasizes the complexity of human action and the need to understand action in terms of how people associated with sports define situations through their relationships with others.

Those using interactionist theory would call for changes in sports that more fully represent the perspectives and identities of those who play sports. This could involve restructuring sports

---

[1]Peter Donnelly and I edited a book entitled *Inside Sports* (1999), in which examples of this type of research are described specifically for students interested in studying sports to learn about the social world.

organizations, so that all participants have opportunities to raise issues about the purposes and conditions of sport participation. Therefore, interactionists would support sport organizations that are open and democratic.

For example, in the case of youth sports, those using interactionist theory would call for changes in games that reflect the needs and interests of children, rather than the needs and interests of adults. They would caution parents and coaches about problems that occur when young people develop identities and relationships that overemphasize sports to the exclusion of other identities and relationships. In the case of other sports, they would call for changes that discourage athletes from defining pain and injury as normal parts of the sport experience. They would see the use of performance-enhancing substances as connected with identity and sport cultures, and they would argue that controlling the use of these substances demands changes in the norms and culture of sports. They would say that identifying users as "bad apples" and punishing them as individuals will not change the culture in which athletes learn to sacrifice their own bodies for the sake of the team and their sport.

Weaknesses of Interactionist Theory

Interactionist theory has inspired many informative studies of meaning, identity, interaction, and cultures in sports. However, it has weaknesses. First, it focuses our attention almost exclusively on relationships and personal definitions of reality without explaining how interaction processes and the construction of meaning in sports are related to social structures and material conditions in society. Interactionist research has generally ignored connections between sport experiences and sport cultures, on the one hand, and the systems of power and inequality that exist in societies, communities, organizations, families, and small groups on the other hand. Therefore, interactionist theory does not tell us much about how sports and sport experiences are related to

issues of power and power relations in society as a whole. Second, interactionist theory does not provide us with a critical vision of what society could and should be when it comes to social organization.

Issues of power and critical visions of what society could and should be are central concerns among people who use *critical* and *feminist theories*.

CRITICAL THEORIES: HOW ARE SPORTS INVOLVED IN CREATING AND CHANGING CULTURE AND SOCIAL RELATIONS?

Most people who study sports in society today use critical theories. Although critical theories take many forms, they focus primarily on explanations of culture, power, and social relations.[2] They consist of various approaches

---

[2]Because this chapter is written as a basic introduction to using theories, I present "critical theories" as a general category. My goal is to give a brief, general description of the valuable analyses being done by those engaged in critically analyzing sports in society. Therefore, I attempt to pull together major ideas from the following theories and theoretical frameworks: *neo-Marxist theories*, *traditional critical theory* (combining ideas of Marx and Freud), *hegemony theory* (based on the ideas of Italian political theorist Antonio Gramsci), *cultural studies* (based on ideas about culture, power, and ideology as they are contested and struggled over in everyday life), *feminist theories* (primarily those informed by critical theory, cultural studies, or poststructuralism), *poststructuralism* (based on cultural studies, semiotics, and forms of literary analysis dealing with language and the construction of power, meaning, representation, and consciousness under the unstable, fluid, fragmented, and often contradictory conditions of postmodern life), and *queer theory* (combining feminist cultural studies and poststructuralism). Of course, none of these frameworks is done justice in my summary. However, my goal is to highlight the exciting issues and questions that various scholars have discussed and analyzed while using one or more of these critical theoretical approaches, as well as to give you a basis for entering these discussions and analyses and learning more about sports, culture, and society in the process.

REFLECT ON
SPORTS

Sports Are More Than Reflections of Society

When people study the social aspects of sports, they often say that "sports are reflections of society." This idea is helpful to someone who is just beginning to think about sports as parts of society and culture. However, it is not very helpful to those of us who want to do in-depth studies of sports. The problem with assuming that sports are reflections of society can be demonstrated by shifting our attention away from sports and to another sphere of social life, such as the family.

Like sports, families are reflections of society, but our personal experience tells us that everyday family life is more than that. Families are the creations of people interacting with one another in many ways, depending on their abilities, resources, power, and definitions of family life. Of course, the opportunities and choices available to the members of any particular family are influenced by factors in the larger society, including laws; economic conditions; government policies; general beliefs about how husbands, wives, parents, and children should relate to one another; and even the words we use when we talk about families. This means that there are similarities among many families in the same society, but it does not mean that all families are destined to be the same or to be mere reflections of society.

Society serves as a context in which individuals produce, define, and reproduce specific family practices. Families are not shaped by society. In reality, they are sets of relationships that are produced by people in society. This is why each family has its own unique way of life. People create families, and they reproduce or challenge ideas about family every day as they go about their lives.

At times, families become sites (social locations) for raising questions about how family life should be organized. Some of these questions force people to rethink larger issues related to cultural values and the organization of society as a whole. In this way, what we do in our families becomes part of a general process of cultural production, the impact of which goes far beyond family life. For example, during the midtwentieth century, when people in the United States asked questions about individual rights, marriage, and family, there were discussions that ultimately led to changes in divorce laws. These and other discussions also encouraged

designed to understand where power comes from, how it operates in social life, and how it shifts and changes as people struggle over the many issues that affect their lives and their relationships with each other (McDonald and Birrell, 1999; Tomlinson, 1998).

Critical theories also offer a range of explanations of the following: (1) how culture is produced and reproduced, (2) how power relations operate in the processes of cultural production and reproduction, and (3) how people struggle over the ideas and meanings they use to make sense out of the world, form identities, interact with others, and transform the conditions of their lives.

People using functionalist and conflict theories often say, "Sport is a reflection of society,"

but those using critical theories explain that sports are much more than that. They say that sports are social places (sites) where society and culture are produced and reproduced, and this makes them much more important than they would be if they were mere reflections of society. This issue is discussed in the box "Sports Are More Than Reflections of Society."

Unlike people who use functionalist or conflict theory, those using critical theories do not believe that it is possible to discover a universal explanation of social life, which we can use to understand all societies at all points in the past, present, and future. In fact, they feel that such a goal inevitably leads us to ignore the diversity, complexity, contradictions, and changes that are people to rethink their ideas about intimate relationships, gender, women's rights, parent-child relationships, children's rights, and even the ways in which community social services should be organized and delivered. In other words, families have always been much more than reflections of society. They are the creations of human beings, as well as sites for producing and transforming the ways of life that constitute culture.

This means that human beings are agents in the construction of social worlds—not just in their immediate family lives but also in the larger social settings in which they live. Through the things they do in their families, people produce and reproduce the culture and society of which they are a part.

So it is with sports and all of those associated with sports. Sports are more than reflections of society. They are constructed as people interact with one another. No voice comes out of the sky and says, "I am society, and this is the way sports should be." Of course, social conditions have an impact on the structure and dynamics of sports, but, within the parameters set by those conditions, people can change sports or keep them the way they are. In fact, it is even possible for

people to create and define sports in ways that differ from or even defy dominant ideas and norms and, in the process, to turn sports into sites for the transformation of the very culture of which they are a part.

This is a helpful way of thinking about sports in society. It recognizes that sports can have both positive and negative effects on participants, that people define and create sports in their own lives, and that sports are involved in reproducing culture as well as standing in opposing and transforming it.

This means that sports are very important in a sociological sense. Instead of being mirrors that simply reflect society, they are the actual "social stuff" out of which society and culture come to be what they are. When we understand this, we become aware of our capacity as agents of social and cultural production. This awareness helps us realize that we are not destined to do sports in a particular way or define sports as they are defined in the images promoted by Coca-Cola, Nike, or Budweiser. We can create culture and sports, if we make the effort. *What do you think?*

• •

inherent in all forms of social life. Furthermore, they realize that there are many perspectives and standpoints from which to study and understand social life and that the search for general social laws or social truths about society and social life is fruitless. This makes them very different from those who use functionalist and conflict theories, even though they may borrow ideas from these theories as they extend and revise their own ideas.

According to critical theories, the relationship between sports and society is never set once and for all time: sports change as historical conditions and political and economic forces change. Sports change with new developments in government, education, the media, religion,

and the family. Sports change with new ideas about masculinity and femininity, race, ethnicity, age, sexual orientation, and physical ability. And sports change with new ways of thinking and talking that offer visions of culture and social life, which people use to make sense of the world around them.

Critical theories are also about action and political involvement. All critical theories have grown out of desires among social scientists to identify issues and problems and to make social life more fair, democratic, and open to diversity. Critical theories have been valuable tools in identifying and studying specific social problems and in thinking about and putting into action practical programs and processes that eliminate oppression and exploitation and promote equity, fairness, and openness.

Most people who use critical theories are interested in explaining that all social relationships are grounded in political struggles over how social life should be defined and organized. They realize that dominant forms of sports in most societies have been socially constructed in ways that systematically and arbitrarily privilege some people over others. Their goals are to study and explain all the ways that this occurs, to expose them, and to inspire new ways of talking about, defining, organizing, and playing sports.

Critical Theories and Research on Sports

Critical theories are diverse and deal with many dimensions of our lives. Therefore, they have inspired and guided a wide range of discussions and research on sports in society.

Those who use critical theories to study sports generally focus on one or more of the following issues:

1. Whose ideas about the meaning and organization of sports are most important when it comes to determining what sports will be funded, who will participate in them, how they will be covered in the media, and how they will be used for social, political, and economic purposes?
2. How are sports and sport experiences (as parts of culture) tied to various forms of power relations in society and to overall processes of social development?
3. When do sports reproduce systems of power and privilege and whom do sports privilege or disadvantage in society?
4. How are sports related to popular ideas about economic success or failure, work and fun, physical health and well-being, gender, race and ethnicity, sexual orientation, physical ability and disability, and what is natural or "deviant" in society?
5. What are the ways that people struggle over the organization and meanings of sports in their lives?
6. When do sports become sites for challenging, resisting, and even transforming how social life is organized?
7. What are the narratives and images that people use to construct sports and to connect sports and sport experiences to their lives and to culture in general?
8. Whose voices are represented and whose perspectives are used to frame how we think and talk about sports and whose voices and perspectives are not represented?
9. How might systems of power relations, as well as everyday narratives and images, be disrupted and transformed to give voice to those who lack power and representation in societies, communities, organizations, or groups?

One or more of these issues are discussed in each chapter in this book. I give priority to these issues because I think that critical theories inspire the most interesting and provocative discussions and analyses of sports in society. Research guided by critical theories emphasizes that sports are more than mere reflections of society. This research is based on the assumptions that sports have never been developed in a neatly ordered, rational manner and that there are no simple or general rules for explaining sports as social phenomena. The intent of research based on critical theories is to expose how the structure, organization, and meaning of sports vary with changing relationships in and between groups that possess different amounts of power and resources over time and from one social setting to another.

Critical theorists also study how sports affect the processes through which people develop and maintain **cultural ideology**—that is, the interrelated orientations and beliefs they use to explain what happens in their lives. Critical theorists want to know how and when sports become sites for questioning, opposing, and challenging dominant forms of cultural ideology and for transforming how people see and interpret the social world around them. One of the mottos of critical theorists (see Hargreaves and MacDonald, 2000) is a statement made by C. L. R. James, a native of the West Indies, who learned to play cricket after the British colonized his homeland. James said, "What do they know of cricket who only cricket know?" (James, 1984, preface). Critical theorists would answer this question by saying, "We know nothing about sports if sports is all we know." In other words, if we want to know about sports, we must also know about the social and cultural contexts in which they exist.

Using Critical Theories in Everyday Life

Critical theories are based on concerns for fairness and desires to understand, confront, and transform systems of exploitation and oppression in social life. They lead to concerns about how sports either reproduce or transform the societies in which they exist.

Those using critical theories emphasize that changes in sports depend on more than simply shifting the control of sports to the participants themselves. They note that many people are aware of who controls sports in their societies and have learned to accept those systems of control and to define them as correct. Therefore, policies based on critical theories would usually call for an increase in the number and diversity of sport participation alternatives available in society. The goal of such policies would be to provide people with opportunities to participate in many sports and, in the process, create the critical abilities that could lead to progressive transformations in their relationships, organizations, communities, and societies.

Critical theorists also raise questions about the stories told about sports in a culture. They challenge those whose voices and perspectives dominate those stories, and they make space for voices that have been silenced and for perspectives that are not represented in those stories.

Critical theories force us to question what sports are and to think of what they might be from a variety of standpoints and perspectives. This can be either exciting or threatening, depending on your willingness to see sports in new and different ways.

Weaknesses of Critical Theories

There are many variations of critical theories, so it is difficult to neatly summarize their weaknesses. However, there are general weaknesses across the variations.

First, most critical theories do not provide clear guidelines for determining when sports reproduce dominant forms of social relations in society and when they become sites for resisting and transforming social relations. Although research based on critical theories has focused on cases in which sports are sites for resistance, it has not identified general guidelines for promoting the forms of resistance that lead to social transformations in sports or social relations. This is partly because most critical theorists give a higher priority to analyzing problems and taking political action to promote change than they do to building a general theory of social life. They say that all knowledge and truth depend on the cultural and social perspective through which they are constructed. Therefore, different problems and conflicts always call for different strategies and different forms of intervention. Of course, this can be a useful approach when dealing with a particular problem, conflict, or injustice, but it does not encourage the building of social theories that might be useful across many different situations.

Second, because critical theories emphasize resistance and transgression, there is a tendency among those who use them to see value in all resistant discourses and all actions that do not conform to dominant norms, especially when they represent the interests of marginalized people in

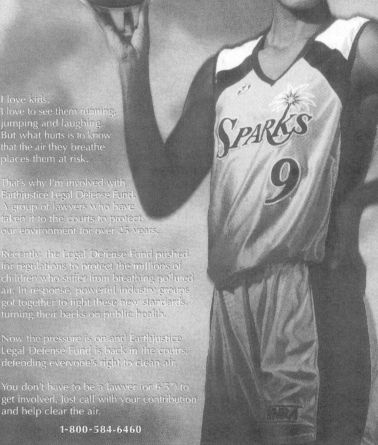

Critical theories call attention to the possibility that sports can be sites for transforming social life. WNBA player Lisa Leslie supported cultural transformation when she endorsed EARTHJUSTICE Legal Defense Fund in the late 1990s. (Provided by EARTHJUSTICE)

society. However, it is clear that dominant norms are not always unfair or oppressive and that the voices and perspectives of some marginalized and disadvantaged groups are not based on concerns about fairness, liberation, and tolerance of differences. It is important to respect the voices and creative potential of marginalized and oppressed groups, but it is not politically or morally wise to assume that the contributions made by all groups have equal value when it comes to transforming social life. Many critical theorists have not identified criteria to prioritize ideas and interventions that have an impact on people's lives. Therefore, they have a difficult time assessing the social and moral value of ideas and actions from one situation to the next.

Third, critical theories are so diverse that it is often difficult to understand their similarities and differences. Some use vocabularies that are confusing and that interfere with merging different critical ideas into more useful frameworks for social intervention and social change. Fortunately, some critical theorists are aware of this weakness and advocate coordinated critical analyses that reveal the dynamics of power relations in various cultural contexts and that can serve as a basis for effective forms of social intervention (McDonald and Birrell, 1999).

FEMINIST THEORIES: WHAT ARE THE CONNECTIONS BETWEEN GENDER AND SPORTS?

Feminist theories represent a diverse set of interpretive frameworks. However, they are all based on the assumption that, if we want to understand people's actions and social life, we must understand the meanings that people give to gender and the ways that those meanings are incorporated into social experience and the organization of society.

Feminist theories in all disciplines grew out of a general dissatisfaction with the intellectual traditions that base knowledge on the values and experiences of men and ignore women or do not take seriously the experiences and insights of women. Feminist theories are grounded in the awareness that women have been systematically devalued and oppressed in many societies and that there is a need to develop political strategies to eliminate oppression and to empower women to transform the cultures in which they are devalued.

Critical feminist theories are used by many people in the sociology of sport. Critical feminists are concerned primarily with issues of power and the dynamics of gender relations in social life. They give close attention to how gender relations privilege men over women and some men over other men (see figure 2.2). They study how gender ideology (i.e., ideas about masculinity and femininity) is formed, reproduced, resisted, and transformed in and through the everyday experiences of men and women.

Critical feminist approaches to sports in society are based on the assumption that sports are *gendered activities*. In other words, the meaning,

"HOW CAN FEMINISTS SAY THAT SPORTS ARE BASED ON THE VALUES AND INTERESTS OF MEN WITH POWER?"

FIGURE 2.2   The man in this cartoon does not agree with feminist theorists who argue that dominant sports are organized to reproduce cultural ideas that work to the advantage of men with power and influence in society. However, research on gender and sports is supportive of the ideas of feminists.

organization, and purpose of sports are grounded in the values and experiences of men and are defined to celebrate the attributes and skills associated with dominant forms of masculinity in society (Birrell, 2000; Burstyn, 1999). Therefore, in the world of sports, a person is defined as "qualified" as an athlete, a coach, or an administrator if he or she is tough, aggressive, and emotionally focused on competitive success. If a person is kind, caring, supportive, and emotionally responsive to others, he or she is qualified only to be a cheerleader, a volunteer worker for the booster club, or possibly an assistant in marketing and public relations; these qualities, often associated with women and weak men, are not valued qualities in most sport organizations.

Critical Feminist Theories and Research on Sports

Critical feminist theories emphasize the need to assess critically and transform the ideology and organization of sports, so that sports give voice to and represent the perspectives and experiences of women in society. Those who use these feminist theories argue that, unless ideological and organizational changes are made, there will never be true gender equity in sports or in society as a whole.

Research done by those who use critical feminist theories generally focuses on one or more of the following issues (see Birrell, 2000):

1. How have girls and women been excluded from or discouraged from participating in sports and how can gender equity be achieved without promoting sports that privilege some girls and women over others or jeopardizing the health and physical well-being of girls and women who play sports?
2. How are sports involved in the production of ideas about what it means to be a man in society, as well as in the production of a system of gender relations that privileges tough and aggressive men?

3. How are women and men represented in media coverage of sports and how do those representations reproduce dominant ideas about gender in society?
4. What strategies can people use to resist or challenge the dominant gender ideology that is promoted and reproduced through most organized competitive sports?
5. How are sports and sport participation involved in the production of gendered ideas about physicality, sexuality, and the body?

When critical feminists do research, they often have clear political goals: they want to use sports as sites for challenging and transforming oppressive forms of gender relations, and they want to expose and resist expressions of sexism and homophobia in sports. For many critical feminists, the goal is to change the meaning, organization, and purpose of sports to emphasize the notion of partnership and competition *with* others; they are opposed to sports that emphasize the notion of dominating and competing *against* others.

Using Critical Feminist Theories in Everyday Life

Critical feminist theories have had a major impact on all of us who study sports in society. They have increased our understanding of sports as a part of culture, and they have made us aware of many other important questions to ask about gender and sports. For example, why do so many men around the world continue to resist efforts to promote gender equity in sports? Why do some women fear being called lesbians if they are strong and powerful athletes? Why are some men's locker rooms full of homophobia, gay-bashing jokes, and comments that demean women? Why don't we become concerned when 40,000 young men get carried off football fields every year with serious knee injuries? Why do church-going mothers and fathers who support "get tough" anticrime policies take their children to football games and cheer for young men charged and sometimes convicted of physical and sexual assault? Why do so many people assume that men who play sports must be heterosexual? Why has an openly gay male athlete never been featured on the cover of *Sports Illustrated?* Why are so many women's high school and college teams called "Lady this" and "Lady that"? These questions, inspired by critical feminist theories, are worth serious attention. They deal with issues that affect our lives every day. In fact, if we do not have thoughtful responses to these questions, we really don't know much about sports in society.

Weaknesses of Critical Feminist Theories

Critical feminist theories are not without weaknesses. In fact, they have most of the same weaknesses of critical theories. Additionally, because of their focus on gender as a category of experience, they have sometimes given too little attention to other categories of experience that are connected with gender in important ways. These include age, race and ethnicity, social class, disability, religion, and nationality. Recent research (Hargreaves, 2000) has focused on the intersections of gender, race, and social class, but much remains to be done to explore the experiences of and problems faced by women of different ages, abilities, religions (for example, Muslim women), and nationalities.

FIGURATIONAL THEORY: UNDERSTANDING SPORTS IN TERMS OF HISTORICAL AND GLOBAL PROCESSES

Because the roots of figurational theory are based in intellectual traditions in Europe, most social scientists who study sports in North America are not familiar with it. However, it is a comprehensive theory that has been used for many years as a guide to forming hypotheses, doing research, and synthesizing research findings about social life and about sports in society (Dunning, 1999).

Figurational theory is based on the notion that social life consists of networks of interdependent people. Those who use this theory focus on the historical processes through which these networks, or sets of interconnections, between people emerge and change over time. These sets of interconnections are called "figurations."

Figurational theory assumes that human beings are "more or less dependent on each other first by nature and then through social learning, through education, socialization, and socially generated reciprocal needs" (Elias, 1978, p. 261). In other words, people exist because of and through their connections with others, and, if we wish to understand social life, we must study the social figurations that emerge and change as social connections between people emerge and change. According to figurational theory, human beings "can be understood only in terms of the various figurations to which they have belonged in the past and which they continue to form in the present" (Gouldsblom, 1977, p. 7).

Those who use figurational theory study the long-term processes through which the relatively autonomous actions of many individuals and collections of people influence and constrain each other. These processes are complex and dynamic, and they involve a wide range of outcomes, which no single individual or group has chosen, designed, planned, or intended. These outcomes may be enabling or constraining for different individuals and groups, but they are never permanent. They shift and change as power within figurations shifts and changes over time. Power tends to shift and change over time in connection with constantly emerging economic, political, and emotional dimensions of social life (Murphy et al., 2000).[3]

---

[3]Figurational theory grew out of the work of Norbert Elias, a German Jew who fled Nazi Germany in 1933 and continued his sociological research in England until he died in 1990. Elias' theory of civilizing processes in western Europe is based on extensive historical research (see Elias, 1978, 1982). When Elias turned his attention to sports and leisure, much of his work was done with Eric Dunning (Elias and Dunning, 1986). Dunning has influenced students around the world through his writing and his lectures at Leicester University in England and many other universities.

Figurational Theory and Research on Sports

Figurational theory has inspired much research and discussion about sports in society. Although most of the research has been done in England and parts of northern and western Europe, it offers useful analyses of the following topics:

1. What are the historical, economic, political, and emotional factors that account for the emergence of modern sports during the eighteenth and nineteenth centuries in much of Europe?
2. What are the historical and social processes through which sport participation became increasingly serious in people's lives and through which sports became professionalized and commercialized in various societies during the twentieth century?
3. What are the historical and social dynamics of violence and efforts to control violence in sports, especially in connection with soccer in England and around the world?
4. What are the relationships among sports, national identity, and the dynamics of globalization processes in which the media, economic expansion, and consumerism play important roles?

Figurational theorists have acknowledged the importance of sports in society. Sports are important because they are "collective inventions," which provide people, especially men, in highly regulated, modern societies with forms of enjoyable excitement that reduce boredom while limiting the excessive and destructive violence that characterized many folk games in premodern Europe (Dunning, 1999).

Furthermore, the concept of figurations has been especially useful in studies of the complex economic, political, and social processes associated with global sports. Figurational research on the global migration of elite athletes, the global sports industry, global media-sports relation-ships, the impact of global sports on identity, and the manner that sports are incorporated simultaneously into local cultures and global processes have helped us understand sports in a global perspective (Maguire, 1999).

Using Figurational Theory in Everyday Life

Figurational theory is based on the ideas that knowledge about social life is cumulative and that the goal of knowledge is to enable people to control expressions of violence, exploitation, and power-driven relationships in their lives. Figurational theorists also emphasize that the application of knowledge in everyday social life is tricky, because applications are bound to produce unintended consequences, which could subvert intended positive and progressive outcomes. This, along with their desire to avoid the influence of ideology in their research, has led them to be cautious when it comes to social action and political intervention.

Most figurational theorists say that their role in social action is to generate valid forms of knowledge and to pass it on to others in a critical manner, so that people can use it as a basis for meaningful participation in social life. When it comes to problem solving, they have recommended policies that increase meaningful participation among those who have historically lacked access to power. In the case of sports, they have made general recommendations that support participation opportunities for women, working-class people, and ethnic minorities, but they have not made recommendations in explicit or assertive terms.

Weaknesses of Figurational Theory

The primary weakness of figurational theory is that its focus on long-term, historical interconnections between people minimizes attention to the immediate issues, current problems, and day-to-day struggles that are the "social stuff" of people's everyday lives. The historical framework that is the backbone of figurational theory tends to diffuse the urgency and painfulness of everyday issues and problems, because it frames them in terms of complex, long-term processes. This is frustrating to those who want to deal with the here-and-now problems and issues that affect people's lives.

Another weakness of figurational theory is that it focuses so much on interdependence between people that it understates the immediate personal consequences of oppressive power relationships and the need for concerted political actions to change the balance of power in particular spheres of social life. For example, figurational research has explained how modern sports are a "male preserve" and how they have reproduced an ideology of masculinity and male power in many societies, but it has traditionally ignored the experiences of women in sports and the need for changes in the inequitable gender relations that characterize sport organizations. This has prevented figurational theory from being combined with critical feminist theories, and it has discouraged many action-oriented critical theorists from working with figurational theorists.

IS THERE A BEST THEORETICAL APPROACH TO USE WHEN STUDYING SPORTS?

In my experience as an involved citizen, a sociologist, and a person who has played and watched sports with friends and family, I have found all the theories discussed in this chapter useful. Each has made me aware of questions and issues that are important in my life or in the lives of those with whom I work and play.

In much of my own research, I have used *interactionist theory* because I have wanted to view sports from the inside, from the perspectives of those who make decisions to play or not to play and who integrate sport participation into their lives in various ways. However, as I have done interactionist research, I have been influenced very much by *critical theories* and *critical feminist theories*. This combination has helped me become more aware of the social and cultural contexts in which people make decisions about sport participation, and it has enabled me to see how access to participation opportunities is influenced by economic, political, and cultural factors. Furthermore, *critical* and *critical feminist theories* have helped me think about very practical issues, such as how to vote on proposals to fund new parks or to fund a new stadium for a professional football team. They have helped me think about policies related to organizing sport programs for at-risk youth and to selecting candidates for coaching jobs at my university.

Functionalist theory helps me understand how other people think about sports in society, but it does not help me identify the social issues and controversies connected with sports in my community and in the sport organizations where I work with coaches and administrators.

Conflict theory alerts me to social class and economic issues, but *critical theories* help me combine those issues with issues related to gender, race and ethnicity, disability, sexuality, and media coverage of sports and sports figures.

Figurational theory has helped me understand historical and global issues more clearly, and I have used figurational research findings to help me think about power and politics in a global perspective.

Critical and *critical feminist theories* offer useful frameworks for thinking about how to change sports and to make sport participation more accessible to a wider range of people in society. I am much more interested in increasing choices and alternatives for people in sports than I am in making sports a more efficient means of maintaining the status quo in society (a goal of *functionalist theory*) or in dismantling sports altogether (a goal of *conflict theory*). I think that many aspects of the status quo in the United States and

Social life is so complex that it should be viewed from multiple perspectives as we study it. Each theory in this chapter could be used to ask sociological questions about this scene. Afghan boys (no girls) are playing Little League baseball organized by U.S. ground troops after Afghanistan had been heavily bombed by the U.S. military as it sought out terrorists. Adult refugees watch the game. (Wally Santana; AP/Wide World Photo)

in other societies are in need of change and that sports can be useful sites for making people aware of the changes that are needed and the forms that those changes might take.

Creating alternative ways of doing sports requires an awareness of the values underlying dominant sports in society today, as well as a vocabulary for thinking about creative possibilities for the future. A combination of *critical* and *critical feminist theories* is especially helpful in critically assessing those values and providing the vocabulary we need to assess existing sport forms and to develop new forms that offer human beings new possibilities for organizing their thoughts about the world and their connections with each other.

My theoretical preferences often conflict with the preferences expressed by students and people who work for sport organizations. Students who would like to work in sport organizations know that most of the people in those organiza-

tions see sports in functionalist terms, so they sometimes prefer *functionalist theory*. However, I remind these students that, if they become familiar with issues of power and culture, they will be able to critically assess organizational policies in terms of their impact on various groups of employees in the organization and on various segments of the surrounding community. When I work with coaches and sports administrators, they often tell me that my critical approach has helped them see things in their lives in new and helpful ways.

Finally, I believe that true empowerment involves enabling people to be critically informed actors, so that they can effectively "challenge and change unequal power relationships" (Mahiri, 1998). As I try to live by this belief, I find that critical and critical feminist theories, combined with interactionist theory, are especially helpful.

SUMMARY

HOW CAN SOCIAL THEORIES HELP US STUDY SPORTS IN SOCIETY?

Theories are tools that enable us to ask questions, identify problems, gather information, explain social life, prioritize strategies to deal with problems, and anticipate the consequences of our actions and interventions. There are many theories that we can use to understand sports and society, and each offers a slightly different angle on or perspective for viewing the connections between them. In this chapter, we have focused on functionalist theory, conflict theory, interactionist theory, critical theories, critical feminist theories, and figurational theory.

The purpose of the chapter is to show that each theory provides a framework to think about sports in society. For example, functionalist theory offers an explanation for positive consequences associated with sport involvement in the lives of both athletes and spectators. Conflict theory identifies serious problems in sports and explains how and why players and spectators are oppressed and exploited for economic purposes. Interactionist theory suggests that an understanding of sports requires an understanding of the meanings, identities, and interaction associated with sport involvement. Critical theories suggest that sports are connected with social relations and culture in complex and diverse ways and that sports change as power and resources shift and as there are changes in social, political, and economic relations in society. Critical feminist theories emphasize gender as a category of experience and sports as sites for producing, reproducing, and transforming ideas about gender and the structure of gender relations in society. Figurational theory identifies the complex and long-term social processes through which modern sports have emerged and changed in societies.

It is also useful to realize that each theoretical perspective has its weaknesses. Functionalist theory leads to exaggerated accounts of the positive consequences of sports and sport participation; it mistakenly assumes that there are no conflicts of interest between groups within society, and it ignores the powerful historical and economic factors that have influenced social events and social relationships. Conflict theory overstates the importance of social class and economic factors in society, and it focuses most of its attention on top-level spectator sports, which make up only a part of sports in any society. Interactionist theory does a poor job of relating issues of meaning, identity, and experience in sports to general social conditions and patterns of social inequality in society as a whole. Critical theories provide no explicit guidelines for determining when sports are sources of opposition to the interests of powerful groups within society, and they lack clearly defined criteria for assessing the value of oppositional ideas and actions from one situation to the next. Critical feminist theories have not sufficiently explored connections between gender and other categories of experience, including age, race, religion, nationality, and disability. Figurational theory unintentionally diffuses the urgency of social problems by framing them in terms of complex, long-term processes and historical accounts of the changing balance of power in social relations.

Despite their limitations and weaknesses, social theories are helpful as we explore issues and controversies in sports and as we assess research and ideas about sports in society. We don't have to be theorists to use theory to help us organize our thoughts and become more informed citizens in our schools and communities.

SUGGESTED READINGS

Functionalist Theory

Loy, J., and D. Booth. 2000. Functionalism, sport and society. In *Handbook of sports studies* (pp. 9–27), edited by J. Coakley and E. Dunning. London: Sage (overview of of functionalism and research informed by functionalism in the sociology of sport).

Conflict Theory

Rigauer, B. 2000. Marxist theories. In *Handbook of sports studies* (pp. 28–47), edited by J. Coakley and E. Dunning. London: Sage (overview of Marxist theory and research in the study of sports; special emphasis on sport as a form of work in capitalist societies).

Interactionist Theory

Coakley, J., and P. Donnelly. 1999. *Inside sports*. London: Routledge (many of the twenty-two articles in this collection use interactionist theory to guide qualitative research on sport participation and sport experiences; highlights processes of becoming involved in sports, developing an athlete identity, participating in sports, and making the transition out of sports).

Donnelly, P. 2000. Interpretive approaches to the sociology of sports. In *Handbook of sports studies* (pp. 77–91), edited by J. Coakley and E. Dunning. London: Sage (overview of interactionist and other interpretive approaches to studying sports).

Critical Theories

Hargreaves, J., and I. MacDonald. 2000. Cultural studies and the sociology of sport. In *Handbook of sports studies* (pp. 48–60), edited by J. Coakley and E. Dunning. London: Sage (overview of critical theories and research informed by Gramsci and cultural studies in the study of sports).

Rail, G., ed. 1998. *Sport and postmodern times*. Albany: State University of New York Press (seventeen articles representing a range of postmodernist and poststructuralist analyses of sports; the general focus is on the significance of sports in the construction and diffusion of cultural meanings and values).

Sage, G. H. 1998. *Power and ideology in American sport: A critical perspective*. 2d ed. Champaign, IL: Human Kinetics (clearly written, informative critical analysis of dominant sport forms in the United States; excellent book to use as an introduction to critical theories).

Critical Feminist Theories

Birrell, S. 2000. Feminist theories for sport. In *Handbook of sports studies* (pp. 61–76), edited by J. Coakley and E. Dunning. London: Sage (overview of how feminist theories have been used in sport studies; traces the history of this use and discusses critical feminist cultural studies as used by many people in recent years).

Edwards, J., and J. Hargreaves. 2001. Feminism. In *International encyclopedia of women and sports* (pp. 395–402), edited by K. Christensen, A. Guttmann, and G. Pfister. New York: Macmillan Reference USA (excellent discussion of how feminism has influenced sports since the late 1960s and inspired political efforts that account for many of the sport participation opportunities available to girls and women today)

Hargreaves, J. 2000. *Heroines of sport: The politics of difference and identity*. London/New York: Routledge (uses critical feminist theory as a basis for discussing groups of women whose stories have been excluded from many previous feminist analyses of sports in society; informative and insightful discussions of women from South Africa, Muslim nations in East Asia, and Aboriginal groups in Australia and Canada, as well as lesbians and women with disabilities from around the world).

Figurational Theory

Dunning, E. 1999. *Sport matters: Sociological studies of sport, violence, and civilization*. London: Routledge (definitive introduction to the study of modern sports from a figurational perspective; figurational theory is clearly distinguished from other theoretical approaches in each of the chapters).

Murphy, P., K. Sheard, and I. Waddington. 2000. Figurational sociology and its application to sports. In *Handbook of sports studies* (pp. 92–105), edited by J. Coakley and E. Dunning. London: Sage (overview of figurational sociology in the study of sports and society).

 **WEBSITE RESOURCES**

Note: Websites often change. The following URLs were current when this book was printed. Please check our website (www.mhhe.com/coakley8e) for updates and additions.

www.mhhe.com/coakley8e Click on chapter 2 for summaries of studies based on some of the theories discussed in this chapter.

www.socsci.mcmaster.ca/w3virtsoclib/theories.html Research source for information on sociological theory and theorists; it is not sports-related, but it provides numerous links to sites around the world.

www.socqrl.niu.edu/FYI/theory.htm Valuable links to helpful sites on social theory.

www.tryoung.com/archives/108sports.html Contains a clear statement of how sport are viewed and analyzed when using a Marxist-based conflict theory as a guiding framework.

www.sussex.ac.uk/Units/CST An advanced critical theory site.

www.feminist.org/research/sports2.html Special coverage of "Empowering Women in Sports"; this site not only is a good example of applied feminist theories but also highlights the issues that are most important in a feminist analysis of sports.

www.usyd.edu.au/su/social/elias.html Site devoted to Norbert Elias and figurational theory; provides links to many European sources.

(Jay Coakley)

Studying the Past

Does It Help Us Understand Sports Today?

Online Learning Center Resources

Visit *Sports in Society*'s Online Learning Center
at **www.mhhe.com/coakley8e** for additional
information and study material for this chapter,
including

* Self-grading quizzes
* Learning objectives
* Related websites
* Additional readings

OF THE THOUSANDS of evils . . . in Greece there
is no greater evil than the race of athletes. . . .
Since they have not formed good habits, they
face problems with difficulty.

—**Euripides, Greek dramatist (fifth century B.C.)**

A complete outline is available online at www.mhhe.com/coakley8e.

THEY WHO LAID the intellectual foundations of the Western world were the most fanatical players and organizers of games that the world has ever known.

—C. L. R. James, West Indian writer and cricket player (1963)

To understand sports as social phenomena in today's world, we should have a sense of what physical games, contests, and sport activities were like in past times. Therefore, this chapter presents brief overviews of sport activities in different cultural and historical settings. My intent is *not* to provide an integrated overall history of sports. Such a history would look at the development and organization of physical activities and games across all continents from one cultural group to another over time. This would be an ambitious and worthy project, but it is far beyond the scope of this chapter.

This chapter will focus on (1) the ancient Greeks, (2) the Roman Empire, (3) the Middle Ages in parts of Europe, (4) the Renaissance through the Enlightenment in parts of Europe, and (5) the Industrial Revolution through recent times, with special emphasis on the United States. I have chosen these times and places because they are familiar to many of us, and they provide good examples of how sports are social constructions connected clearly with the social and cultural contexts in which they exist.

The goal of this chapter is to show that, for each of these times and places, our understanding of sports depends on what we know about the social lives of the people who created, defined, played, and integrated them into their everyday experiences. As critical theories suggest, it is especially important to know how people used their power and resources as they struggled with one another to create and participate in physical activities that fit their needs and interests.

When we view sports history in this way, dates and names are not the most important pieces of information. Instead, we focus primarily on what sport activities tell us about social relationships and everyday life among people at particular times and places. This will be the focus in this chapter.

UNDERSTANDING HISTORY WHILE STUDYING SPORTS IN SOCIETY

When we think about history, many of us think about chronological sequences of events, which build on each other and gradually lead to a better, or more "modern," society. Even the terminology used in many discussions of history leads us to think this way. For example, many historical accounts are full of references to societies that are traditional or modern, primitive or civilized, underdeveloped or developed, preindustrial or industrial. This terminology implies that history is moving in a particular direction and that, as it moves, things are improving and getting more modern and developed. In other words, history is frequently presented as linear and progressive—always following a line that moves forward and up.

This approach enables some people today to feel superior because they conclude that they are the most modern, civilized, and developed people in history. However, this conclusion is not historically accurate. In the case of sports, there are literally thousands of "histories" of physical activities among thousands of human populations in different places around the world. These histories involve patterns of changes that many people would not describe as progressive. Furthermore, even the definitions of *progress* that different people use are products of particular cultural experiences.

Historical evidence suggests that physical activities and games have existed in all cultures. The specific forms of these activities and games, along with the meanings that people gave to them, were shaped through struggles over the organization and purpose of the activities, over who should play them, and over how they should be integrated into people's lives. To say that physical activities and games over the years have evolved to fit a pattern of progress, or modernization, is to distort the life experiences of people all over the world (Gruneau, 1988). There may be fewer contrasts among the games that different people play today, but this does not mean that sports are evolving to fit a grand scheme for how physical activities should be organized or what they should mean in people's lives (Maguire, 1999). Instead, fewer contrasts around the globe are due to processes of cultural diffusion combined with recent concentrations of global power among nation states and corporations. Certain nations and corporations now have the power to define, organize, and present through the media particular sport forms.

According to this approach, the inclusion of beach volleyball as a new sport in the 1996 Summer Olympics in Atlanta was not a case of historical progress. Instead, it was an example of how people from wealthy countries are able to promote the sport through international travel, social connections, and access to resources. This enhanced their ability to secure corporate sponsorships and media coverage. In the process, beach volleyball became attractive to the International Olympic Committee—not as part of a general pattern of progress in the history of sports but as part of global influence and power relations.

Therefore, do not conclude that this chapter is a story of progress. Instead, read it as a set of stories about people at different times and places struggling over and coming to terms with what they wanted their physical activities to be and how they wished to include them in their lives. Certainly, there is some historical continuity in these processes and struggles in particular cultures, but continuity does not always mean that the structure and organization of sports equally represent the interests of all people in a culture. Human history does not follow any grand plan of progress. When progressive things do happen, it is because people have made them happen at a particular time, and these people usually realize that, unless they keep an eye on things, the progress will be only temporary.

SPORTS VARY BY TIME AND PLACE

People in all cultures have engaged in physical activities and have used human movement as a part of their ritual life. As we look at cultural variations, it is necessary to remember that few cultures have had physical games that resembled the highly organized, rule-governed competitive games that most of us describe as sports today.

In prehistoric times, for example, there were no sports as we know them today. Physical activities were tied directly to the challenge of survival and the expression of religious beliefs (see figure 3.1). People hunted for food and sometimes used their physical abilities to defend themselves or to establish social control and power over others. Archaeological evidence suggests

SIDELINES

©1982 M.T.F.-T.W.S.-Lakewood, CO

"How can you stop to shoot pool on the way home when it won't be invented for another 10 million years?"
....

FIGURE 3.1   In early human history, there were no sports as we define and play them today. People used their physical abilities for survival. Physical activities occasionally were included in community and religious rituals, but their purpose probably was to appease the gods, rather than to entertain or build character.

that people on each continent of the globe created unique forms of physical challenges for the purpose of appeasing their gods. These activities involved acting out events that had important symbolic or real meaning in their everyday lives, and, even though they may have taken the form of organized games, they were inseparable from sacred rituals and ceremonies. In fact, they often were performed as forms of religious worship, and sometimes their outcomes were determined by religious necessity rather than the physical abilities of the people involved (Guttmann, 1978).

The first forms of organized games around the world probably emerged from this combination of physical challenges and religious rituals. From what we can tell, these games were connected closely with the social structures, social relations, and belief systems of the societies in which they existed, and they usually recreated and reaffirmed dominant cultural practices in those societies. But this was not always the case. Sometimes they served as sources of protest or opposition against dominant ways of thinking about and doing things in particular groups or societies.

Historical and cultural variations in the form and dynamics of physical activities remind us that all cultural practices, even sports, can serve a variety of social purposes. This raises the question of how the definition and organization of sports in any society promote the interests of various groups within that society. People create sport activities within the constraints of the social worlds in which they live. Therefore, not everyone has an equal say in how those activities are defined and organized. People with the strongest vested interests and the most *power* in a group or society generally have the greatest impact on how sports are defined, organized, and played in that group or society. Sport activities do not totally reflect their desires, but sports represent the interests of the powerful more than they represent the interests of other groups in society.

This approach to studying sports in history is based on critical theory. It calls attention to the existence and consequences of social inequality in societies. Social inequality has always had a significant impact on how sport activities are organized and played in any situation. The most influential forms of social inequality are those related to wealth, political power, social status, gender, age, and race and ethnicity. We will pay special attention to these in the following discussions of times and places.

CONTESTS AND GAMES IN ANCIENT GREECE: BEYOND THE MYTHS (1000 B.C. TO 100 B.C.)

The games played by the early Greeks (circa 900 B.C.) were grounded in mythology and religious beliefs. They usually were held in conjunction with festivals, which combined prayer, sacrifices, and religious services, along with music, dancing, and ritual feasts. Competitors in these early games were from wealthy, respected Greek families. They were the only people who could afford to hire trainers and coaches and who had the time and resources to travel to various games. Events were based on the interests of young males. They consisted primarily of warrior sports, such as chariot racing, wrestling and boxing, javelin and discus throwing, foot racing, archery, and long jumping. Violence and serious injuries were commonplace, in comparison with today's sport events (Elias, 1986; Kidd, 1984, 1996b). Greek women, children, and older people occasionally played sports in these festivals, but they never played in the games held at Olympia.

The locations and dates of the Greek festivals also were linked to religious beliefs. For example, Olympia was chosen as one of the festival sites because it was associated with the achievements and activities of celebrated Greek gods and mythological characters. In fact, Olympia was dedicated as a shrine to the god Zeus about

1000 B.C. Although permanent buildings and playing fields were not constructed until 550 B.C., the games at Olympia were held every four years. Additional festivals involving athletic contests were also held at other locations throughout Greece, but the Olympic Games became the most prestigious of all athletic events.

Women were prohibited from participating as athletes in or spectators at the Olympic Games. However, women held their own games at Olympia. Dedicated to the goddess Hera, the sister-wife of Zeus, these games grew out of Greek fertility rites. According to some estimates, the Heraean Games even predated the exclusively male Olympic Games.

Serious women athletes often risked their reputations in the eyes of males when they engaged in sports. Physical prowess was not consistent with dominant definitions of heterosexual femininity among the Greeks, so many people raised questions about the sexuality of strong and physically skilled women, including the goddesses in Greek mythology (Kidd, 1984).

> **Just as the dominant class writes history, so that same class writes the story of sport.**
>
> —James Riordan, social historian
> and former soccer player (1996)

The discrimination against women who participated in sports was rooted in a patriarchal family structure in which females had no legal rights and only limited opportunities for experiences outside their households. Although some women from powerful Greek families did become regular participants in games at certain sites, their involvement was limited and their achievements were usually ignored.

The men's games at Olympia took on political significance as they grew in visibility and popularity. Winning became connected with the glory of city-states, and physically skilled slaves and young men from lower-class backgrounds were forced to become athletes, or wealthy patrons and government officials hired them to train for the Olympics and other games. Victories brought prizes of cash and subsidies for living expenses for many of these slaves and hired athletes. Victories also earned them reputations, which they could convert into monetary rewards when competing in other popular Greek games. Contrary to widely believed myths about the amateur ideals held by the Greeks, these male athletes saw themselves as professionals. During the second century B.C., they even organized athletic guilds, so that they might bargain for rights, control over the conditions of their sport participation, and material security when they had to retire from competition (Baker, 1988).

Greek athletes were so specialized in their physical skills that they made poor soldiers. They engaged in warrior sports, but they lacked the generalized skills of warriors. Furthermore, they concentrated so much on athletic training that they ignored intellectual development. This evoked widespread criticism from Greek philosophers, who saw the games as brutal and dehumanizing and the athletes as useless and ignorant citizens.

Unfortunately, representatives of the modern Olympics have romanticized and perpetuated myths about Greek games in an attempt to connect the modern Olympics to a positive legacy from the past. Although Plato may have philosophized about connections between mind and body, Greek athletes often maimed or killed one another in the pursuit of victories and the rewards that came with them. Fairness was not as important as honor, violence was common, and athletic contests were closely connected with a cultural emphasis on warfare (Dunning, 1999).

Physical contests and games in Greek culture influenced art, philosophy, and the everyday lives of many people, especially those wealthy enough to train, hire professionals, and travel to games. However, Greek contests and games were different from the organized competitive sports of today (see the box "Dominant Sport Forms Today: What Makes Them Unique?"). First, they were grounded in religion; second, they lacked

Dominant Sport Forms Today
What Makes Them Unique?

The organized competitive sports so popular in many parts of the world today are very different from the physical activities and games played in the past. Allen Guttmann's study of sport activities through history shows that *dominant sport forms (DSFs)* today have seven interrelated characteristics, which have never before appeared together in previous physical activities and games. These characteristics are

1. *Secularism.* Today's DSFs are not directly linked to religious beliefs or rituals. They are sources of diversion and entertainment, not worship. They are played for personal gains, not the appeasement of gods. They embody the immediacy of the material world, not the mysticism of the supernatural.

2. *Equality.* Today's DSFs are based on the ideas that participation should be open to everyone regardless of family or social background and that all contestants in a sport event should face the same competitive conditions.

3. *Specialization.* Today's DSFs involve athletes dedicated exclusively to participation in a single event or position within an event. Excellence is defined in terms of specialized skills, rather than all-around physical abilities.

4. *Rationalization.* Today's DSFs consist of complex sets of rules and strategies. Rules regulate action, equipment and the conditions of participation. Participation involves rationally controlled training methods, guided by "sport sciences."

5. *Bureaucratization.* Today's DSFs are controlled by complex organizations on the international, national, and local levels. Officials in these organizations oversee and sanction athletes, teams, and events. They also enforce rules, organize events, and certify records.

6. *Quantification.* Today's DSFs involve numerous measurements and statistics. Times, distances, and scores are measured and recorded. Achievements are discussed in measurable

Organized competitive sports are characterized by an emphasis on quantification, among other things. Everything that can be defined in terms of time, distance, or scores is measured and recorded. The clock is key in sports, although clocks such as this one have been replaced by timing devices that measure hundredths of seconds. (Bob Jackson, *Colorado Springs Gazette*)

terms, and statistics are used as proof of achievements.

7. *Records.* Today's DSFs emphasize setting and breaking records. Performances are compared and records are published. Most important, of course, are world records.

One or some of these characteristics have existed in the physical activities and games of previous historical periods, but not until the nineteenth century did all seven appear together in what some people have called *modern* sports (Dunning, 1999; Dunning and Sheard, 1979; Guttmann, 1978). This does not mean that today's organized competitive sports are somehow superior to the games and activities of the past. It means only that they are different in the way they are organized and integrated into people's lives. Sociologists study these differences in terms of their impact on the organization and dynamics of social life.

Table 3.1 summarizes Guttmann's comparison of games, contests, and sport activities in each of the places and time periods discussed in this chapter. The table shows that the dominant sport forms that exist in many post-industrial societies today are different from the "sports" played by people in times past. However, it does not explain why the differences exist or the social implications of the differences.

Finally, we should remember that the seven characteristics identified by Guttmann are not found in all sports today. Sports are social constructions. They change as social, economic, and political forces change and as people seek and develop alternatives to dominant sport forms. In fact, the dominant sport forms that exist fifty years from now may have characteristics that are different from these seven characteristics. *What do you think?*

Table 3.1   Historical comparison of organized games, contests, and sport activities*

Characteristic	Greek Contests and Games (1000 B.C. to 100 B.C.)	Roman Contests and Games (100 B.C. to A.D. 500)	Medieval Tournaments and Games (500 to 1300)	Renaissance, Reformation, and Enlightenment Games (1300 to 1800)	"Modern" Sports
Secularism	Yes and no**	Yes and no	Yes and no	Yes and no	Yes
Equality	Yes and no	Yes and no	No	Yes and no	Yes
Specialization	Yes	Yes	No	Yes and no	Yes
Rationalization	Yes	Yes	No	No	Yes
Bureaucratization	Yes and no	Yes	No	No	Yes
Quantification	No	Yes	No	Yes and no	Yes
Records	No	No	No	Yes and no	Yes

*Modified version table 2 in Guttmann (1978).
**This characteristic existed in some sports during this time, but not in others.

complex administrative structures; and, third, they did not involve measurements and record keeping from event to event. However, there is one major similarity: they often reproduced dominant patterns of social relations in the society as a whole. The power and advantages that went with being wealthy, male, and young in Greek society shaped the games and contests in ways that limited the participation of women, older people, and those without economic resources. In fact, the definitions of excellence used to evaluate performance even reflected the abilities of young males. This meant that the abilities of others were substandard by definition—if you could not do it as a young Greek man could do it, then you could not do it the right way.

ROMAN CONTESTS AND GAMES: SPECTACLES AND GLADIATORS (100 B.C. TO A.D. 500)

Roman leaders used physical contests and games to train soldiers and provide mass entertainment spectacles. They borrowed events from Greek contests and games, but they geared athletic training to the preparation of obedient military men. They were critical of the Greek emphasis on individualism and the development of specialized physical skills that were useless in battle. They packaged their physical activities in ways that would appeal to spectators.

Through the first century A.D., Roman contests and games increasingly took the form of circuses and gladiatorial combat. Chariot races were the most popular events during the spectacles. Wealthy Romans recruited slaves as charioteers. Spectators bet heavily on the races and, when they became bored or unruly, the emperors passed around free food to keep them from getting too hostile. In some cases, free "raffle tickets" for prizes were distributed to spectators to prevent riots. This tactic pacified the crowds and allowed the emperors to use the spectator

events as occasions to celebrate themselves and their positions of power. Government officials throughout the Roman Empire used similar events to maintain control in their communities.

As the power and influence of the Roman Empire grew, these spectacles, consisting of contests and games, became increasingly important as diversions for the masses. By A.D. 300, half of the days on the Roman calendar had become public holidays. Many workers held only part-time jobs, and unemployment was extremely high. Activities other than the standard chariot races, boxing matches, and other such contests were needed to keep events interesting. Bearbaiting, bullbaiting, and animal fights were added to capture spectator interest. Men and women were forced into the arena to engage in mortal combat with lions, tigers, and panthers. Condemned criminals were sometimes dressed in sheepskins and thrown in with partially starved wild animals. Gladiators, armed with a variety of weapons, were pitted against one another in gory fights to the death. These spectacles achieved two purposes for the Romans: they entertained an idle populace and disposed of socially "undesirable" people, such as thieves, murderers, and Christians (Baker, 1988).

Some Romans criticized these spectacles as tasteless activities, devoid of cultural value. However, the criticisms were not based on concerns for human rights as much as they were based on an objection to events in which the upper and lower social classes mingled together. Other than some outspoken Christians, few people objected to the spectacles on moral or humanitarian grounds. The objections coming from the Christians had little effect on the fate of the events. In fact, the demise of Roman spectacles went hand in hand with the fall of the Roman Empire. As the Roman economy went deeper and deeper into depression, and as wealthy people moved away from cities, there were not enough resources to support such spectacles (Baker, 1988).

Women were seldom involved in Roman contests and games. They were allowed in the arenas to watch and cheer male athletes, but few had opportunities to develop their own athletic skills. Within the Roman family, women were legally subservient to and rigidly controlled by men. Like women in ancient Greece, they were discouraged from pursuing interests beyond the household.

Although local folk games and other physical activities existed in the Roman Empire, we know little about how they were organized and played and what they meant in people's lives. The gladiatorial spectacles did not capture everyone's interest but they attracted considerable attention in major population centers.

Roman contests and games differed from organized sports today in that they sometimes were connected with religious rituals, and they seldom involved the quantification of athletic achievements or the recording of outstanding accomplishments (review the box "Dominant Sport Forms Today," page 66–67).

TOURNAMENTS AND GAMES IN MEDIEVAL EUROPE: SEPARATION OF THE MASTERS AND THE MASSES (500 TO 1300)

Sport activities during medieval Europe consisted of folk games played by local peasants, tournaments staged for knights and nobles, archery contests, and activities in which animals were brutalized (Dunning, 1999). The folk games, often violent and dangerous, and activities that involved the maiming or killing of animals emerged in connection with local peasant customs. The tournaments and archery contests were tied to military training and the desire for entertainment among the feudal aristocracy and those who served them.

Some of the local games of this period have interesting histories. As Roman soldiers and government officials moved throughout Europe during the fourth and fifth centuries, they built bathing facilities to use during their leisure time.

AT YOUR FINGERTIPS For more information on sports and religion, see pages 456–485.

To loosen up before their baths, they engaged in various forms of ball play. Local peasants during the early medieval period picked up on the Roman activities and gradually developed their own forms of ball games. They often integrated these games into local religious ceremonies. For example, tossing a ball back and forth sometimes represented the conflict between good and evil, light and darkness, or life and death. As the influence of the Roman Catholic Church spread through Europe during the early years of the medieval period, these symbolic rituals were redefined in terms of Roman Catholic beliefs. In these cases, sports and religion were closely connected with each other.

During most of the medieval period, the Roman Catholic Church accepted peasant ball games, even though they occasionally involved violence. In fact, local priests encouraged games by opening church grounds on holidays and Sunday afternoons to groups of participants, so the games became a basic part of village life. People played them whenever there were festive community gatherings. They were included with the music, dancing, and religious services held in conjunction with seasonal ceremonies and saints' feast days. These local ball games contained the roots for many contemporary games, such as soccer, field hockey, football, rugby, bowling, curling, baseball, and cricket. However, the games played in peasant villages had little structure and few rules. Local traditions guided play, and these traditions varied from one community to the next.

The upper classes in medieval Europe paid little attention to and seldom interfered in the leisure of peasants. They saw peasant games and festivities as safety valves defusing mass social discontent. The sport activities of the upper classes were distinctively different from those of the peasants. Access to specialized equipment and facilities allowed the nobility to develop early versions of billiards, shuffleboard, tennis, handball, and jai alai. Ownership of horses allowed them to develop various forms of horse racing, while their stable hands developed a version of horseshoes. On horseback, they also participated in hunting and hawking. Owning property and possessing money and servants clearly influenced their sports.

Through much of the medieval period, the popular sporting events among upper-class males were tournaments consisting of war games designed to keep knights and nobles ready for battle. Some tournaments differed very little from actual battlefield confrontations. Deaths and serious injuries occurred, victors carried off their opponents' possessions, and losers often were taken as prisoners and used as hostages to demand ransoms from opposing camps. Later versions of tournaments were not quite so serious, but they still involved injuries and occasional deaths. Gradually, colorful ceremonies and pageantry softened the warlike tournaments, and entertainment and chivalry took priority over military preparation and the use of extreme violence.

Throughout the period, women were less apt to be involved in physical games and sport activities than men were. Gender restrictions were grounded in a combination of religious dogma (the Roman Catholic Church taught that women had inferior status) and a male-centered family structure. A woman's duty was to be obedient and submissive. This orientation did not change much through the medieval period; however, peasant women were involved in some of the games and physical activities associated with the regular rounds of village events during the year.

Among the aristocracy, gender relations were patterned so that men's activities and women's activities were clearly differentiated. Aristocratic women did little outside the walls of their dwellings, and their activities seldom involved rigorous physical exertion for self-entertainment. Women in the upper classes sometimes engaged in "ladylike" games and physical activities, but, because women were subject to men's control and often viewed as sex objects and models of beauty, their involvement in active pursuits was limited. Feminine beauty during this time was defined in passive terms: the less active a woman, the more likely she was perceived as beautiful. In meeting expectations for beauty, women of privilege avoided all but very limited involvement in physical exercise.

Even though some sports in Europe and North America today can trace their roots back to the contests and games of the medieval period, the tournaments and games of that time were not much like today's organized sports. They lacked specialization and organization, they never involved the measurement and recording of athletic achievements, and they were not based on a commitment to equal and open competition among athletes from diverse backgrounds (review the box "Dominant Sport Forms Today," page 66–67). Historian Allen Guttmann has vividly described this last point:

> In medieval times, jousts and tournaments were limited to the nobility. Knights who sullied their honor by inferior marriages—to peasant girls, for instance—were disbarred. If they were bold enough to enter a tournament despite this loss of status, and were discovered, they were beaten and their weapons were broken. Peasants reckless enough to emulate the sport of their masters were punished by death. (1978, p. 30)

Although some characteristics of medieval sport activities can be seen in the games and contests of the Renaissance, Reformation, and Enlightenment periods, these later periods involved important social transformations, which shaped the forms and meanings of physical activities and games.

THE RENAISSANCE, REFORMATION, AND ENLIGHTENMENT: GAMES AS DIVERSIONS (1300 TO 1800)

The Renaissance

Wars throughout Europe during the fourteenth and fifteenth centuries encouraged some monarchs, government officials, and church authorities to increase their military strength. To do this, they often enacted new rules prohibiting popular peasant pastimes. Those in authority saw the time peasants spent playing games as time they could spend learning to defend the lands and lives of their masters. But, despite the pronouncements of bishops and kings, the peasants did not readily give up their games. In fact, the games sometimes became rallying points for opposition to government and church authority.

About the same time that the peasants were being subjected to increased controls in many locations, the "scholar-athlete" became the ideal among many of the aristocrats and the affluent. This "Renaissance man" was "socially adept, sensitive to aesthetic values, skilled in weaponry, strong of body, and learned in letters" (Baker, 1988, p. 59).

Throughout the Renaissance period, women had relatively few opportunities to be involved in tournaments and sport activities. Although peasant women sometimes played physical games, their lives were restricted by the demands of work in and out of the home. They often did hard physical labor, but they were not encouraged to engage in public activities that called special attention to their physical abilities and accomplishments.

Upper-class women sometimes participated in activities such as bowling, croquet, archery, and tennis, but their involvement was limited because women were seen during this time as "naturally" weak and passive. Some of these "Renaissance women" may have been pampered and put on proverbial pedestals, but men maintained their power by tightly controlling the lives of women, partly by promoting the idea that women were too fragile to leave the home and do things on their own.

The Reformation

During the Protestant Reformation, a growth in negative attitudes regarding games and sport activities adversely affected the participation of both men and women, especially where either Calvinism or Puritanism was popular. For example, between the early 1500s and the late 1600s, the English Puritans worked hard to eliminate or control leisure activities, including physical contests and games, in everyday life in England. The Puritans were devoted to the work ethic and, according to one social historian, this is how they viewed sports:

> [Sports] were thought to be profane and licentious—they were occasions of worldly indulgence that tempted men from a godly life; being rooted in pagan and popish practices, they were rich in the sort of ceremony and ritual that poorly suited the Protestant conscience; they frequently involved a desecration of the Sabbath and an interference with the worship of the true believers; they disrupted the peaceable order of society, distracting men from their basic social duties—hard work, thrift, personal restraint, devotion to family, [and] a sober carriage. (Malcolmson, 1984, p. 67)

The primary targets of the Puritans were the pastimes and games of the peasants. Peasants didn't own property, so their festivities occurred in public settings and attracted large crowds. Thus, they were easy for the Puritans to attack and criticize. The Puritans did their best to eliminate them—especially festivities scheduled on Sunday afternoons. It was not that the Puritans objected to the games themselves, but they

> **Sports may be among the most powerful human expressions in all history.**
>
> —Gerald Early, Distinguished Professor, Washington University, St. Louis (1998)

Lessons from History
Who Tells Us About the Past?

History is much more than a chronological series of events. Historical research should take us inside the lives of people who have lived before us. It should give us a sense of how people lived and how they gave meaning to their experiences and the events of their times. Therefore, when we study sports, we should be aware of whose voices and perspectives are used to construct historical accounts, as well as whose voices and perspectives are missing.

History that represents the voices and perspectives of people who lack power is generally scarce in most societies. There may be statistics about who has participated in what, but there is little in-depth information about the meanings given to participation or how it was integrated into their lives. This is especially true when it comes to the physical activities, games, and sports of Native Peoples in North America.

Prior to the arrival of Columbus and other Europeans, the histories of Native Peoples were kept in oral rather than written forms; they were local and personal histories. It was not until the late eighteenth century that much information about the lives and cultures of Native Peoples was recorded in English. However, most of that information was written from the perspectives of Europeans with limited knowledge of the diverse languages, cultures, and complex social arrangements that made up the lives of nearly 500 unique cultural groups of Native Peoples in North America. This diversity was often obscured by general accounts describing the lives and customs of "Indians," as if they were all the same.

These general accounts provide very limited descriptions of the diverse games and sports played by Native Peoples. In many cases, the descriptions were written after the lives of the Native People had been disrupted and influenced by European explorers and settlers. This history provides little accurate information about traditional games and sports and how they were integrated into the diverse cultures that existed on the North American continent through most of the nineteenth century.

For the most part, it was impossible for Europeans to observe authentic expressions of traditional native cultures. When they did make observations, it was often under strained circumstances, and Native Peoples were unwilling to reveal their customs spontaneously while being watched by outsiders who often viewed them as "oddities." The fact that the most important games

disapproved of the drinking and partying that accompanied the games and did not like the idea of promoting physical pleasure on the Sabbath. The physical activities and games of the affluent were less subject to Puritan interference. Activities such as horse racing, hunting, tennis, and bowling took place on the private property of the wealthy, making it difficult for the Puritans to enforce their prohibitions. As in other times and places, power relations had much to do with who played what activities under what conditions.

Despite the Puritans and social changes affecting the economic structure and stability of English village life, many peasant people maintained their participation in games and sports.

This was especially the case where Martin Luther's ideas had been more influential than John Calvin's ideas. However, some traditional peasant activities were altered, so that they could be played in less public settings.

During the early 1600s, King James I formally challenged Puritan influence in England by issuing *The King's Book of Sports*. This book, reissued in 1633 by Charles I, emphasized that Puritan ministers and officials should not discourage lawful recreational pursuits among English people. Charles I and his successors ushered in a new day for English sporting life. They revived traditional festivals and actively promoted and supported public games and sport activities. A few sport activities, including cricket, played by many groups of Native Peoples were connected with religious rites made it even less likely that Europeans would be allowed to observe the games in their authentic, traditional forms or understand the meanings associated with them. By the time Native Peoples had described their own activities in English, their cultures had changed in appreciable ways, and few people were willing to listen to their stories and publish them in forms that were considered "real history." In the meantime, experiences and meanings were lost forever.

The fact that we know little about the many histories of games and sports among Native Peoples highlights the fact that social, political, and economic forces influence what we know about the history of sports. For example, if we wish to understand the importance of an event, such as the establishment of the Iroquois National Lacrosse Team in 1983, we must know about the following:

- The histories and cultures of specific Native American nations and the six nations of the Iroquois Confederation
- The formal and informal political relationships between groups of Native Americans and the U.S. government

- The experiences of Native Peoples in North America as they struggled to maintain their cultures and to survive as powerful others tried to strip them of their dignity, language, religion, and customs

Knowing these three things enables us to begin an investigation of the significance of the Iroquois National Lacrosse Team in terms of those who formed it, participate on it, and follow its matches.

This scarcity of historical information based on the perspectives of those who have traditionally lacked power diminishes our awareness of sports history around the world. As social historian James Riordan (1996 p. vii) has said, "Just as the dominant class writes history, so that same class writes the story of sport". This means that, when our knowledge of the past does not go beyond the experiences and perspectives of those with the power to tell their own stories, it is always incomplete. In the worst case, such stories can be dangerous, because they may be presented in ways that reproduce stereotypes and justify discrimination against those without power. This is why some people call for a revision of history books and curricula in high schools and universities. *What do you think?*

horse racing, yachting, fencing, golf, and boxing, became highly organized during the late 1600s and the 1700s, although participation patterns reflected and reproduced social class divisions in society.

In colonial America, Puritan influence was strong at the time the colonies were established through the eighteenth century. Many of the colonists were not playful people; hard work was necessary for survival. However, as the lifestyles of the colonists became established and as free time became available, Puritan beliefs became less important than the desire to include games from the past into life in the colonies. Towns gradually abandoned laws that prohibited games and sports, and this made it possible

for leisure activities, including sports, to grow in popularity.

During this time, the games of Native Peoples were not directly affected by Puritan beliefs and cultural practices. Native Peoples in the East and Northeast continued to play the games that had been a part of their cultures for centuries. In fact, sports and sport participation have many histories across North America. This reminds us whose voices and perspectives are represented in various historical accounts of games, contests, and sports. The box "Lessons from History" emphasizes that we should be skeptical of historical accounts that do not represent the experiences and perspectives of those who lack the power to tell their stories in a public forum.

The Enlightenment

During the Enlightenment period (1700 to 1800), many games and sport activities in parts of Europe and North America began to resemble sport forms that we are familiar with today (Guttmann, 1978). With some exceptions, they were no longer grounded in religious ritual and ceremony; they involved some specialization and some degree of organization; achievements sometimes were measured; and records occasionally were kept. Furthermore, the idea that events should be open to all competitors, regardless of background, became increasingly popular. This commitment to equality and open participation gave rise to world-changing revolutions in France and the United States.

However, sport activities during the Enlightenment period were different from the dominant sport forms of today in at least one important respect: they were defined strictly as diversions—as interesting and often challenging ways to pass free time. People did not see them as having any utility for athletes in particular or society in general. No one thought that sports and sport participation could change how people developed or acted or how social life was organized. Therefore, there were no reasons for people to organize sport activities for others or to build sport organizations to oversee participants or events. A few people formed sport clubs, and they occasionally scheduled contests with other groups, but they did not form leagues or national and international associations. But things began to change during the Industrial Revolution.

THE INDUSTRIAL REVOLUTION: THE EMERGENCE OF ORGANIZED COMPETITIVE SPORTS (1780 TO 1920)

It would be an oversimplification to say that the organized competitive sports of today are simply a product of the Industrial Revolution (Dunning, 1999; Gruneau, 1988). They clearly emerged during the process of industrialization, but they were actually social constructions of people themselves—people who were trying to play their games and maintain their sport activities while they coped with the realities of everyday life in their rapidly changing families, communities, and societies. Of course, the realities of everyday life included economic, political, and social forces, which either enabled or constrained people, depending on their position in society.

It is difficult to pinpoint the beginning of the Industrial Revolution. It is not marked by a single event but a combination of the development of factories, the mass production of consumer goods, the growth of cities, and increased dependence on technology. It involved changes in the organization and control of work and community life and was generally accompanied by an increase in the number of middle-class people in the societies in which it occurred. The Industrial Revolution first began in England around 1780. Shortly after that time, it became a part of life in other European countries. In the United States and Canada, it started around 1820.

The Early Years: Limited Time and Space

During the early years of the Industrial Revolution, few people enjoyed opportunities to play games and sport activities regularly. Those who worked on farms and in factories had little free time. The workdays, even for many child workers, were often long and tiring. People who lived in cities had few open spaces where they could play sports. Production took priority over play in the plans of industrialists and city leaders. Parks and public play spaces did not exist. Furthermore, working people were discouraged from getting together in large groups outside the workplace. People in authority perceived such gatherings as dangerous because they wasted time that could be used for work and because they provided opportunities for workers to organize themselves and challenge the power of factory owners (Goodman, 1979; Mrozek, 1983).

In most industrializing countries, the clergy also endorsed restrictions on popular games and gatherings. Ministers preached about the moral value of work and the immorality of play and idleness. Many even banned sports on Sundays and accused anyone who was not totally committed to work of being lazy. In the religious belief systems of the time, work was a sign of goodness. Not everyone agreed with this, but working people had few choices. For them, survival depended on working long hours, regardless of what they thought about work, and they had little power to change the reality of what they needed to do to survive.

In most countries, games and sport activities during this period existed *despite* the Industrial Revolution, *not* because of it. People in small towns and farm communities still had opportunities to play games and sport activities during their seasonal festivities, holidays, and public ceremonies. Most city people had few opportunities to organize their own games and sports, although people with great wealth maintained highly publicized "lives of leisure" (Veblen, 1899). Among the working classes, sport involvement seldom went beyond being spectators at new forms of commercialized sport events. Of course, there were variations from one country to the next, but urban workers tended to watch a combination of cricket, horse racing, boxing and wrestling, footraces, rowing and yachting races, cockfighting, bullbaiting, and circus acts, among other things.

Rules against gathering in large crowds often were suspended when people participated in controlled commercialized spectator events. Local neighborhood events that attracted crowds were often defined as illegal, but organized commercial events were approved in most industrial societies, even when they attracted large crowds. These events were controlled and organized to benefit the interests of those with power and influence in society.

Some sport participation did occur among urban workers, but it was relatively rare during the early days of the Industrial Revolution. In the United States, for example, it usually was limited to activities such as bowling and billiards, played mostly by men. The constraints of work and the lack of money and facilities made it difficult for working-class people to engage in anything but informal games and physical activities. There were exceptions to this pattern, but they were rare.

Similarly, African slaves, who constituted 20 percent of the U.S. population during the early 1800s, had few opportunities to engage in any games or sports beyond what the slaveholders permitted. The dancing and other physical activities that occurred in slave quarters emphasized cooperation and community spirit—qualities required for survival (Wiggins, 1994). These activities took forms based on African traditions and efforts to cope with the experience of slavery. According to former slave and noted abolitionist Frederick Douglass, the games and holidays that the slaveholders permitted "were among the most effective means . . . of keeping down the spirit of insurrection among the slaves" (in Ashe, 1993, p. 10).

Around the middle of the nineteenth century, things began to change. During the first part of the century, people in parts of Europe and North America become concerned about the physical health of workers. Some of this concern was based on the awareness that workers were being exploited, and some was based on the recognition that weak and sickly workers could not be productive, so people began calling for new open spaces and externally sponsored "healthy" leisure pursuits. Fitness became highly publicized, and there was an emphasis on calisthenics, gymnastics, and outdoor exercises. In the United States, for example, these fitness activities did not necessarily include sports, but they definitely excluded hanging around in pool halls, bowling alleys, and bars. Furthermore, the Emancipation Proclamation and the Civil War made it possible for 4.5 million former slaves to participate in a range of sport activities.

In the middle of the nineteenth century, there was an emphasis on exercise and fitness among some people. Exercises were often done by groups of men who worked together or had other community-based relationships with each other. There was no emphasis on organized competition or record keeping of achievements.

The emergence of formally organized competitive sports would require more than increased freedom and limited support for healthy leisure activities, but this was the time during which the foundations for organized sports were established. In discussing more recent issues related to sports in society, we will focus in the next section on events in the United States.

The Later Years: Changing Interests, Values, and Opportunities

From the late nineteenth century until today, there has been a growing emphasis on rationality and organization in American society. For example, during the mid-1800s, common interests in sport activities led to the establishment of organized clubs, which sponsored and controlled sport participation. Club membership usually was limited to wealthy people in urban areas and college students at the exclusive Eastern schools. However, the clubs did sponsor competitions, which often attracted spectators from all social classes. The YMCA, founded in 1844 in England and shortly thereafter in the United States, did much to change the popular notion that physical conditioning through exercise and sports was anti-Christian.

The games and sport activities of working-class people did not usually occur under the sponsorship of clubs or organizations, and they seldom received any publicity. An exception to this pattern involved baseball. Working-class male participation in baseball was relatively widespread and, after the Civil War, baseball games were organized, sponsored, and publicized in many communities throughout the East and Midwest. Leagues were established at various levels of competition, and professional baseball became increasingly popular. Professional women's teams existed, but they seldom received the sponsorship they needed to grow in popularity. African Americans developed teams and leagues around the country, despite the racism that prevented them from playing in many white-dominated communities in the South.

As sport activities became more organized, they generally reinforced existing class distinctions in society. Upper-class clubs emphasized achievement and "gentlemanly" involvement—an orientation that ultimately provided the basis for later definitions of amateurism (which originated in England). These definitions of the *amateur* then became tools for excluding working-class people from the sport events organized to express the interests of upper-class participants (Eitzen, 1988, 2003). The activities of the working classes, by contrast, were much more likely to involve folk games and commercialized sports—a combination that ultimately led to professionalization. This two-phased development of amateurism and professionalization occurred in slightly different ways in different countries (Dunning, 1999).

The Seeds of New Meanings   Underlying the growing organization of sport activities during the second half of the nineteenth century was a new emphasis on the seriousness of sports. Instead of defining sports simply as enjoyable diversions, people gradually came to see physically strenuous, organized competitive games as tools for achieving economic progress and social development. Many people linked sport participation with economic productivity, national loyalty,

and the development of admirable character traits, especially among males. This new way of looking at organized sports was grounded in a wide array of changes in every segment of industrial society: the economy, politics, family life, religion, education, science, philosophy, and technology. Review the box "Dominant Sport Forms Today," page 66–67, for the characteristics of high-profile organized competitive sports.

The Growth of Organized Sports in the United States: 1880 to 1920

POWER AND WEALTH IN ACTION   The years between 1880 and 1920 were crucial for the development of organized sports in the United States (Cavallo, 1981; Mrozek, 1983). During this time, wealthy people developed lives of leisure, in which sport activities played a major part. In fact, the rich used participation in certain sports to prove to the world that they were successful enough to have the luxury of "wasting" time by engaging in frivolous, nonproductive activities (Veblen, 1899). Although the wealthy often used sports to reinforce status distinctions between themselves and the rest of the population, they also influenced how sports were played and organized by others, especially those in the middle class who aspired to enter the ranks of the rich and powerful.

Upper-class influence affected various dimensions of sports, including the norms for players and spectators, the standards for facilities and equipment, and the way in which people in lower social classes defined sports and integrated them into their lives. Specifically, wealthy people used their economic resources to encourage others to define sports as *consumer activities* to be played in *proper* attire, using the *proper* equipment in a *proper* facility, and preceded or followed by *proper* social occasions separated from employment and the workplace. Through this process of "encouragement" and the development of consensus about the forms and meanings of sports (described as *hegemony* by sociologists; see chapter 4, page 119), sports became connected with and supportive of the economy. The connection was subtle because sports involved widespread consumption and a commitment to rules and productivity, while also being popularly defined as "nonwork" activities, separate from the economy.

The emergence of these ideas about how sports "should be" played was important, because it enabled people with power to reproduce their privilege in society without overtly coercing workers to think and do certain things. Instead of maintaining their privilege by being nasty, people with economic power promoted sport forms that were entertaining and fun while reinforcing the values and orientations that promoted capitalist business expansion. As critical theories have emphasized, this is a good example of how sports can be political and economic activities, even though most people see them just as fun physical activities and events.

From 1880 to 1920, middle- and working-class people, especially white males, had increased opportunities to play sports. Labor unions, progressive government legislation, and economic expansion combined to improve working and living conditions—except among many African Americans, who faced new forms of racism and segregation beginning in the mid-1880s, as a white backlash to Reconstruction occurred. The efforts of unions and social reformers gradually led to increases in the free time and the material resources available to many working-class people. This process was complemented by the expansion of the middle class, a collection of people with at least some leisure resources. The spirit of reform around the turn of the twentieth century also was associated with the development of parks, recreation programs, and organized playground activities for urban residents, especially children.

IDEAS ABOUT SPORT PARTICIPATION AND "CHARACTER DEVELOPMENT"   Early in the twentieth century, opportunities for sport involvement increased, but the opportunities available to most

people were shaped by factors beyond the interests of the participants themselves. Important new ideas about human behavior, individual development, and social life led to an emphasis on organized competitive sports as "character-building" activities.

Until the latter part of the nineteenth century, most people believed human behavior was unrelated to environmental factors. They believed that fate or supernatural forces dictated individual development and that social life was established by a combination of God's will, necessity, and coincidence. However, these ideas began to change as people discovered that the social environment influenced people's actions and that it was possible to change people's actions by altering the organization of social life.

This new way of thinking was a crucial catalyst in the growth of modern sports. It made sports into something more than just enjoyable pastimes. Gradually, sports were defined as potential educational experiences—experiences with important consequences for individuals and society as a whole. This change, based on functionalist and evolutionary theories, which were dominant at the time, provided a new basis for organizing and promoting sport participation. For the first time in history, people saw sports as tools for changing behavior, shaping character, building unity and cohesion in an ethnically diverse population, and creating national loyalty.

People began to think about the meaning and purpose of sports in new and serious terms. For example, some religious groups, later referred to as "muscular Christians" (see chapter 15), suggested a link between physical strength and the ability to do good works; they promoted sport involvement as an avenue for spiritual growth. Others saw sports as tools for teaching immigrant children lessons that would turn them into contributing members of a corporate-bureaucratic-democratic society. These people also promoted organized playground programs that used team sports to undermine traditional ethnic values and replace them with an Americanized way of looking at the world. People interested in economic expansion tended to see organized sports as tools for generating profits and introducing untrained workers to activities emphasizing teamwork, obedience to rules, planning, organization, and production; they promoted sports for the purpose of creating good workers who could tolerate stressful working conditions.

In large part, organized sports became important because influential people believed that they could be used to train loyal, hardworking people dedicated to achievement and production for the glory of God and country. Sports were socially constructed and defined in ways that were believed to promote this type of character development. In the United States, this was done through new "Americanized" sports such as football, baseball, and basketball. Soccer, very popular among many central and southern European immigrants at the turn of the twentieth century, was believed to perpetuate potentially dangerous links with "foreign" cultures. Therefore, those who wanted to encourage new American identities among immigrants viewed soccer negatively. These views were so strong that it has taken nearly eighty years for soccer to make a comeback in the United States.

ORGANIZED SPORTS AND IDEAS ABOUT MASCULINITY AND FEMININITY   The new belief that sport participation built character was applied primarily to males. Those who organized and sponsored new programs thought they could use organized sports, especially team sports, to tame what they perceived as the savage, undisciplined character of young, lower-class males. Their intent was to create orderly citizens and cooperative workers. At the same time, they used sports for young males from middle-class backgrounds to counteract what many believed was the negative influence of female-dominated home lives. Their goal was to turn "overfeminized" middle-class boys into assertive, competitive, achievement-oriented young men, who would become effective leaders in business, politics, and the military. In these ways, contemporary sports were heavily grounded in the desire of those in the dominant social classes to exercise control over the working classes, while preparing their own sons to inherit their positions of power and influence (Burstyn, 1999; Kidd, 1996b).

Although an increasing number of women participated in sport activities between 1880 and 1920, many sport programs ignored females. Organizers and sponsors did not see sport participation as an important factor in the character development of girls and women. They sometimes included young girls with boys in the organized games in playground programs, but they discouraged sex-integrated sport activities for children nearing the age of puberty. There were strong fears that, if boys and girls played sports with one another, they could become good friends and that, if they were friends, their relationships would lose the mystery that would motivate them to marry, have children, and maintain dominant ideas about gender.

Whereas boys were taught to play a number of sports on the playgrounds after the turn of the century, girls often were given shady places, where they could rest and preserve their energy. Medical doctors warned that playing sports would sap the energy that young women needed to conceive and bear healthy children. Luther Gulick, the primary shaper of the YMCA's philosophy on recreation at that time, wrote, "It is clear that athletics have never been either a test or a large factor in the survival of women; athletics do not test womanliness as they test manliness" (1906, p. 158). Gulick also felt that strenuous activity was harmful to the minds and bodies of females. This was the gender ideology of the time.

Therefore, organized activities for girls often consisted of domestic science classes designed to make them good homemakers and mothers. When playground organizers did provide opportunities for girls to play games and sports, they designed activities that would cultivate "lady-like" traits, such as poise and body control. This is why so many girls participated in gymnastics, figure skating, and other "grace and beauty" sports (Burstyn, 1999; Hart, 1981). Another goal of the activities was to make young women healthy for bearing children. Competition was eliminated or controlled, and the activities emphasized personal health, the dignity of beauty, and good form. In some cases, the only reason games and sports were included in girls' activities was to provide the knowledge they would need in the future to introduce their sons to active games.

Limited opportunities and a lack of encouragement did not stop women from participating in sports, but they certainly restricted the extent of their involvement (Vertinsky, 1994). Some middle- and upper-class women engaged in popular physical exercises and recreational sport activities, but, apart from a limited number of intercollegiate games and private tournaments, they had few opportunities to engage in formal competitive events. The participation of girls and women from lower-income groups was restricted to informal street games, a few supervised exercise classes, and field days in public schools. Ideas about femininity changed between 1880 and 1920, but traditional gender ideology and numerous misconceptions about the physical and mental effects of strenuous activities on females prevented the "new woman" of the early twentieth century from enjoying the same participation opportunities and encouragement received by males (Lenskyj, 1986). In fact, medical beliefs did more to subvert the health of women during these years than to improve it (Vertinsky, 1987).

ORGANIZED SPORTS AND IDEAS ABOUT SKIN COLOR AND ETHNICITY After the Civil War, African Americans in the United States became increasingly involved in sports. Much of their participation occurred in segregated settings, but participation with whites gradually increased until the 1880s. Then whites established new forms of segregation and racism, designed to slow the changes that were upsetting a social order that had been built and based on white privilege. Whites in both the North and South became increasingly uncomfortable with changes in race relations, and they drafted Jim Crow laws, which clearly divided people into the categories of "white" and "black" and restricted the rights and opportunities of African Americans.

The widespread belief among whites that blacks were intellectually and physically inferior led many whites to view black athletes as a curiosity. Then, as black athletes gradually demonstrated their skills in certain sports, whites developed increasingly detailed genetic explanations for black achievements. The more blacks achieved in sports, the more whites used those achievements as "proof" that blacks had animal-like characteristics, which made them socially inferior. This powerful form of racial ideology became so deeply ingrained in U.S. culture that it continues to exist today.

White ethnics (Irish, Italians, Germans, and others) during this time also experienced forms of discrimination that limited their sport participation and forced them to play their native games in ethnically segregated clubs. Public schools became the settings in which many young men from these ethnic groups came to learn Americanized sports and enjoy participation to such an extent that many excelled in them.

ORGANIZED SPORTS AND IDEAS ABOUT AGE AND DISABILITY Aging involves biological changes, but the connection between aging and sport participation depends on the social meanings given to those changes. Because developmental theory around the turn of the twentieth century emphasized that development occurred during childhood and adolescence, sport programs were created and sponsored for young people, not for older people. Theories suggested that older people were already developed: they were "grown up," and their characters could no longer be shaped.

The leisure activities of the wealthy at the turn of the twentieth century included sports. Systems of gender exclusion in sports have varied through history and from one sport to another. Sports played by girls and women during the nineteenth and twentieth centuries often involved balance and coordination, which were defined as "ladylike" qualities, and they often included nets or other barriers, so that there would be no physical contact between female players. (H. Armstrong Roberts)

Medical knowledge at the time also discouraged older people from engaging in sports. Many people believed that strenuous activities put too many demands on the heart and other muscles in aging bodies. This did not stop older people from participating in certain sport activities, but it did prevent the establishment of organized sport programs for older people. Furthermore, when older people did participate, it was usually in age-segregated settings.

People with most forms of physical or mental disability during this time were either denied the opportunity to participate in or were actively discouraged from engaging in most physical activities, especially sports. People were unsure about the effects of strenuous exercise on their actions and state of mind and body. Definitions of mental and physical disability often gave rise to fears and prejudices. Some people thought it was risky for people with disabilities to become physically active or excited. Therefore, programs to build their bodies were discouraged. This policy meant that people with disabilities were often isolated and seen as unworthy of any serious attention related to their physical development.

1880 TO 1920—A KEY PERIOD   Although opportunities for participation in organized sports between 1880 and 1920 were not equally distributed by social class, gender, skin color, ethnicity, age, or ability, participation among most categories of people increased dramatically. This was the case in most industrializing societies. In North America and Europe, the organizational attributes that we associate with today's high-profile organized sports became clearly established during this time. The games people played featured a combination of secularism, a growing commitment to expanding participation opportunities, increased specialization, rationalization, bureaucratization, quantification, and the quest for records. As noted in the box "Dominant Sport Forms Today," page 66–67, these are some of the sociologically relevant characteristics that have become the foundation of what many people define as sports today.

Since 1920, the resources devoted to organized competitive sports have increased in many societies around the world. Technology has been used to change sport experiences for participants and spectators, and tremendous growth has occurred in sport-related industries and the government sponsorship of sports. Many of today's struggles about the organization, meaning, and purpose of sports and how sports should be integrated into people's lives were visible in some form eighty years ago.

SINCE 1920: STRUGGLES CONTINUE

By 1920, major connections between sports and American culture and society had been firmly established. Sports were a growing part of people's everyday lives, and they were linked to major social institutions, such as the family, religion, education, the economy, the government, and the media.

Since 1920, there has been an intensification of the rate of change and an expansion of the visibility and importance of sports in people's lives. The past eight decades have been a time of many "firsts" in U.S. sports. They have also been a time for continuing struggles over the

AT YOUR FINGERTIPS For more information on sports as social constructions and contested activities, see pages 5, 26–27.

following:

1. The meaning, purpose, and organization of sports
2. Who plays sports under what conditions
3. How and why sports are sponsored

As explained in chapter 1, sports are social constructions *and* contested activities. Therefore, we can outline social trends and patterns in recent history by focusing on issues and events related to these three realms of struggle. They serve as useful reference points for discussing social history, and I use them to guide my choice of materials in nearly all the following chapters. They create a framework for thinking about patterns and trends during the twentieth century.

Table 3.2 highlights events related to major struggles and changes in sports, providing a feel for the social side of what has happened in recent sports history. Of course, the timing, dynamics, and outcomes of these struggles and changes were related to larger historical events and trends. A few of these include

- The Great Depression (1929–1941)
- Increased rationalization and the use of science to organize social life and formulate policies in public-governmental and private-business spheres of life (1920–present)
- WWII (1941–1945) and the Korean War (1950–1953)
- Growth of the power and influence of nation states and growth of the power and influence of the United States (1920–present)
- The Cold War, during which the United States and its capitalist allies were aligned against the Soviet Union and its socialist/communist allies (1945–1991)
- Suburbanization and the baby boom (1946–1964)

In the 1920s, the women's suffrage movement was strong, and many women pushed the boundaries of gender. Attempts to challenge and transform society included playing what then were defined as "men's sports." Women's soccer and baseball games often drew large crowds, even though some people believed that participation in these sports was contrary to nature and morality. (Sally Fox)

- Expansion of the middle class and a growing emphasis on the importance of leisure and entertainment in the lives of Americans (1920–present)
- Growing emphasis on education and a strong cultural focus on child development
- Expansion of the media, especially the electronic media (1920–present)
- The civil rights movement and the women's movement (1960–present)
- Growth of the power and influence of large corporations, especially those headquartered in the United States
- Cultural shift from lives organized around production to lives organized around consumption (1950–present)
- Increased rate of development in communications and transportation technologies (1920–present)
- Increased globalization across all spheres of life (1920–present)

Connections between the recent history of sports and these trends and events are too complex to discuss in this chapter. But it is possible to outline some of the major struggles that have occurred since 1920.

Table 3.2   U.S. Social History Time Line, 1920–1990

This selective list of events provides a general sense of the chronology and complexity of recent sports history in the United States. Since 1920, thousands of sports organizations have come and gone, hundreds of legal decisions have regulated and deregulated sports, and thousands of important struggles have occurred over (1) the meaning, purpose, and organization of sports; (2) who plays sports under what conditions; and (3) how and why sports are sponsored. This list highlights events related to the issues and controversies discussed in chapters 4 through 15.

1920	Formation of a baseball league for black players; formation of the National Football League
1921	The NCAA sponsors the first national college sport championship (in track and field)
1922	Supreme Court rules that professional sports are not a form of "commerce" and exempts them from antitrust laws; first Women's Olympic Games held (in response to the exclusion of women in many Olympic events)
1923	Eastern Colored League for black men is founded (goes broke in 1928)
1924	First live radio coverage of the Olympics (from Chamonix, France)
1926	Babe Ruth suffers from gonorrhea and it is reported as "stomach cramps" in the media; formation of the American Basketball League for men (bankrupt in 1931)
1927	Socialists and communists form the Labor Sports Union of America and sponsor soccer and other sports
1929	Carnegie Foundation for the Advancement of Teaching publishes a report critical of commercialization and professionalization in college athletics
1932	Summer Olympics held in Los Angeles; Babe Didrikson sets two world records and wins two medals; alternative Olympics for working people sponsored in Chicago by The Labor Sports Union of America
1935	African American boxer Joe Louis defeats Italian champion Primo Carnera in a world heavyweight title bout before 60,000 people in Yankee Stadium
1936	Olympic Games held in Berlin; Jesse Owens wins four gold medals and challenges Hitler's ideas about race and white supremacy
1939	Little League Baseball founded; boxing becomes the first sport to receive regular TV coverage
1943	All-American Girls' Professional Baseball League founded (dissolved in 1954)
1946	NCAA holds a major conference and drafts a "Sanity Code" to restore honesty and integrity to intercollegiate athletics; American Football Conference formed (bankrupt in 1950)
1947	Jackie Robinson signs with Brooklyn Dodgers to become the first black since the nineteenth century to play in major league baseball; first Little League World Series tournament
1948	Last baseball season played by Negro National League
1949	Ladies Profession Golf Association and National Basketball Association formed; Mexican American Richard "Poncho" Gonzalez wins U.S. Open Tennis Championship
1951	American Council on Education study reports that college sports are too commercialized and professionalized
1952	Soviet Union competes in the Olympic Games held in Helsinki, Finland; Sports Ambassadors, an evangelical Christian sport organization, founded
1953	Little League World Series televised for the first time
1954	First issue of *Sports Illustrated* published; formation of the Fellowship of Christian Athletes (FCA)
1957	Althea Gibson is the first black player to win a title at Wimbledon; Monterrey, Mexico becomes the first non-U.S. team to win the Little League World Series (they win again in 1958)
1960	Wilma Rudolph wins three gold medals at the Olympic Games in Rome, and Cassius Clay (Muhammad Ali) wins the gold medal in boxing; American Football League formed; ABC is the first U.S. television company to pay for the rights to broadcast the Olympic Games in Rome ($4 million); first Paralympic Games for athletes with physical disabilities are held following the Summer Olympic Games in Rome; Charlie Sifford is the first black to play in a pro golf tournament; the NFL Dallas Cowboys are bought for $500,000; Negro American League goes broke

1964	Olympic Games in Tokyo are the first ever to be televised; Cassius Clay (Muhammad Ali) wins world heavyweight boxing title; Billy Mills, an Oglala Sioux from the Pine Ridge reservation, wins the gold medal in the 10,000 meters in the Olympics in Tokyo; *Sports Illustrated* publishes its first "swimsuit edition"
1965	First fully domed stadium, the Houston Astrodome, opens
1966	Major League Baseball Players' Association formed; Athletes in Action formed as an extension of the Campus Crusade for Christ
1967	Green Bay Packers of the NFL defeat the Kansas City Chiefs of the AFL in the first Super Bowl, played at the Los Angeles Coliseum; the IOC defines and bans doping; the average annual salary of Major League Baseball players is $19,000; Muhammad Ali stripped of his heavyweight boxing title for refusing induction into the army; Katherine Switzer registers as "K. Switzer" and runs the all-male Boston Marathon, even though men try to remove her physically from the course
1968	Many black athletes boycott the Olympic Games in Mexico City in protest against racial discrimination; Mexican students protest against using public money for the Olympic Games and police kill over 30 protestors; Tommy Smith and John Carlos support the boycott by raising their gloved fists on the victory podium at Olympics; Olympic drug testing begins; first Special Olympics held for athletes with mental retardation; women athletes in the Olympics forced to verify their gender by submitting to a mandatory chromosome-based sex test; Arthur Ashe becomes the first and only African American man to ever win the U.S. Open Tennis title
1969	AFL and NFL merge to create one pro football league; Arthur Ashe and others form the Association of Tennis Professionals to represent the rights and interests of players; Poncho Gonzalez defeats Puerto Rican American Charlie Pasarell in the longest match in Wimbledon history
1970	First *Monday Night Football* game is played and televised on ABC
1971	An estimated 294,000 girls play varsity high school sports (1 out of every 27 female students); creation of the Association for Intercollegiate Athletics for Women (AIAW) to organize and administer varsity college sports for women; women officially allowed to run the Boston Marathon for the first time
1972	Title IX, making gender discrimination illegal in educational institutions that receive federal money, signed into law by President Richard Nixon; the NCAA attempts to subvert Title IX; Mark Spitz wins seven gold medals in the Olympic Games in Munich, Germany; Palestinian terrorists capture eleven Israeli team members at the Olympic Village in Munich, they kill two, and the nine others are killed during a botched rescue attempt.
1973	Billie Jean King defeats Bobby Riggs in a made-for-TV "Battle of the Sexes" tennis match; Harry Edwards publishes the first sociology of sport textbook in the United States; the NCAA establishes Divisions I, II, and II and defines all athletic scholarships in Divisions I and II as one-year renewable contracts; tests are developed to detect steroid use among athletes
1974	World Team Tennis founded; World Football League founded (bankrupt in 1975); the NCAA lobbies to exclude college athletic programs from coverage under Title IX; Little League forms a softball programs for girls; an American Council on Education reports that college sports are too commercialized and professionalized; Lee Elder is first black man to play in The Master's golf tournament
1975	President Gerald Ford amends Title IX to specifically prohibit sex discrimination in school-sponsored sports
1976	The "reserve clause" in major league baseball is declared illegal and players become free agents; the ABA and NBA merge to form one pro basketball league; twenty-nine nations, mostly from Africa and Asia, boycott the Olympic Games in Montreal to protest New Zealand's sporting ties with white supremacist South Africa; the NCAA passes Proposition 48, listing new academic requirements that apply to athletes in Division I schools

(Continued)

Table 3.2 *(Continued)*

1977	Janet Guthrie is the first woman driver in the Indianapolis 500; the all-male International Olympic Committee (IOC) declares that women would not be allowed to run in the 3,000-meter race (about 2 miles) because it was too demanding for women's bodies
1978	U.S. Congress passes the Amateur Sports Act, establishing the United States Olympic Committee (USOC) as the central governing body of amateur sports; the North American Society for the Sociology of Sport is founded; three sociology of sport textbooks are published, including the first edition of *Sport in Society: Issues and Controversies*
1979	The Office for Civil Rights of the U.S. Department of Education defines the legal meaning of Title IX and presents enforcement guidelines; ESPN, an all-sports cable television company goes on air; Stanford University changes its name from the Indians to the Cardinal
1980	U.S Men's Hockey team defeats the heavily favored Soviet Union team to win the gold medal at the Winter Olympic Games in Lake Placid, New York, in February; in July, the United States and more than fifty other nations boycott the Summer Olympic Games in Moscow because the Soviet Union invaded Afghanistan in 1979
1981	First midseason strike by major league baseball players (average annual salary for players was about $185,000)
1982	NFL players go on strike for nine weeks (average annual salary for players was about $90,000); Association for Intercollegiate Athletics for Women (AIAW) dissolved as National Collegiate Athletic Association (NCAA) takes over women's sports; first Gay Games held in San Francisco; testosterone added to IOC banned substance list; IOC allows amateur athletes to accept money from sponsors, which enabled the U.S. athletes to compete with state-supported athletes in socialist nations
1983	United States Football League (USFL) plays it first game (bankrupt in 1986)
1984	Soviet Union and thirteen other nations boycott the Olympic Games in Los Angeles; these Olympic Games were the first to show a profit for the host city and this intensified competition among cities bidding to host future games; U.S. Supreme Court restricts Title IX by ruling that it applies only to those programs that directly receive federal money in a school; Little League Baseball charter is rewritten to allow girls to play (after dozens of class action lawsuits brought by girls against Little League); Texas State Legislature approves "no pass, no play" rules governing eligibility in Texas high school sports
1985	In connection with Super Bowl XIX, ABC sells the first million-dollar minute of advertising in television history
1986	Lynette Woodward is the first women to play on a men's pro basketball team, The Harlem Globetrotters
1988	U.S. Congress passes the Civil Rights Restoration Act and reaffirms that Title IX applies to entire schools, not just individual programs; Congress passes the Olympic Coin Act, allowing the USOC to sell silver and gold commemorative coins minted by the U.S. Treasury; Carl Lewis wins the gold medal in 100-meter dash after the medal is stripped from Canadian sprinter Ben Johnson, who sets a world record but tests positive for steroids
1990	NCAA passes Proposition 42 to strengthen and extend the academic standards stated in Prop 48; Olympic sports begin to abolish distinctions between amateur and professional athletes; Congress approves Student Right-to-Know Act, which requires public disclosure of graduation rates for varsity athletes and the general student body*

*Of course, struggles and changes have continued since 1990. For Example, there were temporary changes in the meanings and purposes of sports in the wake of the attacks of 9/11/01. There have continued to be notable "firsts" in connection with race and ethnicity, gender, sexuality, and disability: Venus and Serena Williams and Tiger Woods have contributed to these "firsts"; so have many women, including those who have participated in the Olympics and Soccer's World Cup Tournament; so have the gay and lesbian athletes who have contributed to a range of sports and teams; and so have athletes in the Paralympics, the Special Olympics, and other events that have presented sport participation opportunities for people with disabilities. At the same time, corporate sponsorships have continued to become a major influence in nearly all sports.

Struggles over Meaning, Purpose, and Organization

Meaning of Sports   Struggles over the meaning of sports occur in many spheres of social life. The result has been that sports have always had multiple meanings, and these meanings have changed over time. In fact, the meanings of sports change over the lifetimes of individuals and throughout the histories of organizations, communities, and societies. They even change in connection with global developments.

As in many other nations, national identity is a central realm of meaning connected with sports in the United States. Since 1920, certain sports and athletes have been associated with "Americanness." Through the 1960s, baseball was widely referred to as "America's pastime," and it was associated with apple pie and motherhood. Both men and women played baseball through the 1930s but, after World War II, baseball became primarily a man's game and has remained that way ever since. Gender is another realm of meaning that has been closely connected with the meaning of sports.

In the 1960s, football emerged as the classic American sport. It emphasized strength, power, confrontation, and strategy—all of which were very consistent with dominant values and cultural orientations during the Cold War between the United States and the Soviet Union. Men played football and defended turf, just as men in the military protected the country from communist threats. Furthermore, college football became increasingly visible during the 1960s as baby boomers began to fill classrooms in record numbers. Campuses used football as a public relations tool, and students used it as a ritualized occasion for taking a break from coursework.

Both baseball and football were played by the sons of immigrants as they sought to establish and reaffirm their assimilation into American culture. Sports such as rugby and soccer, born in England and nurtured in Europe, were never

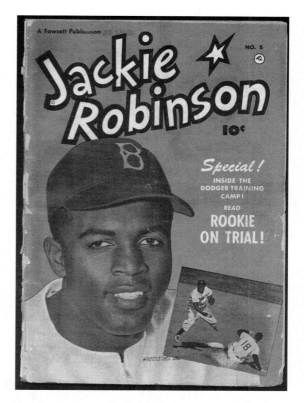

This is the cover of a Jackie Robinson comic book published in 1951. The headline, "Rookie on Trial," indicates that Robinson's performance in baseball was evaluated in connection with issues of racial desegregation in sports. The pressure that Robinson endured has been felt by many others who have been "firsts" in their sports. (American Memory Collection)

associated with national identity in the United States in the same way that baseball and football were. Soccer teams and leagues came and went during much of the twentieth century, but the sport was generally associated with ethnic communities, workers seeking to form labor unions, or elite college students familiar with European sports. It was not until the 1970s and 1980s that soccer gained popularity among boys and girls in white, middle-class families. But soccer remains more of an international game than an American game in the minds of most people, and it has never become closely tied to national identity among more than a small segment of the U.S. population.

Regional identities have also been closely connected with certain sports during recent history. Stock car racing and the National Association for Stock Car Auto Racing (NASCAR) emerged and grew in southern states and represented values, traditions, and histories common to the South. Rodeo has traditionally had special meaning in midwestern and western rural areas, where livestock and horses have been important to local economies and people's everyday lives (Pearson and Haney, 1999).

The meanings given to sports generally reaffirm the values and lifestyles of those who play and watch them, and this certainly was true after 1920. As cities grew, so did basketball, often described as the city game (Axthelm, 1970). As black men came to dominate the highest levels of basketball, the game became defined by many as a "black game." In the process, basketball took on special meaning in many black communities. At the same time, basketball had different meanings for white boys growing up in Indiana, where "Hoosier Hysteria" occurred every fall during the state high school basketball tournament, and it had other meanings for the girls who played high school basketball in Iowa, where for a number of years girls' basketball was more popular than the boys' game.

We will not go into detail about how meanings have varied and changed with dozens of sports among numerous segments of the population. However, as we consider changes in sports since 1920, it is necessary to remember that our understanding of recent sports history depends partly on our knowledge of what sports have meant to those who have played, watched, and sponsored them.

Purpose of Sports   Meaning and purpose have always been closely aligned. Struggles over the

purpose of sports also occur in many spheres of social life. On a very general level, the central purpose of most sports between the 1920s and 1960s was to foster fitness and fair play. At the same time, however, most sports were organized around various forms of exclusion and segregation based on race, ethnicity, gender, age, and (dis)ability.

As occupational success and social mobility became increasingly important in a growing capitalist economy during the 1950s, there was a gradual turn toward an emphasis on competitive success and wins in sports. Competitive sports were seen to build the kind of character that many people felt was essential to American prosperity. As sports teams and sports events became linked to schools, communities, and nations, the primary purpose of sports continued to shift from participation and fair play to wins and prestige for sponsors. By the 1960s, "winning is not the most important thing—it is the ONLY thing" had become a slogan accepted by many people. The main focus in the Olympics, for example, were the medal counts, especially gold medal counts, as people used wins to measure the relative status of the United States and the Soviet Union. The popularity of many sports came to be fueled by an emphasis on winning, not play.

Beginning in the 1970s and the growth of sports coverage in the electronic media, entertainment became an increasingly important purpose of sports. As this occurred, the styles and personas of athletes became widely publicized, and teams worked to develop public relations profiles built around values and identities that resonated with audience segments or large collections of spectators. This is when the Dallas Cowboys came to be known as "America's Team," while the Chicago Bears and the Detroit Lions were known as hard-hitting, "blue-collar" teams that emphasized the fundamentals of traditional midwestern culture. Entertainment and winning were closely linked because winners

SIDELINES

"Why don't we settle this in a civilized way? We'll charge admission to watch!"

FIGURE 3.2 Dominant sport forms in many societies have been organized to celebrate a particular form of masculinity, emphasizing aggression, conquest, and dominance.

filled stadiums and generated revenues for sponsors and owners.

Of course, through recent history, there has never been complete agreement on the purpose of sports. Physical educators often have emphasized fitness and health, whereas people associated with the commercial media have emphasized entertainment. This and other disagreements are highlighted in the recent histories of sports in schools and community recreation programs. These struggles over purpose continue today.

Organization of Sports   Since 1920, there has been a clear trend toward organizing sports in formal and "official" ways. Mainstream sports have become characterized by increasingly standardized rules and control by official governing bodies. Professional sport leagues along with college and high school conferences have been formed. Youth sports have become highly organized since the founding of Little League Baseball in 1939. The general emphasis across most sports has been on establishing rules, standardizing events, and

becoming organized in efficient and, when possible, profitable ways.

Some people have resisted increased organization and rationalization, but resistance has not slowed or reversed this trend. Even most alternative and recreational sports have become increasingly organized as people have tried to make them safer, more accessible to potential participants, or more commercially profitable. Free-spirited surfers and skateboarders may have resisted organized competition, but they have also saved their money to buy high-tech boards with features that enabled them to have new experiences in their sports. In other words, they have accepted the underlying emphasis on rationalization and the use of science and technology that has served as the cultural foundation for the increased organization of most sports.

A good part of the recent history of sports has involved the increased organization of sports (review table 3.2). Hundreds of sport organizations have come and gone, but the emphasis on getting organized has only become stronger and more influential over the years. As this has occurred, there have been classic and sometimes bitter struggles over what organization should control various sports. In fact, the recent histories of most sports contain detailed stories about those struggles.

Struggles over Who Will Participate Under What Conditions

Some of the most contentious struggles in sports since the 1920s have revolved around who participates in formally organized, mainstream sport programs. Men from relatively well-to-do Anglo-Saxon families have generally had the greatest access to sport participation opportunities, even though sport participation patterns vary with the lifestyles characteristic of different social classes, groups, and communities.

As in other time periods, gender, race and ethnicity, age, and physical abilities have been related

During the twentieth century, sports clearly were linked to political and racial ideologies. At the 1936 Olympic Games in Berlin, Hitler and the Nazi Party used the games to promote their ideas about the superiority of the "Nordic race." This historic photo shows a German official giving the Nazi salute and Jesse Owens, the African American sprinter who won four gold medals during the games giving the U.S. salute. Owens' success challenged Hitler's ideas about Nordic, i.e., white, supremacy in sports. (USOC Archives)

to participation patterns through recent history. Since 1920, there have been constant struggles to expand participation opportunities for women, people from low-income families and neighborhoods, ethnic minorities, people with physical and mental disabilities, and people labeled as gay or lesbian. There are complex histories associated with each of these struggles, but the general trend since 1920 has been to open sport participation to more people, especially in the case of sports that are funded by public money and played in public facilities. Many private clubs have maintained

exclusionary membership policies over the years, and some continue to do so today.

Struggles over who participates under what conditions have been further complicated by the diversity of goals among the people involved. Some people have fought to be integrated fully into organized, mainstream sports, whereas others have fought to have separate opportunities that meet their specific needs and interests. In a sense, there has been disagreement over whether everyone's needs and interests could be met in sports developed and organized around the interests and experiences of able-bodied, white, heterosexual males.

Struggles over the conditions of sport participation have also been common. Professional athletes have formed players' associations to represent their interests in struggles related to the conditions of their sport participation. College students have sometimes struggled to have their club teams recognized and funded as official varsity teams. Some high school students have wanted expanded intramural programs, and many children have resisted the sports organized by adults in favor of alternative sports played under conditions more of their own choosing. Struggles since 1920 have also involved issues of eligibility, the allocation of rewards, and the funding of certain types of sport participation opportunities. This brings us to struggles over how and why sports are sponsored.

Struggles over How and Why Sports Are Sponsored

Struggles over sponsorship issues are difficult to detect in the items listed in table 3.2. The Great Depression of the 1930s generally interfered with the funding and sponsorship of many sports. However, as government policies and programs were developed to cope with the consequences of the depression, there was an emphasis on the public sponsorship of sports, especially youth sports. After World War II, most communities in the United States embraced the idea that tax money should be used to provide a range of sport participation opportunities, especially for boys.

The growth of anti-biggovernment sentiments in the late 1970s, combined with the growth of the power and wealth of corporations in the 1980s and 1990s, led to a shift in sponsorship patterns. After more than thirty years of growing public sponsorship of sports, public programs began to lose their funding. New programs in the 1980s increasingly depended on private money and corporate sponsorships. Although many of us simply took these changes for granted, they had a major impact on how sports grew, which sports became popular, and who had opportunities to participate in sports.

Instead of being based on ideas about the public or common good, sports today often are sponsored in connection with the commercial interests of corporations. Struggles in recent history over issues related to who should sponsor sports are complex in many communities, school districts, and intercollegiate athletic programs. An awareness of these sponsorship issues and how people have struggled over them in the past makes us more informed citizens as we participate in our own communities and decide on who should sponsor sports and why. Some of these issues are discussed in chapter 5 and chapters 10–14.

Thinking About Recent History

As we think about the past, it is important to remember that each struggle has occurred in a particular social, political, and economic context. Sports history does not just happen; it has always depended on the actions of people working with each other to construct sports to match their ideals of what sports should be in our lives. Many people in recent history have ignored what others say is practical or realistic and have pursued choices that are based on unrealistic ideals. These are the people who have inspired changes related to racial desegregation in sports, new opportunities for girls and women, new programs for people with disabilities, and the recognition and acceptance of gay and lesbian athletes. Table 3.2 does not do justice to those people and their struggles to make their visions of what sports should be into reality. Each of those struggles has its own history.

During World War II, many women had opportunities to play sports sponsored by the military. After the war, however, there were few sport programs for girls and women. Instead, the government emphasized the importance of domestic roles for women. In the process, many women who played sports in the 1950s were labeled as "dykes," and many girls grew up thinking that cheerleading was more attractive than playing sports.

SUMMARY

CAN WE USE HISTORY TO UNDERSTAND SPORTS TODAY?

Our selective look at different times and places shows us that physical games, contests, and sports activities are integrally related to social relations and social forces in societies. As social life changes and power shifts in any society, there are changes in the organization and meanings of games and sport activities, as well as in the people who participate in and sponsor them.

In ancient Greece, games and contests were grounded in mythology and religious beliefs.

They focused on the interests of young males from wealthy segments of society. As the outcomes of organized games took on political and social implications beyond the events, athletes were recruited from the lower classes and paid for their participation. The existence of professional athletes, the use of violence during contests and games, the heavy emphasis on victory, and the low priority given to fairness show us a side of sports in ancient Greece that contradicts many popular beliefs. They also indicate that fairness and democracy are not achieved in sports without commitment and effort.

Roman contests and games emphasized mass entertainment. They were designed to celebrate and preserve the power of political leaders and to pacify masses of unemployed and underemployed workers in Roman cities and towns. Many athletes in Roman events were slaves recruited for the events or "troublemakers" coerced into jeopardizing their lives in battle with one another or with wild animals. These spectacles faded with the demise of the Roman Empire. Critically assessing the spectacle-like contests and games of this period makes us more aware of the interests that powerful people may have in promoting large sport events.

Folk games and tournaments in medieval times clearly reflected and reproduced gender and social class differences in European cultures. The peasants played local versions of folk games in connection with seasonal events in village life. The knights and nobles engaged in tournaments and jousts. Other members of the upper classes, including the clergy, often used their resources to develop games and sport activities to occupy their leisure time. Studying this time period alerts us to the importance of gender and class differences in our efforts to understand sports and sport experiences today.

The patterns from the medieval period continued through the Renaissance in parts of Europe, although the Protestant Reformation generated negative attitudes about any activities that interfered with work and religious worship. The peasants felt the impact of these attitudes most sharply, because they did not have the resources to avoid the restrictive controls imposed by government officials who were inspired by a Calvinist or Puritan orientation. The games and sports of the wealthy generally continued within the safe confines of their private grounds. The Enlightenment was associated with increased political rights and freedom to engage in diversionary games and physical activities. Studying these historical periods alerts us to the importance of cultural ideology and government policies when it comes to who plays sports under what conditions.

During the early days of the Industrial Revolution, the influence of the Puritans faded in both Europe and North America, but the demands of work and the absence of spaces for play generally limited sport involvement to the wealthy and to people in rural areas. This pattern began to change in the United States from the mid-1800s to the early 1900s, when the combined influence of labor unions, progressive legislation, and economic expansion led to the creation of new ideas about the consequences of sport participation and new opportunities for involvement. However, opportunities for involvement were shaped primarily by the needs of an economy emphasizing mass production and mass consumption. It was in this context that people developed what we now refer to as organized competitive sports. Studying this period shows us that the origins of today's sports were tied closely to complex social, political, and economic factors.

Sports history since 1920 has revolved around continuing struggles over the meaning, purpose, and organization of sports; who participates in sports under what conditions; and who sponsors sports and why. These struggles have occurred in connection with major historical events, trends, and patterns. In most cases, powerful economic and political interests have prevailed in these struggles, but, in a few cases, people motivated by idealistic visions of what sports could and should be like have prevailed. Every now and then their visions have become reality for some time, but the struggles never end.

Those of us who study sports in society are concerned with these struggles and the contexts in which they occur. As we try to understand current struggles, our awareness of past struggles is useful. This will become increasingly clear in the following chapters.

SUGGESTED READINGS

Ashe, A. 1993. *A hard road to glory*. 3 vols. New York: Amistad (overview and analysis of the history of sport participation among blacks in the United

States; little attention is given to black women's participation in any form of sport activity).

Baker, W. J. 1988. *Sports in the western world.* Urbana: University of Illinois Press (survey and analysis of European and North American sports, starting with the ancient Greeks and ending with contemporary commercial sports).

Cahn, S. K. 1994. *Coming on strong: Gender and sexuality in twentieth-century women's sports.* New York: The Free Press (focuses on the struggles women have engaged in as they have become increasingly involved in sports since the turn of the twentieth century).

Cavallo, D. 1981. *Muscles and morals: Organized playgrounds and urban reform, 1880–1920.* Philadelphia: University of Pennsylvania Press (excellent discussion of how sports became connected with American values around the turn of the twentieth century).

Dunning, E. 1999. *Sport matters: Sociological studies of sport, violence, and civilization.* London: Routledge (development and change in sport are viewed in connection with historical developments and changes; clear examples of how figurational sociology uses historical data as integral to a sociological analysis of civilizing processes and sport).

Gruneau, R. 1988. Modernization or hegemony: Two views of sport and social development. In *Not just a game*, edited by J. Harvey and H. Cantelon. Ottawa, Ontario: University of Ottawa Press (concise critique of conceptual approaches to the history of sports; read this article before reading any of the "historical accounts" of sport events in this list).

Guttmann, A. 1978. *From ritual to record: The nature of modern sports.* New York: Columbia University Press (comparative analysis of the characteristics of sports in different historical periods).

Guttmann, A. 1988. *A whole new ball game: An interpretation of American sports.* Chapel Hill: University of North Carolina Press (readable interpretation of sports within the social context of U.S. history; includes chapters on sports and Native Americans, Puritans, and Southerners, among other topics).

Guttmann, A. 1991. *Women's sports: A history.* New York: Columbia University Press (overview of women's sport participation in ancient civilizations through the present, with special emphasis on the nineteenth and twentieth centuries).

Kidd, B. 1997. *The struggle for Canadian sport.* Toronto: University of Toronto Press (focuses on key struggles over the meaning and organization of Canadian sports, primarily during the first half of the twentieth century; analysis centers on four major sport organizations and how they fared in connection with major social and cultural transformations).

Kruger, A., and J. Riordan, eds. 1996. *The story of worker sport.* Champaign, IL: Human Kinetics (overview and ten accounts of the history of the worker sport movement, which, between 1912 and the late 1940s, provided for workers around the world an alternative to sport forms emerging in connection with capitalist economic expansion).

Mrozek, D. J. 1983. *Sport and American mentality, 1880–1920.* Knoxville: The University of Tennessee Press (excellent social historical analysis of the origins of organized sports in the United States).

Ruck, R. *Sandlot seasons: Sport in black Pittsburgh.* Urbana: University of Illinois Press (unique look at the sporting life and the meanings of sports in the community life of blacks in Pittsburgh in the early twentieth century).

Struna, N. 2000. Social history and sport. In *Handbook of sports studies*, edited by J. Coakley and E. Dunning. London: Sage (critical overview of historical studies of sports; emphasizes the need to view sports as social practices and social formations that are constitutive of societies over time).

Wiggins, D. K., ed. 1995. *Sport in America: From wicked amusement to national obsession.* Champaign, IL: Human Kinetics (nineteen essays focusing on sports activities from colonial times to the 1990s).

 **WEBSITE RESOURCES**

Note: Websites often change. The following URLs were current when this book was printed. Please check our website (www.mhhe.com/coakley8e) for updates and additions.

www.mhhe.com/coakley8e Click on chapter 3.

www.studies.org The Institute for Mediterranean Studies; site summarizes and sells audiotapes on the Olympic Games in ancient Greece and on sports in the Roman world.

http://depthome.brooklyn.cuny.edu/classics/gladiatr/index.htm Site developed by Roger Dunkle, an expert on Roman sports; excellent information and visuals related to the spectacles in which gladiators participated.

www.umist.ac.uk/sport/ishpes.html International Society for the History of Physical Education and Sport provides links to many other sites for sports history.

www.nassh.org North American Society for Sport History.

www.sover.net/~spectrum/index.html Site of the American Soccer History Archives; excellent histories of both men's and women's soccer.

Colorado Springs Gazette

Sports and Socialization

Who Plays and What Happens To Them?

SPORTS HAVE GIVEN me my foundation. . . . I'm an athlete inside and out. It's not something I try to be, it is who I am. I can't remember a time when I didn't play sports. It's truly all I know.

—Danielle Martin, multisport athlete (2002)

 Online Learning Center Resources

Visit *Sports in Society*'s Online Learning Center at **www.mhhe.com/coakley8e** for additional information and study material for this chapter, including

- Self-grading quizzes
- Learning objectives
- Related websites
- Additional readings

A complete outline is available online at
www.mhhe.com/coakley8e.

WHAT DO KIDS know about us? They only know that we play sports. They don't know who we are as people. You don't learn the important things about life by watching a person play football.

—Emmitt Smith, NFL player (1996)

Socialization is a popular topic today in discussions about sports. When we ask any of the following questions, we are concerned about sports and socialization issues:

- Why are some people fanatically interested in playing and/or watching sports, whereas others don't seem to care about sports?
- How and why do some people see themselves as athletes and dedicate themselves to playing particular sports?
- When and why do people stop playing competitive sports and what happens to them when they do?
- What impact do sports and sport participation have on people's lives?

Many of us in the sociology of sport have done research to find answers to one or more of these questions. The search for answers has taken us in different directions, depending on the theoretical frameworks we have used to guide our thinking about sports and sport participation. The influence of theoretical perspectives will be discussed in the first section of this chapter. Then we will consider three topics that are central to discussions of sports and socialization:

1. The process of becoming involved and staying involved in sports
2. The process of changing or ending sport participation
3. The impact of being involved in sports

In connection with these topics, I will explain how the questions previously listed have been answered in the sociology of sport. As you read the chapter, you will see that most of the answers are incomplete and many others are so complex that discussions about them will carry over into other chapters.

The chapter closes with information about new approaches to socialization. These approaches are based on critical theories that emphasize socialization as a community and cultural process rather than only an individual and personal process.

WHAT IS SOCIALIZATION?

Socialization is an active process of learning and social development, which occurs as we interact with one another and become acquainted with the social world in which we live. It involves the formation of ideas about who we are and what is important in our lives. We are *not* simply passive learners in the socialization process. We actively participate in our own socialization as we influence those who influence us. We actively interpret what we see and hear, and we accept, resist, or revise the messages we receive about who we are, about the world, and about what we should do as we make our way in the world. Therefore, socialization is *not* a one-way process of social influence through which we are molded and shaped. Instead, it is an interactive process through which we actively connect with others, synthesize information, and *make decisions* that shape our own lives and the social world around us.

This definition of *socialization*, which I use to guide my research, is based on a combination of *critical* and *interactionist* theories. Therefore, not all sociologists would agree with it. Those using functionalist or conflict theory approaches, for example, would define *socialization* in slightly different terms. Their definitions have an impact on how they do research and the questions they ask about sports and socialization.

A Functionalist Approach to Socialization

When *functionalist theory* is used to guide research, socialization is viewed as a process through which we develop the social characteristics that enable us to fit into society and contribute to its operation. Functionalists assume that socialization conforms to an *internalization model* (see Coakley, 1993a, b). In other words, as we grow up in our families, go to school, interact with peers, and receive messages from the media, we learn the rules we should follow and the roles we should play in society.

When researchers use an internalization model to guide their studies, they focus attention on three things: (1) the characteristics of those being socialized, (2) the people and social institutions that *do* the socializing, and (3) the specific *outcomes*, or results, of socialization. In most studies of sports and socialization, researchers focus on athletes as the people being socialized. The studies are designed to identify *who* socializes athletes. The primary agents of socialization include fathers, mothers, brothers, sisters, teachers, coaches, peers, and occasionally certain role models. The most central and influential socializers are described as **significant others.** In some cases, socializing institutions, such as the family, education, and the media, are also studied in connection with sport participation. The socialization outcomes, or results, that are studied include the personal attitudes, values, and skills that are considered functional for the society as a whole.

Those who use a functionalist approach have often studied who and what *causes* people to participate in sports and how participation prepares young people to be productive members of society. These studies primarily have used quantitative research methods. Numerous functionalist studies have been done and thousands of questionnaires have been sent to people, especially children and high school students, in an effort to find out how people become involved in sports and what they learn when they play sports. The analyses in these studies have compared those who play organized sports with those who do not play organized sports. The researchers have tried to identify (1) who or what might influence a person to play sports and (2) what personal characteristics might be developed in connection with sport participation (see figure 4.1).

Some of these studies have helped us understand certain aspects of sports and socialization, but many of them have presented inconsistent and contradictory findings. With notable exceptions,[1]

"I know this is starting early, but I can't let him get too far behind the other kids if he's ever going to make a team in high school."

FIGURE 4.1 Research guided by functionalist theory has focused on who influences the sport participation patterns of children. Fathers and other family members have usually been identified as *significant others* when it comes to influencing when, how, and where children play sports.

data on the causes and benefits of playing sports have tended to be superficial, and they have told us little about sport socialization as an ongoing process in people's lives. They have given us fuzzy snapshots, rather than clear videos, of socialization.

A Conflict Theory Approach to Socialization

Studies based on conflict theory have also used an internalization model of socialization. However, they have emphasized how socialization processes in sports serve the economic needs of capitalist systems by influencing people in society to become compliant workers and eager consumers of goods and services. Conflict theorists assume that people with economic power direct and use economic forces to maintain their

---

[1]The exceptions include the following: Beller and Stoll, 1995; Decker and Lasley, 1995; Miller et al., 1999; President's Council on Physical Fitness and Sports, 1997; Sabo et al., 1998; Spreitzer, 1995.

privileged positions in society. Therefore, studies based on this theoretical approach have focused on research issues such as these: (1) Does participation in organized competitive sports create apolitical, militaristic, sexist, and racist orientations among players and spectators? (2) Are people from low-income and working-class backgrounds systematically denied opportunities to play sports on their own terms and in their own ways? (3) Are athletes, especially those from poor, minority backgrounds, victims of a profit-driven, win-at-all-cost sport system in which they have no rights? (4) Do people with money and power control the conditions of sport participation and exploit others to make money and maintain their own interests?

Overall, these studies have emphasized how elitist, oppressively organized sport programs and autocratic, military-style coaches produced athletes who were obedient, politically conservative, and willing to engage in violence to achieve goals approved by those with power in the society. Some of these studies also have described how sport participation has jeopardized the health of athletes and has alienated athletes from their own bodies to the point that they have been willing to play while injured or numbed by drugs.

New Approaches to Socialization

Many sociologists have become dissatisfied with the assumptions inherent in the internalization model of socialization used in research by functionalists and conflict theorists. They are not comfortable with the idea that we humans are either products of society and its system needs or victims of economic forces. Therefore, many researchers have turned to *interactionist models* of socialization and use new methods to study socialization processes.

Recent research on sports and socialization tends to be based on various combinations of critical and interactionist theories. Therefore, socialization is defined as an interactive process of learning about the social world and our

participation in it. The researchers who study socialization in these terms are likely to use qualitative rather than quantitative research methods. Instead of using questionnaires to obtain statistical data from large numbers of people, they are more likely to use in-depth interviews and field observations. Their goal is to obtain detailed descriptions of sport experiences as they occur in people's lives. They seek information on how people actively make decisions about their sport participation and about how they derive meaning from playing sports. Finally, they seek to connect those meanings with the larger cultural context in which sports and sport participation exist. The rest of this chapter will draw on both old and new approaches in an effort to outline what we know about sports and socialization today.

BECOMING INVOLVED AND STAYING INVOLVED IN SPORTS

Research based on functionalist theory tells us that sport participation is related to three factors: (1) a person's abilities and characteristics; (2) the influence of significant others, including parents, siblings, teachers, and peers; and (3) the availability of opportunities to play and experience success in sports. These are the snapshots that we have of *socialization into sports*. However, a fuller description of the ongoing process of becoming and staying involved in sports emerges when we obtain detailed stories from people about their sport participation. These stories are more like videos than snapshots.

Studies using in-depth interviews, fieldwork, participant observations, and strategic conversations indicate that sport participation is connected with many ongoing processes that make up people's lives, and it occurs as people actively make decisions about their lives in connection with those processes. In other words, people continually make decisions about sport participation; they don't make decisions once and for all time. As social conditions change, so do people's decisions. Furthermore, as people stay involved in sports, their reasons for participating on one day may be different from their reasons for participating on the next day or the next. When there is no reason, they may discontinue or change their sport participation.

We can best understand the process of becoming and staying involved in sports by looking at examples of research. The following studies give us sociological videos of how people have integrated sport participation into their lives on an everyday basis. These videos help us develop a sense of socialization processes in people's lives.

Example 1: The Process of Becoming an Elite Athlete

Chris Stevenson is a sport sociologist interested in how people become athletes. Using a symbolic interactionist approach, he interviewed and collected stories from elite athletes about how they were introduced to their sports and became committed to sport participation. As he analyzed the stories, he noticed that they sounded much like descriptions of careers. In other words, they had identifiable beginnings, followed by a process of development, and ultimately an end. Stevenson felt that he could understand these careers in terms of the decisions the people had made about sport participation in connection with other things that were important in their lives over time.

In one of his studies, Stevenson (1999) interviewed twenty-nine Canadian and British international athletes. At first, he was struck by the diversity of the stories the athletes told him. But then he detected two processes that were common in the stories. First, there was a process of **introduction and involvement,** during which young people received support as they tried certain sports. His interviewees talked about being introduced to sports bit-by-bit over time through important relationships in their lives. Gradually, they chose to specialize in a particular sport based on an evaluation of their potential for success

and on how much they felt personally connected to the people associated with the sport. Second, there was a process of **developing a commitment** to sport participation. This process occurred as the athletes formed a web of personal relationships connected with their participation and gradually established personal reputations and identities as athletes in their sports. Their relationships and identities figured prominently in how they set priorities and made decisions about sport participation. Their participation over time depended on active and thoughtful efforts to develop identities as athletes. As this happened, and as people who were important in the lives of these young people gave them recognition and respect as athletes, they became more deeply committed to their sports and to living the life of an athlete.

Stevenson found that these processes did *not* occur automatically. The young people themselves helped them happen. Becoming and staying involved in sports was a complex process. The young people realized that they could not take for granted the social support they received for playing sports and being athletes. They knew that the resources needed for participation could disappear or that changes in other parts of their lives could force them to alter the importance of sport participation. Therefore, they made decisions to stay involved in sports day after day, and, as they stayed involved, they impressed and influenced those who supported and influenced them.

Stevenson's research shows that the socialization process is *interactive* and that each of us actively participates in our own socialization.

Example 2: The Process of Being Accepted as an Athlete

Peter Donnelly and Kevin Young are sociologists who have studied sports as "social worlds," or subcultures in which people develop their own ways of doing things and relating to another. In their research, they have paid special attention to how people become a part of those

Participation in sports usually is sponsored through important social relationships. This girl's participation in competitive climbing football is tied to her relationship with her father and her coach. Her continued participation will depend on developing a commitment to the sport. Commitment depends on sponsorship combined with the establishment of important social connections related to the sport. (Jay Coakley)

subcultures. They have taken a closer look at some of the things studied by Stevenson (Donnelly and Young, 1999).

On the basis of stories that Donnelly collected from rock climbers and Young collected from rugby players, they have determined that playing sports occurs in connection with complex processes of identity formation. They explain that entering and becoming an athlete in a particular sport subculture occurs through a four-phase process:

1. Acquiring knowledge about the sport
2. Associating with people involved in the sport
3. Learning how those people think about their sport and what they do and expect from each other
4. Becoming recognized and fully accepted into the sport group as a fellow athlete

This description of sport socialization extends our understanding of what is involved in developing a commitment to a sport. Donnelly and Young discovered that becoming involved in a sport depends on learning to "talk the talk and walk the walk," so that one is identified and accepted as an athlete by others who are athletes. This process of identification and acceptance does not happen once and for all time; it is continuous. When we lose touch and are no longer able to talk the talk and walk the walk, acceptance wanes, our identities become difficult to maintain, and overall support for our participation becomes weak. We are not athletes forever.

To discover part of what Donnelly and Young found in their study, just observe a sport group, such as skateboarders ("street skaters," "ramp skaters," or "curbheads"), in-line skaters, snowboarders, or beach volleyball players. Each group has its own vocabulary and its own way of referring to its members and what they do. The terms they use are not found in dictionaries. They also have unique ways of thinking about and doing their sports, and they have special understandings of what they can expect from others in their groups. New participants in these sports may be tested and "pushed" by the "veterans" before being accepted and defined as true skaters, riders, or volleyball athletes. Vocabularies may change over time, but this process of becoming accepted and gaining support for participation exists in basketball, hockey, gymnastics, and golf—in every sport. Many people have discovered that, if they do not establish social connections and acceptance in a sport, their sport participation may not be very regular or long term. Becoming involved in sports clearly is part of a complex, *interactive* socialization process.

Example 3: To Participate or Not to Participate

Anita White is a sport sociologist and former director of sport development at the British Sports Council. Before she began working at the Sports Council, Anita and I did a study of sport participation patterns among British adolescents in a working-class area east of London (Coakley and White, 1999). Our goal was to provide coaches and program organizers information on why some young people participated in council-sponsored sport programs, whereas most did not.

Our in-depth interviews with thirty-four young men and twenty-six young women indicated that their participation or lack of participation in sports was the result of decisions based on a combination of factors. In the lives of British teenagers, these factors included the following:

> **Athletics play an important role in shaping our character and values.**
>
> —Bill Clinton, former President of the United States (1999)

1. Their ideas about how sport participation was related to other interests and goals in their lives
2. Their desires to develop and display competence in ways that would gain them recognition and respect from others
3. Social support for participation and access to the resources needed for participation (time, transportation, equipment, and money)
4. Memories of past experiences with physical activities and sports
5. General sport-related cultural images and messages that they had in their minds

We found that the young people made decisions to play sports when it helped them extend control over their lives, become what they wanted to be, and present themselves to others as competent. We also found that the young women were less likely than the young men to imagine that sport participation could do these things for them. Therefore, the young women participated in organized sports less often and less seriously.

The young people in our study did not simply respond to the world around them. Instead, they actively thought about how sports might fit with the rest of their lives and what they wanted out of their lives in the future. Their decisions were based on their conclusions. Their sport participation patterns shifted over time, depending on their access to opportunities, changes in their lives, and changes in the way they saw themselves and their connections to the world. Therefore, socialization into sports was a *continuous, interactive process* grounded in the social and cultural contexts in which the young people lived.

The stories we heard in our study showed that people make decisions to participate in sports for different reasons at different points in their lives. This fits with theories telling us that developmental tasks and challenges change as we move through childhood, adolescence, young adulthood, and adulthood. Therefore, the issues considered by seven-year-olds who make decisions about sport participation are different from the issues considered by fourteen-year-olds, forty-year-olds (see Porterfield, 1999), or sixty-year-olds (C.L. Stevenson, 2002). Furthermore, when seven-year-olds make decisions about sport participation today, they do so in a different cultural context than the context in which seven-year-olds lived in 1970 or will live in 2020.

Sport participation decisions at all points during the life course and through history also are tied to the perceived cultural importance of sports and the links between playing sports, gaining general social acceptance, and achieving personal goals. Therefore, studies of socialization into sports must take into account the ways in which sport participation is related to individual development, the organization of social life, and the ideologies that are prevalent in a culture (Ingham et al., 1999).

In summary, this study and the two previously discussed provide three videos about becoming and staying involved in sports. They show that sport participation is grounded in decision-making processes involving self-reflection, social support, social acceptance, and cultural factors. People never make decisions about sport participation once and for all time. They make them day after day as they consider how sports are related to their lives. In fact, they sometimes make them moment-by-moment when coaches are making them run wind sprints and they are sucking air at the starting line! These decisions are mediated by the social and cultural contexts in which the people live. Therefore, the social meanings attached to gender, class, race, age, and physical (dis)abilities influence decision-making processes, and political, economic, social, and cultural forces influence social meanings.

CHANGING OR ENDING SPORT PARTICIPATION

Questions about becoming and staying involved in sports often are followed by questions about changing or ending involvement. Much of the research on this latter issue has been guided by "role theories" inspired by functionalist theory or "alienation theories" inspired by conflict theory (see Coakley, 1993b).

Researchers using *functionalist theory* have been concerned with identifying who is dropping out of sports and what can be done to keep them in sports, so that they would learn the positive lessons that come with sport participation. This was a very popular research topic when millions of baby boomers were flooding playgrounds and elementary schools, and parents wanted to know how to control and build character in their children. Research based on functionalist approaches also has focused on how to make sport programs more efficient in developing skills and

preparing young people to move to higher levels of competition. This remains a popular topic among people in sports, since they have an interest in creating winners on interscholastic, international, and professional teams.

Researchers using *conflict theory* generally focused on the possibility that rigidly organized, win-oriented programs turned children off to participation. It was hypothesized that these programs, along with autocratic, command-style coaches, alienated many young athletes and caused them to drop out. Older athletes dropped out because of injuries or alienation caused by years of exploitation. Research explored how athletes in elite sports were victims of exploitation and how specialized, long-term sport participation itself could be a socially alienating experience, causing athletes to drop out and to have serious personal problems when they ended participation.

After reviewing dozens of these studies grounded in functionalism and conflict theory, I've concluded that they tell us the following important things:

- When people drop out of particular sports, they don't drop out of all sports forever, nor do they cut all ties with sports. In fact, many play different and less competitive sports or move into other sport roles, such as coach, program organizer or administrator, or sports businessperson.
- Dropping out of sports is usually part of a process involving changes and transitions in the rest of a person's life (changing schools, graduating, getting a job, getting married, having children, etc.).
- Dropping out of sports is not always the result of victimization or exploitation, although injuries and negative experiences can and do influence decisions to change or end participation.
- Problems may occur for those who end long careers in sports, especially those who have no identity apart from sports or who lack the social and material resources they need to

Although people may drop out of sports at one point in the life course, they may return at a later point. This team of women, all over seventy years old, is playing an exhibition game against a group of younger women. The team is raising funds to travel to the national finals in the Senior Games. (Jay Coakley)

make transitions into other careers and social settings.

Recent studies, especially those using qualitative methods and informed by critical interactionist models of socialization, have built on these findings and extended our understanding. Following are three examples of these studies.

Example 1: Burnout Among Young Athletes

My work with coaches combined with my interest in identity issues led me to do a study of young people who, after being age-group champions with the potential to succeed in their sports, had made the decision to quit playing their sports (Coakley, 1992). Since the term *burnout* often was used to describe this phenomenon, I decided to interview former elite athletes identified by themselves or others as cases of burnout; all were adolescents.

Data from in-depth interviews led me to conclude that burnout was grounded in the organization of the high-performance sports in which these young people had played. It occurred when the young people felt they had lost control over their lives and felt they could not explore and develop identities apart from sports. The athletes associated this combination of having no control and having a unidimensional identity with high levels of stress and a decline in the amount of fun they had in their sports. As stress increased and fun decreased, they burned out.

This study showed that stress and fun were connected with how sport programs were organized and how sport experiences were connected with developmental issues during adolescence. When being a young athlete, especially a highly successful one, interfered with accomplishing important developmental tasks during adolescence, burnout was likely. Teaching young athletes how to manage stress is important in preventing burnout, but it is also important to empower athletes and change the social organization of the sport contexts in which they train and compete (Gould et al., 1997).

Example 2: Getting out of Sports and Getting on with Life

Konstantinos Koukouris (1994) is a physical educator from Greece who wanted to know how and why people who had been committed to sports had decided to end or seriously reduce their participation. After analyzing questionnaire data from 157 former athletes in track and field, rowing, and volleyball, Koukouris identified 34 who had ceased or reduced sport participation between the ages of 18 and 24. In-depth interviews with these people enabled him to construct case studies illustrating the process of disengaging from sports.

Stories told by the athletes indicated that they had voluntarily decided to end or change their participation. They had done this over a period of time, during which they had stopped playing and then started again more than once; they hadn't gone "cold turkey" as they cut their sport involvement. The decision to end or change sport participation had been associated primarily with the need to get a job and support themselves, but also with realistic judgments about their own sport skills and their chances to move to higher

levels of competition. As they graduated from high school or college, they had been faced with the expectation that they should be responsible for their own lives. As they got jobs, they didn't have the time needed to train and play sports at a serious level, and, as they spent money to establish adult lifestyles, they didn't have enough left to pay for serious training. Furthermore, sport programs enabling them to train had not been available or had been organized so rigidly that training didn't fit into their new adult lives.

As serious training ended, many of these young adults sought other ways to be physically active or connected with sports. They sometimes experienced problems, but, as they faced new challenges, most of them grew and developed in positive ways, much like people who had never been serious athletes. Disengagement from serious sport training had been inevitable, necessary, and usually beneficial in the lives of these young adults.

Example 3: Changing Personal Investments in Sport Careers

Garry Wheeler from the University of Alberta is concerned with the careers of athletes with disabilities and what happens when their playing careers end. Building on a study he and others had done with Canadian paralympic athletes (Wheeler et al., 1996), Wheeler and his fellow researchers gathered data through interviews with forty athletes from Israel, the United Kingdom, Canada, and the United States (Wheeler et al., 1999). Data indicated that patterns among the athletes with disabilities were similar in each of the countries. The athletes tended to become deeply involved in their sport participation, and they often achieved a high level of success in a relatively short time. Through sports, they found meaning, developed a sense of personal competence, and established identities as elite athletes. Their intense investment in sport participation and their sport identity brought both rewards and costs.

AT YOUR FINGERTIPS   For more information, on post-retirement adjustment issues, see pages 354–358.

Withdrawal from participation and the transition into the rest of life presented challenges for many. About one in ten experienced serious emotional problems during this process. Retirement often came quite suddenly and was accompanied by a process of reinvesting time and energy into other spheres of their lives. There was a focus on reconnecting with family members and friends, going back to school, and getting on with occupational careers. However, most stayed connected with sports and sport organizations as coaches, administrators, or recreational athletes. Those few who hoped they might compete again often experienced difficulties during the retirement transition, but most accepted and adjusted to ending their competitive careers.

In summary, research shows that ending or changing sport participation often involves the same interactive and decision-making processes that underlie becoming and staying involved in sports. Just as people are not simply socialized into sports, neither are they simply socialized out of sports. Changes in participation are grounded in decision-making processes tied to the lives, life courses, and social worlds of those involved. It is difficult to explain changes in sport participation without knowing about the identity issues and the developmental and life course issues that are involved (Dacyshyn, 1999; Drahota and Eitzen, 1998; Swain, 1999). It also is important to know about the resources that athletes possess and can use as they make transitions to other relationships, activities, and careers. Some people have problems when they retire from sports, but, to understand those problems, we need information about how sports fit into their lives. My conclusion is that, if sport participation expands a person's identity, experiences, relationships, and resources, the retirement transition will be smooth. Difficulties are most likely to occur when a person has never had the desire or the chance to live outside the culture of elite sports (Messner, 1992; Murphy et al., 1996).

BEING INVOLVED IN SPORTS: WHAT HAPPENS?

Do Sports Build Character?

Although beliefs about the consequences of sport participation vary from culture to culture, the belief that playing sports builds character has been widely accepted in many cultures. It has been used as a basis for encouraging children to play sports, funding sports programs, building stadiums, promoting teams and leagues, and sponsoring events such as the Olympic Games.

For nearly fifty years, people have done research to test the validity of the "sport builds character" belief. Much of this research has involved comparisons of the traits, attitudes, and behaviors of people who participate in particular organized competitive sports at a particular time with the traits, attitudes, and behaviors of those who do not. Most of these comparisons have looked at differences between the members of U.S. high school varsity teams and other students, who are not on varsity teams, at a particular time. These snapshot comparisons have provided inconsistent and confusing results. This is because "character" is difficult to measure, and researchers have used multiple definitions of *character* in their studies (Stoll and Beller, 1998). Furthermore, many researchers have based their studies on two faulty assumptions about sports and sport experiences (McCormack and Chalip, 1988). First, researchers have wrongly assumed that *all* organized competitive sports involve similar character-shaping experiences for *all* athletes. Second, they have wrongly assumed that the character-shaping experiences in organized sports are so unique that people who don't play sports do not have opportunities to develop certain positive traits, attitudes, and behaviors.

Many factors can encourage people to decide to drop out of sports or shift their participation from one sport to another. Identity changes, access to resources, and life course issues are involved. As circumstances change, so do our ideas about ourselves and about sports and sport participation. (Travis Spradling, *Colorado Springs Gazette*)

Over the years, these faulty assumptions have led many researchers to overlook the following important things when they have used statistical comparisons of athletes and nonathletes to study sports and socialization:

1. Sports are organized in vastly different ways across programs, teams, and situations and therefore offer many *different experiences* to participants. Therefore, sport participation involves a wide range of possible socialization experiences, both positive and negative. (I explain this point in the box "Power and Performance Versus Pleasure and Participation.")

2. People who choose or are selected to participate in sports may already have different traits than those who do not choose or are not selected to participate. Therefore, sports may not *build* character as much as they are organized to *select* people who already have character traits valued by coaches.

3. Different people define sport experiences in different ways, even when they are in the same programs or on the same teams. Therefore, the lessons learned in sports and the applications of those lessons to everyday life vary from one person to the next.

4. The meanings that people give to sport experiences often change over time as people

grow older and change how they view themselves and the world. Therefore, the lessons that people learn while playing sports may change in the future as they learn new ways to evaluate their past experiences, including experiences in sports.

5. Socialization occurs through the social interaction that accompanies sport participation. Therefore, the meaning and importance of playing sports are derived through a person's social relationships and the social and cultural contexts in which participation occurs.

6. The socialization that occurs in sports may also occur in other activities. Therefore, people who do not play sports may participate in other activities that involve valuable socialization experiences.

Due to these oversights, studies that have compared so-called athletes with so-called nonathletes have not provided consistent evidence about the complex socialization processes that occur in connection with sports and sport participation.

My review of these studies leads me to conclude that sport participation is most likely to have positive effects on people's lives when it is associated with the following:

- Opportunities for testing and developing identities apart from playing sports
- Knowledge of the world and how it works
- Experiences that go beyond the locker room and the playing field
- Formation of new relationships, including relationships outside of sports
- Clear lessons about how sport experiences can be used as a basis for dealing with challenges outside of sports
- Opportunities for other people to see, define, and deal with a person as more than just an athlete
- Opportunities to develop competence and become responsible in activities outside of sports

On the other hand, when playing sports *constricts* a person's opportunities, knowledge, experiences, and relationships, we can expect that negative socialization consequences will accompany participation. Neither good nor bad socialization outcomes occur automatically in connection with sport participation. In fact, the impact of all our experiences in sports is mediated by the social and cultural contexts in which we live.

The mere fact that people do or do not play sports tells us little about their overall lives and how they develop their sense of who they are, how they are connected with others, and what is important in their lives. This is why hundreds of studies have not given us the evidence we need to determine whether sports do or do not build character (Miracle and Rees, 1994; Sage, 1998a; Shields and Bredemeier, 1995; Stoll and Beller, 1998). The snapshots provided by comparisons of so-called athletes and nonathletes have helped us develop hypotheses about what happens in sports, but they have not provided the videos we need to understand all the positive and negative things that can occur in such dynamic socialization contexts.

The failure to find consistent, measurable effects of sport participation on specific character traits *does not mean* that sports and sport experiences have no impact on people's lives. We know that the discourses, images, and experiences associated with sports in many parts of the world are vivid and powerful. Sports do have an impact on us and the world around us. However, we cannot separate that impact from the meanings we give sports and the ways we integrate sport experiences into our lives, relationships, and culture. Therefore, if we want to know what happens in sports, we must study sport experiences in the social and cultural contexts in which they occur. This type of research is exciting, and it provides helpful insights into the many ways that sports are involved in socialization processes. See the box "Power and Performance Versus Pleasure and Participation," for a discussion of the differences in sports experiences.

Power and Performance Versus Pleasure and Participation
Different Sports, Different Experiences, Different Consequences

Sport experiences vary with the conditions under which sports are organized and played. To assume that all sports are organized around the same goals and emphasize the same orientations and behaviors is a mistake. In North America, for example, there are highly organized competitive sports, informal sports, adventure sports, recreational sports, extreme sports, alternative sports, cooperative sports, folk sports, contact sports, artistic sports, team sports, individual sports, and so on, and there are various combinations of these types. However, at this time, it seems that the dominant sport form in many societies is organized around what I will call a **power and performance model.**

Power and performance sports are highly organized and competitive. Generally, they emphasize the following:

- The use of strength, speed, and power to push human limits and aggressively dominate opponents in the quest for victories and championships
- The idea that excellence is proved through competitive success and achieved through intense dedication and hard work, combined with making sacrifices, risking one's personal well-being, and playing in pain
- The importance of setting records, defining the body as a machine, and using technology to control and monitor the body
- Selection systems based on physical skills and competitive success
- Hierarchical authority structures, in which athletes are subordinate to coaches and coaches are subordinate to owners and administrators
- Antagonism to the point that opponents are defined as enemies

Of course, becoming involved in and playing sports with these characteristics would be different from becoming involved in and playing sports with other characteristics.

Although power and performance sports have become the standard for determining what sports should

Power and performance sports involve the use of strength, speed, and power to dominate opponents in the quest for competitive victories. (Bob Jackson, *Colorado Springs Gazette*)

be in many countries, they have not been accepted by everyone. In fact, some people have maintained or developed other forms of sports grounded in a wide range of values and experiences. Some of these are revisions of dominant forms, whereas others represent alternative or even oppositional sport forms. These alternative and oppositional forms are diverse, but many fit what I will call a **pleasure and participation model.**

Pleasure and participation sports represent a diverse collection of physical activities, but they generally emphasize the following:

- Active participation revolving around a combination of types of connections—connections between people, between mind and body, and between physical activity and the environment
- An ethic of personal expression, enjoyment, growth, good health, and mutual concern and support for teammates and opponents
- Empowerment (not power) created by experiencing the body as a source of pleasure and well-being
- Inclusive participation based on an accommodation of differences in physical skills
- Democratic decision-making structures characterized by cooperation, the sharing of power, and give-and-take relationships between coaches and athletes
- Interpersonal support around the idea of competing *with*, not against, others; opponents are not enemies but those who test each other

These two sport forms do *not* encompass all the ways that sports might be organized and played. In fact, some people play sports that contain elements of both forms and reflect many ideas about what is important in physical activities. However, power and performance sports remain dominant today in the sense that they receive the most attention and support. When people play or watch these sports, their experiences are different than when they play or watch pleasure and participation sports. Not all sports are the same when it comes to socialization.

Why are power and performance sports dominant today? Using critical theories, the answer to this question is that sports are parts of culture, and people with power and resources usually want sports in their cultures to be organized and played in ways that promote their interests. They want sports to fit with how they see the world. They want sports to celebrate the relationships, orientations, and values that will reproduce their privileged positions in society. Today, power and

Pleasure and participation sports may involve competition, but the primary emphasis is on connections between people and on personal expression through participation. (Susanne Tregarthen/Educational Photo Stock)

performance sports fit the interests of people with power and resources.

Powerful and wealthy people in societies around the world maintain their privileged positions through many means. Some use coercive strategies through their control of military force, but most use cultural strategies designed to create the belief that power and wealth are distributed in legitimate and acceptable ways in society. For example, in countries with monarchies, the privilege of the royal family usually is explained in terms of its birthright. The monarchies exist as long as people in the society believe that birthrights represent legitimate claims to wealth and power. This is why the church and state have been so close in most societies with monarchies—kings and queens have used their association with powerful external forces, such as God or gods, to legitimize their power and wealth.

REFLECT ON SPORTS

Power and Performance Versus Pleasure and Participation (continued)

In democratic countries, most people use merit as a standard when judging whether power and wealth are legitimate. Thus, power and wealth in democracies can be maintained only when most people believe that rewards go to those who have earned them. When there is widespread inequality in a democratic society, those with power and wealth must promote the idea that they have earned their privileged positions through intelligence and hard work and that poverty and powerlessness are the result of a lack of intelligence and hard work. One way to promote this idea is to emphasize *competition* as a natural part of social life and as a fair means of determining who gets what in the society. If people believe this, then they will believe that those with power and wealth deserve what they have.

This connection between power relations and an emphasis on competition helps us understand why power and performance sports are so widely promoted and supported in North America and in many countries around the world today. These sports are based on a class ideology that celebrates winners and idealizes the domination of some people over others. These sports also promote the ideas that the only fair and natural way to distribute rewards is through competition and that those with the most power and wealth deserve more than what other people have because they have competed successfully—they are the winners.

This is how power and performance sports have come to be dominant in democratic societies in which there are extensive inequalities among people. In fact, the global expansion of these sports is based on similar factors. Powerful and wealthy transnational corporations spend billions of dollars annually on the sponsorship of power and performance sports because they want to promote widespread agreement that life should involve competition. They want people to agree that rewards should go to winners, that the winners deserve power and wealth, and that the ranking of people on the basis of power and wealth is not only fair but natural. In other words, their sponsorships are based on concerns about ideology as well as financial profits that might be generated by sports.

Pleasure and participation sports, as well as other sport forms that challenge or oppose the ideology that underlies power and performance sports, may be popular among some people, but they generally do not receive sponsorships and support from those with power and wealth in democratic societies. In fact, sponsorships and support go primarily to forms of alternative sports that have been converted to fit the power and performance model. When ESPN created the XGames, its goal was to represent alternative sport forms in a power and performance model that fits the interests of wealthy corporate sponsors, *not* the interests of participants and spectators. *What do you think?*

How Do Sports Affect Our Lives?

Sports and sport participation have an impact on people's lives. We are learning more about this impact through three types of studies based on a combination of critical, critical feminist, and interactionist theories:

1. Studies of sport experiences as explained through the voices of sport participants
2. Studies of the social worlds that are created around sports
3. Studies of sports as sites for the formation of ideology and struggles over ideological issues

Taken together, these studies have led many of us who are concerned with sports in society to rethink socialization issues. Now we view sports as *sites for socialization experiences*, rather than as *causes of specific socialization outcomes*. This is an important distinction. It highlights two things. First, sports are social locations rich in their potential for providing memorable and meaningful personal, social, and cultural experiences. Second, sports *by themselves do not cause particular changes in the character traits, attitudes, and behaviors of athletes and spectators*. In other words, when positive or negative socialization occurs in association with sports, we cannot just say it is caused by sports; instead, we treat sports as sites for experiences and then search for and explain the specific social processes through which socialization occurs.

A summary of some of this research illustrates how it helps us understand what happens in sports and how sports are connected with larger social issues in society.

Real-Life Experiences: Sport Stories from Athletes

The following examples provide socialization videos. They illustrate what happens in sports from the perspectives of the participants themselves, and they show us how people make sense out of sport experiences and integrate them into their lives on their own terms.

Example 1: The Moral Lessons of Little League
Sociologist Gary Alan Fine (1987) spent three years studying boys in Little League baseball. Fine focused on the moral socialization that occurred as the boys interacted with one another, with coaches, and with parents. He found that the moral messages presented to the boys by the coaches and parents were based on adult views of the world. But the boys heard and interpreted these messages in terms of their views as eleven-year-old males who were concerned primarily with being accepted by peers and learning what it means to be a man in U.S. culture. Thus, socialization was an interactive process in which the boys played key roles in what and how they learned. What happened to the boys as they played baseball resulted from a combination of adult influence, the developmental issues associated with preadolescence, and the social reality of being eleven-year-old boys in U.S. culture during the late 1980s.

Among other things, the boys learned to define *masculinity* in terms of toughness and dominance and to express disdain for females and any boys seen as weak or unwilling to take risks on or off the playing field. They also learned

other things, but their emerging ideas about manhood were influential in how they saw themselves and their connections to the world. Playing baseball did not *cause* the boys to define *masculinity* in a particular way, but their Little League teams were one of the social sites where they began to consider various ideas about what it means to be men and how to act as men.

What made baseball significant was that these emerging ideas about being tough and aggressive received endorsement from the coaches, parents, and peers. In fact, these people actually promoted toughness and aggression in connection with team strategies, player evaluations, and peer acceptance. The impact of this social feedback was accentuated because it generally reinforced other cultural messages the boys received in their lives. Therefore, playing baseball was a heavily gendered experience for them—it involved a connection between their identities as males in U.S. culture and their identities as athletes. A more recent study by Ingham and Dewar (1999) reported very similar findings in the case of fourteen- to fifteen-year-old boys in an organized ice hockey league.

Example 2: Lessons In the Locker Room
Sociologist Nancy Theberge (1999, 2000b) spent two years studying an elite women's ice hockey team in Canada. As she observed and interviewed team members, she noted that their experiences and orientations were related to the fact that men controlled the team, the league, and the sport itself. Within this overall sport structure, the women developed a professional approach to participation. They focused on hockey and were serious about being successful on the ice. In the process, they developed close connections with one another. The team became a community, with its own dynamics and internal organization. Within the context of this constructed community, the athletes learned things about hockey, about themselves, and about one another. The definitions and meanings that the players gave to their hockey experiences and the ways they linked them to their

lives emerged as they interacted with one another on and off the ice.

The locker room was a key place for the interaction through which the team members bonded with each other and worked out their personal definitions and meanings of sport participation. The emotional climate of the locker room, especially *after* a practice or game, encouraged talk that focused on who the athletes were as people and how they saw their connections with the world. This talk gave shape and meaning to what they did on the ice, to their sport experiences. It also served as a means for expressing feelings and thoughts about men, sexuality/homosexuality, male partners and female partners, and families. The women talked and joked about men but didn't degrade or reduce them to body parts in their comments. They made references to sex and sexuality in their conversations, but the substance of these references promoted inclusiveness rather than hostility or stereotypes. This was very different from what has reportedly occurred in many men's locker rooms (Curry, 1993).

Theberge's study shows us that playing sports is a social as much as a physical experience. The socialization that occurs in sports occurs *through social relationships*. Theberge focused on relationships between the athletes, but also important were their relationships with coaches, managers, trainers, friends, family members, sport reporters, and even fans. If we want to know what happens in sports, we must understand what happens in all those relationships. It is through them that players give meaning to what happens on the playing field, regardless of whether they win or lose, play well or make mistakes.

Example 3: Stories About Gay Male Athletes

The meanings given to sport experiences emerge in connection with social relationships. Meanings vary from one person to another because social relationships are influenced by social definitions given to age, gender, socioeconomic status, ethnicity, skin color, (dis)abilities, and sexuality. This is one of the points highlighted in Dan Woog's (1998) book about gay male athletes in the United States. Woog, a journalist, felt it was important to give voice to gay men in sports and to hear what they had to say about themselves and their sport experiences. Using data collected in interviews, Woog tells twenty-eight stories about athletes, coaches, referees, administrators, and others in sports.

The stories indicate that the social worlds created around sports hinder the coming out process. Successfully combining a gay identity with an athlete identity was a challenging process for nearly all the interviewees. Woog observed that the social contexts and relationships associated with individual sports, such as running and swimming, generally were more gay-friendly than team sports, although a cosmopolitan sport, such as soccer, provided a more gay-friendly context than "a mechanized, play-by-rote game like football." Being out was liberating for most of the gay men, but it was also dangerous for some of them. These men cared deeply about sports, and they often feared that being out might lead others to exclude them from sports teams and programs. Positive experiences for the gay athletes were enhanced when there were organizations that acknowledged and supported them on and off the field, when there was overt support from family and friends, and when someone in their sport, such as a teammate or coach, served as their advocate.

Of course, there are many similarities between the experiences of gay men and those of straight men in sports. However, the meanings given to those experiences and the ways in which they are integrated into people's lives differ in important ways because of how *heterosexuality* and *homosexuality* are defined by many people in the United States and other societies. Those definitions influence what happens in sports and how people are affected by their sports experiences (see also Anderson, 2000, 2002).

In summary, people define and give meaning to their sports experiences in connection with their social relationships. Meanings given to sports experiences are also grounded in the cultural context in which they occur. Prevailing definitions of social characteristics often influence the importance of sports in people's lives. As these definitions change, so do the meanings of sports experiences.

Social Worlds: Living in Sports

Although sociologists study sports mostly as parts of the societies and cultures in which they exist, some research has focused on sports as **social worlds,** a term used in interactionist theory to refer to a way of life and an associated mindset that revolve around a particular set of activities and envelop all the people and relationships connected with the activities.[2] I use this term to explain that we can't understand who athletes are, what they do, and how sports influence their lives unless we view them in two contexts: (1) the social worlds of their sports and (2) the overall society and culture in which the sports world exists. Unless we know about these contexts, we have difficulty making sense of sport experiences and their impact on people. This is especially the case when we study people whose lives revolve completely around a particular sport—that is, when the social world of their sport is their entire world.

Studies of social worlds that are created in connection with specific sports provide useful information about socialization processes and experiences. Following are a few examples.

Example 1: Learning to Be a Hero   Sociologists Patti and Peter Adler spent nearly ten years studying the social world of a high-profile college basketball team. Much of their data, presented in the book *Backboards and Blackboards* (1991), focuses on how the self-conceptions of

varsity college athletes changed as they played college basketball. The Adlers found that the young men, about 70 percent of whom were African Americans, usually became deeply engulfed in their athlete roles after they entered the social world of big-time college basketball. Their roles as athletes deeply affected how they viewed themselves and how they allocated time to basketball, social life, and academic matters. This "role engulfment" occurred as the young men made commitments to identities based exclusively on playing basketball. Coaches, students, fans, community members, the media, and teammates all supported and reinforced these commitments. Thus, the social world of intercollegiate basketball became the context in which the young men viewed the rest of the world, set goals, and evaluated and defined themselves.

The Adlers felt that these young men learned something about setting goals, focusing their attention on specific tasks, and making sacrifices to pursue their goals while they played basketball. However, the Adlers found nothing to suggest that the athletes carried over these lessons into the rest of their lives. It seemed that the social world of basketball separated the men so much from the rest of life that the lessons they learned in that world stayed there.

This lack of carryover between sports and the rest of life may be more common among men than among women, because the social worlds that revolve around women's intercollegiate sports are not so isolated from the rest of the athletes' lives. It may be more common for black men than for white men because of the ethnic dynamics on many predominantly white college campuses. These are important issues to be explored in future research on sports and socialization.

Example 2: Realizing Image Isn't Everything
Anthropologist Alan Klein studied the social world of competitive bodybuilding for seven years. In his book *Little Big Men* (1993), he explains that much of the lives of the bodybuilders revolved around issues of gender and sexuality.

---

[2]I use the term *social world* in the same way that many of my colleagues use the term *subculture* (see Crosset and Beal, 1997; Donnelly, 1988b).

The bodybuilders, both male and female, learned to project public images of power and strength, although privately they experienced serious doubts about their identities and self-worth. The social world of bodybuilding seemed to foster a desperate need for attention and approval from others, especially fellow bodybuilders. Ideas about masculinity within the social world of bodybuilding were so narrow and one-dimensional that the male bodybuilders developed homophobic attitudes and went to great lengths to assert their heterosexuality in public. Also, the focus on body size and hardness created such insecurities that the men learned to present and even define themselves in terms of exaggerated caricatures of masculinity—like comic-book depictions of men. Overall, bodybuilding was a site for powerful socialization experiences in their lives. However, due to gender relations in the culture at large, these experiences took on different meanings for the women bodybuilders than they did for the men (see the box "Women Bodybuilders," in chapter 8, pages 270–271).

Example 3: Living in the Shadow of a Man's World   Sociologist Todd Crosset (1995) spent fourteen months studying the social world of women's professional golf. He found that being on the LPGA tour created and, in fact, required a complete mindset revolving around the commitment to using physical competence as a basis for evaluating self and others on the tour. He described this mindset as "an ethic of prowess." This ethic of prowess existed partly because the women were very concerned about neutralizing the potentially negative effects that dominant ideas about gender could have if these ideas were to enter the social world of women's professional golf. One golfer he interviewed said that much of what she did in her life was a response to the notion that "*athlete* is almost a masculine noun" in this society. The impact of being a pro golfer was summarized by one woman, who said, "We are different than the typical married lady with a house full of kids in what we think and do."

Crosset's study emphasized that we can understand the meaning of this statement only in the context of the social world of the LPGA and that we can understand the social world of the LPGA only in the context of gender relations in U.S. culture.

Example 4: Surviving in a Ghetto   Sociologist Loïc Wacquant (1992) spent three years studying the social world of boxers in a ghetto gym in Chicago. His observations, interviews, and experiences as a boxer helped him uncover the ideas and meanings that underly the life and craft of boxing. He explains that the social world of the boxing gym is very complex: it is created in connection with the social forces in the black ghetto and its masculine street culture, but it also shelters black men from the full destructive impact of those forces. In order to learn the "social art" of boxing, the men at the gym engaged in an intense regime of body regulation focused on the physical, visual, and mental requirements of boxing. They had to "eat, drink, sleep and live boxing," and, in the process, they developed what Wacquant described as a *socialized lived body*, which was at the very core of their identities and behavior. This experience of living in the social world of the boxing gym separated them from their peers and kept them alive as they tried to navigate their lives in dangerous neighborhoods devoid of hope or opportunity. For these men, boxing was, indeed, a powerful socialization experience, but it cannot be understood apart from the context of their everyday lives.

Example 5: Sport Worlds Portrayed in the Media   Joan Ryan (1995) and Christine Brennan (1996) are journalists who have studied and written about the social worlds of elite, competitive women's gymnastics and men's and women's figure skating. Their research methods and writing styles are different from those of academic scholars, but they contribute to what we know about socialization experiences in these two sports. For example, Ryan's descriptions of the social world of

Sports in many cultures are no longer seen as exclusively masculine activities. However, traditional gender definitions and associated clothing may still keep some girls out of the action. (Jay Coakley)

elite women's gymnastics provide a basis for understanding why girls and young women in that world frequently develop disordered-eating behaviors. Although parents, coaches, and fellow athletes do not explicitly teach these behaviors, the young women often come to see them as part of being a gymnast, part of life in the social world of gymnastics. As we know from a few highly publicized cases, when relationships and routines in sports foster eating disorders, they can be fatal. This is body socialization in an extreme form.

In summary, the social worlds of sports are *sites* for powerful forms of socialization. A full understanding of socialization processes and experiences requires knowledge of those worlds and the connection between them and the culture as a whole. Once we deeply understand a sports world, once we are able to delve into it through good research, the things that athletes think and do become meaningful and understandable to us, regardless of how they appear to those who are not part of those worlds.

Ideology: Sports as Sites for Struggling over How We Think and What We Do

Socialization research has focused mostly on what occurs in the lives of individuals and small groups. However, as researchers have combined critical theories with cultural studies and post-structuralism,[3] they have done creative studies of *socialization as a community and cultural process.* Their research goes beyond looking at the experiences and characteristics of athletes. Instead, it focuses on sports as sites where many people in society create and learn "stories," which they can use as they make sense out of the world and their lives. The stories that revolve around sports and athletes have their own vocabularies and images; their meanings shift, depending on the settings in which people tell them and hear them, and they often identify important cultural issues in people's lives. Researchers try to identify these stories and then determine how they fit into the culture and how people use them in connection with what they think and do.

Researchers also are concerned with whose stories about sports

> In his own way, [Michael] Jordan did spread an ideology. It was that sports are not just games but tools for advertisers. It was that basketball isn't a playground thing, but a corporate thing.
>
> —Jay Weiner, *BusinessWeek* (1999)

become dominant in the culture, since there are so many stories that could be told about sports. These stories are culturally important because they identify what is natural, normal, and legitimate and therefore give priority to ideas and orientations that tend to privilege some people more than others, some interests more than other interests. For example, the stories and vocabulary frequently used in discourse about sports revolve around heroic figures who are big, strong, aggressive, record-setting champions. Political scientist Varda Burstyn (1999, p. 23) says that these stories celebrate the notion of "higher, faster, stronger" that today serves the interests of capitalist expansion and traditional manly values associated with conquest. This is an important way in which socialization occurs in connection with sports.

Researchers are also concerned with whose stories are not told and with who is silenced or even "erased" from the stories that are told in the dominant culture. For example, researchers may study media coverage to learn about what is *not* contained in narratives and images as much as what is contained in them. After all, we can learn about culture by seeing what *is not* represented in cultural discourses and images as well as by seeing what is represented.

Research on this form of socialization is difficult to do, because it requires a knowledge of history and a deep understanding of the settings in which sports and sport stories come to be a part of people's lives. But this research is important, because it deals with the influence of sports in the culture as a whole, rather than just in the lives of individuals and small groups.

The Politics of Socialization as a Community and Cultural Process   Research on socialization as a community and cultural process is partly inspired by the ideas of Italian political theorist

---

[3]Poststructuralism is a theoretical and methodological perspective based on the assumption that culture today revolves around language, representations of things and ideas, and rapidly changing media and computer images. Structuralists, including functionalists, conflict theorists, and some critical theorists consider material production and material reality to be the key dynamic around which culture is created and maintained. Those using a poststructuralist perspective focus on language, including both written and spoken discourse, because they assume that social life in today's postmodern culture is constantly negotiated, constructed, challenged, and changed through language and discourse. Research done by poststructuralists often deals with the media and focuses on how images, identities, symbols, and meanings are fabricated through the media and then serve as the contexts for our lives. Poststructuralists often do scholarly work that disrupts these media-generated discourses and increases critical sensibilities in the culture as a whole.

Antonio Gramsci. When fascists in Italy imprisoned Gramsci for speaking out against their political ideas, he spent time in prison (1928–1935), thinking about why people had not revolted against repressive forms of capitalism in Western societies. Gramsci concluded that it was important to understand how people in a society form definitions of common sense and ideas about how society ought to be organized socially, politically, and economically. He thought that one of the most effective ways for powerful people to influence popular definitions and ideas, and thereby win support from the general population in a society, is to sponsor and control major sources of pleasure and joy in people's lives.

Gramsci suspected that most people use the cultural messages associated with everyday pleasure and joy in their lives to inform their ideas about the organization and operation of society as a whole. Therefore, if dominant groups in a society can influence the language, images, and messages tied to the fun and excitement in people's lives, they can encourage agreement with their ideas, or at least defuse the extent to which people might disagree with them. Therefore, the sponsorship and control of sports and other sources of entertainment is a useful strategy for maintaining power and privilege.

Gramsci's analysis helps us understand why large corporations spend millions of dollars to sponsor sports and to advertise in connection with sports. For example, when Coca-Cola spent over $500 million in connection with the 1996 Olympics in Atlanta and was willing to spend even greater amounts to sponsor the 2000 Sydney Games, is it only because Coca-Cola executives thought that advertising in connection with sports would make them more money? Of course, this was an important consideration, but, more important for Coca-Cola, General Motors, and other corporations is the fact that they can use the Olympics and other sports as vehicles for delivering cultural messages they want people in the world to hear. They want people watching the Olympics to agree that competition is the best way to allocate rewards in life and that successful and powerful people (and corporations) really deserve their money and power.

The people who run Coca-Cola and General Motors want people to drink Coke and drive Chevy trucks, but they also want people to develop an approach to life that associates pleasure with consumption, and social status with corporate logos. They want people to say, "These large companies are important in our lives, because without them we would not have the sports we love so dearly." They want people to think that enjoyment and pleasure in life depend on large corporations and their products. They want to establish consumption as a way of life, as the foundation for culture itself. Their profits and power depend on it, and their marketing people know it. They are selling a whole way of life and an ideology in which people express their identities through competitive success and consumption. To the extent that people in society adopt this way of viewing the world and their relationship to it, corporate interests gain more power in society. Many sociologists refer to this process of forming consent around a particular ideology as the process of establishing **hegemony.**

The cultural messages associated with sports have become a part of our lives at the beginning of twenty-first century. It is difficult to determine how these messages are heard around the world, but it is clear that major corporations see sports as important vehicles for delivering them. People in corporations know that their interests depend on establishing "ideological outposts" in people's heads. Sports, because they are pleasurable activities for so many people, are logical avenues through which these outposts can be built. Once established, these outposts are useful to corporations. In fact, they become terminals through which a range of corporate messages can be delivered effectively. To paraphrase Gramsci's conclusion about hegemony, it is difficult to fight an enemy that has outposts in your head.

When corporations spend money to have their names, logos, and products associated with sports, they are looking for more than sales. In the long run, their executives hope that people will believe that their enjoyment of sports depends on the corporations. If this happens, people are more likely to support and less likely to interfere with corporate interests. Sport sponsorships were especially important after 2002, when accounting scandals and CEO excesses damaged corporate credibility. (Jay Coakley)

Research on Socialization as a Community and Cultural Process   It is difficult to understand socialization as a community and cultural process unless we see it in action. The following examples of research highlight this informative approach to sports and socialization.

Anthropologist Doug Foley (1999a) studied the connection between sports and community socialization processes in a small Texas town. His findings showed that high school football was important in the lives of many individuals in the small town he studied. However, the stories created around football and those who played it, coached it, cheered for it, and watched it reaffirmed established ways of thinking and doing things. In the process, sports became a means for maintaining the forms of social inequality that made life good for a few and difficult for many in the town. For example, even though a young Mexicana could become popular as a cheerleader and a young Mexicano from a poor family could be a star on the team, this had no effect on the political and economic standing of women, Mexican Americans, or low-income people in the town. People's experiences in connection with football did not lead them to challenge inequalities related to gender, ethnicity, and social class. Instead, their experiences reproduced the ideas that supported those inequalities, even though individual lives sometimes were changed in connection with sports.

Mike Messner's (1992) interviews with former elite male athletes showed that sports were sites where these athletes created identities that influenced how they presented themselves in public, how they related to women, and how they defined and evaluated themselves (go to the Online Learning Center for a summary of this study). These identities and the stories associated with them then became part of popular culture in the

United States and reproduced dominant ideas about manhood. Messner concluded that, as people struggle over issues related to gender, sports are important because they provide vocabularies and images that perpetuate thoughts and actions that privilege most men over most women and some men over others.

Susan Birrell and Diana Richter's (1994) observations of softball teams and in-depth interviews with players showed that the feminist consciousness of women can be used to alter the ways organized sports are played. The stories that emerged in connection with the women's experiences came with vocabularies and images that empowered the players in feminist terms. This made their experiences very different from the experiences of most people who play power and performance sports. This study showed that sports don't always reproduce dominant ways of thinking and doing things. Sometimes, sports can be played or organized in ways that clearly push the limits of what is traditionally accepted and acceptable in society. When this happens, socialization in sports may involve changes in how entire groups of people think about what is important in life and how social relationships can and should be organized.

Other studies also have approached the issue of socialization through the concept of ideology. They have focused on how popular images connected with sports become influential cultural symbols as they are represented in the media and everyday conversations. For example, David Andrews (1996b) has used a combination of critical theories to study the connection between racial ideology in the United States and the cultural stories created around Michael Jordan between 1982 and 1995. Andrews' analysis of commercials and other media coverage show how the "Jordan persona" was severed from African American experiences and culture, so that white America, seeking evidence that it was colorblind and open to all, could comfortably identify with him. Andrews uses historical information about race and depictions of the Jordan persona in media commercials to argue that, even though

race and skin color were erased from Jordan's public persona, we cannot understand Jordan's status and impact as a cultural icon without knowing how racism operates in the United States.

Andrews' research and similar studies done by others emphasize that *none of us lives outside the influence of ideology* (Andrews, 1996a, b; Burstyn, 1999; Paraschak, 1997). This research is based on the premise that sports, because they are popular sources of pleasure in people's lives, are significant avenues through which people learn and possibly question ideology. This research holds the promise of showing us how sports influence

Nike-sponsored images of Michael Jordan were used around the world in the 1990s. This one appeared on a building in Paris. Nike and other corporations worked hard to sever the Jordan persona from connections with African American experiences. This allowed people to comfortably ignore the legacies of colonialism and racism, which still affect economic, political, and social lives today among people of color around the world. (Jay Coakley)

widely held ideas in a culture and how people can disrupt that influence if it promotes stereotypes and exploitation (see Andrews and Jackson, 2001).

WHAT SOCIALIZATION RESEARCH DOESN'T TELL US

Existing research doesn't tell us all we want to know about sports and socialization. We have many research snapshots and a few short videos to help us understand parts of socialization processes related to sports. But we lack information on how these processes operate in the lives of people from various ethnic groups and social classes. In North America, research on Asian Americans, Latinos, Native Americans, and French-Canadians in sports is especially needed. We also need studies of sport participation in high-income and low-income communities, as well as among wealthy and poor individuals and families.

We know that an eleven-year-old white girl from a wealthy Euro-American family playing tennis in an exclusive suburban club has different sport experiences than a Latino boy from a Mexican migrant worker family playing soccer on a dusty road next to fields of lettuce in California. Clearly, we need to know more about variations in sport experiences and how people from different social and cultural backgrounds give those experiences meaning and integrate them into their lives at various points in their life course. We cannot talk about the socialization consequences of sports without putting sport experiences into real-life contexts (see figure 4.2). That's why your sport participation has had a different impact on you than mine has had on me, and that's why it is senseless to argue about whether all sports build character or whether all athletes are role models. Neither socialization nor sports are that simple, and research cannot give us unconditional yes or no answers about what sports do to us or to our communities and societies.

We also need research on sport participation careers among children and on how those careers

"I don't think these guys agree about the meaning of boxing."

FIGURE 4.2   Meanings given to sports vary from one person to another. However, many power and performance sports are organized to encourage orientations that emphasize domination over others. Those who do not hold this orientation may not fit very well in these sports.

are linked to overall social development, especially among girls, children with disabilities, and children from ethnic minority backgrounds. Similarly, we need research on older people, especially those considering or trying sports for the first time or the first time in a long while.

We need research on how people make participation decisions about different types of sports. Sports come in many forms, and the socialization processes related to power and performance sports are different from experiences related to pleasure and participation sports (see "Power and Performance versus Pleasure and Participation," pages 110–112).

If we knew more about each of these topics, we could provide sport participation opportunities that fit into the lives of a greater number of people. This would help us make sports more democratic and less subject to the commercial forces that make them exclusive and elitist (Donnelly, 1993, 1996b).

We also need research on the emotional dimensions of socialization processes. Few sociologists have considered emotions in their research, but most of us know that decisions about sport participation are clearly connected with our feelings, fears, and anxieties. For example, decisions may be tied to what people in sports refer to as "psyching up": the emotional experience of forming expectations about what they will encounter in sports. These expectations are based on memories, as well as the images about sports that exist in the culture as a whole.

Stories about the emotional side of sports have been collected by social psychologists who have studied "flow experiences" among athletes (Jackson and Csikszentmihalyi, 1999). Flow occurs when we become so engrossed in what we are doing that we lose track of time and get carried along by the activity itself. Runner's high, peak experiences, and "that game when everything just seems to click" are examples of flow in action. Even though flow is a personal experience, it is tied to sociological issues, such as how activities are organized and the amount of control that participants have over their involvement in those activities.

Finally, we need more research on how the vocabulary used in certain sports influences sport participation decisions and the meanings given to sport experiences. When words constantly refer to opposition, hostility, rivalries, confrontations, warriors, domination, and mastery over others, they set the stage for memories, fantasies, and identifications that serve as powerful sources of personal identity and social dynamics. This vocabulary tells us much about the way that sports are organized and played. For example, given the words that many people use when they talk about sports it is not surprising that young women in U.S. high schools are less likely than their male counterparts to try out for and stay on varsity teams. If the language of sports is based on traditionally masculine images and orientations, many girls and women may not find certain sports very appealing. Furthermore, what types of boys and men are likely to be attracted to sports described as forms of "warfare," requiring aggression, toughness, and the desire to dominate others? Sociologists, especially those interested in gender equity and gender relations, would like to know answers to these questions.

On the practical side of things, when we learn more things about sports and socialization, we can become wiser parents, coaches, teachers, managers, and sport administrators. Then we can create sports that offer a wider array of challenging and satisfying experiences.

SUMMARY

WHO PLAYS AND WHAT HAPPENS?

Socialization is a complex, interactive process through which people form ideas about the social world, who they are, and how they are connected to the world around them. This process occurs in connection with sports and other activities and experiences in people's lives. Research indicates that playing sports is a social experience as well as a physical one.

Becoming involved and staying involved in sports occur in connection with general socialization processes in people's lives. Decisions to play sports are influenced by the availability of opportunities, the existence of social support, processes of identity formation, and the cultural context in which decisions are made.

Studies of socialization into sports show that sport participation decisions are related to processes of individual development, the organization of social life, and cultural ideology. People do not make decisions about sport participation once and for all time. They make them day after day, as they set and revise priorities in their lives.

Studies of socialization into sports have told us a few things about first experiences in sports and about who may have influenced and supported those experiences, but becoming involved and staying involved in sports is a long-term process. Influential factors and people change over time as people's lives change, and it is important to do studies that capture the complexities of these processes.

Changing or ending active sport participation also occurs in connection with general socialization processes. Again, these processes are interactive and are influenced by many personal, social, and cultural factors. Changes in sport participation are usually tied to a combination of identity, developmental, and life course issues.

Ending sport participation usually involves transition processes, during which athletes redefine their identities, reconnect with friends and family members, and use available resources to become involved in other activities and careers. Just as people are not socialized into sports, they are not simply socialized out of sports. We have good information illustrating that changing and ending a career as a competitive athlete occurs over time and is often tied to events and life course issues outside of sports. These connections are best studied through methods that enable us to describe long-term transition processes.

Efforts to understand what happens to people when they play sports have been sidetracked by the popular belief that sports build character. This belief is grounded in an oversimplified conception of sports, sport experiences, and socialization. We know that, when people live much of their lives in and around sports, their characters and actions, positive or negative, are related to sport participation in some way.

When we consider sports and socialization, it is helpful to know that different sports involve different experiences and consequences. For example, what occurs in connection with power and performance sports is quite different from what occurs in connection with pleasure and participation sports. The visibility and popularity of power and performance sports are related to issues of power and ideology: these sports fit the interests of people who have the power and wealth to sponsor and promote sports.

The most informative research on what happens in sports deals with (1) the everyday experiences of people who play sports, (2) the social worlds created around sports, and (3) community and cultural processes, especially in connection with the ideological messages associated with sports in society. As we listen to the voices of those who participate in sports, study how they live their lives in connection with sports, and pay special attention to the ideological messages associated with sports, we learn more about sports and socialization.

Most scholars who study sports in society now see sports as sites for socialization experiences, rather than as causes of specific socialization outcomes. This distinction recognizes that powerful and memorable experiences may occur in connection with sports, and it recognizes that these experiences take on meaning only through social relationships that occur in particular social and cultural contexts. Therefore, the most useful research in the sociology of sport focuses on the social processes through which socialization occurs.

SUGGESTED READINGS

Note: In addition to the following readings, readers should consult the studies summarized in this chapter; many have good discussions of socialization issues and bibliographies that identify other useful sources.

Andrews, D. L., and S. J. Jackson. 2001. *Sport stars: The cultural politics of sporting celebrity.* London/New York: Routledge (sixteen articles focusing on the cultural, political, economic, and technological factors that influence sport celebrity around the world and how sport celebrities influence culture and the everyday lives of people around the world).

Coakley, J., and P. Donnelly, eds. 1999. *Inside sports.* London: Routledge (twenty-two articles that summarize qualitative research projects on socialization and sports; written especially for beginning students, these original articles focus on the processes of becoming involved in sports, developing an identity as an athlete, doing sports, and then facing life beyond the playing field).

Fine, G. A. 1987. *With the boys: Little League baseball and preadolescent culture.* Chicago: University of Chicago Press (one of the best analyses of the processes of moral socialization that occur on youth sport teams; using an interactionist perspective, this study shows how young boys are involved in their own socialization).

Foley, D. 1990. *Learning capitalist culture.* Philadelphia: University of Pennsylvania Press (ethnographic study of sports and socialization in the context of a community's way of life; deals with issues of class, gender, and ethnicity in connection with the local high school, the varsity football team, and the socialization processes associated with high school sports in the town).

Klein, A. 1993. *Little big men: Bodybuilding subculture and gender construction.* Albany: State University of New York Press (inside look at training experiences associated with competitive bodybuilding; focuses on how gender and gender relations are involved in what happens during training and competition, as well as what happens to the athletes themselves).

Lavalee, D., and P. Wylleman. eds. 2000. *Career transitions in sport: International perspectives.* Morgantown, WV: Fitness Information Technology (written by and for sport psychologists, the thirteen articles deal with how people from a number of countries make the transition from sports careers to the rest of their lives; good information for sociologists as well).

Lafeber, W. 2000. *Michael Jordan and the new global capitalism.* New York: W. W. Norton (critical look at how Michael Jordan's product endorsements have been used to export U.S. products to more than 100 countries around the world and, in the process, to influence consumption patterns and cultures).

Miracle, A. W., and C. R. Rees. 1994. *Lessons of the locker room: The myth of school sports.* Amherst, NY: Prometheus Books (overview of research on what happens to participants in high school sports in the United States; discusses the implications of research findings for school policy).

Theberge, N. 2000. *Higher goals: Women's ice hockey and the politics of gender.* Albany: State University of New York Press (based on two seasons of observations and interviews with the members of an elite women's hockey team, the analysis provides a valuable look inside the locker room at how women give meaning to their sport experiences and integrate those experiences into their lives).

Woog, D. 1998. *Jocks: True stories of America's gay athletes.* Los Angeles: Alyson Books (breaks the silence about gay men in sports; twenty-eight biographical accounts focus on many issues, especially coming out and living life as an out gay athlete, coach, referee, or sports administrator in the context of late-twentieth-century U.S. sports and society).

WEBSITE RESOURCES

Note: Websites often change. The following URLs were current when this book was printed. Please check our website (www.mhhe.com/coakley8e) for updates and additions.

www.mhhe.com/coakley8e Click on chapter 4; see information on the concept of competition, the relationship between competition and culture, and the persistent belief that sports build character.

www.charactercounts.org/sports/sports.htm A loosely organized coalition of individuals and organizations committed to the idea that sports should build positive character; the goal of the coalition is to change how sports are played, coached, and watched by individuals.

www.sportsmanship.org A loosely organized coalition of organizations with the goal of fostering changes, so that sports will build positive character traits; the focus is on changing individuals rather than organizations.

www.nd.edu/~cscc Site of The Mendelson Center for Sport, Character & Culture; established by the University of Notre Dame, the center focuses on promoting social justice through sports and through a critical analysis of the relationships between sports and culture; see resources link for other sites related to socialization and development in and through sports.

www.sportsethicsinstitute.org Go to Youth Sports and other topics on the Sports ethics issues page; this site highlights ethical issues at all levels of sports.

(Jay Coakley)

Sports and Children

Are Organized Programs Worth the Effort?

SPORTS ARE A GREAT way to teach kids to be successful, to teach them life lessons, and they can apply that to every level of their life.

—Glen Kozlowski, youth sport coach, parent, and former NFL player (2000)

Online Learning Center Resources

Visit *Sports in Society*'s Online Learning Center at **www.mhhe.com/coakley8e** for additional information and study material for this chapter, including

- Self-grading quizzes
- Learning objectives
- Related websites
- Additional readings

A complete outline is available online at
www.mhhe.com/coakley8e.

KIDS DON'T GO to the playground anymore. When they practice there's a coach telling them what to do and how to do it. What happens to the kids' passion and heart in all this?

—**Ken Ravizza, sport psychologist (2002)**

When, how, and to what end children play sports are issues that concern families, neighborhoods, communities, and even national and international organizations. When sociologists study these issues, they focus on how children's experiences vary with the types of programs or settings in which they play sports and with the cultural contexts in which they play. Since the early 1970s, the research done by sociologists and others has had a strong impact on how people think about and organize youth sports. Parents, coaches, and program administrators today are much more aware of the questions and issues they must consider when evaluating organized youth sport programs. Many of these people have used research findings to create and change organized programs to serve better the interests of children.

This chapter will deal with five major topics:

1. The origin and development of organized youth sports
2. Major trends in youth sports today
3. Differences between informal, player-controlled sports and formally organized, adult-controlled sports
4. Commonly asked sociological questions about youth sports, including
   - When are children ready to play organized competitive sports?
   - What are the dynamics of family relationships in connection with organized youth sports?
   - How do social factors influence youth sport experiences?
5. Recommendations for changing children's sports

Throughout the chapter, the underlying question that will guide our discussion is this: are organized youth sports worth all the time, money, and effort put into them? I asked this question as my son and daughter moved through childhood, and I continue to ask it as I talk with parents and work with coaches and policymakers who have made extensive commitments to youth sports.

ORIGIN AND DEVELOPMENT OF ORGANIZED YOUTH SPORTS

During the latter half of the nineteenth century, people in Europe and North America began to realize that the social environment influences the character and behavior of children. This encouraged many people to try to control the environment as much as possible and to organize children's lives, so that boys and girls would develop into productive adults in rapidly expanding capitalist economies.

It wasn't long before sport activities were organized for young boys in schools, on playgrounds, and in church groups. The organizers hoped that sports, especially team sports, would teach boys from working-class families how to work together. They also hoped that sports would turn boys in middle- and upper-class families into strong, assertive, competitive men by providing them with experiences to counterbalance what they thought were "feminized" values learned at home. At the same time, girls were provided with activities that would teach them to be good mothers and homemakers. Most people believed that it was more important for girls to learn domestic skills than to learn sport skills, and they organized the school curriculum and playground activities to reflect this belief.

Of course, there were exceptions to these patterns, but this was the general cultural context in which organized youth sport programs were developed after World War II in most industrialized countries. As the first wave of the baby boom generation moved through childhood during the 1950s and 1960s, organized youth sports grew dramatically, especially in the United States. Programs in the United States were funded by a combination of public, private, and commercial sponsors. Parents also entered the scene, eager to have the characters of their sons built through organized competitive sports. Fathers became coaches, managers, and league administrators. Mothers did laundry and became chauffeurs and short-order cooks, so that their sons were always ready for practices and games.

Most programs were for boys eight to fourteen years old and emphasized competition as preparation for future occupational success. Until the 1970s, girls' interests in sports were largely ignored in most countries. Girls were relegated to the bleachers during their brothers' games and, in the United States, given the hope of becoming high school cheerleaders. Then the women's movement, the fitness movement, and government legislation prohibiting sex discrimination all came together to stimulate the development of new sport programs for girls (see chapter 8). During the 1970s and early 1980s, these programs grew rapidly, to the point that girls had nearly as many opportunities as boys. However, their participation rates have remained lower than rates for boys—for reasons we will discuss in the section, "How Do Social Factors Influence Youth Sport Experiences?" (and in chapter 8).

Participation in organized youth sports is now an accepted part of the process of growing up in most wealthy nations, especially among the middle and upper classes, in which family and community resources enable adults to sponsor, organize, and administer many programs for their children. Most parents now encourage both sons and daughters to participate in sports. Some parents may question the merits of programs in which winning seems to be more important than overall child development, whereas other parents look for the win-oriented programs, hoping their children will become the winners.

Of course, some parents also encourage their children to engage in noncompetitive physical activities outside of organized programs, and many children participate in these activities as alternatives to adult-supervised organized sports. Physical educators have studied the recreational forms of these activities, and social scientists have begun to study alternative sports, which have become increasingly popular in the lives of children in many countries (Midol and Broyer,

1995; Rinehart, 2000; Rinehart and Grenfell, 2002; Rinehart and Syndor, 2003).

Since the 1950s, an increasing amount of children's free time and sport participation has occurred in organized programs supervised by adults (Adler and Adler, 1998). This growth is related, in part, to changes in how we view family and childhood in contemporary culture. The following five changes are especially relevant.

First, the number of families with both parents working outside the home has increased dramatically, especially since the early 1970s. This has created a growing demand for organized and adult-supervised after-school and summertime programs. Organized sports are especially popular among the activities provided in these programs, because many parents think that sports offer their children opportunities to simultaneously have fun, learn adult values, and acquire skills valued in their peer groups.

Second, since the early 1980s, there have been significant changes in what it means to be a "good parent." Good parents, in the minds of many people today, are those who can account for the whereabouts and behavior of their children twenty-four hours a day. This expectation is a new component of parenting ideology, and in recent years it has led many parents to seek organized, adult-supervised programs for their children. Organized sports are favored because they emphasize the control and leadership of adult coaches, they have predictable schedules, and they provide parents with measurable indicators of their children's accomplishments. When their children succeed, parents can claim that they are meeting their responsibilities.

Third, there has been a growing belief that informal, child-controlled activities often provide occasions for children to cause trouble. In its extreme form, this belief leads adults to view children as threats to social order. Many adults see organized sports as ideal activities for keeping active children constructively occupied, out of trouble, and under the control of adults.

Fourth, many parents have come to see the world outside the home as a dangerous place for children. They regard organized sports as safe alternatives to informal activities that occur away from home. This belief is so strong that it often persists in the face of information about coercive coaching methods, the predatory behavior of some coaches (Nack and Yaeger, 1999), and occasionally high injury rates in organized youth sports (American Academy of Pediatrics, 2000; Lyman et al., 1998; Ryan 1995).

Fifth, the visibility of high-performance and professional sports has increased people's awareness of organized sports as a part of culture. As children watch sports on television, listen to parents and friends talk about sports, and hear about the wealth and fame of popular athletes, they often become interested in playing the sports that others define as official and important. For this reason, organized sports with expert, adult coaches become attractive to many children. When children say they want to be gymnasts or basketball players, parents often look for the nearest organized program (see figure 5.1). Therefore, organized youth sports are popular because children enjoy them and see them as activities that will gain them acceptance from peers and parents alike.

Together, these five changes in family and childhood account for much of the increased popularity of organized youth sports. Furthermore, these changes help us understand why parents are willing to invest so many family resources into the organized sports participation of their children. Many of these programs are quite expensive. The amount of money that parents spend on participation fees, equipment, and other things defined as necessary in many programs has skyrocketed in recent years (Ferguson, 1999; Moore, 2002). For example, when my students

FIGURE 5.1 When children have schedules that are full of organized youth sports, they have little time to be with their parents. The irony is that many parents spend more time making it possible for their children to play sports than they spend with their children.

and I interviewed the parents of elite youth hockey players who had traveled to Colorado for a major tournament in 2002, we discovered that the families had spent at least $5,000 and up to nearly $20,000 per year to support their sons' hockey participation. As they informed us about their expenses for fees, equipment, travel, and other things, many of them shook their heads and said, "I can't believe we're spending this much, but we are." In a *Washington Post* article on this topic, one single mother of a twelve-year-old boy explained, "Yes, it's expensive, [but I] want to give [my son] every advantage. . . . I know I overspend . . . but he's always wanted to be a baseball player, and to attain that takes money (Wee, 1995, p. A1).

These five changes also help us explain other forms of parental commitment to organized sports. When children participate in these programs, parents often become personal chauffeurs and support personnel. They serve as coaches, referees, and umpires. They launder uniforms, keep track of equipment, prepare special meals, alter work and holiday schedules, and sit in bad weather and stuffy sport facilities to watch their children.

One of the negative consequences of some of these changes is that parents in working-class and lower-income households may be defined as irresponsible or careless parents because they are unable to pay the financial price for controlling their children, as wealthier parents do. Furthermore, they are not as likely to have the time and other resources needed to participate in and provide the labor for organized sport programs. In this way, organized sports for children become linked to ideological and political issues and debates about low-income parents and how they measure up to ideas about "family values" in society.

MAJOR TRENDS IN YOUTH SPORTS TODAY

In addition to their growing popularity, youth sports are changing in at least five other socially significant ways. *First*, organized programs have become increasingly privatized. This means that more youth sports today are sponsored by private and commercial organizations, and fewer are sponsored by public, tax-supported organizations.

Second, organized programs are increasingly likely to emphasize the "performance ethic." This means that participants in youth sports, even in low-key, recreational programs, are encouraged to evaluate their experiences in terms of developing technical skills and progressing to higher personal levels of achievement in one or more sports.

Third, there has been an increase in the number of elite sport training facilities, which are dedicated to producing highly skilled and specialized athletes who can move up through increasingly difficult levels of competition.

Fourth, parents are becoming more involved in and concerned about the participation and success of their children in organized youth sports. In the process, youth sports are increasingly serious in the lives of adults and children, and adults are now more likely to act in extreme ways in connection with youth sports.

Fifth, participation in alternative and "extreme" sports has increased. This means that many young people prefer unstructured, participant-controlled sports, such as skateboarding, in-line skating, snowboarding, BMX biking, and other physical activities that have local or regional relevance for children.

These five trends have an impact on who participates in organized youth sports and what kinds of experiences children have when they do participate. I will explain this throughout this chapter and in the box "Organized Youth Sports and the Goals of Sponsors."

The Privatization of Organized Programs

Privatization is an interesting and sometimes alarming trend in youth sports today. Although organized sports have become more popular, there has been a decline in the number of publicly funded programs with free and open participation policies. When local governments face

REFLECT ON SPORTS

Organized Youth Sports and the Goals of Sponsors
How Do Politics Affect Sport Participation?

The purposes of organized youth sports often vary with the goals of sponsors. Forms of sponsorship differ from one program to another, but they generally fall into one of the following four categories:

1. *Public, tax-supported community recreation organizations.* This includes local parks and recreation departments and community centers, which traditionally have offered a range of free or low-cost organized sport programs for children. These programs are usually inclusive and emphasize overall participation and general physical skill development as it relates to health and enjoyment.

2. *Public, nonprofit community organizations.* These include the YMCA, the Boys and Girls Club, the Police Athletic League (PAL), and other community-based clubs, which traditionally have provided a limited range of free or low-fee organized sport programs for children. The goals of these programs are diverse, including everything from providing children from particular neighborhoods a "wholesome, Christian atmosphere" for playing sports to providing at-risk children with activities to keep them off the streets. Some professional sport franchises and wealthy pro athletes in a few U.S. cities are now funding these organizations out of their profits and salaries.

3. *Private, nonprofit sport organizations.* These include organizations such as the nationwide Little League, Inc., and local organizations operating independently or through connections with larger sport organizations, such as national federations. These organizations usually offer more exclusive opportunities to selective groups of children, generally those with special skills from families who can afford relatively costly participation fees.

4. *Private commercial clubs.* These include gymnastics, tennis, skating, soccer, and many other sport clubs and training programs. Many of these organizations have costly membership and participation fees, and some emphasize intense training, progressive and specialized skill development, and elite competition.

Since these sponsors exist for different purposes, the youth sports they provide are likely to appeal to different people and offer different types of experiences. Therefore, their impact on children and families is also likely to vary. This makes it difficult to generalize about what happens in organized youth sports and how participation affects child development and family dynamics.

When there are cuts in government spending, one of the first things to be dropped or scaled back is public, tax-supported youth sport programs—the type in category 1. Wealthy people seldom object to this because they have the money to fund private programs and to pay membership fees in commercial programs. However, cutting public programs has a range of effects. *First,* it limits opportunities available to children from low-income families and funnels those with strong interests and top skills into one or two sports for which public programs remain. *Second,* it creates a market for private, commercial programs that cater to those with the money to pay for their services.

This information shows how local and national politics have an impact on who participates in organized youth sports and on the type of participation opportunities available. Many communities continue to face the question of whether organized youth sports ought to be funded through local taxes. *What do you think?*

budget crises, various social services, including youth sports, often are cut back or eliminated. In the face of cutbacks, local parks and recreation departments and other public agencies sometimes have tried to maintain youth sport programs by imposing participation fees to cover expenses. But many have been forced to drop programs altogether.

In response to this turn of events, concerned parents with resources have organized privately sponsored leagues for their children. These leagues depend on fund-raising, participation fees, and corporate sponsorships. They offer many of the same kinds of sport opportunities that have existed in public programs. However, they usually exist in well-to-do suburbs and communities, they are expensive, and they tend to attract children from middle- and upper-middle-income families. Even when there is a willingness to waive fees for children from low-income families, few participate.

Commercial sport providers also have entered the youth sport scene in growing numbers as public programs have declined. The private commercial programs are usually selective and exclusive, and they provide few opportunities for children from low-income households. The technical instruction in these programs is very good, and they provide children from wealthier families with many opportunities to develop skills. Through these commercial programs, parents with enough money even hire private coaches for their children at rates of $35–$150 per hour (Moore, 2002; Patrick, 2002a).

At least two negative consequences are associated with this trend. *First*, privatized youth sports reproduce the economic and ethnic inequalities that exist in the larger society. Unlike public programs, they depend on money paid by participants. Low-income and single-parent families often do not have the money to pay fees. This, in turn, accentuates various forms of ethnic segregation and exclusion, as well as social class divisions, in communities. *Second*, as public parks and recreation departments cease to offer programs, they often become brokers of public parks for private organized sport programs. The private programs that use public parks may not have commitments to gender equity and affirmative action, which are mandated in public programs. If 83 percent of the participants in these programs are boys and 17 percent are girls, as was the case in Los Angeles in the late 1990s, what can be done to prevent the taxpayers from indirectly funding the perpetuation of gender inequity? As you can see, a number of challenges are associated with privatization.

Emphasis on the Performance Ethic

The performance ethic has become increasingly important in many organized youth sport programs. This means that performance becomes a measured outcome and an indicator of the quality of the sport experience. *Fun* in these programs comes to be defined in terms of becoming a better athlete, becoming more competitive, and being promoted into more highly skilled training categories. Often, the categories have names that identify skill levels, so there may be gold, silver, and bronze groups to indicate where a child is placed in the program. Many parents find this attractive because it enables them to judge their child's progress and to feel that they are meeting their parental expectations. (Review the box "Organized Youth Sports and the Goals of Sponsors," page 132.)

Private programs generally emphasize the performance ethic to a greater degree than do public programs, and many market themselves as "centers of athletic excellence." Such an approach attracts parents willing to pay high membership, participation, and instructional fees. Another way to sell a private program to parents who can afford the cost is to highlight successful athletes and coaches who have trained or worked in the program.

Parents of physically skilled children often are attracted to organized programs emphasizing the performance ethic. They sometimes define fees and equipment expenses, which can be shockingly high, as *investments* in their children's future. They are concerned with skill development, and, as their children get older, they use performance-oriented programs as sources of information about college sports, scholarships,

As publicly funded youth sports are downsized or eliminated, private clubs provide participation opportunities. Unfortunately, membership fees in these club-based programs are too expensive for many families. Additionally, many children may not enjoy the emphasis on the performance ethic that is common in many club programs. (Travis Spradling, *Colorado Springs Gazette*)

and networks for contacting coaches and sport organizations. They approach their children's sport participation rationally and see clear connections between childhood sport participation and future development, educational opportunities, and success in adult life. Of course, the application of the performance ethic is not limited to organized sports; it influences a range of organized children's activities (Mannon, 1997). Childhood in some societies has been changed from an age of exploration and freedom to an age of preparation and controlled learning. Children's sports reflect this trend.

New Elite, Specialized Sport Training Programs

The emphasis on performance is also tied to a third trend in youth sports—the development of elite, specialized training programs. Many private and commercial programs encourage exclusive attention to a single sport, because it is in the interest of program owners and staff to capture year-round fees for memberships. Commercial programs pay salaries to staff, rent facilities, and pay for other operating expenses year-round, so they need membership fees through the year to meet expenses and make money. Therefore, they demand year-round commitments and participation, and they justify their demands with the claim that staying competitive and moving up to higher levels of competition require a year-round commitment to training.

As more parents accept this claim, there has been an increase in the number of "high-performance" training schools, clubs, and programs for child athletes. Organized programs in gymnastics, figure skating, ice hockey, soccer, tennis, and other sports now boast an explicit emphasis on making children into headline-grabbing, revenue-producing sport machines. Children in these programs may become symbols of conspicuous consumption for the parents, who pay the bills and brag to friends about their children's accomplishments (Mahany, 1999; Rinehart and Grenfell, 1999).

Children in these high-performance training programs work at their sports for long hours week after week and year after year. They compete regularly and often generate revenues (directly and indirectly) for their coaches and families. They appear on commercial television, they attract people to expensive spectator events to watch them perform, and they are used to endorse products. In a sense, they become child laborers, because the livelihoods of coaches and other adults often depend on their performances. All this occurs without government regulations, which might protect the child athletes' interests, bodies, health, and overall psychosocial development.

Existing child labor laws in many postindustrial societies prevent adults from using children as sources of financial gain in other occupations and in the film and advertising industries, but there are no enforceable standards regulating what child athletes do or what happens to them. Coaches need no credentials. They can use fear, intimidation, and coercion to turn a few children into medal-winning athletes; they may destroy

> I can't believe how you're playing! You're giving these guys hope; your job is to destroy their hope!
>
> —Football coach to eleven-year-old players (2001)

others in the process. Parents can live off their children's earnings, and commercial events can be scheduled around their talents. The results of this situation are sometimes frightening (Ryan, 1995).

When Bela Karolyi was hired in late 1999 to coordinate the U.S. women's gymnastics team, one of his former student-performers, 1996 Olympic medal winner Kerri Strug said this about her former coach:

> He knows how to get the most out of each child. I think a lot of his motivation is fear. When I messed up, I was more worried about what he would think than about messing up. (in Raboin, 1999, p. 2A)

Strug fought through pain in her final vault to help the U.S. team win a gold medal in the 1996 Summer Olympics. In 1999, she had second thoughts about her life as a gymnast:

> Bela had complete control of everything in your life—your workouts, your eating, your sleeping. . . . I look back now and say, "That was crazy. That's not America." But it was Bela's way or no way. And he was a coach who got you where you wanted to go. (Strug, 1999, p. 73)

Dominique Moceanu, another member of the 1996 team, had a slightly different story to tell. In 1998, she disclosed that her father-coach had subjected her to mental and physical abuse as she trained. She said, "Most of the time . . . he'd hit me because I was gaining weight or wasn't doing well in the gym" (in Raboin, 1998, p. 2C). (Moceanu's troubles were accentuated because her father had lost nearly all of the money she had earned as a gymnast-laborer.) Karolyi tried to explain how this extreme system of handling children actually makes sense. As he coached the young athletes on the 1992 U.S. gymnastics team, he said,

> Sometimes the preparation is so hard, so intense . . . [t]he crying, the screaming. . . . We are not in the gym to be having fun. The fun comes at the end, with the winning and the medals. (in O'Brien, 1992, p. 52)

Are there ethical issues that should be considered in connection with this approach to sport participation? Are children being used and abused? Are children being harmed physically, psychologically, and socially? Sociologists, some parents, and others now are asking serious questions about how this trend affects the health and development of children.

Increased Involvement and Concerns Among Parents

Youth sports have become serious business in many families. The notion that good parents today must control the actions of their children twenty-four hours a day and carefully promote and monitor their children's development has changed parents' lives over the past two generations. Many parents now feel compelled to find the best organized youth sport programs for their children and to actively ensure that their children's interests are being met in those programs.

Even though many factors influence child development today, many people attribute the success or failure of children entirely to their parents. When children are successful in sports, their parents are seen to be doing the right thing as parents. When Tiger Woods began winning tournaments, everyone labeled Earl Woods, his father, as a good and wise parent. The same thing occurred with Richard Williams, the father of Venus and Serena Williams. When children succeed, parents are labeled "good parents" and even asked by other parents how they did it. When children fail, people raise questions about parents' actions and characters.

Under these conditions, a child's success in sports is especially important for many parents, because what children do in sports is visible to many people. Youth sports become sites where dads and moms can establish and prove their moral worth as parents. This increases the stakes associated with youth sports. This link between parents' moral worth and their children's achievements in sports, leads many parents to take youth sports very seriously.

The stakes associated with youth sports are increased even further among parents who hope that their children might use sports to earn college scholarships, professional contracts as athletes, or social acceptance and popularity in school and among peers. When parents think in these terms, the success of their children in youth sports is linked to anticipated financial and social payoffs. In some families, this also turns youth sports into very serious business.

As the moral, financial, and social stakes associated with youth sport participation have increased, youth sports have become sites for extreme actions among some adults (Engh, 1999; Nack and Munson, 2000). Parents may be assertive and disruptive as they advocate the interests of their child with coaches and youth sport program administrators. Some are obnoxious and offensive as they scream criticisms of coaches, referees, players, and their own children. A few have even attacked other people over sport-related disagreements.

In the most extreme case, a father from Reading, Massachusetts, attacked and beat to death another father in connection with events that occurred during an open skating session at an ice rink. This case was defined as an example of "rink rage" and covered in terms of one hockey dad killing another hockey dad. Subsequent coverage of extreme, disruptive, or belligerent actions by parents has led many people to think that there is a general epidemic of out-of-control youth sport parents.

Another highly publicized case of parent and coach misconduct occurred in 2001, when a father and the coach of a Little League team from the Bronx falsified the birth records of the team's star player, born in the Dominican Republic. Instead of being twelve years old, the boy was fourteen. His team, after winning district, sectional, and regional tournaments and placing third in the highly publicized Little League World Series, was forced to forfeit all its wins.

The father was widely criticized, and the team, the coach, and organizer of the local league in the Bronx were banned from the Little League organization.

These and other cases have led many people to call for parent education combined with new rules and enforcement procedures designed to control adults associated with youth sports. These are appropriate strategies. Parents and other adults must be held accountable for their actions. They should not be seen as "victims of society." At the same time, it is important to recognize and understand the context in which parenting occurs today. We can expect that, as long as parents' moral worth is linked with the achievements of children in youth sports, and as long as other perceived financial and social payoffs are associated with success in sports, parents will be heavily involved in and concerned about their children's youth sport participation. After all, if parents don't look after their children's interests, who will? According to the prevailing ideology, it takes only a family to raise a child. Until this ideology is questioned and parents receive more support from community institutions, we can expect many of them to be focused on control and actively engaged in advocating the interests of their children, even to the point of being obnoxious.

This set of social and cultural circumstances has surely influenced youth sports and the experiences of the children who play them. In a growing number of cases, it has turned children off to organized programs and led them to seek alternatives outside the control of parents and coaches. In these alternative activities, they learn, display, and even teach physical skills apart from the watchful eyes of parents, the whistles of coaches, and the inflexible schedules of incessant practices and competitive events that come to be more important than they should be.

Increased Interest in Alternative Sports

As organized programs have become increasingly exclusive, structured, performance-oriented, and elitist, some young people have sought alternatives, which allow them to engage freely in physical activities on their own terms. Because organized youth sports are the most visible settings for children's sport participation, these unstructured and participant-controlled activities are referred to as alternative sports—alternatives, that is, to organized sports. Alternative sports encompass an infinite array of physical activities done individually or with groups. Their popularity is based, in part, on children's reactions against the highly structured character of adult-controlled, organized sports (see Beal, 1995).

When I observe children in many of these activities, I am regularly amazed by the physical skills they have developed without adult coaches and scheduled practices and contests. Although I am concerned about injury rates and about the sexism so common in the social dynamics of these activities, I am impressed at the discipline and dedication of children who seek challenges apart from adult-controlled sport settings.

The norms in these participant-controlled activities are complex, and they vary from one location to another (Rinehart and Grenfell, 2002). A widely accepted norm that has made many of these activities attractive to children is explained by Mark Shaw, winner of the first International Mountain Board Championships in 2000. He says that, when he goes to areas where there are other skateboarders and mountain boarders, he feels that it is important to be "a positive influence as a skater." He teaches tricks, gives helpful hints to less experienced riders, and values the friendships and sense of community created around the sports. He explains, "I look forward to helping young skaters . . . at the park each weekend almost as much as I look forward to skating and my own progression on the board" (2002, p. 3). Many children find this orientation to be more engaging than what they perceive in competitive youth sport programs.

This trend of participation in alternative sports is so widespread that media companies and other large corporations that sell things to

As children have sought physical activities that involve large amounts of action as well as participant control over the action, many of them, especially boys, have gravitated to alternative sports. Many of these are related to the "extreme" sports seen in televised events and in the videotapes that are made, duplicated, and circulated by the participants themselves. When you make your own ramp (part of the fun) and your sisters watch as you work on your moves, you have an experience very different from that of organized youth sports. (Ric Francis; AP/Wide World Photos)

children have invented competitive forms of these sports and present advertising images that highlight risk and the "extreme" challenges associated with some of the activities. They have sponsored events, such as the XGames and the Gravity games, that provide exposure and material support for those who are willing to display their skills in a televised competitive format that is or at least appears to be highly organized and structured. Although the participants in these events are teens and young adults, many of the spectators are children. These children use the images from these media events to inform what they do when they play these sports, but we need research on this issue. So far, adult intervention in these activities has been limited to the provision of facilities,

such as skateboard parks and occasional words of advice regarding safety (Merrill, 2002). Will the future bring adult skateboard coaches and organized programs for participation? I'd bet on it, but I'd also bet that children will always seek opportunities to play sports on their own terms.

DIFFERENT EXPERIENCES: INFORMAL, PLAYER-CONTROLLED SPORTS VERSUS ORGANIZED, ADULT-CONTROLLED SPORTS

Since the late 1970s, my students and I have talked with many children about their sport experiences and have watched children play sports in different settings. We've learned that individual children define and interpret personal experiences in various ways. But we've also discovered that experiences among children differ, depending on whether sports are informally organized and controlled by the players themselves or are formally organized and controlled by adults.

Our findings indicate that informal, player-controlled sports are primarily action-centered, whereas formal, adult-controlled sports are primarily rule-centered. This means that, when children get together and make up their own activities and games, they emphasize movement and excitement. When children play sports that are organized and controlled by adults, the adults emphasize learning and following rules, so that games and game outcomes can be considered "official" within the larger structure of a league or tournament. The following sections provide more complete descriptions of these two types of participation settings.

Informal, Player-Controlled Sports

Students and I have observed informally organized, player-controlled sports in backyards, parks, vacant lots, and school playgrounds. We have talked with hundreds of children in connection with observed games. The observations and conversations have indicated consistently that, when children get together and play on their own, they are interested in four things:

1. Action, especially action leading to scoring
2. Personal involvement in the action
3. A challenging or exciting experience (for example, a close score in a competitive contest)
4. Opportunities to reaffirm friendships during games

The informal games we observed usually had two to twelve players. The players often knew one another from games played on previous occasions. In most cases, they formed teams quickly. Skill differences and friendship patterns were the criteria used to choose teams. Starting games and keeping them going was usually a complex operation; success depended on how good the players were at managing interpersonal relationships and making effective decisions.

The games and game rules often resembled those used in organized programs, but they contained many modifications to maximize action, scoring, and personal involvement, while keeping the scores close. Free throws were eliminated in basketball, throw-ins were kept to a minimum in soccer, yardage penalties were dropped from football, and the pitcher's mound in baseball and softball was moved closer to the batter, so that weak batters could hit the ball. Similar types of action-producing rules were found in other informal games. Further proof of the importance of action was the extremely high scores in most of these games.

Personal involvement was often maximized through clever rule qualifications and handicap systems. The children sometimes used restrictive handicaps to keep highly skilled players from dominating games. Other handicaps advantaged less skilled players. Furthermore, less skilled players often used special rules in their own favor. They were most likely to use "do-over" or "interference" calls to get another chance or compensate for the effects of their mistakes on the outcomes of games. This saved them personal embarrassment and preserved their integrity as contributing members of their teams. It also kept game scores close. The overuse of these special rules was usually discouraged informally, through jests and teasing.

Personal involvement was also promoted by unique game rules. In baseball, there was often a rule against called strikes, so that everyone had a chance to hit—which meant that fielders had chances to make catches and other action-packed plays. In football, every team member was usually eligible to receive a pass on any play. When children were asked to name the biggest source of fun in their games, they almost always referred to hitting, catching, kicking, scoring, or another form of action in which they were personally involved. Children sought to be a crucial part of what was going on in the games.

Maintaining order in informal games depended on the extent to which players were committed to maintaining action. Usually, when children were personally involved in the game, they were more committed to maintaining action. Tactics to control behavior were used most often to keep players from disrupting action in the games. Players joked around, and even ignored rules, but these forms of deviance were ignored unless they interfered with the flow of action.

Our observations of these games uncovered many performance styles and moves, and these were accepted as normal if they did not disrupt

action in the games. The players with the greatest skill also had the most freedom to use creative styles and moves, because they usually could do so without upsetting game action or interfering with the personal involvement of other players.

Prestige and social status among players was important, because it determined which individuals became involved in decision-making processes during the games. The older players or those with the greatest skills usually had the highest status. Arguments, even though they did occur, were usually handled in creative ways and did not often destroy the games. When children played together often, they became more skilled at solving conflicts.

Informal games usually emphasize action, personal involvement, close scores, and the reaffirmation of friendships. These boys and girls often play games with each other, and they have developed creative strategies for resolving conflicts. (Jay Coakley)

A word of caution: these summary descriptions of informal sports do not apply to all occasions when children create their own games. Problems in informal games do occur. Bigger and stronger children may exploit smaller and weaker ones. Girls may be patronized or dismissed when they try to play with groups of boys, and those children excluded from games often feel rejected by their peers.

Additionally, the dynamics of activities and games usually vary with the availability of play spaces and equipment. For example, when a large group uses the only basketball court in a neighborhood, the games exclude many children who want to play. The team that wins takes on challengers, rather than giving up the court to others, and those with less developed skills are not given concessions when it comes to participation. Taking turns is rare when there are more players than spaces to play. However, when there are many courts and only a few players, the goal is often to accommodate everyone's interests, so that nobody leaves and forces the game to end. This is a major reason that the informal games of children in low-income areas with few facilities and resources are often different from the games played by children in higher-income areas, where facilities are more plentiful and there is little or no competition for space (Carlston, 1986).

Clearly, then, external conditions in the society as a whole have important effects on the way children play informal games. Most of the children we observed and interviewed in our projects were from neighborhoods where competition for space was not a major issue.

Formal, Adult-Controlled Sports

Our observations and interviews done in connection with formally organized, adult-controlled sports focused on children between eight and twelve years old. The data we collected indicated that, even though the children valued action and personal involvement, they were likely to be serious and concerned with playing well and winning games. Most apparent in these games was that the action, personal involvement, and behavior were strictly regulated by formal rules. Adults, including coaches, managers, umpires, referees, scorekeepers, timekeepers, and other game officials, enforced these rules.

The children in these sports often were concerned with the formal positions they played on their teams. They even referred to themselves in terms of those positions and took pride in describing themselves as "defensive halfbacks" or "offensive ends," as "centers" or "left wingers," as "catchers" or "right fielders." The importance of positions was also emphasized by the coaches and spectators, who often encouraged players to "stay in position" during games. This happened regularly in basketball, soccer, hockey, and other sports in which the players were constantly on the move.

Adult-controlled schedules governed the duration and play of organized sports, although the weather and the setting of the sun were also factors. Individual playing time varied by players' skill levels. Most often, the smaller, visibly timid, and less skilled children sat on the sidelines. Although everyone usually played for at least a short time, the children whose playing time was low often maintained only a token interest in the games. While these substitute players were on the sidelines, they were usually bored with the whole situation or interested in things unrelated to the games. The highly skilled players were most likely to show strong interest in the games and to express disappointment when they were taken out of the lineup.

A consequence of adult control and organization was the visible absence of arguments and overt displays of hostility between players from opposing teams. The few arguments we have seen over the years were between adult officials (or spectators and officials) or between players on the same team. Arguments between team members usually were connected with a player's inability to remember game rules, stay in position, play a position efficiently, or carry out the strategies developed by the adults.

Adult control and *formal structure* (that is, *rules plus positions*) kept children organized, but they also seemed to limit visible displays of affection and friendship during the games. This made it difficult to determine who were friends. However, interpersonal relationships among the players had little to do with how the games were played, because players made so few decisions.

The major purpose of game rules was the standardization of competition and the control of player behavior. Rules and rule enforcement regularly caused breaks in the action, but the players did not seem to resent these breaks. The only signs of displeasure came when delays were caused by penalties called against a player's team. Rule enforcement (social control) in these games was based on the players' self-control and obedience, but it ultimately rested in the hands of adults: coaches, referees, and game officials. These adults usually applied the rules universally and seldom made exceptions, even when there were differences in players' abilities and characteristics. The coaches' strict application of the rules restricted the players' freedom, but compliance with the rules and coaches' expectations were extremely high among the players.

When deviance occurred, it was more often caused by players forgetting or not knowing what to do than by players blatantly ignoring the rules. On the playing field, rule infractions usually were accompanied by formal sanctions, even if they did not have an effect on game action or outcomes. Off the field, rules varied from one team to another, and violations usually involved "joking around" or exhibiting a lack of interest in the game or the team. Responses to these behaviors also varied. Coaches and parents used verbal and nonverbal sanctions. They used the game rules, team rules, and sanctions to control behavior and preserve the organization of the game and the values underlying the authority of the referees and coaches.

Our observations and interviews indicated that the children in organized sports were serious about their games. They wanted to win, although usually they were not obsessed with winning. Those most concerned with winning were the highly skilled players and members of the most successful teams. Although they had other goals, the principal goal of participation was to have fun. However, they always knew their win-loss record and their place in the league standings. The players were most likely to be disappointed when they did not log the playing time they thought they deserved. Playing time was very important, because it was related to the children's reputations among peers.

Status on organized teams depended largely on the coaches' assessments of the players' physical skills and value to the team. The better players were sometimes given more responsibility and more latitude in determining what they did during games. Physical skills and approval from the coaches were the basis of status and autonomy among the players, and approval from the coaches came most often when the players followed team rules.

Finally, the games in organized sports were extremely stable. They did not end until the rules said they were over, regardless of the quality of play or enjoyment among the players. Adults' whistles, along with verbal encouragement, commands, and advice, were ever present in these games.

Analysis of Differences

The personal experiences of the children in these two sport forms are very different. Informal sports are generally action-centered, whereas organized sports are rule-centered.

Which of these experiences is more valuable in the development of children? The answer to this question is important not only to the children involved but also to the adults who invest so much time, money, and energy in organized programs.

After doing years of research on this issue, I believe that each experience makes different contributions to the lives of children, and both have problems. However, people traditionally overrate the contributions of participation in organized sports and underrate the contributions of participation in informal sports (Schultz, 1999).

Playing informal sports clearly involves the use of interpersonal and decision-making skills. Children must be creative to organize games and keep them going. They encounter dozens of unanticipated challenges requiring on-the-spot decisions and interpersonal abilities. Long-time sports journalist Leonard Koppett said that the most important part of informal sports is "learning how to set up the game, choose sides, agree with your peers, make compromises, figure out answers, [and] submit to self-directed rulings so that the game can continue" (1994, p. 294). He added that these experiences have "important civilizing functions," which aren't found in adult-controlled organized sports.

Patricia and Peter Adler's (1998) eight-year study of the everyday lives of children and adolescents in their own community led them to conclude that informal sports provide experiences involving cooperation, planning, organizing, negotiating, problem solving, flexibility, and improvisation. Their examples of how children do these things are impressive. Although we do not know how or to what extent the learning that occurs in these informal sports carries over to other settings, we can assume that children are influenced by their experiences.

Playing organized sports, on the other hand, involves a different set of experiences. Organized sports demand that children be able to manage their relationships with adult authority figures. Children also learn the rules and strategies used in activities that are highly visible and important within the culture, and through their participation they often gain status, which carries over to the rest of their lives. When they play organized sports, they see bureaucracy and hierarchy in action, and they become acquainted with forms of rule-governed teamwork and adult models of work and achievement (Adler and Adler, 1998). A possible negative outcome of too much participation in organized sports is that children may learn to view the world in passive terms, as something that is given rather than created. If this is true, children may grow up thinking they are powerless to change the world in which they live.

In this discussion, I have ignored the fact that some games fall between the two types I have described. Certainly, there are informal games in which an adult provides subtle guidance to the children, who are controlling most of what occurs. There are also organized games in which adults take a low profile and let children handle many things on their own. My sense is that these hybrids are valuable contexts for learning a variety of things. The adults who are involved in such games often say that it takes tact and considerable patience to put up with children's mistakes and oversights. They also say that it is a joy to see the creativity and compassion shown by many children, who respond to adult suggestions and subtle encouragement.

As we adults organize and intervene in the games of children, we should consider the advice given by a parent writing about children's activities:

> Sometimes I think that by being so involved in our kids' sports, we dilute their experience. After all, it's not *their* win, it's *our* win. Do all the valuable lessons—losing, striking out, missing the winning shot—have the same impact when Mom and Dad are there to immediately say it's okay? . . . As parents, we know that at some point we need to make it *their* game, *their* recital, *their* grades. If we share every element of their lives, we're cheating them out of part of it. . . . As hard as it is to risk missing her first home run, or not being there to comfort him after the missed foul shot, at some point we need to take ourselves out of their ball game. Because that is what good parents do. (Keri, 2000, p. 55)

In organized sport programs for children, it is the adults who determine and enforce the rules,

plan strategies and call plays,

solve problems,

and wait anxiously for results. (Jay Coakley)

SOCIOLOGICAL QUESTIONS ABOUT YOUTH SPORTS

When Are Children Ready to Play Organized Competitive Sports?

Parents ask readiness questions often. They wonder: should they sign their three-year-olds up for T-ball teams, put their five-year-olds on swim teams, and let their eight-year-olds participate in state gymnastics competitions? Some want to give their children an early start on an imagined path to athletic glory; others don't want their children to fall behind peers in skills development; still others just want their children to have healthy fun and feel good about their bodies.

Answers to readiness questions are available in the fields of motor learning, physical education, exercise physiology, psychology, and sociology. When sociologists respond to readiness questions, their answers often reflect interaction-ist research done by scholars who study social development during childhood. This work suggests that, at about eight years of age, children begin to develop the cognitive and social abilities they need to understand fully the complex social relationships involved in most competitive sports. These abilities are not fully developed until about twelve years of age for most children.

Anyone who has ever watched two teams of eight-year-old soccer players knows about these developmental issues. Most children younger than twelve play what I call "beehive soccer": after the opening kick, there are twenty bodies and forty legs surrounding the ball, and they follow the ball around the playing field like a swarm of bees following its queen. Everyone is out of position, and all the players usually stay that way for the entire game. Meanwhile, the coaches and parents loudly plead with them to "Stay in position!" and "Get back where you belong!"

However, determining where you belong in most sports is difficult. Positions change, depending on the placement of teammates and opponents relative to the location of the ball. Understanding the concept of position requires the ability to do three things simultaneously: (1) mentally visualize the ever-changing placements of teammates and opponents over the entire field, (2) assess their relationships to each other and to the ball, and (3) then decide where you belong. The ability to think through these three things and accurately determine where you should be on the field develops gradually in connection with social experience and individual maturation.

Parents and coaches often are frustrated when children fail to understand positions or follow strategies. When adults don't know about cognitive and social development during childhood, they may accuse preteen children who are out of position of not thinking or trying hard

> I play to win. I don't play to play. If I find out I have a team that's going to be 0–8, I'll go with a different team.
>
> —Nick, age ten, hockey player, Lake Forest, IL (1999)

enough or of having a bad attitude. This frustrates children who *are* thinking and trying as best they can at their stage of development. Their attitude is *not* the issue.

"Beehive soccer" and its equivalents in other sports can be avoided in two ways. *First*, the games children play can be altered to focus on skills and expression, rather than competition and team strategies. In other words, games can be revised to fit the children's needs and abilities (Morris and Stiehl, 1989; Torbert, 2000). This is a preferred strategy. *Second*, children can be systematically conditioned to respond in certain ways to certain situations during competitive games and matches. This requires practices during which coaches create various game situations and then have each player rehearse individual tactical responses to each situation. Doing this with every player for even a few basic strategies is very tedious. It may win games, but it is not a preferred strategy, because it often destroys much of the action and personal involvement that children value in sports. When action is destroyed, it causes some children to wonder if sports are worth their time and effort.

Just imagine how many ground balls a coach must hit to infielders on a children's baseball or softball team to teach them where to throw the ball with different numbers of outs and different numbers of opponents on base. I tell my students that I will buy dinner for any one of them and three of their friends if they can find me a ten-year-old who can determine without adult guidance what to do in the following situation: The child is playing left field. There is one out, with opposing runners at first and second base. The batter hits a long line drive, which falls beyond and between the right fielder and the center fielder. Everyone on the team now has a position to which he or she should move. Where should the left fielder go? If the left fielder had the ability to put him- or herself simultaneously in the positions of eight teammates and three base-runners, he or she would run in toward third base to back up the third base person. This would be done in case of an overthrow from the second base person, who should have moved to the relay position in short right-center field. Ten-year-olds cannot figure this out by themselves. They must be conditioned to do it, because they do not yet have the abilities needed to fully understand complex sets of relationships among three or more people. By the way, where should the pitcher go in this situation? How about the first base person? Can a coach teach all these things without making baseball boring for children?

Children are not born with the ability to compete or cooperate with others, nor are they born able to visualize complex sets of social relationships between teammates and opponents. They must learn these things, and the learning depends on a combination of social experience and the development of abstract thinking and interpersonal abilities. This learning cannot be forced. It occurs only as children move from a stage in which they see the world from their own limited viewpoint to a stage in which they can see the world from third-party perspectives. A **third-party perspective** is one that goes beyond their own views and the view of any other person they know. Third-party perspectives gradually emerge between the ages of eight and twelve years in most children. Therefore, organized sports for preteens should be controlled in ways that accommodate this gradually emerging ability; the highest emphasis should be on developing physical skills and basic cooperation. After all, children must learn to cooperate before they can compete with one another in positive ways. If they don't know how to cooperate, competitions can get nasty and brutish.

Finally, those of us who ask the question "When should children play organized competitive sports?" generally live in cultures in which scientific approaches to childhood development are popular and people have the time and

resources to organize children's activities. Youth sports are a luxury. They cost money and take time; therefore, many people cannot afford them. This is true even in wealthy countries among families with few resources. Many children around the world simply include movement and physical play in their lives as they learn how to be boys or girls in their cultures and learn to fit into social class and occupational structures. When to begin organized sports is not an issue for them or their parents. How, where, when, and what they play are seriously constrained by the material conditions of their lives. As we think about organized youth sports, it is important to be aware of poverty and its impact on children within and between societies.

What Are the Dynamics of Family Relationships in Connection with Organized Youth Sports?

Organized youth sports require time, money, and organizational skills, and these usually come from parents. Therefore, playing organized sports is often a family affair; however, few sociologists have done research on how youth sport participation affects family relationships.

Anecdotal information indicates that youth sports serve as sites for bringing family members together in supportive ways. However, problems do occur. Parents may act in ways that damage their relationships with their children, and they may become so emotionally involved with sports that they put pressure on their children or fail to see that their children perceive their encouragement as pressure. When children feel pressure in either of these forms, they face a triple dilemma: (1) if they quit sports, they fear that their parents may withdraw support and attention; (2) if they play sports but do not perform well, they fear their parents will criticize them; (3) if they perform well, they fear that their parents will treat them like "little pros" instead of children.

When sociologist Mike Messner (1992) interviewed former elite male athletes, he heard

There is an interesting parental division of labor associated with youth sports. Mothers provide a wide range of off-the-field support, whereas fathers do the coaching and league administration. (Jay Coakley)

about similar dilemmas. Many men in his study remembered that early sport experiences enabled them to connect with their fathers, who were otherwise away from home and emotionally distant from them. As young boys, they had wanted to please and receive attention from their fathers. However, they often found that the togetherness they had in sports did not involve real intimacy, and it did not carry over into their lives away from sports. Despite this, many of the men remembered feeling that they had to stay in sports and become good athletes to maintain relationships with their fathers.

Organized youth sports have an impact on families and family relationships in other ways as well. Studies by Janet Chafetz and Joe Kotarba (1999) in the United States and Shona Thompson (1999a, b) in Australia highlight the fact that organized sport programs for children could not exist without the volunteer labor of parents, especially mothers. Their research shows that

mothers drive children to practices and games, fix meals at convenient times, launder dirty training clothes and uniforms, and make sure equipment is ready. Mothers raise funds for teams and leagues. They purchase, prepare, and serve food during road trips and at postgame get-togethers. They form and serve on committees that supervise off-the-field social activities and make phone calls about schedules and schedule changes. They manage the activities of brothers and sisters who do not play in the programs, and they provide emotional support for their child-athletes when they play poorly or when coaches or fathers criticize how they play. Fathers also provide labor, but it is devoted primarily to on-the-field and administrative matters, such as coaching, field maintenance, and league administration.

The analysis in both these studies focuses on the extent to which parent labor in organized youth sports reproduces a gendered division of labor in the family and the community, as well as in the minds of the children, especially of the boys who play organized sports. The studies highlight the labor of mothers because this topic has been widely ignored by many who study sports in society. It is now important to build on this research and delve more deeply into the family dynamics that exist in connection with youth sports.

How Do Social Factors Influence Youth Sport Experiences?

Children make choices about playing sports, but they have little control over the context in which they make their choices. Many factors, including parents, peers, and the general social and cultural contexts in which they live, influence the alternatives from which they choose and how they define and give meaning to their choices. For example, children from low-income, inner-city backgrounds generally have many fewer sport participation opportunities than other children have. Children with able bodies have more opportunities and receive more encouragement to play sports than do children with disabilities. Choosing to play a contact sport, such as football, is seen by most people around the world to be more appropriate for boys than for girls. Boys who want to figure skate generally do not receive the same encouragement from peers as girls receive. When African American boys choose to play certain sports, many people in the United States are more likely to identify them in terms of their athletic skills than in terms of their other characteristics, such as academic achievements.

None of these statements is earthshaking. People know these things. They know that, as children make sport choices and give meaning to their sport experiences, they and the people around them are influenced by prevailing cultural beliefs about age, gender, sexuality, race and ethnicity, ability and disability, and social class. This is how social forces influence youth sport experiences.

Research by Patti and Peter Adler (1998) provides vivid examples of how social forces influence children and their sport choices and experiences. During their eight years of observing, interviewing, and hanging out with children in their community, the Adlers discovered that playing sports fit into the lives of the boys and girls in very different ways. For example, athletic ability, coolness, toughness, and being "smooth" in social relationships were key determinants of the popularity of the boys. Very high or very low academic performance often subverted popularity among the boys. The popularity of the girls depended primarily on their families' social status, the freedoms granted to them by their families, their physical appearance and grooming behavior, their abilities to manage relationships with boys and with female peers, and their grades in school. The Adlers emphasize that their research focused on children in a predominantly white, upper-middle-class community and that the criteria for popularity sometimes shift slightly when young people enter junior high school (about age twelve in most U.S. school districts).

These popularity criteria were linked with sport participation choices in interesting ways. Both the boys and the girls in this community had numerous choices when it came to playing informal sports as well as organized sports at recreational to elite levels of competition. The girls and groups of girls were less likely than their male counterparts to play informal and alternative sports. In preadolescent culture, girls do not receive as much encouragement, approval, and social rewards for doing these activities as boys receive. Furthermore, boys often control the way informal games are organized and played, and they may not treat girls as equals in these settings. In the Adlers' study, the girls played organized sports almost at the same rate as the boys. However, as the children moved into junior high school, the girls dropped out of sports at a higher rate than the boys did. The girls who excelled at sports tended to stay involved, but many of those with average or mediocre physical skills dropped out. Overall, the girls felt that playing sports was not required for acceptance and status among peers (Creager, 1999).

Other research also highlights that sport choices and experiences are influenced by dominant definitions of gender in society. These definitions influence early childhood experiences when it comes to physical activities (White et al., 1992). For example, in the United States, fathers play with their sons more often and in more physically active ways than they play with their daughters. Furthermore, the physical activity messages that most young boys receive differ from the messages many young girls receive, both inside and outside family settings (Beal, 1994; Greendorfer, 1993; Hargreaves, 1994; Hasbrook, 1999; Lenskyj, 1986; Nelson, 1991).

One result of these messages is that, before most children take their first physical education class or play their first organized sport, they have clear ideas about their physical skills and potential. Boys are more likely to see themselves as being physically skilled than girls are, even though measurable gender differences in actual skill levels are small or nonexistent (Nelson, 1990, p. 9). Boys are more likely than girls to *think* they are better than they actually are when it comes to sports skills. This has an effect on their self-confidence and willingness to use and test their bodies in active ways and to participate voluntarily in physical activities. Girls learn to minimize the physical space they occupy, sexualize their bodies through modifying their appearance and movement, and accept the notion that boys are physically superior to them. At the same time, boys learn to present themselves as physically big and strong, to act in ways that claim physical space around them, and to expect to exert power and control over girls (Hasbrook, 1999; Hasbrook and Harris, 1999).

Physical self-concepts come to be connected with gender, because many people expect different levels of sport-related skills from girls and boys; a similar dynamic exists when it comes to ethnicity and skin color: blacks often are expected to be more interested in and better at sports than whites are (L. Harrison, 1995; Harrison et al., 1999). Gender-related expectations may be one of the reasons boys' ball games often dominate the space on elementary school playgrounds and in other public places. This pattern extends through the life course—observe the extent to which young men appropriate space for themselves on the open playing fields of most U.S. college campuses. Of course, many people actively discourage such gender-based patterns, but it is often difficult to change them, because they are deeply rooted in the culture as a whole.

The influence of social forces on youth sports has been identified in many studies. Research by Ingham and Dewar (1999) shows how dominant ideas about masculinity influence the meanings that boys give to their experiences in a youth hockey program. I have done research into how dominant ideas about ethnicity and social class influence the funding and program orientations of youth sport programs in minority areas in inner cities and in white suburban areas (Coakley, 2002). Howard Nixon (2000) discusses the exclusion and the participation barriers faced by children with certain disabilities, and he outlines the complex and contentious issues surrounding the segregation and integration of people with disabilities in sports competitions. As we read these studies, it is important to focus on the experiences of children, rather than simply looking for differences by gender, ethnicity, ability, and social class. As we see how experiences vary, we learn how social forces interact with each other and influence children's lives on and off the playing field.

RECOMMENDATIONS FOR CHANGING CHILDREN'S SPORTS

Changing Informal and Alternative Sports

Informal and participant-controlled alternative sports are unique because they are not controlled directly by adults. In fact, many children opt for such sports, because they want to avoid the organized structures of adult-controlled teams and programs. However, adults can become indirectly involved in ways that increase the safety of these sports and that maximize children's opportunities to participate in them.

This means that, instead of passing laws to suppress sports such as skateboarding or in-line skating, adults should work with young people to provide safe settings for them to create their own activities. If adults do not become supportive of new informal and alternative sport forms, their children will use the extreme models of the XGames, Gravity Games, and other made-for-TV spectacles as primary sources of inspiration. The challenge for adults is to be supportive and to provide subtle guidance without being controlling. Children need their own space, in which they can be creative and expressive while they play sports. Adult guidance can be helpful in making that space as safe as possible and by making it open to as many children as possible, boys and girls as well as children with disabilities and from various ethnic and social class backgrounds.

Changing Organized Sports

There are a wide variety of organized sport programs for children. This is especially true in countries that have no centralized state authority through which youth programs are funded, controlled, and administered. Programs vary from one sport to another, from community to community, and from league to league. However, those in charge could improve conditions in most programs, maximizing positive experiences and minimizing negative experiences for participants. This is true in other parts of the world as well as in North America.

In making recommendations for change, most people agree that organized programs should meet the needs of the children who participate in them. This means that the children themselves are a valuable source of information, which adults can use as they organize and administer

youth sports. If children seek fun in their own games by emphasizing action, involvement, close scores, and friendships, it makes sense that organized programs also should emphasize these things. The recommendations in the following discussion are based on this assumption.

Increasing Action   Children emphasize *action* in their own games. Much activity occurs around the scoring area, and scoring is usually so frequent that it is difficult to keep personal performance statistics. Organized sports, although they do contain action, strongly emphasize rules, order, standardized conditions, and predictability. The strategy of many organized teams is to prevent action, rather than stimulate it. Parents and coaches sometimes describe high-scoring games as undisciplined free-for-alls caused by poor defensive play. The desired strategy in the minds of many adults is to stop action: to strike out the batter (baseball and softball), to stall the game when you are in the lead (soccer and basketball), and to use a safe running play for a 3-yard gain (football). These tactics may win some games, but they limit the most exciting aspects of most games: action and scoring.

It's usually easy to increase action and scoring in organized sports, as long as adults do not view game models as sacred and unchangeable. Bigger goals, smaller playing areas, and fewer rules are the best means to increase action. Why not double the width of goals in soccer and hockey, make all players eligible to receive passes and carry the ball in football, and use a 6-foot basket in a half-court basketball game? Of course, care must be taken in sports such as soccer and hockey not to put goalkeepers at a disadvantage. Therefore, it might be appropriate to eliminate this position in some cases and to rotate it among players in other cases. Many adults resist changes they think will alter game models—that is, the models used in elite, adult sports. They want children to play "the real thing." They forget that children are more interested in having fun than in playing as adults do.

Many sport programs for younger children have decreased the size of playing fields and teams. This soccer program has 3-on-3 teams, there are no goalies, and no scores are recorded, although some parents keep track of scores and team records. The four- and five-year-olds in the league are most interested in running around and kicking the ball somewhere, even if it's in the wrong direction. (Jay Coakley)

Increasing Personal Involvement   Children do not sit on the bench in informal games. They use rule qualifications and handicap systems to maximize their involvement and to promote action. Smaller or less skilled players may not contribute to the action as much as their bigger and more skilled peers do, but they play the whole game. If they are treated badly or excluded, they leave without being branded as quitters or being lectured to on commitment by their parents.

In organized games, playing time is often seriously limited for all but the most skilled players, and the substitution process is a constant source of problems for the coach and pressure for the players. Specialization by position further restricts the range of involvement. When ten-year-olds describe themselves as left defensive tackles, center fielders, left wingers, or center halfbacks, it is a sure sign that the range of personal involvement is limited.

Coaches and other leaders could extend personal involvement in organized sport programs by rotating players to different positions and by coordinating group substitutions with opposing teams. They could alter team size to allow more players on the field, or they could reduce rosters so that there were more teams with fewer subs. Batting lineups for baseball and softball could include all team members, regardless of which ones were playing the nine or ten positions in the field. In ice hockey, the games could be played across the width of the rink, and portable dividers and lightweight goals could be used; this would allow three times as many teams to compete at the same time. In basketball, the first-string teams could play a half-court game at one basket, while the second-string teams played each other at the other basket. A combined score could determine the winner. These and many other similar changes would increase personal involvement.

Creating Close Scores   "Good games" are those for which the outcomes are in doubt until the last play; double overtime games are the best. Lopsided scores destroy the excitement of competition. Children realize this, so they keep their informal games close.[1] Since motivation partially depends on how people perceive their chances for success, a close game usually keeps players motivated and satisfied. Just like adults who use handicaps to keep the competition interesting in bowling, golf, and other sports, children adjust their games to keep them close.

In organized games, lopsided scores are common and team records are often very uneven. Keeping players motivated under these circumstances is difficult. Coaches are forced to appeal to pride and respect to keep children motivated in the face of lopsided scores and long, losing seasons. Ironically, coaches also urge their teams and players to take big leads during games. This makes no sense, because it destroys motivation.

Adults who control organized youth sports are usually hesitant to make changes affecting the outcomes of games, but they might consider some possibilities. For example, they could encourage close scores by altering team rosters or by using handicap systems during games. The underdog could be given an advantage, such as extra players or the right to use five downs, five outs, or a bigger goal. Numerous changes could keep games close; however, when game models are viewed as unchangeable, possible changes are never even discussed.

Maintaining friendships   When children play informal and alternative sports, the reaffirmation of friendships is important. Friendships influence the ways in which teams are chosen and the dynamics of the problem-solving processes during games. Organized sports may provide useful contexts for making friends, but players need more opportunities to nurture relationships with teammates and with children on other teams.

Coaches and managers could ask groups of players in organized sports to plan game strategies or coach practice sessions. They could encourage players to talk with opponents, help them when they were knocked down, and congratulate them when they did something commendable. Too often, relationships between opposing players are cold and impersonal. Players should learn that games have a human component, which they can recognize during play. Most important, players should be expected to enforce most of the rules themselves during games. Through self-enforcement, they would learn why rules are necessary and how collective action depends on taking other people and the expectations of others into consideration. Many people argue that self-enforcement would never work (although it does work in tennis)—however, if organized programs do not teach young people how to cooperate to the extent needed to play games with their friends, then those programs are not worth our time and effort.

Other changes are also needed. For example, Shane Murphy (1999), a psychologist who has worked with many athletes and families in his clinical practice, suggests that programs include education for all participants, including parents, coaches, and players. He suggests involving children in decisions about youth sport programs, designing programs to teach life skills as well as sport skills, and using social goals to inform the philosophies of organized programs. Finally, he suggests developing and enforcing codes of conduct for parents, coaches, and players.

Changing High-Performance Sport Programs

Many of the worst problems in youth sports occur in high-performance programs. To deal

---

[1]Close scores may be sacrificed when close friends want to be on the same team; playing with friends is sometimes more important than having evenly balanced teams.

with these problems, sociologist Peter Donnelly (1993) has called on sport governing bodies to do two things:

1. Change their policies, procedures, and rules to account for the rights and interests of children
2. Create less controlling sport environments designed to promote children's growth, development, and empowerment

Because people in sport organizations often have vested interests in keeping things as they are now, Donnelly advocates that some form of child labor laws be applied to high-performance youth sports and be enforced when the health and well-being of children are in jeopardy (see figure 5.2). Journalist Joan Ryan picked up on Donnelly's points when she studied girls in elite

gymnastics and figure skating. She suggested the following:

> Since those charged with protecting young athletes so often fail their responsibility, it is time the government drops the fantasy that certain sports are merely games and takes a hard look at legislation aimed at protecting elite child athletes. (1995, p. 15)

This is a suggestion that all of us should all take seriously. When the livelihoods of adults depend on the work or performance of children, it is likely that the children need formal protection.

PROSPECTS FOR CHANGE

Many organized youth sport programs have made changes that reflect a concern for the needs and well-being of children. In fact, there are many excellent models for thinking about and making changes in youth sports (Chalip and Green, 1998; Morris and Stiehl, 1989; Murphy, 1999; Torbert, 2000). However, the approach most often used to guide changes in youth sport programs is grounded in a functionalist theoretical perspective (see chapter 2). In other words, adults are most concerned with changes that will increase efficiency and organization in youth sports and that will increase the skill levels of child-athletes. Thus, we see more training programs for coaches, more formal rules regulating the behavior of parents and spectators, and more rules for what is expected from players and coaches. There are more promotional brochures and advertising in the local media, more emphasis on the performance ethic, and more tournaments, playoffs, and championships.

As organized youth sports become increasingly affiliated with national organizations and sport governing bodies, the chance that these bodies will consider critical changes in game models and the structure of youth sports becomes increasingly remote. Changes occasionally may

"How many times have I told you to practice your basketball before you even think about homework?"

....

FIGURE 5.2 The fame and fortune of some professional athletes may encourage some parents to overemphasize youth sports in the lives of their children. Might this turn young athletes into "child workers"?

be considered at local levels, but even local sport programs are not likely to change official game models or program structures. Such changes would threaten the relationships of local programs with the influential state and national organizations that many of the players' parents have paid to join.

Changes are also slow to come because many adults who administer and support organized sport programs have vested interests in keeping them as they are. They know the programs are not perfect, but they are afraid changes in them will eliminate many of the good things they have accomplished in the past. In the absence of critical structural changes in youth sports, important incremental changes can occur if parents and coaches watch and listen closely to the children in their lives (see figure 5.3).

"Have you ever considered that maybe I'd like this to remain a repressed childhood memory?"
....

FIGURE 5.3   Many children who play sports do not enjoy videotapes of their games, meets, and matches. They would rather remember their experiences in their own terms. Too often, the tapes are used to identify mistakes and make youth sports more important than children want them to be.

Coaching education programs will continue to grow. Existing programs in many countries provide coaches with information on how to (1) deal with young people responsively and safely and (2) be more effective in organizing their practices and in teaching skills to young people. Most coaching education programs emphasize putting athletes' needs ahead of winning, but none of them teaches coaches how to critically assess the sports programs in which they work with young people. None presents information on how to make structural changes in the programs themselves or on how to create alternatives to existing programs. Coaching education materials generally are based on the functionalist assumption that existing sports programs are pretty good, but they could be better if coaches were to use more applied sport science as they work with child athletes.

Although coaching education is important, I worry that some programs ultimately will foster a "technoscience approach" to youth sports. A technoscience approach emphasizes issues of control and skill development, rather than an overall understanding of young people as human beings. If this happens, coaches are defined as "sports efficiency experts," rather than teachers who provide young people with opportunities to become autonomous and responsible decision makers who control their own lives.

Most coaching education programs have contributed to responsible coaching in youth sport programs. But, as we examine coaching education programs and critically assess their place at all levels of sport, it would be good to remember that the former East Germany had one of the most efficient and highly respected coaching education programs in the world. However, its program was based on a technoscience approach and did little to contribute to the overall development of young people as human beings. The East German experience reminds us that, without critical self-reflection, the application of sport science knowledge to coaching will not necessarily make youth sports or the world any better. If coaching education were informed by critical self-reflection, it could lead to many positive changes in sport programs for people of all ages.

SUMMARY

ARE ORGANIZED YOUTH SPORT PROGRAMS WORTH THE EFFORT?

Children in all societies participate in various forms of movement and physical activity. For the most part, these activities take place in informal settings and are characterized by freedom and spontaneity. However, they do not occur in social and cultural vacuums. In fact, the forms and dynamics of children's physical activities are connected indirectly with larger socialization processes, through which participants learn how to be girls and boys and learn about the systems of social relations and cultural beliefs that exist in their families, communities, and nation-states. These processes vary from society to society and across cultural settings within societies.

Although movement and physical activities exist in all cultures, organized youth sports are a luxury. They require resources and discretionary time among children and adults. They exist only when children are not required to work and only when there is a widespread belief in society that experiences during childhood influence a person's development and character. Youth sports have a unique history in every society in which they exist. However, they always have been constructed to emphasize experiences and values defined as important in the societies in which they exist.

The growth of organized sports in North America and much of Europe is associated with the changes in the family that occurred during the latter half of the twentieth century. Many parents now see organized sports as important extensions of their control over their children and as settings in which their children gain important developmental experiences.

Major trends in youth sports today include the privatization of organized programs, an emphasis on the performance ethic, the development of high-performance training programs, and more involvement by and concern among parents. In response to these trends, some children have turned to informal and alternative sports, including the highly visible extreme versions of alternative sports.

Children's sport experiences vary with levels of formal organization and with the extent to which they are participant-controlled or adult-controlled. The dynamics of sport participation, as well as what children may learn from their experiences, are different in informal games than in organized youth sport programs. Involvement across a range of participation settings is important in the developmental experiences of children.

Research in the sociology of sport can be used to answer many of the commonly asked questions about youth sports. Studies guided by symbolic interactionism help us understand that, prior to eight years old, children do not have the developmental abilities needed to understand the social dynamics of organized competitive sports, especially team sports in which complex strategies are used. Such abilities do not become fully developed until twelve years of age in most children. Studies guided primarily by critical feminist theories have begun to describe and explain some of the family dynamics associated with organized youth sports, especially in terms of how they affect family relationships, family schedules, and the lives of mothers and fathers. Studies often guided by a range of critical theories illustrate how social factors influence youth sport experiences, including the participation choices available to children and the meanings given to various sport experiences.

Recommendations for changing children's sports could be formulated by using the characteristics of children's informal games as a guide. This would call for changes in the structure and organization of many youth sport programs. These changes would emphasize increased action and involvement among all participants. They also would emphasize changes to keep game scores close and to give children opportunities to formulate and nurture friendships with team-mates and opponents.

The prospects for change in organized youth sport programs are inhibited by the vested inter-ests of many adults in programs as they are cur-rently organized. This is especially true in high-performance sport programs, even though these are the programs in which changes are most needed. Coaching education programs could fa-cilitate changes if they were to deal with youth sports in more critical terms.

Of course, no program can guarantee that it will make children into models of virtue, but the adults who organize programs can change them to minimize problems. This means that orga-nized sport programs for children *are* worth the effort—when the adults controlling them put the children's interests ahead of the pro-grams' organizational needs and their own needs to gain status through their association with child athletes.

 ## SUGGESTED READINGS

Adler, Patricia, A., and Peter Adler. 1998. *Peer power: Preadolescent culture and identity*. New Brunswick, NJ: Rutgers University Press (the authors collected data over eight years on the lives of children in an upper-middle-class town; excellent information about how play, informal games, recreational activities, and organized sports fit into the social lives of children).

Coakley, J., and P. Donnelly, eds. 1999. *Inside sports*. London: Routledge (accessible articles on sport experiences; articles by Hasbrook, Ingham and Dewar, and Chafetz and Kotarba deal directly with youth sports).

DeKnop, P., B. Skirstad, L.-M. Engstrom, and M. Weiss, eds. 1996. *Worldwide trends in youth sport*. Champaign, IL: Human Kinetics (background material on comparative research; information about youth sports in twenty countries; summarizes research on youth sports in terms of global patterns, trends, problems, and policies).

Fine, G. A. 1987. *With the boys: Little League baseball and preadolescent culture*. Chicago: University of Chicago Press (classic study of youth sports for boys; in-depth qualitative data on eleven-year-old boys illustrate how boys create their own ways of experiencing organized sports).

Murphy, S. 1999. *The cheers and the tears: A healthy alternative to the dark side of youth sports today*. San Francisco: Jossey-Bass (years of clinical experiences with athletes in elite and community-based programs inform this critique of youth sports; information about families and parents, as well as suggestions for change).

Rinehart, R., and S. Syndor, eds. 2003. *To the extreme: Alternative sports, inside and out*. Albany: State University of New York Press (twenty-five articles by scholars and noted athletes in alternative sports; articles do not focus on children, but they capture the spirit and experiences that attract many children to alternative, extreme, and action sports).

Ryan, J. 1995. *Little girls in pretty boxes: The making and breaking of elite gymnasts and figure skating*. New York: Doubleday (in-depth journalistic account and exposé of the lives of U.S. girls and young women in elite gymnastics and figure skating).

WEBSITE RESOURCES

Note: Websites often change. The following URLs were current when this book was printed. Please check our website (www.mhhe.com/coakley8e) for updates and additions.

www.mhhe.com/coakley8e Information on studying gender in children's sports, observation guide for studying a youth sport event; in-depth discussion of when children are ready to play sports; materials on parent-child relationships and youth sports; discussion of social factors influencing youth sports.

http://ed-web3.educ.msu.edu/ysi Site for The Institute for the Study of Youth Sports at

Michigan State University; the institute sponsors research on the benefits and detriments of participation in youth sports, produces educational materials, and provides educational programs for coaches, officials, administrators, and parents; useful links to other sites.

www.nays.org Site for the National Alliance for Youth Sports, a nonprofit organization with the goal of making sports safe and positive for America's youth; links to other youth sport sites.

www.sportsparenting.org/csp Site for the Center for Sports Parenting, a Web-based program that offers immediate and practical guidance to parents, coaches, educators, administrators, officials, and others involved in youth sports.

www.momsteam.com Information at this parents' site is designed to create a safer, saner, less stressful, and more inclusive youth sports experience; it is directed at mothers of children in organized youth sport programs.

www.sportinsociety.org/uys.html Site for the Urban Youth Sports Program of the Center for the Study of Sport in Society; focuses on issues in Boston, but it provides a useful conceptual model for what might be done in other cities to overcome barriers that limit youth sport participation and to increase opportunities for healthy development.

www.youth-sports.com General site for information, advice, and instructional products for parents, coaches, and children involved in youth sports.

(Mark Reis, *Colorado Springs Gazette*)

Deviance in Sports

Is It Out of Control?

WHERE DO ACCEPTABLE practices end and cheating begin? Why is it okay for a cyclist to sleep in an oxygen tent but not okay to inject EPO?

—**Paula Parrish, journalist (2002)**

OLC

Online Learning Center Resources

Visit *Sports in Society*'s Online Learning Center at **www.mhhe.com/coakley8e** for additional information and study material for this chapter, including

- Self-grading quizzes
- Learning objectives
- Related websites
- Additional readings

A complete outline is available online at
www.mhhe.com/coakley8e.

IT'S NO SECRET what's going on in baseball. At least half the guys are using steroids. They talk about it. They joke about it. . . . At first I felt like a cheater. But I looked around, and everybody was doing it.

—Ken Caminiti, Major League Baseball player (2002)

Cases of deviance among athletes, coaches, agents, and others connected with sports have attracted widespread attention in recent years. Regular media coverage of on-the-field rule violations and off-the-field criminal actions has led some people to conclude that deviance in sports is out of control.

Publicity given to criminal charges against athletes has come with continuing information about widespread behind-the-scenes drug and substance use among athletes. Disclosures of performance-enhancing substance and drug use among elite athletes appears regularly in sports news. Statements by Olympic insiders claim that it is rare for anyone to win gold medals without taking performance-enhancing substances. Athletes in many sports avoid positive tests by using substances for which tests are not yet developed or approved. As the former director of drug testing for the United States Olympic Committee (USOC) has said, "Athletes are a walking lab, and the Olympics have become a proving ground for chemists" (in Bamberber and Yaeger, 1997, p. 62).

Because popular beliefs have emphasized sport participation as a character-building experience, these highly publicized cases of deviance among athletes, coaches, and others in sports have shocked and disappointed many people. In their disappointment, some have concluded that the moral fabric of society itself is eroding. Their explanations are nearly always the same: too much money and greed, too little discipline and self-control. The result, they say, is that the purity of sport is gone and sportsmanship is dead.

In light of this conclusion, the purpose of this chapter is to look at the issue of whether deviance is, indeed, out of control in sports. We will focus on four questions as we deal with this issue:

1. What problems do we face when we study deviance in sports?
2. What is the most useful way to define *deviance* when studying sports in society?

3. Are rates of deviant actions among athletes (on and off the field), coaches, and others connected with sports out of control?
4. Why do some athletes use performance-enhancing substances and is it possible to control the use of these substances in sports?

These questions direct our attention to important issues in the study of sports in society.

PROBLEMS FACED WHEN STUDYING DEVIANCE IN SPORTS

Studying deviance in sports presents special problems for four reasons. *First, the forms and causes of deviance in sports are so diverse that no single theory can explain all of them.* For example, think of the forms of deviance that have been engaged in by at least some male college athletes: talking back to a coach at practice, running wind sprints to the point of vomiting, violating rules or committing fouls on the playing field during a match or game, taking megadoses of performance-enhancing substances in the locker room, hazing rookie team members by demeaning them and forcing them to do illegal things, binge drinking and getting into occasional fights in local bars, harassing women at bars, engaging in group sex, committing sexual assault, turning in coursework prepared by others, betting on sports with student bookies, playing with painful injuries and using painkillers to stay on the field, destroying hotel property during a road trip after an embarrassing loss or a difficult win, and going home over a holiday to meet agents who have given big checks to their mothers and have left fancy cars for them to use for the next year. This diverse list includes only a sample of the types of deviance reported for one group of athletes at one level of competition over the past decade. The list would be more diverse if we were to include all athletes and if we were to list forms of deviance by coaches, administrators, team owners, and spectators.

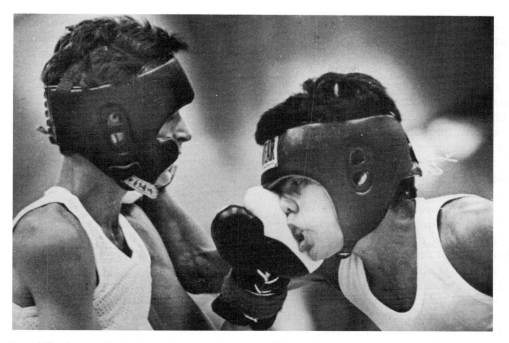

It is difficult to study deviance in sports because athletes often engage in actions that would not be accepted in other settings. For example, actions that are acceptable in boxing, hockey, football, and other sports would get you arrested or sued if you were to engage in them off the field. (*Colorado Springs Gazette*)

Second, what is accepted in sports may be deviant in other spheres of society. Athletes are allowed and even encouraged to act in ways that are prohibited or defined as criminal in other settings. For example, the actions of athletes in contact sports would be classified as felony assault if they were to occur on the streets; boxers would be criminals outside the ring. . . Ice hockey players would be arrested for actions they define as normal during their games. Racecar drivers would be ticketed for speeding and careless driving. Speed skiers and motocross racers would often be defined as deviant outside their sports. However, even when serious injuries or deaths occur in sports, criminal charges usually are not filed, and civil lawsuits asking for financial compensation are generally unsuccessful.

The use of hatred as a source of motivation in sports clearly deviates from the norms most people use to guide their actions in families, religious congregations, classrooms, and work settings. On the other hand, male teammates may embrace one another, touch each other supportively, hold hands, and cry with each other in sports, although the same actions in other settings would violate widely accepted traditional norms about masculinity.

Coaches treat players in ways that most of us would define as deviant if teachers treated students or employers treated employees similarly. Team owners in North American professional sports clearly violate the antitrust laws that apply to other business owners. Fans act in ways that would quickly alienate friends and family members in other settings or lead people to define them as mentally deranged.

These examples show that, when we study deviance, the social worlds created around sports often are different from other social worlds. Norms do exist in sport worlds, but, when athletes and others push normative limits, responses are often different than they would be in other settings. Engaging in extreme actions that risk health and well-being and inflict pain and injury on others are not as quickly condemned in sports as they are in other activities. We tend to view the motives of people in sports, especially athletes, as positive, because their actions are directed toward the achievement of success for their team, school, community, country, or corporate sponsor. Therefore, those actions, even when they clearly overstep accepted limits, may be tolerated or even praised, rather than condemned. Athletes and even coaches are seen as different and deviant in ways that evoke fascination and awe, rather than automatic condemnation. Most sociological theories about deviance have no way of explaining such a phenomenon.

Third, deviance in sports often involves an unquestioned acceptance of norms, rather than a rejection of norms. It is important to note that much of the deviance in sports does not involve a rejection of commonly accepted norms and expectations for action. In the case of athletes, sports involve a combination of exciting experiences and powerful social processes, which encourage extreme actions. These actions are deviant because they fall outside of what most people would consider a normally accepted range, but they may not be punished because they reaffirm normative ideals in the society at large. In fact, this may even lead some athletes to define themselves as morally upstanding, and even righteous, as they push or exceed limits.

Unlike deviance in other settings, deviance in sports often involves an unquestioned acceptance of and extreme conformity to norms and expectations. For example, most North Americans see playing football as a positive activity. Young

men are encouraged to "be all they can be" as football players and to live by slogans such as "There is no *I* in t-e-a-m." They are encouraged to increase their weight and strength, so that they can play more effectively and contribute to the success of their teams. When young men go too far in their acceptance of expectations to become bigger and stronger, when they are so committed to playing football and improving their skills on the field that they use muscle-building drugs, they become deviant (Neyer, 2000).

This type of "overdoing-it-deviance" is dangerous, but it is grounded in completely different social dynamics from the dynamics that occur in the "antisocial deviance" enacted by alienated young people who have no hope for the future, reject commonly accepted rules and expectations, and use substances such as heroin to deaden their awareness of the world. Athletes accept without question the norms that define what it means to be an athlete, and it is overconformity to those norms, not a rejection of them, that often leads to extreme actions.

We must take into account this difference between a rejection of norms and an uncritical overconformity to norms when we study deviance in sports. Social processes in sports, especially high-performance sports, often encourage extreme forms of action that represent normative overconformity. We must study these processes if we wish to understand much of the deviance that exists among athletes today.

Fourth, training and performance in sports have become "medicalized." Training and performance in sports are seen increasingly in medical and sport science terms. People now regard medical treatments previously reserved for those in poor health as tools for meeting the everyday challenges of training and competition in sports. Many people now believe that ingesting substances thought to enhance performance is a necessary part of being an athlete. Just go to a store that sells nutritional supplements to see all the products that can be purchased by anyone interested in improved sport performance. Count the ads for performance-enhancing substances in any recent issue of the magazines *Muscle Media* and *Muscle and Fitness*. The motto for these ads seems to be "Strength and high performance are just a swallow away"! Of course, corporations encourage this approach when they use athletes' bodies to promote products and corporate profiles presented in terms of strength and efficiency (Hoberman, 1995). In the meantime, it has become much more difficult to determine just what actions are deviant and what actions are accepted parts of athletic training.

DEFINING AND STUDYING DEVIANCE IN SPORTS: THREE APPROACHES

Using Functionalist Theory: Deviance Disrupts Shared Values

According to functionalist theory, social order is based on shared values. Shared values give rise to shared cultural goals and shared ideas about how to achieve those goals. Deviance occurs when people engage in actions that involve a rejection of cultural goals and/or the accepted means of achieving them. In other words, deviance involves a departure from cultural ideals: the greater the departure, the more disruptive the action, the greater the deviance. Conversely, the greater the conformity to cultural ideals, the greater the reaffirmation of the social order, the better the action: in other words, conformity = morality.

Most functionalists see deviance as a result of faulty socialization or inconsistencies in the organization of society. In other words, deviance occurs because people have not learned and internalized cultural values and norms or because there are conflicts and strains in society. Therefore, controlling deviance would call for more efficient socialization processes and an elimination of conflicts, strains, and inconsistencies in society.

In the case of sports, deviance would involve a rejection of cultural goals and/or a rejection of

AT YOUR FINGERTIPS For more information, on violent actions in sports, see pages 203–221.

the approved means of attaining those goals. For example, deviance would occur if a person in a sport were to reject the goal of improving one's skills or reject the notion that commitment and hard work are the means to achieve that goal.

One problem with this approach is that, if there is a lack of agreement about the importance of various goals, it is difficult to identify deviance. For example, if I think the ultimate goal in sports is to engage in fair play but you think it is to win, then I will see any violation of the rules as deviant, whereas you will see some violations as "good fouls" that contribute to winning. If I regard sports as a form of play in which intrinsic satisfaction is the primary reason for participation but you regard sports as "war without weapons" fought for external rewards, such as trophies and cash prizes, then I will see violent actions as deviant, whereas you will see them as signs of courage and commitment. Because we don't see eye to eye on the goals and ideals of sports, we will not define *deviance* in the same way.

Another problem with this approach is that it leads many people to think that controlling deviance always calls for increasing conformity. Their control strategies involve establishing more rules, making rules more strict and consistent, developing a more comprehensive system of detecting and punishing rule violators, and making everyone more aware of the rules and what happens to those who don't follow them (see figure 6.1). Of course, this subverts creativity and change, and it assumes that all conformity, even extreme conformity, is a cultural ideal. This assumption is questionable, because conformity is sometimes dangerous, and extreme conformity can lead to forms of fascism—certainly an undesirable outcome.

"We need more rules to stop this stuff."

FIGURE 6.1 Many people use a functionalist approach when they think about deviance in sports. They call for more rules and better enforcement. This approach has only limited usefulness in sports today.

Despite these problems, many people use a framework based on functionalist theory when they discuss deviance in sports. Therefore, when they see actions that do not match cultural ideals, they define these actions and those who engage in them as deviant. Most often their recommendation is to "get tough," throw the "bad apples" out, develop codes of conduct, and make the rules more strict and the punishments more severe. This approach also leads to the idea that people violate rules because they lack moral character, intelligence, or sanity and that good, normal, healthy people wouldn't do such things.

This approach may be useful when people are unaware of the existence of norms. However, it ignores the influence of powerful social processes in sports and leads people to label athletes unjustly as moral failures when, in fact, most athletes are "hyperconformers" whose main fault is that they do not critically assess the norms that they have been taught in connection with sport participation. We will say more about this throughout the chapter.

Using Conflict Theory: Deviance Interferes with the Interests of People with Economic Power

According to conflict theory, social order is based on economic interests and the use of economic power to exploit labor. Social norms reflect the interests of people with power and wealth, and any action or person violating those norms is defined as deviant.

Those who use this theory assume that all people act in their own interests and that people in power use their position and influence to make sure their definitions of what is good or bad become the official definitions of what is normal or deviant in the society as a whole. Those who lack power in society are at a disadvantage, because they have nothing to say about the content or enforcement of rules. Therefore, the actions of people who lack power are labeled as deviant more often than the actions of people with power. To make matters worse, people who lack power don't have the resources to resist being labeled as deviant when their actions do not conform to the standards of the rule makers.

Conflict theorists assume that rules in sport organizations reflect the interests of owners and sponsors and ignore the interests of athletes. Therefore, they see deviance among athletes as the result of rules that not only discriminate against them but also force them to deny their own interests and follow the expectations of those in power, even though their health and well-being may be harmed in the process. When this approach is used, athletes are viewed as victims of a profit-driven system, in which progressive change depends only on disrupting the rules and rebelling against them.

A problem with this approach is that it leads to the conclusion that all deviance in sports is the result of biased norms and the exploitive enforcement of those norms by those who have power. This conclusion is difficult to defend when many forms of deviance that exist in big-time intercollegiate and professional sports also exist in nonrevenue-producing sports, where the athletes themselves may be in positions of power and control. For example, the statement that the use of dangerous growth hormones in elite track and field is the result of rules through which athletes are forced to risk their health for colleges, countries, and corporate sponsors does not hold up, since similar forms of drug use exist among athletes who are not subject to the coercive tactics used by the economically powerful people who control revenue-producing sports.

In other words, it is unlikely that all bad things in sports today would disappear if athletes were in charge. This, however, does not mean that athletes should not have more control over the conditions of their sport participation; they should. But the point is that, since much of the deviance in sports involves unquestioned acceptance of norms and extreme conformity to them, it is unrealistic to expect that most athletes have the critical consciousness needed to transform the meaning, organization, and purpose of sports in society today. Athletes certainly need to have their consciousness raised and to play a crucial role in transforming sports, but those using conflict theory are naïve when they assume that all the causes of deviance in sports would automatically disappear if profit motives were eliminated and athletes had the power to make and enforce all rules in sports.

Those using conflict theory have another problem: they see all established forms of social control as oppressive, and they see no hope for change until social systems are radically restructured. Only then will athletes stop engaging in destructive and dehumanizing actions when they play sports. This is why those who use this theory have talked often about the need to change society as a whole in order to control deviance in sports. This may be an admirable long-term goal, but deviance is grounded in things other than profit-driven exploitation processes. Therefore, there are good reasons to explore other factors related to deviance and other means of controlling the actions that jeopardize the health and well-being of people who play sports.

Using Interactionist and Critical Theories: Deviance Is Based in Social Processes and Power Relations

Those who use functionalist theory define *deviance* as a failure to conform, and they see rule violators as disruptive and morally bankrupt. Those who use conflict theory define *deviance* as behavior that violates the interests of people with economic power, and they see rule violators as exploited victims.

The main flaws in these approaches are that they ignore deviance that involves overconformity to rules and expectations and they do not take into account the norms in sports cultures and the ways in which athletes use those norms to evaluate themselves and others. It is clear that most people who violate rules in sports can't be classified either as morally bankrupt or exploited. For example, it is not accurate to say that young people lack moral character when they go overboard in accepting and overconforming to ideas about what it means to be an athlete. Nor is it accurate to define all athletes who engage in deviance as passive victims of an exploitive, profit-driven sport system. Of course, athletes don't control all the conditions of their sport participation, but they do play an important part in the creation and maintenance of the norms that guide their own decisions and actions in sports. According to critical theories, people make choices and changes in their lives and in the cultures of which they are a part.

In light of these factors, Bob Hughes and I (Hughes and Coakley, 1991) have suggested that our understanding of deviance in sports could be expanded if we assumed two things:

1. Social norms emerge in connection with complex and powerful forms of social relations in sports and in society as a whole.
2. Actions, ideas, and characteristics usually fall into a normally accepted range, and those that do not fall into this range involve either overconformity or underconformity.

The best way to illustrate these two points is by using a graph that depicts a normal bell-shaped curve (see figure 6.2). The horizontal line below the curve represents a continuum of actions, ideas, and characteristics, which ranges from cases of extreme underconformity on the left to cases of extreme overconformity on the right. Actions, ideas, and characteristics that fall into a normally accepted range are located in the middle of the bell curve to show that they occur with

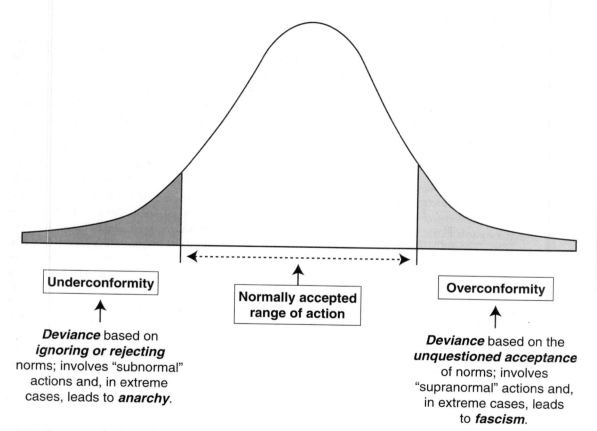

Underconformity

Deviance based on *ignoring or rejecting* norms; involves "subnormal" actions and, in extreme cases, leads to *anarchy*.

Normally accepted range of action

Overconformity

Deviance based on the *unquestioned acceptance* of norms; involves "supranormal" actions and, in extreme cases, leads to *fascism*.

FIGURE 6.2   Two types of deviance in sports. Most actions in sports falls within a normally accepted range in society. Deviance occurs when actions, ideas, and characteristics go beyond the boundaries on both sides of this range. Deviance involving underconformity is grounded in different dynamics than deviance involving overconformity. Most people discuss deviance in sports in terms of athletes or coaches who ignore or reject norms; they do not identify deviance in terms of athletes and coaches who overconform to norms. In fact, deviance grounded in overconformity is often identified as an indication of commitment and dedication, even though it may be dangerous and have serious consequences for the health and well-being of self and others.

the most frequency. The height of the curve represents the frequency of actions, ideas, and characteristics along the continuum. The shaded areas at each end of the continuum represent deviance—that is, actions, ideas, and characteristics that fall outside the boundaries of what is normally acceptable. In other words, **deviance** *consists of actions, ideas, and characteristics that fall outside a normally accepted range, because they involve extreme cases of overconformity or extreme cases of underconformity.*

Deviant underconformity consists of actions that involve a rejection or lack of awareness of norms, whereas **deviant overconformity** consist of actions that involve an uncritical acceptance of rules. Both types of deviance can be dangerous.[1] For example, widespread underconformity pushed to an extreme would create conditions of anarchy or lawlessness in a group or society, whereas widespread overconformity pushed to an extreme would create conditions of fascism or blind faith in an ideal embodied in a rigid belief system or a charismatic leader. Both anarchy and fascism are dangerous.

Research shows that deviant overconformity occurs in sports. For example, when Keith Ewald and Robert Jiobu (1985) studied men seriously involved in bodybuilding or competitive distance running, they concluded that some of the men displayed classic characteristics of deviance in the form of addiction-like overconformity to the norms in their sport. Many of the bodybuilders and distance runners followed training norms to such an extent that their family relationships, work responsibilities, and/or physical health were affected negatively, yet they never questioned what they were doing or why they were doing it.

This is not unique. Many elite athletes prepare so intensely for their sports that the needs of family members are ignored. As former NFL player Matt Millen says, "You have to be selfish, getting ready for a game that only a handful of people understand. It's tough on the people around you. . . . It's the most unspoken but powerful part of the game, that deep-seated desire to be better at all costs, even if it means alienating your family or friends." Millen also says that, whenever athletes enter high-level sports, they want to make the cut and stay involved, and "they will doing anything to accomplish that goal, even if it means sacrificing their own physical or mental well being" (Freeman, 1998, p. 1). Bette McKenzie (1999), a daughter of an NHL player and a former wife of an NFL player, agrees. She notes that her ex-husband's deviant overconformity to the norms of professional football interfered with family relationships so much that it was a key factor in their divorce.

Research has identified other forms of deviant overconformity, such as self-injurious overtraining among distance runners (Nash, 1987); unhealthy eating behaviors and weight-control strategies among women athletes in intercollegiate and other elite amateur sports, and among men in wrestling;[2] extremely rigid and exclusive dedication to training and competition among ultra marathon bicyclists (Wasielewski, 1991) and triathletes (Hilliard and Hilliard, 1990); and uncritical commitment to playing sports with pain and injury.[3]

When we use this critical approach to define and study deviance in sports, we see how important it is to distinguish between actions that show indifference toward or a rejection of norms in

---

[1]Some social scientists have used the terms *negative deviance* and *positive deviance* to refer to deviant underconformity and deviant overconformity, respectively. The term *positive deviance* does *not* imply that such deviance is good or beneficial to self or others. In fact, positive deviance involves extreme actions, ideas, and characteristics that can be very dangerous.

[2]See Beals, 2000; Davis, 1999; Donnelly, 1993; Franseen and McCann, 1996; Hawes, 2001; Johns, 1992, 1996, 1997; Johns and Johns, 2000; Sundgot-Borgen, 2001; Thompson and Sherman, 1999; also see Wilmore, 1996, for a review of thirty-five studies.

[3]See Curry, 1993; Curry and Strauss, 1994; Grant, 2002a, b; Lyon, 2002; Nixon, 1993a, b, 1994a, b, 1996a, b; White and Young, 1997; Young and White, 1995; Young et al., 1994.

sports, on the one hand, and actions that show an uncritical acceptance and overconformity to norms on the other hand. This approach also forces us to examine the value systems and social processes that exist in sports cultures. For example, the value system in high-performance sports often encourages overconformity to a set of norms or guidelines that athletes use to evaluate themselves and others as they train and compete (Donnelly, 1996b; Ingham et al., 1999; Johns, 1997). Because of this, much of the deviance among athletes (and coaches) involves *unquestioned acceptance of* and *conformity to* the value system embodied in the sport ethic.

The Sport Ethic and Deviance in Sports The **sport ethic** *is a set of norms that many people in power and performance sports have accepted as the dominant criteria for defining what it means to be an athlete and to successfully claim an identity as an athlete.* The sport ethics constitutes the normative core of high-performance sport culture. As Bob Hughes and I have collected information from and about athletes and coaches, we have concluded that the following four norms make up the core of the sport ethic:

1. *An athlete makes sacrifices for "the game."* This norm stresses that athletes must love "the game" above all else and prove it by giving the game priority over other interests. To establish identities as athletes, individuals must have the proper attitude, demonstrate unwavering commitment to their sports, live up to the expectations of fellow athletes, and make the sacrifices necessary to stay in the game. In other words, being an athlete involves meeting the expectations of fellow athletes, meeting the demands of competition without question, making sacrifices without question, and being willing to pay the price to play their sport. Coaches' pep talks and locker room slogans are full of references to this norm.

A college football player who had ten knee operations in six years and continued to play the game he loved between each operation explained this norm with these words: "I've told a hundred people that if I got a chance to play in the NFL, I'd play for free. It's never been about money. It's never been about anything but playing the game" (in Wieberg, 1994, p. 8C). Respected NBA coach Phil Jackson emphasized this norm when he said, "Whether they're willing to acknowledge it or not, what drives most players is not the money or the adulation, but their love of the game" (in Sandomir, 1996, p. 7). There are numerous examples of athletes who make sacrifices to continue playing the game because they love it; even retired athletes talk about giving back to the game because they care so much about it.

2. *An athlete strives for distinction.* The Olympic motto "Citius, Altius, Fortius" (swifter, higher, stronger) captures the meaning of this norm. Being an athlete means constantly seeking to improve and to achieve perfection. Winning symbolizes improvement and establishes distinction; losing is tolerated because it's part of learning how to win. Breaking records is the ultimate standard of achievement, because athletes are a special group dedicated to climbing the pyramid, reaching for the top, pushing limits, excelling, exceeding others, and being the best they can be.

   This norm was highlighted by a former U.S. gymnast who explained, "The harder you train, the more pounding the body takes. . . . We're clearly pushing the envelope. All it takes is one or two gutsy guys to exceed the difficulty level, then everyone tries it" (in Becker, 1999, p. 4E).

3. *An athlete accepts risks and plays through pain.* According to this norm, an athlete does not give in to pressure, pain, or fear. The voluntary acceptance of risks is a sign of

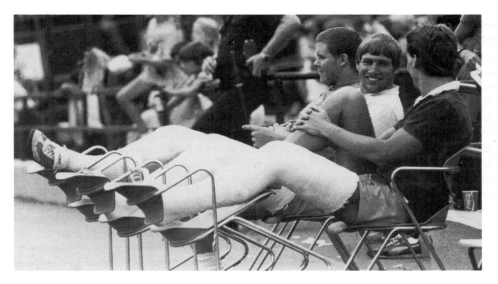

Athletes may overconform to the norms of the sports ethic to demonstrate their moral and physical courage. This often leads to high rates of injury in certain sports. Of course, these athletes do not see their overconforming actions as deviant, even if they result in torn ligaments and broken bones. Coaches and teammates praise their unquestioned acceptance of the norms of the sport ethic. (Bobette Brecker, University of Colorado Media Relations)

courage and dedication among athletes; playing under pressure is expected. The idea is that athletes don't back down from any challenge; standing up to challenges involves moral and physical courage. Being an athlete means that a person willingly confronts and overcomes the fear and the challenge of competition and accepts the increasing risk of failure and injury as he or she moves up the competitive pyramid.

The language used in sports is full of references to this norm. When asked about playing with serious injuries and pain, NFL running back Ricky Williams explained that "every Sunday, an NFL player plays through pain that would make the average human cry and stay home from work for a few days. . . . The measure of a football player isn't how well he performs on Sunday but how well he performs in pain" (in Williams, 1999, p. 80). Similarly, U.S. gymnast Blaine

Wilson said, "You're not a gymnast if you're not sore" (in Becker, 1999, p. 4E). When NBA player Allen Iverson was asked about playing with disabling shoulder pain he said, "This is what I do. It kills me to sit and watch a game. It kills me. . . . My teammates need me . . . they just need me. . . . And I need to be with my teammates" (in *Denver Post*, 2 March, 2000, p. 4D). Brian Burke, director of operations in the NHL, noted, "The code among our athletes is, if you have a pulse you play. There is no logical explanation for their pain threshold" (in *Denver Post*, 1999, p. 7D). He also explained that coaches in hockey and other sports look for players willing to take risks and play through pain; they like injured players in the lineup because these players show teammates that overconformity to the norms of the sports ethic is a taken-for-granted part of being an athlete.

4. *An athlete accepts no limits in the pursuit of possibilities.* This norm stresses "the dream" and the obligation to pursue it without question. An athlete doesn't accept a situation without trying to change it, overcome it, and beat the odds. Those who successfully claim an identity as an athlete believe that sports make up a sphere of life in which anything is possible—*if* a person is dedicated enough. They feel obligated to pursue dreams without reservation; they ignore external limits as they attempt to achieve success. Of course, external rewards may influence athletes, but their pursuit of possibilities is driven primarily by what they believe they must do as athletes, apart from money.

This norm was clearly illustrated by Buddy Lazier, who won the Indianapolis 500 while driving with a broken back. Despite his injury, he trained four hours a day, seven days a week. After the race, his father said, "He absolutely never said quit. He was not going to be robbed of this opportunity" (in Ballard, 1996, p. A1). Lazier accepted no limits in pursuing his dream; surgery on the crushed disks pressing on his nerves waited until after the race.

These four norms of the sport ethic are deeply rooted in the culture of today's power and performance sports. At first glance, they call to mind slogans hanging on locker room walls and written in self-help and motivation books. By themselves, these norms call for actions and orientations valued by people in society as a whole: making commitments and sacrifices, striving for improvement, pushing yourself even when things are difficult or painful, and pursuing dreams. However, deviance occurs when the norms of the sport ethic are accepted uncritically, without question and qualification, and then followed without limits, without setting or acknowledging boundaries.

Alberto Salazar, a great marathoner, discussed the dangerous consequences of deviant overconformity when he coached middle-distance runner

Mary Decker Slaney during the mid-1990s. Slaney had undergone nineteen sport-related surgeries and was living in constant pain at the time. Salazar explained that

> [t]he greatest athletes want it so much, they run themselves to death. You've got to have an obsession, but if unchecked, it's destructive. That's what it is with [Slaney]. She'll kill herself unless you pull the reins back. (in Longman, 1996, p. B11)

Salazar's warning shows that dangerous forms of deviance occur when athletes do not critically question the sport ethic and set boundaries that limit their conformity to its norms. Controlling these forms of deviance may be the biggest challenge facing sports today.

This is not to say that deviant underconformity is not a problem; however, when athletes reject norms or refuse to take them seriously, they are likely to be cut by coaches or others who control sports. When players are unwilling to make sacrifices for the game and refuse to strive for distinction, play through pain, and fight through limits as they pursue dreams, they do not last long in high-performance sports. Their underconformity is not tolerated, and their careers are terminated.

Reactions to deviant overconformity are different. When players go to extremes in conforming to the norms of the sport ethic, when they follow the norms to the point of risking their own safety and well-being, they are praised and hailed as heroes. Media commentators glorify athletes who overconform to the sport ethic; they praise athletes who play with broken bones and torn ligaments, have surgery after surgery to play the game, and request or submit to injections of huge doses of painkilling drugs to play through pain. Spectators also glorify athletes who are willing to overconform to the sport ethic. According to Dr. Robert Huizinga, a former NFL team physician and past president of the NFL Physicians Society, many sport fans today "want people to play hurt, and when someone doesn't play hurt, he's no longer our hero" (in King, 1996, p. 27). Therefore, it is not surprising that many athletes go overboard in their acceptance of the sport ethic and overconform to its norms without question or qualification, even when overconformity creates problems, causes pain, disrupts family life, jeopardizes health and safety, or even shortens life itself. This type of deviance is dangerous; even so, it is widely ignored (Berger, 2002; Grant, 2002a, b).

Why Do Athletes Engage in Deviant Overconformity? Not all athletes overconform to the norms of the sport ethic, but many do. The following are the three main reasons for overconformity:

1. Athletes find their experiences in sports so exhilarating that they want to continue participating as long as possible; they love their sports and will do almost anything to stay involved.
2. The likelihood of being chosen or sponsored for continued participation in sports increases when athletes overconform to the sport ethic. Coaches often praise athletes who conform without question and make them models on their teams.
3. Exceeding normative boundaries infuses drama and excitement into people's lives; it increases the stakes associated with their sports and bonds them strongly to fellow athletes willing to do the same thing.

For these reasons, many athletes use deviant overconformity to define and evaluate their sport experiences. Nike even has used it in TV commercials (see the box "Just (Over)do It") by highlighting athletes who throw up, shed blood, collapse from exhaustion, and break bones as part of regular training and competition. "Just doing it" is fine, even commendable, but "just overdoing it" until you vomit, bleed, lose consciousness, or need surgery is deviant. However, most athletes don't see overconformity to the sport ethic as deviance. Instead, they see it as reaffirming their identities as athletes and their membership in select sport groups. This can be very important to them, especially when their continued participation and success in sports take on deep personal and social meanings.

Of course, not all athletes are equally likely to overconform to the sport ethic. Bob Hughes and I hypothesize that those most likely to do so include

1. Athletes who have low self-esteem or are so eager to be accepted as athletes by their peers in sports that they will make whatever sacrifices and go to whatever extremes they think others would like to see
2. Athletes who see achievement in sports as their only way to get ahead, make themselves a name, and become important in the world

> **I feel like I've been coached that way my whole life—to play dirty and to play mean.**
>
> —Jeremy Shockey, NFL player, 2003 (in Lieber, 2003, p. 1C)

In other words, the athletes whose identities or future chances for success and significance are exclusively dependent on their sport participation are most likely to engage in deviant overconformity. In fact, they may use overconformity to the sport ethic to demonstrate their worthiness for continued membership and status within their sport groups. An athlete's vulnerability to group demands, combined with the desire to gain or reaffirm group membership, is a critical factor underlying deviant overconformity.

This may be why certain coaches create environments that keep athletes in a perpetual state of adolescence. This leads athletes to strive continually to confirm their identities and eliminate self-doubts by engaging in behaviors that please their coaches and teammate-peers. When this dependency-based commitment occurs, overconformity to the sport ethic becomes increasingly common, and many young people become willing to sacrifice their bodies and play with reckless abandon in the pursuit of affirmation and approval. When coaches encourage this, intentionally or naïvely, they promote dangerous forms of deviance. If coaches were concerned

Just (Over)do It
The Sport Ethic in Nike Ads

Nike and other corporations have adopted advertising strategies in which they depict and glorify deviant overconformity to the norms of the sport ethic. They assume that this form of deviance attracts attention and sells products.

In 1996, during coverage of the Olympic Games in Atlanta, a Nike ad in *Sports Illustrated* asked boldly, "Who the Hell Do You Think You Are? Are You an Athlete?" The text in the ad answered this question with words that echo the norms of the sport ethic:

> Because if you are [an athlete], then you know what it means to want to be better, to want to be the best. And if you are [an athlete], then you understand it's not enough to just want to be the best. You can't just sit around and BS about how much you want it. Show me how much you want it. . . . Dare to do what it takes to be the best. And then, whether you win, lose, or collapse on the finish line, at worst you'll know exactly who you are.
>
> If You Can't Stand the Heat, Get Out of Atlanta!

In 1999, Nike ran ads showing the disfigured bodies of athletes who had pushed limits in their sports.

The background tune, Joe Cocker's "You Are So Beautiful," was chosen to glorify these bodies, which were seriously injured and left permanently scarred or broken. Of course, the ad showed only the bodies of athletes who had recovered enough to play again. Erased from the images were athletes whose injuries had ended their careers and possibly left them so disabled that they cannot walk without pain or play actively with their friends and children.

More recent ads have shown young people, usually young men, in extreme sports engaging in actions that clearly fall outside the boundaries of generally accepted norms. The images and narratives in these ads show that the advertising people at Nike and other corporations understand the sport ethic and the tendency among athletes to overconform to its norms. I can't prove it, but I think that these ads and others like them glorify and encourage dangerous forms of deviance. *What do you think?*

with controlling deviance in sports, they would help athletes set boundaries and limits when it comes to conformity to the norms of the sport ethic; they would also encourage athletes to ask themselves why they do what they do and how their lives as athletes are connected with the rest of their lives.

Deviant Overconformity and Group Dynamics

Being an athlete is a social as well as a physical experience. At elite levels of competition, special bonds form between athletes as they follow the norms of the sport ethic—as they express their commitment to the game and make sacrifices, strive for success, play in pain, and pursue dreams together. These special bonds serve as a context in which overconformity to the norms of the sport ethic is encouraged and comes to be

seen as part of what a person does to reaffirm his or her identity as an athlete, as well as to be accepted by other athletes as "one of them."

In other words, the actions, ideas, and characteristics that demonstrate unqualified commitment to the sport ethic become "normalized" in sports, although they remain clearly deviant in society as a whole. This is the same social dynamic that serves as a foundation for motivation among athletes in high-risk sports (Hunt, 1995). As athletes in high-performance and high-risk sports collectively overconform to the norms of the sport ethic, the bonds between them become extraordinarily powerful, so powerful that they often separate the athletes from the rest of the community. After all, "normal" people in the community cannot understand what it's really like to be an elite athlete. They may view elite athletes with admiration, but they don't really know what it takes to pay the price day after day, to face risk and pain, to subordinate one's body and being to the needs of the team, and to practice and sacrifice to improve skills and stay among a select few who can perform as no others in the world can when it comes to their sports. Only other athletes can understand this.

This separation between athletes and the rest of the community makes the group dynamics associated with participation in high-performance sports very powerful. However, they are not unique. Other select groups, usually groups of men, experience similar dynamics. Examples can be found in the military, especially among Special Forces units. Former soldiers frequently talk about these dynamics and the powerful social bonds formed while they faced danger and death as members of groups that trained together as fighting teams. Examples also exist among test pilots and astronauts, as vividly described by journalist Tom Wolfe (1979) in his book *The Right Stuff*. He explains that pushing the envelope in a jet and trusting your life to fellow pilots as you do so is certain to create special bonds, along with feelings that you and the entire group are special. Similar bonds even exist in certain fraternities and sororities, where "pledges" voluntarily submit to systematic hazing processes designed to emphasize that all must pay the price to become members of such special groups of people. In fact, hazing rituals have long been a part of the identity formation and member selection processes that occur in many groups that are defined as special. Sport teams often have preseason hazing rituals, during which rookies are expected to follow the commands of team veterans, no matter how demeaning, sickening, painful, or illegal the "mandated" actions (Alfred University, 1999; Bryshun and Young, 1999; Hawes, 1999a; Wieberg, 2000a, b).

As high-performance athletes endure the challenges of maintaining their membership in select groups and teams at the highest level of accomplishment in their sports, they develop not only extremely strong feelings of unity with other athletes but also the sense that they are unique and extraordinary people. After all, they are told this day after day by everyone from coaches to team boosters to autograph seekers. They read it in newspapers and magazines, and they see it on TV and the Internet.

When the sense of being unique and extraordinary becomes extreme, as it does among many high-profile athletes in certain settings, it may be expressed in terms of pride-driven arrogance, an inflated sense of power and importance, and a public persona that communicates superiority and even insolence. The Greeks used the word **hubris** to describe this expression of uniqueness and the accompanying sense of being separate from and above the rest of the community. My colleague Bob Hughes and I think that many elite athletes today exhibit hubris. In fact, for some athletes it has become a key dimension of their public personas—they even market it and use it to attract attention and make people remember them.

The point in this section is that the social processes that exist in many sports, especially elite power and performance sports, do three things:

1. They bond athletes together in ways that encourage and even normalize deviant overconformity in many sports.
2. They separate athletes from the rest of the community while they inspire awe and admiration from people in the community.
3. They lead athletes to develop hubris, which is expressed in ways that simultaneously bond athletes together and further separate them as a group from the rest of the community.

As we understand the impact of these social processes on athletes, we see that much of the deviance in sports is not motivated primarily by the desire to win or to make money. Instead, it is motivated by desires to play the game, to be an athlete, and to maintain membership in an elite

FIGURE 6.3   This cartoon illustrates that winning is not irrelevant to athletes. However, many athletes who will never make it to the victory podium engage in deviant overconformity. Their goal is not to win as much as it is to be defined and accepted as athletes.

athletic in-group. This is not to say that winning and money are irrelevant to athletes; they *are* important and powerful motivators. But we must remember that many athletes who know they will not win championships or make money from their athletic accomplishments frequently engage in deviant overconformity (see figure 6.3). These athletes, just like their more talented and money-making peers, are motivated by the belief that being a "real athlete" means taking risks, making sacrifices, and paying the price to develop skills and stay in the game.

This means that the roots of deviance go deeper than individual desires to win or make money. In fact, these roots are grounded in the very values promoted through the sport ethic itself. Therefore, much of the deviance in sports is most accurately identified as a social issue rather than just a personal problem of individual athletes. For this reason, it is especially difficult to control. Fines and jail sentences do little to slow it down. Throwing out the so-called bad apples may help in the short run, but the social processes that operate in the social world of many sports

guarantee that next season there will be another bunch of bad apples in the same orchard.

Deviant Overconformity and Deviant Underconformity: Is There a Connection?   This analysis of deviant overconformity raises questions about other forms of deviance that exist in sports and among athletes—for example,

- If the social bonds created in sports are powerful enough to normalize the forms of deviant overconformity that jeopardize health and well-being, are they also powerful enough to foster other forms of deviance?
- If the extreme behaviors, ideas, and characteristics of athletes separate them from the rest of the community, do athletes come to disdain nonathletes to the point that they might be likely to harass or assault them?
- If athletes develop extreme degrees of hubris, might they feel that they live in a special zone, where normal community standards and rules do not apply to them or their fellow athletes?
- If people in the community view athletes with awe and admiration because of their extreme actions, ideas, and characteristics, might this view interfere with the enforcement of community standards and rules when athletes, especially high-profile athletes, violate them?

Research is needed on each of the issues raised in these questions. My sense is that long-term overconformity to the sport ethic creates social conditions and group dynamics in sports that encourage notable forms of deviant underconformity, such as binge drinking, academic cheating, group theft and property destruction, drunken and careless driving, sexual harassment, physical assault, spouse abuse, and sexual assault.

The possible connection between these two types of deviance came to mind when an NFL football player said, "Hey, I have no problem sharing women with my teammates. These guys go to battle with me" (in Nelson, 1994, p. 144).

This player's comment may be shocking, but it is consistent with other cases. For example, in a number of cases, male high school or college athletes did not break group silence after witnessing teammates gang rape a woman (Curry, 1991, 1996, 1998; Lefkowitz, 1997). Groups of athletes have mercilessly taunted and harassed other students, whom they defined as "unworthy" of respect because of how they looked or dressed (ESPN, 1999). Hazing rituals have subjected prospective teammates to demeaning and even criminal treatment—coercing rookies to steal, drink to the point of passing out, harass others, urinate on each other, drink urine, hold each other's genitals, appear nude in public, and endure various forms of sodomy, beatings, and brandings (Hawes, 1999).

The awe and admiration accorded to athletes who entertain others as they push limits and engage in deviant overconformity on the field have clearly interfered with the enforcement of community standards and rules off the field. Kathy Redmond, founder of the National Coalition Against Violent Athletes, has noted that people in society do not "want to admit that this athlete whom we live vicariously through . . . is capable of deviant behavior" (*USA Today*, 1998, p. C3). For example, boosters and fans who normally preach a "get-tough-on-crime" philosophy have threatened women who have filed well-documented assault and rape charges against high-profile athletes (Benedict, 1997; Lipsyte, 1998). Police officers have asked athletes who are being arrested to sign autographs for their children, and judges have made favorable decisions involving athletes who play on teams representing their alma mater or teams for which the judges have season tickets.

Controlling Deviant Overconformity in Sports

Deviant overconformity presents special social control problems in sports. Coaches, managers, owners, and sponsors—people who exercise control of sports—often benefit when athletes blindly accept and overconform to the sport ethic. These people often see athletes who willingly engage in deviant overconformity as a blessing, not a curse. The fact that athletes often use their overconformity to the sport ethic as proof of their personal commitment and courage works to the advantage of all who benefit from winning records and high TV ratings. This is why those who control sports are unwilling to discourage this type of deviance—even when it involves using performance-enhancing substances.

The issue of social control is further complicated by the tendency to promote overconformers to the sport ethic into positions of power and influence in sports. Because these people have proved they are willing to pay the price and use the sport ethic without reservation, they are seen as ideal candidates for certain jobs in sports, especially coaching jobs. This creates a situation in which deviance and ethical problems among athletes are rooted in the organization of sports, in athletes' relationships with one another and with coaches and managers.

Controlling deviant overconformity is not easy. It requires a willingness and commitment among parents, coaches, and sport administrators to teach athletes about the importance of setting and respecting limits as they play sports. This, of course, goes against the existing norms of the sport ethic. Controlling deviant underconformity is less difficult. Rejecting rules and regulations is quickly identified by authority figures, and everyone understands that it is likely to be punished when it occurs. Deviant overconformity, however, is more subversive, because it is widely ignored. For example, when a fourteen-year-old gymnast is late for practice, a coach immediately identifies this type of deviance and acts on the spot to eliminate it. However, when the same gymnast engages in unhealthy eating behaviors to lose weight as she strives for distinction and pursues her dream, many coaches, parents, and gym owners don't see this deviance, or they don't want to interfere with the mindset of a champion and the culture of the gym—until, of course, stress fractures interfere with competition and weight loss puts their athlete and daughter in a hospital.

The control of deviant overconformity demands that athletes, coaches, commentators, and fans raise critical questions about the meaning, organization, and purpose of sports, as well as about the sport ethic itself. In the absence of these questions, athletes will continue to think and act in ways that threaten the health and well-being of themselves and others. Furthermore, the common motivational strategy of convincing athletes that their teams are families and that teammates must put their bodies on the line for each other because they go to battle together clearly promotes the hubris and the athlete-community separation that perpetuate deviant overconformity.

This type of social separation leads some athletes to conclude that "outsiders are out to get us" and that "we have to stick together because nobody else understands us." Their hubris is reaffirmed and strengthened in the process, and they further disconnect from the community whose standards apply to their lives. Of course, if these dynamics were changed and deviant overconformity declined, there might not be as many gladiator-type athletes to entertain us as we sit safely in front of our TVs and watch people put their bodies on the line for our viewing pleasure.

All social life contains tensions between overconformity and underconformity. In the case of sports, these tensions are especially evident because of the processes that encourage overconformity to norms. This means that special efforts are needed to strike a balance between accepting rules and questioning rules. The more everyone in sports is involved in questioning and qualifying norms and rules, the more effective they will be in controlling deviant overconformity, although the control will never be perfect or permanent. My sense is that controlling deviant overconformity is also an important step in controlling deviant underconformity. The ultimate goals are to diminish the separation between athletes and the rest of the community, to alter social processes so that athletes will be less likely to feel above the law, and to make the community aware of the need to deal with athletes without letting awe and admiration interfere. Athletes must be held accountable for their deviance, regardless of their popularity and celebrity status in the community and the rest of society.

RESEARCH ON DEVIANCE AMONG ATHLETES

Headlines and media coverage of deviance among athletes are common, but systematic studies of deviance among athletes are rare. Publishing lists of arrest records and charges filed against athletes attracts attention, but it doesn't tell us much about whether deviance is out of control in sports, whether there is more deviance today than there was in the past, whether deviance involves overconformity or underconformity, or whether it is rooted in the characters of athletes, the culture and organization of sports, or factors that exist outside of sports. Most media reports conclude that deviance is caused by character weaknesses and a lack of discipline among athletes or that it is the result of money and an overemphasis on winning. Few reports discuss the possibility that deviance is related to the culture and organization of sports or to social dynamics that exist in the social worlds created around sports.

When we review accounts of deviance among athletes, it is important to distinguish deviance that occurs on the field and in sport settings from deviance that occurs off the field and away from sports. They are related to different types of norms and rules, and they have different causes and consequences.

Deviance on the Field and in Sport Settings

Deviance on the field and in sport settings includes cheating (such as using the spitball or corking a bat in baseball), gambling, shaving points, throwing games or matches, engaging in unsportsman-like conduct, fighting, taking performance-enhancing drugs, and generally finding ways to avoid rules. Some people claim that these types of deviance have become serious today because the personal and financial stakes have become so great in sports.

Most long-term historical analyses, however, suggest that cheating, dirty play, fighting, and the use of violence are less common today than they were in the days before television coverage and high-stakes commercialization (Dunning, 1999; Maguire, 1988; Scheinin, 1994). These analyses make the case that sports today are more rule-governed than they were in the past and that instances of on-the-field deviance are more likely to be punished with formal sanctions within sports and criticized by observers outside of sports. Therefore, it may be a mistake to blame deviance in sports today on money and TV, as some people are inclined to do.

Short-term data collected by the NCAA (1999) supports this conclusion: compared with responses given in 1996, fewer Division I athletes said in 1999 that teammates would expect them to cheat to win games, fewer said they would retaliate in response to flagrant fouls on the field, and fewer said that sportsmanship had become less important to them since entering college.

Actually, it is very difficult to track and study rates of on-the-field deviance among athletes, because rules change over time and rules are enforced in different ways at different points in time. Research does suggest that athletes in most sports interpret rules very loosely during games and that they often create informal norms, which stretch official rules (Shields and Bredemeier, 1995). However, this is not new. Athletes have done this ever since umpires and referees have been enforcing rules. In fact, athletes in organized sports traditionally have played to the level permitted by umpires and referees—they adjust their actions according to how tightly the referees are calling a game. But this does not mean that the players ignore rules or that deviance is out of hand. Nor does it mean that we ought to ignore deviance when it occurs.

The perception that rates of on-the-field and sport-related deviance are increasing also may exist because there are more rules today than ever before, and sports are more rule-governed than they were in the past. A look at the rulebooks of sport organizations clearly shows that there are literally thousands of rules today that did not exist twenty years ago in sports. For example, the National Collegiate Athletic Association (NCAA) and other sport governing organizations have hundreds of rules and regulations in official handbooks, and every year more rules are added. International sport organizations now list thousands of banned substances. There are more ways than ever before of becoming deviant in sports! Furthermore, the forms of surveillance used today and the increased emphasis on rule enforcement means that more rule violators are caught today.

Finally, there is evidence that athletes in certain sports simply come to expect and engage in certain on-the-field rule violations, such as, "good fouls", and "cheating when you can get away with it" (Anonymous, 1999; Pilz, 1996; Shields et al., 1995). This approach seems to be more prevalent at higher levels of competition and to increase with time spent participating in a sport. It is also more common among men than women, and it is especially strong among members of winning teams and nonstarters. This finding is consistent with other research suggesting that playing most forms of power and performance sports does not promote moral development and moral decision making (Stoll and Beller, 1998; 2000).

However, in the absence of good historical data, my sense is that most on-the-field and sport-related rule violations are not more common today than they were in the past and they are not out of control. Deviance does exist; *it is a problem.* It ought to be studied, and efforts should be made to control it without violating the principles of due process and justice. The form of sport-related deviance that may be more prevalent today is the use of banned performance-enhancing substances. This is clearly a serious

Even though many people think that deviance is out of control in certain sports today, there is no evidence that rates of deviance are higher today than in the past. What is different today is the media coverage and video technology, which enable us to see deviance in slow motion, stop action, and replay after replay after replay. (Peter Cosgrove; AP/Wide World Photos)

problem, and it will be discussed later in the section on "Performance-Enhancing Substances: Deviant Overconformity in Sports".

Deviance off the Field and Away from Sports

Off-the-field deviance receives widespread media attention. When athletes are arrested or linked to criminal activity, they make headlines and become lead stories on the evening news. Media reports of bar fights and assault charges appear regularly (Starr and Samuels, 2000).

Research on these forms of deviance has not provided clear conclusions about whether rates have gone up or down, or whether they are higher than rates among comparable segments of people in the general population. However, it is clear that felonies are a problem whenever they occur. They do harm that cannot be lessened by data showing that rates are lower today than yesterday or that rates among athletes are lower than rates for comparable people from similar backgrounds. A DUI is a potentially fatal act, and a sexual assault does extreme harm to a woman, regardless of who does them and how "the case" fits with rates for various groups or over time. Those who commit these crimes, athletes or not, must be held accountable—even if it means losing the big game next week.

At present, there are data from studies of delinquency and sport participation among high school students, from a few studies of academic cheating and excessive alcohol use among high school and college athletes, and from a very few studies of felony rates.

Delinquency Rates Current research on delinquency and sport participation is scarce, but past studies generally contradict attention-grabbing headlines about athletes. For example, when rates of off-the-field delinquent and deviant actions among varsity athletes have been compared with rates among other students, the rates for athletes almost always have been found to be lower than those for other students from similar backgrounds. With a couple of exceptions, this general finding seems to hold for athletes in various sports, athletes in different societies, and both boys and girls from various racial and social class backgrounds (see Miracle and Rees, 1994, for a summary of these studies).

Of course, these findings may reflect the fact that students with histories of deviant actions do not usually try out for sport teams, that coaches cut them when they do try out, or that athletes receive preferential treatment, which keeps them out of court and jail when they are deviant. It is also possible that forms of deviance among some athletes are obscured by a façade of conformity (Miracle and Rees, 1994).

Until we know more about off-the-field actions, it is difficult to argue that athletes have higher rates of delinquency than comparable nonathletes. Of course, as noted in chapter 4,

sport experiences vary from program to program, and sport participation constitutes only a part of a person's experiences. Therefore, it is misleading to make generalizations about how sport participation affects all actions. At present, it seems safe to say that sport participation turns young people neither into models of virtue nor into delinquents in any systematic way.

Academic Cheating Despite highly publicized cases of high-profile varsity athletes in big-time revenue-producing intercollegiate programs having their coursework written by "academic support" staff, the charge that college athletes engage in academic cheating more than other students has never been examined thoroughly. In fact, data are hard to come by.

If we compared athletes with members of other closely knit groups of college students, I think we would find rates of cheating to be comparable. A varsity athlete might be more likely to hand in a paper written by an "academic tutor" hired by the athletic department, whereas a student in a fraternity or a dorm might use an Internet site to buy or "borrow" a paper written by a professional writer. Of course, both cases involve cheating, but, when a regular student is caught buying papers on the Internet, the case will not make national news, nor will the student be rebuked publicly by people all over the country, nor will the reputation of the university be questioned in the national media, nor will faculty be fired because they didn't police their students more carefully.

Might varsity athletes cheat more often because the stakes associated with making particular grades are so much higher for them than for other students? This is possible, but we need studies comparing athletes with similar other students who would lose scholarships or job opportunities if they did not maintain minimum grade point averages. Might some varsity athletes cheat less because they are watched more closely and have more to lose if they are caught? This, too, is possible.

Differences between the academic actions of varsity athletes and those of other groups of students have not been documented enough for us to make definitive conclusions. Such documentation should include careful assessments of the academic experiences of a range of students from various backgrounds.

Alcohol Use and Binge Drinking   As most of us know from our own experience, underage and excessive alcohol consumption in high school and college is not limited to athletes. Data collected during the early and mid-1990s indicate that male and female intercollegiate athletes engage in more alcohol use, abuse, and binge drinking than other men and women students (Naughton, 1996; Wechsler et al., 1997). Recent data collected from junior and senior high school students in the United States suggest that rates of alcohol use may be lower among twelve- to seventeen-year-olds who play on sport teams than among those who do not (SAMHSA, 2002). This may mean that norms related to alcohol use are different among younger athletes or that young people under eighteen years old who play sports are monitored and controlled by their parents and other adults more closely than are other young people or college athletes.

These research findings are important because alcohol use and abuse may be related to other forms of deviance. More studies are needed to see if the group dynamics of alcohol use and binge drinking at the college level are related to the dynamics underlying overconformity to other group norms among athletes. Slamming drinks and getting drunk with fellow athletes may not be very different, sociologically speaking, from playing with pain to meet the expectations of teammates: "Have another shot of tequila—it's what we teammates who take risks together are doing tonight; are you a part of this special group or not?" Again, research is needed to see if, why, when, and how often this occurs.

Felony Rates   Widely publicized cases of assault, hard drug use, and drug trafficking in which male athletes are the offenders have created a growing

sense of urgency about the need for systematic studies of these forms of deviance. Commentaries, theoretical analyses, and empirical studies have begun to focus on whether participation in certain sports goes hand in hand with high felony rates. However, systematic empirical research is scarce, and the studies that do exist report mixed findings (see Crossett, 1999, for a review and critique of research on sexual assault, in particular).

Another problem with studies of felony rates is that the data on the arrest rates for athletes are seldom compared with arrest rates in the general population and in populations comparable to the athletes in age and race. For example, after a study by Jeff Benedict and Don Yaeger (1998) reported that 21.4 percent of a sample of NFL players had been arrested at least once for something more serious than minor crimes since the year they started college, most people were horrified. However, a follow-up study by crime statistics experts Alfred Blumstein and Jeff Benedict (1999) showed that 23 percent of the males living in cities of 250,000 or more people are arrested for a serious crime at some point in their lives, usually during young adulthood; for whites it is 14 percent and for blacks it is 51 percent. When they focused on the crimes of domestic violence and nondomestic assault and compared NFL players with young adult males from similar racial backgrounds, Blumstein and Benedict discovered that the annual arrest rates for NFL players were less than half the arrest rates for males in the general population, and this pattern was nearly the same when rates for whites were compared with whites and rates for blacks with blacks. However, we do not know if the official data reflect the reality of athlete actions when it comes to assault and sexual assault.

When Blumstein and Benedict compared arrest rates for property crimes, NFL players had distinctively lower rates than the rest of the population, a finding the researchers explained partly in terms of the salaries made by NFL players.

However, their overall conclusion was that, when NFL players are compared with young men in the general population, their off-the-field deviance does not seem to be out of control. Of course, this does not mean that deviance among athletes is not a problem or that professional sport leagues and universities should not take actions to control it.

The incidence of assault and sexual assault among male athletes is an especially important topic and will be discussed in detail in chapter 7.

Off-the-Field Deviance: A Final Comment

The point of this section on off-the-field deviance among athletes is that athletes do not seem to be out of control. This does *not* mean that off-the-field deviance is not a problem; it is a problem, and both athletes and sport organizations must take responsibility for controlling it. Research suggests that the delinquency and crime rates of athletes may not be higher than they are for comparable peers. There are exceptions to this in the case of alcohol abuse and binge drinking and possibly in the case of other forms of deviance, including certain forms of assault. However, research is needed to establish if and why athletes measure higher on various forms of deviance than do other groups and individuals in society as a whole.

Finally, it is important to recognize that, whereas some people claim that off-the-field deviance among athletes is out of control, others claim that sport participation can be used to control deviance among young people. Although this latter claim also needs further testing, it is discussed in the box "Is Sport Participation a Cure for Deviant Behavior?"

Why Focus Only on Deviance Among Athletes?

This chapter focuses almost exclusively on deviance among athletes. This is an important issue. However, athletes are not the only people in sports who violate norms. The following

AT YOUR FINGERTIPS For more information, on Title IX, see pages 238–242.

are a few other examples of deviance related to sports:

- Coaches who hit players, treat them inhumanely, use male players' insecurities about masculinity as a basis for motivating them, sexually harass women in and out of sports, subvert efforts to provide women with equal participation opportunities in sports, and violate NCAA or other organizational rules

- High school and college program administrators who ignore or try to subvert Title IX law in the United States, operate sport programs that do not provide athletes with proper health and accident insurance, or ignore infractions of university or NCAA rules (Zimbalist, 1999); the *NCAA Register* (published with *The NCAA News*), for example, presents a multipage monthly collection of reports of "institutional deviance" on the part of NCAA schools and only a portion of the offenses that occur

- Sport team owners who stretch or violate antitrust laws, collude with each other to depress player salaries, and deliberately mislead city officials and voters in connection with stadium bond and construction issues

- Sport administrators (including those on the International Olympic Committee and related organizations) who take bribes and gifts in return for favors and who violate public trust and organizational principles by making decisions clearly based on their personal interests (see Jennings, 1996a, b; Jennings and Sambrook, 2000); this has been so common that Olympic corporate sponsors now demand that a morals clause be included in their sponsorship contracts (Dodd, 2000)

REFLECT ON SPORTS   Is Sport Participation a Cure for Deviant Behavior?

We often hear that sports keep kids off the streets and out of trouble and build character in the process, and then we hear about athletes who get into trouble and prove that years of playing sports have not kept them from being deviant. How do we make sense out of this conflicting information? Fortunately, research can help.

A study by sociologist Michael Trulson (1986) suggests that *only certain types of sports and sport participation* can lower delinquency rates among young people. Trulson worked with thirty-four young men, ages thirteen to seventeen, who had been classified as delinquents, tested them for aggression and personality adjustment, and divided them into three groups matched on important background characteristics. For six months, each group met three times a week for training sessions with the same instructor. Group 1 received traditional Tae Kwon Do training, taught with

a philosophy emphasizing respect for self and others, the importance of physical fitness, self-control, patience, perseverance, responsibility, and honor. Group 2 received "modern" martial arts training, emphasizing free-sparring and self-defense techniques; the coach provided no philosophy in connection with the physical training. Group 3 received no martial arts training but jogged and played basketball and football under the instructor's coaching and supervision.

Trulson's findings indicated clear changes in Group 1. After six months, the young men in this group had fewer delinquent tendencies, less anxiety and aggression, improved self-esteem and social skills, and more awareness of commonly held values. Those in Group 2 had increased delinquent tendencies and were more aggressive and less adjusted than when the study began. Those in Group 3 showed no change

Off-the-field deviance among athletes may decrease if athletes are taught a philosophy of nonviolence, respect for self and opponents, self-control, confidence in their abilities, and responsibility. This can happen in a variety of sports, even those involving heavy physical contact. (*Colorado Springs Gazette*)

in delinquent tendencies or on most personality measures, but their scores on self-esteem and social skills improved over the six months.

THE MORAL OF THE STORY

Sport participation might keep kids out of trouble when it emphasizes (1) a philosophy of nonviolence, (2) respect for self and others, (3) the importance of fitness and control over self, (4) confidence in physical skills, and (5) a sense of responsibility. When these five things are absent, sport participation will seldom keep young people out of trouble. Simply taking kids off the streets is just the beginning. If they play sports that emphasize exhibiting hostility, dominating others, using their bodies as weapons, and defining masculinity in terms of conquest, we *cannot* expect rates of deviance to decrease.

Changing behavior is a complex process, and to do it in connection with sport participation requires a clear program of intervention in the lives of young people. This doesn't mean that all sports must be turned into treatment programs, but it does mean that playing sports can't be expected to keep kids out of trouble unless participation connects them with other people in supportive and positive ways.

A WORD OF CAUTION

A study by sociologist Eldon Snyder (1994) suggests that, when athletes form special bonds with each other, become arrogant about their unity and uniqueness, and become subjectively separated from the rest of the community, their sport participation may foster deviant behaviors. Snyder did a qualitative analysis of a case in which nine varsity athletes at a large university were arrested after committing dozens of burglaries over two years. Seven of the athletes were on the men's swim team, one was on the track and field team, and one was a former member of the women's swim team (and currently dating one of the men); they all came from middle-class families.

Snyder examined records, testimony, and court documents in the case, including statements by athletes, parents, lawyers, and others. He did *not* conclude that sport participation had *caused* these young people to be deviant. Instead, he concluded that playing sports had created the bonds and dynamics out of which the deviance of this group of college athletes emerged. Snyder had no final explanation for why these young people did what they did, but he noted that sport participation certainly did not serve as a deterrent to deviance.

This general conclusion is consistent with Peter Donnelly's (1993) research showing that certain forms of binge deviance are relatively common among elite athletes, especially after major competitions, at the end of their seasons, and following retirement. Donnelly interviewed recently retired national-level athletes in Canada and found that, when they had breaks in their training, they often felt, as one former athlete explained, that they "had to make the most of it. Go for it. Do everything to the max!" Another said that, "when you partied, you just partied your face off [because] you knew that you would have to get into the grind tomorrow or the next day." Others explained that after the season they went on a binge by "eating, popping, drinking, injecting, and sniffing everything that wasn't nailed down."

A FINAL NOTE

These studies show that neither virtue nor deviance is *caused* by sports and sport participation. Sports are sites where young people often have powerful and exciting physical and social experiences. When they are organized so that young people can receive thoughtful guidance from adults who are sensitive to what young people need to develop self-respect and become connected to the rest of the community, good outcomes are likely. However, when playing sports separates athletes from the rest of the community and fosters overconformity to the norms of the sport ethic, good outcomes are unlikely. The bonds formed among athletes can take them in many directions, including deviant ones. Sport programs are effective only when they enable people to live more satisfying lives in the community; simply taking people off the streets for a few hours a week, so that they can bounce basketballs does little more than provide temporary shelter. *What do you think?*

Athletes are not the only sports participants who engage in deviant acts. Bobby Knight, a long-time college basketball coach has engaged in repeated acts of deviance on and off the court. Here he is throwing a chair on the court to protest a referee's call. Despite his deviance, he has had a long career in coaching, and he has been praised for his ability to control the actions of his players. (AP/Wide World Photos)

- Judges and other officials in events such as figure skating, gymnastics, and boxing who take bribes or make agreements with others to alter the outcomes of events
- Team managers and player personnel staff who ignore the dynamics of race and ethnicity when they recruit, evaluate, hire, and promote administrative staff and coaches
- Media promoters and commentators who deliberately distort and misrepresent sport events, so that they can generate high television ratings or newspaper/magazine sales
- Agents who mislead athletes, misrepresent themselves, or violate rules as they solicit college student-athletes and represent professional athletes
- Parent/spectators who berate, taunt, and fight with each other, referees, and players as they watch their children in youth sports (Engh, 1999)
- Spectators who endanger athletes by throwing objects onto the field of play, verbally attack athletes, fight with one another, destroy property in anger after losses and in "joy" after wins, place illegal bets on sports, and forge and sell autographs of athletes

Some of these and other examples of deviance are discussed in chapters 5, 7, 8, and 11–14.

As I think about this list, I am reminded of the case when Latrell Spreewell, then a player on the NBA's Golden State Warriors, choked his coach, P. J. Carlesimo. Spreewell was out of line, and he paid for it with fines and a suspension, which cost him one year of his career and over $6 million in salary and endorsement revenue. As people debated whether Spreewell should have been punished even more, few asked why his coach had never been punished for regularly harassing and demeaning his players in ways that would have led him to be fired if he had been a supervisor or manager in most other U.S. organizations. Some people said Carlesimo was a jerk, but there were no studies of how coaches harass and mistreat athletes and no discussions of whether they violate organizational or community rules when they do so. Spreewell's actions were wrong, and they deserved to be punished, but he was not the only person who overstepped normative boundaries.

PERFORMANCE-ENHANCING SUBSTANCES: DEVIANT OVERCONFORMITY IN SPORTS

Stories about athletes using performance-enhancing substances are no longer shocking; they appear regularly in the media. However, many people do not know that drug and substance use in sports has a long history.[4] Athletes have taken a wide variety of everyday and exotic substances over the years, and substance use has never been limited to elite athletes. Data suggest that, if today's drugs had been available in past centuries, athletes back then would have used them as frequently as athletes use them today (Hoberman, 1992; Todd, 1987). This makes it difficult to blame all drug use on the profit motive, commercial interests, television, and the erosion of traditional values.

The historical data also suggest that drug and substance use by athletes generally is not the result of defective socialization or lack of moral character. After all, users and abusers often are the most dedicated and committed athletes in sports! Nor are all substance users helpless victims of coaches and trainers who lack moral character, although coaches and trainers who push the sport ethic without question may indirectly encourage

the use of performance-enhancing substances. Instead, most substance use and abuse seem to be an expression of overcommitment to the norms of the sport ethic. Therefore, it is grounded in overconformity—the same type of overconformity that occurs when injured distance runners continue training, even when training may cause serious injuries; when young female gymnasts control weight by cutting their food intake to dangerous levels; and when American football players use painkilling drugs and risk their already injured and surgically repaired bodies week after painful week in the NFL (Freeman, 2002).

Apparently, many athletes enjoy playing their sports so much that they will do whatever it takes to stay involved and meet the expectations of their fellow athletes. Of course, they seek on-the-field success, enabling them to avoid being cut or eliminated, but the desire to win is usually secondary to the desire to play and be accepted as an athlete. This means that, as long as some athletes are willing to take performance-enhancing substances to gain the edge they need to continue playing at the highest possible level of competence, others will conclude that they also must use similar substances to stay competitive at that level, even if it's against their better judgment. These dynamics, all connected with overconformity to the sport ethic, operate at various levels of sports—from local gyms, where high school athletes work out, to the locker rooms of professional sport teams—and among women and men across a wide variety of sport events, from the 100-meter sprint to the marathon and from tennis to football.

The important points to remember are that using performance-enhancing substances is not a new thing in sports, the use of these substances usually involves deviant overconformity, and the search for and use of these substances has continued despite antidoping regulations and drug-testing policies. The usefulness of these points becomes clear when we examine efforts to define, ban, test for, and control the use of performance-enhancing substances.

---

[4]See the *Sports in Society* website (www.mhhe.com/coakley8e) for a summary of this history.

"Is this what those hormones are supposed to do, Carl?"

FIGURE 6.4 The negative side effects of various combinations of substances are difficult to identify. Controlled studies of banned substances are difficult to do, because it may not be ethical to experiment with the same dosages that athletes use. This means that the side effects of many substances are unknown.

Defining and Banning Performance-Enhancing Substances

Defining *performance-enhancing substances* is difficult. They can include anything from aspirin to heroin; they may be legal or illegal, harmless or dangerous, natural or synthetic, socially acceptable or unacceptable, commonly used or exotic. Furthermore, they may produce real physical changes, psychological changes, or both (see figure 6.4).

Problems with definitions are faced whenever a sport organization develops an antidrug or no-doping program. For example, until 1999, the International Olympic Committee (IOC) defined doping in this way:

> [Doping is] the administration of or use by a competing athlete of any substance *foreign* to the body or any *physiological substance* taken in *abnormal quantity* or taken by an *abnormal route of entry* into the body with the *sole intention* of increasing in an *artificial* and *unfair* manner his/her performance in competition. When necessity demands *medical treatment* with any substance that, because of its nature, dosage, or application, is able to boost the

athlete's performance in competition in an artificial and unfair manner, this too is regarded by the IOC as doping. (USOC, 1992, p. 1; italics added to emphasize key terms)

This definition may sound good, but the IOC had difficulty defining all the terms in italics. For example, what is a substance "foreign" to the body, and why are the "foreign" substances of aspirin and ibuprofen not banned, whereas the "natural" hormone testosterone is banned? What is an "abnormal" quantity or an "abnormal" route of entry? Why are megadoses of vitamins not banned, whereas small amounts of many decongestants are banned? Why can athletes be stripped of medals when they swallow medications without intending to enhance performance, whereas other athletes are legally rehydrated with IV needles inserted into veins?

With new scientific discoveries being made every day and applied to sports, what is artificial and what is unfair? Why are needles permitted to inject certain painkillers but are considered dangerous and artificial when used to inject an athlete's own red blood cells into a vein (blood boosting)? Why isn't the electronic stimulation of muscles banned? Isn't it artificial? Is it fair to compete with knees that have surgically inserted synthetic ligaments because "natural" ligaments were destroyed? Why are biofeedback and other psychological technologies defined as "natural" and "fair," whereas certain forms of "natural" herbal tea are defined as "unnatural" and "unfair"? Are vitamins natural? amino acids? caffeine? human growth hormone? Gatorade? marijuana? How about so-called natural herbs, chemicals, and compounds now stacked floor to ceiling in stores that sell nutritional supplements with the promise of performance enhancement?

Is it natural to deprive yourself of food to make weight or meet the demands of a coach who measures body fat every week and punishes athletes who eat "normal" diets? Should athletes who binge and purge or become anorexic or exercise in rubber suits to lose weight be considered normal? In fact, what is normal about all of the social, psychological, biomechanical, environmental, and technological methods of manipulating athletes' bodies in today's high-performance sports?

Are big-time college football players deviant when saline solutions are dripped into their veins through intravenous needles in a pregame locker room to minimize the threat of dehydration on a hot playing field? Isn't this a performance-enhancing procedure? Is it normal, safe? How about twelve-year-old gymnasts who pop a dozen anti-inflammatory pills every day, so that they can train through pain? Are they deviant? Are they different from hockey players who pop a half-dozen Sudafed pills (containing pseudoephedrine) to get "up" for the game?

How about NFL players who became addicted to painkillers after being regularly injected by physicians hired by team owners? Why do we call athletes heroes when they use an IV procedure to play in ungodly heat or take large injections of painkilling drugs to keep them training and playing and then condemn the same athletes when they take drugs to help them build muscles damaged by overtraining or other drugs to help them relax and recover after their bodies and minds have been pushed beyond limits in the pursuit of dreams?

Why do many athletes see the use of drugs as a noble act of commitment and dedication, whereas many spectators see it as a reprehensible act of deviance yet pay big money to watch athletes do superhuman things requiring extreme training regimes and strategies made possible by drugs?

These and hundreds of other questions about what is artificial, natural, foreign, fair, and abnormal show that any definition of *doping* will lead to endless debates about the technical and legal meaning of terms. For this reason, the IOC changed its definition of doping in 1999. Now the Olympic Movement Anti-Doping Code defines doping as:

> (1) the use of an expedient (substance or method) which is potentially harmful to athletes' health and/or capable of enhancing their performance, or (2) the presence in the athlete's body of a Prohibited Substance or evidence of the use thereof or evidence of the use of a Prohibited Method. (USADA, 2001, p. 4)

However, even this simplified definition, along with the thirty pages in which prohibited substances and prohibited methods are described, raises many questions. Meanwhile, physicians, pharmacists, chemists, inventors, and athletes continue to develop new and different aids to performance—chemical, "natural," and otherwise. This creates an endless game of scientific hide and seek, which shows no sign of letting up, regardless of definitions. In fact, we can expect it to get more heated and controversial as scientists manipulate the brain and nervous system and try to use genetic engineering to improve athletic performance. How will we define, identify, and deal with doping and drugs in light of all these possibilities? Drug use among athletes seems to be only one of many issues related to technology and the manipulation of athletes' bodies; soon we will be forced to deal with issues much more contentious than so-called doping.

> **We've taught illegal tactics to survive.**
>
> —Billy Tubbs, basketball coach, Texas Christian University, 2003 (in Wolff, 2000, p. 47)

Further complicating decisions about which substances to ban is confusion about their effects on athletic performance. Ethical and legal considerations have constrained researchers who study the impact of super-high doses and multiple combinations of substances that are "stacked and cycled" by athletes. Athletes learn things in locker rooms faster than scientists learn them in the lab, although the validity of locker room knowledge is frequently suspect. Furthermore, by the time researchers have good information about a substance, athletes have moved on to others, which have not been tested. This is why most athletes ignore "official statements" about the consequences and dangers of doping—the statements are about two to five years behind the "inventors" who supply new substances.

Sport organizations often withhold information about substances because they think that knowledge among athletes might encourage use. However, most athletes now get information in the locker room, at the local gym, and in both mainstream and underground publications that claim to provide a sound basis for making informed choices about substance use (see any issue of *Muscle Media*; Phillips, 1997; www.bigsport.com; www.elitefitness.com). Most athletes in international sports, such as the Olympics, also realize that the IOC and other sport organizations withhold information because they don't want to jeopardize the billions of dollars that corporate sponsors and TV networks pay for what they want to present to the world as a clean and wholesome event (Jennings, 1996a; Jennings and Sambrook, 2000).

There are literally hundreds of antidoping and antidrug policies. Every professional sport league has its own policy, and they all differ in terms of banned substances and testing procedures. The NCAA has its own policy, as do hundreds of high school districts. However, most policies are at least partially based on the belief that these substances are dangerous to the health of athletes. Although this is true in some cases, it is tough to argue this point to athletes who already make sacrifices, pay the price, and take many health risks as they strive for distinction and pursue dreams in their sports. For example, when athletes who have dedicated between four and fifteen years of their youth to make a national team or play a pro sport are told that taking certain hormones could shorten their lives by a few years or do damage to their livers or hearts, they don't listen very closely. Such messages don't scare many of them; they know that being an athlete means that you take risks and sometimes suffer in the process. Furthermore, when they are not encouraged to question the extreme commitment that promotes other dangerous forms of overconformity to the sport ethic, how can they be convinced to avoid substances that may negatively affect their health? After all, athletes know that participation in power and performance sports is itself a threat to their health (Waddington, 2000a, b)!

Finally, some people ask why drugs should be banned in sports when they are widely accepted in society and used to improve performance or treat conditions that interfere with performance at home or on the job. The majority of adults in most wealthy, high-tech societies use tranquilizers, pain controllers, mood controllers, antidepressants, decongestants, diet pills, birth control pills, caffeine, nicotine, sleep aids, and alcohol. Doctors now prescribe or suggest for their patients various health-related hormone-drug-supplement therapies designed to improve strength and counteract the negative effects of aging; these include testosterone, various anabolic steroids, human growth hormone (HGH), HGH stimulants, androstenedione, DHEA, and creatine.[5] Every six months, the list changes and grows longer as new discoveries are made and new supplements manufactured. In fact, if people really did say no to drugs, life in most Western societies would change dramatically. When a fifty-five-year-old man takes HGH to maintain strength so he can perform on the job, why shouldn't his twenty-five-year-old son do the same thing in the NFL?

These facts give rise to an important question. Why bother to control athletes in ways that other people are not controlled? After all, do colleges have rules banning caffeine used to enable students to study all night for a test? Do teachers make students sign an oath to avoid drugs that might enable them to do their coursework? Do employers tell executives not to use hormone therapies to keep them fit for work? Do wives tell their husbands not to take Viagra, the performance-enhancing drug that boosts sexual arousal? Why should athletes have to do these things, when

---

[5]Dehydroepiandrosterone (DHEA) is a hormone widely available over the counter in most countries. It is a product of the adrenal glands, and it stimulates the production of testosterone. Some athletes and people over age forty take it to maintain lean body mass. At this time, it is not a banned substance for athletes. Creatine is a compound produced by the liver, kidneys, and pancreas. It facilitates the renewal of anaerobic energy reserves, delays the onset of fatigue during intense exercise, and cuts recovery time between workouts (Kearney, 1999).

others competing or working for valued rewards do not? As these questions are asked, it remains difficult to define drugs, doping, and substance abuse in sports.

Why Is the Challenge of Substance Control So Great in Sports Today?

Many factors contribute to the tendency among today's athletes to look to various substances for the edge they need to pursue their dreams and stay involved in the sports from which they derive enjoyment and other benefits, including material rewards. These factors include the following:

1. *The visibility and resources associated with sports today have fueled massive research and development efforts devoted to performance-enhancing substances.* Numerous individual entrepreneurs and corporations have tied the development of performance-enhancing substances to the general realm of "alternative medicine" and have seen it as a way to make quick and substantial profits. The market for these substances is especially attractive because aging baby boomers (the massive population cohorts born between 1946 and 1964) see these substances as health aids. When these baby boomers are combined with athletes from all levels of competition, the potential for profits in the supplement industry is greater today than ever before. Therefore, the availability and diversity of substances are greater today than ever before.

2. *There is a deep fascination in most postindustrial cultures with technology and how it can be used to push or extend human limits.* This fascination has also been fostered by advertising slogans that promote the notion of uncritical hyperconsumption in society as a whole. Athletes, because they live in social worlds characterized by a "culture of excellence," hear those corporate messages more loudly than many others. The athletes are dedicated

to the notion that they should be the best they can be in a social world where they hear over and over that they can be anything they want to be—if they overconform to the norms of the sport ethic.

3. *The rationalization of the body has influenced how people conceptualize the relationship between the body and mind.* People in most postindustrial societies see the body as a malleable tool serving the interests of the mind. Separating the body from the mind is common in cultures with Judeo-Christian religious beliefs, and it opens the door for people to seek substances to improve the body. At the same time, athletes are expected to use their minds to ignore bodies suffering from pain and injury (Grant, 2002a, b).

4. *There is a growing emphasis on self-medication.* People in wealthy postindustrial societies increasingly seek alternatives to remedies prescribed by mainstream medical practitioners. They depend on friends, ads, and websites for medical information. In the process, they have become more open to trying a wide range of health- and performance-enhancing substances that can be purchased over the counter without licensed medical advice or approval. Furthermore, the Dietary Supplement Health and Education Act of 1994 exempted a wide range of "nutritional" and performance-enhancing substances from testing and approval by the U.S. Food and Drug Administration (FDA). As long as this act remains as it is now written, people may manufacture and sell many untested substances without being regulated or accountable. This has flooded the market with over-the-counter products and has promoted an emphasis on self-medication.

5. *Gender relations are changing in contemporary society.* As traditional ideas about masculinity and femininity have been challenged, the threat of change has fueled a desire among

This photo, taken in late 2002, will already be out of date when you see it. It presents just a few of the "nutritional supplements" that athletes take without prescriptions. Some athletes spend hundreds of dollars a month on supplements; professional and elite amateur athletes may spend much more. Since 2000, many positive drug tests have occurred in cases in which athletes had taken substances containing the steroid nandrolone or another banned substance that was not listed among the ingredients of certain supplements. Despite this, substance use continues to be a widespread part of high-performance sport culture.

some males to do whatever it takes to develop a physique that reaffirms an ideology of male strength and power. At the same time, the promise of change has fueled a desire among many women to revise their notions of femininity, to do whatever it takes to achieve strength, power, and physical ability and to lose weight at the same time. Therefore, both men and women are likely to define performance-enhancing substances as valuable in their quests to preserve or challenge prevailing gender ideology.

6. *The organization of power and performance sports encourages athletes to overconform to the norms of the sport ethic.* Many contemporary sports are organized so that continued participation at the level needed to sustain an "athlete identity" requires winning in the form of outdoing others—making the

cut, so to speak. The desire to maintain participation fuels the search for performance-enhancing substances.

7. *Coaches, sponsors, administrators, and fans clearly encourage most forms of deviant overconformity.* Athletes who make sacrifices and put their bodies on the line for the sake of the team, the school, the community, the nation, and so on are held up as heroes. Athletes realize this, and many willingly take substances to "do their duty."

8. *The performance of athletes is closely monitored within the social structure of elite sports.* Elite sports today emphasize control, especially control over the body; conformity, especially to the demands of a coach; and guilt, especially when one does not meet the expectations of fellow athletes and those who sponsor participation (such as parents, sport clubs, and corporations). The combination of the desire to control one's body, the need to meet expectations for improving performance, and the existence of potential guilt over letting teammates and fans down is a powerful incentive to do whatever it takes to remain an elite athlete.

When these eight factors are combined, it is easy to see why substance use is greater today than ever and why it is more difficult to control than ever.

Drug Testing as a Deterrent

Drug testing is controversial. This is because there are powerful arguments against it and powerful arguments for it. The arguments against it are these:

1. Testing is generally ineffective because athletes are often one step ahead of the rule makers and the testers when it comes to choosing and using substances (see figure 6.5). By the time certain substances are banned and tests are developed to detect them, athletes have moved on to other substances. Drug tests provide an incentive

"Don't worry, honey. Most of these are legal, some can't be tested for, others mask the ones they can test for, and some are too new for the tests!"

FIGURE 6.5 Some athletes take vast amounts of various substances in many combinations. The industries that produce performance-enhancing substances have stayed ahead of the testers in sports, and they will probably continue to stay ahead.

for people to develop new synthetic versions of drugs that tests are not calibrated to detect (Zorpette, 2000).

2. Requiring people to submit to drug tests without cause violates rights to privacy and sets precedents for invasive testing programs that produce medical and biological information that could be used against a person's interest apart from sports (Malley and Zaky, 2002). The protocols for future tests will probably require blood samples, muscle biopsies, genetic testing, and DNA analysis; test results could lead some people to be stigmatized as "impure," "contaminated," or abnormal for medical or biological reasons.

3. Drug tests are expensive and drain resources that could be used for health education programs for athletes. The test administered to athletes in Olympic sports by the recently formed United States Anti-Doping Agency (USADA) and the World Anti-Doping Agency (WADA) costs about $300 per athlete every time it is administered. Testing 100,000 potential Olympic athletes around the world once a year would cost about $30 million, and athletes taking substances are unlikely to be deterred by a test administered only once a year. High schools face similar cost issues. In a school district with 10,000 high school students, in which 4,000 students play sports, a basic test for illegal

street drugs would cost $15 per student, or $60,000 for the district. A test for a range of performance-enhancing substances given once per year would cost about $250,000, and athletes could still take the substances in the off season while they train and then stop prior to the season when they would be tested. Instead of paying for tests, these funds could pay for health education programs for athletes.

4. Drug tests are generally ineffective for substances that are naturally produced by the body. EPO (erythropoietin), HGH (human growth hormone), IGF-1 (insulin-like growth factor-1), and testosterone are all powerful performance enhancers produced by the body, and normal levels of these substances vary from one person to the next.[6] This makes it difficult to determine an amount of each substance that would be considered illegal for all bodies. And, once legal levels are determined, athletes who test positive frequently use lawsuits to challenge the limits in individual cases (Zorpette, 2000).

5. Drug tests provide an incentive for people to develop forms of genetic engineering designed to alter a wide array of physical characteristics related to performance (Longman, 2001a; Parrish, 2002; Swift and Yaeger, 2001; Zorpette, 2000). When genetic engineering occurs, it will make steroids and other drugs obsolete. Genetic manipulation

will be difficult, if not impossible, to detect, and tests will cost at least $1,000 per athlete. Chuck Yesalis, a professor at Penn State who has studied drugs in sports for many years, argues that drug testing "won't change a damn thing. Two, four, six years from now, this whole conversation could be passé due to genetic engineering" (in Patrick, 2002b, p. 6C).

The arguments in favor of testing are equally powerful. They include the following:

1. Drug testing is needed to protect the health of athletes and to relieve athletes of the pressures they feel to take potentially dangerous substances to keep up with competitors. In elite cycling, the blood-boosting drug EPO has been implicated in the deaths of about twenty riders from Europe since 1988 (Zorpette, 2000). EPO causes a person's blood to thicken and clot, and it can be fatal when taken in high doses. In the World Wrestling Federation (now World Wrestling Entertainment—WWE), steroids are suspected in forty deaths among wrestlers under the age of forty between 1997 and mid-2002; ten of those deaths occurred in the first six months of 2002 (Marvez, 2002). Furthermore, the use of steroids and other substances may partially account for the rising injury toll in certain sports in which severe muscle and tendon tears and bone fractures are common (Verducci, 2002). Other serious health risks are associated with various substances, including ephedrine; steroid precursors, such as androstenedione; diuretics; epogen; and beta-blockers (Meyer, 2002a).

2. Drug testing is needed to guarantee a level playing field where competitive outcomes reflect skills and training rather than access to substances. Although it is difficult to prove, many athletes and some spectators believe that the winners of important athletic events owe their success to drugs and supplements as much as to training. This

---

[6]EPO (erythropoietin) is a protein hormone that is produced by cells in the kidneys. It promotes the production of red blood cells, the cells that carry oxygen. Therefore, it can be useful to endurance athletes looking to increase the oxygen-carrying capacity of their blood. HGH (human growth hormone) is a hormone produced naturally by the pituitary gland, and it stimulates physical growth in children. However, it can be used to increase muscle mass and overall strength in adults, and some adults take it in the belief that it slows the aging process. IGF-1 (insulin-like growth factor-1) is a protein that helps muscles grow and repair themselves when they are damaged. It can be used to reduce muscle-recovery time after strenuous workouts.

Most fans favor drug testing, but these two fans demonstrated that they were also aware of other forms of deviance in sports. These fans were concerned with the judging scandal that occurred during the figure skating pairs competition at the 2002 Winter Olympic Games in Salt Lake City. (Lionel Cironneau; AP/Wide World Photos)

damages the integrity of sports and jeopardizes sponsorships, television rights fees, and the interest of spectators.

3. Requiring people to submit to drug tests is legally justified because the actions of those who take substances affect the lives of other people. Furthermore, the U.S. Supreme Court ruled in 2002 that schools could conduct drug tests on all students involved in sports and other extracurricular activities because drug use by schoolchildren is a serious national problem and because schools have "custodial responsibilities" for their students (Lewin, 2002).

4. Drug testing is a part of normal law enforcement because drug use is illegal and must be controlled, as are other criminal acts. This means that punishments must be

clearly explained, fairly administered, and severe enough to deter future substance use.

5. Drug tests must be expanded to anticipate genetic engineering because the use of genetic engineering will change the meaning of athletic performance. Bengt Saltin, a Swedish physiologist on the World Anti-Doping Agency's special committee on "gene doping," says that genetic manipulation will mean "the end of sport as we know it. Sport will be a circus of unbelievable performances" (in Swift and Yaeger, 2001, p. 91). Unless testing is used to discourage genetic manipulation, sports will be replaced by spectacle, and athletes will become pawns in video game-like contests controlled by "body-ware developers."

In the face of the arguments against and for drug testing, many athletes have mixed feelings about testing policies and programs. They realize that political and economic interests can cloud the validity and reliability of testing programs. They also know that drug testing is an enormously complicated bureaucratic process and that mistakes can occur at many points. This has already provoked legal challenges to test results. These challenges are complicated, because they often cross national borders, where judicial processes and definitions of individual rights and due process are inconsistent. In the meantime, athletes know that fellow athletes continue to be willing to overconform to the sport ethic and continue to seek creative ways to push their bodies to new limits in the pursuit of dreams.

Mixed feelings about testing continue because most testing is done by sport organizations that have vested interests in test results or, in some cases, reasons to manipulate test results. To counteract these possibilities, international athletes in Olympic sports are tested by "independent" agencies formed in 1999. The World Anti-Doping Agency (WADA) conducts random, unannounced tests around the world. The United States Anti-Doping Agency (USADA) conducts similar tests on U.S. athletes wherever they are training around the world. These two agencies work together. However, part of the funding for the USADA comes from the United States Olympic Committee. This causes some people to wonder about how independent the agency is, despite clear statements about agency integrity made by the spokespeople for the USADA and WADA. Fortunately, both agencies have an educational emphasis, and this can be more important than the tests they conduct, if educational programs are expanded to emphasize the control of all forms of deviant overconformity in elite sports. Unfortunately, this is unlikely.

Controlling Substance Use in Sports: Where to Start

Today's athletes, like their counterparts in the past, seek continued participation and excellence in sports. When they overconform to norms promoting sacrifice and risk in the pursuit of distinction and dreams, they are not likely to define the use of performance-enhancing substances as deviant. Even Ben Johnson, the Canadian sprinter who lost his gold medal for the 100-meter sprint in the 1988 Seoul Olympics, said this in 1993: "You can never clean it up. People are always gonna be doing something. They feel good about themselves, and they feel it's right to do it" (in Fish, 1993, p. A12). Johnson's point is made in another way by a physician who works with athletes; he observes that "athletes don't use drugs to escape reality—they use them to enforce the reality that surrounds them" (DiPasquale, 1992, p. 2).

A central point in this chapter is that athletes use performance-enhancing substances not because they lack character, intelligence, or sanity, as might be concluded when using functionalist theory; nor do they use them because they are victims of biased and coercive rules, as might be concluded when using conflict theory. The solutions based in these theoretical approaches are also unsatisfactory. Tougher rules and increased testing have not and will not be effective; nor will changing the system so that athletes make all the rules.

As long as athletes accept without question or qualification the norms of the sport ethic, they will voluntarily try or take anything to remain in sports. Moral panics over drug use and over-simplified solutions will not make athletes stop using substances they see as essential in maintaining their identities and their experience of participation.

Drug use and future forms of genetic manipulation can be controlled only when the people associated with sports critically assess the norms of the sport ethic in ways that lead them to set limits on conformity to those norms (Shogan and Ford, 2000).

In light of this approach, recommendations for controlling substance use in sports should begin with the following changes:

- *Critically examine the deep hypocrisy involved in elite power and performance sports.* How is it possible to encourage athletes to limit their use of performance-enhancing substances when federations and teams formally or informally approve the use of legal performance-enhancing drugs and procedures? Using painkillers; using massive injections of vitamin B-12, artificial hydration, pure oxygen, and so on; playing with pins in broken bones or with high-tech "casts" to hold broken bones in place during competition; and using special harnesses to restrict the movement of injured joints all foster a sport culture in which the use of performance-enhancing substances is defined not only as logical but courageous.
- *Establish rules indicating clearly that certain risks to health are undesirable and unnecessary in sports.* When fourteen-year-old girls who compete with training-induced stress fractures in elite gymnastics are turned into national heroes and poster children for corporate sponsors, we promote deviant overconformity in sports. This sets up athletes for permanent injuries and disabilities. Is this necessary for entertainment in our lives?

- *Establish rules stating that injured athletes should not be allowed to play until certified as "well" (not simply "able to compete") by an independent physician outside the team or program in which the athlete is involved.* Too many team physicians and trainers have divided loyalties because they are paid by teams or by medical organizations that have contracted with teams or leagues (Pipe, 1998; Polsky, 1998). Trainers and physicians also must be able to identify the ways that athletes hide injuries in an effort to get back on the field.
- *Establish educational programs for young athletes.* Young people should learn to define *courage* in terms of recognizing limits and accepting the discipline necessary to accurately and responsibly acknowledge the consequences of sports injuries. Learning to be in tune with one's body rather than to deny the body is important in controlling the use of potentially dangerous performance-enhancing substances.
- *Establish codes of ethics for sport scientists.* Too many sport scientists devote their professional attention to assisting athletes to overconform to the norms of the sport ethic, rather than helping them raise critical questions about how deviant overconformity is dangerous to their health and development. When they do this, they become "high-tech dopers." For example, sport psychology should be used to help athletes understand the consequences of their choices to play sports and to reduce the extent to which guilt, shame, and pathology influence participation and training decisions. This is the alternative to the technique of "psycho-doping," which encourages deviant overconformity by making athletes more likely to give body and soul to their sports without carefully answering critical questions about *why* they are doing what they are doing and what it means in their lives.

This is an "Athlete Anti-Doping Passport" used by the United States Anti-Doping Agency and the World Anti-Doping Agency— independent testing organizations contracted to conduct tests for all Olympic sports. The passport must be carried by Olympic athletes and presented to the doping control officer who conducts tests. All test results are recorded in this document. It also contains the athlete's photo and a signed pledge not to violate the ideals of the Olympic movement. (Jay Coakley)

- *Make drug education part of larger deviance and health education programs.* Parents, coaches, league administrators, managers, trainers, and athletes should participate in formal educational programs in which they consider and discuss the norms of the sport ethic and how to prevent deviant overconformity to those norms. Unless all these people understand their roles in reproducing a culture supportive of substance abuse, the problems will continue. Such a program would involve training to do the following:
  - Create norms regulating the use of new and powerful technology and medical knowledge that go beyond the use of drugs

- Question and critically examine values and norms in sports, as well as set limits on conformity to those values and norms
- Redefine the meaning of achievement in sports in light of available new forms of performance-enhancing technologies
- Teach athletes to think critically about sports, so that they understand that what happens in sports is a matter of choice and that changes in the current culture of sport is possible at all levels of competition
- Provide parents, coaches, and athletes with the best and most recent information available on performance-enhancing technologies, so that they can make informed decisions about whether or not and how they will be used

As it is now, we face a future without any clearly defined ideas about the meaning of achievement in sports in light of: (1) new financial incentives to set records and win events; (2) the new importance of sport participation in the lives and identities of many young athletes; (3) the new technologies, which clearly enhance performance; and (4) the new forms of corporate sponsorship, which make image as important as ability. Therefore, we need *new* approaches and guidelines. Old approaches and guidelines combined with increasingly coercive enforcement methods will not work. Efforts to make sports into what we believe they were in the past are fruitless. We cannot go back to the past. We face new issues and challenges, which call for new approaches.

Widespread involvement in this process of facing new issues and challenges is needed, or powerful entities, such as transnational corporations, will appropriate sport culture and the bodies of athletes as sites for delivering their messages about success, performance, efficiency, winning, and pain for the sake of achieving goals. We are already headed in that direction, and we are traveling at a rapid pace.

SUMMARY

IS DEVIANCE IN SPORTS OUT OF CONTROL?

The study of deviance in sports presents interesting challenges. This is due to four factors: (1) the forms and causes of deviance in sports are so diverse that no single theory can explain all of them; (2) actions, ideas, and characteristics accepted in sports may be defined as deviant in the rest of society; (3) deviance in sports often involves an uncritical acceptance of norms, rather than a rejection of them; and (4) training in sports has become medicalized to the point that athletes use medical technology in ways that push normative limits.

Widely used conceptual frameworks in sociology don't offer useful explanations of the full range of deviance in sports, nor do they offer much help in devising ways to control it. Problems are encountered when functionalist theory is used—*deviance* is defined, according to functionalists, as failing to conform to ideals, and deviants are seen as lacking moral character. But ideals are difficult to identify, and athletes may violate norms because they go overboard in their acceptance of them, not because they lack character.

Similarly, problems occur when conflict theory is used—*deviance* is defined by conflict theorists as behaviors that violate the interests of people with money and power, and deviants are seen as exploited victims of economic power. But people with power and money don't control all sports, and not all athletes can be described as exploited victims.

An approach using interactionist and critical theories seems to be most useful when explaining much of the deviance in sports today. Such an approach emphasizes that the dynamics of sport participation are grounded in the social worlds created around sports and that people in sports make choices and can act as agents of change in sports and the culture as a whole.

The use of interactionist and critical theories in this chapter highlights the distinctions between cases of deviance that involve extreme underconformity and those that involve extreme overconformity. Such distinctions are important because the most serious forms of deviance in sports occur when athletes, coaches, and others overconform to the norms of the sport ethic. The sport ethic is a cluster of norms that emphasizes making sacrifices, striving for distinction, taking risks, playing with pain, and pursuing dreams. When little concern is given to limiting conformity to these norms, deviant overconformity becomes a problem.

Research supports this explanation. Most on-the-field and sport-related behaviors among athletes fall within a normal range of acceptability; when they fall outside this range, they often involve overconformity to the norms of the sport ethic. Rates of off-the-field deviance among athletes are generally comparable with rates among peers in the general population; when rates are high, they often are connected with the dynamics and consequences of overconformity to the sport ethic.

The use of performance-enhancing substances is a form of deviance that is reportedly widespread among athletes, despite new rules, testing programs, educational and treatment programs, and strong punishments for violators. Historical evidence suggests that recent increases in rates of use are due primarily to increases in the supply and range of available substances, rather than to changes in the values and moral characters of athletes or increased exploitation of athletes. Most athletes through history have sought ways to improve their skills, maintain their athlete identity, and continue playing their sports, but today their search is more likely to involve the use of widely available performance-enhancing substances.

Despite expanding lists of banned substances, athletes have generally stayed one jump ahead of the rule makers and testers. When one drug is banned, athletes use another, even if it is more dangerous. If a new test is developed, athletes switch to an undetectable drug or use masking drugs to confuse testers. The use of HGH, blood doping, certain levels of testosterone, and many new substances still escape detection, and testing programs are often problematic because they are so costly and many violate privacy rights or cultural norms in many societies. However, many people are strongly committed to testing, and new testing procedures have been developed. The prospect of performance-enhancing genetic manipulation will present significant challenges for testing in the future. In the meantime, testers are struggling to stay ahead of athletes who continue to overconform to the norms of the sport ethic.

Controlling deviant overconformity requires a critical assessment of norms in sports. A balance must be struck between accepting and questioning norms and rules; people in sports must critically qualify norms and rules and set limits on conformity, so that athletes who engage in self-destructive actions are not presented as heroes. Everyone in sports should question existing norms and create new norms related to the use of medical science and technology. The meaning of achievement in sports today must be revised if deviant overconformity is to be controlled. After all, what would happen if someone were to discover how to safely stimulate the brain, so that the body produced hormones that would increase size and strength and dramatically change performance potential?

An effective transformation of sports also requires that all participants be involved in a continual process of critical reflection about the meaning, organization, and purpose of sports. Controlling deviance requires a critical examination of the values and norms in sports, as well as a restructuring of the organizations controlling and sponsoring sports. This critical examination should involve everyone, from athletes to fans. It is idealistic, but it is worth trying.

SUGGESTED READINGS

Benedict, J., and D. Yaeger. 1998. *Pros and cons: The criminals who play in the NFL*. New York: Warner Books (descriptions of the criminal activity and arrests in the biographies of NFL players; presents information showing that 21 percent of a sample of 509 NFL players had been arrested for relatively serious offenses).

Blumstein, A., and J. Benedict. 1999. Criminal violence of NFL players compared to the general population. *Chance* 12 (3): 12–15 (provocative statistical analysis concluding that the arrest rate for NFL players is clearly below the rate for a comparable segment of the general population).

Eitzen, D. S. 2001. Sport and social control. In *Handbook of sports studies* (pp. 370–81), edited by J. Coakley and E. Dunning. London: Sage (although not dealing directly with deviance, this article outlines useful information on the ways that sports are related to the dynamics of social control in society).

Hoberman, J. 1992. *Mortal engines: The science of performance and the dehumanization of sport*. New York: The Free Press (analysis of the use of sport science in the quest of extending human limits; raises questions about deviance and the medicalization of sport culture).

Jennings, A., and C. Sambrook. 2000. *The great Olympic swindle: When the world wanted its games back*. London: Simon and Schuster International (the third book in a classic trilogy devoted to exposing forms of deviance among members of the IOC and others associated with elite amateur sports around the world; journalistic presentation based on meticulous investigative research).

Miracle, A. W., and C. R. Rees. 1994. *Lessons of the locker room: The myth of school sports*. Amherst, NY: Prometheus Books (chapter 5, pp. 101–25, "School Sports and Delinquency," summarizes research on sport participation in U.S. high schools and deviance).

Waddington, I. 2000. *Sport, health and drugs: A critical sociological perspective*. London: Routledge (unlike other books on drugs in sports, this one uses a sociological perspective to look at the connections among drugs, health, culture, and public policy).

Yesalis, C. E., and V. E. Cowart. 1998. *The steroids game: An expert's inside look at anabolic steroid use in sports*. Champaign, IL: Human Kinetics (accessible discussion of how steroids are used in sports and how they are related to performance and health; explanation of testing issues and how steroid users have stayed ahead of the testers).

WEBSITE RESOURCES

Note: Websites often change. The following URLs were current when this book was printed. Please check our website (www.mhhe.com/coakley8e) for updates and additions.

www.mhhe.com/coakley8e Click on chapter 6 for information on the history of performance-enhancing drug use and drug testing in high-performance sports, information on recent cases of athletes testing positive for certain drugs.

www.sportslaw.org The Sports Lawyers Association often refers to deviance in sports in terms of the legal issues raised; this site lists articles and recent cases.

www.ajennings.8m.com Jennings has exposed deviance in the IOC, and this site highlights his work and the work of others who have written articles on deviance in elite international sports.

www.alfred.edu/news/html/hazing_study.html Report of the National Survey of Initiation Rites and Athletics for NCAA Sports; excellent source of data from U.S. colleges, universities and high schools.

www.physsportsmed.com/issues/1998/06jun/pipe.htm Article calling for physicians to act assertively to control deviance in sports by reviving ethics in sports and encouraging athletes to minimize risk-taking behaviors on the field.

www.feminist.org/research/sports7.html Short summary of research dealing with contact sports and violence against women; the goal of this site is to empower women in sports.

www.ncava.org National Coalition Against Violent Athletes; provides news, statistics, updates, and information about prevention programs.

www.sports.findlaw.com Contains a list of the "Tarnished 20" rankings, which identify universities where people associated with sport programs have violated rules; has a Student-Athlete Center where NCAA rules are simplified.

www.usantidoping.org Site of the official substance-testing agency in the United States; online materials illustrate how the agency is presenting regulatory and educational materials to athletes and others.

www.wada-ama.org Site of the official worldwide drug- and substance-testing agency; online materials illustrate how the agency is presenting regulatory and educational materials.

www.bigsport.com Underground source of information about performance-enhancing substances, especially *anabolic* steroids.

www.SportsEthicsInstitute.org Nonprofit corporation that fosters critical information and discussions about ethical issues in sports; site provides news, information, and links to online resources.

www.espn.go.com/special/s/drugsandsports Provides basic information on a variety of drugs used by athletes; ESPN regularly includes on its site information about deviance in sports as it hits the news.

(Tony Gutierrez; AP/Wide World Photos)

Violence in Sports

How Does It Affect Our Lives?

 Online Learning Center Resources

Visit *Sports in Society*'s Online Learning Center at **www.mhhe.com/coakley8e** for additional information and study material for this chapter, including

- Self-grading quizzes
- Learning objectives
- Related websites
- Additional readings

WITH THE SMART COACH, fighting is a tool . . . . Fighting can be used to inspire your team, send a message, change momentum.

—**Barry Melrose, ESPN hockey announcer (2002) in Fatsis, 2002, p. W6**

A complete outline is available online at
www.mhhe.com/coakley8e.

[DURING THE DRAFT, what the coach] is looking
for are cold-blooded defenders who smile when
quarterbacks bleed.

—Mark Kiszla, *The Denver Post* sport journalist
(2001) p. 3D

I DON'T WANT TO SOUND LIKE I'm bragging,
because I'm not, but back [in the 1960s, when
I played basketball] the violence was much more
intense.

—Satch Sanders, former NBA player (1999) in
Latimer, 1999, p. 31C

Discussions of violence in sports, like discussions of deviance, are often connected with people's ideas about the moral condition of society as a whole. When violence occurs in sports, many people are quick to use it as an indicator that the moral foundation of society is eroding and that people, especially children, are learning a warped sense of morality as they watch athletes and use them as models for their own behavior.

Statements about violence in sports are often confusing because they are so contradictory. Some people say that violence is an inherent part of many games, whereas others say that violence in any form destroys the dynamics of games. Some people say that violence in sports reflects natural tendencies among males in society, whereas others say that men use violence in sports to promote the idea that physical size and strength is a legitimate basis for maintaining power over others. Some say that violence in sports has increased to intolerable levels, whereas others say it is not as frequent or as brutal as it was in the past.

Contradictory statements and conclusions about violence in sports often occur for four reasons. *First,* many people don't define important terms in their discussions. They use words such as *physical, assertive, tough, rough, competitive, intense, intimidating, risky, aggressive, destructive,* and *violent* interchangeably. *Second,* they may not distinguish players from spectators, even though the dynamics of aggressive behavior and violence in these two groups differ. Third, they may lump all sports together, regardless of differences in meaning, organization, purpose, and amount of physical contact involved. Fourth, they may not distinguish the immediate, short-term effects of playing or watching sports from the more permanent, long-term effects on patterns of violence among individuals and groups.

The goal of this chapter is to enable you to include information based on research and theories in your discussions of violence in sports. Chapter content focuses on five topics:

1. A practical definition of *violence* and related terms

AT YOUR FINGERTIPS For more information on deviance in sports, see pages 160–197.

2. A brief historical overview of violence in sports
3. On-the-field violence among players in various sports
4. Off-the-field violence among players and the impact of violence in sports on people's lives apart from sports
5. Violence among spectators who watch media coverage of sports, attend events in person, and play sport video games

In connection with the last three topics, I will make suggestions about how to control violence and limit its consequences on and off the field.

WHAT IS VIOLENCE?

Violence *is the use of excessive physical force, which causes or has the potential to cause harm or destruction.* We often think of violence as actions that are illegal or unsanctioned, but there are situations in which the use of violence is encouraged or approved in most groups or societies. When violence occurs in connection with deviant underconformity or a rejection of norms in society, it is often classified as illegal and is sanctioned severely. When violence occurs in connection with the enforcement of norms, the protection of people and property, or deviant overconformity to widely accepted norms, it may be approved and even lauded as necessary to preserve order, reaffirm important social norms, or entertain spectators. Therefore, violence is often, but not always, accepted and defined as legitimate, as when it is used by soldiers, police, and athletes pursuing victories as they represent communities or the ideals cherished by powerful people in those communities.

When violence occurs in connection with the widespread rejection of norms, it is often described as anarchy. When it occurs in connection with the use of extreme forms of social control or extreme overconformity to norms, it may be associated with a spirit of moral righteousness and the feeling that, even though violence produces harmful or destructive consequences, it is being done for the right reasons and should be rewarded. Under certain social and cultural conditions, this type of violence is an expression of fascism.

In the case of sports, pushing a referee who has just penalized you or choking your coach in anger is violence based on a rejection of norms. These forms of violence would be defined as illegal and punished severely by teams and sport organizations, even if the referee or coach were not seriously injured. However, if a football player were to deliver a punishing tackle, which broke the ribs or blew out the knee of an opposing running back after his coach had told him to be aggressive and put his body on the line for the team, the violence would be based on extreme conformity to norms. Such violence is often defined as part of the job and seen as justified by most fans, highlighted on video replays, and approved by teammates and even many opponents. The player might even feel righteous in his actions, despite their harmful consequences and would do them again, even if it meant doing harm to his own body or the bodies of others. His violence would not be punished, because it conformed to current perceptions of how football should be played. Furthermore, it would be used to affirm his identity as an athlete and a football player.

The term **aggression** will be used in this chapter to refer to *verbal or physical actions grounded in an intent to dominate, control, or do harm to another person.* Aggression is often involved in violence, but some violence occurs without aggressive intent. This definition allows us to distinguish aggressive actions from other actions we might describe as assertive, competitive, or achievement-oriented. For example, a very competitive person may use violence during a game without the intent to dominate, control, or harm others. However, there is often a difference between being aggressive and simply being assertive or trying hard to win or achieve other goals. The term **intimidation** will be used to refer to *words, gestures, and actions that threaten violence or aggression.* Like aggression, intimidation is used as a means to dominate and control another person. These definitions will help focus our discussion, but they will not eliminate all conceptual problems.

VIOLENCE IN SPORTS THROUGH HISTORY

Violence is certainly not new to physical activities and sports (Dunning, 1999; Guttmann, 1998). As noted in chapter 3, so-called blood sports were popular among the ancient Greeks and throughout the Roman Empire. Deaths occurred regularly in connection with ritual games among the Mayans and Aztecs. Tournaments during medieval and early modern Europe were designed as training for war and often had warlike consequences. Folk games were only loosely governed by rules, and they produced injuries and deaths at rates that would shock and disgust people today. Bearbaiting, cock fighting, dog fighting, and other "sporting" activities during those periods involved the treatment of animals that most people today would define as brutal and violent.

Research by figurational sociologists indicates that, as part of an overall civilizing process in Europe and North America, modern sports were developed as more rule-governed activities than the physical games in previous eras (see figure 7.1). As sports became formally organized, official rules prohibited certain forms of violence that had been common in many folk games. Bloodshed decreased, and there was a greater emphasis on self-control to restrict physical contact and the expression of aggressive impulses often inspired by the emotional heat of competition (Dunning, 1999).

SIDELINES

"Now that we've invented violence, we need a sport to use it in."

FIGURE 7.1 The existence of violence in sports is not new. However, this does not mean that violence is a part of nature or an inevitable part of sports.

As figurational theorists have studied these changes, they have noted that rates of sports violence do not automatically decrease over time. In fact, as people's actions and emotional expression in societies become more regulated and controlled, many players and spectators are more likely to experience violence and aggression in sports as pleasurable and exciting. Furthermore, the processes of commercialization, professionalization, and globalization have given rise to new forms of instrumental and "dramatic" violence in many sports. In other words, expressive violence has decreased over time, whereas goal-oriented and entertainment-directed violence has increased, at least temporarily, in many Western societies. Sociologist Eric Dunning (1999) notes that violence remains a crucial social issue in modern sports because sports are activities designed to create tension rather than relieve or discharge it, and sports continue to serve, in patriarchal societies, as an arena in which aggression is used to reproduce an ideology of male privilege. Finally, Dunning and other figurational sociologists point out that sports and actions in sport are given different meanings by different groups and individuals and that violence in sports can be understood only in relation to the social and cultural contexts in which it occurs. Scholars using interactionist, critical, and critical feminist theories agree with these points.

VIOLENCE ON THE FIELD

Types of Violence

The most frequently used typology of on-the-field violence among players is one developed by Mike Smith, a Canadian sociologist (1983; see Young, 2000, 2002a). Smith identified four categories of violence associated with playing sports:

1. *Brutal body contact.* This includes physical practices that are common in certain sports and accepted by athletes as part of the action and risk in their sport participation. Examples are collisions, hits, tackles, blocks, body checks, and other forms of forceful physical contact that can produce injuries. Most people in society would define this forceful physical contact as extreme, although this form of violence is not punished or defined as illegal or criminal. Coaches often encourage this form of violence. As one coach said after a big playoff victory in high school football, "We preached to the kids all week that we had to get back to what we do best—playing smash-mouth football" (in Trivett, 1999, p. 30C).

2. *Borderline violence.* This includes practices that violate the rules of the game but are accepted by most players and coaches as conforming to the norms of the sport ethic and to commonly used competitive strategies. Examples are the "brush back" pitch in baseball, the forcefully placed elbow in soccer and basketball, the strategic bump used by runners to put another runner off stride, the fistfight in ice hockey, and the forearm to the ribs of a quarterback in football. Although these actions may be expected, they sometimes provoke retaliation by other players. Official

sanctions and fines have not been severe for cases of borderline violence. However, public pressure to increase the severity of sanctions has grown in recent years, and the severity of punishments has increased in some cases.

3. *Quasi-criminal violence.* This includes practices that violate the formal rules of the game, public laws, and even the informal norms used by players. Examples are cheap shots, late hits, sucker punches, and flagrant fouls that endanger the players' bodies and reject the norm of respecting the game. Fines and suspensions are usually imposed on players who engage in such violence. Players usually condemn this form of violence and see it as a rejection of the informal norms of the game and what it means to be an athlete.

4. *Criminal violence.* This includes practices that are clearly outside the law to the point that athletes condemn them without question and law enforcement officials may even prosecute them as crimes. Examples are assaults that occur after a game and assaults during a game that appear to be premeditated and violent enough to kill or seriously disable a player. These are relatively rare and are seldom prosecuted. However, there seems to be growing support for the notion that criminal charges are appropriate in these cases. This support grew in early 2000 when a hockey player intentionally smashed an opponent's head with his stick. The act was such a blatant and dangerous assault that a fellow player known for his on-ice violence said, "He's lost the respect of every player in the league."

Sociologist Kevin Young (2000, 2002a) has noted that this is a useful general typology but that the lines separating the four types of violence shift over time as norms change in sports and society at large. Furthermore, the typology fails to address the origins of violence and how violent acts are related to the sport ethic, gender ideology, and the commercialization of sports. Despite these weaknesses, I will use this typology to make distinctions among various types of violence in sports as they are discussed through the chapter.

Violence as Deviant Overconformity to the Norms of the Sport Ethic

In Pat Conroy's novel *The Prince of Tides* (1986), there is a classic scene in which the coach addresses his team and describes the ideal football player. He uses words that many athletes in heavy contact sports have heard during their careers:

> Now a real hitter is a headhunter who puts his head in the chest of his opponents and ain't happy if his opponent is still breathing after the play. A real hitter doesn't know what fear is except when he sees it in the eyes of a ball carrier he's about to split in half. A real hitter loves pain, loves the screaming and the sweating and the brawling and the hatred of life down in the trenches. He likes to be at the spot where the blood flows and the teeth get kicked out. That's what this sport's about, men. It's war, pure and simple. (p. 384)

Not all coaches use vocabulary that is so vividly descriptive, and some avoid it because they know it might inspire dangerous forms of violent deviance. However, there are many coaches, team administrators, and owners in contact sports who privately dream of having a team full of athletes who think this way.

When athletes do think this way, levels of violence in sports are generally high and they attract attention. In fact, journalists describe it, sociologists and psychologists try to explain it, and athletes brag or complain about it. When an athlete dies or is paralyzed by this type of brutal body contact or borderline violence, the media usually present stories on violence in sports, asking if we've gone too far, if there is a need to pull in the reins, and if violence is rampant in sports and in society. Then they run multiple replays or photos of violent acts and watch their ratings points and sales increase.

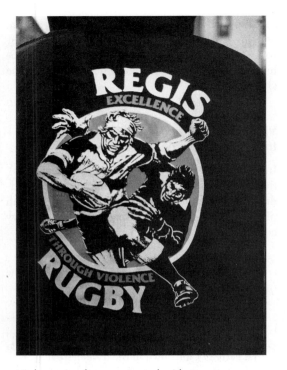

Violence is often connected with overconformity to the norms of the sport ethic. This high school rugby jacket presents violence as a key part of team culture. By associating violence with excellence, players learn what is expected on the field, even if they do not feel comfortable with brutal body contact and borderline violence. (Jay Coakley)

Although players do not always feel comfortable with the amount of brutal body contact and borderline violence in their sports, they generally accept these forms of violence, and even those who don't like them may use them to improve or maintain their status on teams and their popularity with spectators. Athletes whose violence involves overconformity to the sport ethic become legends on and off the field. Athletes who engage in quasi- and criminal violence often are marginalized in sports, and they may face criminal charges, although prosecuting such

charges has been difficult and convictions are almost nonexistent (Young, 2000, 2002a).

Violence as deviant overconformity is also related to the insecurity of life in a high-performance sport. Athletes learn that "you're only as good as your last game," and they know that their feelings of self-worth, their identities as athletes, and their status as team members are constantly under question. Therefore, many athletes are willing to take extreme measures to prove themselves, even if those measures involve violence. Violence becomes a means to prove self-worth and reaffirm membership in the subcultural in-group of those who play the game at a high level. This is why athletes who don't play in pain are defined as failures and why those who do play in pain and with injuries are defined as courageous. After all, playing in pain and with injuries honors the importance of the game and expresses dedication to teammates.

It is important to understand that violence grounded in overconformity to the sport ethic is not limited to men, although it is certainly more common in men's games than in women's games. Women also overconform to the norms of the sport ethic, and, when they play contact sports, they face the challenge of drawing the line between physicality and violence. For example, when sociologist Nancy Theberge (1999) spent a full season studying the sport experiences of women on an elite ice hockey team in Canada, she discovered that the women loved the physicality of hockey and the body contact that occurred, even though body checking was not allowed. As one woman said,

> I like a physical game. You get more fired up. I think when you get hit . . . like when you're fighting for a puck in the corner, when you're both fighting so you're both working hard and maybe the elbows are flying, that just makes you put more effort into it. (in Theberge, 1999, p. 147)

The experience of dealing with the physicality of contact sports and facing its consequences creates drama and excitement, strong emotions, and special interpersonal bonds among women athletes, as it does among men. Despite the risk and reality of pain and injuries, many women in contact sports feel that the physical intensity and body contact in their sports make them feel alive and aware. Although many women currently are committed to controlling brutal body contact and other forms of violence in their sports, their love of the physicality of the game often makes this difficult to do. After all, they also accept the norms of the sport ethic.

In the case of male athletes in contact sports, the love of physicality is connected with issues of masculinity in ways that lead overconformity to the norms of the sport ethic to be expressed through violence. Although elite women athletes who play contact sports do overconform to the norms of the sport ethic, their love of physicality is not connected with gender issues in ways that encourage them to define violence in positive terms. Some women may do so, but they do not receive the same support and rewards that men receive when they do violence in sports—unless they wrestle in the WWE or skate on a Roller Jam team.

Commercialization and Violence in Sports

There is no doubt that some athletes in power and performance sports are paid to do violence. Some are paid handsomely. However, many violent athletes in the past were not paid very well, and most athletes in high schools, colleges, and sport clubs today are paid nothing to do violence, yet many of them have accepted on-the-field violence, despite what it has cost them in pain and injury.

Commercialization and money in sports have clearly expanded the opportunities to play certain contact sports in some societies, and sponsorship money attracts the media coverage that makes these sports and the violence they contain more visible to more people than ever before. Children watch this coverage, and they sometimes imitate violent athletes when they play informal games

and organized youth sports. This is a problem, and it is related to commercialization and money, but it does not justify the conclusion that commercialization is the major cause of violence in sports.

We must remember that football players and other athletes in contact sports engaged in violence on the field long before television coverage and the promise of big salaries. In fact, players at all levels of organized football killed and maimed each other at *rates* that were higher than the death and injury rates in football today. There are more injuries today because there are more people playing football. Of course, this makes injuries and the violence that causes them very serious problems that must be dealt with, but to think that these problems are caused mainly by commercialization and money is a mistake.

This is an important point, because many people who criticize sports today blame all problems in sports, including violence, on money and greed. They state in one form or another that, if only athletes were true amateurs and played for a love of the game instead of money, they would be less violent. This conclusion is naïve, and it distracts attention away from the deep cultural and ideological roots of violence in sports and in society as a whole. Taking money away from athletes would be relatively easy—U.S. universities have done it for nearly a century! What is *not* easy is changing the culture in which athletes, especially male athletes, learn to value and use violence in sports.

Suggesting that we must make changes in culture causes many people to be uncomfortable, because it places the responsibility for change on all of us. It is much easier to blame "all those wealthy and greedy team owners, athletes, and TV people who destroy the purity and goodness of sports to make money." It is much more difficult for people to critically examine the culture of sports and the patterns of overconformity to the sport ethic, which many of them love to watch and discuss. Similarly, it is difficult for people to critically examine the definitions of *masculinity* and the structure of gender relations that they have long accepted as a part of nature and goodness. But we must do these things if we want do understand violence in sports.

Commercialization and money, however, are not irrelevant when it comes to violence in sports. Consider the following statements made by a boxer and a football player:

> I'm challenging Laila Ali. . . . Kicking [her] butt will be a walk in the park. . . . And if she wants a rematch, I'll dust her off again. (Jacqui Frazier-Lyde in Farhood, 2000, online)

> I want to hurt him. . . . I love to see people bleed. I do my talking [in the NFL] by hitting my man, throwing him on the ground, jumping on him. (Orlando Brown in Montville, 1999, p. 100)

These are two among dozens of similar statements from recent sports publications. They have become an increasingly common part of the language and rhetoric used in certain sports. They resemble the promotional rhetoric used by professional wrestlers. Therefore, when we hear images of intimidation used by Jacqui Frazier-Lyde (daughter of former heavyweight boxing champion Joe Frazier) as she challenges Laila Ali (daughter of Muhammad Ali) to a money-making bout and when we read that NFL players have told a *Sports Illustrated* reporter that they want to hurt each other and watch opponents bleed (Montville, 1999), we should wonder if their violent rhetoric tells us about how they *really play sports* or whether it tells us about how they *want us to think they play sports*.

Commercialization clearly has inspired, at least in some cultures, a promotional and heroic rhetoric that presents images of revenge, retaliation, hate, hostility, intimidation, aggression, violence, domination, and destruction. It is obvious that such images attract attention and serve commercial purposes. The NFL, the NHL, and even the NBA have used these images for many years to promote their games. They even sell videos full of carefully edited footage, which isolates, presents, and glorifies violence in sports

AT YOUR FINGERTIPS   For more information, on commercialization, see pages 374–382.

in slow-motion close-ups accompanied by the actual sounds of bodies colliding, bones and tendons snapping on impact, and players gasping in agony and pain. Of course, in true promotional fashion, the same media companies that sell these videos also publish articles that condemn violence and players who are "too violent." Violence sells, and antiviolence sells!

Does this commercially inspired rhetoric represent the real on-the-field orientations of athletes, or does it represent efforts to create personas and attract attention, which have commercial value, even though most athletes don't really want to hurt opponents and make them bleed on the field? Research is needed on this, and a good place to start might be with professional wrestling, a realm of physical performance in which the rhetoric of violence has been perfected to an art form and used effectively to enhance the commercial appeal of events. Does this rhetoric tell us about real violence and aggression in wrestling, or does it present carefully crafted images that are part of an overall entertainment package that heightens the dramatic effect of wrestling performances? Maybe it does both. Research is needed on wrestling and on so-called mainstream sports that sell violent images and narratives as a part of an entertainment package that also includes dramatic storylines delivered by paid announcers, sexy cheerleaders and halftime dancers, action toys, and play tomahawks for the symbolic "chopping" of opponents.

Violence and Masculinity

Violence in sports is not limited to men. However, critical and critical feminist research has shown clearly that, *if we want to understand violence in sports, we must understand gender ideology and issues of masculinity in culture.* Sociologist Mike Messner explains:

> Young males come to sport with identities that lead them to define their athletic experience differently than females do. Despite the fact that few males truly enjoy hitting and being hit, and that one has to be socialized into participating in much of the violence commonplace in sport, males often view aggression, within the rule-bound structure of sport, as legitimate and "natural." (1992, p. 67)

In fact, Messner explains that many male athletes learn to define injurious acts as a necessary part of the game, rather than as violence, as long as they are within the rules of the game and within the informal norms the players use to judge and evaluate each other.

Across many cultures, playing power and performance sports has become an important way to prove masculinity. Boys discover that, if they play these sports and come to be seen as people who can do violence, they can avoid social labels such as *pussy, lady, fag, wimp,* and *sissy* (Ingham and Dewar, 1999). In fact, after reviewing a long history of research on this issue, Phil White and Kevin Young (1997) noted that, if a boy or young man avoids these sports, he risks estrangement from his male peers.

Boys and men who play power and performance sports learn quickly that they are evaluated in terms of their ability to use violence in combination with physical skills. This learning begins in youth sports, and, by the time young

Both men and women are capable of violence on and off the playing field. However, women may not connect violent actions to their identities in the same way that some men do. Prevailing definitions of *masculinity* lead many people to feel that violence is more "natural" for men than for women, and it may lead men to feel comfortable with violence in their sports. (Beth A. Keiser; AP/Wide World photos)

men have become immersed in the social world of most power and performance sports, brutal body contact and borderline violence are being encouraged by teammates and coaches, sometimes by parents (fathers more than mothers), and always by spectators. These young men learn that their status in the eyes of coaches and their identities as men in the eyes of their peers and the community at large often come to depend on their ability to do violence on the field (Weinstein et al., 1995).

The connection between violence and acceptance by peers in contact sports is illustrated in team rituals in which established players subject rookies to various forms of violent and aggressive treatment. The goal of these rituals is to "see if a would-be player has what it takes to be one of us." Learning to "take it and give it back" is an expression of a player's manhood and his membership in a select fraternity of athletes. For example, when NHL player Bryan Marchment was asked how he felt about the consequences of his violence on the ice, he said, "Hey, it's a man's game. If you can't play, get out and play tennis." Of course, this orientation makes certain power and performance sports especially dangerous activities, but many men choose to play them because they have learned to define *masculinity* in terms of being tough enough to participate in the give-and-take of violent confrontations.

After reviewing dozens of studies on this topic, Phil White and Kevin Young (1997) concluded that power and performance sports emphasize an orientation that clearly "confirms and consolidates violent physicality as one of the cornerstones of masculinity" (p. 9).

A dramatic and tragic example of the complex connection between masculinity and violence in sports occurred in Reading, Massachusetts, in July 2000. As a number of boys were practicing their hockey skills during an informal skating session at a local rink, the father of one of the boys became angry when his son failed to stick up for himself as other boys pushed him around on the ice. The father entered the rink and told

his son that he had to "be a man" on the ice, and he continued to harass his son as the boy went to the locker room. Another father passed by and told him to ease up because it wasn't a big deal. This further irritated the already angry father, who then attacked the other father. After landing a punch, he exited the rink, but he came back, found the father he had hit, and beat him to death in front of the children, a few stunned mothers, and an employee at the rink.

Although this highly publicized case was covered in the media as an extreme example of parental "rink rage" and linked to other cases of parental misconduct at youth sports, it also should be linked to the masculinity issues associated with certain sports. The father, who was later convicted of voluntary manslaughter, first became enraged when his son failed to meet his definition of what a man should be on the ice, and then he killed another man who had said that the issue was not that important. This case signals the problems associated with a gender ideology that leads people to think that masculinity is proved on the field by doing violence. I always think of this when I hear a coach say, "Let's go out and prove who the better men are."

Violence, Gender, Social Class, and Race

When it comes to understanding violence in sports, we must also understand the complex interconnections of gender, social class, and race. For example, when sociologist Mike Messner interviewed men who had been elite athletes, he discovered that the men from lower-income families and minority-group backgrounds placed special importance on the *respect* they received when they played sports and when they used intimidation, aggression, and violence on the field. The men from these backgrounds were more likely than their white counterparts from middle- and upper-class families to encounter limited opportunities and to be channeled into sports in which brutal body contact and borderline violence were a part of the game. As athletes in these sports, they sought respect by physically dominating others. Being a "superstud" was an important part of establishing an identity as a man worthy of respect in the face of how people in society perceived the meaning of being minority men from poor families.

Messner also identified some black male athletes who had capitalized on the racist stereotypes held by whites. These men discovered that, by presenting a menacing and violent image on the field, they could intimidate competitors, especially those who thought black males were physically gifted and naturally prone to violence. One of the men Messner interviewed explained it this way:

> I'm tall, I'm thin, I'm a black person with a shaved head, and I'm fearful [looking]. You have to intimidate mentally. . . . [Y]ou've got to talk shit in this game, you have to say, . . . "If you come close to me, I'm gonna hurt you!" (1992, p. 83)

This statement and other findings in Messner's study illustrate a few ways that gender, social class, and race have come to be linked in the experiences of athletes, and it shows that such links may be related to the incidence of violence in sports.

The Institutionalization of Violence in Sports

Learning to Use Violence as a Strategy: Noncontact Sports   In some noncontact sports, participants may try to intimidate opponents, but violence is rare. For example, tennis players have been fined for slamming a ball to the ground in protest or talking to an official or opponent in a menacing manner. Players in noncontact sports are seldom, if ever, rewarded for violent actions. Therefore, it is doubtful that playing or watching these sports teaches people to use violence as a strategy on the field.

Some athletes may use violent images as they describe competition, but they don't have actual opportunities to convert their words into deeds. For example, sprint cyclist and 1996 Olympic silver medalist Marty Nothstein used violent images as he described his approach to a race:

> I am really aggressive out there. I pretty much hate the guy I'm racing. It wouldn't matter if it were my brother. . . . I want to destroy the guy. End it quick. Boom. One knockout punch. (in Becker, 1996, p. 4E)

Of course, cycling does not allow him to physically destroy or punch a competitor, but the language used in sports, even in noncontact sports, often has violence built right into it.

Men who play noncontact sports use violent images in their descriptions of competition much more often than women use them. The use of a language of violence is clearly linked to masculinity in most cultures. This does not mean that women do not use it, but it does mean that men use it more frequently. Apparently, many women realize that violent language reaffirms an ideology that works against their interests, as well as against their health and well-being in society as a whole.

Learning to Use Violence as a Strategy: Men's Contact Sports   Athletes in power and performance sports involving heavy physical contact learn to use intimidation, aggression, and violence as on-the-field strategies. Success in these sports depends on the use of brutal body contact and borderline violence. Research shows that male athletes in contact sports readily accept certain forms of violence, even when they involve rule-violating behaviors, and that, as the amount of contact increases in a sport, so does this acceptance (Pilz, 1996; Shields and Bredemeier, 1995; Weinstein et al., 1995; White and Young, 1997). These athletes routinely disapprove of quasi-criminal and criminal violence, but they accept brutal body contact and borderline violence done within the rules of the game. They may not intend to hurt, but this does not prevent them from putting opponents' bodies in jeopardy by doing what they feel they must do to "take the guy out," "break up the double play," "stop the drive to the basket," and so on.

"When are you gonna learn when it's necessary to use unnecessary roughness?"

FIGURE 7.2   In men's contact sports, players sometimes learn physical intimidation and violent behaviors as strategies. Both have been used to win games and build reputations.

In heavy contact sports (boxing, football, ice hockey, rugby, etc.), intimidation and violence have become widely used as strategies for winning games, promoting individual careers, increasing drama for spectators, and making money for athletes and sponsors (see figure 7.2). Athletes in these sports are quick to say that they do whatever it takes: whatever it takes to stop the other guy and whatever it takes to win. They realize that they are paid to do this, even if it causes harm to themselves and others. This was illustrated when highly successful NBA coach Pat Riley fined his players $1,500 if they did not give a hard foul to an opponent driving to the basket or if they helped an opponent up after knocking him to the floor. His message was clear: be violent or be punished. In the 1990s, his message caused considerable controversy among people in the United States, but some coaches continue to demand brutal body contact and borderline violence from their players. When players cross the line and use quasi-criminal violence, they may be fined by the league, but not by their coaches or teams.

Violence has also been incorporated into game strategies in certain heavy contact sports when coaches have used players as designated agents of intimidation and violence for their teams. In hockey, these players have been called "enforcers," "goons," and "hit men." They are expected to protect teammates and strategically assist their teams by intimidating, provoking, fighting with, and even disabling opponents. In fact, they are paid to do these things.

The violence of these enforcers and goons is well known to other players. For example, one hockey player described such a player this way: "His job is to hurt people. He goes for the knees a lot. He takes runs at you, and really all he's trying to do is hurt you and knock you out of the game" (in Scher, 1993). Rick Fox of the Los Angeles Lakers in the NBA has regularly played the role of enforcer on the basketball court. To do it right, he says, "You have to look within and find the evil that's inside of you. It's not the kind of talk you want your kids to hear, but we're grown men" (in AP, 2000).

For many years, the violence of enforcers was accepted widely. Some people associated with hockey even claimed that this violence controlled other forms of violence that might be even more dangerous. However, the validity of this claim has been challenged recently as highly paid superstars with entertaining and nonviolent physical skills have been sidelined by injuries caused by enforcers on opposing teams.

Some players continue to act as enforcers, and they are still paid for doing violence. However, every time they come close to killing someone on the ice, court, or playing field, people raise questions about the wisdom of institutionalizing violence in sports in this manner. Hockey has gradually taken action to control the violence used by enforcers and the fighting that is usually a part of their violence. However, the use of enforcers is such an institutionalized part of hockey strategy that change has been slow.

Learning to Use Violence as a Strategy: Women's Contact Sports   Information on violence among girls and women in contact sports remains scarce. It seems that there are more cases of violence in some women's sports than there were in the past, but there are few studies that tell us if this is true and why it has happened.

Women's programs have undergone many changes over the past twenty-five years. They have become more competitive, they are more likely to involve an emphasis on power and performance, and the stakes associated with success have increased considerably. Today, as the level of competition rises, and as women become increasingly immersed in the social world of elite sports, they become more tolerant of rule violations and aggressive actions on the playing field, but this pattern is less clear among women than it is among men (Nixon, 1996a, b; Shields and Bredemeier, 1995; Shields et al., 1995).

Some women use intimidation and violence in sports, and "there is no known biological reason that women cannot be as physically aggressive as men" (Dunn, 1994), but most girls and women become involved in and learn to play sports in ways that differ from the ways in which most boys and men become involved in and learn to play sports. As women compete at higher and higher levels, they often become similar to men in the way they embrace the sport ethic and use it to frame their self-definitions as athletes. Like men, they are willing to take risks, make sacrifices, pay the price, and play with pain and injury; however, unlike men, they do not link toughness, physicality, and aggression to their gender identities. In other words, women do not link violence to definitions of what it means to be a woman in society. Similarly coaches don't try to motivate women athletes by urging them to "go out and prove who the better woman is" on the field. Therefore, at this point in time, women are less likely than men to do violence on the field or to see it as appropriate (Tucker and Parks, 2001).

Do elite women athletes develop the same form of hubris (pride-based arrogance) that many elite male athletes develop? If so, how is it linked to their identities, and how do they express it in sports? Do women athletes use a rhetoric of violence when they talk about sports? Research suggests that they don't (Nelson, 1994,

1998; Theberge, 1999; Young and White, 1995), but more information is needed. A good place to start might be with the women now playing heavy contact sports or participating in dramatic spectacles, such as professional wrestling.

Pain and Injury as the Price of Violence

Many people think about sports in a paradoxical way: they accept violence as a part of sports, although they are concerned about the injuries caused by that violence. They seem to want violence without consequences—like the fictionalized violence they see in the media and video games, in which people are hit but not really injured. However, sports violence is real, and it does cause pain, injury, disability, and even death.

Research on pain and injury among athletes has increased in recent years. Sociologists Howard Nixon (2000) in the United States, Kevin Young and his colleagues in Canada (White and Young, 1997, 1999; Young, 2000), and Ivan Waddington in England (2000a, b) have studied pain, injury, and health issues in sports. Nixon's research suggests that over 80 percent of the men and women in top-level intercollegiate sports in the United States sustain at least one serious injury while playing their sport, and nearly 70 percent are disabled for two or more weeks. Nearly all players, both men and women, say that they play while they are hurt, and many experience chronic pain. Nixon notes that the rate of disabling injuries in the NFL is over three times greater than the rate among workers in high-risk construction jobs. The rates of disabling injuries vary from sport to sport, but they are high enough in many sports to constitute a health and medical problem as well as a social issue.

Young's research focuses on professional sport participation as work, and his data indicate that pro sports involving brutal body contact are the most violent and dangerous workplaces in the occupational world (Young, 1993). The "normal" experiences of elite male athletes in sports such as football, rugby, soccer, and ice hockey regularly lead to arthritis, concussions, bone fractures, torn ligaments, partial blindness, partial and full paralysis, and even death. Men and women athletes conform to norms about playing with pain and injury, but prevailing ideas about masculinity in many cultures create an emphasis on violence and risk-taking that makes men more vulnerable to serious injuries in sports (White and Young, 1997, 1999).

Waddington's research shows that the health benefits of playing sports are highest when participation involves rhythmic movements under conditions that can be controlled by the athletes themselves. The health costs are highest when participation occurs in highly competitive contact sports played under conditions that are outside the athletes' control. In other words, the violence inherent in power and performance sports takes a definite toll on the health of athletes.

Much of this research shows a close connection between dominant ideas about masculinity and the high rate of injuries in many sports. As one NHL coach explained, playing with pain and injuries is not only part of the ethos of power and performance sports but "at times your manhood is up for grabs. Playing hurt is a status thing. It's the simplest way of getting the respect of teammates, opponents, coaches" (in Farber, 1998b, p. 94). Furthermore, when the give-and-take of violence leads to injury and pain, some men learn to "suck it up" and stay in the game— partly because of what it means to be an athlete and partly because of what it means to be a man in their social world. Men who have learned to define *masculinity* so that they fear weakness and avoid emotional concern for others often use violence to avoid labels that challenge their masculinity. In fact, they sacrifice their bodies to live by this code of manhood. As long as some athletes continue to uncritically accept the norms of the sport ethic combined with dominance-based ideas about masculinity, they will define *violence* as action that adds "value" to their lives, rather than defining it as restricting, limiting, and sometimes life-threatening.

Controlling on-the-Field Violence

The roots of violence on the playing field are deep. They are grounded in overconformity to the sport ethic, processes of commercialization, and definitions of *masculinity*. Therefore, many men in power and performance sports resist efforts to control violence. They have come to think that their identities as athletes and men depend on doing violence and that success and financial rewards on the field depend on strategic violence.

The most difficult type of violence to control in sports is brutal body contact. It is grounded in the culture of power and performance sports and is tied strongly to a gender ideology that emphasizes physical dominance over others as important to manhood. Unfortunately, about 90 percent of the serious injuries in power and performance sports occur *within the rules* of those sports. This means that many men pay the price for their destructive definitions of *sports* and *masculinity*.

Efforts to control brutal body contact require changes in the culture of power and performance sports and the gender ideology that supports that culture. The best strategy to do this is to be relentless in calling attention to the dangers and absurdity of the actions and the language that men and women use to reproduce that culture. We need to keep accurate records and publish information on injuries and then tell parents about them before they enlist their children in the service of reproducing patriarchy and a gender ideology that jeopardizes health and development. We should calculate the cost of injuries due to brutal body contact and other types of violence in terms of medical expenses, lost work time and wages, days missed in college classes, disability payments, family problems, and even loss in life expectancy.

Controlling brutal body contact and certain forms of borderline violence is difficult. In basketball, for example, there is a fine line between a "hard foul," as encouraged by many coaches, and a flagrant or intentional foul, as defined by league rules. However, when enforced consistently, rules can limit some forms of violence. (Chuck Burton; AP/Wide World Photos)

It is easier to control borderline, quasi-criminal, and criminal violence in sports, although many people continue to resist taking necessary actions. Enforcers should be eliminated. How? Suspend them (and cut salaries) for at least three games for borderline violence and at least half the season for more serious types. Have the suspensions carry over into the next season if necessary, prevent teams from replacing suspended players on their rosters, and fine team owners and put the money into research on sports violence and injuries. Unless owners are fined and teams punished, they will simply replace one head-hunter with another. Owners and coaches know that some people will pay to see violence, so what is their incentive for controlling it unless they lose money when their players cross the line?

Assessing fines for violent players is generally ineffective. Fines of $5,000 mean nothing to a player who makes $1 million a year brutalizing people. They spend that much on phone calls telling their buddies about their latest victims. Don't fine—use unpaid suspensions. Suspensions prevent players from doing what they love to do. Suspensions separate them from the game that sustains their identities as athletes, and, if they cannot be replaced on rosters, the suspensions also hurt coaches and team owners, and they are the ones that have the power to discourage violence.

VIOLENCE OFF THE FIELD

When athletes in contact sports are arrested for violent crimes, many people assume that their violence off the field is related to the violent strategies they have learned and are rewarded for on the field. For example, *New York Times* columnist Robert Lipsyte says,

> Felony arrests among pro and college [male] athletes may or may not be rising, but better reporting makes it clear that many of them cannot turn off their aggressive behavior at the buzzer. (1999, p. 11)

Jessie Armstead, a linebacker in the NFL, says making the transition from a violent playing field to life off the field is not easy for many players:

> When you think about it, it is a strange thing that we do. During a game we want to kill each other. Then we're told to shake hands and drive home safely. Then a week later we try to kill each other again. (in Freeman, 1998, p. 1)

John Niland, a former NFL player, supports this:

> Any athlete who thinks he can be as violent as you can be playing football, and leave it all on the field, is kidding himself. (Falk, 1995, p. 12)

These quotes suggest that the violence used strategically on the field carries over into athletes' lives off the field. However, research on the carryover issue is difficult to do, and studies are rare. Even if data in a study show a high rate of off-the-field violence among athletes, this does not prove that carryover has occurred. People inclined to use violence in their lives may choose to play power and performance sports more often than other people do, or certain athletes may have had more nonsport experiences emphasizing violence as a way to cope with problems and conflicts. In other words, inclinations to use violence to solve problems may be high among certain people and may have little to do with playing contact sports.

Off-the-field violence among athletes may also be due to unique situational factors encountered by some athletes. For example, athletes with reputations for being tough on the playing field might receive encouragement from others to be tough on the streets. They may even be challenged to fights because of their reputations in sports. Athletes who grew up in neighborhoods with high crime rates may find that, when they return home, they are identified as "marks" by locals who push drugs or run scams to make money. If they hang out in those neighborhoods, they may attract locals who define them as "sellouts" to big money and corporate sponsors. Some of these locals would like nothing better than to take the athletes down a notch or two. If trouble occurs and an athlete is arrested for fighting in these circumstances, it is not accurate to say that it is due to violent actions learned in sports.

Research suggests that male athletes who have many years of experience in power and performance sports are more likely than recreational players or nonplayers to approve of off-the-field violence and to use violence when they play other sports (Bloom and Smith, 1996). These results are helpful, but they still do not say whether violence in hockey is a cause or an effect of violence that occurs in other spheres of the players' lives.

Assaults and Sexual Assaults by Athletes

Highly publicized cases of assault, sexual assault, rape, gang rape, and even murder that involve athletes who play power and performance sports have led many people to think that the violence in those sports carries over to personal relationships off the field, especially relationships with women. Information about the cases, including reliable statements made by assault and rape victims, often contains references to the athletic status and sport participation of the perpetrators (Benedict, 1997, 1998; Lefkowitz, 1997; Robinson, 1998). Furthermore, research on the conversations and biographies of athletes has presented powerful and shocking information suggesting that the social worlds created around men's power and performance sports subvert respect for women and promote the image of women as "game" to be pursued and conquered (Curry, 1991, 1996, 1998; Lefkowitz, 1997; Messner and Stevens, 2002; Nack and Munson, 1995; Reid, 1997). However, as noted in chapter 6, data on the arrest records of NFL players do not support the carryover hypothesis (Blumstein and Benedict, 1999).

How do we make sense of this? In a critical assessment of the debate about male athletes' violence against women, sport sociologist Todd Crosset (1999) reviewed all the published research on the issue. His review indicated that male intercollegiate athletes, in particular, seem to be involved in more sexual assaults than other male students, but the differences are not significant in any study, and they are often related to other factors, which makes differences difficult to interpret. Crosset concludes that trying to explain the violence of male athletes against women in terms of carryover from the violent, hypermasculine world of men's power and performance sports leads us to overlook important cultural and ideological issues as we study the problem of sexual assault. He also concludes that comparing assault rates of athletes with those of nonathletes distracts us from the following important points:

- Violence against women does occur.
- It is a serious problem.
- Male athletes are among the perpetrators of this violence.
- We must understand the problem within the context of sports if we wish to deter assaults perpetrated by athletes.

Building on the framework developed by Crosset, and combining it with other research on patterns of violence in all-male groups, I hypothesize that a combination of the following factors accounts for male athletes' violence against women:

1. Support from teammates and fellow athletes for the use of force as a strategy for "doing" masculinity in their lives and being a man in their relationships with women
2. Perceived cultural support for an emphasis on physical domination as a source of status in the community and as a basis for identity as a man and an athlete
3. Deviant overconformity to the norms of the sport ethic, to the point that it creates strong social bonds among teammates, strong feelings that others cannot understand them or their experiences in sports, and a strong sense of hubris (i.e., pride-driven arrogance)
4. Collective hubris among team members supporting the notions that those outside the fraternity of elite athletes do not deserve respect, that elite athletes can expect outsiders to defer to their wishes and demands, and that elite athletes live outside the norms of the general community
5. Support within their social world for the belief that women (apart from their own mothers and sisters) are "groupies" seeking status through relationships with elite athletes and that athletes need not take responsibility for the consequences of relationships with women

6. Institutional (team, athletic department, university, community) support for elite athletes, regardless of their actions
7. Institutional failure to hold elite athletes accountable when they violate community norms and rules

Research is needed on the relevance of these factors in an overall theory of assault and sexual assault perpetrated by male athletes. It is clear that male athletes do not target political leaders, corporate executives, and team owners in their off-the-field violence. With rare exceptions, they do not target mothers, coaches, or one another. Most often, the targets of violence are the people whom athletes define as unworthy of their respect, the people who athletes think cannot understand the meaning of their lives in elite sports, and the people who have characteristics directly opposed to the athletes' definitions of their own worth as athletes and as men. Therefore, common targets include many women, gay men, and "cocky straight" men in the community who publicly challenge an athlete's assumed status and privilege. Athletes' rates of violence may or may not be higher than those of other men, but our goal should be to understand violence *in the full social and cultural contexts in which it occurs.*

As noted in chapter 6, the norms and group dynamics in certain all-male sport groups encourage athletes to demean and humiliate those who don't come close to matching what they see as their own unique, elite status. In other words, off-the-field violence is not simply on-the-field violence that carries over to the rest of life. Instead, it is behavior grounded in complex social processes related to the social worlds in which athletes live, define their identities as athletes and as men, and deal with their social relationships. As athletes are increasingly being separated from the rest of the community, these processes become more important, if we wish to explain assault rates among athletes. The fact that elite athletes today are more separate from the rest of the community (on campus and in town) than ever before is an important issue. Until this separation is eliminated, assault will continue to be a problem, even if teams hire psychologists to assist athletes. This is a public issue in society as much as it is a personal problem among male athletes.

Control Versus Carryover

What about the possibility that athletes in power and performance sports learn to control expressions of off-the-field violence? Could it be that sport participation teaches people to control violent actions related to stress, defeat, hardship, and pain and enables them to avoid being violent off the field when they face adversity?

This possibility was explored in research that found a decrease in aggressive tendencies among male juvenile delinquents who received training in the philosophy and techniques of Tae Kwon Do (Trulson, 1986; summarized in chapter 6). The philosophy emphasized respect for self and others, confidence, physical fitness, self-control, honor, patience, and responsibility. Similar young men who received martial arts training *without* the philosophy actually measured higher on aggressive tendencies after a training period, and young men who participated in running, basketball, and football with standard adult supervision didn't change at all in terms of their aggressive tendencies.

French sociologist Loic Wacquant did one of the most provocative studies on this topic. For over three years, Wacquant trained and "hung out" at a traditional, highly structured, and reputable boxing gym in a black ghetto area in Chicago. During that time, he observed, interviewed, and documented the experiences and lives of more than fifty men who trained as professional boxers at the gym. He not only learned the craft of boxing but also became immersed in the social world in which the boxers trained. He found that the social world formed around this gym was one in which the boxers learned to value their craft and to become dedicated to the idea of being a professional boxer; they also learned to respect their fellow boxers and to accept the rules of sportsmanship that governed boxing as a profession. In a neighborhood where poverty and hopelessness promoted intimidation and violence all around them, these boxers accepted taboos against fighting outside the ring, they avoided street fights, and they internalized the controls necessary to follow a highly disciplined daily training schedule.

When Wacquant (1995a) asked the boxers about the connection between boxing and violence, the responses he heard challenged popular beliefs. Three of those responses were as follows:

> Boxin' doesn't jus' teach you violence. I think, boxin' teaches you discipline an' self-respect an' it's also teachin' you how to defen' yourself. . . . Anybody who feels that it teaches you violence is a person tha's really a, a *real incompetent mind* I think. (Twenty-four-year-old night security guard from a black neighborhood who had trained at the gym for eight years pp. 494–95)

> It's a skill. . . . I don't think violence and all, [shakes his head vigorously] I don't agree with that. I tell ya the truth: ever since I started boxing, I've been more of a mellow person. I've been more relaxed. . . . All my aggressions are taken out. In the gym I work out, I come home, someone come up to me and say "yer an asshole," I'm like, [with a smirk] "you're right!" You know, I'm *mellowed out.* (Twenty-four-year-old truck driver from a white ethnic neighborhood, p. 498)

> Man, the sports commentators an' the writers and stuff, they don't know nuthin' abou' the boxin' game. *They ignorant.* I be embarrassed to let somebody hear me say [chuckles in disbelief], "Boxing teach you violence." . . . Tha's showin' *their* ignorance. For one thin', they lookin' at it from a spectator point of view . . . on the *outsi' lookin' in,* but [the boxer's] *insi' lookin out.* (Twenty-eight-year-old part-time janitor, seven years in the ring, p. 489)

I do not include these statements here to promote professional boxing, a sport I think ought to be banned for health reasons. However, the

statements, along with other findings in the studies by Trulson and Wacquant, suggest that participation in sports, even martial arts and boxing, can encourage individuals to control violence. However, this control depends greatly on the conditions under which sport-participation occurs. *If* the social world formed around a sport promotes a mindset and norms emphasizing nonviolence, self-control, respect for self and others, physical fitness, patience, responsibility, and humility (the opposite of hubris), then athletes *may* learn to control violent behavior off the

Some sports, even at the youth level, use symbols and language that encourage orientations supportive of violence. The skull and crossbones decals on this player's helmet are awarded by coaches to players who make "big hits" and intimidate the opposition. (Jay Coakley)

REFLECT ON SPORTS

Violence on the Field
Does It Distort Our Ideas About Gender?

"Men are naturally superior to women": this statement arouses anger among many people today. However, many others still believe it. Furthermore, the hierarchical structure of gender relations in many cultures depends on this belief.

Political scientist Varda Burstyn (1999) argues that the "hypermasculine ideology of coercive entitlement" represented by boxers, football players, and other men in heavy contact sports links them and their sports to millions of other men around the world. Violence on the field, she says, reaffirms an ideology that assumes hierarchical distinctions between men and women and people of different races, ethnicities, and social classes.

Power and performance sports emphasize *difference* in terms of power and might, they emphasize *control* through the domination of others, and they emphasize *status* as dependent on victories over others. In fact, in the minds of many people, power and performance sports "naturalize" differences, which take the form of rankings, and present hierarchical differences as inevitable—as the way things are and should be in the world. These people say that success depends on being "ranked." They use the ritualized actions and narratives of power and performance sports as the basis for the stories they tell about themselves, social arrangements, and what is important in life. They may

not play these sports, but their lives are influenced by the ideology that is promoted by myths about large, strong, record-setting, and often violent champions (Burstyn, 1999).

This ideology is so important in U.S. culture that male boxers are paid up to $50 million dollars for three to thirty-six minutes of brutalizing each other. Why are heavyweight boxers paid more than any other athletes in the world for what they do? Apparently, people will pay big money to promote the idea that one-on-one violent confrontations are "nature in action," and, when it comes to basic human survival, only the fittest, strongest, and most violent are left standing (even though they may have lost millions of brain cells in the process).

Boxing, along with other power and performance sports, celebrate, among other things, the use of strength and violence in a quest for victory over others. At the same time, they reproduce an ideology of masculinity stressing the same factors.

The irony in this approach is that, if gender were really grounded in biology and nature, there would be no need for such ideas about males and females to be taught and preserved through sports—they would just come naturally to boys and girls without our painting their bedrooms different colors before they are born.

· ·

field. Those most likely to benefit seem to be young men who need structured challenges and firm guidance dedicated to making them respect themselves when they do avoid violence.

Unfortunately, these conditions are rare in many sports. Instead, most sport cultures emphasize hostility, physical domination, and a willingness to sacrifice one's body and well-being for competitive success. They are also organized to produce hubris, separate athletes from the community, and encourage athletes to think that others do not deserve their respect.

More studies are needed, especially those that dig into the social worlds of athletes in particular sports and outline the meanings athletes attach to their actions and to the place of violence in their worlds. Studies should also focus on issues of identity, group dynamics among athletes, ideological issues, and social factors associated with the incidence of violence. The aggression and violence learned in certain sports do not inevitably carry over to other relationships and settings, nor does sport participation automatically teach people to control violence. Instead of

But the behaviors of males and females don't come naturally, so those whose privilege depends on maintaining a gender ideology that emphasizes difference see power and performance sports as consistent with their interests.

Sociologist Michael Messner discovered this when he asked a thirty-two-year-old man in a professional job what he thought about the recent promotion of a woman to a high position in his organization. The man replied with these words:

> A woman can do the same job I do—maybe even be my boss. But I'll be *damned* if she can go out on the [football] field and take a hit from Ronnie Lott. (1992, p. 168; note that Lott was a football player with a reputation for hitting others very hard)

Messner noted that, even though this man could not "take a hit" from Lott either, he identified with Lott as a man, and then he used that identification to claim that men are superior to women because of men's "superior" ability to do violence.

This is why some men celebrate sports in which aggression is commonplace. They want to keep alive the notion of difference because it privileges them in the gender order. These are usually the same people who reject rules against fighting. For example, when rules were passed in the 1990s to partially limit fighting in hockey, Tie Domi, a player with a reputation for doing violence complained:

> If you take out fighting, what comes next? Do we eliminate checking? Pretty soon, we will all be out there in dresses and skirts. (Domi, 1992, p. C3)

Domi's point was that, unless men can do violence in hockey, there will be nothing that makes them different from women, and the perception is that nothing is worse for a man than being like women—except, perhaps, being gay.

What happens to gender ideology when women play power and performance sports and use violence on the field? On the one hand, this contradicts the ideological notion that women are frail and vulnerable. On the other hand, it reaffirms values and experiences that have worked to the disadvantage of many women. This means that women should be careful not to buy into the same emphasis on physical domination used by some men in sports. It is important for women to find ways to be strong and assertive without being aggressive and violent.

The social impact of the ideology reproduced in connection with sports goes far beyond the off-the-field behavior of the athletes themselves. It affects the cultural context in which we all live—sometimes in destructive ways. *What do you think?*

- -

looking for examples of carryover or control, perhaps we should be looking for cultural connections between sports and ideologies associated with high rates of violence. This is discussed in the box "Violence on the Field."

VIOLENCE AMONG SPECTATORS

Do sports incite violence among spectators? This question is important, because sports and sport events capture considerable public attention in communities around the world. Spectators number in the billions. To answer this question, we must distinguish between watching sports on television and attending events in person.

Violence Among Television Viewers

Most sport watching occurs in front of the television. Television viewers may be emotionally expressive during games and matches. They may even get angry, but we know little about whether their anger is expressed through violence directed at friends and family members at home.

We also do not know much about violence among those who watch sports in more public settings, such as bars and pubs. My sense is that most viewers are supportive of one another and restrict their emotional expressions to verbal comments. When they do express anger, they nearly always direct it at the characters in the mediated event, rather than at fellow viewers. Even when fellow viewers define outbursts of emotions as too loud or inappropriate, their efforts to settle a fan down are supportive rather than aggressive. When fans from opposing teams are in the same bar, there are usually other sources of mutual identification, which keep them from identifying each other as targets of aggression, and they tend to confine expressions of their differences to verbal comments.

There have been cases when people, usually men, watching sports in a bar or other public place have joined in celebratory violence following victories in championship games. However, there are no studies of this phenomenon or of how watching the event on television may influence celebratory actions.

Violence at Sport Events

Spectators attending noncontact sport events seldom engage in violence. They may be emotionally expressive, but violence directed at fellow fans, players, coaches, referees, ushers, or police are very rare. The attack and wounding of Monica Seles in 1993 stands out as one of the only violent incidents at a noncontact sport event, and that had more to do with celebrity stalking than with sports. Of course, there are occasions when fans use hostile words or engage in minor skirmishes when a drink is dropped onto another's head, but such cases of violence are often controlled quickly by the fans themselves.

Spectators attending contact sports tend to be vocal and emotional, but most of them have not been involved in violent actions (see figure 7.3).

"Hey, watch it, pal! You stepped on my foot."

FIGURE 7.3   The language used by some spectators often refers to violence, but it is not known if such language actually incites violent actions.

However, crowd violence does occur, and it has occurred with enough regularity and seriousness in certain sports to be defined as a problem for law enforcement, as well as a social problem involving personal injuries, deaths, and property destruction. This is true for the United States and Canada, as well as for other parts of the world (Young, 2002 b).

Historical Background   Media reports of violent actions at sport events around the world, especially at soccer matches, have increased our awareness of crowd violence. However, crowd violence is not new. Although data documenting the actions of sport spectators through the ages is scarce, research suggests that spectator violence did occur in the past and that much of it would make crowd violence today seem rare and tame in comparison (Dunning, 1999; Guttmann, 1986, 1998; Scheinin, 1994; Young, 2000). Roman events during the first five centuries of the first Christian millennium contained especially brutal examples of crowd violence (Guttmann, 1986, 1998). Spectators during the medieval period were not much better, although levels of violence decreased in the late medieval period. With the emergence of modern sports, violence among sport spectators decreased further, but it remained common by today's standards. For example, a baseball game in 1900 was described in this way:

> Thousands of gunslinging Chicago Cubs fans turned a Fourth of July doubleheader into a shoot-out at the OK Corral, endangering the lives of players and fellow spectators. Bullets sang, darted, and whizzed over players' heads as the rambunctious fans fired round after round whenever the Cubs scored against the gun-shy Philadelphia Phillies. The visiting team was so intimidated it lost both games . . . at Chicago's West Side Grounds. (Nash and Zullo, 1986, p. 133)

The account continues to explain that, when the Cubs scored six runs in the sixth inning of the first game, guns were fired around the stadium to the point that gunsmoke made it difficult to see the field. When the Cubs tied the score in the ninth inning, fans again fired guns, and hundreds of them shot holes in the roof of the grandstand, causing splinters to fly onto their heads. As the game remained tied during three extra innings, fans pounded the seats with the butts of their guns and fired in unison every time the Phillies' pitcher began his windup to throw a pitch. It rattled him so much that the Cubs scored on a wild pitch. After the score, a vocal and heavily armed Cub fan stood up and shouted, "Load! Load at will! Fire!" Fans around the stadium emptied the rest of their ammunition in a final explosive volley.

Between 1900 and the early 1940s, crowd violence was common: bottles and other objects were thrown at players and umpires, and World Series games were disrupted by fans angered by umpires' calls or the actions of opposing players (Scheinin, 1994). Players feared being injured by spectators as much as they feared the "bean balls" thrown regularly at their heads by opposing pitchers. During the 1950s and 1960s, high school basketball and football games in some U.S. cities were the sites of local youth gang wars. Spectators, including students, used chains, switchblade knives, brass knuckles, and tire irons to attack each other. During the late 1960s and early 1970s, some high school games in Chicago were closed to the public and played early on Saturday mornings, because the regularly scheduled games had become common sites for crowd violence, much of it related to racial and ethnic tensions.

These examples are not meant to minimize the existence or seriousness of crowd violence today. They are mentioned here to counter the argument that violence is a bigger problem today than it was in the past and that coercive social control tactics are needed to prevent what some people see as a growing decline of civility among fans. There are obnoxious and violent fans today, and they present problems, but they should not be viewed as unprecedented threats to the social order.

Celebratory Violence Oddly enough, some of the most serious forms of crowd violence associated with sports occur in connection with the celebrations that follow victories in important games. When these occur inside stadiums, as in the case of middle-class, white college students tearing down expensive goalposts after football victories or ransacking seats and throwing seat pads and other objects on the field, they often are defined as displays of youthful exuberance and loyalty to the university or community. However, as property destruction moves outside the stadium into the surrounding community and involves large crowds of people, including those who did not attend the games, violence becomes more serious and is defined as a major law enforcement problem.

Unfortunately, scholars in the sociology of sport have not studied this type of violence (see figure 7.4). Little is known about it other than what is contained in newspaper reports, and there have been no systematic attempts to collect data and develop theories about the social dynamics of celebratory violence.

Research and Theories About Crowd Violence
Ironically, researchers in the United States have

FIGURE 7.4   We need research on so-called celebratory riots. Research on other forms of collective action suggests that celebratory riots may not be as spontaneous and unplanned as many people think.

generally ignored violence at sport events, even though violence is more common in the United States than in other industrial countries. Apparently, violence at sport events has not been seen as significant enough, relative to other forms of violence, to attract research attention. The research that does exist has focused primarily on issues of race relations, and little attention has been given to other issues.

British and other European scholars have done most of the research on crowd violence, and most of their studies have focused on soccer and "soccer hooliganism." Studies grounded in social psychological theories have emphasized that displays of intimidation and aggression at soccer matches have involved ritual violence, consisting of fantasy-driven status posturing by young males who want to be defined as tough and manly (Marsh, 1982; Marsh and Campbell, 1982). These studies are interesting, and they describe classic examples of ritualistic forms of "aggro" (as it is called in the studies), but they sometimes understate the serious and occasionally deadly violence perpetrated by soccer fans, especially during pre- and postgame activities.

Research inspired by various forms of conflict theory has emphasized that violence at soccer matches is an expression of the alienation of disenfranchised working-class men (Taylor, 1982a, b, 1987). In addition to losing control over the conditions of their work lives, these men also feel they have lost control of the recently commercialized clubs that sponsor elite soccer in England. This research helps us understand that violence may be associated with class conflict in society, but it does not explain why violence at soccer matches has not increased proportionately in connection with the declining power of the working class in England.

Research inspired by interactionist and critical theories has emphasized a variety of factors, including the importance of understanding the history and dynamics of the working-class and youth subcultures in British society and how those subcultures have been influenced by the professionalization and commercialization of society as a whole, and soccer in particular (Clarke, 1978; Critcher, 1979). However, the data presented in this research are not very strong, and more work is needed to develop critical analyses of crowd violence across various situations.

Figurational theory has inspired the most research on crowd violence. The work of those using a figurational approach represents a synthesis of approaches grounded in biology, psychology, sociology, and history. Much of this work, summarized by Dunning (1999) and Young (2000) emphasizes that soccer hooliganism is grounded in long-term historical changes, which have affected working-class men, their relationships with each other and their families, and their definitions of community, violence, and masculinity. Taken together, these changes have created a context in which soccer has come to represent the collective turf and identity of people in local communities and the identity of the British people as a whole. In either case, soccer becomes a site for defending and/or asserting community and identity through violence. Figurational research has provided valuable historical information and thoughtful analyses of the complex social processes of which soccer hooliganism is a part. It has also been used as a reference for those who have formulated some of the recent policies of social control related to soccer crowds in England and around Europe.[1]

General Factors Related to Violence at Sport Events   Crowd violence at sport events is a complex social phenomenon related to three factors:

1. The action in the sport event itself
2. The crowd dynamics and the situation in which the spectators watch the event
3. The historical, social, economic, and political contexts in which the event is planned and played

---

[1]The causes of crowd violence at British soccer games, and at games in Europe and South America, are far too complex to explain in this chapter. Those interested in this phenomenon should consult the following: Adang, 1993; Armstrong, 1998; Dunning, 1999; Giulianotti, 1994; Giulianotti et al., 1994; Haynes, 1993; Murphy et al., 1990; Pilz, 1996; Roversi, 1994; Taylor, 1982a, b, 1987; Weed, 2002.

VIOLENCE AND ACTION IN THE EVENT   If spectators perceive players' actions on the field as violent, they are more likely to engage in violent acts during and after games (Smith, 1983). This point is important, because spectators' perceptions often are influenced by the way in which events are promoted. If an event is hyped in terms of violent images, spectators are more likely to perceive violence during the event itself, and then they are more likely to be violent themselves. This leads some people to argue that promoters and the media have a responsibility to advertise events in terms of the action and drama expected, not the blood and violence.

Another important factor in the event is the actions of the officials. Data suggest that, when fans believe that a crucial goal or a victory has been "stolen" by an unfair or a clearly incompetent decision made by a referee or an umpire, the likelihood of violence during and following the event increases (Murphy et al., 1990). This is why it is important to have competent officials at crucial games and matches and why it is important for them to control game events, so that actions perceived as violent are held to a minimum. The knowledge that fan aggression may be precipitated by a crucial call late in a close, important contest puts heavy responsibility on the officials' shoulders.

VIOLENCE, CROWD DYNAMICS, AND SITUATIONAL FACTORS   The characteristics of a crowd and the immediate situation associated with a sport event also influence patterns of action among spectators. Spectator violence is likely to vary with one or more of the following factors:

- Crowd size and the standing or seating patterns among spectators
- Composition of the crowd in terms of age, sex, social class, and racial/ethnic mix
- Meaning and importance of the event for spectators
- History of the relationship between the teams and between spectators

- Crowd-control strategies used at the event (police, attack dogs, surveillance cameras, or other security measures)
- Alcohol consumption by the spectators
- Location of the event (neutral site or home site of one of the opponents)
- Spectators' reasons for attending the event and what they want to happen at the event
- Importance of the team as a source of identity for spectators (class identity, ethnic or national identity, regional or local identity, club or gang identity, etc.)

We will not discuss each of these factors in detail, but the following comparison of two game situations illustrates how many of them might be related to spectator violence.

The *location of an event* is important because it influences who attends and how they travel. If the stadium is generally accessed by car, if spectators for the visiting team are limited due to travel expense, and if tickets are expensive, it is likely that people attending the game have a vested interest in maintaining order and avoiding violence. On the other hand, if large groups of people travel to the game in buses or trains, and if tickets are relatively cheap and many of the spectators are young people more interested in having a memorable experience than in maintaining the status quo, confrontations between people looking for exciting action increase, and so does the possibility of violence. If groups of fans looking for excitement have consumed large amounts of alcohol, the possibility of violence increases greatly.

If spectators are respected as patrons rather than treated as bodies to be controlled, and if stadium norms emphasize service as opposed to social control, people are less likely to engage in defensive and confrontational actions, which could lead to violence. If the stadium or arena is crowded and if the crowd itself is comprised mostly of young men rather than couples and families, there is a greater chance for confrontations and violence, especially if the event is seen as a special rivalry whose outcome has status implications for the schools, communities, or nations represented by the teams.

Spectator violence, when it does occur, takes many forms. There have been celebratory riots among the fans of the winning team, fights between fans of opposing teams, random property destruction carried out by fans of the losing team as they leave town, panics incited by a perceived threat unrelated to the contest itself, and planned confrontations between groups using the event as a convenient place to face off with each other as they seek to enhance their status and reputation or as they reaffirm their ethnic, political, class, national, local, or gang identities.

Whenever thousands of people get together for an occasion intended to generate collective emotions and excitement, it is not surprising that crowd dynamics and circumstances influence the actions of individuals and groups. This is especially true at sport events where collective action is easily fueled by what social psychologists call *emotional contagion*. Under conditions of emotional contagion, norms are formed rapidly and may be followed in a nearly spontaneous manner by large numbers of people. Although this does not always lead to violence, it increases the possibility of potentially violent confrontations between groups of fans and between fans and agents of social control, such as the police.

VIOLENCE AND THE OVERALL CONTEXT IN WHICH EVENTS OCCUR   Sport events do not occur in social vacuums. When spectators attend events, they take with them the histories, issues, controversies, and ideologies of the communities and cultures in which they live. They may be racists who want to harass those they identify as targets for discrimination. They may come from ethnic neighborhoods and want to express and reaffirm their ethnicity. They may resent negative circumstances in their lives and want to express their bitterness. They may be members of groups or gangs in which status is gained partly through fighting. They may be powerless and

Crowds at sport events are often characterized by strong emotions. When these emotions are expressed in violent ways, other fans may intervene to control violence. (John Leyba, *The Denver Post*)

alienated and looking for ways to be noticed and defined as socially important. They may be young men who believe that manhood is achieved through violence and domination over others. Or they may be living lives so devoid of significance and excitement that they want to create a memorable occasion they can discuss boastfully with friends for years to come. In other words, when thousands of spectators attend a sport event, their behaviors are grounded in factors far beyond the event and the stadium.

When tension and conflict are intense and widespread in a community or society, sport events may become sites for confrontations. For example, some of the worst spectator violence in the United States has been grounded in racial tensions aggravated by highly publicized rivalries between high schools whose students come from different racial or ethnic backgrounds (Guttmann, 1986). Where housing segregation has led to heavily segregated schools, the racial and ethnic conflicts within communities have contributed to confrontations before, during, and after games. Gangs, some of whose members have weapons, may stake out territories around a sport stadium, so that sport events become scenes for displays of gang power. Similarly, when the "ultras," organized groups of fans prevalent in Italy during the 1990s, attended soccer games, they often used violence to express their loyalty to peers and the teams they followed (Roversi, 1994).

In his classic book *Power and Innocence: A Search for the Sources of Violence*, Rollo May

REFLECT ON SPORTS

Terrorism
Planned Political Violence at Sport Events

The visibility of certain sport events, and the density of the crowds attending many events, make sport venues a possible target of terrorist attacks. After the murderous 9/11 attacks on the World Trade Center and the Pentagon, people in the United States have a greatly heightened awareness of terrorism and its possible impact on their lives.

Since 9/11, those in charge of sport events have initiated security measures at arenas and stadiums. People now may be searched as they enter venues, and there are new rules regulating what spectators may bring to events. However, most security changes have taken place behind the scenes in the form of bomb searches, electronic surveillance, and undercover tactics.

As sport teams and venues deal with security issues, their costs have increased between a few thousand dollars at smaller venues to well over $50,000 per event at larger venues. Furthermore, professional teams and some college teams face massive increases in their insurance bills. For example, an NFL stadium that once paid $250,000 annually for insurance could now have an annual bill that exceeds $1 million (Hiestand, 2002). During the 2004 Summer Olympic Games in Athens, about $600 million was budgeted for security.

Although the threat of political terrorism may be new in the minds of people in the United States, others around the world have long lived with the threat and reality of terrorism in their everyday lives. Furthermore, terrorism is not new to sports. Just over

thirty years ago during the early morning hours of September 5, 1972, members of a Palestinian terrorist group called Black September entered the Olympic Village in Munich, Germany. Dressed in athletic warm-up suits and carrying sport bags full of grenades and automatic weapons, they made their way to a bedroom that housed Israeli athletes participating in the Summer Olympic Games. They broke into the room, shot and killed a wrestling coach and a weightlifter from Israel, and captured nine Israeli athletes, one of whom lived in the United States.

After a twenty-one-hour standoff and a poorly planned rescue attempt, seventeen people were dead—ten Israeli athletes and one coach, one West German police officer, and five terrorists. Other terrorists involved were sought out and killed by Israeli commandos. The Olympics were suspended for a day, but events resumed and the Olympics were completed with the planned closing ceremonies. About $2 million had been spent on security during the Olympics in Munich.

Although this case of terrorism has been remembered by those responsible for planning subsequent Olympic Games, it has not been formally remembered in the media coverage of subsequent Olympics. The reasons for overlooking this event are complex, but it is clear that many people do not want their favorite sport events disrupted or defined in connection with the nasty realities of everyday life, even though

(1972) observed that all human beings need a means of achieving a sense of personal significance. Significance, he said, is best achieved when people are in control of their lives, but, when people are powerless and without resources, "violence may be the only way [they] can achieve a sense of significance." This may partially explain the violent behavior of young, predominantly male soccer fans around the world. At least some of these young spectators

perceive violence as a means of achieving a sense of significance. After all, violence forces others to take notice and respond to the perpetrator's existence. This is certainly not the only factor underlying violence among fans, but it is part of a historical, social, political, and economic context that we must understand when explaining violence among spectators.

Finally, it must be noted that nearly all crowd violence involves men. This suggests that future

This seven-year-old girl is playing catch on the sidelines of a boys' baseball game in Afghanistan. She is learning early in life that sports cannot be separated from the violence in her everyday life. (Wally Santana; AP/Wide World Photos)

sports cannot be separated from the world in which they exist.

Politically based terrorism is now a part of our lives, and sports cannot be separated from the policies, events, and material conditions of life that create deeply felt resentment and hatred around the world. This means that it is important for all of us to learn more about the world in which we live and how we can transform it to make peace more likely. This will take time and commitment on our part, and it won't be easy to change the conditions that precipitate terrorism. In the meantime, none of us can escape the threat of terrorism, not even at the sport events we attend. *What do you think?*

research on this topic must consider the role of masculinity in crowd dynamics and the actions of particular segments of crowds (Hughson, 2000). Female fans generally do not tip over cars and set them on fire or throw chairs through windows during so-called celebratory riots. They may become involved in fights, but not nearly to the same extent as men do. Crowd violence may be as much a gender issue as it is a racial or social class issue, and controlling it may involve changing notions of masculinity as much as hiring additional police to patrol the sidelines at the next game.

Control of Crowd Violence Effective efforts to control spectator violence are based on an awareness of each of the three factors previously listed. *First,* the fact that perceived violence on the field positively influences crowd violence indicates a need to control violence among players during events. If fans do not define the actions of players as violent, the likelihood of crowd violence decreases. Furthermore, fans' perceptions of violence are likely to decrease if events are not hyped as violent confrontations between hostile opponents. Players and coaches could be used to make public announcements that defuse hostility and emphasize the skills of the athletes involved in the event. High-profile fans for each team could make similar announcements. The use of competent and professionally trained officials is also important. When officials maintain control of a game and make calls the spectators see as fair, they decrease the likelihood of spectator violence grounded in anger and perceived injustice. These referees also could meet with both teams before the event and calmly explain the need to leave hostilities in the locker rooms. Team officials could organize pregame unity rituals involving an exchange of team symbols and displays of respect between opponents. These rituals could be given media coverage, so that fans could see that athletes do not view opponents with hostility.

Second, an awareness of crowd dynamics and the conditions that precipitate violence is critical. Preventive measures are important. The needs and rights of spectators must be known and respected. Crowd-control officials must be well trained, so that they know how to intervene in potentially disruptive situations without creating defensive reactions and increasing the chances of violence. Alcohol consumption should be regulated realistically, as has been done in many facilities around the world. Facilities should be safe and organized, to enable spectators to move around while limiting contact between hostile fans of opposing teams. Exits should be accessible and clearly marked, and spectators should not be herded like animals before or after games. Encouraging attendance by families is important in lowering the incidence of violence.

Third, an awareness of the historical, social, economic, and political issues that often underlie crowd violence is also important. Restrictive law-and-order responses to crowd violence may be temporarily effective, but they will not eliminate the underlying tensions and conflicts that often fuel violence. Policies dealing with oppressive forms of inequality, economic problems, unemployment, a lack of political representation, racism, and distorted definitions of *masculinity* in the community and in society as a whole are needed. These are the factors often at the root of tensions, conflicts, and violence. As noted in the box "Terrorism," dealing with the threat of political terrorism at sports events also requires an awareness of these factors on a global level.

Also needed are efforts to establish connections between teams and the communities in which they are located. These connections can be used to defuse potentially dangerous feelings or plans among groups of spectators or community residents. This does not mean that teams merely need better public relations. There must be *actual* connections among the teams, the facilities, and the communities in which they exist. Players and coaches need to be engaged in community service. Owners must be visible supporters of community events and programs. Teams must develop programs to assist in the development of local neighborhoods, especially those around their home stadium or arena.

The goal of these guidelines is to assist in the creation of antiviolence norms among spectators. This is difficult to do, but not impossible. Over the long run, it is more effective than using metal detectors, moving games to distant locations away from either team's home, hiring scores of police, patrolling the stands, using video cameras for surveillance, and scheduling games in the early morning on Saturdays so that crowds will be sparse. Of course, some of these tactics can be effective, but they destroy part of the enjoyment of attending events, and they restrict attendance access for many people. I see them as last resorts or temporary measures taken only to provide time to promote the development of new spectator norms.

SUMMARY

DOES VIOLENCE IN SPORTS AFFECT OUR LIVES?

Violence in sports is an important and highly publicized topic. Violence in the form of excessive physical force that causes or has the potential to cause harm or destruction is not new to sports; however, as people see it as something that can be controlled, they deal with it as a problem.

Violence in sports ranges from brutal body contact to criminal violence, and it is linked with deviant overconformity to the sport ethic, money and commercialization, and cultural definitions of *masculinity*. It has become institutionalized in most contact sports for both men and women as a strategy for competitive success, despite the fact that it causes considerable pain and injury among athletes. The use of enforcers is an example of the extreme form of this institutionalization. Controlling on-the-field violence has been difficult, especially in men's contact sports, because it is often tied to the way athletes see themselves as athletes and as men.

Male athletes in contact sports learn to use violence and intimidation as strategic tools, but it is not known if they carry over these strategies into off-the-field settings and relationships. Among males, learning to use violence as a tool within a sport is frequently tied to the reaffirmation of a form of masculinity that emphasizes a willingness to risk personal safety and a desire to intimidate others. If males who participate in certain sports learn to perceive this orientation as natural or appropriate, then sports may intensify serious forms of off-the-field violence, including assault and sexual assault. However, such learning is not automatic, and men may, under certain circumstances, even learn to control violence as they play sports.

The most important impact of violence in sports may be how people use it to reaffirm an ideology of the "natural superiority of men," based in the belief that an ability to engage in violence is part of the essence of being a man.

Female athletes in contact sports also engage in aggressive acts, but little is known about how those acts and the willingness to engage in them are linked to the identities of women athletes at different levels of competition. At this time, many women seem to prefer an emphasis on supportive connections between teammates and opponents, as well as on pleasure and participation in sports. Therefore, aggression and violence do not occur as often or in connection with the same dynamics in their sports as in men's sports.

Violence among spectators is influenced by violence on the field of play, crowd dynamics, the situation at the event itself, and the overall historical and cultural contexts in which spectators live. Isolated cases of violence probably are best controlled by improved crowd management, but chronic violence among spectators usually signals that something needs to be changed in the way certain sports are defined and played or in the actual social, economic, or political structures of the community or society.

Terrorism in the form of planned political violence at sport events is rare, but the threat of terrorism has altered the policies and procedures at many sport venues. The terrorist attack at the 1972 Olympic Games reminds us that global issues influence our lives, even when we attend our favorite sport events. Just as violence in sports affects our lives, the social conditions in the rest of our lives affect violence in sports.

 ## SUGGESTED READINGS

Benedict, J. 1997. *Public heroes, private felons: Athletes and crimes against women.* Boston: Northeastern University Press (exposé providing information about sexual assaults perpetrated primarily by professional and college football players in the United States; analysis condemns sport organizations for coddling deviant athletes but says little about how the culture of sports is related to deviance).

Burstyn, V. 1999. *The rites of men: Manhood, politics, and the culture of sport.* Toronto: University of Toronto Press (chapter 4, "Organized Violence and Men's Sport," and chapter 5, "The Reproduction of Hypermasculinity" represent a feminist discussion of why many sports are violent and how violent sports affect the lives of both men and women).

Crosset, T. W., J. R. Benedict, and M. A. McDonald. 1995. Male student-athletes reported for sexual assault: Survey of campus police departments and judicial affairs offices. *Journal of Sport and Social Issues* 19 (2): 126–40 (contains original data from U.S. universities and provides an overview and critique of published accounts of sexual assault and sports; very helpful in discussions of this topic).

Dunning, E. 1999. *Sport matters: Sociological studies of sport, violence, and civilization.* London: Routledge (in chapters 6 and 7, figurational theory is used to guide an analysis of soccer hooliganism around the world and sports crowd violence in North America).

Messner, M. A., and M. A. Stevens. 2002. Scoring without consent: Confronting male athletes' violence against women. In *Paradoxes of youth and sport* (pp. 225–40), edited by M. Gatz, M. A. Messner, and S. J. Ball-Rokeach. Albany, NY: State University of New York Press (brief but thorough and thoughtful overview of issues and research related to male athletes' violence against women).

Robinson, L. 1998. *Crossing the line: Violence and sexual assault in Canada's national sport.* Toronto: McClelland & Stewart (journalistic exposé of the forms of violence that exist on and off the ice in Canadian hockey; general critique of the rape culture of the hockey locker room and a hockey culture that supports expressions of violence by players and coaches).

Sugden, J. 1996. *Boxing and society: An international analysis.* Manchester, NY: University of Manchester Press (detailed, insightful analysis of boxing as an element of cultures around the world; the analysis puts the violence of boxing into context as it focuses on the sport's social, economic, and historical roots and the

moral, ethical, and political debates that it has evoked).

Young, K. 2000. Sport and violence. In *Handbook of sports studies* (pp. 382–407), edited by J. Coakley and E. Dunning. London: Sage (overview of manifestations and explanations of sports violence among spectators and players; excellent analysis of issues related to policing sports violence).

Young, K. 2002. From "sports violence" to "sports crime": Aspects of violence, law, and gender in the sports process. In *Paradoxes of youth and sport* (pp. 207–24), edited by M. Gatz, M. A. Messner, and S. J. Ball-Rokeach. Albany, NY: State University of New York Press (comprehensive yet concise review of cases and studies of athlete/participant violence in North America; references to nearly all major work on this topic).

Young, K. 2002. Standard deviations: An update on North American crowd disorder. *Sociology of Sport Journal* 19 (3): 237–75 (comprehensive yet concise review of cases and studies of spectator violence in North America; references to nearly all major work on this topic).

WEBSITE RESOURCES

Note: Websites often change. The following URLs were current when this book was printed. Please check our website (www.mhhe.com/coakley8e) for updates and additions.

www.mhhe.com/coakley8e Information and critique of instinct theory and frustration-aggression theory as applied to violence in sports; discussion of cultural patterning theory and violence associated with sports.

www.sportinsociety.org/mvp.html The Mentors in Violence Prevention—MVP—Program is a gender violence prevention and education program based at Northeastern University's Center for the Study of Sport in Society; it is designed to enlist high school, collegiate, and professional athletes in the effort to prevent all forms of men's violence against women.

www.ed.gov/databases/ERIC_Digests/ed316547.html Summary of basic information about violence in sports; created by ERIC, the Educational Resources Information Center.

www.ncava.org National Coalition Against Violent Athletes; news, statistics, updates, and information about prevention programs.

www.harassmentinsport.com Sport Canada sponsors this site, which provides information and links to sites on sexual harassment in sports.

http://conventions.coe.int/Treaty/EN/cadreprincipal. htm Site for the Council of Europe; Document 120 contains the council's official position on "spectator violence and misbehavior at sports events and in particular at football matches."

www.noviolence.com Presents a campaign to curb fan violence in soccer stadiums; links to other useful sites, as well as information about the campaign.

www.footballhooligans.org.uk Links and commentary discussing the myths and the reality of disruptive and violent actions in connection with soccer around the world, especially in Europe.

(Marc Piscotty; Rocky Mountain News)

Gender and Sports

Does Equity Require Ideological Changes?

EVERY GIRL SHOULD BE given the opportunity to participate in a sport she loves. The experience will teach her valuable lessons . . . and will give her confidence to strive for success in sport and life.

—Julie Foudy, captain of the U.S. National Soccer Team and President of the Women's Sports Foundation

 Online Learning Center Resources

Visit *Sports in Society*'s Online Learning Center at **www.mhhe.com/coakley8e** for additional information and study material for this chapter, including

- Self-grading quizzes
- Learning objectives
- Related websites
- Additional readings

A complete outline is available online at
www.mhhe.com/coakley8e.

. . . ALL MY LIFE, I believed that I couldn't show weakness. I couldn't pull myself out if I was hurt, I couldn't let people say, "She's just a girl." . . . I had to be tougher [than men], because only then did you get respect.

—**Lauren Arase, Goalie for NCAA soccer champions**

Gender and gender relations are central topics for those of us who study sports in society. We realize that it is important to explain why most sports around the world have been defined as men's activities, why half the world's population generally was excluded or discouraged from participating in many sports through most of the twentieth century, and why there have been such major changes in women's participation since the mid-1970s. We also want to explain the relationship between sports and popular beliefs about masculinity and femininity and homosexuality and heterosexuality. Although gender issues underlie many topics discussed in this book, a separate chapter is necessary to identify the full significance of gender relations and sports.

When people discuss gender relations and sports, they usually focus on issues related to fairness and equity, as well as to ideology and culture. *Fairness and equity issues* revolve around topics such as

- Sport participation patterns among women
- Gender inequities in participation opportunities, support for athletes, and jobs in coaching and administration
- Strategies for achieving equal opportunities for girls and women

Ideological and cultural issues revolve around topics such as

- The production and reproduction of gender ideology in connection with sports
- The ways in which prevailing gender ideology constrains the lives of women and men and subverts the achievement of gender equity
- The cultural changes required to achieve gender equity and democratic access to participation in sports

The goal of this chapter is to discuss these two sets of issues and to show that, even though many people deal with them separately, they go hand in hand in real life. We cannot ignore either one if we are seeking fairness as we interact with others and as we do sports in our lives.

PARTICIPATION AND EQUITY ISSUES

The single most dramatic change in the world of sports over the past generation has been the increased participation of girls and women. This has occurred mostly in wealthy postindustrial nations. Changes have occurred in traditional, labor-intensive, poor nations as well, but many factors have kept them from being revolutionary in scope. Despite resistance in some countries, girls and women around the world now participate in a variety of school, community, and club programs, which did not exist thirty-five years ago.

Reasons for Increased Participation

Since the early 1970s, five factors have accounted for dramatic increases in sport participation among girls and women:

1. New opportunities
2. Government equal rights legislation
3. The global women's rights movement
4. The health and fitness movement
5. Increased media coverage of women in sports

New Opportunities   New participation opportunities account for most of the increased sports participation among girls and women over the past three decades. Prior to the mid-1970s, many girls and women did not play sports for one simple reason: teams and programs did not exist. Young women today may not realize it, but the opportunities they enjoy in their schools and communities were not available to most of their mothers. Teams and programs developed since the late 1970s have uncovered and cultivated interests ignored in the past. Girls and women still do not receive an equal share of sport resources in most organizations and communities, but their increased participation clearly has gone hand in hand with the development of new opportunities. Most of these new opportunities owe their existence to some form of political pressure or government legislation.

Government Equal Rights Legislation People often complain about government regulations, but literally millions of girls and women would not be playing sports today if it were not for local and national legislation mandating equal rights. Many policies and rules exist today because of concerted efforts to raise legal issues and to pressure political representatives. The individuals and groups making these efforts have been committed to the struggle to achieve fairness in sports. For example, the U.S. Congress passed Title IX of the Educational Amendments in 1972 only after years of lobbying by concerned citizens. Title IX declared *no person in the United States shall, on the basis of sex, be excluded from participation in, be denied the benefits of, or be subjected to discrimination under any educational program or activity receiving federal financial assistance.*

The men who controlled athletic programs in high schools and colleges objected to this "radical" idea of treating girls and women equally, and they delayed the enforcement of Title IX for five years after it became law. Many men and some women claimed that equity was impractical and unfair because men would have to share the privilege and resources they had come to think rightfully belonged to them. This is discussed in the box "Title IX."

Governments in many nations have passed laws and formulated policies promoting equal rights for girls and women in sports. Women around the world have formed the International Working Group on Women and Sport (the IWG; see www.iwg-gti.org) to promote the enforcement of these laws and policies and to pressure resistant governments and international groups to pass equal rights legislation of their own. Official power in these nations and organizations rests in the hands of men, and they often see women's sport participation as disruptive of the social or moral order.

The women and men striving to produce changes in these settings have had to be persistent and politically creative to produce even minor changes. Progress has been made in some nations, but at least half the women in the world lack regular access to sport participation opportunities.

The Global Women's Rights Movement The global women's movement over the past thirty years has emphasized that females are enhanced as human beings when they develop their intellectual *and* physical abilities. This idea has encouraged women of all ages to pursue their interests in sports, and it has led to the creation of new interests among those who, in the past, never would have thought of playing sports (Fasting, 1996). The women's movement also has helped redefine occupational and family roles for women, and this has provided more women the time and resources they need to play sports.

As the ideals of the women's movement have become more widely accepted, and as male control over the lives and bodies of women has weakened, more women have chosen to play sports. More changes are needed, however, especially in poor nations and among low-income women in wealthy nations, but the choices now available to women are less restricted than they once were.

The global women's movement has fueled both national and international political action. Many politically influential women's sport organizations have emerged in connection with the women's movement. For example, the Women's Sport Foundation in the United States and similar groups in other nations have become important lobbying groups for change. The IWG emerged from a 1994 conference, which brought women delegates from eighty countries to Brighton, England, to discuss "women, sport,

REFLECT ON SPORTS

Title IX
Can a Law Create Gender Equity?

Title IX is a law prohibiting gender discrimination in schools that receive funds from the federal government. The law, passed in 1972, applies to all schools receiving federal funds through grants, scholarships, or other support for students, academic and extracurricular programs, or research. It says that federal funds can be withdrawn from a school if it is shown to discriminate intentionally against either gender in the provision of curriculum, counseling, academic support, or general educational opportunities; this includes interscholastic or varsity sports.

On the thirtieth anniversary of this law, a reporter asked tennis star Jennifer Caprioti what she thought of Title IX. Caprioti looked puzzled and said that she had never heard of it. This surprised many people because the law has been a central factor accounting for the dramatic growth of sport participation opportunities for girls and women in the United States. But Caprioti, twenty-six years old in 2002, was born four years after Title IX passed. She has grown up living with the benefits of the law without realizing its existence or its impact on her life.

BEFORE TITLE IX: PLAY DAYS AND CHEERLEADERS

Prior to 1972, sports were almost exclusively a "guy thing" in American schools. In 1971, there were nearly 3.7 million boys playing varsity high school sports. At the same time, about 295,000 girls were playing—for every 12.5 boys on teams, there was 1 girl on a team. Similarly, out of every dollar spent on high school varsity sports, girls received about 1 cent, whereas boys received 99 cents.

At the same time, an estimated 180,000 men and 32,000 women were playing intercollegiate sports. This means that, in 1971, 10.5 percent of the men and 1.5 percent of the women in college played intercollegiate sports. Women's intercollegiate programs at the time received about 1 percent of the money spent by athletic departments, even though the student fees of women students and the tax money of female workers were being used to fund a good proportion of the intercollegiate athletic programs.

In the pre–Title IX era, most girls and women played sports only on annual "play days" when track and field events were scheduled for them. Of course, girls did have opportunities to be cheerleaders for the boys' and men's teams, and they could be in pep clubs and attend games as spectators. But very few had chances to play on any team that resembled the teams provided for boys and men. If you know women over the age of forty-eight (in 2005), ask them to tell you about those days.

TITLE IX: A HISTORY OF RESISTANCE AND PROGRESS

In 1972, when Richard M. Nixon was president, Congress decided to update and clarify the 1964 Civil Rights Act, which prohibited discrimination based on "race, color, religion, or national origin" in public education, public facilities, publicly funded programs, and private companies engaged in interstate commerce. The members of Congress were especially concerned about extending the law to prohibit gender discrimination in public education, so they passed the Education Amendments to the Civil Rights Act, and President Nixon signed it.

Title IX was a section of the Education Amendments that applied directly to educational opportunities in schools; its purpose was to eliminate gender-based barriers to educational programs and experiences.

When Title IX was passed, it wasn't very controversial. The women's movement and the civil rights movement were in full swing, and most people wanted their daughters to have the same educational opportunities as their sons. But, when people realized that Title IX could be applied to sport programs, sparks began to fly.

Gender equity sounded good in theory, but, when people associated with interscholastic sports realized what it could mean in practice, many of them objected to and raised questions about Title IX. What was meant, they wanted to know, by *equity*? Did the law mean that boys and men must share the 99 percent of the athletic budget that they used for their programs? How much of the 99 percent would they have to share? Equity did not mean a 50/50 split, did it? Was it fair to make boys and men share if it meant giving up opportunities they had come to expect and define as "rightfully" and "naturally" theirs? Did it mean that girls and women should have the same number of sport teams that boys and men had? Should just as many girls and women be playing on varsity teams as boys and men?

In the general world of education, gender equity was highly valued. But, in the world of sports and athletic programs, where men had nearly all the opportunities and had organized things around their interests, equity was generally seen as radical, subversive, disruptive, and potentially destructive.

As men complained that they didn't know the legal meaning of *equity*, the U.S. Department of Education's Office of Civil Rights (OCR) developed a clarification of Title IX. In the meantime, the NCAA tried to subvert the law because it knew it would be required to take gender equity seriously; the NCAA certainly did not want equity to mean that everything should be divided by half! Treating women as equals would threaten what men had come to expect.

After receiving nearly 10,000 comments, questions, and complaints about Title IX, the OCR published legal clarifications in 1975. Officials told high schools that they had one year to comply with the regulations, whereas universities were given three years to comply. But many people associated with established sport programs continued to complain that they did not know how the OCR was going to decide if equity really existed in their programs. In response, the OCR in 1979 established three legal tests to be used to assess compliance with Title IX. According to OCR enforcement guidelines, a school is in compliance with Title IX if it meets *any one* of the following three tests:

1. *Proportionality test.* This requires a school to provide sport participation opportunities for each gender that are generally proportionate to its full-time undergraduate enrollment. This means that, if 49 percent of students in the school are female, no less than 44 percent and no more than 54 percent of the student-athletes should be female. A 5-percentage-point deviation from exact equality has been the guideline used to determine if a school is within the law.

2. *History of progress test.* This requires a school to show that it has a history and continuing practice of expanding the women's athletic program. Most crucial to this test are the actions and progress that have been made over the past three years.

Despite the success and popularity of Title IX, it has been a controversial law among those who think that men should not be asked to share or give up what they had come to expect during nearly a century of excluding women from sport programs and marginalizing women's teams. (*Colorado Springs Gazette*)

Title IX   (continued)
Can a Law Create Gender Equity?

3. *Accommodation of interest test.* This requires a school to show that its programs and teams have fully accommodated the interests and abilities of members of the traditionally underrepresented sex. In other words, the school must prove that women (or men) students do not have the ability or interest to sustain any new sport teams or that new teams would not have reasonable opportunities to compete against other teams (most likely because other teams do not exist).

The existence of this precisely defined three-part test did not eliminate resistance to Title IX. But it did give women a legal basis for individually filing lawsuits against schools that they claimed did not provide them equitable opportunities to play sports. This, in turn, caused more resistance to the law.

Title IX opponents lobbied Congress, contacted President Ronald Reagan, and filed suits to subvert the law. In 1984, one of those suits reached the U.S. Supreme Court. The conservative justices ruled that Title IX applied only to programs that directly received money from the federal government and, since varsity sports did not directly receive federal funds, the law did not apply to them. Immediately, the OCR dropped its investigations of nearly 800 complaints against schools charged with violating the law.

Title IX was not enforced between 1984 and 1987. Then the U.S. Congress passed the Civil Rights Restoration Act in 1987. Among other things, this act declared that Congress intended Title IX to apply to sport programs. President Reagan promptly vetoed the law, but Congress overrode Reagan's veto in 1988.

In 1990, the OCR provided a detailed guide that specified what *equity* meant in connection with particular aspects of athletic programs, such as scholarships, facilities, scheduling, coaching, and other forms of support for athletes and athletic programs.

In 1992, there was court case in which it was ruled that a plaintiff filing a Title IX complaint could be awarded monetary damages if she (or he) won the case. This marked a major turning point for Title IX enforcement because it meant that schools could be mandated to pay damages if they lost a case. Prior to 1992, it was expected that, if schools lost a Title IX case, they would just be required to rectify certain inequities without paying for any past discrimination. (The fact that no school has ever lost federal funds even when Title IX has been clearly violated suggests that the OCR has been reasonable, if not lenient, in the way it has enforced the law.)

Title IX became easier to enforce and gained credibility in the general consciousness of Americans in 1994 when Congress passed the Equity in Athletics Disclosure Act. This act required any university with students receiving financial aid from the federal government to provide an annual report containing data on athletic participation, staffing, and revenues and expenses for all men's and women's sports. The purpose of this report was to enable prospective students to see the actual numbers related to equity in schools that they might choose to attend. These data, available online at www.ed.gov/offices/OPE/PPI/eada.html, have shined a bright light on universities and have made their equity/inequity records public.

Since 1994, there have been steady moves toward gender equity at both the high school and college levels, although equity has been fully achieved by very few schools at any level. Resistance to Title IX has continued to be strong among those with vested interests in certain men's sports. Brown University objected on legal grounds to the three-part test, but the appropriateness of the test was upheld in a 1996 court decision. After the case, the OCR further clarified the meaning of the three-part test to answer questions from university and athletic administrators. In 1997, Title IX prohibitions against sexual harassment in schools were clarified. More clarifications about equity in athletic scholarships were published in 1998.

Resistance hit a peak in 2001, after the election of George W. Bush. Some Bush supporters thought that he would be supportive of a critical review of Title IX and how it was being enforced. They joined with others, including representatives of men's teams that had been cut from intercollegiate sport programs since 1981. They argued that Title IX had created a system of "preferences" for girls and women and had hurt men's sports in the process. Men had been hurt, they argued, when athletic departments cut men's teams to meet the terms of the proportionality test. The assumption underlying their argument was that men should not be asked to give up resources or opportunities as schools strive to achieve gender equity.

Rod Paige, President Bush's Secretary of Education, responded to those objecting to Title IX by forming a fifteen-member Commission on Athletic Opportunity (CAO) charged with investigating whether the law might be modified to increase opportunities for women without negatively impacting opportunities for men. The CAO often had heated discussions during its eight months of meetings, and when it issued its report and recommendations in early 2003, it created considerable controversy. Several of the twenty-five recommendations in the report were contradictory, and many focused on altering the proportionality test so that schools would have more flexibility in complying with Title IX.

Advocates of girls' and women's sports criticized the report and the methods used by the commission as it formulated recommendations. Advocates for reforming Title IX hoped that the recommendations would lead to policies that prohibited schools from cutting men's teams to achieve gender equity and allowed schools more freedom in determining how they complied with the law.

As people debated the meaning and implications of the commission's recommendations, Ted Leland, athletics director at Stanford University and co-chair of the commission said, "Let us remember, the commission is not the last word on Title IX. Rather, [it] is the first step in what will be a long process." What Leland did not say was that the process of achieving gender equity through Title IX was already thirty years old in 2003, and that hundreds of steps had already been taken.

THE SOCIOLOGY OF TITLE IX

As you read this, the story of Title IX continues. Up to this point, the story demonstrates that the law can be a powerful tool in bringing about changes in society. Between 1971 and 2002, the number of girls playing varsity high school sports increased from 295,000 to about 2.8 million—almost a 1,000 percent increase. Instead of 1 of every 27 high school girls playing on teams, now 1 in 3 play. The number of women playing on intercollegiate teams has increased from 32,000 to about 160,000—well over a 500 percent increase.

Today, over 5 percent of all women in college play intercollegiate sports. At the same time, there are nearly 4 million boys playing high school sports and 240,000 men playing in college (see chapter 14 for data on participation over time). Also important is that many of these boys and men have learned to see and respect women as athletes—something that boys and men in 1971 seldom had a chance to learn.

The story of Title IX also demonstrates that laws do not exist in a social and cultural vacuum. Laws depend on popular support and a commitment to enforce them. When laws threaten vested interests, ideology, or deeply held principles, people will resist them, especially if they have the power to do so. This means that the histories of certain laws involve extended struggles over what is important to us and how our lives should be organized. Developing consensus about these things is seldom easy.

The fact that laws, like sports, are social constructions means that they can be changed as society and culture change. When Title IX was passed in 1972, the time was right to make the case for gender equity. Many people were ready and eager to embrace it. But enforcement was bound to evoke resistance among those whose privilege would be threatened. Sport programs have generally reaffirmed and reproduced male privilege, so it is not surprising that resistance to gender equity has been strong over the history of Title IX. Nor is it surprising that people have continued to raise questions about Title IX.

As progress toward gender equity has slowed since the mid-1990s, some people have argued that there is nothing left to be done, whereas others say more changes are needed. In the process, people have questioned the merits of the proportionality test, saying that boys and men will always be more interested in sports than girls and women are. Others respond that we need to create more encouragement and developmental opportunities for girls, because our culture contains strong participation incentives for boys and men but mixed messages for girls and women.

Some say that cheerleading has changed and should now be considered a sport. They argue that, if cheerleaders were counted as athletes, most schools would be very close to proportional participation for males

Title IX   (continued)
Can a Law Create Gender Equity?

Although highly sexualized images of cheerleaders are presented in men's professional sports, many young women at the high school level view cheerleading as a sport in its own right. If cheerleaders were considered athletes, it would help many schools reach or come closer to achieving gender equity. However, in some schools, such a change might reaffirm the very definitions of *femininity* that perpetuate inequities. (Mary Bowden [left]; Dennis Coakley [right])

and females. Others say that cheerleading still reaffirms traditional definitions of femininity and discourages the very cultural changes that are needed to support increased interest in sports among girls and women. Some want to know why boys' and men's teams should be cut when girls' and women's teams sometimes must recruit players. Others say that, as long as girls and women receive mixed messages about the value of sport participation, there will always be differential interests.

Therefore, we must work to change ideas about femininity and alter sports to make them more compatible with the values and experiences of girls and women.

We will discuss these issues throughout this chapter. However, my sense is that sports remain sites that privilege men over women and where existing social arrangements continue to favor boys and men. That means that struggles over Title IX will last long into the future. *What do you think?*

Note: Materials in this section are based on many sources, including the following government reports: Government Accounting Office. 2000. *Gender equity: Men's and women's participation in higher education.* Report number *GAO-01-128* (December 15); online www.gao.gov—go to "GAO Reports" and then to "Find GAO Reports." Government Accounting Office. 2001. *Intercollegiate athletics: Four-year colleges' experiences adding and discontinuing teams.* Report number *GAO-01-297* (March 8); online www.gao.gov—go to "GAO Reports" and then to "Find GAO Reports."

The global women's rights movement has enabled some women to become world-class athletes. The skills of top women athletes are demonstrated clearly in major international events such as soccer's World Cup and the Olympic Games. (Michael Caulfield; AP/Wide World Photos)

and the challenge of change." After three days of discussion and debate, the delegates unanimously passed a set of global gender equity principles now known as the "Brighton Declaration." This document, updated at world conferences in Windhoek, Namibia, in 1998 and Montreal, Canada, in 2002, continues to be used by people as they apply pressure on governments and sport organizations to make new spaces for girls and women in sports.

Lobbying efforts by representatives from these and other groups led to the inclusion of statements related to sports and physical education in the official Platform for Action of the U.N.'s Fourth World Conference on Women, held in Beijing, China, in 1996. These statements called for new efforts to provide sport and physical education opportunities to promote the education, health, and human rights of girls and women in countries around the world. What began as inspiration based in the women's movement has become a widely accepted global effort to promote and guarantee sport participation opportunities for girls and women.

The Health and Fitness Movement   Since the mid-1970s, research has made many people around the world more aware of the health benefits of physical activities. This awareness has encouraged women to seek opportunities to exercise and play sports. Although much of the publicity associated with this movement has been influenced by traditional ideas about femininity and has been tied to the prevailing feminine ideal of being thin and sexually attractive to men, there also has been an emphasis on the *development of physical strength and competence.* Muscles have become more widely accepted as desirable attributes for women of all ages. Traditional standards remain, as illustrated by many of the clothing fashions and marketing strategies associated with women's fitness, but many women have moved beyond those standards and have focused on physical competence and the good feelings that go with it, rather than trying to look like anorexic models in fashion magazines.

Furthermore, many companies that produce sporting goods and apparel have jumped from the women's *fitness and appearance* bandwagon to the *fitness and sports* bandwagon. Their ads are designed to sell clothes, shoes, and even sweat-proof makeup, but they also present strong messages intended to appeal to women who see sports as a symbol of independence and power. In the process, they have encouraged and

AT YOUR FINGERTIPS   For more information on the media coverage of women in sports, see pages 428–431.

supported sport participation among girls and women.

Increased Media Coverage of Women in Sports
Even though women's sports are not covered as often or in the same detail as men's sports, girls and women now can see and read about the achievements of women athletes in a wider range of sports than ever before. Seeing women athletes on television and reading about them in newspapers and magazines encourage girls and women to be active as athletes themselves. This was clearly evident in the United States after its national soccer team won the World Cup in 1999. The media images in the coverage of that event were very powerful and inspirational to girls and women.

As girls grow up, they often want to see what is possible before they experiment with and develop their own athletic skills. This is the case because many of them still receive mixed messages about becoming serious athletes. For example, their visions of being an athlete can be clouded by swimsuit models in *Sports Illustrated*—powerful images connecting thinness and vulnerability with sex appeal—and by homophobic fears about becoming too strong and too "malelike." Despite mixed messages, the media coverage of everything from professional women's basketball to synchronized swimming helps girls and young women conclude that sports are human activities, not male activities (see figure 8.1).

Media companies, like their corporate counterparts that sell sporting goods, have begun to realize that women make up half the world's population and, therefore, half the world's consumers. NBC, the company that televised the 1996 Olympic Games in Atlanta, experienced high ratings when it targeted women during its 175 hours of coverage. Many men complained

"Hey, dad—who's that tall guy with Mia Hamma?"

FIGURE 8.1 The media coverage of women's sports has an impact on boys and girls. A youth soccer coach recently said that one of the seven-year-old boys on her team said he wanted to be as good as Mia Hamm when he grew up. How many boys see women athletes as their heroes?

about this new approach; they liked it better when the media catered to their interests alone. Despite these complaints, women's sports will continue to be covered in the media, and that coverage will change the images that all of us associate with sports and athletic achievement.

In summary, these five factors have fostered increased sport participation among girls and women and the awareness that gender equity in sports is a worthwhile goal. Gender equity is far from being achieved, but there is no turning back to the days of excluding girls and women—at least not without a fight!

Reasons to Be Cautious When Predicting Future Participation Increases

Increases in the sport participation rates of girls and women have not come easily. They are the result of the dedicated efforts of many individuals and groups. Progress has been remarkable, but gender equity does not exist yet in many sport programs in most areas around the world. Furthermore, there are seven reasons to be cautious about the pace and extent of future sport participation increases:

1. Budget cutbacks and the privatization of sport programs
2. Resistance to government regulations
3. Backlash among those who resent changes favoring strong women
4. Underrepresentation of women in decision-making positions in sports
5. Continued emphasis on "cosmetic fitness"
6. Trivialization of women's sports
7. Homophobia and the threat of being labeled "lesbian"

Budget Cutbacks and the Privatization of Sport Programs Efforts to achieve gender equity are often subverted by budget cutbacks. Compared with programs for boys and men, programs for girls and women are often vulnerable to cuts, because they are less well established, they have less administrative and community support, and they have less revenue-generating potential. Overall, they often are seen as less important for the future of sponsoring organizations. As one woman said, "It seems like the only time women's programs are treated equally is when cuts must be made."

Another issue related to budget cutbacks is that sport programs for girls and women are often new programs, and they have start-up costs that long-standing and well-established programs for boys and men do not have. Therefore, budget cuts may cause women's programs to fail at a faster pace than men's programs, because they have never had the chance to develop name recognition and market presence. Many programs for boys and men are less vulnerable, because they have enjoyed consistent support and development for nearly a century, and they are now in a position to raise funds to sustain themselves.

As public, tax-supported programs are cut, sport participation becomes increasingly dependent on private support and sponsorship. This trend often has a negative impact on the provision of sport participation opportunities for girls and women, especially those who live in low-income households. Public programs are accountable to voters, and they are regulated by government rules related to equal rights and opportunities. Private programs are accountable to the needs of their dues-paying members, regulated by market forces, and they are seldom mandated to provide equal rights or opportunities.

When free and affordable public programs are cut, people must buy sport participation from private providers. This is no problem for females from well-to-do backgrounds: they just buy what they want. In fact, private providers seek their business and make efforts to attract it. "Free enterprise sports" are great things for people with money, but not very good for those on tight budgets; nor are they good for women, who generally have lower salaries and less discretionary money than men. Private providers don't serve those who can't buy what they sell. When money talks, poor people are able only to whisper, and poor women often are silenced. Therefore, future participation increases may be unevenly distributed among girls and women; in fact, those who lack resources will probably suffer participation setbacks in the future.

Setbacks have already occurred in some U.S. public schools as they cut sports, especially in low-income areas. In some schools where cuts have occurred, booster organizations provide funds and facilities for boys' sports, such as football, but they often ignore girls' sports. They don't follow Title IX law because they are private organizations and receive no support from the federal government. Similarly, when the city of Los Angeles cut some of its public sport programs and let private organizations run sport programs in public parks, the new programs served four times as many boys as girls. The organizations claimed that boys wanted to play sports but girls did not. Los Angeles has struggled to deal fairly with this equity dilemma.

Resistance to Government Legislation   Those who benefit from the status quo often resist government legislation that mandates changes. This is certainly true in the case of legislation calling for gender equity in sports. For example, many people in the United States continue to resist the application of Title IX in sport programs. They claim that there is too much government interference in everyday life. Of course, they have operated programs for boys and men for over a century without ever considering the needs and interests of girls and women, so it is easy to see why they would resist "government interference" demanding that they open their eyes. These people cannot turn back the clock when it comes to changes already made, but they can slow future changes.

Backlash Among Those Who Resent Changes Favoring Strong Women   When women play certain sports, they become strong. Strong women challenge the prevailing gender ideology that underlies the norms, legal definitions, and opportunity structures that frame and set the conditions under which men and women form identities, live their lives, and relate to each other. The people who are privileged by the prevailing gender ideology in society see strong women as a threat. They do all they can to discredit most women's sports and strong women athletes, and they call for a return to the "good ol' days," when men played sports and women watched and cheered.

A notable example of backlash by an individual occurred in 2002 after Martha Burk, head of the National Council of Women's Organizations, which represents 6 million members and 160 organizations, wrote to Hootie Johnson, chairman of the Augusta National Golf Club. Burk asked Johnson to open the Augusta Club to women members. The all-male club is very prestigious. It hosts the annual Masters golf tournament, and its members receive public attention and have their status boosted by worldwide media coverage of the Masters event. Johnson used the following words to describe how he felt about Burk's request:

> We will not be bullied, threatened or intimidated. We do not intend to become a trophy in their display case. . . . There may well come a day when women will be invited to join our membership, but that timetable will be ours, and not at the point of a bayonet. (in Brennan, 2002 p. 3C).

It was clear that Johnson felt strongly about a woman's organization asking his club to abandon its tradition of maintaining an all-male membership. His response suggested that he did not want people to see him and other men giving in to a request by women. If his golf club was to "allow" women to play golf, it would be on a time table and terms set by the men, not by women.

Regardless of how we might feel about the rights of private clubs to maintain policies of gender exclusion, Johnson's response was indicative of backlash by a powerful man in a sport organization against equity claims asserted by women. To the extent that other men in positions of power in male-controlled sport organizations feel as Johnson did, progress toward gender equity can be slowed down by their reactionary approaches to change.

Backlash also contributes to the mixed messages girls and women receive about sports, and it fuels the trivialization of women's sports and the marginalization of strong women athletes. If this is occurring, future increases in sport participation rates will be slowed.

Underrepresentation of Women in Decision-Making Positions in Sports   Despite large increases in the number of sport participation opportunities for girls and women since the mid-1970s, women have suffered setbacks in the ranks of coaching and sport administration in women's programs. For example, in the years immediately following the passage of Title IX

in the United States, there was an actual decline in the number and proportion of women head coaches and administrators (Parkhouse and Williams, 1986). As women's sports changed and became more important in high schools and colleges, women coaches and administrators were replaced by men.

Of course, it is possible for men to do a good job in these positions; however, unless girls and young women see women in decision-making positions in their programs, they will be reluctant to define sports and sport participation as important in their futures. If women are not visible as leaders in sport programs, some people conclude that women's abilities and contributions in sports are less valued than men's. This conclusion certainly limits progress toward gender equity in sports (Ligutom-Kimura, 1995).

Continued Emphasis on "Cosmetic Fitness"
There are competing images of female bodies in many cultures today. Many girls and women hear confusing cultural messages that they should be "firm but shapely, fit but sexy, strong but thin" (Markula, 1995). Although they see images of powerful women athletes, they cannot escape the images of fashion models whose reputations depend on a body shape that women can match only by depriving themselves of the nourishment they need to be strong. These fashion images highlight thinness, bust size, waist size, lip shape, hairstyles, body hair removal, complexion, allure, and the clothes and accessories that together "make" the woman. Girls and women also hear that physical power and competence are important, but they see disproportionate rewards going to women who look young and vulnerable. They are advised to "get strong but lose weight." They get the impression that muscles are good but too many muscles are unfeminine. They are told that men now like competent women, but they see men attracted to the NFL and NBA cheerleaders and the latest celebrity models with breast implants and workout videos, rather than to accomplished women athletes.

AT YOUR FINGERTIPS   For more information visit www.mhhe.com/coakley8e.

Despite cultural messages that promote athletic images for females, powerful cultural messages also promote the "beauty myth" (Hargreaves, 1994; Heywood, 1998; Wolf, 1991). Effective commercial messages for everything from makeup to clothing are premised on the assumption that, if women have positive body images, they will not spend as much money on products whose sales depend on insecurities about appearance. The ads are clear: "heterosexualized hard bodies" are valued, especially when they are displayed in the latest leotards and high-fashion sports gear.

"Yes, buff is beautiful—but only as long as its function is to be gawked at by guys" (in Solomon, 2000). For example, as the U.S. Women's Soccer team was described as "Babe City" by a popular U.S. TV talk show host, it was clear that, underlying all the adulation of strong, physically competent women, there was also an effort to remind people that men still retain the prerogative to judge women on how they look and to assess women's bodies as objects of men's pleasure (Solomon, 2000). Even when Brandi Chastain tore off her shirt in spontaneous jubilation after scoring a shootout goal to win the 1999 World Cup and revealed a sport top, which women have been wearing for years on tracks, on jogging trails, and in gyms, reporters around the world desperately wanted to read her act as a form of striptease that titillated the masses. As Solomon (2000) notes, many people in 1999 still did not have a frame of reference to make sense out of Chastain's gesture without sexualizing her body.

These messages about heterosexualized hard bodies are so powerful that some women don't want to play sports until they are thin enough to look "right" and to wear the "right" clothes; other girls and women combine participation

These Barbie dolls are a classic example of sport images mixed with the notion of cosmetic fitness. The beauty myth remains strong in popular ideas about femininity. Does Barbie reproduce those myths? (Jay Coakley)

with pathogenic weight-control strategies. For example, studies show that an alarming number of women athletes use laxatives, diet pills, diuretics, self-induced vomiting, binges, and starvation diets in conjunction with their training (Beals, 2000; Hawes, 2001a; Johns, 1996, 1997; Tofler et al., 1996; Wilmore, 1996). This increases the probability of injuries, jeopardizes health, and keeps alive the idea that women must either conform to the beauty myth or be rejected by men and by women who subscribe to the myth and use it to evaluate other females of all ages.

Finally, when the goal of playing sports is cosmetic fitness, some women may limit their workouts to avoid too much muscularity, or they may tie workouts to eating. In research on body image among female exercisers and athletes, Vicki Krane and her colleagues (2001) found that women concerned with achieving an unrealistic body image often defined their workouts in connection with eating: when they worked out strenuously, "they gave themselves permission to eat and if they ate too much they punished themselves with exercise." In my own conversations with young women, I found a related phenomenon connected with weight control. When the goal of sport participation is cosmetic fitness, some young women drop out of sports if they gain weight while they train, and others drop out after they achieve weight-loss goals. In nearly all cases, an emphasis on cosmetic fitness interfered with participation in sports.

Trivialization of Women's Sports

"Okay, women play sports, but they are not as good as men and people won't pay to watch them." Statements like this are based on the assumptions that "real" sports involve "manly" things, such as intimidation, violence, and physical domination over others and that the measure of a sport is determined by spectator appeal. Therefore, if sports involve grace, balance, and coordination or do not attract spectators, they are second-rate. This orientation is widespread enough that it continues to interfere with the achievement of gender equity in sports.

Power and performance sports are grounded in the values and experiences of men, and they imply evaluative standards that work to the disadvantage of women. Of course, highly accomplished women athletes are challenging these standards and establishing new ways to be excellent on the playing field without being violent or physically overpowering opponents. They have shown that basketball can be played with finesse and passing and does not have to involve monster dunks and heavy body contact. They have shown that exciting hockey can be played without bone-jarring body checks, and exciting soccer can be played without macho posturing on the field. These new ways to play sports are beginning to make sense for many people, but others continue to insist that, as long as women can't outplay men, they don't deserve the same support that men receive to play sports.

Homophobia and the Threat of Being Labeled "Lesbian"

Homophobia is a generalized fear or intolerance of lesbians, gay men, and bisexual people (Griffin, 1998). It may be expressed in terms of prejudice, discrimination, harassment, and violence toward those identified or believed to be homosexual or bisexual. It is a powerful cultural factor that has, among other things, discouraged many girls and women from playing sports or making sports an important part of their lives.

Homophobia causes some parents to steer their daughters away from sports they believe attract lesbians and away from teams or programs where lesbians are believed to play or coach. Homophobia and public expressions of homophobic discourse influence and often limit the sport participation choices available to women (Veri, 1999). When women fear the label of *lesbian*, or fear being associated with lesbians, they may avoid certain sports or limit their commitment to playing sports. These fears may be grounded in personal homophobia or in an awareness of homophobia among others and how others express it. These fears influence both heterosexual women and lesbians.

Some women athletes find that peers accuse them of being lesbians when they play certain sports or take sports very seriously. Some

> Parity in funding must be more than a goal. It must be a reality. That means more money for operating women's sports programs. . . . Justice often comes with a price tag.
>
> —Donna Shalala, former U.S. Secretary of Health and Human Services (2002)

heterosexual women fear these accusations, and they may become defensive or even hide their athletic identities when they interact with homophobic others (Blinde and Taub, 1992). Closeted lesbians may fear the loss of secrecy, limit their relationships with others, and become lonely and isolated in the process (Bredemeier et al., 1999).

Heterosexual and lesbian athletes often fear harassment and discrimination motivated by the homophobia of others. Heterosexual men may use homophobic discourse to tease women athletes and control all women who are intimidated by it. This continues to occur regularly in some high schools and colleges in North America. When this causes women to become defensive and give sport participation a lower profile in their lives, homophobia subverts gender equity. Challenging homophobic discourse and forcing others to confront their homophobia is a daunting task. Some open lesbians have become effective at doing this, but most other women lack the experience to do it effectively.

In the meantime, many women athletes go out of their way to emphasize traditional feminine attributes and even say in interviews that being an athlete is not nearly as important as eventually getting married, settling down, having children, and becoming a nurturing homemaker. Homophobia affects all women, lesbian and straight alike; it creates fears, it pressures women to conform to traditional gender roles, and it silences and makes invisible the lesbians who manage, coach, and play sports (Griffin, 1998; Lenskyj, 1999; Nelson, 1998). All of these things can limit increases in sport participation among girls and women.

In summary, sport participation among girls and women will not continue to increase automatically. Just as the participation of men has been nurtured and developed through support and popular images of men in sports, so must it be for women. Without continued support and encouragement, without powerful new images, some of the progress of the past could be jeopardized.

However, we will never backslide to the extreme inequality that existed before 1970.

Gender and Fairness Issues in Sports

Participation Opportunities The history of gender inequities in sports was illustrated in powerful terms in late 1999, when news and sport publications presented their lists of top athletes of the twentieth century. Some lists had no women on them; others had a few, but I saw no list with more than 5 percent women athletes. Of course, men developed these lists, and they used their memories and experiences to identify and rank athletes. They undoubtedly had less knowledge of the accomplishments of women athletes, but they had few women from which to choose. Women had few opportunities to play sports for the first eighty years of the century. Those who had noteworthy accomplishments often were "activists," known as much for breaking social barriers as for setting records. Apparently, breaking the barriers that privileged men did not count for much among those who cast votes for athletes of the century; they defined *excellence* in ways that fit their values and experiences.

The types of sport participation opportunities available for girls and women always are related to dominant definitions of *femininity* in a culture. Prior to the early 1970s, many people believed that females were naturally frail and inclined toward graceful movements. When girls and women were encouraged to play sports, they were steered into figure skating, ice dancing, gymnastics, swimming, tennis, golf, and other sports that people thought were unrelated to strength, power, and speed—the traits associated with masculinity. Some girls and women ignored barriers. They played sports involving strength, power, and speed, and lived with the consequences. However, opportunities for sport participation were limited.

Over the past fifty years, some women athletes have demonstrated clearly that notions of female frailty were grounded in ideology, rather than nature. This has led to gradual changes in popular ideas about what girls and women can and should do in sports. Today the vast majority of people in North America and many other regions agree that women should have the same participation opportunities as men. However, some people continue to argue that women should not wrestle, box, play on men's contact sport teams, or ask men to share equally the resources that fund sports.

Inequities in participation opportunities continue to exist in international sports. For example, there are still fewer sports for women than for men in the Olympics and other international events. Although important changes have occurred since the early 1980s, women athletes remain underrepresented in international competitions. The data in figure 8.2 and table 8.1 illustrate that women in the modern Summer Olympic Games have always had fewer events than men have had, and there have always been fewer women participants than men. The International Olympic Committee (IOC), which from 1894 to 1981 had no women members, did

not approve a women's 1500-meter run until the 1972 Games in Munich. It was not until the 1984 Games in Los Angeles that women had the opportunity to run the marathon. Women waited until 1988 to run the Olympic 10,000-meter race and until 1996 to run the 5,000-meter race. The men on the IOC have justified these restrictions by claiming that "women need to be protected from such demanding events." Opportunities have increased over the past century, but gender equity has not been achieved. In fact, some nations continue to send only male athletes to the Olympic Games. This led the French Minister of Sports to state in 2000 that "women's involvement in sports [around the world] is characterized by deep inequalities."

Equity sometimes is difficult to achieve because of fundamentalist religious beliefs in certain cultures. For example, strict Islamic beliefs forbid women from publicly exposing any surface of their bodies to the sight of men. Women in traditionally Catholic nations have not faced moral restrictions, but they have lacked the power and resources to make choices to play

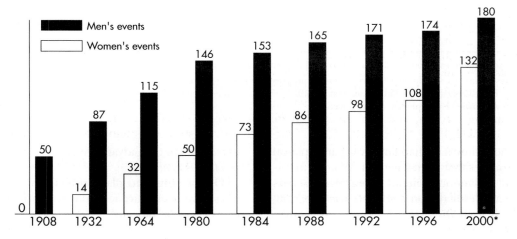

*Twelve events in 2000 were mixed, or open to both men and women. These twelve have been added to both totals for men and women. This procedure of adding mixed events to the total events for women and men was also used for each of the other Olympics in this graph.

FIGURE 8.2   Number of Summer Olympic events open to women and to men.

Table 8.1   Male and female athletes in the modern Summer Olympic Games, 1896–2000

Year	Place	Countries Represented	Male Athletes	Female Athletes	Percent Female
1896	Athens	13	311	0	0.00
1900	Paris	22	1,319	11	0.01
1904	St. Louis	12	617	8	1.30
1908	London	22	1,999	36	1.80
1912	Stockholm	28	2,490	57	2.20
1916	Olympics scheduled for Berlin canceled (World War I)				
1920	Antwerp	29	2,543	64	2.50
1924	Paris	44	2,956	136	4.40
1928	Amsterdam	46	2,724	290	9.60
1932	Los Angeles	47	1,281	127	9.00
1936	Berlin	49	3,738	328	8.10
1940	Olympics scheduled for Tokyo canceled (World War II)				
1944	Olympics canceled (World War II)				
1948	London	59	3,714	385	9.40
1952	Helsinki	69	4,407	518	10.50
1956	Melbourne	71	2,958	384	11.50
1960	Rome	83	4,738	610	11.40
1964	Tokyo	93	4,457	683	13.30
1968	Mexico City	112	4,750	781	14.10
1972	Munich	122	6,077	1,070	17.60
1976	Montreal	88	4,915	1,274	20.60
1980	Moscow	81	4,238	1,088	20.40
1984	Los Angeles	140	5,458	1,620	22.80
1988	Seoul	160	7,105	2,476	25.80
1992	Barcelona	170	7,555	3,008	28.50
1996	Atlanta	197	7,059	3,684	34.00*
2000	Sydney	199	6,582	4,069	38.20

*Twenty-six countries sent only male athletes to the 1996 Summer Games.

Note: These data show one hundred years of gradual progress toward the goal of gender equity. If this progress continues at past rates, one half the participants will be women at the 2012 Summer Games. The number of athletes participating in 1976, 1980, and 1984 was lower than expected, due to boycotts.

sports, and they have had far fewer participation opportunities than men have had. Women in traditional and poor societies often face barriers that preclude or discourage sport participation, as well as limit the extent to which any woman could take sports seriously enough to train at an elite level. These barriers are both ideological and structural. In other words, they are related to *ideas* about what is and isn't appropriate (*ideology*) and to the organization of *opportunities* and access

to *resources* to take advantage of those opportunities (*social structure*).

Opportunities to play professional sports always have been scare for women. Until recently, many people did not believe that spectators would pay to watch women play anything but "ladylike" sports, in which they competed alone (golf) or with nets separating the opponents and preventing physical contact (tennis). Norms in some countries began to change in the 1980s, but many people still doubted that spectators would pay to watch women play sports that went beyond the limits of dominant definitions of *femininity*. Although these limits have been pushed and broken, there remains "cultural encouragement" to highlight traditional notions of femininity. Therefore, many women athletes are still referred to as "ladies," and any recognition of the participation of lesbians has been carefully erased in the media profiles of teams and leagues. The media emphasis is on heterosexual habits, lifestyles, and "looks"; children and husbands are made visible and discussed often. Homophobia has shaped the public image of women's sports, and lesbians have been made invisible, despite their strong presence in many sports. Participation opportunities for women will never match those enjoyed by men until ideological and cultural factors such as these are challenged and changed.

Support for Athletes   Female athletes in most North American high schools and colleges seldom receive the same support enjoyed by the boys and men. This is also the case in sport-sponsoring organizations around the world. Historically, there have been serious inequities in the following areas:

- Access to facilities
- Quality of facilities (playing surfaces, locker rooms, showers, etc.)
- Availability of scholarships*
- Program operating expenses
- Provision and maintenance of equipment and supplies
- Recruiting budgets*
- Scheduling of games and practice times
- Travel and per diem expenses
- Opportunity to receive academic tutoring*
- Numbers of coaches assigned to teams
- Salaries for administrators, coaches, trainers, and other staff

---

*These apply primarily to U.S. colleges and universities.

- Provision of medical and training services and facilities
- Publicity for individuals, teams, and events

Inequities in some of these areas remain a problem in schools at all levels of education, but they also are a problem in many community programs. When they exist in community programs, they often go undetected unless someone digs through data from public, nonprofit, and private programs. Access to facilities, the number of programs available, and the staff assigned to programs are the most likely areas of inequity in community-based sports in North America and around the world.

Most people today realize that a lack of support for women athletes subverts sport participation among girls and women. For well over a century, men have built their programs, shaped them to fit their interests and values, generated interest in participation, sold them to sponsors, and marketed them to potential spectators. During this time, public funds, student fees, and private sponsorships have been used to start and maintain programs for boys and men. Girls and women want only the same treatment. Mary Jo Kane, director of the University of Minnesota's Tucker Center for Research on Girls and Women, says,

> Women are not asking for a handout, we're just asking for an investment. Just put the same investment in us that you put into men. Then we'll see what happens. (in Lamb, 2000, p. 57)

For those who believe in fairness, it is difficult to argue with this position.

Jobs for Women in Coaching and Administration   Most sport programs are controlled by men. Although women's sport programs have increased in number and importance around the globe, women often have lost power over those programs. Data at all levels of competition show that women do not have equal opportunities when it comes to jobs in coaching and administration. Women are especially underrepresented at the highest levels of power in sports. A twenty-five-year study by Vivian Acosta and Linda Carpenter (2002) documents gender trends for U.S. college coaching and administration:

- When Title IX became law in 1972, women coached 90 percent of women's teams; by the time the enforcement of Title IX had begun in 1978, the proportion had dropped to 58 percent; by 2002, it had dropped to 44 percent.
- Between 2000 and 2002, there were 361 new jobs for head coaches of women's teams; men received 326 (90.3 percent) of these jobs, whereas women received 35 (9.7 percent).
- Women administered 90 percent of women's athletic programs in 1972; women administered only 18 percent of those programs in 2002, and 19 percent of all women's programs had *no* women administrators.
- In 2002, there were 3,210 administrative jobs in NCAA *women's athletic programs*. Men held (60 percent) of those jobs, whereas women held 40 percent.

- The women's programs that had women athletic directors in 2002 also had a higher proportion of women coaches.
- The decline in the proportion of women coaches and administrators generally has been most dramatic at the highest levels of competition and in the highest-paying jobs.
- Women held only 12.3 percent of the full-time sports information director positions in universities in 2002 and 28 percent of athletic trainer positions.
- Women held about 2 percent of coaching positions in men's programs, and most of those were coaches of combined teams in swimming, cross-country, or tennis.

Table 8.2 presents longitudinal data on the proportion of women coaches for the ten most popular women's intercollegiate sports. Only soccer had a higher proportion of women coaches in 2002 than they had in 1977. Seven of the other nine sports showed at least a fifteen percentage-point decline in the proportion of women coaches between 1977 and 2002.

What would men say if nearly 60 percent of the coaches and administrators *in men's programs*

Table 8.2   Percentage of women coaches for the ten most popular women's intercollegiate sports in all NCAA divisions, 1977–2002

Sport	1977	1987	1997	2002	Percentage Point Change, 1977–2002
Basketball	79.4	59.9	65.2	62.8	−16.6
Volleyball	86.6	70.2	67.8	57.3	−29.3
Tennis	72.9	54.9	40.9	34.5	−38.4
Softball	83.5	67.5	65.2	65.1	−18.4
Cross-country	35.2	18.7	20.7	21.3	−13.9
Track	52.3	20.8	16.4	19.0	−33.3
Swimming/diving	53.6	31.2	33.7	23.0	−30.6
Field hockey	99.1	96.8	97.6	96.8	−2.3
Golf	54.6	37.5	45.2	39.2	−15.4
Soccer	29.4	24.1	33.1	30.7	+1.3

Modified from Acosta and Carpenter (2002). In 2002, 44 percent of the coaches of women's teams were women. This is the lowest representation of women as coaches of women's teams in the history of college sports. In 1972, 90 percent of all women's teams were coached by women, but there were far fewer teams.

were women, whereas men held only 2 percent of the coaching jobs in women's programs? They would be outraged! They would certainly call for major affirmative action programs to achieve fairness, and they would be justified in doing so.

The coaching and administration situation is much the same in other nations and on a global level (see McKay, 1997, for Australia, Canada, and New Zealand). Systematic data on coaches are not easy to collect from nation to nation, but over 90 percent of all national team coaches are men. The International Olympic Committee (IOC), probably the most powerful administrative body in global sports, has a membership of 127 men and 10 women. There were *no* women on the IOC from 1896 until the 1980s. Between 1990 and 1996, forty of forty-two new appointments went to men. The IOC did not meet its goal of having women make up 10 percent of its membership in 2000. Unfortunately, many national olympic committee and international and national sport federations have even worse records than the IOC when it comes to progress toward gender equity, especially in positions of power and influence. The goal of having women in 20 percent of the top decision-making positions in sport organizations around the world by 2005 will not be reached at the current rate of progress. At current rates of change, job equality in most sport organizations will not come until today's twenty-year-olds are grandparents.

The reasons for the underrepresentation of women in coaching and administrative positions in women's sports have been widely debated and studied (McKay, 1997, 1999; Pastore et al., 1996; Wilkerson, 1996). The major reasons for this underrepresentation appear to include the following:

- Men have used well-established connections with other men in sport organizations to help them during the job search and hiring process.
- Compared with men, most women applicants for coaching and administrative jobs do not have the strategic professional connections

and networks that they need to compete with male candidates.
- Job search committees often use subjective evaluative criteria, making it more likely that women applicants for coaching and administrative jobs will be seen as less qualified than men applicants.
- Support systems and professional development opportunities continue to be scarce for women who want to be coaches or administrators, as well as for women already in coaching and administrative jobs.
- Many women have the perception that athletic departments and sport organizations have corporate cultures that don't provide much space for those who see and think about sports differently than men do (see figure 8.3).
- Sport organizations are seldom organized to be sensitive to the family responsibilities of coaches and administrators.
- Sexual harassment is more likely to be anticipated and experienced by women than by men, and women coaches and administrators often feel they are judged by more demanding standards than men are.

SIDELINES

FIGURE 8.3 Women traditionally have been expected to play support roles for men in sports, as well as in society at large. This is changing, but these roles are still present in the gender ideology of many societies.

AT YOUR FINGERTIPS   For more information on social class, gender, and sports, see pages 436–441.

These factors affect aspirations and opportunities, who applies for jobs, how applicants fare during the selection process, how coaches and administrators are evaluated after they obtain jobs, who enjoys his or her job, and who is promoted into a higher-paying job with more responsibility.

People on job search committees seek, evaluate, and hire candidates they think will be successful as coaches and administrators in sport organizations emphasizing power and performance. After looking at all the objectively measurable qualifications, such as years of experience and win-loss records, the search committee members try to subjectively assess such things as a candidate's abilities to recruit and motivate players, raise money, command respect on the team and in the surrounding community, build toughness and character among players, maintain team discipline, and interact effectively with others in the athletic department or sport organization.

Of course, none of these subjective assessments occur in a vacuum. They are influenced by ideas about men and women and the goals and organization of sport programs. Although people on search committees do not agree on all things, most think in subjective terms that favor men over women (Hovden, 2000). This is because coaching and other forms of leadership in sports often are seen in terms that are consistent with traditional ideas about masculinity: if you "coach like a girl," you are doing it wrong; if you "coach like a man," you are doing it right.

Under these conditions, women get jobs only when they present compelling objective evidence of their qualifications, combined with other evidence that they can do things the way successful men have done them in the past. In some cases, women are considered for jobs when there are so few women coaches in a sport or athletic department that administrators feel that they may be accused of discrimination if they do not hire a woman.

When women are hired, they are less likely than men to feel that the sport organizations in which they are working are organized to be open and inclusive, and this has a negative impact on their job satisfaction (Pastore et al., 1996). In other words, many women feel that the culture of most sport organizations leaves little space and provides little support for those who see the world from different vantage points than those of the white men who have shaped that culture over many years. This is one reason that turnover among women in sport organizations is higher than it is among men.

Also important is the fact that the roles of coach and athletic administrator have been developed over the years by men, most of whom have had wives who have raised their children, provided them and their teams with emotional support, hosted social events for their teams and boosters, coordinated their social schedules, handled household finances and maintenance, made sure they were not distracted by nonsport family and household issues, and faithfully attended games season after season. Of course, not all the men in sport jobs have had such wives, but many of the successful coaches and administrators have. Women coaches and administrators seldom have husbands willing to do what wives have traditionally done to advance the coaching and administrative careers of their spouses. Furthermore, sport organizations are not family-friendly; child care is not provided for coaches' children, and schedules are not designed to accommodate responsibilities away from sports (McKay, 1999).

Finally, sport organizations have been notoriously negligent in controlling sexual harassment and responding to complaints from women coaches and administrators who have expectations that are different from the expectations of the men who have shaped organizational cultures. This means that, unless there are changes in the cultures of sport organizations, gender equity will never be achieved in the ranks of coaching and administration.

Access to Informal and Alternative Sports

Gender and fairness issues are not limited to formally organized, mainstream sports. Informal games are often characterized by gender dynamics that present girls and women with special challenges when it comes to gaining access to participation and claiming identities as athletes. Similar challenges often exist in alternative sports settings, both informal and formal. Boys and men generally control participation access and the processes through which participants come to be accepted as fellow athletes.

Whether participation occurs in backyards, on driveways, in local parks, in the gyms and on playing fields of high schools and universities, or on streets and elementary school playgrounds, if participation is gender-mixed, boys and men generally control who plays and who is defined as an athlete. This often leads girls and women to withdraw from participation voluntarily, and it creates a situation in which girls and women must be exceptionally good athletes and have clever inclusion strategies to be given the chance to play and be defined as an athlete by other participants. In some cases, the best strategy is to be "sponsored" by an influential boy or man who vouches for girl's or a woman's "right" to demonstrate what she can do as an athlete.

Forms of excluding and restricting the participation of girls and women in these settings has

Women have been eager participants in some alternative sports. Climbing has been reasonably open to girls and women. However, in many of the new "action sports," boys and men control who plays and who is defined as an athlete, and girls and women have a difficult time being treated seriously in those sports. (Jay Coakley)

received only limited research attention in the sociology of sport. However, we do know that girls and women face unique participation and identity challenges in both informal and alternative sports and that there are equity and fairness issues related to who plays under what conditions. The most important consequence of these issues is that many girls and women feel that they are not welcome to develop and display their skills. Then boys and men say that they should receive priority when it comes to participation access and the use of resources because girls and women are not interested in playing. It's a Catch-22 situation for girls and women, or, as a sociologist would say, it's a gender-based double standard in action.

Laws such as Title IX do not apply to these settings. This means that changes often come more slowly than they do in formal sport settings, such as school-sponsored varsity sports. However, as certain alternative sports become increasingly organized and are sponsored by governing bodies and corporations, young women are expressing their displeasure at being excluded or treated as sexy diversions during events. This has occurred in connection with participation in the XGames, in which the emphasis is on being "hard and aggressive" (Kilvert, 2002). Women have found that they must be accepted on the terms set by men or must try to make "cultural space" for different definitions of achievement and excellence. Consequently, equity and fairness remain elusive.

Strategies to Achieve Equity and Fairness

Equity is about who gets what. Appeals to fairness have not been very effective in creating gender equity in sports. Everyone supports fairness, but many don't want to give up what they already have to achieve it. This certainly has been the pattern in sport programs in which men control most of the power and resources. Most men support the idea of gender equity, but few of them are willing to achieve it by sacrificing their privileges related to participation, support, or jobs.

This resistance has forced proponents of gender equity to ask governments for assistance or to file lawsuits. Governments have been helpful, but they often are slow to respond. Legal actions have been effective, but lawsuits involve costly legal fees and long-term commitments. So far, only a few women have been willing to take on debt and give up years of their lives to see if they can force a sport program to be fair. Only when women have been legally able to sue for personal damages to compensate them for legal fees and lost opportunities have legal actions been a consistently effective means for achieving equity.

According to Donna Lopiano, executive director of the Women's Sport Foundation (WSF), equity can be achieved only through strategic political organization and pressure. She has called for the development of grass-roots organizations to systematically support and publicize sport programs for girls and women. As these organizations publicly recognize the achievements of female athletes and their sponsors, more people will see the value of women's sports and join their efforts to achieve equity. The WSF and other organizations have facilitated this process with its resources, and they have been effective in bringing about progressive changes.

Lopiano (1991) also has urged people in sport organizations to use the following strategies to promote gender equity:

- Confront discriminatory practices in your organization and become an advocate for women athletes and women coaches and administrators.
- Be an advocate and a watchdog and insist on fair and open employment practices in your organization.
- Keep track of data in your organization and have an independent group issue a "gender equity report card" every year to the media.

- Learn and educate others about the history of discrimination in sports and how to recognize the subtle forms of discrimination that operate in sports today.
- Object to and alert the media to any policies that would result in a decrease in women's sport participation or participation opportunities.
- Package and promote women's sports as revenue producers, so that there will be financial incentives to increase participation opportunities for women.
- Recruit women athletes into coaching and establish internships and other programs to recruit and train women to enter jobs at all levels in your organization.
- Use women's hiring networks when looking for coaches and administrators in all sport programs.
- Create a supportive work climate for women in your organization and establish policies to eliminate sexual harassment.

These are useful suggestions. They emphasize a combination of public relations, political lobbying, pressure, education, and advocacy. They are based on the assumption that increased participation and opportunities for women will not come without struggle and that favorable outcomes depend on organization and persistence. More important, they have produced varying degrees of change in many organizations. However, it is important that those who struggle for gender equity understand the origins of inequities and critically assess the ideology that has shaped dominant forms of sport in their society.

If women participate in existing sports and sport organizations without understanding the connections among sports, gender relations, and dominant definitions of *masculinity* in society, they often reproduce ideas about social life that privilege men, guaranteeing that women will never achieve full equity in sports. Striving for equity in activities and organizations that have been shaped over the years by the values and experiences of men *will not* eliminate the most important problems women face as they play and work in sports.

Equity is an important goal, but participation in sports based on a commercialized, media-driven version of the power and performance model should be critically assessed. Those who use critical and critical feminist theories to study sports in society have argued that real gender equity can never be achieved in sport activities and organizations shaped exclusively by the values and experiences of men interested in control, conquest, and domination. They say that real equity requires the development of new models of sport participation, as well as new organizations shaped by the values and experiences of women and of men who do not see themselves in terms of dominant definitions of *masculinity* (Birrell, 2000; Nelson, 1998; Theberge, 2000a). This is discussed in detail in the section "Ideological and Cultural Issues."

Girls and Women as Agents of Change   Some people have assumed that women are empowered when they play sports and that empowered women are effective agents of fairness and equity in sports and in society as a whole. For example, author and former pro basketball player Mariah Burton Nelson says, "Sport is a women's issue because female sport participation empowers women, thereby inexorably changing everything" (1994, p. 9). Research supports Nelson's claim, but only to a point.

Sport participation does provide girls and women with opportunities to connect and reconnect with the power of their own bodies. This is important, because social life sometimes is organized to encourage girls and women to see themselves as weak, dependent, and powerless.

Many images of women in society present the female body as an object to be viewed, evaluated, and consumed, and many girls and women even learn to objectify their own bodies as they apply these images to themselves. Because one's physical identity and sense of power are grounded in a person's body and body image, sport participation can help women overcome the feeling that their bodies are objects. Developing physical skills can give women the confidence that comes from knowing that their bodies can perform with physical competence and power. Furthermore, the physical strength often gained through sport participation goes beyond simply helping a woman feel fit. It also can make her feel less vulnerable, more independent, and more in control of her physical safety and psychological well-being (see Birrell and Richter, 1994; Blinde et al., 1993, 1994; Nelson, 1994, 1998; Theberge, 2000a; Young and White, 1995).

Playing sports also can change how girls and women relate to males. For example, when Fabiola, a standout aggressive in-line skater, was asked how men viewed her, she said, "Men say, 'Oh, girls suck,' and I hate that. I want to show them that girls are really strong" (in Berger, 1999, p. 129). Fabiola does just that, and she is proud of being able to out-skate most men in the world. A seventeen-year-old working-class woman interviewed in England expressed similar feelings about her own weight training:

> I think mainly I want to be . . . equal with the blokes because I think too many girls get pushed around by blokes. They get called names and things. I think that's wrong. They say "a girl can't do this, a girl can't do that," and I don't like it at all. I'd rather be, you know, equal. (in Coakley and White, 1999, p. 80)

Developing physical skills gives women a lift and enables them to be in control of their bodies. In many cases, this helps women feel empowered and less vulnerable, but it does not automatically make them more concerned about women's issues or with equity outside of sports. (Barry Gutierrez; Rocky Mountain News)

These women and many others have used their competence in sports to express a sense of personal empowerment relative to men. However, this sense of empowerment does not occur automatically, nor is it always associated with a form of consciousness that would lead a girl or woman to actively promote fairness and equity issues in sports or other spheres of life. Feeling competence as an athlete does not guarantee that women will critically assess gender ideology and gender relations or work for fairness and equity in sports or anywhere else. For example, after interviewing women intercollegiate athletes in U.S. universities, Elaine Blinde and her colleagues reached this conclusion:

> Women's participation in sport may challenge traditional notions of women's capabilities and provide positive role models for girls and women. However, sport does not appear to be an effective vehicle for developing the athlete's consciousness as a woman or encouraging activism regarding the concerns of women (1994, p. 57).

In fact, some women athletes express negative attitudes toward the idea of feminism, and they make a point to distance themselves from social activism related to women's issues. In other words, those who play elite-level sports are not likely to be "boat rockers" critical of the gender order (McClung and Blinde, 1998; Young and White, 1995). There are four possible reasons for this:

1. Women athletes may feel they have much to lose if they are associated with civil and human rights issues for women, because others might identify them as ungrateful or marginalize them by tagging them with labels such as *feminist, man-hater,* and *lesbian* (Crosset, 1995).
2. The corporation-driven "celebrity feminism" promoted through highly visible women's sports today focuses on individualism and consumption, rather than everyday struggles faced by ordinary girls and women who want to play pleasure and participation sports, as well as ordinary women in need of child care, health care, and a decent job (Cole, 2000a).
3. The "empowerment discourses" associated with fitness and sports tend to emphasize individual self-empowerment through physical changes that improve heterosexual attractiveness (Eskes et al., 1998; MacNeill, 1999).
4. Women athletes, even those with high media profiles and powerful bodies, have little control over their own sport participation and little political voice in their sports or in society as a whole (Lowe, 1998).

Similarly, women hired and promoted into leadership positions in major sport organizations are expected to advance the status of power and performance sports in society. The men who control many sport organizations usually are not eager to hire women who put women's issues on the same level as sport issues. Of course, not all women in these positions become uncritical cheerleaders for power and performance approaches to sports and to life in general. However, it takes effort and courage to engage in a critical analysis of sports and then use the power of those positions to actually change the structure and organization of sports. Without this effort and courage, gender equity comes more slowly.

Boys and Men as Agents of Change   Gender equity is not just a women's issue; equity also involves creating options for men to play sports that are not based on an extreme power and performance model. Sports that emphasize aggression and domination often lead to self-destructive orientations in the forms of chronic injuries, an inability to relate to women, fears of intimacy with other men, homophobia, and a compulsive concern with comparing oneself with other men in terms of what might be called "life success scores" (Burstyn, 1999; White and Young, 1997).

Some men understand that, as they seek rewards in sport organizations in which success is defined in terms of dominating other men, they ultimately constrain and distort their relationships with each other as well as with women. Bruce Kidd, a former Olympic runner and now a physical educator and social scientist, has pointed this out:

> Through sports, men learn to cooperate with, care for, and love other men, in [many] ways, but they rarely learn to be intimate with each other or emotionally honest. On the contrary, the only way many of us express fondness for other men is by teasing or mock fighting. (1987, p. 259)

Men who want to get beyond an expression of fondness based on teasing and mock fighting have good reason to join with those women concerned with critically assessing dominant sport forms in their society (Pronger, 1999).

In summary, some men and women realize that achieving gender equity in a full sense requires fundamental changes in our ideas about gender *and* sports.

Facing Football: A Challenge for Equity Strategies   In the box "Title IX" on page 238–242, I did not mention that one of the primary obstacles to achieving gender equity in high school and college sport programs is the organization and culture of high-profile football teams. Strategies for achieving equity and fairness often come up short in the face of football.

High schools and colleges with large football programs often fail to meet equity goals because of the size and cost of football teams. When football teams have 80 to 120 team members, award 85 scholarships, employ multiple coaches, and have high operational costs, it is impossible for a women's sport program to match the men's program in terms of the budget and number of athletes. For example, only 15 Division 1 universities spend more on all sport teams for women than they spend on football alone (Keating, 2002).

This means that football is the major reason that very few universities meet the Title IX proportionality test. Despite this, university officials resist cutting the size and budgets of football teams—even though many big-time football programs and nearly all other football programs lose money every year. This management decision puts officials in a position in which it is easiest to achieve gender equity by cutting men's teams in nonrevenue-producing sports.

Of course, the men whose teams are cut feel that they are victims of Title IX. But they are actually victims of a management strategy based on giving priority to the current structure and culture of big-time football. It seems that challenging Title IX is easier than challenging football. After all, the structure and culture of the athletic department revolve around football, whereas women's sports are relatively powerless in comparison. Furthermore, defining the loss of men's teams as a men versus women gender battle makes more sense to many men than challenging the sport that represents ideas about masculinity that many of them have used to define their identities and status since they were boys.

When football is the "structural and cultural centerpiece" in schools and their surrounding communities, gender equity is chronically out of reach. The ironic exception to this is that some of the best-funded intercollegiate women's sport programs exist in the fifty to sixty universities where big-time Division 1 football generates so much money that the athletic department is resource-rich. However, most football teams do not make money, and they are supported by boosters whose identities are deeply grounded in a gender ideology reproduced by football. This ideology is not consistent with strategies to achieve gender equity. For example, when a booster of a Georgia high school football team was asked about participation opportunities for girls in the high school, he had this to say:

> We got girls in the band. The cheerleaders are girls. Half the people in the stands are girls. We hold graduation in the stadium, and half the graduates are girls. Our managers are girls; our statisticians are girls. (in Fish and Milliron, 1999)

When football dominates a school's sports program, gender equity often is difficult to achieve. The size and cost of a football team may rival the size and cost of the entire women's sports program in the school. (Joe Mahoney/Rocky Mountain News)

According to his gender ideology, football put everyone in his or her proper place in the school: boys on the field, physically battling for competitive success, with girls on the sidelines, cheering them on and keeping track of what they do. Of course, many people do not agree with this booster. But, when those who agree with him have control over resources for sports, the strategies for achieving equity and fairness must focus on ideological and cultural issues associated with sports.

IDEOLOGICAL AND CULTURAL ISSUES

Cultural ideology refers to sets of interrelated ideas that people use to explain individual action and social life. Ideology is so deeply rooted in our cultural being that we seldom think about it and almost never raise questions about it. We just take it for granted and use it as a form of "cultural logic" to make sense of the world. This is especially the case with gender ideology. Gender is a central organizing principle of social life, and gender ideology influences how we think

of ourselves and others, how we relate to others, and how social life is organized at all levels, from families to societies. It influences what we wear, how we walk, how we present ourselves to others, and how we think about and plan for our future. Most people take gender ideology as a "given" in their lives; they do not question it because it is so deeply rooted in their psyches and the way they live their lives.

The tendency to ignore ideology is a serious problem when we deal with fairness and equity issues in sports. This is because complete fairness and equity cannot be achieved in sports unless we change the gender ideology that has been used in the past to organize, play, and make sense of sports. Therefore, it is important to critically examine the prevailing gender ideology in society, its affects on our lives, its connection with sports, and some strategies for changing it.

Gender Ideology in Society

Gender ideology varies from culture to culture. In most societies in which men have been

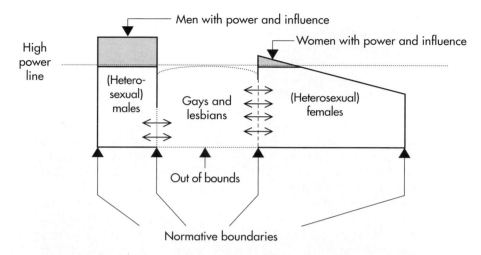

Note: The short double arrows (⟷) indicate two processes: (1) movement into and out of the categories of heterosexual male and female and gay/lesbian and (2) efforts to push normative boundaries to make more space for different ways of "doing" masculinity and femininity.

The "high power line" indicates that, in society as a whole, men occupy a greater number of high power and influence positions, such as heads of state, members of the senate/congress/parliament, CEOs, and top-level leaders and decision makers in religious organizations, education, sports, and the media. A few women in certain societies have pushed the upper limits of gender categories to enter top power positions. However, the "glass ceiling" remains, even though it has been cracked.

FIGURE 8.4   The two-category gender classification system: a representation of gender construction in U.S. culture.

privileged in terms of legal status, formal authority, political and economic power, and access to resources, gender ideology is based on a *simple binary classification system*. According to this system, all people are classified into one of two **sex** categories: male or female (see figure 8.4). These categories are defined in biological terms, and they are conceptualized to highlight difference and opposition; in fact, they are called "opposite sexes." Everyone in the male category is believed to be naturally different from everyone in the female category, and they are held to different normative expectations when it comes to feelings, thoughts, and actions. These expectations outline the basis for how people define and identify **gender**—that is, what is masculine and what is feminine. This classification and interpreta-

tion system is so central to the way many people see the world that they feel they cannot revise or abandon it.

It takes dedication and hard work to maintain a simple binary classification system, because it is inconsistent with evidence showing that anatomy, hormones, chromosomes, and secondary sex characteristics vary in complex ways and cannot be divided neatly into two sex categories, one male and one female. As biologist Anne Fausto-Sterling (2000) explains, "A body's sex is simply too complex. There is no either/or. Rather, there are shades of difference" (p. 3). Real bodies have physiological and biological traits, which are distributed along continua related to these dimensions of physiology.

Of course, this natural sexual/biological variation does not fit with a binary classification system. Therefore, when people are born with physical traits that don't fit our definitions of *male* and *female*, genitals and reproductive organs usually are surgically "fixed" to make them fit (Fausto-Sterling, 2000).

Hormones vary from one person to the next, and both men and women have testosterone and estrogen present in their bodies. However, testosterone is identified as a "male hormone" and estrogen as a "female hormone." This way of thinking about and referring to hormones is misleading, but it enables people to maintain their two-category gender classification system without asking critical questions about it.

Even chromosomal patterns do not always fit neatly into two distinct categories. Nor do secondary sex characteristics, which vary greatly. But we do our best to cover the variations with sex-appropriate clothes and various forms of body management emphasizing characteristics that identify us as male or female. In fact, most people spend considerable time, energy, and money to ensure that their physical characteristics and appearance fit general expectations based on the two-category gender classification system. Those who ignore these expectations risk being marginalized or treated as if they are out of gender bounds. A woman who does not remove natural hair growth above her upper lip or on other parts of her body risks being ridiculed, and a slender man with "fine" features who does not avoid wearing clothes defined as effeminate risks more than ridicule.

Physical variation is real, and to say that all variation can be reduced to two separate and "opposite" categories forces biology to fit popular social definitions of what males and females are "supposed to be" in physical terms.

Being "Out of Bounds": A Problem for Gays and Lesbians

Another problem with a binary classification system is that it comes with relatively fixed ideas and expectations about how men and women are each supposed to feel, think, and act. These ideas and expectations emphasize difference, and they are the foundation for *gender*. A binary gender classification system is based on the assumption that heterosexuality is natural and normal and that those who express feelings, thoughts, and actions that do not fit neatly into the two socially constructed categories of masculine and feminine are "out of bounds" when it comes to gender (review figure 8.2).

When gender ideology is based on this classification system, many people, including gay men, lesbians, and bisexuals, don't fit into either of the two categories, so they usually are defined as deviant. A two-category system provides no social space or recognition for those who are neither heterosexual males nor heterosexual females. This, in turn, serves as a foundation for homophobia, a general fear and/or intolerance felt for those who are "out of bounds" in the classification system.

Power in Society: Gender Ideology in Action

Another important aspect of a binary classification system is that the two categories are seldom equal. As represented in figure 8.2, males have access to higher levels of privilege, power, and influence than females have, and men occupy the highest levels of power and influence in greater numbers than women do. However, there is a social and personal cost with this access to and possession of power.

When a two-category gender classification system exists in cultures where there is an emphasis on equal rights and freedom of expression, the accepted range of feelings, thoughts, and actions for men often is more restricted than it is for women. This means that the normative boundaries associated with masculinity are more restrictive and more closely regulated than the normative boundaries associated with femininity.

Because masculinity comes with greater chances of reaching a high level of power and influence, men have more to lose collectively if they do not conform to gender expectations.

Therefore, they strictly patrol and police their boundaries and sanction those who don't stay within them. Women, on the other hand, have less to lose and more to gain if they push boundaries, although they must do so carefully. What this means in everyday life is that men have less social permission to express the feelings, attitudes, and actions associated with femininity than woman have to express the feelings, thoughts, and actions associated with masculinity. This is why boys are teased for being "sissies," whereas girls are praised for being "tomboys"; it's also why male ballet dancers and interior designers are less likely to be socially accepted in society than are female wrestlers and women in Congress (Laberge and Albert, 1999).

To demonstrate this point, ask the women in a gender-mixed group how many of them have bought clothing for themselves in a men's department of a store; most will say they have done so. Then ask the men how many of them have bought clothing for themselves in a women's department, and listen to the laughter caused by the tension of even thinking about the question. The responses illustrate that men face more restrictive normative boundaries related to gender than women face. However, the payoff for men is that they have more access to power, although not all men gain high levels of power.

Challenging Gender Ideology: Blurring the Old Boundaries

One of the characteristics of a binary classification system is that normative boundaries are socially constructed. However, not everyone accepts or conforms to them. The double arrows in figure 8.2 represent efforts by men and women to push and revise normative boundaries. Of course, women do more pushing than men, although there are potential costs associated with boundary pushing (and "gender bending"). However, normative boundaries often shift over time as the boundary pushers raise issues that lead to revised definitions of *masculinity* and *femininity*. Revisions come slowly, because so many people have vested interests

and identities based in the two-category gender classification system; they use the system as their guide for perceiving and making sense of the social world.

Gender Ideology in Sports

Celebrating Masculinity

Gender is not fixed in nature. Therefore, gender ideology grounded in a binary classification system can be preserved only if people work hard to police gender boundaries and maintain them through myths, rituals, and everyday cultural practices. People must "practice" gender to keep the system viable, and the system is most effectively maintained when gender categories become embodied dimensions of people's lives—that is, when they are built into the way people move and experience the world with and through their bodies. This is how and why sports become important in connection with gender.

Sports have been important sites and activities for preserving gender ideology in many cultures. The meaning of gender and its application in people's lives have been symbolized and powerfully presented in the bodily performances that occur in sports. Men's achievements in power and performance sports have been used as evidence of men's aggressive nature, their superiority over women, and their rights to claim social and physical space as their own. Big, tough, and powerful male athletes are symbolic proof of traditional gender ideology.

When we take a critical look at dominant sport forms in many societies around the world, we see that they often involve actions highlighting masculine virility, power, and toughness—the attributes associated with dominant ideas about masculinity in those societies (Burstyn, 1999). Sport spectacles often celebrate an interpretation of the world that privileges men and perpetuates their power to organize social life to fit their interests. This is why Bruce Kidd (1987) has described sports stadiums and domed arenas as "men's cultural centers." These facilities, often

Traditional gender ideology is reproduced in many men's sports. Some of those sports inspire fantasies and symbols of a heroic manhood, in which playing the role of warrior is the substance of being a man. Do these fantasies and symbols influence how these boys define *masculinity?* (Jay Coakley)

built with public funds, cater to the interests of men, and they host sports in which men "kill," "whip," "roll over," "punish," and "annihilate" other men while others, both men and women, cheer them on. (People often cheer when they see their binary classification system being reaffirmed in such powerful terms!) The images associated with these sports are images of a manhood based on aggression, physical power, and the ability to intimidate and dominate others; they emphasize a concern with ranking people in terms of their ability to dominate. As a Major League Baseball coach noted when asked about hitting strategies used by many players, he noted,

"The bottom line is . . . you're dealing with the male ego. It's not just about winning. . . . It's about dominating" (in Armstrong, 2000, p. 3D). In this way, sports reinforce and perpetuate a gender ideology that favors the interests of men over the interests of women.

Political scientist and cultural critic Varda Burstyn (1999) argues convincingly that the major men's sports in most societies provide a fictive master narrative through which a reality of diverse and contradictory masculinities are homogenized through the fantasies and symbols of a heroic manhood, in which playing the role of warrior becomes the substance of being a man. She notes how sports are a realm of confrontation and domination that provokes a combination of "memories, fantasies, and identifications," which are powerful sources of personal identity and group life among men (see Bricknell, 1999); many men organize their relationships around sports. Furthermore, the masculinized culture of sports takes on serious political implications, because it celebrates values that privilege men and marginalize women. After all, being tough, disciplined, and physically strong enough to dominate others often is the central criterion for evaluating everyone from coaches to business executives: "doing it like a man" is usually the way to gain power and influence.

Girls and Women as Invaders   The participation of girls and women in sports has always presented a threat to the preservation of traditional gender ideology. This is why girls and women have been excluded from playing many sports, or why they have been encouraged to play only sports that emphasize grace, beauty, and coordination. Through most of the twentieth century, this exclusion was rationalized by experts and educators, who told women that they would damage their uteruses and breasts and would experience other physical problems endangering their abilities to have children if they were to play sports. Today's college students laugh at these myths from the past, because young women now have access to information that refutes them. However, it has taken many years to destroy the myths and challenge traditional gender ideology; in fact, myths continue to exist in cultures where literacy rates are low and men control the production and distribution of knowledge.

The legacy of traditional gender ideology still remains strong, even in postindustrial societies. Children learn it in their families, play groups, and schools (Harrison et al., 1999; Hasbrook and Harris, 1999). Journalist Joan Ryan writes about the legacy of traditional gender ideology as it is so vividly demonstrated in the highly popular sports of women's gymnastics and figure skating:

> Talent counts, but so do beauty, class, weight, clothes and politics. The anachronistic lack of ambivalence about femininity in both sports is part of their attraction, harkening back to a simpler time when girls were girls, when women were girls for that matter: coquettish, malleable, eager to please. In figure skating especially, we want our athletes thin, graceful, deferential and cover-girl pretty. We want eyeliner, lipstick and hair ribbons. . . . [We want athletes presented to us] free of the sticky issues of power, sexual orientation and aggression that encumber female athletes in sports [other than figure skating and gymnastics]. (1995, pp. 5, 68)

Living with these ideas about gender is not easy. When U.S. women's figure skating champion Tara Lipinski was fifteen years old and training for the 1998 Nagano Olympics, she said that her most difficult challenge was maintaining the strength and power needed to do seven triple jumps in a routine while still looking cute, soft, and feminine.

Many girls and women have challenged traditional gender ideology and have pushed gender boundaries to make more cultural space for girls and women in sports. As co-captain of the 1999 Women's World Cup team, Julie Foudy says, "Tomboy. All right call me a tomboy. Tomboys get medals. Tomboys win championships. Tomboys can fly. Oh, and tomboys aren't boys" (*WOSPORT Weekly*, 1999). Foudy's statement is encouraging, and it is indicative of changes for women in sports.

Despite changes, remnants of old boundaries continue to exist. For example, as girls get older and their bodies are sexualized in terms of traditional ideas about femininity, they often hear powerful cultural messages that being a tomboy may interfere with meeting expectations for heterosexual attractiveness, lifestyles, and the presentation of themselves. Playing sports is accepted, but the cuteness of being a tomboy during childhood usually disappears during adolescence. If young women do not conform to dominant definitions of *femininity* as they play sports, especially contact and power sports, they may still be socially marginalized and face homophobia in their social lives. Of course, if they have just won a world championship, this may not matter.

FOREVER "LADIES"?   Women athletes deal with the consequences of traditional gender ideology in various ways (Cox and Thompson, 2000). For example, those who play contact and power sports sometimes discover that, unless they are careful to act in "ladylike" ways, the label *tomboy* may change to *lesbian*. Therefore, they sometimes try to be more feminine by wearing hair ribbons, ponytails, makeup, dresses, hose, heels, or engagement or wedding rings; by saying how they like to party (with heterosexuals in heterosexual clubs); and by making statements about boyfriends or husbands and their desire to settle down eventually and have children (Mennesson, 2000). If women athletes in contact and power sports don't do these things, some people define them as threats to the ideas about "nature" and morality that are based on the two-category gender classification system. This is one of the ways that homophobia enters sports and the lives of women athletes (Griffin, 1998; Krane, 1996). The dynamics of this process are discussed in the box "Women Bodybuilders."

The pressure to be "forever ladies" was intensified in the mid-1960s through the late 1990s, when many international sport events, including the Olympics, demanded that women competitors take "gender tests" to prove they were women (see www.pponline.co.uk/encyc/0082.htm). The assumption was that, if they were really good in sports, they may not be real women! At first,

> It's unfortunate that [some golf clubs have policies that exclude women and minorities], but it's just the way it is.
>
> —Tiger Woods, pro golfer, 2002
> (in Dodd, 2002, p. 1C)

the women athletes were required to undress and present themselves, naked, to a panel of doctors. But the women complained that this was degrading.

At the 1968 Olympics in Mexico City, the "testing protocol" changed, and women were required to allow a technician to take cells from the inside of their mouths, so that Olympic testing could run a Barr body test to see if they had "proper" chromosome profiles. But chromosome profiles don't always match the socially constructed two-gender classification system used by IOC officials. This meant that some athletes who had lived their entire lives as women were disqualified for failing the Barr body test. This surprised their husbands (in some cases) and fellow competitors who knew they were women. Most women athletes continued to object to gender testing, and the tests were eliminated by most sport organizations in the 1990s, but 3,500 women athletes at the Olympic Games in Atlanta still remember the anxiety of submitting to the tests to prove they were women. If they wanted to compete, they had to possess their "fem card" certifying their sex.

DOUBLE STANDARDS   Another manifestation of traditional gender ideology is the existence of gender-based double standards for evaluating the behavior of athletes. For example, what would people say if soccer star Mia Hamm were to beat up a man or a couple of women in a bar fight? What if a women's rugby team were to drop their boxer shorts and "moon" some tourists in a public setting? What if WNBA player Sheryl Swoopes were to talk about how she had "accommodated" more than 2,000 men during the past few years (as Magic Johnson did in the early 1990s)? Or what if she had had four children with four different fathers? What if players on a women's university basketball team were to

REFLECT ON SPORTS

Women Bodybuilders
Expanding Definitions of Feminity?

Women bodybuilders have been described as powerful women, unfeminine freaks, the ultimate sexualized hard bodies, new women, gender benders, entertainers, and sideshows for real sports. Descriptions have varied over time and from one group to another as gender ideology has changed.

Until the late 1970s, there was no such thing as competitive women's bodybuilding. It didn't exist, because it so totally contradicted dominant definitions of *femininity* and what people saw as "natural" muscular development for women. The first bodybuilders challenged those definitions of *femininity*, pushed the boundaries of social acceptance, and raised questions about what is natural when it comes to the bodies of women.

Many people continue to see women bodybuilders as rebels or deviants, as freaks of nature. According to the gender ideology used by most people, females are the "weaker sex" when it comes to muscles and strength. Leslie Heywood, a lifelong athlete and currently a professor of English and a bodybuilder, has explained that women bodybuilders challenge this ideology and threaten dominant ideas about gender and nature. She describes women's bodybuilding as

> an in-your-face confrontation with traditional roles, an unavoidable assertion of . . . unequivocal self-expression, an indication of women's right to *be*, for themselves . . . not for anyone else. In a culture that still mostly defines women's purpose as service for others, no wonder female bodybuilding is so controversial. (1998, p. 171)

Therefore, bodybuilders have been accused of being unfeminine, because they are "too muscular," too like men. Of course, not everyone accepts this gender ideology, and, for those seeking new or expanded definitions of *femininity*, women's bodybuilding has provided exciting new images. These images challenge notions of "female frailty" and raise questions about the biology of gender difference.

Like others who challenge the prevailing gender ideology, women bodybuilders often face the constraints of dominant definitions of *femininity*. The

first women bodybuilders were careful not to be too good at building muscles. They emphasized a toned, symmetrical body displayed through carefully

In women's bodybuilding, there is clear tension between muscularity and traditional ideas about femininity. Success in contests demands a combination of muscles and "femininity insignias." The women are more heavily muscled than nearly all men, but they must also take care to smile cutely at judges, pose gracefully in brightly colored bikinis, wear long hair and pony tails, polish their nails, and wear "feminine" jewelry. (Steve Wennerstrom; *Women's Physique World Magazine*)

choreographed graceful moves. Their goal was to stay within the boundaries of femininity as determined by contest judges. However, even this presented problems, because definitions of *femininity* have never been set permanently. Definitions changed, and judges could not provide absolute guidelines for what was too muscular or how much body symmetry was needed to look feminine.

Many women bodybuilders have been frustrated as they have tried to anticipate changing guidelines. For example, one bodybuilder observed,

> When you compete, your muscularity is all, but the judges insist on [our] looking womanly. They try to fudge the issue with garbage about symmetry, proportion and definition. What they really want is tits and ass. (Cammie Lusko in Bolin, 1992a)

Some bodybuilders try to live with the confusion caused by prevailing ideas about gender by making clear distinctions between how they present themselves during competitive posing and what they do in their workouts (Bolin, 1992b, 1998). In the gym, they focus on bodywork and musclebuilding. As Heywood notes, "The gym remains a place where the female body, unlike other places, can, by getting strong, earn a little respect" (1998, p. 187). Serious training overrides concerns about how *gender* is defined outside the gym. Workouts are not "gendered," and bodybuilders, both women and men, train in similar ways.

The public arena of competitive posing is different, and the women try to neutralize the socially imposed stigma of having too many muscles. They use "femininity insignias" to carefully construct a presentation of self that highlights the "look" of dominant femininity as it is defined today. They may dye their hair blonde; wear it in a long, fluffy style; and adorn it with a ribbon. They manicure and polish fingernails or glue on false fingernails. They employ makeup artists, carefully choose posing bikinis for color and material, wear earring studs and an engagement or wedding ring, shave all body hair, and perhaps use plastic surgery to soften the contours of their faces. When they pose, they may walk on their toes, use graceful dance moves, and smile incessantly. They try to be seen with husbands or male friends, and they cautiously flirt with male judges. They do all this to appear "natural" in terms of dominant ideas about femininity (this process is described in Bolin, 1998).

Of course, none of this is natural. When women bodybuilders walk on stage, the femininity insignias they inscribe on their bodies contrast with their muscularity to such an extent that it is difficult for anyone who sees them not to realize that femininity is a social construction rather than a biological fact. The contestants in women's events today are clearly more muscled than 98 percent of the men in the world, and they challenge the notions that women are the weaker sex and that femininity implies frailty and vulnerability.

Those who benefit from traditional gender ideology and definitions of *femininity* have tried to erase images of heavily muscled women and present images of "heterosexualized hard bodies"—bodies desired by men and dependent on men for sexual satisfaction. They use airbrushed photos of bodybuilders in soft-porn poses that highlight vulnerability and accessibility (Heywood, 1998). Muscles are softened, or the women are photographed leaning on or looking up to even more muscular men. Women often go along with this heterosexualized image, so that they can obtain publicity, endorsement contracts, appearance fees, and a chance to be on the cover of *Muscle and Fitness* magazine. Back at the gym, however, they train in ways that contradict the photos.

Even though the public part of women's bodybuilding has been commercially manipulated to fit with traditional ideas about gender, women bodybuilders have made it possible for women to view the development of muscles and strength as a source of personal empowerment. This empowerment focuses on personal change, rather than the development of progressive and collective politics among women, but those personal changes challenge dominant definitions of *femininity*. Isn't this one of the positive things that happens in sports? *What do you think?*

have prominent tattoos on their arms (and they were not butterflies and flowers)? What if *ESPN Magazine* were to publish photographs of Anna Kournikova surrounded by men wearing skimpy bathing suits and looking at her lustfully? Would these women athletes be judged more critically than male athletes behaving or represented in the same way? They probably would be.

This hypothesis does not contradict the points made in the previous discussion of normative boundaries for men and women. When male athletes have bar fights, "flash a moon" in public, admit numerous sexual relationships with women, display macho tattoos, and are pictured in magazines with "available" women draped all over them, they are defined by many people as "tough studs" acting as men act, acting within traditional normative boundaries for men. However, if the men were to say they were gay or were to talk about their intimate relationship with a male partner, they would be judged more harshly than women who have done the same. For example, when NBA star Magic Johnson said he was HIV-positive in 1991, most sport fans were upset, but they expressed great relief when Johnson said he had contracted the virus in one or more of his 2,000 sexual relationships with women. As long as he hadn't contracted it during a sexual encounter with a man, people saw him and his behavior within the bounds of traditional masculinity. Similarly, if a woman athlete were to say she wears men's boxer shorts around the house and under her street clothes, nobody would define this as out of bounds, but, if a male athlete were to say he wears women's underwear, he would face serious social sanctions, and jokes about his identity would be made in the media.

SPORTS AS SITES FOR CHANGE   Although women athletes still live with the consequences of traditional gender ideology, the growing achievements of many women in sports have challenged that ideology and have forced many people to think in new ways about masculinity, femininity, and gender relations (Theberge, 2000a). In fact,

some women's sports have been important sites for pushing the normative boundaries for girls and women and questioning definitions of *femininity*. In some cases, women athletes have even encouraged people to raise questions about the validity of the two-category gender classification system and to rethink the meaning of gender in society.

Gender Ideology: The Challenge of Being Gay or Lesbian in Sports

When a two-category gender classification system is the foundation for defining *gender* in a society, gay men, lesbians, bisexuals, and transgendered people are seen as being outside of normative boundaries. Therefore, they are feared, ignored, or marginalized. They may be harassed and, in extreme cases, physically attacked. Discussions about the identities and lives of those who live outside traditional gender boundaries often evoke strong emotions, defensive reactions, and moral judgments. Exceptions to this exist among people who have questioned the use of a two-category gender classification system and have defined *gender* in less rigidly bounded terms (see figure 8.5).

The same is true in sports: gay men and lesbians are not accepted, homophobia is widespread, and people in sports avoid the topic of homosexuality for fear that the walls of their two-category gender classification system might crumble if they were to acknowledge and talk about it. The silence about gays and lesbians in sports is deafening (Lenskyj, 1999; Nelson, 1991; Pronger, 1999). The silence about homophobia is downright dangerous.

People know that gay men and lesbians play sports, but discussions that acknowledge this are avoided. The exceptions to this exist among openly gay men and lesbians who play and watch sports, as well as among women and men who play on teams and in programs that have developed an open and inclusive culture in which lesbian and gay coaches and teammates are

FIGURE 8.5 Gender ideology is changing. However, when men or women become seriously involved in sports that challenge the two-category gender classification system, some people may tease or discourage them.

accepted. The irony of the silence about sexuality and homophobia is that sports often focus our attention on finely conditioned, attractive bodies at the same time that we carefully discuss sports in asexual or nonsexual terms. The beauty and eroticism of bodies in sports are seldom acknowledged, except in whispered voices (Burstyn, 1999; Pronger, 1999).

Lesbians in Sports Pat Griffin's groundbreaking book *Strong Women, Deep Closets: Lesbians and Homophobia in Sports* (1998) provides clear evidence that "sports and lesbians have always gone together" (p. ix). She notes that this evidence has been ignored and that widespread homophobia has led to the creation of many myths about lesbians. In fact, the myth that all female athletes are lesbians has been used for nearly a century to exclude and discourage all women from playing sports. Today, lesbians play sports, but their identities have been erased as much as possible from the publicity and media coverage of women's sports.

Myths about lesbians have a range of consequences in sports. They have created among many lesbian athletes a sense of loneliness and isolation, combined with fears about being outed. They have created forms of discrimination experienced by lesbians seeking jobs or promotions as coaches and administrators. They have created fears among heterosexual women about relating to lesbian teammates and coaches. Finally, they have created a situation in which lesbians must carefully choose and use one of the following six identity-management strategies:

1. Being completely closeted
2. Passing as heterosexual
3. Covering lesbian identity
4. Being "out" by not covering identity in all situations
5. Being "out" by revealing identity only to trusted others
6. Being an open lesbian in sports and the rest of their lives (Griffin, 1998)

Many women's sports are characterized by a "don't ask, don't tell" atmosphere. Some heterosexuals are uncomfortable dealing with the idea and reality of lesbians in sports, and lesbians often choose a "don't rock the boat" strategy, which enables them to play the sports they love to play without being harassed. However, such a strategy has its costs, and it does not encourage changes that might defuse and even eliminate homophobia in women's sports. Ethics educator Pat Griffin makes a good case for being open and truthful about sexual identity, but she also notes that open lesbians must be prepared to handle everything from hostility to cautious acceptance. She notes that handling challenges is made easier when there are friends, teammates, and coaches who provide support; when organizations exist to challenge expressions of homophobia and advocate tolerance; and when there is institutionalized legal protection for gays and lesbians in organizations, communities, and society.

Gay Men in Sports   Men's sports have always been key sites for celebrating and reproducing dominant ideas about masculinity. Playing sports has been a rite of passage for boys to become men, and many people define male athletes in contact and power sports as the epitome of what it means to be a heterosexual man in society. Therefore, there is much at stake in maintaining the silence about gay men in sports and in discouraging gay male athletes from revealing their identities. This is clearly explained by Canadian physical educator Brian Pronger:

> Sport practice is . . . an important expression of orthodox masculinity. Because homosexuality is a departure from sexual orthodoxy, homosexual athletes tend to be feared, mistrusted, and stigmatized. They are perceived as "letting down the team" by sabotaging the types of masculinity that sport tends to celebrate. (1999, p. 187)

This is why the normative boundaries of gender are actively patrolled and strictly policed in men's sports. Pushing or crossing those boundaries jeopardizes the cultural legitimacy of the two-category gender classification system and the access to power and influence that men have in connection with that system. The message to boys and men in sports is loud and clear: "don't be a fag" and "don't play like a girl." The message to gay men of all ages is also clear: don't challenge the two-category gender classification system because it works for us men and has given some of us privilege and power in sports and in society.

These messages have created deep fears of homosexuality in men's sports. Heterosexual men have developed threatening antigay locker room discourse—forms of verbal gay bashing that would keep gay men in the closet forever and keep heterosexual men silent about homosexuality and fearful of doing anything that could be labeled "gay." Of course, this is the goal, and it has been achieved with frightening efficiency. Stories about gay male athletes are nearly nonexistent; heterosexual men have kept quiet, even when coaches have sexually abused them (Donnelly and Sparks, 1997; Nack and Yaeger, 1999; Robinson, 1998), and most men will sacrifice their bodies to maintain the myth that real men are tough, no matter what the consequences (White and Young, 1997).

The dual silence about homosexuality and homophobia creates a context in which boys and men feel ashamed about feelings of affection toward other men and feel that they must mimic violent caricatures of masculinity to avoid being accused of being "fags" (Messner, 1996). After all, real men play with pain and injuries; they don't admit they are afraid; and they don't confide affectionately in other men, even the teammates they care about deeply. Instead, connections between men in football are expressed through bell-ringing head-butts, belly bashers, shoulder pad slams, arm punches, posttouchdown tackles in the end zone, military-like salutes, and other ritualistic behaviors. Fists are clenched and forearms bumped after home runs in baseball. Other men's sports have their own masculinity rituals. In some cases, these rituals would be funny if they didn't symbolize an approach to manhood that can make certain sports a dangerous place to be. Furthermore, coaches know athletes fear any association with homosexuality, and some coaches even call male athletes "ladies" or "fags" to take advantage of institutionalized homophobia and turn it into a willingness to be aggressive and violent on the playing field.

A significant effort to break the silence about gay men in sports is the book *Jocks: True Stories of America's Gay Male Athletes*. Written by gay journalist and former coach Dan Woog (1998), the book tells the stories of twenty-eight gay men who play, coach, or work in sports. All the men are out to some degree, and Woog tells their stories in a deeply personal, informative, and emotionally moving way. Some of the stories are positive and hopeful, whereas others are sad and depressing. The words of a former college football player represent the spirit of many of the stories:

> We're on your teams. We're next to you. And we're hurting. We need places to be homophobia-free so we can keep playing, so we don't drop out, so we don't kill ourselves. (in Woog, 1998, p. 151)

Gay coaches and administrators also face challenges. Woog notes that "many coaches equate coming out with touching the third rail [of an electric train track]: It brings shock, perhaps [career] death."

Eric Anderson (2000), an openly gay track coach in a California high school has followed Woog's lead and interviewed eighteen self-identified gay male high school and college athletes in the United States. His data support a statement made by one of Woog's interviewees:

> It's not that people in athletics are innately more homophobic than others. But athletics is an area in which they're given permission to dislike and exclude gays. (in Woog, 1998, p. 231)

This point is important, because heterosexual male athletes should *not* be defined as the cause of problems for gay athletes. Problems are caused by definitions of *gender* grounded in a two-category gender classification system. Solutions rest in finding new ways to view gender and gender relations.

Strategies for Changing Ideology and Culture

Fairness and gender equity in sports require a complete rethinking of our definitions of *masculinity* and *femininity*, as well as our ideas about the purposes and goals of sports and sport organizations. This is a complex and challenging task; the following pages offer a few suggestions for how it might be undertaken.

***Alternative Definitions of* Masculinity** We need new definitions of *masculinity* in society. As things are now, dominant forms of sport tend to normalize the idea that masculinity involves aggressiveness and a desire to physically dominate others. In fact, some people associate men's behavior in sports with biological nature and conclude that traditional definitions of *masculinity* are "natural." Strong and aggressive men are lionized and made into heroes in sports, whereas weak or passive men are marginalized and emasculated.

As boys and men apply this ideology to their lives, they learn to view manhood in terms of things that jeopardize the safety and well-being of themselves and others. They may ride the tops of elevators, drive cars at breakneck speeds, play various forms of "chicken," drink each other under the table, get into fights, use violence in sports as indicators of manhood, use dangerous substances to build muscles, avoid interacting with women as equals, keep sexual scores in heterosexual relationships, beat up girlfriends or wives, rape, or kill "unfaithful" women. Some men learn that size and toughness allow them to get away with violating norms and that status depends on making others fear or depend on them. If men take this ideology far enough, they may get in the habit of "forcing their way" on others through physical intimidation or coercion.

Even though this ideology of masculinity can be dangerous and socially isolating, male athletes are seldom criticized for using it to guide their behavior in sports. For example, I've never heard coaches scold athletes for hitting someone too hard or showing no feeling when they have blown out someone's knee, have knocked someone unconscious, or have paralyzed or even killed an opponent (as in boxing). Is it dangerous to teach young men not to hesitate to hurt people or not to express remorse when they do? Does this destroy their ability to empathize with others and feel their pain? If boys are taught to be tough and to dominate others, will they be able to develop intimate and supportive relationships with other men or with women? How will they handle their relationships with women? Will their rates of assault and sexual assault be high?

The frightening record of men's violent and destructive behavior suggests that there is definitely a need to answer these questions and to develop additional and alternative definitions of *masculinity*. The dominant definition of *masculinity* and the idea that "boys will be boys" are closely associated with seriously dangerous actions in many societies around the world—in other spheres of everyday life as well as sports (Miedzian, 1991). However, dominant forms of sport in today's society seem to prevent people from raising questions about gender ideology. The study of sports in society has an important role to play in the raising of these questions.

Alternative Definitions of **Femininity**   The experiences of many women athletes also suggest a need to develop additional definitions of *femininity*. This process has already begun; however, until there is widespread acceptance of alternatives to dominant definitions of *femininity*, women will continue to face problems in connection with playing certain sports. These problems can take many forms, and they often begin early in life. For example, some girls still do not receive the same kind of encouragement as their brothers to be socially independent and physically active in play activities and sports. As infants, they are handled more gently and protectively than boys. Boys are thrown into the air

more often, given more toys requiring active play and the use of motor skills, and allowed to explore more of their physical environment before being cautioned and constrained by their parents. Girls are watched over more closely, even before they start to walk. This pattern of protectiveness and constraint continues through childhood and limits girls' participation in sport activities.

The need for alternative definitions of *femininity* should not be taken to mean that girls and women should adopt behaviors that express traditional ideas about masculinity. It is important for girls and women to explore and connect with the power of their bodies and to do so in competitive sports as well as other physical activities. Therefore, there is a need for definitions of *femininity* that embrace the notions of competing with other women in sports, competing with men, and striving for victories while respecting opponents (Nelson, 1998). Finally, there is a need for definitions of *femininity* that include and support visibly strong women. There are still people who see strong women and say, "Do you think she is really female?" (Caudwell, 1999); apparently, they have no space in their two-gender classification system to include a woman who is strong.

Strong women have always challenged that system, and there is a need for new femininities that recognize and support those women. The same is true for lesbian women. New spaces must be created to recognize and support their identities in sports and in society as a whole.

Changing The Way We Do Sports   Gender equity involves more than inventing new ways to define and perform masculinity and femininity. It also depends on changes in how sports are defined, organized, and played. We need new types of sport programs, new vocabularies to describe those programs, new images that people can associate with sports, and new ways to evaluate success and the enjoyment of sport experiences (Burstyn, 1999; Hargreaves, 2000; Nelson, 1998).

As new ideas about femininity have been accepted, girls and women have become involved in sport settings where they were previously excluded. Only a small number of parents and coaches in this youth football league had problems when this girl excelled as a defensive end on one of the teams. (Jay Coakley)

At the same time, we need women and men who can critically assess sports to become a part of existing programs and work to change sports from inside. (See chapter 16.)

One strategy for achieving fairness and gender equity is to develop new sport programs that change how we do sports. Some of the possibilities include the following:

1. Programs promoting lifetime sport participation and emphasizing combinations of competition and partnership, individual expression and teamwork, and health and skill development

2. Programs reflecting an ethic of care and connection between teammates and opponents (Duquin, 1993)

3. Programs providing coaching and administrative opportunities for women, thereby creating more experiences that generate feelings of empowerment among women and the opportunities to put those feelings into action, like those that men have had for many years in sports

4. Programs bringing boys and girls and men and women together in shared sport experiences that promote new ideas about gender

The creation of new sport programs should not be the only strategy used to achieve equity. New programs are useful, but they may present political problems when it comes to gender equity issues—for example,

1. When women's sport programs are structured differently than men's programs, it can be difficult to determine if there are equal opportunities for girls and women.
2. New sport programs that are different from those already in existence run the risk of being perceived as "second class," thereby perpetuating notions of female inferiority.
3. New sport programs are more difficult to promote than programs based on existing models, and it is much easier to apply pressure for equal resources within schools and other organizations when asking for comparable programs than when asking for new programs.
4. Sports that cannot be used to reproduce masculinity often are devalued and defined as "not real" and are treated accordingly.

The point here is that efforts to create new sport programs run the risk of inadequate funding and the loss of some community support. On the other hand, the approach in which girls and women simply participate in dominant sport forms has risks as well: girls could be discouraged from playing sports, ideals could be compromised, and problems tied to beliefs about male superiority could be reproduced.

In the long run, it may be most effective for those interested in promoting fairness and gender equity to maintain both approaches simultaneously. This means that those who strive to participate in existing sports should continue to be aware of alternatives for the future. Then, as they gain power in sports, they will have a vision of how participation opportunities might be maximized for all people. Likewise, those who envision new sport forms should recognize that women could use their participation in existing sports and sport organizations to establish credibility and gain access to the power and resources needed to make changes.

All of us can encourage ideological and cultural change by critically assessing how we talk about sports. We could eliminate the language of difference and domination associated with sports and sport participation. Labels such as *sissy*, *tomboy*, *fag*, and *wimp* inscribe gender into sports in ways that interfere with gender equity. Motivating young men by telling them to go out and prove their masculinity on the playing field has similar consequences. Locker-room language that bashes gays and demeans women also subverts the achievement of gender equity; the listener who stands by and says nothing in response to this language perpetuates inequities. The use of military metaphors to describe what happens in sports is another way that sports are masculinized: "throwing long bombs" and "killing the opposition" are just two examples of metaphors based on the experiences of men, not women (Segrave, 1994; Trujillo, 1995).

Structural and ideological changes promoting gender equity also could be encouraged through rule changes in sports. For example, there is a need for rules to eliminate violence in such sports as hockey, football, rugby, and soccer. Men will object to such rules by saying they make sports into "girls' games," but such comments only reaffirm that the rules are necessary. Sports also need more rituals that bring opponents together in ways that emphasize partnership rather than hostility and rivalry.

Gender equity depends on redesigning sports from both the outside and the inside, as well as on developing new sports that reflect the values and experiences of women and of men who don't identify themselves in terms of the dominant definition of *masculinity*. As we think about gender equity it is important to decide if the goal is to have girls and women play sports just as men have played them, or if the goal is to provide a wide range of choices for women and men when it comes to organizing, playing, and giving meaning to sports.

SUMMARY

DOES EQUITY REQUIRE IDEOLOGICAL CHANGES?

Sport participation among females has increased dramatically since the late 1970s. This has been primarily the result of a growth in opportunities fueled by equal rights legislation, the women's movement, the health and fitness movement, and increased publicity given to women athletes.

Despite this trend of increased participation, future increases in sport participation among girls and women will not be automatic. In fact, there are reasons to be cautious when we predict increases. These reasons include budget cuts and privatization of sports, resistance to government policies and legislation, backlash in response to changes favoring strong women, a relative lack of women coaches and administrators, a cultural emphasis on cosmetic fitness among women, the trivialization of women's sports, and the existence of homophobia.

More women than ever are playing sports and working in sport organizations, but gender inequities continue to exist in participation opportunities, support for athletes, jobs for women in coaching and administration, and informal and alternative sports.

Even when sport participation leads to feelings of personal empowerment among women, the achievement of full gender equity is impossible without a critical analysis of the gender ideology used in sports and society as a whole. This critical analysis is important, because it not only gives direction to women's efforts to achieve fairness and equity but also shows that there are reasons for men to join women who are trying to achieve equity.

The major point of this chapter is that gender equity in sports is integrally tied to ideological and cultural issues. Gender equity will never be complete or permanent without changes in how people think about masculinity and femininity and in how sports are organized and played.

Dominant sport forms in society are currently based on a two-category gender classification system, which leads to the conclusion that girls and women are, by definition, inferior to boys and men. The gender ideology based on this classification system includes beliefs about male-female differences that "naturalize" the superiority of men over women and erase the existence of gay men and lesbians from cultural images about sports and athletes. Therefore, sports celebrate a form of masculinity that leads to the social marginalization of women and many men. As this form of masculinity is celebrated through sports, homophobia and misogyny are built right into the structure of sports and sport organizations.

Because of prevailing gender ideology and the fact that sports have been shaped by the values and experiences of men, real and lasting gender equity depends on changing dominant definitions of *masculinity* and *femininity* and the way we do sports. New sports and sport organizations need to be created, whereas existing ones need to be changed both from the inside and through outside pressure.

Change in sports can be accomplished through a combination of strategies: using new ways to talk about sports; developing new rules to control violence and injuries and to foster safety for all players; and creating new rituals and orientations based on the pleasure and participation approach to sports, rather than the power and performance approach. Unless ideology changes, fairness and gender equity will never be completely and permanently achieved. This is the reason those interested in gender equity in sports should be interested also in gender and gender relations issues outside of sports.

 SUGGESTED READINGS

Burstyn, V. 1999. *The rites of men: Manhood, politics, and the culture of sport.* Toronto: University of Toronto Press (critical feminist analysis of gender ideology, masculinity, and sports; focuses on history, media, commercialization, violence, drugs, and social change).

Fausto-Sterling, A. 2000. *Sexing the body: Gender politics and the construction of sexuality*. New York: Basic Books (analysis of the "science of the body," showing how and why two-sex/gender classifications systems are neither natural nor cultural universals; written by a biologist who knows the history and sociology of sex and gender).

Griffin, P. 1998. *Strong women, deep closets: Lesbians and homophobia in sports*. Champaign, IL: Human Kinetics (explores the experiences of lesbians in sports; written by an educator with personal, professional concerns about ethics and equity in sports).

Hargreaves, J. 2000. *Heroines of sport: The politics of difference and identity*. London: Routledge (analysis of women's sports that focuses on the experiences of particular groups of women around the world—South African women, Muslim women in western Asia, Aboriginal women from Australia and Canada, lesbians, and women with disabilities; the global scope of the analysis highlights issues seldom discussed in connection with gender).

Messner, M. A. 2002. *Taking the field: Women, men, and sports*. Minneapolis: University of Minnesota Press (analysis of gender as it is incorporated into the everyday lives of sport participants, the structures of sport organizations, and the ideologies and belief systems transmitted through the media).

Theberge, N. 2000. *Higher goals: Women's ice hockey and the politics of gender*. Albany: State University of New York Press (research based on two seasons of observations and interviews with the members of an elite women's hockey team; the author provides a valuable inside-the-locker-room look at how women define and give meaning to their sport experiences).

Thompson, S. 1999. *Mother's taxi: Sport and women's labor*. Albany: State University of New York Press (research on how sports in many situations depend on behind-the-scenes free work done by mothers, wives, and girlfriends; data were gathered in Australia, but the analysis is relevant for other postindustrial countries where adult leagues and youth sports are a prominent part of community life).

Whannel, G. 2002. *Media sport stars: Masculinities and moralities*. London/New York: Routledge (analysis of how the media have created sport stars around particular images of masculinity and in connection with what many people believe to be a general crisis of masculinity in society).

White, P., and K. Young, eds. 1999. *Sport and gender in Canada*. Don Mills, Ontario: Oxford University Press (the sixteen chapters in this collection provide analyses of current issues; discussions of gender relations and power, sexuality, homophobia, harassment and abuse, aging, disabilities, race and ethnicity, and the organization of sports).

Woog, D. 1998. *Jocks: The true story of America's gay male athletes*. Los Angeles: Alyson Books (twenty-eight stories that give voice to gay men who play, coach, referee, and work in sports; written by a journalist sensitive to the need to break the silence about gay men in sports).

 **WEBSITE RESOURCES**

Note: Websites often change. The following URLs were current when this book was printed. Please check our website (www.mhhe.com/coakley8e) for updates and additions.

www.mhhe.com/coakley8e Discussion of cheerleaders and gender issues.

http://raw.rutgers.edu/womenandsports Valuable gateway site for women in sports links.

http://chronicle.com/indepth/titleix Classic source for information on Title IX.

http://education.umn.edu/tuckercenter/default.htm Site of the Tucker Center for Research on Girls and Women in Sports, directed by Mary Jo Kane; describes the center and provides numerous links to women in sports sites.

www.de.psu.edu/wsi/contacts.htm Site for WomenSports International; provides links to sites about women's sports in Australia, Canada, Japan, United Kingdom, and the United States.

www.de.psu.edu/wsi/wsweb.htm Site for Women's Sports on the web; links to sites about women's sports around the world; see especially the link to *Women in the Olympic Movement*.

www.feminist.org/research/sports2.html Special coverage of "empowering women in sports"; this site has useful links and information about issues related to gender relations and women in sports.

www.feminist.org/gateway/sp_exec2.html Numerous links to sites dealing with girls and women in sports; links include many sites related to gender equity.

www.iwg-gti.org Site of the International Working Group on Women and Sport; contains information on programs, policy issues, and problems faced by girls and women in more than 100 nations.

www.ajc.com Site for the *Atlanta Journal Constitution*—go to Archives and search for Mike Fish's eight-day series, "The Gender Gap"; discusses gender inequities in Georgia High Schools in 1999.

www.aahperd.org/nagws/publications-related sites.html The National Association for Girls and Women in Sport is an active organization advancing gender equity in U.S. schools; excellent information on Title IX, plus a link to Acosta and Carpenter's twenty-five-year study of woman in intercollegiate sports programs.

www.sportinsociety.org Center for the Study of Sport in Society; click on Urban Youth Sports and SportsCAP; both of these programs are designed to increase participation and job opportunities for girls and women in sports; also click on the Racial and Gender Report Card to find data on the affirmative action records of major U.S. professional sport leagues and Division I intercollegiate sports in the United States.

(Jay Coakley)

Race and Ethnicity

Are They Important in Sports?

SPORTS CAN BRING KIDS together. It can also pull them apart by feeding the misconception that race predetermines what athletes can or cannot do.

—Michael Dobie, journalist (2000, p. 335)

 **Online Learning Center Resources**

Visit *Sports in Society*'s Online Learning Center at **www.mhhe.com/coakley8e** for additional information and study material for this chapter, including

- Self-grading quizzes
- Learning objectives
- Related websites
- Additional readings

A complete outline is available online at www.mhhe.com/coakley8e.

THE SPORTS INDUSTRY is a white and male-dominated institution. Historically, black women have [not been] a real threat to the system, because we are women, and women do not have real power.

—Colette D. Winlock, former U.S. track star (2000)

Sports involve complex issues related to race and ethnicity. These issues have increasing social relevance as global migration and political changes bring together people from different racial and ethnic backgrounds and create new challenges for living, working, and playing together. The challenges created by racial and ethnic diversity are among the most important ones we face in the twenty-first century (Edwards, 2000).

Cultural beliefs about race and ethnicity influence social relationships and the organization of social life. Sports not only reflect this influence but also are sites where people challenge or reproduce dominant beliefs and forms of racial and ethnic relations in a society. As people make sense of sports and give meaning to their experiences as athletes and spectators, and to the experiences of others, they often take into account ideas about skin color and ethnicity.

Not surprisingly, the social meanings and the experiences associated with skin color and ethnic background influence access to sport participation, decisions about playing sports, and the ways in which sports are integrated into everyday life. People in some racial and ethnic groups use sport participation to express their cultural identity and even their sense of biological and cultural destiny. In some cases, people may be identified and evaluated as athletes because of the meanings given to their skin color or ethnic background.

Sports also are cultural sites where people formulate or change their ideas about skin color and ethnic heritage. These ideas often are carried over and used in other parts of people's lives. This is why sports are more than mere reflections of racial and ethnic relations in society and why it is important to study them if we want to understand the dynamics of racial and ethnic relations in society.

In light of these factors, this chapter will focus on the following topics:

1. Definitions of *race* and *ethnicity*, as well as the origins of ideas about race in culture

2. Racial classification systems and the use of racial ideology in sports
3. Sport participation patterns among racial and ethnic minorities in the United States
4. The dynamics of racial and ethnic relations in sports

DEFINITIONS OF *RACE, ETHNICITY,* AND *MINORITY GROUP*

Discussions about race and ethnicity can be confusing when people do not define their terms. In this chapter, **race** refers to a category of people regarded as socially distinct because they share genetically transmitted traits believed to be important by people with power and influence in a society. When people identify a racial group, they use or infer a classification system that divides all human beings into distinct categories, which share physical traits passed from one generation to the next through genes. Therefore, race involves a reference to physical traits, but it is ultimately based on a socially constructed classification system developed around the meanings that people have given to particular physical traits (see the section "Origins and Implications of the Concept of Race" for further explanation).

Ethnicity is different from race in that it refers to the cultural heritage of a particular group of people. Ethnicity is *not* based on biology or genetically determined traits; instead, it is based on characteristics associated with cultural traditions and background. An **ethnic group** is a category of people regarded as socially distinct because they share a way of life and a commitment to the ideas, norms, and material things that constitute that way of life.

Confusion is created when people use *race* and *ethnicity* interchangeably as they deal with social and behavioral issues. One reason some people use these terms interchangeably is that most racial and ethnic groups are assumed to be "minority groups." However, this is not always accurate. **Minority group** is a sociological term used to refer to a socially identified collection of people who experience discrimination, suffer social disadvantages because of discrimination, and have a strong self-consciousness based on their shared experiences of discriminatory treatment. Of course, not all minority groups are racial or ethnic groups, and not all racial or ethnic groups are minority groups. For example, whites in the United States may be identified as a racial group, but they would not be a minority group unless another racial group had the power to subject them to systematic discrimination, which would put them at a collective disadvantage in the social, economic, and political life of U.S. society. Similarly, Polish people in the United States may be considered an ethnic group, but they are not a minority group. Mexican Americans, on the other hand, are clearly an ethnic group that also is a minority group.

Another reason for confusion is that some people define African Americans as an ethnic group because of their shared cultural heritage, whereas others define African Americans as a racial group because the physical trait of skin color has been given important social meaning in U.S. culture. Of course, there are many cases when race and ethnicity overlap. This, combined with problems associated with the validity of racial classification systems, has led many scholars to focus their research and vocabulary on ethnicity rather than race.

In summary, it is important to remember that the definition of *race* focuses on biologically based traits and characteristics, whereas the definition of *ethnicity* focuses on culturally based orientations and behaviors. The definition of *minority group* focuses on an identifiable collection of people who suffer disadvantages at the hands of others who define them as inferior or unworthy and have the power to affect their lives negatively.

> Science has a long and disreputable history of making false extrapolations from inconclusive hard data— extrapolations that merely parrot the prejudices of the age.
> —Gary Kamiya, Executive Editor, *Solon* (2000, online)

Origins and Implications of the Concept of Race

When people divide human beings into racial categories, they use classification systems based on social meanings given to particular biological traits. The racial categories that people use today are cultural creations, and they are not indicators of deep underlying biological truths about human beings and their similarities and differences. The physical traits that people use to identify races are traits that have been given special meaning among a particular group of people. This meaning often is tied to complex beliefs about the deep importance and implications of a particular trait. In other words, the trait comes to symbolize something about the genetic ancestry and the underlying character of the person who has it.

Over the past three centuries, there have been numerous attempts to develop valid biological classification systems that divide humans into distinct racial groups. Scientists have used classifications based on many factors, including mental characteristics, brain size, skin color, and many combinations of head shape, hair texture, stature, and nose shape, combined with skin color. In the process, they have "discovered" dozens of races, subraces, collateral races, and collateral subraces—as they have been labeled in various racial classification systems. In fact, they have found that differences among people are so numerous and overlapping that it is impossible to fit humans into distinct biological categories that do not overlap in many ways; instead, dozens of categories are needed, and, even then, many populations of people fall between or around categories.

Popularly used racial classification systems are confusing, because they are based on *continuous traits*, such as skin color or other biological characteristics that exist to some degree in everyone. Height is a good example of a continuous trait: everyone has some height, people vary from short to tall, and it is impossible to use biological criteria for separating people into distinct "height groups." Height falls along a continuum, with the shortest person in the world on one end of the continuum, the tallest person on the other, and everyone else in between. If we want to divide people into height groups, we have to agree about where one group ends and the next begins. Therefore, height groups would be based on social agreement, rather than biological fact—even though height is a physical characteristic.

The same is true for skin color, which also is a continuous physical trait. Skin color varies from *snow white* to *midnight black*, with an infinite array of color shades in between. When skin color is used to identify racial groups, the trick is determining where lines should be drawn to distinguish one racial group from others. Lines can be drawn anywhere and everywhere. There can be 2 lines or 2,000 lines. There are no biological rules for where to draw lines or how many to draw. Even after lines are drawn at particular points along the continuum, someone else may decide to draw them in other places! The decisions on where to draw the lines and how many lines to draw are based on social decisions about biological characteristics. This is why many scientists have abandoned the search for a biology-based racial classification system.[1]

Geneticist Luigi Cavalli-Sforza from Stanford University explains that racial classification systems have little biological utility because

> the characteristics we see with the naked eye that help us distinguish individuals from different continents are, in reality, skin-deep. Whenever we look under the veneer, we find that the differences that seem so conspicuous to us are really trivial. (in Boyd, 1996: A14; see also Cavalli-Sforza and Cavalli-Sforza, 1995, chapter 9)

However, people around the world continue to use racial classification systems to identify and mark themselves and others in social relationships and everyday life. These systems vary from one culture to another, because different cultures use different definitions of *race*. Thus, a person might be classified as "black" in the United States, but not in Brazil, Haiti, or Egypt, where the meanings and uses of race are different. For example, former tennis player Yannick Noah explains that in his native France he is considered black, but in Africa he is considered white. In Brazil, he would be classified in yet another way, because people there use up to 135 terms when asked to classify their race. Only 4 percent of Brazilians classify themselves as black, even though half of all Brazilians would be "black" according to prevailing racial definitions in the United States. Also confusing is that not all racial classification systems use skin color as the primary distinguishing trait.

Race in the United States

Biological variations exist among certain human populations, but traditional racial classification systems distort and oversimplify those variations. The racial classification system used by many people in U.S. culture is based on widely shared and culturally unique social meanings associated with skin color. Historically, the key principle underlying this classification system has been the "one drop rule," or the rule of *hypo-descent*. This rule was developed by white men to ensure that

---

[1]This conclusion needs to be qualified. Using genetics to identify and understand disease patterns in certain human populations has been successful. However, the "races" identified through these attempts do not correspond to the racial definitions and classifications popularly used by Europeans and North Americans today and in the past. In fact, these new, medically useful "genetic populations" often group blacks and whites together. For example, there is evidence of a "sickle-cell race," but it includes Greeks, Italians, and Africans living close to the equator (see Begley, 1995).

Tiger Woods is only one-quarter African American, yet he is often identified as black because of how race has been defined by most people in the United States. Annika Sorenstam, a highly talented Swedish golfer, is defined as white, even though her physical characteristics are quite different from those of Italians, Greeks, and others commonly described as whites according to the racial classification system used by many people in the United States. (Mark J. Terrill; AP/Wide World Photos)

the "white race" would remain "pure" and that property ownership would remain in the hands of white males, even when children were born to one black and one white parent. As long as a person had "one drop of black blood," he or she was defined as black. There was no middle ground, according to prevailing social and legal definitions, although, in biological terms, there were many "mixed-race" people. There was no social recognition of racially mixed parentage, and people were classified as black even though they had white ancestry. This helped preserve the institution of slavery, it kept assets and estates in the hands of white men, and it discouraged white women from having sexual relationships with black men because the children born of those relationships would be considered black, and the women would face discrimination and the prospect of being socially separated from their children.

The legal definitions of *race* have changed over the past 300 years, but the legacy of the "one drop rule" still creates confusing social and identity issues. For example, when golfer Tiger Woods was identified by others as black, he noted that he was actually "Cablinasian"—a term he invented to describe the fact that he is one-fourth Thai, one-fourth Chinese, one-fourth African American, one-eighth Native American, and one-eighth white European (Ca-bl-in-asian = *Ca*ucasian + *Bl*ack + *In*dian + *Asian*). Other mixed-race persons in sports are constantly referred to as black, even though one of their parents or grandparents is white.

As a *cultural creation*, race has been a powerful force around the world. Race is not a valid biological concept, but it continues to have life-and-death implications for many people, and it is tied to systems of privilege and discrimination that affect all people. This makes race and race theories important topics for study if we want to understand human actions and social relationships. However, when it comes to using racial classifications in our personal lives, we should recognize that the human race contains many combinations of changing physical similarities and differences and that *traditional racial categories are based on the social meanings given to those similarities and differences, not on biology.*

RACIAL CLASSIFICATION SYSTEMS AND RACIAL IDEOLOGY IN SPORTS

Racial Ideology in Euro-American History

Racial classification systems and ideas about the meaning of race were developed in the 1700s, as white Europeans who were exploring and colonizing territories around the globe tried to explain why everyone in the world did not look or act as they did. They assumed that their own appearance and actions were normal and that any variations were strange, deviant, immoral, irrational, or primitive. In this way, whiteness became the standard against which all other things were measured and evaluated.

Between the seventeenth and early twentieth centuries, this approach led to beliefs among whites that people of color around the world were primitive beings driven by brawn rather than brains, instincts rather than moral codes, and impulse rather than rationality. These beliefs were used to justify the colonization and subsequent exploitation of these peoples.

White Europeans and North Americans also developed racial theories leading them to conclude that any expressions of physicality and physical skills among people with dark skin were signs of intellectual inferiority and arrested development. Such theories, wrongheaded as they were, fit neatly with an oversimplified Darwinian model of human evolution, in which mental traits were seen to be superior to physical traits among humans and other primates. This approach led to the conclusion that white-skinned people were superior beings who deserved to be in positions of power and control around the world (this belief is called Social Darwinism). To whites, these ideas about race made perfect sense, because they had "facts" to support it.

The belief that white-skinned people were intellectually superior, whereas people of color were "animal-like savages" was very convenient to white colonial powers (Hoberman, 1992). Although it led some whites to view blacks as pagans who needed to be "civilized" and have their souls saved, and hence were the "white man's burden," it enabled other whites both to kill dark-skinned natives without guilt and to subjugate them as slaves and indentured servants. Because it was so convenient, these ideas eventually became institutionalized in the form of a complex racial ideology about skin color, intelligence, character, and physical characteristics and skills.

As noted in chapter 1, racial ideology is an interrelated set of ideas that people use to give meaning to skin color and to evaluate people in terms of racial classifications. Racial ideologies vary around the world and change over time. But, over the past three centuries, they have been powerful forces in the social lives of many people. They continue to be used to place people into racial categories, interpret actions and relationships, and construct social practices and policies that affect people's lives.

This racial ideology has been revised continually over the years to fit new circumstances, explain contradictions, and justify new forms of racial discrimination. For example, just after the Civil War, a surgeon in New Orleans who treated "colored" soldiers wounded in the war noted that "at present, [my black patients are] too animal to have moral courage or endurance" (in Hoberman, 1992, p. 44). His conclusions suggested that maybe "colored people" would eventually evolve into something less animal-like.

Then, when Africans and other people of color engaged in clearly courageous acts, most whites used racial ideology to point out that such behavior among blacks was a sign of ignorance and desperation, rather than *real* character. In fact, some white people went so far as to say that people of color did not feel pain in the same way whites did and that this permitted dark-skinned people to engage in superhuman physical feats. Whites concluded that those feats were meaningless acts driven by animal instincts, instead of heroic acts driven by human moral character. Of course, when whites did extraordinary physical things, racial ideology led many whites to see their actions as indications of fortitude, intelligence, moral character, and a "civilized" nature.

Whites in the United States and many colonized areas used this ideology to justify slavery and the physical mistreatment of African slaves. During the early part of the twentieth century, they used it to explain the success of African American boxers and other athletes (see figure 9.1). For example, black males were believed to have unique physical stamina and skills grounded in an absence of deep human feelings and intellectual awareness. In fact, many whites even thought the skulls of black people were so thick that they could not be bruised or broken by a white man's fist (Hoberman, 1992). Thus, when black boxers were successful, this racial ideology was used to explain their success.

A clear example of the racial ideology used during much of the twentieth century is illustrated by the media coverage of the highly publicized championship boxing match between Joe Louis, the legendary African American heavyweight champion, and Italian champion Primo Carnera. After Lewis defeated Carnera before 60,000 people in Yankee Stadium in 1935, sportswriters in the United States described him

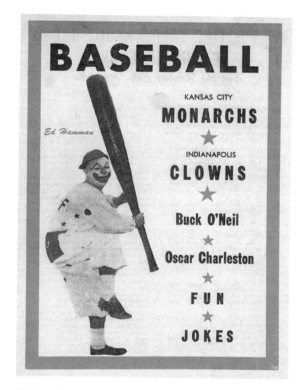

FIGURE 9.1 African American athletes were not taken seriously by most white people through much of the twentieth century. To make money playing sports, they often had to present themselves to fit the racial stereotypes held by whites. The Indianapolis Clowns baseball team and the Harlem Globetrotters basketball team joked around and acted in childlike ways so that whites would pay to watch them. Racism seemed to allow cultural space for blacks to be entertainers for the enjoyment of whites. (American Memory Collection)

as "savage and animalistic." A major news service story sent all over the country began this way:

> Something sly and sinister and perhaps not quite human came out of the African jungle last night to strike down and utterly demolish . . . Primo Carnera. (Mead, 1985, p. 91)

Noted sportswriter Grantland Rice referred to Louis' quickness as "the speed of the jungle, the instinctive speed of the wild" (in Mead, 1985, p. 91). Before another Louis fight, *New York Times* sports editor Paul Gallico wrote a nation-wide syndicated column in which he described Louis in this way:

> The magnificent animal. . . . He eats. He sleeps. He fights. . . . Is he all instinct, all animal? Or have a hundred million years left a fold upon his brain? I see in this colored man something so cold, so hard, so cruel that I wonder as to his bravery. Courage in the animal is desperation. Courage in the human is something incalculable and divine. (in Mead, 1985, p. 92)

Despite hundreds of these stories, Joe Louis remained dedicated to representing African Americans as an ambassador of goodwill to whites. However, despite his dedication and gentlemanly behavior, he was still described as "a natural athlete . . . born to listen to jazz . . . eat a lot of fried chicken, play ball with the gang on the corner and never do a lick of heavy work he could escape" (from a story in a New York paper, in Mead, 1985, p. 96). Racial ideology can be powerful, because it influences what people see and how they interpret the world.

Recent history in predominantly white societies indicates that racial ideology encourages people to see the world in terms of black and white. Many people learn to use a form of racial profiling as they try to make sense of people, actions, relationships, and social life, especially when people of color are involved. Racial ideology elevates skin color and racial classification to a position of prominence when it comes to perceiving and interpreting information in the world around us. It makes skin color different from eye color, height, weight, hair color, shoe size, and other physical traits when it comes to identifying and understanding human beings.

This racializing of the world sometimes is difficult for white people to understand, because whiteness has become normalized in predominantly white cultures to the point that whites often do not think of themselves in racial terms or as having "color". Few whites mention "whiteness" in their self-descriptions, although references to skin color are clearly given a high priority in the identity statements of most blacks in the United States and in many other predominantly white cultures. When white people look in the mirror, they tend to see human beings, or maybe men or women. When black people look in the mirror, they often see *black* men or *black* women. Whiteness has become colorless to the point that one of the privileges of being white in society is "never having to think about race, if you don't want to"—unless, of course, your sports in society textbook forces you to think about it. A black person does not have this privilege, unless he or she lives in a setting where everyone else is black and where nobody is affected by the actions of whites.

Racial Ideology in Sports Today

The use of racial ideology today is complex and often subtle, but it revolves around the assumption of racial differences and the related assumption that differences are ultimately grounded in biological factors. A more subtle assumption underlying dominant ideas about race in societies where whites traditionally have power and influence is that whiteness is the norm and that any variation from this norm constitutes something out of the ordinary, something problematic or deviant, and something that requires study and explanation. Sports provide many examples of this.

"Seeing" Sport Performances in Black-and-White   Skiers from Austria and Switzerland, countries that together are half the geographical size of the state of Colorado, with populations that together are one-twentieth the size of the U.S. population, have won many more World Cup championships than U.S. skiers. Even though this occurs year after year, people do not look to race-based genetic ancestry to discover why the Austrians and Swiss are such good

skiers. Everyone already knows why: they live in the Alps, they learn to ski before they go to preschool, they grow up in a culture in which skiing is highly valued, they have many opportunities to ski, all their friends ski and talk about skiing, they see fellow Austrian and Swiss skiers winning races and making money in highly publicized (in Europe) World Cup competitions, and their cultural heroes are skiers. Racial ideology focuses attention on these *cultural* factors when the athletes are white; thus, there has been no search for "ski genes" that can be traced to the white ancestors of Austrian and Swiss skiers.

Dominant racial ideology has not led to studies looking for race-related genetic explanations for the success of athletes packaged in white skin, even when the shades of white and genetic histories vary among so-called Caucasians around the world. There have been no claims that white Canadians owe their success in hockey to naturally strong ankle joints, instinctive eye-hand-foot coordination, or an innate tendency not to sweat, so they can retain body heat in cold weather. When event after event in the Olympic Nordic skiing finals involve white men and women, few people think about explaining performance success in terms of the race-related genetic ancestry and the racial similarity of the cross-country skiers. The "fact" of white success in these sports is not studied from a racial starting point; whiteness is not "seen" because prevailing ideas about race have made it the taken-for-granted standard against which everything else is viewed.

However, when athletes with black skin excel or fail at a certain sport, regardless of where they come from in the world, many people look for genetic explanations consistent with dominant racial ideology. They seek to explain the successes and failures of black athletes in terms of natural or instinctive qualities or weaknesses, rather than experience, strategy, motivation, and intelligence. When the skin color of athletes is a shade of "dark," the discussion quickly turns to race-related questions, and people embark on

searches for *the* physical traits possessed by *those* people, even when success clearly involves a combination of physical, psychological, and cognitive skills across different sports and even when the athletes come in different sizes and shapes and have racially mixed genetic ancestries. In the process, there is a tendency for many people to ignore, discount, or understate the influence of social and cultural factors in the lives of people of color. Of course, this is convenient for whites, because those factors often are tied to ugly histories of colonialism, oppression, slavery, discrimination, and racism (see figure 9.2).

When people with dark skin dominated two or three highly visible spectator sports, the editors at *Sports Illustrated* defined this worthy of a

"*Of course, white folks are good at this. After 500 years of colonizing the world by sea, they've been bred to have exceptional sailing genes!*"

FIGURE 9.2 This statement may sound laughable when made about whites. However, some whites have made similar statements about blacks, and racial ideology has encouraged some scientists to use these statements as a basis for developing research hypotheses. This is one way that culturally based ideas about race influence research.

long article, "What Happened to the White Athlete?" (in Price, 1997). According to prevailing ideas about race, when blacks beat whites, it is an issue that must be studied and explained. Again, racial categories serve as the starting point for asking questions, and the search for racial differences begins; if differences are found, they are assumed to be the cause of success among dark-skinned athletes.

This is how racial ideology creeps into science and influences how studies are done and how data are interpreted. Of course, scientists claim to be seeking truth, but truth depends on the facts they choose to examine, the classification systems they use to categorize the facts, and the theoretical frameworks they use to interpret the facts. When racial ideology influences the identification of facts, the classification of the facts identified, or the interpretations of the relationships among the facts, science reproduces a view of the world that emphasizes racial difference rather than shared humanity. This leads some people to wonder if scientists ought to be more critically self-reflective about how and why they do what they do. This is discussed in the box "'Jumping Genes' in Black Bodies."

Noted African American author Nate McCall has summarized how many blacks think about sports and ideological issues with this statement:

> I love basketball, but I hate the grotesque contradictions we Americans bring to the game. . . . [Many blacks and whites] are driven by a crude assumption that's so firmly embedded in our psyches we don't even see it half the time: It's the deep-rooted belief that blacks are more gifted as athletes than whites but that God somehow shortchanged brothers on brains. (1997, p. 9)

McCall's observations are taken a step further by prize-winning author John Edgar Wideman—the father of Jamila Wideman, who played basketball at Stanford and in the WNBA. He says,

> Basketball also functions to embody racist fantasies, to prove and perpetuate "essential" differences between blacks and whites, to justify

the idea of white supremacy and rationalize an unfair balance of power . . . between blacks and whites. (in Lipsyte, 2001a, p. 513).

McCall and Wideman are thoughtful observers of the racial scene in U.S. culture, but they should not have the last word about the impact of racial ideology on how people "see" sport performances in black-and-white. Ideologies are complex and often internally contradictory. They are expressed in different ways in different contexts. But we must be aware of them and take them seriously, because they exert a powerful influence on how we interpret the world around us.

Racial Ideology and a Sense of Destiny Among African American Men   Does racial ideology influence how African Americans interpret their own physical abilities and potential as athletes? This is a controversial question. My guess is that many young black men and women in the United States today grow up believing that the black body is special and superior when it comes to physical abilities in certain sports. This belief might inspire some young people to think that playing certain sports and playing them better than anyone else in the world is part of their biological and cultural destiny. This inspiration might be especially strong if young blacks felt that their future might involve low-wage, dead-end jobs on the one hand or big money and respect gained from slam-dunks, end zone catches, or Olympic sprint victories on the other hand. Even boxing might look better than a demeaning, minimum-wage job!

Figure 9.3 outlines a hypothesized sociological explanation of the athletic achievements of African American male athletes. A look at U.S. history shows that dominant racial ideology has fostered stereotypes that emphasize black male physicality and black athletic superiority. At the same time, racial segregation and discrimination have limited life chances for black men in most spheres of life. However, there have been growing opportunities for black males of all ages to develop skills and achieve immense status and

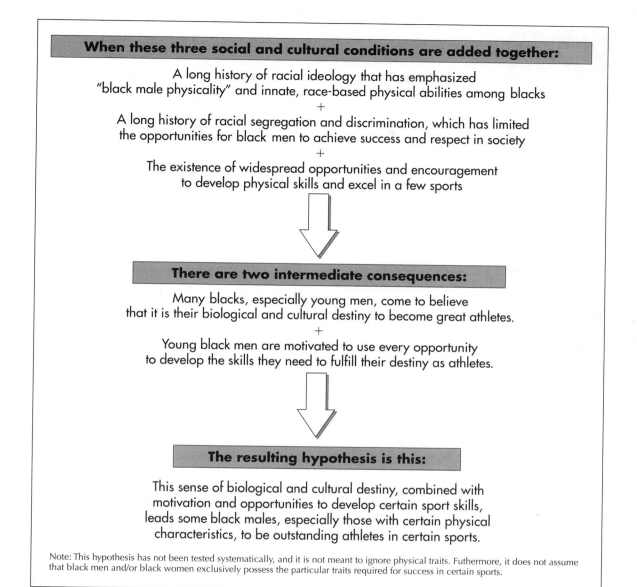

When these three social and cultural conditions are added together:

A long history of racial ideology that has emphasized
"black male physicality" and innate, race-based physical abilities among blacks

+

A long history of racial segregation and discrimination, which has limited
the opportunities for black men to achieve success and respect in society

+

The existence of widespread opportunities and encouragement
to develop physical skills and excel in a few sports

There are two intermediate consequences:

Many blacks, especially young men, come to believe
that it is their biological and cultural destiny to become great athletes.

+

Young black men are motivated to use every opportunity
to develop the skills they need to fulfill their destiny as athletes.

The resulting hypothesis is this:

This sense of biological and cultural destiny, combined with
motivation and opportunities to develop certain sport skills,
leads some black males, especially those with certain physical
characteristics, to be outstanding athletes in certain sports.

Note: This hypothesis has not been tested systematically, and it is not meant to ignore physical traits. Futhermore, it does not assume
that black men and/or black women exclusively possess the particular traits required for success in certain sports.

FIGURE 9.3   A sociological hypothesis for explaining the achievements of black male athletes.

money in a few sports, and there has been widespread encouragement for them to take advantage of those opportunities.

When you put these things together, you can certainly understand why many African American males grow up thinking that it is their biological and cultural destiny to become great athletes in certain sports. They would view as heroes others who had fulfilled that destiny and then use them as models as they dedicate

"Jumping Genes" in Black Bodies
Why Do People Look for Them and What Will They Say If They Find Them?

When people set off on a quest to find a gene or combination of genes that explains the success of black athletes, many of us who study sports in society have doubts about why their search begins and where it will take us. The search for jumping genes is a good example. There are three major reasons for our doubts about this search: (1) ideas about the operation and effects of genes are oversimplified among many people in postindustrial cultures, (2) jumping is much more than a simple physical activity, and (3) skin color is never a good starting point for research.

OVERSIMPLIFIED IDEAS ABOUT GENES

Many people in postindustrial societies have great hopes for genetic research. They see genes as the ultimate building blocks of life and believe that knowledge about genes will enable us to explain and control everything from food supplies to human behavior. Therefore, when people are violent, they search for "violence genes"; when people are smart, they search for "intelligence genes"; when people run fast or far, they search for "power or endurance genes"; and, when people jump high, they search for "jumping genes." These searches lead many people to expect that, if we can find the gene, we can explain why people do what they do and possibly even control the actions supported by the gene.

According to Robert Sapolsky (2000), a professor of biology and neurology at Stanford University, this notion of the primacy of the genes leads to deterministic and reductionist views of human behavior and social problems in the world. His point is that human biology and behavior cannot be reduced to genetic causes and that, even though genes are important, they do not work independently of the environment. In fact, research shows that genes are activated and suppressed by many environmental factors, and the effects of genes in our bodies are influenced by environmental factors as well.

In other words, genes are neither autonomous nor the sole causes of important real life outcomes associated with our bodies and behaviors. Genes are regulated by chemicals that exist in cells and by chemicals, such as hormones, that come from other parts of the body; furthermore, many genes are regulated by many external environmental factors. Sapolsky notes that, even when a mother rat licks and grooms her infant, these environmental factors begin a series of biochemical events, which turn on and influence the effects of genes related to the physical growth of the infant rat. In other words, genes cannot be disassociated from the environment that turns them on and off, and the effects of genes cannot be disassociated from the environment in which other factors influence the expression of those effects. Sapolsky is hopeful about genetic research, but he explains that, as we learn more about genes, we also will learn more about the environment and the connections between the two.

Genes do not exist and operate in environmental vacuums. This is true for genes related to diseases and genes related to jumping. Just because they are there does not mean they will be turned on, and, when they are turned on, their effects may vary from one environment to another. At this point, nobody has discovered jumping genes, and, if such genes are discovered in the future, we also will learn about the various environmental factors, in and outside the human body, that turn them on or off and influence how they affect the body's potential for being propelled off the ground. This will be an exciting series of discoveries, but to assume that the existence and operation of jumping genes is related to the color of a person's skin is not warranted at this time.

JUMPING IS NOT SIMPLY A PHYSICAL ACTIVITY

Many people think that jumping is a basic physical behavior to study and explain. However, jumping is not simply a mechanical, springlike action initiated by a few leg muscles exploding with power. Instead, it is a total body movement involving the neck, shoulders, arms, wrists, hands, torso, waist, hips, thighs, knees, calves, ankles, and toes. Jumping also involves a timed coordination of the upper and lower body, a particular type of flexibility, a "kinesthetic feel," and a total body rhythm. It is an act of grace as much as power, a rhythmic act as much as a sudden muscular burst, an individual expression as much as an exertion, and it is tied to the notion of the body in harmony with space as much as simply the overcoming of resistance with the application of physical force.

In the case of jumping in sports, different athletes jump in different ways. Gymnasts, volleyball players, figure skaters, skateboarders, basketball players, ski jumpers, high jumpers, and pole vaulters all jump, but techniques and styles vary greatly from sport to sport and person to person in each sport.

Furthermore, the act of jumping in societies where skin color and ethnic heritage have important social meanings is even more complex, because race and ethnicity are types of performance in their own ways (Early, 1998). These performances involve physical expressions and body movements that are integrally related to the cultural-kinesthetic histories of particular groups. As Gerald Early (1998) has noted in his provocative article "Performance and Reality: Race, Sports, and the Modern World," even playing sports is something racial and ethnic in those societies.

We also know that the relevance and meaning of jumping vary from one cultural context to another. Jumping is irrelevant to the performances of world leaders, CEOs of major corporations, sport team owners, coaches, doctors, and college professors. The power and influence possessed by these people and the rewards they receive are not dependent on jumping abilities. This is why the statement that "white men can't jump" is irrelevant to most whites (Myers, 2000). Outside of a few sports, jumping ability has nothing to do with success and the achievement of power and influence in the world today; white CEOs making million of dollars a year don't care that someone says they can't jump.

Jumping, sprinting, and distance running are important in certain sports and in certain cultural settings around the world. This is why those who study sports in society are concerned with understanding the historical, cultural, social, and economic circumstances that make jumping and running important in some people's lives and why some people work so hard to develop their jumping and running abilities. After all, if we did not know these things, how could we understand why some people are so good at sports, why patterns of success vary from group to group, and why those patterns of success change over time in different ways from one culture to another? It is clear that the search for jumping genes is part of the total science of jumping.

Although there are probably a number of genes related to jumping potential and ability, they have not been identified in scientific research. It is not wrong to assume they exist, but it is naïve to assume that they operate independent of environmental factors or that they are tied to skin color or a socially constructed racial classification system. At this point, nothing is known about the environmental factors, either internal or external to the human body, that might turn those genes on or off or influence the effects of the genes on a body and its potential to jump. Furthermore, it is doubtful that anyone will ever identify genes related to different types and styles of jumping in sports. Genes will never tell us much about the complex physical and cultural performance of slam dunks orchestrated by NBA players Vince Carter and Kobe Bryant.

SKIN COLOR IS NOT A GOOD STARTING POINT FOR RESEARCH ON HUMAN PERFORMANCE

When someone says, "White men can't jump" or "Blacks are great jumpers," he or she is inferring a comparison based on a socially constructed racial classification system. This inference and the racial categories used in the comparison are related to long histories of race relations and racism in the United States and many other societies. Although some people think it is important to study jumping and jumping ability, it is not a good idea to initiate research based on racial classification systems, which have been developed and changed in connection with complex social and cultural factors.

Research based on racial comparisons has inherent methodological problems. For example, if the jumping

"Jumping Genes" in Black Bodies   (continued)
*Why Do People Look for Them and What Will
They Say If They Find Them?*

abilities of blacks and whites are compared and average group differences are found, additional studies are done to determine if blacks have physical traits that enable them to jump higher than whites. If such traits are found, there is a tendency to assume that they are grounded in race-related genetic differences and that it is important to trace the genetic ancestry of racial groups, especially certain people of color, to further document the existence of racial characteristics and differences.

This overall approach is problematic. It involves a search for physical differences that begins with questions based on a socially constructed racial classification system and ends with data about whether jumping is related to that classification system. This tells us little about jumping and human performance independent of social notions about race. No matter what

is found in the research, the racial classification system used by the researchers is central to their understanding of jumping and their interpretation of jumping behavior. Such research does more to reproduce various forms of racial separation than it does to produce a scientific understanding of human performance.

To avoid this outcome, scientists must know about the racial ideologies that permeate the cultures in which they live and do their research. This enables them to assess the validity and usefulness of the facts they choose to study and the findings they report and publish. If they don't do this, their research will deepen our sense of racial separateness in the world instead of deepen our knowledge about the complexity of human behavior and the full range of human genetic variation. This is a potentially dangerous way to do science. *What do you think?*

· ·

themselves to their own quest for athletic stardom. Since public school sport programs offer coaching, equipment, facilities, and opportunities to develop skills in basketball, football, and track, the pursuit of their perceived destiny is possible, even in the absence of the material resources needed to play other sports.

This combination of factors has created a powerful force in the lives of millions of young people. This force has driven more than a few young African American males to dedicate the very fabric of their being to achieving greatness in certain sports. Is this what has led to the notable achievements of African Americans in basketball, football, track, and boxing? Is this the reason African American men have been winning gold medals in the Olympics for many years? Is this why young African American women are following in their brothers' footsteps in certain sports? When a group of people feel destined to greatness in an activity, when their feelings are grounded in a racial ideology emphasizing the naturalness of their achievements, and when their

social worlds are structured so that those feelings make sense in their lives, *it shouldn't be surprising when they achieve notable things.*

The role of this powerful sense of destiny in the lives of African Americans in the United States has been widely debated. Former NBA player Charles Barkley, an outspoken observer of sports in U.S. culture, claims the following:

> Sports are a detriment to blacks . . . not a positive. You have a society now where every black kid in the country thinks the only way he can be successful is through athletics. People look at athletes and entertainers as the sum total of black America. That is a terrible, terrible thing, because that ain't even one-tenth of what we are. (in McCallum, 2002, p. 34)

A similar conclusion has been expressed by Gerald Early:

> The blind pursuit of attainment in sports is having a devastating effect on our people. Imbued with a belief that our principle avenue to fame and profit is through sports, . . . far too many black kids treat

In U.S. culture, many African American men grow up taking sports, especially basketball and football, very seriously. This youth player learned by age eleven not to smile when presenting himself as an athlete. His father told him to look serious and tough in the photo. (Jay Coakley)

basketball courts and football fields as if they were classrooms in an alternative school system. "OK, I flunked English," a young athlete will say. "But I got an A plus in slam-dunking." (Early, 1991, p. 87)

Regardless of whether you agree with Barkley and Early or think that their statements must be qualified, it is clear that racial ideology is powerful, especially when it is combined with other factors that lead it to be used as a framework for self-evaluation and self-motivation. Three centuries ago, white Western Europeans felt it was their biological and cultural destiny to explore and colonize other parts of the world. This sense of destiny was so powerful that it drove them to control over three-fourths of the globe! This frightening and notable achievement was not due to the genetic ancestry of white Europeans, although some of them would like to think it was.

The Challenge of Escaping Racial Ideology   In racially and ethnically diverse settings, where people from different backgrounds interact frequently and in many contexts, racial ideology often is defused as people deal with each other as individuals and discover that they have many similar and different characteristics and abilities. However, in some U.S. schools where blacks are a distinct numerical minority, there is a tendency for black male varsity-athletes to be "tagged" in a way that subverts their success in claiming other identities. For example, educator Amanda Godley (1999b) studied student interactions in a California high school and discovered that, when black male student-athletes excelled in academic work and were placed in honors classes, their identity in the culture of the school and their interactions with teachers and fellow students, even in the honors classroom, focused on their athlete status. Other students in honors classes, even the Asian and white students who played on varsity teams were identified as honor students rather than as athletes. Data on black women varsity-athletes in honors classes were inconclusive, but black women honor students who did not play varsity sports were identified by others and by themselves as honors students, rather than in any race-related manner.

University of Michigan professor Keith Harrison has found similar identity dynamics on major university campuses. As two black male athletes in his study noted, "Everyone around perceives us being there only for our physical talents," and "Everything is white [on campus], only sports [are] for blacks" (1998, p. 72). This is not a new phenomenon (Adler and Adler, 1991), but its consequences are still frustrating for black men who want to expand their social identities beyond sports.

More research is needed on this issue, but it seems that, when being a black male is combined with playing sports, it may become difficult for some men to escape the subtle racial ideology that encourages people to bind race and sports together in the identity politics that exist in certain settings. If this means that high school culture enforces a student-versus-athlete dichotomy for certain people, and that black males and some black females who excel at sports face academic marginalization in the cultures of some schools, racial ideology subtly constricts how these individuals connect with fellow students, teachers, and the institution of the school. We need to know more about when this does or does not occur and how it affects everyone involved.

Racial Ideology and Sport Choices Among Whites   A few years ago, I invited five children to be on a youth sports panel in my sports in society course; all were ten- to twelve-year-olds, heavily involved in sports, and white. During the discussion with the college students, a sixth-grade boy known in his nearly all-white elementary school for his sprinting and basketball skills was asked if he planned to try out for those sports when he went to junior high school. Surprisingly, he said no. When asked to explain, he said, "I won't have a chance because all the black kids at the junior high will beat me out." He went on to point out that this did not upset him, because he was a good soccer player and distance runner, too. He said he would try out for those sports instead of sprinting and basketball. He also said he had never played with black or Latino children while in elementary school.

About the same time this sixth-grader was using his ideas about race to make important sport participation decisions, a white male high school student with outstanding skills in football and basketball was asked by a local sportswriter what sport he planned to play in college. The young man, who was being heavily recruited in both sports by many top universities, said, "I guess, right now, I'd take football because it's

more unique to be a 6-6 quarterback . . . than a 6-6 *white* forward." This young man was taking into account his whiteness and his ideas about race as he assessed his chances for success as a college athlete.

Both of these young people watched sports on television, listened to people talk about the abilities of athletes, and in the process developed their own ideas about race, physical abilities, and chances for success in various sports. Their whiteness, a taken-for-granted characteristic in the rest of their lives, had a major influence on their decisions about their athletic futures. In fact, they voluntarily limited their options because of their skin color.

Systematic data on this issue are scarce, but some studies indicate that whites in certain situations do avoid participation in sports in which blacks predominate, or, if whites do participate, they don't think they have a chance to excel relative to the blacks they compete with. This may be why the times of white runners in certain sprints and long-distance road races have actually become slower over the years; whites' genes have not changed, but whites' choices and motivation have changed (Bloom, 1998; George, 1994; Merron, 1999; Weir, 2000).

When Tim Layden, a *Sports Illustrated* journalist, returned to the high school that served as the inspiration for the 2000 film *Remember the Titans*, he noted that the football team at the school no longer had a roster characterized by the racial togetherness portrayed in the film. Things had changed since 1971. One of the players on the 2002 team observed that white students seldom contributed to the team anymore. He said, "Most white kids around here wouldn't even think of coming out for football. They think it's a black sport" (Layden, 2002, p. 79).

The connection between racial ideology and sports participation choices is an issue that needs to be studied. As racial ideology becomes wrapped up and disguised by other issues and then expressed in more subtle and indirect ways, researchers must become more sensitive to a

Racial ideology operates in complex and diverse ways. In some cases, it influences whites to avoid the sports in which blacks have a record of excellence. This way of thinking did not influence the white teenager on this team.

fuller range of dynamics in social life. Past expressions of racial ideology were quite easy to document; current forms are more difficult to identify, although they remain subversive forces in organizations and social life as a whole.

Racial Ideology, Gender, and Social Class

There are complex interconnections between racial and gender ideologies in the social world of sports. For example, research suggests that the implications of racial ideology are different for black men than for black women (Corbett and Johnson, 2000; Daniels, 2000; Majors, 1998; Messner, 1992; Y. Smith, 2000; A. Solomon, 2000; Winlock, 2000). This is true partly because the bodies of black men have been socially constructed and viewed differently than the bodies of black women over the years.

Whites in the United States have grown up fearing the power of black male bodies, being anxious about the sexual capacities of those bodies, and being fascinated with their movements. Ironically, this has created circumstances in which black male bodies have come to be valuable entertainment commodities, first on stage in music and vaudeville theater, later on athletic fields. Black female bodies, on the other hand, have undergone different social constructions (Corbett and Johnson, 2000; Winlock, 2000). They've been sexualized in the image of the promiscuous welfare queen, but not feared; they've been defined in terms of domestic labor, but not defined in ways that would make black women uniquely valuable entertainment commodities on athletic fields.

Richard Majors (1998), founder of the *Journal of African American Men*, has suggested that, as black males have struggled to establish their masculinity in terms recognized in U.S. culture, some have developed a presentation of self described as "cool pose." Majors explains that black men in the United States have accepted the dominant definition of *masculinity* in American culture. They have bought into the idea that men should be strong breadwinners and protectors in their families and dominant in their relationships with women. However, their chances for success in institutional spheres, such as education, politics, and the economy, where they might establish who they are as men in the terms that other males have used, have been limited by dominant ideas about race and the discrimination associated with those ideas.

As African American men over the years have faced limited life chances, they have experienced a combination of frustration, self-doubt, anger, and even emotional withdrawal from schools, families, and the mainstream economy. Black males in U.S. culture have coped with these things "by channeling their creative energies into the construction of unique, expressive, and conspicuous styles of demeanor, speech, gesture, clothing, hairstyle, walk, stance, and handshake" (Majors, 1998, p. 17). These expressive styles are the forms of interpersonal self-presentation that Majors describes as cool pose.

Cool pose is all about achieving a sense of significance and respect through *interpersonal* strategies when one cannot achieve significance and success in jobs, politics, and education. Cool pose is also about being in control, tough, and detached. Cool pose says different things to different people. To the white man, it says, "Although you may have tried to hurt me time and time again, I can take it (and if I am hurting or weak, I'll never let you know)." It also says, "See me, touch me, hear me, but, white man, you can't copy me" (Majors, 1986, pp. 184–85). In general, cool pose is one of the ways in which black males who face status threats in the culture have used physicality in the production of masculinity. This occurs even among first- and second-graders in inner-city U.S. schools (Hasbrook, 1999; Hasbrook and Harris, 1999).

Majors suggests that cool pose has become part of the public personas of many black males in the United States and an integral part of the sports in which many athletes are black men. Is this how style has become a big part of basketball? Is this why some black athletes are known for their "talk" as well as physical skills? Do black men use cool pose to intimidate white opponents? Does cool pose sell tickets and create spectator interest in college basketball, the NBA, and football? Do people go to see dunks and other moves inscribed with the personas of the men who perform them? Is cool pose the result of what happens when black men face a combination of racial and gender ideology and the realities of class relations in the American economy? Majors says yes, and his point is worth considering (see Wilson, 1999).

Black women athletes face some of the same challenges faced by black men. However, Donna Daniels, an African American studies scholar from Duke University, suggests that aesthetic norms for females in predominantly white cultures have been racialized, so that black women athletes exist outside the norm. Therefore, they must carefully "monitor and strategize about how they are seen and understood by a public not used to their physical presence or intellect, whether on the court, field, or peddling a product" (2000, p. 26). If they are not careful, there is a danger that people will interpret their confidence and intelligence as arrogance and cockiness. This means that they must tone down their toughness and appear amicable and nonthreatening, lest they be defined as outsiders.

The marketing people at the WNBA were so sensitive to this issue that, when they first promoted the league, they presented ad after ad highlighting black players who had modeling contracts or newborn babies (Banet-Weiser, 1999; A. Solomon, 2000). When lip gloss and babies were not used, the ads depicted nicely groomed black women players in nurturing and supportive roles, especially with children.

Even the intense training and thoughtful strategizing of Venus and Serena Williams were frequently overlooked when they first entered the pro tennis scene. Many commentators could not focus on anything but the Williams sisters' "natural abilities" and "all those strange beads" in their hair. Journalists and tennis spectators seemed to have a difficult time fitting these women into their racialized ideas about beauty and femininity in U.S. culture. Meanwhile, many of them clicked onto the website for Anna Kournikova, the blonde Russian-born player, to find images more consistent with dominant aesthetic norms for females, or they just watched figure skating or gymnastics, in which nearly all the images were consistent with those norms.

SPORT PARTICIPATION AMONG RACIAL AND ETHNIC MINORITIES IN THE UNITED STATES

Sports in the United States have long histories of racial and ethnic exclusion (Abney, 1999; Bretón, 2000; Brooks and Althouse, 2000b; Corbett and Johnson, 2000; Eisen and Wiggins, 1994; Harrison, 1998; Shropshire, 1996; Wiggins, 2000). Men and women in all ethnic minorities traditionally have been underrepresented at all levels of competition and management in most competitive sports, even in high schools and community programs. Prior to the 1950s, the organizations that sponsored sport teams and events seldom opened their doors fully to blacks, Latinos, Native Americans, and Asian Americans. When members of minority groups played sports, they usually played among themselves in segregated games and events.

Sport Participation Among African Americans

Prior to the 1950s, most whites in the United States consistently avoided playing with and against blacks. Blacks were systematically excluded from participation in white-controlled sport programs and organizations. Blacks formed their own baseball and basketball leagues. Occasional games with white teams were held behind closed doors, but they were not considered official, and they did not affect the records of white teams. Because black teams sometimes beat even the best white teams and because whites rationalized the exclusion of blacks from white leagues with the notion that blacks didn't have the character or fortitude to compete with whites, these games received no coverage in the white press.

Since the 1950s, the sport participation of blacks has been concentrated in a limited range of sports. Even as we begin the twenty-first century, the 36.7 (as of July 2003) million African Americans are underrepresented in or absent from most sports at most levels of competition. This is often overlooked, because those who watch boxing, track and field, college and professional football and basketball, and Major League Baseball see many black athletes. However, these sports make up only four of the forty-four men's and women's sports played in college, four of the dozens of sports played at the international amateur level, and five of the many professional sports in the United States. There is a similar pattern in

Canada and in European countries with strong sporting traditions.

Many people forget that there is a virtual absence of black athletes—male or female—in archery, auto racing, badminton, bowling, canoeing/kayaking, cycling, diving, equestrian events, field hockey, figure skating, golf, gymnastics, hockey, motocross, rodeo, rowing, sailing, shooting, alpine and Nordic skiing, soccer, softball, swimming, table tennis, team handball, tennis, volleyball, water polo, yachting, and many field events in track and field. How many black medal winners have there been in the Winter Olympics? When have black athletes been profiled in the XGames and NASCAR auto racing, two of the most rapidly growing media sports today?

The exceptions to this pattern stand out because they *are* exceptions. In fact, the underrepresentation of blacks in this long list of sports is much greater than the underrepresentation of whites in sports such as basketball and football: there are many more whites who play basketball and football in high school and college than there are blacks who play tennis or golf at those levels. Finding black drivers at an Indy-car or NASCAR race is impossible, and, even though all the drivers, support personnel, and nearly 100 percent of the spectators are white, nobody refers to these races as white events.

Throughout U.S. sports history, the participation of black females has been severely limited and has received little attention, apart from that given to occasional Olympic medal winners in track events. Black women suffer the consequences of gender and racial ideologies. Apart from a handful of studies, little is known about the unique experiences of African American women athletes, even those participating today

African Americans are visible in a few high-profile sports in the United States but are underrepresented in most sports. The participation patterns and experiences of African American women in sports seldom have been studied, so little is known about the combined influence of gender and racial ideologies in their lives. (USA Volleyball)

(Corbett and Johnson, 2000; Green, 2000; Y. Smith, 2000).

Overall, sport participation rates in middle- and upper-middle-income white communities in the United States are much higher than those in the vast majority of predominantly black communities. Racial ideology causes many people to overlook this fact. Many people see only the black male athletes who make high salaries in high-profile sports and then assume that they have "taken over" sports. This exemplifies how dominant racial ideology influences what people see in their social worlds.

Sport Participation Among Native Americans

There are about 2.5 million Native Americans in the United States, and approximately 2 percent of the Canadian population is officially considered Native. Although officially classified as one minority group, Native Americans comprise dozens of diverse cultural groups. The differences among these cultural groups are deep and important. However, most people who are not Native American tend to think of them all as "Indians" and use stereotyped descriptions of their habits and dress. Popular ideas about Native Americans have their own history and have grown out of unique forms of ethnic relations. Furthermore, Native American lifestyles and sport participation patterns are diverse and vary, depending on socioeconomic status and whether people reside on or off reservations. Poverty rates approach 50 percent on some reservations and in many urban areas with high Native American populations.

Many sports in traditional Native American cultures have combined physical activities with ritual and ceremony (Keith, 1999; Nabokov, 1981; Oxendine, 1988). For example, when Native Americans from several western states gathered in southeastern Colorado in November 1999 to commemorate the nearly 200 Cheyenne and Arapaho people who were killed at Sand Creek by regional government troops in 1864, they organized a 187-mile run from the site of the massacre to the state capital in Denver. Forty Northern Arapaho people participated in the run, which was held in connection with a prayer vigil for the men, women, and children who were killed in the surprise attack at dawn (Fraser, 1999).

Although Native Americans have made significant achievements in certain sports over the past century, public acclaim has been limited to those few who have been standout athletes on the football and baseball teams of government-sponsored reservation schools and training schools. For example, when Jim Thorpe and his teammates at the Carlisle School, a segregated government training school, defeated outstanding mainstream college teams in 1911 and 1912, they attracted considerable attention (Bloom, 2000; Oxendine, 1988). Apart from a few successful teams and individual athletes in segregated government schools, Native American participation in most sports has been limited. Where participation is not made impossible because of poverty, poor health, and lack of equipment and programs, it is discouraged by a combination of discrimination, cumbersome government bureaucracy and mismanagement, and a lack of understanding by non-Indians.

Another factor that discourages young people who could play intercollegiate sports is the fear of being cut off from the cultural roots that are at the heart of personal identity for many Native Americans. For example, Billy Mills, gold medalist in the 10,000-meter race at the 1964 Olympics, explained that becoming immersed in sport programs away from one's reservation is "like walking death." He warned, "If you go too far into [white] society, there's a fear of losing your Indianness. There's a spiritual factor that comes into play. To become part of white society you give up half your soul" (in Simpson, 1996, p. 294). Other Native Americans have voiced similar feelings. They say that there is inherent tension between the dominant American culture

Team Names, Logos, and Mascots
When Are They Forms of Bigotry?

Using stereotypes to characterize Native Americans in the United States is so common that most people don't even realize they do it. This has occurred for so long that stereotypes are now widely accepted as valid depictions of Native Peoples. When these stereotypes are used as a basis for team names, mascots, and logos, sports become a site for perpetuating an ideology that exploits, trivializes, and demeans the history and cultural heritage of Native Americans. This may not be the intent of those who use Native American images in this way, but it is often the result. When this is pointed out to them, many people try to excuse their ignorance and insensitivity by saying that using images in this way is just part of tradition, although they seldom say *whose* tradition it is.

Consider the following story from a statement by the group Concerned American Indian Parents:

> An American Indian student attended his school's pep rally in preparation for a football game against a rival school. The rival school's mascot was an American Indian. The pep rally included the burning of an Indian in effigy along with posters and banners labeled "Scalp the Indians," "Kill the Indians," and "Let's burn the Indians at the stake." The student, hurt and embarrassed, tore the banners down. His fellow students couldn't understand his hurt and pain.

This incident occurred in the late 1980s, but this student's pain has not prevented hundreds of sport teams at the high school, college, and professional levels from using stereotypes of Native Americans for team names, logos, and mascots. The pain continues today (Brady, 1999b; Coombe, 1999; Davis, 2002; Hawes, 2001b; King and Springwood, 2001b; Sigelman, 1998; Staurowsky, 1998, 1999, 2000). There are still non-Indians who dress in war bonnets and war paint and run around, brandishing spears and tomahawks or pounding tom-toms. For example, the mascot of the Cleveland Indians, Chief Wahoo, is built on long-accepted stereotypes of Native Americans. Chief Wahoo is one of many examples of disrespectful caricatures used by American sport teams. As Native American Jody Potts wonders (in Garber, 1999), does putting Native Americans in a category with eagles, donkeys, pigs, and an array of vicious beasts and bullies imply that they are subhuman or inferior to whites? She clearly thinks so and asks that whites respect her feelings.

Many people don't realize that names such as Redskins and mascots such as Chief Wahoo tend to perpetuate stereotypes that have contributed to the powerlessness, poverty, unemployment, alcoholism, and dependency of many Native Peoples in the United States. What would people say if the mascot for the San Diego Padres were a fat, self-indulgent missionary who ran around, swinging a rosary and waving a crucifix in a menacing or celebratory way? What if he were to lead the fans in secular renditions of Gregorian chants as hitters came up with runners on base? What if fans were to do a "crucifix carry" as they chanted? Many Christians would object, and rightly so!

If teachers, administrators, and students in U.S. schools had a deep knowledge of the rich and diverse cultures of Native Americans and realized the discrimination native peoples currently face, they would not use names such as Indians, Redskins, Chiefs, Braves, Savages, Tribe, and Redmen for their teams. Nor would they allow Anglo students to entertain fans by culturally cross-dressing as caricatures of Native Americans. Nor would they allow fans to mimic Native American chants or act out demeaning stereotypes of war-whooping, tomahawk-chopping Native Americans.

Schools should not use any Native American name or symbol in connection with sport teams unless they do the following:

1. Sponsor a special curriculum about the history, cultural heritage, and current living conditions of the native group after which their sport teams are named. Unless 70 percent of the students can pass annual tests on this material, schools should drop the names they claim are used to "honor" Native Americans. There cannot be honor without knowledge, and cultural illiteracy is no excuse for insensitivity.

2. Publish at least two press releases per year in which information about the heritage and current circumstances of Native Americans honored by their team names is described and analyzed; publish similar materials annually in school newspapers and yearbooks.
3. At least once per year, during a major sport event, sponsor an educational forum developed by Native Americans in the local area, with the purpose of informing students, faculty, and administrators about the people they say they honor with their team names.

If schools were to do these things, they would be less likely to perpetuate destructive stereotypes. Schools must not distort history through their own team names, logos, and mascots, but schools using Native American names and mascots often ignore history and perpetuate misunderstandings and bigotry in the process. Traditions that insult others should be abandoned, or at least those insulted should be compensated. Pro teams and the Olympics never let anyone use their names and symbols without permission and license fees. Native American names and symbols should receive the same legal status.

If schools were to do these things, their students would think twice before using certain team names. Students would learn that many Native Americans consider the term *redskin* as derogatory as African Americans consider *nigger* and Latinos consider *spic*. The capital city of the government that has broken hundreds of treaties with Native Americans still has a professional football team named Redskins. For many Native Americans, the use of this name, the use of stereotypes for mascots and logos, and the use of historically inaccurate images without permission simply symbolizes a long history of oppression.

Only when Native Peoples have a representative share of power and resources in the United States might the situation be right for using their names and images in association with sport teams. The Irish do not object to Boston's use of the name Celtics or

This poster was developed to illustrate that we would not use the names and images of other racial and ethnic groups as the names and images of Native Americans are used. Presenting caricatures of Native Americans and using symbols of the animistic religions of many Native cultures is insensitive, if not racist. (The National Conference, Minnesota-Dakotas Region)

Team Names, Logos, and Mascots   (continued)
When Are They Forms of Bigotry?

Notre Dame's use of "the Fighting Irish," because they have enough power and influence in U.S. society to not worry about such things or to use them as symbols of a past they have now defined in positive terms.

The poster pictured here was developed to make people question the use of Native American images in sports. If demeaning images of other ethnic groups were used in similar ways, there would be widespread objections. Native American activist and leader Dennis Banks (1993) has asked for nearly thirty years, "Why do these people continue to make mockery of our culture [with tribal names and mascots in sports]?" Other Native People want to know why professional teams, which make millions of dollars using Native American images on products such as jerseys, hats, and coffee cups and selling souvenir tomahawks and mock feathers don't build sport facilities on reservations and fund programs to keep young Native Americans healthy enough that they can play sports. Maybe all those romanticized images on hats and gym walls prevent people from seeing the reality of Native Americans today. And, to make matters worse, isn't using someone else's name and image a form of identity theft? It would be if it happened to people with the power and resources to raise objections. *What do you think?*

....

and Native American cultures, and, when you leave your customs, religious ceremonies, families, community, and history, you must be prepared to live without everything that you have learned is the essence of who you are (Bloom, 2000; Clancy, 1999). This is difficult for many young people.

The challenge of dealing with cultural tensions is especially difficult for a young Native American attending a school or watching games between schools with team names such as Indians, Redskins, Redmen, and Savages and with mascots that run around and mimic white stereotypes of "Indian" behavior. Playing sports under such conditions involves giving up much more than half one's soul (see the box "Team Names, Logos, and Mascots"). To see a distorted or historically inappropriate caricature of a Native American on the gym wall of a school where students have no knowledge of local or regional native cultures means swallowing cultural pride; repressing anger against insensitive, historically ignorant non-Indians; and giving up hope of being understood in terms of personal feelings and cultural heritage.

Native American athletes also have experienced problems when their own cultural orientations have not matched orientations in the power and performance sports of many high schools. Through the years, some white coaches who have worked with Native American students on certain reservations have used systematic strategies to encourage them to abandon their traditional cultural ideologies emphasizing cooperation and to replace them with Euro-American cultural ideology emphasizing competition.

Some coaches frustrated with the nonaggressive orientations of Native Americans on their football and basketball teams even have tried to instill a "killer instinct" in their players. For example, a high school football coach in Arizona complained that students at Hopi High School "aren't used to our win-at-all-costs, beat-the-other-man mentality. Their understanding of what it means to be a good Hopi goes against what it takes to be a good football player." When the coach was asked how he handled the situation, he said, "[I did] exactly what the missionaries tried to do—de-Indianize the Indians" (in Garrity, 1989, p. 12).

It seems that, when Native Americans don't give up their cultural souls voluntarily when they play sports, some white coaches ask for them in the name of winning and cultural assimilation. Fortunately, not all Native American experiences match these. Some Native Americans play sports in contexts in which their ethnic identities are not only respected but also supported by others (Bloom, 2000; Clancy, 1999; King and Springwood, 2001b; Paraschak, 1995, 1999; Schroeder, 1995). In these cases, sports can provide opportunities for students to learn about the cultural backgrounds of others. In other cases, Native Americans have adopted Euro-American ways and have played sports without expressing any evidence of their cultural heritage.

Sport Participation Among Latinos and Hispanics

Hispanic is a generic term used by the U.S. government to group together all people whose ethnic roots can be traced to Spanish-speaking countries around the world; *Latino* and *Latina* are terms often preferred by many Hispanics, especially those whose ancestors are from Latin America, including Central and South America and the Caribbean. Latinos include people from diverse cultures. They may share language, colonial history, or Catholicism, but their cultures and group histories vary greatly. Mexican Americans constitute the largest Hispanic group in the United States, followed by Puerto Ricans, Cubans, other Central and South Americans, and people from Spain. There were about 35.9 million Hispanics in the United States in 2003. This includes some listed as whites and some as blacks, but it does not include undocumented workers or their family members.

Most scholars and journalists in the past have ignored the experiences of Latino athletes. Ethnic stereotypes about Latinos often vary in content and in how frequently they are used from sport to sport and from one region of the United States to another. For example, one Major League Baseball scout explained that most Mexicans and Mexican Americans in Major League Baseball were pitchers because

> Mexicans have bad foot speed. It's a genetic type thing. They have a different body type. Most have good hands and good rhythm. That's why they dance so well. Rhythm is important in baseball, it means agility. (in Beaton, 1993, p. 11)

Of course, millions of fans of the Mexican national soccer team know that foot speed is not a special problem among Mexicans. Another baseball scout, a Latino himself, used a slightly different stereotype about Mexicans when he stated, "Mexicans, because of their Indian blood, can run to New York and not stop. Just not fast" (in Beaton, 1993, p. 11).

Stereotypes about the genetic makeup of Mexican bodies are not applied to Cubans, whose success in baseball extends to many positions and whose success in many sports requiring different physical abilities is legendary. Nor are they applied to baseball players from the Dominican Republic, who are heavily represented in Major League Baseball.

Other racial and ethnic stereotypes are used when people of color can be classified as black rather than Latino. Dark-skinned Latinos from the Caribbean and other parts of Latin America present problems for the obsolete "black or white" racial classification system traditionally used in the United States. Furthermore, stereotypes about Mexican Americans ignore that Mexico itself is a multiethnic society, with about 100 million people who have a combination of Spanish, English, German, French, Indian, and various Central American ancestries.

It is clear that using ethnic stereotypes about physical traits to explain the success or failure of Latino athletes only creates confusion and perpetuates misinformation. These stereotypes are diverse, and they have an impact on sport participation patterns and experiences in diverse ways. They remind us of the need for research on the cultural, political, economic, and social factors affecting the sport experiences of Latinos. In other words, we must focus on ethnic relations issues, not mysterious genetic predispositions and abilities.

Latinos in North American Baseball Anthropologist Alan Klein's (1991) study of baseball in the Dominican Republic describes clearly what happens in the baseball academies sponsored by North American major league teams. He notes that Dominican players who sign contracts and play in the minor or major leagues in North America often face significant cultural adjustments and language problems and must deal with actions based on ethnic stereotypes and a general lack of understanding of their cultural backgrounds. Klein's points have been reaffirmed and updated by journalists Marcos Bretón and José Luis Villegas (1999), who describe the experiences of Latino baseball players who grow up poor and dream of playing at elite levels, especially in the major leagues in North America. These books are timely because Latinos made up 26 percent of the players in Major League Baseball in 2002.

The increase in Latino players is due to the traditional popularity of baseball in many Latin American countries and the efforts of major league teams to develop and cultivate a cheap source of highly talented players. Established Latino stars are well paid, but young players can be signed for a fraction of the amount needed to sign a player born and trained in the United States, regardless of racial or ethnic background. For example, the Texas Rangers signed a young Sammy Sosa in 1986 for $3,500—the same amount paid to Jackie Robinson by the Brooklyn Dodgers in 1946! As a vice president of one major league team noted, teams can sign five Latin American players for what it takes to sign one U.S. player. This, more than any other factor, is the reason that over 40 percent of all major and minor league baseball players in 2003 were Latin Americans, and many of these players were born outside the United States.

North American baseball teams have used this cost-cutting strategy ever since free agency drove up the price for U.S. players. Bretón (2000) refers to it as a "boatload mentality"—designed to buy as many players as possible for as little as possible in the hope that one will be the next Sammy Sosa. However, an estimated 90 to 95 percent of all Latino players who sign contracts never make it to the major leagues, and most don't even play in the minor leagues. Those who do play in the minors often are cut by teams after a year or two. Rather than return home to face the embarrassment of failure, they stay in the United States as undocumented workers, doing low-wage work in New York or other large cities. Bretón notes that "these castoffs represent the . . . rule rather than the exception in the high-stakes recruitment of ball players from Latin America and the Caribbean" (2000, p. 15), but their stories remain untold on the sports pages.

The stories that are told emphasize the recent successes of Latino and Latin American players as they achieve rookie of the year, most valuable player, best pitcher, best hitting, and all-star awards. Such success guarantees that Latinos will continue to be recruited and that those who study sports in society will devote more attention to their involvement in sports in the future.

"Mexicanos" in Texas High School Football Anthropologist Doug Foley gave special attention to Mexicano-Anglo relations in his study of rituals associated with high school football in a small Texas town. He describes the working-class Mexicano[2] males (*vatos*) who rejected sport participation but used sport events as occasions for publicly displaying their "style" (cool pose?) and establishing their social reputations in the community. Foley (1990a, b, 1999a) described how the Mexicanos protested a homecoming ceremony that gave center stage to Anglos and

---

[2]*Mexicano* is the self-reference used by Mexican Americans in Foley's study.

marginalized Mexicanos, how the Mexicano players defied the coaches when the Anglo players were given high-status positions on the team, and how the Mexicano coach resigned in frustration because he could not challenge bigotry and appease powerful Anglo boosters and school board members at the same time.

Foley concluded that, despite these examples of protest against prevailing Anglo ways of doing things in the town, high school football perpetuated the power and privilege of the local Anglos. As long as the Mexicanos saw things and did things the Anglo way, they were accepted; raising issues did nothing to make the Anglos see or do things to accommodate the Mexicanos' values and experiences.

Latinas in U.S. Sports Research on Latinas in the United States shows the diversity of the traditions and norms that revolve around gender and sport participation for girls and women from various Latino cultures (Acosta, 1999; Jamieson, 1998). Some Latinas whose families have recently immigrated to the United States do not receive parental support to play sports, especially if participation might separate them from their cultural traditions. Others, however, may be encouraged by parents and their relatives to play whatever they wish. Kathy Jamieson's (1998) research on Latinas in intercollegiate softball describes some of the unique identity-management experiences of players who constantly face the challenge of bridging the cultural divides they face in their daily lives.

Journalistic accounts have given selective descriptions of the experiences of top Latinas in golf, tennis, and a couple of Olympic sports. However, research is needed as sport participation among Latinas increases. Up to now, many of us who study sports in society have overlooked Latinas because of faulty generalizations about gender dynamics in Latino families and cultural norms that supposedly discourage involvement in competitive physical activities among Latinas.

Research is needed to describe and understand how Latinas manage gender relations in their families, how cultural norms vary when it comes to sport participation, and how sports are related to social class dynamics among various and diverse groups of Latinos.

In summary, research on the experiences of all Latinos is important because they are the fastest growing ethnic population in the United States and because leaders in commercial sports now are trying to attract Latino fans. The economic success of professional soccer in California and other parts of the United States depends on sensitivity to the interests and orientations of Latino athletes and spectators. Latinos are eager to have their diverse cultural heritage recognized and incorporated into sports and sport experiences in the United States and into the awareness of their fellow citizens.

> Diversity does not breed interaction.
>
> —T. Layden, journalist,
> *Sports Illustrated* (2001)

Sport Participation Among Asian Americans

There were about 12.6 million Asian Americans in mid-2003. The global migration of labor has brought people from many Asian cultures to the United States and other nations around the world. In the United States, most Asian Americans live on the West Coast and in cities where they have been attracted by job opportunities. The cultural heritage and the individual histories of Asian Americans are very diverse. To group them together is like grouping all Europeans together and making no distinctions between Irish Americans and Italian Americans. Although this diversity presents major challenges for researchers, there is a need for studies focusing on ethnic relations and sport participation patterns and experiences among various Asian American groups.

The recent success and popularity of a few Asian and Asian American athletes in the United States have raised important issues about ethnic dynamics in sports. For example, the popularity of several Japanese baseball players highlights how many Japanese Americans have embraced baseball, as both spectators and participants. Safeco Field, home of the Seattle Mariners and star player Ichiro Suzuki, now has so many Japanese spectators at baseball games that signs in the stadium are posted in both Japanese and English (Price, 2002a). Research is now needed to examine the impact of these players on ethnic relations in the stadiums and communities where these players live and play.

The success of tennis player Michael Chang, speed skater Apolo Anton Ohno, and figure skaters Kristi Yamaguchi and Michelle Kwan raise questions about the limits to which others in the United States, including Latinos, African Americans, and Euro-Americans will embrace Asian American athletes as cultural heroes and spokespeople for products they endorse. Chang's image has been used and accepted more in China than in the United States, although it was used during the late 1990s in the United States in connection with products and services that were associated with Pacific Rim nations. Yamaguchi and Kwan certainly have been popular as athletes, and as product endorsers, although some advertisers have wondered if the "identification" factor for these athletes is as strong as it would be for athletes from Euro-American backgrounds. Apolo Ohno's mixed ethnic heritage (half Japanese and half Euro-American), combined with his "soul patch" chin whiskers and his unassuming but confident "action sport" persona caught the attention of teen fans and the media during the 2002 Winter Olympics. His popularity, anchored in his exciting athletic performances, may also be tied to how he has seemingly forged a hybrid ethnic identity with which he is comfortable. This is attractive to many people who have done the same or face the challenge of doing so in a society in which living with a mixed ethnic heritage is an increasingly common experience.

At this point, research is needed on how images of Asian and Asian American athletes are taken up and represented in the U.S. media and in the minds of people around the country.

Research is also needed on the dramatic rise in popularity of various martial arts in North America. Karate, judo, Tae Kwon Do, and other sports with Asian origins have become especially popular with U.S. children. Has participation in these martial arts had an impact on children's knowledge and awareness of Asian cultures, on ethnic relations in elementary schools, and on the stereotypes used or challenged among children and others who participate in these sports? Or have these sport forms become so Americanized that their Asian roots are lost or ignored by participants?

The experiences and sport participation patterns of Asian Americans differ, depending on their immigration histories. Chinese Americans whose families have lived in the United States for four or more generations, along with many Japanese Americans, have experiences that are clearly different from those of recent Vietnamese and Cambodian immigrants and their children. Research must be sensitive to these differences and the ways they influence sport participation patterns and experiences. Gender issues also are important to study across a range of sports (Wong, 1999). Applied research is needed to assist coaches in high schools with Asian American students.

Anthropologist Mark Grey (1999) dealt with some of these issues in his study of high school sports and relations between immigrants from Southeast Asia and the established residents of Garden City, Kansas. Grey reports that, despite beliefs about sports serving democratic functions in schools, sports at Garden City High School were organized so that participation could occur only in narrowly defined terms. The immigrant and minority students had to fit in with the dominant system of values and game orientations, and this system was grounded in the experiences of Euro-Americans. The school failed to provide these newcomers with sports they wanted to play, and, when the immigrant students did not

The popularity of Apolo Ohno has been linked to his exciting athletic skills, his "action sport" persona, and his mixed ethnic heritage. He was raised by his Japanese father and is clearly aware of his combined Japanese and Euro-American background. As more people forge their own hybrid ethnic identities, public figures like Ohno may be viewed in positive ways. (Amy Sancetta; AP/Wide World Photos)

try out for football, basketball, baseball, and softball, they were seen as unwilling to become "true Americans."

Over time, the failure of Asian and Asian American students to participate in the major high school sports led them to be socially marginalized in the school and community. The established community residents believed that "if *those people* really wanted to become Americans, they would participate in true American sports." When they didn't participate, new tensions were created and existing tensions were intensified. It is possible that this pattern also exists in other communities, although not enough is known about it or about other possible patterns.

In contrast to Grey's research, third- and fourth-generation Asian American families often are well integrated into community life in the United States and play the same sports that other members of the community play. In fact, some Asian American young people have used sports to express their assimilation into U.S. culture and to reaffirm social relationships with peers. Again, research is needed on how and when this occurs, especially in multiethnic neighborhoods and schools.

THE DYNAMICS OF RACIAL AND ETHNIC RELATIONS IN SPORTS

Many people believe that racial and ethnic problems do not exist in sports today. They think that playing fields are generally level, barriers to participation have been removed, personal prejudices and stereotypes have been controlled, and long-time patterns of discrimination have been eliminated or are disappearing with each passing year.

This conclusion reflects the positive changes that have occurred over the past fifty years in many nations, but it ignores the challenges that are faced now that some sports are becoming more multiracial and multiethnic in terms of participation and popularity. It also overlooks the legacy of past problems and how that legacy still influences what happens in sports today. Overall, race and ethnic relations have improved in many sport settings, but sports are far from being a paradise of racial and ethnic harmony.

Today's challenges related to race and ethnic relations are not the same ones that people faced twenty years ago in sports. Experience has taught us that challenges associated with racial and ethnic relations never disappear once and for all time; they simply change as circumstances change. When one set of problems is solved, the solutions create new situations, which contain new challenges. For example, once racial and ethnic segregation is eliminated, people face the challenge of living, working, and playing together with those who have different experiences and cultures. Meeting this challenge requires more than enforcing rules of fairness and promoting affirmative action. It also involves learning about the perspectives of other people, understanding how they perceive things, and then determining how relationships can be formed and maintained while respecting differences, making compromises, and supporting each other in the pursuit of goals that may not always be shared.

> The challenge in sports in the 21st Century is going to be diversity.
>
> —Harry Edwards,
> sociologist/activist (2000)

Too many people think in fairy tale terms when it comes to racial and ethnic relations: they believe that, once everyone comes together on the same team, in the same classroom, or the same organization, they will live happily ever after. However, coming together is just the first step in a never-ending process of relationship management. Racial and ethnic diversity brings potential vitality and creativity to a team or group, but this potential does not automatically become reality. It takes awareness, commitment, and work to establish and maintain it.

The following sections deal with three of the major challenges related to racial and ethnic relations in sports today: (1) eliminating racial and ethnic exclusion in sport participation, (2) dealing with and managing racial and ethnic diversity in sports, and (3) integrating positions of power in sport organizations. The final section deals with the prospects for successfully meeting these three challenges.

Eliminating Racial and Ethnic Exclusion in Sport Participation

Why are some sports characterized by disproportionately high rates of participation by racial and ethnic minorities, whereas others have little or no racial or ethnic diversity? One answer to this question is that some teams and leagues have commercial incentives to recruit the best players regardless of race or ethnicity, and they are organized so that diversity does not disrupt established power relations or require people in the organization to change their lives in significant ways. For example, forms of discrimination and exclusion in sports are most likely to be challenged and eliminated under the following six conditions (Edwards, 1973):

1. When people with power and control benefit financially if discrimination and exclusion are eliminated
2. When individual performances can be measured precisely and objectively and do

not depend primarily on the subjective assessments of scouts and coaches

3. When members of an entire team benefit from the achievements of teammates
4. When superior performances by athletes do not lead to promotions in the organization or control over fellow players
5. When team success does not depend on friendships and off-the-field social relationships between teammates
6. When athletes are subordinate to the power and authority of coaches, managers, administrators, and owners in the organizational structure of a sport or sport team

Under these six conditions, those who control sport teams can recruit racially and ethnically diverse players without feeling threatened, giving up power and control, or upsetting the existing structure and relationships within the team. Of course, there is no guarantee that policies of discrimination and exclusion will always be eliminated when these conditions exist. Through history, racism and bigotry have been so strong that racial and ethnic barriers were maintained, even when games could be won and money could be made if they were eliminated. Some of these barriers still exist today, although they are more difficult to maintain in the face of increasing concerns about civil rights in many nations.

In the case of revenue-generating sports in the United States, the desire to win and make money, combined with other changes in U.S. society, gradually led to changes in traditional policies of racial discrimination and exclusion in certain team sports. However, for the majority of the twentieth century, most team sports remained racially segregated.

Changes in patterns of discrimination and exclusion come even more slowly in individual and team sports that involve informal, personal, and male-female social contact on or off the field. This is why golf, tennis, swimming, and other sports often learned and played in private clubs have been slow to welcome racial and ethnic diversity. When sport participation is accompanied

by informal and close personal contact between family and friends, people are more likely to enforce various forms of exclusion. When others define these forms of exclusion as unfair and challenge them, racial and ethnic conflict is likely. In fact, there is a history of this conflict in the United States, and policies of discrimination and exclusion in many sport settings have been dropped only as a result of government legislation and/or civil rights lawsuits.

Formal and official policies of racial and ethnic exclusion are illegal in many, but not all, societies today. Informal patterns of exclusion still remain in some private clubs and in sports in which athletic skills are developed in private clubs. This is why in 2003 there were no African American women or men on the LPGA and PGA tours. This is why Tiger Woods, who is one-quarter African American, has received so much publicity since he began to play on the PGA tour. Golf and tennis at all levels of competition are comprised almost exclusively of whites with European backgrounds, and the people associated with those sports are eager to show that the blatant racist and exclusionary policies that were characteristic of the past no longer exist today. However, even in 2003, over fifty-five years after Jackie Robinson began playing Major League Baseball, we look at college and professional golfers and tennis players and see almost no people of color from the United States. Jim Thorpe, an African American playing on the senior professional golf tour, observes that progress in boosting racial diversity in club-based sports has been slow or nonexistent. He points out, "When I came on the [PGA] tour in 1975, there were more African American players than there are today. I think we had 12. Today, we have Tiger Woods. So Tiger has done a lot, but has he opened any doors?" (in Potter, 2002, p. 12C).

When we take a close look at private golf and tennis clubs in the United States, we see many more black, Latino, and Asian people working in low-wage service jobs than playing golf and tennis and watching their children take lessons.

Asian American and Latino athletes are gradually gaining membership in professional golf and tennis organizations, but they generally are citizens of countries where they are not ethnic minorities and where they have open access to club memberships because they come from wealthy families. More rare in these sports are players who represent racial or ethnic *minorities* in various countries. Of course, there are exceptions to this pattern, and these exceptions often receive considerable attention, because they enable people associated with the sports to claim that racism and discrimination have been eliminated.

The forms of racial and ethnic exclusion that are most important today occur at the community level, where they are hidden behind policies that tie participation to fees and access to personal transportation. Some communities claim to have open sport programs, when there are few or no facilities in areas where racial and ethnic minorities live and when fees and convenient access to transportation are required for participation. Furthermore, as public programs are dropped and more sports become organized by nonprofit and private organizations, there is a tendency for class-based patterns of exclusion to have an impact on some racial and ethnic groups more than others. Even though this form of exclusion is not grounded directly in racial and ethnic discrimination, its effects are much the same as those of past forms of exclusion, and they are more difficult to attack on the grounds that they violate civil rights. Eliminating these forms of exclusion will be one of the most difficult racial and ethnic challenges of this century.

Dealing with and Managing Racial and Ethnic Diversity in Sports

As sports become more global, as teams recruit players from around the world, and as global migration creates pressures to develop racially and ethnically sensitive policies related to all aspects of sports, there will be many new racial and ethnic challenges faced by players, coaches, team administrators, and even spectators. It is naïve to think that the racial and ethnic issues that exist around the world today have no impact on sports or that sports can deal with these issues in ways that eliminate them once and for all time. A brief look at sports and racial issues in U.S. Major League Baseball can be used to illustrate this point.

Sports history in the United States shows that, after Branch Rickey signed Jackie Robinson to a contract with the Brooklyn Dodgers in 1946, there was a host of new challenges encountered by Rickey, Robinson, the Dodger organization, players throughout the league, other baseball teams in the National League, and spectators attending baseball games. Rickey had to justify his decision to sign a black player to many people, including his partners in the Dodger organization and other baseball team owners. Robinson had to endure incident after incident of unspeakable racism by opponents, spectators, and racists in the general population. He needed support from Rickey, his coach, and his teammates as he struggled to control his anger and depression.

The Dodgers and other teams had to change their policies of excluding black spectators or segregating them in small sections of seats far from the field. Teammates had to make decisions about if and how they would support their new teammate. The team's coach had to manage a set of interracial dynamics that he had never before experienced. He had to deal with who would be Robinson's roommate on road trips, where the team would stay and eat in cities where hotels and restaurants excluded blacks, and what to say to players who made racist comments that could destroy team morale.

Baseball fans who had never socialized across racial lines were forced to come to terms with sitting next to someone from a different race. Stadium managers had to deal with the prospect of serving food to people with different tastes and traditions, and white, working-class service workers had to come to terms with serving black customers—something that most of them had

Eliminating racial exclusion is important as when Jackie Robinson joined the Brooklyn Dodgers in 1947. However, this does not end the challenges associated with racial and ethnic relations. After desegregation, there are new challenges associated with managing intergroup relations on teams and integrating positions of power in sport organizations. (American Memory Collection)

never done before. Journalists and radio announcers had to decide how they would represent Robinson's experiences in their coverage, whether they would talk about the racism of other players who were fan favorites, or whether they would just pretend that race was not an issue, even though it was crucial in much of what was going on in baseball.

Of course, this is only a partial list of all the new challenges faced *after* the policy of racial exclusion in Major League Baseball was dropped. As these challenges were faced and gradually solved, new and different challenges emerged. As other black players entered Major League Baseball, teammates began to racially segregate themselves in the locker room and in their social lives. Successful black players could not buy homes in segregated white areas of the cities where they played. When black players challenged records set by whites in the past, they

received death threats, and stadium security became an issue. Some teams became racially divided. Black players felt at a disadvantage in team politics, because all the coaches, managers, trainers, and owners were white. Even the positions that blacks and whites played tended to fit patterns that resembled racial traditions and beliefs: blacks played outfield positions, requiring speed and quick reactions to others' actions, whereas whites played the positions that many felt required intelligence along with physical skills. One of the consequences of these position placements, or "stacking," patterns was that they prevented most blacks from playing the positions that might have led them to be identified as good candidates for coaching jobs after they retired.[3]

---

[3]"Stacking" is discussed in detail at the *Sports in Society* website, www.mhhe.com/coakley8e.

In fact, the lack of black general managers and coaches remains a central issue in baseball today.

Currently, one-fourth of the players in major league baseball are Latino, and the number of Asian players is increasing. These changes have created new racial and ethnic challenges for baseball teams and everyone connected with them.

This example of just one professional sport is intended to illustrate how racial and ethnic issues are never settled permanently. Issues faced today present new challenges. For example, some NHL hockey coaches have players on their teams from five or more different national and cultural backgrounds. Many of these players bring potentially disruptive racial and ethnic stereotypes with them, they often speak different languages, and they have different experiences and customs that may be defined as strange by some teammates, team staff, and spectators (see figure 9.4).

"Line dancing in the end-zone? Maybe white boys oughta leave the 'end zone dance' stuff alone."

FIGURE 9.4 Experiences and traditions vary from one racial or ethnic group to another. What happens when people from various groups bring their experiences and traditions to sports and use them to guide how they play or how they celebrate on-the-field success? If white players from the University of Texas did a line dance after scoring a touchdown, would the NCAA make a rule prohibiting it?

Translators are now needed on hockey and baseball teams, many players need cultural diversity training, coaches must learn new ways to communicate effectively, and the marketing departments for teams must learn how to take advantage of racial and ethnic diversity as they market the teams to new groups of potential fans. Ethnic and cultural issues enter into sponsorship considerations and the products sold at games, and cultural and ethnic awareness is an important qualification for employees who handle team advertising and sponsorship deals.

These and related issues are central to the success of many teams in Major League Soccer in the United States, because some teams have a strong base of Latino spectators—well over 25 percent of all the fans for teams in California, Colorado, Florida, Texas, and New York City. In fact, the success of soccer in the United States depends on attracting ethnic spectators to games and television broadcasts. Spanish-speaking announcers are crucial, and deals must be made with radio and television stations that broadcast in Spanish. This also will be one of the challenges faced by the new women's professional soccer league in the United States, even though many of the girls and young women who play soccer in the United States come from white Euro-American families.

Some teams in the NFL and NBA now face situations in which 70 to 85 percent of their players are black, whereas 90 to 98 percent of their season ticket holders are white. Many people are aware of this issue, although there have been few public discussions about it. Race is not something that many people in the United States feel comfortable talking about in public settings, even though they will talk about it in private, often among friends from the same racial or ethnic background. Research shows that this avoidance of the issue of race and certain issues related to ethnicity is not so much due to personal prejudices or underlying racism as it is to a civic etiquette that leads to an avoidance of racial and ethnic issues in public discourse (Eliasoph, 1999). This etiquette makes it difficult to put racial and ethnic issues "on the table" so they can be dealt with through a thoughtful and public exchange of ideas (even in college classrooms).

Many sport teams in Western Europe also have dealt with diversity issues over the years, but new racial and ethnic tensions created by high rates of migration from Africa and Eastern Europe have presented new challenges to teams, players, coaches, and sport organizations. Racial and ethnic issues vary from sport to sport, and they often are connected with related matters of national identity, labor migration, and citizenship status. Populist leaders in some nations have raised questions about allowing immigrants to play on national teams, and some fans have associated players from Africa with social and economic problems in their lives. These issues are not likely to go away anytime soon in Europe, North America, or other parts of the world. Challenges related to managing racial and ethnic relations are here to stay, although they will change over time.

Integrating Positions of Power in Sport Organizations

Despite progressive changes in many sports, the major positions of power and control in sports continue to be held by white, non-Hispanic men. Of course, there are exceptions to this in North America as well as other parts of the world, but these exceptions do not obscure deep, pervasive, and persistent racial and ethnic inequalities when it comes to power and control in sports.

Data on who holds positions of power in sport organizations change every year, and it is difficult to obtain information from many organizations. Fortunately, Richard Lapchick and his staff at the Center for the Study of Sport in Society at Northeastern University have published on a regular basis since the late 1980s a *Racial and Gender Report Card* for sport organizations. This publication contains data on the racial and ethnic composition of players in major professional team sports and an analysis of the number and types of jobs held by women and people of color

in major professional, university, and Olympic sports organizations. The report covers everyone from owners and athletic directors to office staff and athletic trainers.

The data in table 9.1 were drawn from six of the sixty-five tables included in the 2001 *Report Card*. The data, in table 9.1 focus on men's professional sports because patterns in those sports are representative of patterns in other sports organizations. Table 9.1 lists percentages for the racial and ethnic composition of players, assistant coaches, head coaches and managers, chief operating officers and general managers, team chairmen and presidents, and team owners. The data show that only in the NBA, MLB (Major League Baseball), and the MLS (Major League Soccer) did the percentages of black or Latino head coaches or chief operating officers match or surpass the percentage of blacks and Latinos in the general population (13 percent in both cases). In the NBA and MLB, 34 percent and 20 percent of the head coaches were black; in the MLS, Latinos held 25 percent of the head coach jobs. Only in MLB and the MLS did the percentages of black and Latino head coaches surpass the percentages of black and Latino players, respectively. At the top levels of power and control in all the sport organizations, whites held between 87 and 100 percent of the positions; whites were the primary owners of all but 1 of nearly 140 teams, and all but four of those whites were men.

Patterns are the same or worse in most other sport organizations at nearly all levels of competition. For example, during the 2001 WNBA season, 63 percent of the players were black and 3 percent were Latina, but 75 percent of all assistant and head coaches were white. Almost all the top administrators were white. At the same time, about 93 percent of all athletic directors in NCAA colleges and universities were white. Division I basketball has been the only sport in which black men have been well represented in coaching. Among the 117 Division 1 football teams, there were only four black head coaches at the start of the 2002 season—a situation described by Tyrone Willingham, the head coach

Table 9.1   Who plays, who coaches, and who has the power: Race and ethnicity in major men's team sports in North America, 2000–2001.

League	Players (%)	Assistant Coaches (%)	Head Coaches (%)	COO/ General Manager* (%)	Team Chairman or President (%)	Primary Owner (%)
NFL						
Blacks	65	28	10	6	0	0
Latinos	<1	0	0	0	0	0
Others**	<1	0	0	0	0	0
Whites	33	72	90	94	100	100
NBA						
Blacks	78	36	34	21	10	0
Latinos	1	0	0	0	0	0
Others	0	0	0	0	0	0
Whites	21	64	66	79	90	100
MLB						
Blacks	13	19	20	3	0	0
Latinos	26	11	3	0	0	0
Others	1	0	0	0	0	0
Whites	59	70	77	97	100	100
NHL						
Blacks	2	0	0	0	0	0
Latinos	<1	0	0	0	0	0
Others	<1	0	0	0	0	3
Whites	98	100	100	100	100	97
MLS						
Blacks	19	0	0	0	0	NA**
Latinos	20	28	25	8	0	NA
Others	2	3	0	0	0	NA
Whites	59	69	75	92	100	NA

Source: Lapchick and Mathews, 2002.

*These men are responsible for the day-to-day operation of teams.

**Except for players, "Others" in the remaining positions are Asians/Asian Americans. The MLS operates as a total monopoly; it has investor/franchise holders rather than real owners; nearly all are white men.

at the University of Notre Dame, as "criminally wrong, to be honest about it" (in Price, 2002, p. 40). When he made this statement, Willingham realized that, in 2002, blacks held less than 4 percent of all the head coaching jobs at all NCAA schools—1,058 out of 22,895. He and many others felt that, since desegregation was ruled to be illegal a half-century ago, since universities are supposed to be leaders when it comes to diversity, and since African Americans make up 13 percent of the U.S. population and over 20 percent of all varsity-athletes, this record is undeniably embarrassing and in need of immediate attention (this is discussed further in chapter 14).

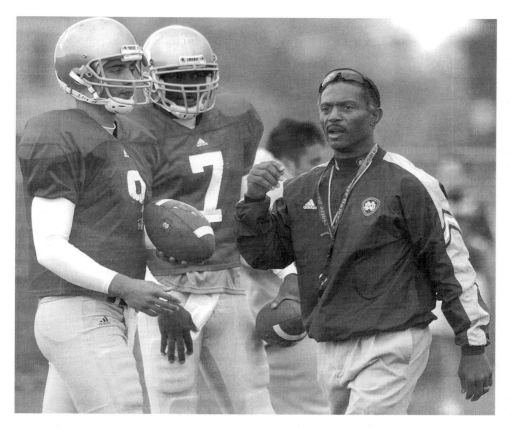

During the 2002 college football season, only 4 of 117 NCAA Division I football teams had African American head coaches. Tyrone Willingham, coach at the University of Notre Dame, described this situation as "criminally wrong." African Americans hold only 1,058 of nearly 23,000 head coaching jobs in NCAA college sports. This makes many people wonder if universities are serious about the goal of fostering diversity. (Joe Raymond; AP/Wide World Photos)

Additionally, African Americans hold less than 15 percent of the top power positions in Olympic sports. This is the case in the USOC and in most of the national governing bodies for particular sports. Black women and members of other ethnic minority populations are underrepresented in nearly all jobs in all sport organizations.

Of course, owners and CEOs can hire anyone they wish, but the patterns of hiring practices indicate that racial and ethnic minorities share little in the control of most sports. The exception is the NBA, in which 80 percent of the players are black and there have been pressures from players to hire black coaches and general managers. There may be changes in the future if current assistant coaches move up the ranks into the positions of head coach and chief operating officer. However, past patterns suggest that this will occur very slowly, if at all.

Black and Latino players at all levels of sports are aware of the percentage distributions in each of the categories in table 9.1. As they see good minority candidates passed over and white candidates selected for important jobs in sport organizations, they raise questions about the attitudes and orientations of owners and other decision makers in sport organizations. These athletes know the difference between the desegregation of sports to make more money and a commitment to full integration to the point of sharing power in sport organizations. The data suggest that full integration has not yet occurred.

Apart from general racial issues in sports, the underrepresentation of blacks and other minorities in coaching and administration jobs has been one of the most widely publicized topics in sports since the mid-1980s. Although this issue will be discussed further in chapter 10, it is important to note that the blacks and Latinos who have been hired as coaches had longer and more productive playing careers than the whites hired as coaches (Rimer, 1996). Many whites hired as coaches had mediocre or unimpressive playing careers, and some have unimpressive past coaching records as well. Meanwhile, minority candidates with similar or better playing careers are routinely passed over as coaching candidates in a range of sports. It seems that, because coaching and administrative abilities cannot be measured as objectively as playing abilities, the subjective feelings of those doing the hiring come into play when coaching and top management candidates are assessed (Lavoie and Leonard, 1994).

Prospects for Change

It is clear that people do not give up racial and ethnic beliefs easily, especially when they come in the form of well-established ideologies rooted deeply in their cultures. Those who have benefited from widely accepted racial ideologies will resist changes in the relationships and social structures that are built on and then reinforce their beliefs. This is why certain expressions of racism and ethnic bigotry have remained a part of sports in the United States and other societies.

Sports may bring people together, but they do not automatically lead them to question how they think about race or ethnicity or how they define and interact with people from other racial or ethnic groups. For example, white team owners, general managers, and athletic directors in the United States worked with black athletes for years before they ever hired black coaches, and it continues to require social and legal pressures to encourage those in power positions to act more affirmatively when it comes to their hiring procedures. In the meantime, blacks and other ethnic minorities are still underrepresented in coaching and administration, because people in power don't easily change the ideologies and social structures that support their power (Shropshire, 1996).

My purpose here is not to argue that sports are unique when it comes to resistance to progressive changes. In fact, many sport organizations are more progressive than other organizations when it comes to certain aspects of racial and ethnic relations. However, these good things do not happen automatically or as often as many think; nor do changes on the personal level automatically lead to changes on an organizational or institutional level. Challenging the negative personal beliefs of other people is one thing; changing the relationships and social structures that have been built on those beliefs is another thing (see figure 9.5). Both forms of change are needed, and neither occurs automatically just because sports bring people together in the same locker rooms and stadiums.

For racial and ethnic relations to be improved through sports, those who control sport teams and sport events must make organized, concerted efforts to bring people together in ways that will encourage them to confront and challenge racial and ethnic issues. These efforts must be initiated and supported by whites as well as members of ethnic minorities, or else they will fail (Oglesby and Schrader, 2000). Of course, it has never been easy for people to deal with racial and ethnic issues. However, if it could be done in connection with sports, it would be significant, because sports attract so much public attention in societies today.

"We will not tolerate any player who demonstrates such racial and ethnic insensitivity!"

FIGURE 9.5   When spokespeople for professional sport organizations condemned a player's insensitive remarks (in 1999) about other people, they clearly came off as hypocrites. Native Americans told them to look in the mirror before offering their sanctimonious and self-righteous statements.

We need a new vocabulary to deal with the existence of racial and ethnic diversity in social life and to promote affirmative action on both personal and organizational levels. We must get away from the notion that skin color or ethnicity signifies a biological essence that shapes character and physical abilities. In connection with sports, we must realize that, when we ask questions about so-called racial performance differences, we are merely reproducing a racial ideology that has caused hatred, turmoil, and confusion in much of the world for nearly 300 years. Now we must ask questions about how people give meaning to physical and cultural characteristics and then use those meanings as a basis for their thoughts and their relations with others. However, even framing questions this way requires a big shift in the way many people view the world.

Sport leaders at all levels of competition should be encouraged to sponsor training sessions on racial and ethnic diversity. Everyone from team owners and athletic directors to the people in training rooms should attend these sessions. Coaches need them, and so do athletes. Even those who are already sensitive to diversity issues should be made aware that there is a formal commitment in their organizations to acting on those sensitivities. Furthermore, there are always new things to learn about the perspectives of those whose experiences and cultures are different from our own. In fact, when the perspectives of racial and ethnic minorities are not used to guide efforts to make things better in society as a whole, those efforts often fail. When making things better means doing things to fit the interests of those with power and influence, real change is unlikely.

SUMMARY

ARE RACE AND ETHNICITY IMPORTANT IN SPORTS?

Racial and ethnic issues exist in sports, just as they exist in most other spheres of social life. As people watch, play, and talk about sports, they often take into account ideas about skin color and ethnicity. The meanings given to skin color and ethnic background have an impact on access to sport participation and the decisions that people make about sports in their lives.

Race refers to a category of people identified through a classification system based on meanings given to physical traits among humans; *ethnicity* refers to collections of people identified in terms of their shared cultural heritage. Racial and ethnic minorities are populations that have endured systematic forms of discrimination in a society.

The concept of race has a complex history. Ideas about race often take the form of racial ideology, which people use to identify and make sense of racial differences. Racial ideology, like other social constructions, changes over time as ideas and relationships change. However, over the past century in the United States, the dominant racial ideology has led many people to assume that there are important biological and even cognitive differences between blacks and whites and that these differences explain the success of blacks in certain sports.

To some degree, racial ideology has influenced how African Americans and many blacks around the world view their own physical abilities, how people identify black males who excel in sports, and how some whites make sport participation decisions. Race, gender, and class relations in American society have combined to create a context in which black males emphasize a personal presentation of self that has been described as "cool pose," or a stylized persona that has not only added to the commodity value of the black male body in sports but also has enabled some black athletes to use widely accepted ideas about race to intimidate opponents, especially white opponents, in sports.

The sport participation patterns among Native American, African American, Latino, and Asian American people have their own histories. Combinations of various ideological, historical, economic, and political factors have influenced those histories. However, the sport participation of any minority group usually occurs under terms set by the dominant group in a community or society. Minority groups seldom have been able to use sports to challenge the power and privilege of the dominant group, even though individual minority-group members may experience great personal success in sports.

The fact that some sports have histories of racially and ethnically mixed participation does not mean that racial and ethnic problems have been eliminated in those sports. In fact, harmonious racial and ethnic relations never occur automatically in any setting. Furthermore, harmony is never established once and for all time. As current problems are confronted and solved, new relationships and new challenges develop. This means that racial and ethnic issues must be given

regular attention in order to anticipate and meet challenges successfully. Success also depends largely on whether members of the dominant group see the value in racial and ethnic diversity and are committed to facing diversity issues alongside those who are different from them.

Sports certainly are not free of problems related to racial and ethnic relations. However, it is important to acknowledge that, despite problems, sports can be sites for challenging racial ideology and transforming race and ethnic relations. This happens only if people in sports plan strategies to encourage critical awareness of ethnic prejudices, racist ideas, and forms of discrimination built into the structures of sport organizations. This awareness is required to eliminate forms of racial and ethnic exclusion in sports, deal with and manage racial and ethnic diversity in sports, and integrate racial and ethnic minorities into the power structures of sport organizations. Without this awareness, these and other problems will become worse in the future.

SUGGESTED READINGS

Bloom, J. 2000. *To show what an Indian can do: Sports at Native American boarding schools.* Minneapolis: University of Minnesota Press (draws on recollections of former students and describes how sports were important in their lives; illustrates that the meaning of sport participation varies by ethnicity and changes over time).

Boyd, T., and K. L. Shropshire, eds. 2001. *Basketball Jones: America above the rim.* New York: New York University Press (eighteen articles focused on the complex connections among, culture, basketball, race, and the celebrity of contemporary professional athletes; issues related to crime, gender, social class, and economics are investigated).

Bretón, M., and J. L. Villegas. 1999. *Away games: The life and times of a Latin American baseball player.* Albuquerque: University of New Mexico Press (journalists tell the story of a young player from the Dominican Republic; they describe the experiences of Latino athletes who dream of playing big-time sports, are hired by U.S. sport organizations, deal with the challenges of working in U.S. culture, and then face the harsh realities of life after sports).

Brooks, D. D., and R. C. Althouse, eds. 1999. *Racism in college athletics: The African-American athletes' experience* (2d ed.). Morgantown, WV: Fitness Information Technology (sixteen essays dealing with problems faced by African Americans in college sports; essays provide historical material; discussion of recruitment, retention, and mobility issues; analysis of the intersection of race and gender in sports; and prospects for change in the future).

Dobie, M. 2000. Race and sports in high school. In *Best newspaper writing* 2000 (pp. 319–87), edited by C. Scanlon. St. Petersburg, FL: The Poynter Institute for Media Studies (this five-part series of reports originally published in *Newsday* received a major national award for newspaper writing about diversity; the reports provide a unique view of race and ethnic relations in a Long Island, New York, high school).

Entine, J. 2000. *Taboo: Why black athletes dominate sports and why we are afraid to talk about it.* New York: Public Affairs (a journalist uses selective research from many disciplines to argue that the success of black athletes in sports that involve sprinting, long-distance running, jumping, and bursts of muscular power is due largely to genetically based characteristics shared by those whose ancestry can be traced to certain West African, East African, and North African regions).

Hoberman, J. 1997. *Darwin's athletes: How sport has damaged black America and preserved the myth of race.* Boston: Houghton Mifflin (controversial discussion of sports in African American culture; focuses on the notion that African Americans have forsaken mainstream routes to social mobility in the quest for fortune and fame in sports and that this has reaffirmed racist ideas about their abilities and potential).

Journal of Physical Education, Recreation and Dance. 1999. 70 (4) (this special issue has brief review articles on African American, Euro-American,
Asian, Hispanic, and Native American women in sports).

King, C. R., and C. F. Springwood. 2001. *Beyond the cheers: Race as a spectacle in college sport.* Albany: State University of New York Press (analyses of racial dimensions of intercollegiate sports, shows how racial ideology has become embedded in the taken-for-granted practices of college campuses).

King, C. R., and C. F. Springwood, eds. 2001. *Team spirits: The Native American mascots controversy.* Lincoln: Bison Books and University of Nebraska Press (fourteen articles by an impressive array of activists and academics take a critical look at the use of Native American images and names by sport teams).

Sailes, G., ed. 1998. *African Americans in sport.* New Brunswick, NJ: Transaction (eighteen articles dealing with cultural issues, media representations, athletic performance, college and professional sports, and racism and discrimination in sports).

WEBSITE RESOURCES

Note: Websites often change. The following URLs were current when this book was printed. Please check our website (www.mhhe.com/coakley8e) for updates and additions.

www.mhhe.com/coakley8e Discussion guides for *Hoop Dreams* and *In Whose Honor;* history of racial desegregation in U.S. sports; discussion of stacking in the NFL and MLB.

www.sportinsociety.org/rgrc.html See the *Racial and Gender Report Card*—research document that analyzes hiring practices in major sports organizations in the United States.

www.sportinsociety.org/ptw.html Project TEAMWORK is a diversity awareness and conflict resolution program that teaches high school students to combat discrimination.

http://racerelations.about.com/cs/raceandsports A general site with links to articles on diversity and other sources that cover race and ethnicity-related issues in sports.

chapter 10

(John Sutherland, *The Denver Post*)

Social Class

Do Money and Power Matter in Sports?

WHEN MEN AND WOMEN compete on the athletics field, socioeconomic status disappears. . . . It's the same way in the stands, where corporate presidents sit next to janitors . . . which makes me wonder if [social class matters] at all.

—Former U. S. President
Ronald Reagan (1990)

 Online Learning Center Resources

Visit *Sports in Society*'s Online Learning Center at **www.mhhe.com/coakley8e** for additional information and study material for this chapter, including

- Self-grading quizzes
- Learning objectives
- Related websites
- Additional readings

A complete outline is available at
www.mhhe.com/coakley8e.

LUXURY BOXES AND CLUB seat sections are the
gated communities of sport stadiums.

    —**Spectator assessing Invesco Field, new stadium
      of the NFL's Denver Broncos (2002)**

325

People like to think that sports transcend issues of money, power, and economic inequalities. They see sports as open to everyone, watch many sports on "free" television, and define success on the field in terms of ability and hard work. However, formally organized sports depend on material resources. The fates of teams, events, and media coverage rest in the hands of wealthy and powerful individuals and corporations.

More than ever before, it takes money to play sports and receive the coaching needed to develop sport skills. Tickets are expensive, and spectators often are segregated by social class in the stadium: the wealthy and well-connected sit in club seats and luxury suites, whereas others are seated in various sections, depending on their ability to pay for premium tickets or buy season tickets. It even takes money to watch sports on television when events air on cable channels that have monthly subscriber fees or a pay-per-view format. This means that sports and sport participation are connected with the distribution of economic, political, and social resources in society. Money and power do matter in sports.

Many people also believe that sports are avenues for economic success among people from all social classes. Rags-to-riches stories are common when people talk about athletes. However, these beliefs and stories distract attention from how sports can subvert economic success and how sports perpetuate existing economic inequalities in society.

This chapter deals with matters of money and wealth, as well as issues related to social class and socioeconomic mobility. Our discussion will focus on the following questions:

1. What is meant by *social class* and *class relations?*
2. How do social class and class relations influence sports and sport participation?
3. Are sports open and democratic in the provision of economic and career opportunities?

4. Does playing sports contribute to occupational success and social mobility among former athletes?

SOCIAL CLASS AND CLASS RELATIONS

Social class and the related concepts of social stratification, socioeconomic status, and life chances are important concepts in the study of society and social life. They are important because economic resources are related to power in society, and economic inequalities influence nearly all aspects of people's lives.

Social class refers to categories of people who share an economic position in society based on a combination of their income, wealth, education, occupation, and social connections. People in a particular social class also share similar **life chances**—that is, they share similar odds for achieving economic success and gaining economic power. Social classes exist in all industrial societies, because there are economic inequalities and differences in life chances among people in those societies.

Social stratification is the concept used to refer to structured forms of economic inequalities that are part of the organization of everyday social life. In other words, people from lower-social-class backgrounds have fewer opportunities to achieve economic success and gain economic power than have people from upper social classes. Children born into wealthy, powerful, and well-connected families are in better positions to become wealthy, powerful, and well-connected adults than are children born into poor families that lack influence and social networks connecting them with educational and career opportunities.

Most of us are very aware of economic inequalities in society, but there are few public discussions about the impact of social class on our views of ourselves and others, our social relationships, and our everyday lives (Perrucci and

Wysong, 2002). In other words, we do not discuss **class relations**—that is, we do not discuss the many ways that social class is incorporated into social processes in society. In schools and the media, we hear about the importance of equal opportunities, but we learn little about how people in upper socioeconomic classes use their income, wealth, and power to maintain privileged positions in society and pass that privilege from one generation to the next. We hear about those who have moved up and out of lower socioeconomic classes through hard work and strong character and about "millionaires next door" and CEOs with big salaries and bonuses, but we learn little about the oppressive effects of poverty and the limited opportunities available to those who lack economic resources, access to good education, and well-placed social connections.

People in many postindustrial societies, and especially in the United States, are uncomfortable with critical discussions of social class and class relations (Sage, 1998b). The myth of equality in many democratic societies discourages such discussions, even though we are aware of class and class relations in our lives. This is especially true when it comes to sports and sport participation.

The discussion of social class and class relations in this chapter is grounded in critical theories. The focus is on how economic inequality is maintained in society, how it serves the interests of those with wealth and economic power, and how it affects what happens in sports and the lives of people associated with sports.

SPORTS AND ECONOMIC INEQUALITY

Money and economic power exert significant influence on the meaning, organization, and purpose of sports in society (Gruneau, 1999; Sugden and Tomlinson, 2000). Many people believe that sports and sport participation are open to all people and that inequalities related to money, position, and influence don't spill over into the organized games we play and watch. However, formally organized sports could not be developed, scheduled, or maintained without economic resources. Those who control money and economic power use their financial clout to organize and sponsor sports. As they do so, they give preference to sport forms that reflect and maintain their own values and interests.

The wealthy aristocrats who organized the Olympic Movement and sponsored the modern Olympic Games even used their power to establish a definition of *amateur* that privileged athletes from wealthy backgrounds around the world. This definition excluded athletes from working-class backgrounds, who could afford to train only if they used their sport skills to help them earn a living. The definition of *amateur* has been revised over the years, so that more people can participate in sports. However, money and economic power now operate in different ways as powerful corporations use the Olympics to expand profits and market share by linking their logos and products to athletes and global sport images. Social class and class relations have been expressed in sports in many ways during the past century.

Elite and powerful groups in society always have had considerable influence over what types of activities will be organized as sports and how those sports will be defined, scheduled, and played. Even as grass-roots games and physical activities become formally organized as sports, they are not widely sponsored or promoted unless they can be used to promote the interests and ideologies of those with money and economic power in society. Similarly, the informal

> We are already in a situation where we are expecting children to play games they cannot afford to watch.
>
> —Harry Edwards, sociologist/social activist (2000)

games played by people of all ages often depend on the availability of facilities, equipment, and safe play spaces. These are more plentiful in the everyday lives of people from upper- and upper-middle-income families and neighborhoods. Low-income families and neighborhoods often lack the resources needed to initiate and sustain informal activities. This is why it is important that we understand the dynamics of class relations when we study sports and patterns of sport participation.

The Dynamics of Class Relations

One way to understand the dynamics of class relations in connection with sports is to think about how age relations are involved in sports and sport participation. Consider this: even though children are capable of creating their own games, adults have intervened and developed youth sport programs. These programs are organized around the ideas and orientations that adults think should be emphasized in the lives of children and in social life generally. As noted in chapter 5, adults possess the *resources* to develop, schedule, and maintain organized youth programs that reflect what they think children should be doing and learning as they play. This does not mean that children do not enjoy adult-controlled sports, but it does mean that their enjoyment occurs in a framework that legitimizes and reproduces the power of adults over the lives of children.

When children's behavior in organized sports deviates from adult expectations, adults use their power to force compliance or convince children that it is in their best interest to play "the right way." When children comply and meet adult expectations, the adults say they possess "character" and reward them accordingly. This is why many people perceive autocratic and controlling coaches as heroes. These coaches reaffirm the cultural belief that the world is a better place when adults have full and strict control over young people and when young people consent to

that control. In this way, sports reproduce a hierarchical form of age relations, in which adult power and privilege are defined as natural and necessary aspects of social life.

Class relations work in similar ways. People in the upper social classes have the resources to organize and promote sports that support their ideas about how social life should be organized. For example, they can play sports in exclusive clubs to emphasize the idea that wealthy and influential people are special in society and deserve special places to play sports. They also can create and sponsor forms of organized sports that reinforce ideologies supportive of existing economic relationships and organization in society. For example, popular spectator sports around the world now are presented in ways that emphasize competition, individualism, highly specialized skills, the use of technology, and dominance over opponents; they are *not* presented in ways that emphasize partnership, sharing, open participation, nurturance, and mutual support. This emphasis in sports ties popular everyday activities and events to an ideology that stresses individual achievement through competition and the use of technology and equipment to outscore and dominate others.

This ideology involves a set of interrelated ideas emphasizing that economic success (winning) serves as proof of individual ability, worth, and character. People who use this ideology to interpret their own lives often set out on an endless quest for individual economic achievement. They measure success in terms of how many "things" they can acquire and how they rank relative to their peers when it comes to economic worth. Things and wealth become symbols of their identity, status, and moral worth.

A key component of the ideology of achievement through competitive success is illustrated by a popular locker-room slogan often repeated by coaches in their pep talks: "When you're satisfied with your performance, you're finished." This and similar ideas stress that achievement is measured in terms of a never-ending quest to

An ideology of achievement through competitive success infers that being wealthy and powerful (winning) is proof of individual abilities, moral worth, and character. Exclusive sports clubs such as this one, highlight this ideology. Therefore, they promote the interests of powerful and wealthy people and, at the same time, provide them with luxurious places to play sports. (Jay Coakley)

improve the "bottom line." This way of thinking drives market economies and enables people with wealth and power in those economies to preserve and extend their resources.

When people in a society adopt an ideology that links competitive success with moral worth, they assume that "you get what you deserve, and you deserve what you get." Consequently, wealthy and powerful people tend to be defined as worthy winners, whereas the poor and powerless tend to be defined as lazy losers. This clearly works to the advantage of those who have more wealth and economic power than others, and it promotes the idea that economic inequality in society is necessary for society to operate efficiently.

This idea is promoted even further when people with resources sponsor sports. The message underlying sponsorship is clear: if people want the enjoyment of playing and watching sports, they must look to the wealthy and powerful for support and sponsorship. When support and sponsorship comes, people tend to accept the ideological strings attached to it. This, of course, is part of the process of how sports are tied to class relations in society.

Class Relations and Who Has Power in Sports

Sport decisions are made at many levels, from neighborhood youth sport programs to the International Olympic Committee. Although scholars who study sports in society are concerned with identifying those who exercise power in various settings, they usually do not develop lists that rank powerful people in sports. But such lists do exist. For example, *The Sporting News*, a national weekly newspaper in the United States, has published a list of "the 100 most powerful people in sports" every year since 1991. The list appears at the end of the calendar year, and it is based on the editors' estimates of which people during the past year had the greatest influence on elite-level sports in the United States. Although people from outside the United States may be included, their rank generally reflects how much influence they have on what happened in the world of sports from a U.S. perspective.

Table 10.1 identifies the *Sporting News* "Top 25" people from the list for 2002 and indicates their ranks in 1990 and 1996. The "Top 100" for 2002 identified 116 people. This is because two or more people were sometimes ranked together as decision-making partners in an organization or business arena. The "Top 100" included 3 women, 6 people of color, and 109 white men. The "Top 25" actually lists 36 people, including three men identified as "emperors" because they have vast power over sports around the world. Of these 36, there are 8 executives from media organizations, 8 from sponsoring corporations; 2 from sport management companies; 16 from sport organizations, including professional sport leagues and college athletic conferences; and 1 athlete. Thirty-four of the thirty-six, or 94 percent, are white men. Tiger Woods, ranked 25th is the only person of color in the Top 25, and Dawn Hudson, President of Pepsi-Cola North America, is the only woman in the Top 25. The 16 white men on the list who control professional and college sport organizations have power partly because they deal with the white men who control media organizations that broadcast games and pay them rights fees. It is clear that in addition to structural factors, such as access to wealth and control of major corporations, gender and racial ideology also influence who has power in sports.

It is interesting that there were no coaches on the list, and only 9 athletes. Few athletes, even when they are highly paid, have influence in sports that matches the influence of people who control sport organizations or control multi-billion-dollar corporations, especially media corporations. As you will read in chapter 16, celebrity athletes are visible and have market status, but they have little power because their images and personas are heavily controlled by people who pay them and cover them in the media.

Table 10.1   The Top 25 in *The Sporting News'* "Power 100," 2002*

Rank	Name	Position	Organization	1990 Rank	1996 Rank
**	Michael Eisner	Chairman/CEO	Disney	NR^	5
**	Rupert Murdoch	Chairman/CEO	News Corp	NR	6
**	Ed Snider	Chairman	Comcast Spectacor	NR	NR
1	George Steinbrenner	Owner	New York Yankees	NR	NR
2	Paul Tagliabue	Commissioner	National Football League	3	16
3	Bud Selig	Commissioner	Major League Baseball	11	22
4	George Bodenheimer	President	ESPN	NR	NR
5	David Stern	Commissioner	National Basketball Assn.	5	8
6	Phil Knight	Chairman/CEO	Nike	46	2
7	Mark McCormack	Chairman & CEO	Int. Mgmt. Group (IMG)	6	4
8	David Hill	Chairman/CEO	Fox Sports Television Group	NR	30
9	August Busch IV &	President	Anheuser-Busch	NR	NR
	Tony Ponturo	V.P., Marketing	Anheuser-Busch	NR	26
10	Gary Bettman	Commissioner	National Hockey League	NR	18
11	Bill France, Jr.	Chairman	NASCAR & ISC	40	NR
12	Dawn Hudson &	President	Pepsi-Cola North America	NR	NR
	John Galloway	Director, Marketing	Pepsi-Cola North America	NR	NR
	Ron Askew	Director, Marketing	Coors Brewing Co.	NR	NR
13	Roger Goodell	Exec. V.P./COO	National Football League	NR	NR
14	Mark Shapiro	Exec. V.P.	ESPN	NR	NR
15	David Baxter	President	Reebok's OnField	NR	NR
16	Bruce McMillan	Exec. V.P.	Electronic Arts (video games)	NR	NR
17	Myles Brand	President/CEO	NCAA	NR	NR
18	Ed Goren	President	Fox Sports	NR	NR
19	Jim Delany	Commissioner	Big Ten Conference	NR	NR
	Thomas Hansen	Commissioner	Pac-10 Conference	NR	NR
	Mike Slive	Commissioner	Southeastern Conference	NR	NR
	John Swofford	Commissioner	Atlantic Athletic Conference	NR	NR
	Michael Tranghese	Commissioner	Big East Conference	NR	NR
	Kevin Weiberg	Commissioner	Big 12 Conference	NR	NR
20	Bob DuPuy	President/COO	Major League Baseball	NR	NR
21	Mike Helton	President	NASCAR	NR	NR
22	Robert Kain	President/CEO	IMG Americas (sport mgmt.)	NR	NR
23	David D'Alessandro	Chairman/CEO	John Hancock Financial Serv.	NR	47
24	Mark Parker	President	Nike Brand	NR	NR
25	Tiger Woods	Pro Golfer	Professional Golf Association	NR	35

*The list ranks the 100 most powerful people in sports during the preceding year. This is done every year. I use rankings published as of January 7, 1991; January 1, 1996; January 8, 2003 in *The Sporting News*.

**These three people were not ranked, but were described as "Emperors" controlling broadcast and cable television empires as well as teams. Their power transcends the everyday decisions in sports, so they were included as a special part of the list, but they were not ranked.

^ NR means "not ranked"

We can see how power operates in sports by taking a closer look at the three men who were identified as "Emperors" by *The Sporting News:* Michael Eisner, Rupert Murdoch, and Ed Snider.

Michael Eisner is the Chairman and CEO of the Walt Disney Company, a corporation that owns ABC, ESPN, ESPN2, Disney channels, other ESPN channels in nearly 150 countries, *ESPN The Magazine*, ESPN Radio, a portion of NFL.com, the Mighty Ducks in the NHL, the Anaheim Angels in MLB, and ESPN Zone (entertainment park), in addition to all the other Disney holdings. When the Anaheim Angels won the 2002 World Series, they had their victory parade in Disneyland with Mickey Mouse sitting next to the coach and Most Valuable Player in the lead parade float decorated in a Disney theme. Of course, it was covered by ABC News and ESPN. The decisions made by Eisner and the executives who work for him influence what millions of children see in cartoons and films, and what adults see in news and sports coverage. Such power has an impact on what we see, the narratives we hear, and how we become sport spectators and fans.

Rupert Murdoch is the Chairman and CEO of NewsCorp, a media corporation that owns Fox, (Fox) FX, Fox News, Television Games Network (horseracing and betting), a portion of the Golf Channel, Fox international sports channels, along with cable, broadcast, and satellite systems and channels in Asia, Europe, Latin America, and Australia. Murdoch's company decides what soccer games will be seen by billions of people in more than 140 nations. The company also owns major newspapers around the world. It owns sport teams, including the New York Knicks (NBA), the New York Rangers (NHL), the New York Liberty (MSL), the Los Angeles Dodgers (MLB), and a number of minor league teams in various sports. It also owns Madison Square Garden, Dodger Stadium, Dodgertown, and the National Rugby League. Fox has television contracts with all the major professional men's sports in the United States,

and it has fueled the national popularity of NASCAR by covering its stockcar racing circuit. NewsCorp also has working relationships with Disney. Murdoch's decisions influence what sports become popular and what sports don't receive media attention. His company makes things happen in sports, and it keeps things from happening in sports.

Ed Snider is Chairman of Comcast Spectacor, a sports and entertainment company that is an emerging power in sports. It owns a major cable system, the Philadelphia Flyers (NHL), the Philadelphia 76ers (NBA), and many minor league baseball teams. It owns Ovation Food Services, and it manages many of the new multi-million dollar sport arenas that pay for those services. The arenas, often built with public money, serve as massive profit machines for those who manage them and own the teams that use them. This is discussed further in the box, "Public Money and Private Profits" on page 336–337. Comcast Spectacor also owns arenas, including First Union Spectrum and First Union Center in Philadelphia. Ed Snider's power is enhanced because subsidiaries of Comcast Spectacor have close working relationships with Disney and NewsCorp (see Harvey, Law, and Cantelon, 2001, and the January 7/14, 2002 issue of *The Nation*, which is devoted to media power).

Finally, *The Sporting News* excluded Paul Allen from its Top 100 list. Allen, co-founder of Microsoft and current owner of much Microsoft stock, might have been the fourth "Emperor" in the list except that he owns *The Sporting News*. The editors of the magazine explain that it might be a conflict of interest if they listed him and outlined all the power he has in sports. This means that issues of power even influence lists about power in sports!

Descriptions of others on the list (www.sportingnews.com/features/powerful2002/index.html) clearly indicate that economic wealth and power matter in sports. Those who control economic resources around the world make decisions that influence the visibility of sports, the ways in which they are organized, and the images and meanings associated with them. Although these decisions do not ignore the interests of people around the world, their main purpose is to establish and expand the power and profitability of the organizations represented by the decision makers. Therefore, sports tend to revolve around the meanings and orientations valued by those with economic resources and power while providing enjoyable and entertaining experiences to people around the world.

This is why some critical theorists have described sports as cultural vehicles for developing ideological "outposts" in the minds of people around the world: when transnational corporations become the primary providers of popular pleasure and entertainment, they can use pleasure and entertainment to deliver many other messages about what should be important in people's lives. This is a clear manifestation of class relations at work.

SOCIAL CLASS AND SPORT PARTICIPATION PATTERNS

In all societies, social class and class relations influence who plays, who watches, who consumes information about sports, and what information is available in the mainstream media. Involvement with sports goes hand in hand with money, power, and privilege. Organized sports are a luxury item in the economies of many nations, and they are most prevalent in wealthy nations where people have discretionary money and time (see chapter 11).

In all societies, it is people in high-income, high-education, and high-status occupational groups that have the highest rates of active sports participation, attendance at sports events, and even watching of sports on television (Booth and Loy, 1999; Donnelly and Harvey, 1999; Scheerder et al., 2002). For example, Olympic athletes and officials always have come from more privileged groups in society (Kidd, 1995). This was noted in connection with an analysis of U.S. Olympic teams across all sports:

A sport by sport breakdown of recent U.S. Olympic teams shows a movement split by both class and race. Although in theory anyone can earn a spot in the Olympics, the reality of the process is far different. Lack of funding and access at the developmental level creates a team and a system tilted toward segregation. (*Atlanta Journal/Constitution*, 1996, p. H7)

This pattern also exists in other top-level sports in the United States and other countries.

Even the health and fitness movement, which often has been described as a grass-roots phenomenon in the United States and Canada, is confined primarily to people who have higher-than average incomes and educations and work in professional or managerial occupations. People in lower-income groups may do physical labor, but they don't run, bicycle, or swim as often as their high-income counterparts. Nor do they play as many organized sports on their lunch hours, after work, on weekends, or during vacations. This pattern holds true throughout the life course, for younger and older age groups, among men and women, among various racial and ethnic groups, and among people with disabilities: social class is related strongly to participation, regardless of the category of people in question.

Other aspects of sports participation patterns can also be explained in terms of class relations. The long-term impact of economic inequality on people's lives has led to connections between certain sports and the lifestyles of people with differing amounts of wealth and power (Bourdieu, 1986; Laberge and Sankoff, 1988). For the most part, these connections reflect patterns of sponsorship and access to opportunities for involvement. For example, wealthy people have lifestyles that routinely include participation in golf, tennis, skiing, sailing, and other sports that are self-funded and played at exclusive clubs and resorts. These sports often involve the use of expensive facilities, equipment, and/or clothing, and they have come to be associated with *class* as people with money and power define it. The people who engage in these sports usually

REFLECT ON SPORTS

Public Money and Private Profits
When Do Sports Perpetuate Social Inequality?

The dynamics of class relations sometimes have ironic twists. This is certainly true in connection with the ways in which sports have been used as vehicles for transferring public monies collected through taxes into the hands of wealthy individuals and corporations in the private sector. For example, during the 1990s, over $15 billion of public money in the United States was used to build sport stadiums and arenas, which generate revenues for wealthy individuals and powerful corporations that own professional sport team franchises and develop real estate around those facilities (Cagan and deMause, 1998; Eitzen, 2000, 2002).

Furthermore, wealthy investors have purchased the tax-free municipal bonds that cities sell to obtain the cash to build these facilities. Thus, city and/or state taxes are collected from the general population to pay off the bonds, wealthy investors who buy the bonds receive tax-free returns, and team owners use the facilities built by taxpayers to make large amounts of money for themselves and their corporations. When sales taxes are used to pay off bonds, people in low- and middle-income brackets pay a higher proportion of their annual incomes to build the stadiums than the people in higher income brackets pay.

According to a U.S. senator who reviewed a study done by the nonpartisan Congressional Research Service, this method of financing stadiums through tax-exempt bonds "amounts to little more than a public housing program for millionaire team owners and their millionaire employees [athletes]" (Welch, 1996, p. A1). He also asked, "Do [Americans] have enough money to finance stadiums for [wealthy team] owners . . . at the same time we are cutting Head Start Programs [for low-income children]?" (in Brady and Howlett, 1996, p. 13C).

To make matters worse, the average residents whose taxes build the facility usually cannot afford to buy tickets (Kuhlemeyer, 1999; Swift, 2000). This is because wealthy ticket purchasers who often buy tickets on corporate accounts are willing to pay higher prices, and ticket prices are increased to match the demand. The fact that corporations and other businesses can save money by claiming tax deductions for part

of their ticket prices contributes to the escalation of prices. Ironically, this means that tax revenues decline and the government has less money to support programs that might benefit average taxpayers. Finally, if average residents do save enough money to buy tickets and attend a game, they find that the luxury suites have pushed the average seats so far away from the action that they have a hard time seeing what's going on (see figure 10.1). Meanwhile, team owners misleadingly blame price increases on players' salaries.

The dynamics of class relations does not stop here. After contributing public money to build nice new

"Oh sure, they told us that 'sports unite ALL the classes,' when they wanted us to PAY for this place!"

FIGURE 10.1   As they sit in the distant bleachers and spot wealthy people in luxury boxes and club seats, these fans discover that the dynamics of social class operate in ways that privilege some people more than others. To say that "sports unite the social classes" is to ignore the dynamics that often separate people from different social class backgrounds.

stadiums and arenas, local and state governments may also give discounted property tax rates to team owners and their real estate partners who develop areas around the facility.

Property taxes are the main source of revenues for public schools, so urban public schools often have to do with less because the teams are making more (Cagan and deMause, 1998). Meanwhile, the teams set up a few charity programs for "inner-city kids" and occasionally send players to speak at the schools. Of course, the local sports media then describe team owners and millionaire athletes as great public servants! When teachers complain about this scam, local editorials and letters to the editor may tell them that schools are irresponsible in how they spend money and that teachers ought to work more and be thankful for what they have.

Ironically, this form of transferring public money into the hands of wealthy people has occurred during a time in U.S. history when legislators and voters have cut many social services for the unemployed and working poor. Apparently, it is difficult to give public money to wealthy team owners and take care of the needy at the same time. When Carl Pohlad, the owner of the Minnesota Twins baseball team, was asked about this, he said, "Sports is a way of life, like eating. People say, 'You should pay to feed the homeless.' But the world doesn't work that way" (Cagan and deMause, 1998: 162). At least Pohlad doesn't think it should work that way!

WHAT ABOUT JOBS CREATED BY SPORTS?

Of course, it is true that jobs are created in connection with sport facilities, but those jobs also would be created if the facilities were privately financed. Furthermore, when cities spend public money to build sport facilities, they create far fewer jobs than they would create through other forms of economic development.

The congressional study cited previously found that *each new job* created in connection with the state-financed $222 million football stadium that opened in Baltimore in 1998 cost about $127,000. Meanwhile, the cost of creating one job through the Maryland eco-nomic development fund was about $6,250. Thus, for each job created by the new stadium, twenty-one jobs could have been created if public money had been invested in other development projects. This is because sport facilities do not employ many people. Stadiums and arenas sit empty most of the time, and most of the jobs they generate are low-paying, seasonal jobs.

WHO ELSE BENEFITS?

Sport team owners are not the only wealthy and powerful people who benefit when tax money is used to construct stadiums and arenas. New publicly financed sport facilities increase property values in urban areas in which major investors and developers can initiate projects, from which they will benefit directly. For example, when Atlanta hosted the Olympics in 1996, the major payoffs associated with the new construction and increased property values went directly to a small proportion of real estate developers and major corporations, which were in position to use the millions of dollars of public money invested in the Atlanta area to their benefit. Of course, others benefited as money trickled down to the rest of the community from the wealthy individuals and organizations associated with the Olympics and the Atlanta Committee for the Olympic Games. But the average taxpayers who helped fund the Olympics will never see the benefits enjoyed by those whose power and wealth gave them the ability to take advantage of public investments. As journalist Andrew Jennings has noted, the emerging pattern in connection with hosting the Olympics is that "the IOC will take its profits, the sponsors and television networks will make theirs and the local taxpayers will foot the bill" (1996a, p. 293). This method of transferring public money to powerful individuals and corporations in the private sector is another clear manifestation of class relations at work in connection with sports. A growing number of people object to them. *What do you think?**

---

*The pros and cons of using public money to build stadiums and arenas are discussed further in chapter 11.

have considerable control over their work lives, so they have the freedom to take the time needed to participate, or they can combine participation with their work and even have someone else pay for it, in some cases!

The lifestyles of middle-income and working-class people, on the other hand, tend to include sports that by tradition are free and open to the public, sponsored by public funds, or available through public schools. When these sports involve the use of expensive equipment or clothing, participation occurs in connection with some form of financial sacrifice: buying a motocross bike means not taking a vacation this year and working overtime for a couple of months.

The lifestyles of low-income people and those living in poverty seldom involve regular forms of sport participation. Life chances vary by social class, and, when people spend much of their time and energy coping with the challenges of everyday life, they have few resources left to develop sport participation traditions as part of their lifestyles. Spending money to play or watch sports is a luxury few can afford. Furthermore, when hard work has not made them winners in the economy, they may have little interest in playing or watching sports popularly associated with an ideology claiming that poverty is associated with laziness and a lack of character. At the same time, those who are successful in the economy are so supportive of that ideology that they are willing to spend thousands of dollars each year to buy their club memberships, season tickets, and luxury suites, so that they can reaffirm the cultural ideas that work to their advantage.

Homemaking, Child Rearing, and Earning a Living: What Happens When Class and Gender Relations Come Together in Women's Lives?

The impact of social class on everyday lives often varies by age, gender, race and ethnicity, and geographical location. For example, women in family situations are less likely than their male counterparts to be able to negotiate the time and resources needed to maintain sport participation (Thompson, 1999a, b).

When a married woman with children decides to join a soccer team that schedules practices late in the afternoon, she may encounter resistance from members of her family. Resistance is certain if she traditionally has served her family as chef, chauffeur, and tutor. "Time off for good behavior" is not a principle that applies to married women with children.

On the other hand, married men with children may not face the same resistance within their families. In fact, when they play softball or soccer after work, their spouses may delay family dinners, keep dinners warm until they arrive home, or even go to the games and watch them play.

Women in middle- and lower-income families most often feel the constraints of homemaking and child rearing. Without money to pay for child care, domestic help, and sport participation expenses, these women simply don't have many opportunities to play sports. Nor do they have time to spare, a car to get them to where sports are played, access to gyms and playing fields in their neighborhoods, or the sense of physical safety they need to leave home and travel to where they can play sports. Furthermore, sports often are social activities occurring among friends, and, if a woman's friends don't have resources enabling them to play, she will have even fewer opportunities and less motivation for involvement (Gems, 1993). Of course, this is also true for men, but women from middle- and lower-income families are more likely than their male counterparts to lack the network of relationships out of which sport interests and participation emerge and come to be supported.

Women from upper-income families often face a different situation. They have the resources to pay for child care, domestic help, carryout dinners, and sport participation. They often participate in sport activities by themselves, with friends, or with family members. They have social networks made up of other

The sports played by young people from low-income households often occur in public spaces, such as this public school playground. Young people from upper-income backgrounds usually have the resources to purchase access to privately owned sport facilities and spaces. This results in different sport experiences and different sport participation patterns from one social class to another in society. (Tini Campbell)

women who also have the resources to maintain high levels of sport participation. Women who have grown up in these families often have played sports during and since their childhoods and have attended schools with good sport programs. They seldom have experienced the same constraints as their lower-income counterparts. Although this is not to say they do not have any problems negotiating time for sport involvement, their rates of successful negotiation are relatively high. Their opportunities are much greater than those of lower-income women, even though they may not be equal to those of upper-income men.

The sport participation of girls and young women also may be limited when they are asked to shoulder adult responsibilities at home. For example, in low-income families, especially single-parent families, teenage daughters often are expected to care for younger siblings after school until after dinner, when their mothers get home from work. According to one girls' team coach in a New York City high school, "It's not at all unusual that on a given day there may be two or three girls who aren't [at practice] because of responsibilities at home" (Dobie, 1987). The coach also explained that child-care duties keep many girls from going out for teams. His solution was to coordinate a cooperative child-care program at practices and games, so that girls from low-income families could meet family expectations *and* play sports. However, when coaches are not so creative or accommodating, some girls drop out of sports to meet responsibilities at home.

Boys and girls from higher-income families seldom have household responsibilities that force them to drop out of sports. Instead, their parents drive them to practices, lessons, and games; make sure they have all the equipment they need to play well; and then give them cars, so that they can drive themselves to practices and games.

The implications of class dynamics become very serious when health and obesity issues are considered. Limited opportunities to exercise safely and play sports are part of a series of factors contributing to a rapid rise in obesity, diabetes, and heart disease, especially among girls and women from low-income households (NHANES, 2002). The availability of facilities, safe spaces, transportation, and sports programs all vary by social class, and the girls and women in low-income households experience the effects of social class in different and more profound ways when it comes to involvement in physical activities and sports.

Getting Respect and Becoming a Man: What Happens When Class and Gender Relations Come Together in Men's Lives?

Boys and young men learn to see and use sports participation as a special and legitimate means of establishing a masculine identity, but specific views and strategies vary by social class. For example, in a qualitative analysis of essays written about sports by fifteen- to sixteen-year-old French Canadian boys in the Montreal area, Suzanne Laberge and Mathieu Albert (1999) discovered that ideas about sports and masculinity varied among the upper-class, middle-class, and working-class boys. The upper-class boys connected sports participation to masculinity because they saw sports as an arena in which they could learn to be leaders, and leadership was a key dimension of masculinity as they defined it. The middle-class boys connected sports participation to masculinity because they saw sports as an arena for sociability and opportunities to gain acceptance in male groups, thereby confirming their manhood. The working-class boys connected sports participation to masculinity because they saw sports as an arena for displaying tough, hypermasculine behaviors, which represented their conception of manhood.

Sociologist Mike Messner has noted that, in U.S. culture, "the more limited a boy's options appear to be, and the more insecure his family situation, the more likely he is to make an early commitment to an athletic career" (1992, p. 40). In other words, the personal stakes associated with sport participation are different and greater for boys from low-income backgrounds than they are for boys from higher-income backgrounds.

Messner found that former elite male athletes from lower-income backgrounds often saw sport participation as a means of obtaining "respect." However, this was not so much the case among males from middle-class backgrounds. One former athlete who later became a junior high school coach explained this in the following way:

> For . . . the poorer kids, [sports are] their major measuring stick. . . . They constantly remind each other what they can't do in the sports arena. It's definitely peer-acceptable if they are good at sports—although they maybe can't read, you know—if they are good at sports, they're one of the boys. Now I know the middle- and upper-class boys, they do sports and they do their books. . . . But as a whole, [they put] less effort into [sports]. (in Messner, 1992, pp. 57–58)

This coach was suggesting that social class factors create social conditions under which young men from lower-income backgrounds often have more at stake when it comes to sport participation. What this coach didn't point out is that the development of sport skills often requires material resources that do not exist in low-income families. Therefore, unless equipment and training are provided in public school athletic programs, young men from low-income groups stand little chance of competing against upper-income peers, who can buy equipment and training if they want to develop skills.

In fact, young people from upper-income backgrounds often have so many opportunities to do different things that they may not focus on one sport to the exclusion of other sports and other activities. For someone who has a car, nice clothes, money for college tuition, and good career contacts for the future, playing sports may be good for bolstering popularity among peers, but it is not perceived as a necessary foundation for an entire identity and economic survival (Messner, 1992). Therefore, young men from middle- and upper-income backgrounds often disengage gradually from exclusive commitments to playing particular sports and striving for careers as athletes. When these young men move through adolescence and into adulthood, opportunities may take them in a variety of directions; playing sports may be important, but not usually in the same ways that it is for young men from working-class and low-income families. This is clearly illustrated in the next section.

Fighting to Survive: What Happens When Class, Gender, and Racial and Ethnic Relations Come Together?

Chris Dundee, a famous boxing promoter, once said, "Any man with a good trade isn't about to get himself knocked on his butt to make a dollar" (in Messner, 1992, p. 82). What he meant was that middle- and upper-class males see no reason to have their brain cells destroyed in a quest to get ahead through a sport such as boxing. Of course, this is why nearly all boxers always come from the lowest and most economically desperate income groups in society and why boxing gyms are located in low-income neighborhoods, especially low-income minority neighborhoods, where desperation is often most intense and life-piercing.

The dynamics of becoming and staying involved in boxing have been studied and described by French sociologist Loïc Wacquant (1992, 1995a, b). As noted in chapter 7, Wacquant spent over three years training and hanging out at a boxing gym in a black ghetto area in Chicago. During that time, he documented the life experiences of fifty professional boxers, most of whom were African Americans. His analysis of those experiences shows that the motivation to dedicate oneself to boxing can be explained only in terms of a combination of class,

Children in suburban areas often have safe streets on which they can play. The boys in this cul-de-sac have access to many portable basketball goals, and they often recruit friends to play full court games in the street. Of course, they also play roller hockey, soccer, baseball, and football, and they water ski behind the boats owned by families in the neighborhood. Sports may be important in their lives, but they are not seen as a means of economic survival. (Jay Coakley)

race, and gender relations. Statements by the boxers themselves illustrate the influence of this combination:

> Right [in the area where I lived] it was definitely rough, it was dog-eat-dog. I had to be a mean dog . . . young guys wan'ed to take yer money and beat ya up an' you jus' had to fight or move out

the neighbo'hood. I couldn't move, so I had to start fightin'. (in Wacquant, 1992, p. 229)

> I used to fight alot when I was younger *anyway so,* my father figure like, you know, [said] "If you gonna fight, well why don't you take it to a gym where you gonna learn, you know, a little more basics to it, maybe make some money, go further and do somethin' . . . insteada jus' bein' on the

streets you know, and fightin' for nothin." (in Wacquant, 1992, p. 229)

The alternative to boxing for young men in this area was often the violence of the streets. When Wacquant asked one boxer where he'd be today if he hadn't started boxing, he said, "Uh, prob'y in jail, dead or on the streets turnin' up a bottle" (1992, p. 230). Other boxers said the following:

> I figure if it weren't for the gym I might be doin' somethin' that I wouldn't wanna do . . . like you know, prob'ly *killin' somebody*, you know, stick up, you know drugs, anythin': you can't never tell! You never know what the world holds. (in Wacquant, 1992, p. 230)
>
> I figure well, the bes' thin' for me to do is chan' my life style 'cause I saw a lot of my frien's git hurt an' kill' from thin's that we were doin'. . . . The gym show me that I coul' do somethin'. The gym show me that I can be my own man. The gym show me that I can do other thin's than the *gang bang, use drugs, steal, rob people, stick people up, or jus' bein' in jail.* (in Wacquant, 1992, pp. 230–31)
>
> [If] I hadn't found boxin', I be in some trade school as a mechanic or some kind of a laborer, or maybe in a factory. 'Cause that's the only thing for me, (joyfully) I mean, *I'm lucky I found boxin'.* 'Cause you know I'll be (with a touch of bitterness) like the rest of the minorities in Chicago, y'know: jus' workin' in some factory or doin' somethin' laboral to make do. (in Wacquant, 1995a, p. 519)

Wacquant explains that most boxers know that, if they had *not* been born as poor minority persons and had been successful in school, they might never have put on boxing gloves. A trainer-coach at the gym explained the connection between social class and boxing when he said, "Don't nobody be out there fightin' with an MBA" (in Wacquant, 1995a, p. 521). In fact, Wacquant sees the men he studied as being tied to boxing in the form of a "coerced affection, a captive love, one ultimately born of racial and class necessity" (1995a, p. 521). And many of the boxers realized that, despite their personal commitment to boxing, their sport involved

exploitation. As one boxer noted, "Fighters is whores and promoters is pimps, the way I sees it" (in Wacquant, 1995a, p. 520).

When Wacquant asked one boxer what he would change in his life, the boxer's answer represented the feelings of many of his peers at the gym:

> I wish I was born taller, I wish I was born in a rich family, I . . . wish I was smart, an' I had the brains to go to school an' really become somebody real important. For me I mean I can't stand the sport, I hate the sport, [but] it's carved inside of me so I can't let it go. (in Wacquant, 1995a, p. 521)

Even though the boxers were attached to their craft, over 80 percent didn't want their children to become boxers. For example, one said,

> No, no fighter wants their son [to box], I mean . . . *that's the reason why you fight, so he won't be able to fight.* . . . It's too hard, jus' too damn hard. . . . If he could *hit the books* an' study an' you know, with me havin' a little background in school an' stuff, I could help him. My parents, I never had nobody helpin' me. (in Wacquant, 1995a, p. 523)

These mixed feelings about boxing were pervasive; the men were simultaneously committed to and repulsed by their trade.

We can understand the sport participation of these men only in terms of the social class contexts in which they lived their lives. For them, boxing and the gym where they practiced their craft provided a refuge from the violence, hopelessness, and indignity of the racism and poverty that had framed their lives since birth (Wacquant, 1995a).

Class Relations in Action: Changing Patterns in Sports Participation Opportunities

In chapter 5, we noted that publicly funded youth sport programs are being cut in U.S. communities facing government budget crises. The same thing is occurring with high school sports in school districts with high proportions of low-income families (see chapter 14). Varsity sport programs are being cut back or eliminated in many poor school districts. When this occurs, fewer young people from low-income backgrounds have opportunities to participate in sports such as baseball and football, each of which requires playing fields that are relatively large and expensive to maintain. Meanwhile, basketball grows in popularity among low-income boys and girls because a school can offer basketball as long as it can maintain a usable gym. However, maintaining a usable gym is a serious problem in some inner-city schools, where overcrowding has caused gyms to be turned into classroom space.

School sport programs in middle- and upper-income areas also may be threatened by financial problems. But, when this occurs, "participation fees" paid by athletes and their families are used to maintain them. These fees, sometimes as high as $250 per sport, guarantee that opportunities to participate in varsity programs will continue for those young people lucky enough to be born into families living in relatively wealthy areas. Furthermore, when school sport programs do not measure up to the expectations of those with economic resources, as is currently the case with soccer, they often vote to use public funds to build dozens of new soccer fields, hire coaches, and run high-profile tournaments, at which college coaches look for athletes they might recruit with scholarships. For young people with economic resources, there is a wide range of sports participation opportunities that can be bought. This trend toward privatization highlights the importance of social class. When it comes to sport participation, the socioeconomic status of the family you are born into has never been more important—participation is a family affair and is driven by family resources.

Boxing has long been a sport for men from low-income groups. Most boxers have mixed feelings about their sport. On the one hand, they see it as one of the few opportunities they have to excel and possibly earn money. On the other hand, they say they do not want their sons to be boxers, because "it's too hard, jus' too damn hard" (in Wacquant, 1995a, p. 523). (*Colorado Springs Gazette*)

When we compare the availability and quality of school and club sport programs by social class, we see forms of what educator Jonathan Kozol (1991, 2002) has described as *savage inequalities.* These inequalities insidiously subvert the life chances of young people living with the legacy of poverty and racism.

The impact of class inequality on sports was clearly noted by Arthur Agee, one of the two young men profiled in the 1994 documentary film *Hoop Dreams.* When Arthur was forced to transfer from a private suburban school, for which he could not afford the tuition, to a public inner-city school in his neighborhood, he saw first-hand the differences between suburban and city basketball. High schools in Chicago's public school league didn't play at night or on weekends, as did the suburban schools; the public schools couldn't afford the overtime janitorial costs, so their games were played on weekday afternoons after school (Joravsky, 1995). Other differences were related to the quality of equipment and practice facilities, the availability of uniforms, the existence of junior varsity teams, the size of the gym and its seating capacity, the locker-room facilities, heating and air conditioning in the gym, transportation to away games, the number of coaches, the number and quality of referees, access to training-room support, and game attendance.

With funds being cut and coaches being laid off, people in poor neighborhoods realize that bake sales and car washes can no longer keep sport programs going. They now are looking to foundations, large corporations, and professional sport leagues and teams to sponsor high school sports. Sponsorships have been forthcoming in some cities, but sometimes strings are attached to the money.

Corporations tend to sponsor only those sports that promote their images. A shoe company may support basketball rather than other sports, because basketball's popularity makes it effective in the company's marketing and advertising programs. Corporate funding usually emphasizes certain sports to generate product visibility through media coverage and high-profile state and national tournaments. NFL funding, for example, emphasizes tackle football for boys. League executives may have some concerns for the lives of poor boys in inner cities, but they also realize that, if the schools are not training the next generation of football players, they must do so with their programs. Sports continue to exist, but they exist on terms that meet the interests of corporate and pro team sponsors. When this happens, the link between sports and class relations becomes especially apparent.

Class Relations in Action: The Cost of Attending Sport Events

It is still possible to attend recreational sports for free. High school and many college events in the United States are affordable for most people, and in some communities the tickets for minor league sports are reasonably priced. But tickets to most major intercollegiate and professional events are now beyond the means of many people, even those whose taxes are being used to pay for the facilities in which the events are played. The cost of attending these events has increased far beyond the rate of inflation over the past decade (Swift, 2000).

Table 10.2 shows that, between 1991 and 2001, the average ticket prices for major league baseball, the NFL, the NBA, and the NHL increased 119 percent, 98 percent, 121 percent, and 99 percent, respectively. During the same time period, inflation was 30 percent. The average ticket price to see a baseball game was relatively low, about $19. Tickets to NFL, NBA, and NHL games had an average cost of $50, $51, and $48, respectively (in 2001 U.S. dollars), and they are likely to increase further as new stadiums are built. New stadiums include expensive luxury suites and sections of club seating, where upper-income spectators have special services available to them: wait staff, special food menus, private restrooms, televisions, telephones, refrigerators, lounge chairs, temperature controls, private entrances with no

Table 10.2   Escalating ticket prices versus inflation, 1991–2001

	AVERAGE TICKET PRICE			Eleven Year Increase (%)
	1991 ($)	1996 ($)	2001 ($)	
Major League Baseball	8.64	11.20	19.00	119
National Football League	25.21	35.74	50.02	98
National Basketball Association	23.24	31.80	51.34	121
National Hockey League	24.00[a]	34.75	47.70	99[a]
			Inflation rate, 1991–2001 =	30%[b]

Source: Adapted from data in Team Marketing Report.

[a]These are estimates, because no NHL data are available prior to 1994.

[b]Ticket prices increased at more than three times the rate of inflation as measured by the Consumer Price Index.

waiting lines or turnstiles, special parking areas, and other things to make attendance at a game resemble going to a private club. For example, when Detroit's new Comerica Park opened in 2000, ticket prices increased 103 percent from what they were in Tiger Stadium in 1999. This is typical of what happens when the taxpayers build a stadium: the owner jacks up prices to attract relatively wealthy fans to the games.

As ticket prices increase and as spectators are increasingly segregated by their ability to pay, social class and class relations become more evident in the stands. Everyone at the games may cheer at the same times and experience similar emotions, but social class differences in society are not transcended at the events; in fact, they are reaffirmed and becoming more apparent.

An interesting fact is that class relations partially account for the failure to organize fans so that they can collectively have more influence over ticket and concession costs at games. People in luxury boxes, club seats, and other exclusive seats are not eager to align themselves with those who cannot attend games or afford the high-priced tickets. In fact, they have used expensive tickets as status symbols with their friends and business associates. They *want* class distinctions to be preserved in connection with attending games, and they are willing to pay, for example,

over $1,500 per ticket for NBA courtside seats in New York and Los Angeles to conspicuously display their status. Attendance and seating at many events, from the opening ceremonies at the Olympics to the NFL Super Bowl, also are tied to conspicuous displays of wealth, status, and influence. As long as this is the case, efforts to organize fans will fail.

In summary, sports, sport participation, and sport spectatorship are closely tied to social class and class relations in societies. Organized sports require material resources, and sport programs and events usually depend on the approval and support of those with power and influence. This creates a tendency for sport programs and events to be organized in ways that recreate and perpetuate existing forms of class relations in a society. Furthermore, patterns of sport participation and spectatorship clearly reflect the distribution of resources and opportunities in a society.

ECONOMIC AND CAREER OPPORTUNITIES IN SPORTS

Do sports and sport organizations provide opportunities for upward social class mobility in society? **Social mobility** is a term used by sociologists to refer to changes in wealth, education, and occupation over a person's lifetime or from one generation to the next in families. Social mobility can occur in either a downward direction or an upward direction. On a general level, it is clear that career and mobility opportunities are offered in and through sports and sport organizations. However, as we consider the impact of sports on mobility in society as a whole, it is important to remember the following things about sport-related opportunities:

1. The number of career opportunities in sports is limited and, for athletes, opportunities are short-term.
2. Opportunities for women are growing but they remain limited.
3. Opportunities for blacks and other minorities are growing but they remain limited.

We will discuss each of these qualifications in the following sections.

Career Opportunities Are Limited

Young athletes often have visions of becoming professional athletes; their parents may have similar visions for them. But the chances of turning these visions into reality are quite low.

Quantitative estimates of a person's chances of becoming a college or professional athlete vary greatly, because of the different methods of computation used. For example, the chances of becoming a professional athlete may be computed for high school or college athletes in a particular sport, for high school or college athletes from particular racial or ethnic groups, or for any male or female in a particular age group of the total population in a society. They may be based on the number of players in the top league in a sport, such as the NHL in hockey, or they may take into account that there are professional hockey leagues in Europe and many "minor league" professional teams throughout North America. They may try to control for the

number of NHL players from different countries, or they may simply assume that international player in-migration and out-migration cancel each other out. In the case of hockey, the "high school to the pros" estimates are inaccurate because of two factors: (1) few future NHL players have ever played on a U.S. high school varsity team, and (2) about 75 percent of the players in the NHL grew up outside the United States, most in Canada.

The point here is that all estimates of the odds of making it in the pros must be qualified, and many estimates reported in the media are inaccurate. The data in table 10.3 represent my best attempt to provide reasonably valid statements of the odds that a high school athlete in certain sports will play his or her sport at the college or professional level and the odds that a college athlete will play at the professional level. As you can see as you read the footnotes to the table, these odds must be qualified in many ways.

As you view the data in table 10.3, here is how to put the numbers in the first row into words: if we consider all the young men playing varsity high school football in 2002, the odds of a player making a college team were about 17 to 1; the odds for the same player to make a pro team were about 1,222 to 1. At the same time, if we consider all those young men playing college football at all levels, the odds of a player making a pro team were about 68 to 1. Because only about 25 percent of all college football players have full athletic scholarships, we can say that the odds of a high school player receiving a football scholarship are about 68 to 1.

As you look at all the data in table 10.3, you can see that playing at the professional level is a long-shot. In fact, if you saw similar odds for a horse at a racetrack, you would never bet on it unless you had money to lose—and, as you placed your bet, most people would look at you as if you had lost your mind.

The odds in other sports, such as soccer, tennis, golf, bowling, volleyball, auto racing, and

Table 10.3 Approximate odds of playing in the major professional leagues, 2002

Sport	NUMBER OF PLAYERS IN			ODDS FOR PLAYERS ADVANCING FROM		
	High School	College[c]	Pros[a]	High School to College[b]	High School to Pros	College to Pros
Football	1,023,712	61,000	805[a]	17:1	1,272:1	76:1
Men's basketball	540,597	19,100	220[a]	28:1	2,457:1	87:1
Women's basketball	456,169	17,500	100[a]	26:1	4,562:1	175:1
Baseball	451,674	30,300	455[a]	15:1	993:1	54:1

Sources: National Federation of State High School Associations; the Government Accounting Office (GAO, 2001), and the NFL, NBA, WNBA, and Major League Baseball.

[a]The numbers for high school and college are for first year through senior year, four years in all. Because pro careers may last more than four years, and the median career length is about four years, only half of the pro athletes turn over every four years. Therefore, I have divided the total number of pro players in each league in half to give a more realistic sense of odds. Furthermore, these odds of playing in the pros are rough estimates. They do not take into account players from other nations who play in U.S. colleges and professional leagues; nor do they take into account players in professional minor leagues or U.S. players in professional leagues outside the United States. Note that 26 percent of Major League Baseball players and about 14 percent of NBA players come from outside the United States.

[b]To estimate the odds of receiving a scholarship to college in each sport, take the odds times 4, so it would be 68:1 in football, 112:1 in men's basketball, 104:1 in women's basketball, and 60:1 in baseball. This is because only 25 percent of all college players in these sports have scholarships.

[c]Extrapolations of 1999 data and recent annual increases (see GAO, 2001).

professional wrestling are worse than the odds for the sports included in table 10.3.

According to computations made by sociologist Wib Leonard (1996), the odds that an American man between the ages of 15 and 39 will be a professional athlete in the NFL, the NBA, the NHL, or Major League Baseball are about 20,000 to 1—if the proportion of baseball and hockey players who come from outside the United States (26 percent and 75 percent, respectively) is taken into account. For all black men between 15 and 39 years old in the United States, the odds of playing in the NFL or NBA are at least 10,000 to 1 and 20,000 to 1, respectively.

Professional sport opportunities are also short-term, averaging three to seven years in team sports and three to twelve years in individual sports. This means that, after a playing career ends, there are about *forty additional years* in a person's work life. Unfortunately, many people, including athletes, coaches, and parents, ignore this fact.

Ideas about careers in professional sports often are distorted by misinterpretations in media coverage (see figure 10.2). The media focus on the best athletes in the most popular sports. The best athletes tend to have longer playing careers than others in their sports. Little coverage is given to those who play for one or two seasons before being cut or forced to quit for other reasons, especially injuries. For example, we hear about the long football careers of popular quarterbacks, but little or no coverage is given to the numerous players whose one-year contracts are not renewed after their first season. The average age of players on the *oldest* NFL team in 2002 was less than twenty-eight. This means that only a few players older than thirty-five are still in the league. Much more typical than thirty-three-year-olds contemplating another season are twenty-four-year-olds trying to deal with the end of their careers as paid athletes.

"Ah, the glamorous life of a spoiled, overpaid professional athlete!"

....

FIGURE 10.2   Only a few professional athletes achieve fame and fortune. Thousands of them play in minor and semipro leagues, where salaries are low and working conditions are poor.

Opportunities for Women Are Growing but Remain Limited

Career opportunities for women athletes are growing, but they are still scarce relative to opportunities for men. Tennis and golf have provided some opportunities for women during the past fifty years. However, the professional tours for these sports now draw athletes from around the world. This means that the competition to make a living in these sports is greater than it has ever been.

There are more than 1,900 players who play in Women's Tennis Association (WTA) tournaments every year, but only 130 of them are from the United States. Among the top 100 money winners on the WTA list of players, 16 are from the United States. In the Ladies Professional Golf Association (LPGA), 89 of 280 players are from nations other than the United States.

There are expanding opportunities in professional basketball, soccer, volleyball, figure skating, bowling, skiing, bicycling, track and field, and rodeo, but the number of professional women athletes remains very low, and only a few women make large amounts of money. For example, it took nineteen years for Aleta Still, the top money winner in the history of bowling, to make $1 million in total earnings for her career (whereas boxer Mike Tyson made that much every ninety seconds during his twenty-three-minute championship bout against Lennox Lewis in 2002, a fact that says much about opportunities, gender, and cultural values).

Professional leagues for women now exist in basketball, soccer, and beach volleyball, but they provide career opportunities for fewer than 400 athletes at any given point in recent years. In the new Women's United Soccer Association (WUSA), there are 8 teams employing about 170 players. Between 35 and 40 of these players are from outside the United States. The average salary is $40,000 per season, and the salary range goes from a low of $24,000 to a high of $85,000. Each team has a salary cap of $800,000. The combined salaries for *all* players during the 2002 season amounted to $6.76 million. This means that all 170 women players made less than the annual salary of most individual star players on European men's teams. Compared with what the men make in the U.S.-based Major Soccer League (MLS), the differences are not as dramatic. The men make average salaries of about $90,000. Therefore, the women make about 40 cents for every dollar that the men make when they play pro soccer in the United States.

In the WNBA, the pay is slightly better, but it is much worse relative to what men in the NBA make. The minimum salary for first-year players in the WNBA is $30,000, whereas the minimum for veterans is $40,000. The average salary for the 200 players in the league is about $46,000 without counting other benefits, although it rises to about $60,000 if all benefits are included. Top players make a maximum of $79,500, and some receive incentive-based pay, which may boost the salaries of the top stars to between $150,000 and $160,000.

Serena and Venus Williams are among the top money winners in women's sports history. In sports such as tennis and golf, the competition for prize money attracts women from around the world. Among the 1,900 WTA players in 2002, only 130 of them were from the United States. As successful as they are, the Williams sisters rank far lower than dozens of men when it comes to annual income related to sports. (*Amy Sancetta; AP/Wide World Photos*)

The combined salaries of all WNBA players in 2002 amounted to about $9.2 million. This constituted an estimated 15 percent of the revenue taken in by the league. The men in the NBA make about 55 percent of total league revenues. Their average salary is $4.5 million. In comparison, it took NBA star Shaquille O'Neal about 4 games during the 2002–2003 season to make what all 200 WNBA players made during the 2002 season. For every dollar that an NBA player makes, a player in the WNBA makes about 1 cent.

Additionally, the futures of the WNBA and WUSA are tenuous. Of course, there are opportunities in Europe in basketball and soccer, but they are limited, and salaries are not impressive. In fact, many high school teachers make as much. Overall, the advice for women who aspire to make a living as professional athletes is "don't quit your real job."

What about other careers in sports? There are jobs for women in coaching, training, officiating, sports medicine, sports information, public relations, marketing, and administration. As noted in chapter 8, most of the jobs in women's sports continue to be held by men, and women seldom have been hired for jobs in men's programs, except in support positions. In the United States, when men's and women's high school or college athletic programs are combined, men become the athletic directors in nearly all cases. Women in most postindustrial nations have challenged the legacy of traditional gender ideology, and some progress has been made in various administrative positions in some sports organizations (Lapchick and Mathews, 2002). However, a heavily gendered division of labor continues to exist in nearly all organizations (McKay, 1997, 1999). In traditional and developing nations, the record of progress is negligible, and very few women hold positions of power in any sports organizations (Rintala and Bischoff, 1997).

For a number of reasons, including the persistence of traditional ideas about gender, job opportunities for women have not increased as rapidly as women's programs have grown. This pattern exists in nearly all job categories and nearly all sport organizations. For example, in U.S. colleges and universities, the men and women who coach women's teams make less money than the men who coach men's teams. This is true in nearly all sports, even those that do not generate revenues.

NCAA Division I data indicate, that, in 2001, the combined salaries of head and assistant coaches for men's teams was about $165 million greater than the combined salaries of the men and women coaching women's teams in 321 Division I schools. It was about $23 million higher in 295 Division II schools and $24 million higher in 423 Division III schools (NCAA, 2002). This means that, as a group, coaches of women's teams in the NCAA during the year 2000 made combined salaries that were about $210 million less than the amount paid to coaches of men's

teams. This does not include incentives and other perks received by some coaches of men's teams. Of course, only 44 percent of all coaches of women's teams are women. This means that men coaching women's teams also experience the effects of this difference.

These differences are a cause for concern. However, prior to 1997, they were so much greater that the U.S. Equal Employment Opportunity Commission (EEOC) issued guidelines for salary equity among college coaches. These guidelines have had a strong impact on salaries. In fact, the data from 2001 used in the previous examples show differences that are much smaller than the differences from 1997 and before.

We can expect that patterns will continue to shift toward equity, but some people will resist real transformation and will impede the deep ideological changes that would open the door to full equity. Job opportunities for women will grow, and we will see more women coaches, sports broadcasters, athletic trainers, administrators, and referees. Changes will occur more rapidly in community-based recreation and fitness programs where financial rewards are low and in certain sport industries that target women as consumers and need women employees to make more money. But the gender ideology used by influential decision makers *inside* many sports organizations will continue to privilege those perceived as tough, strong, and aggressive—and men are more likely to be perceived in such terms.

As it is now, many women who work in sport organizations face the burden of dealing with an organizational culture that they have had little or no role in shaping. This contributes to high turnover among women. Professional development programs, workshops, and coaching clinics have not been widely sponsored for women employees, although some women's organizations, such as the Women's Sport Foundation in the United States and the Canadian Association for the Advancement of Women and Sport (CAAWS), have stepped in to provide assistance and guidance for women working in sports.

Barriers to career opportunities for women in sports are being hurdled and knocked over, but the forces that have limited opportunities in the past still exist. As noted in chapter 8, equity issues and ideological issues are tied together. Hiring more women is only one aspect of the changes needed to achieve real equity; another is changing the cultures of sports and sport organizations and the ideas about masculinity that shaped them. This suggests that real transformation will come when enough men in sports and sport organizations change how they see themselves, how they relate to others, and how they define the terms of their manhood (McKay, 1997).

Opportunities for African Americans and Other Ethnic Minorities Are Growing but Remain Limited

The visibility of black athletes in certain spectator sports often has led to the conclusion that career opportunities for African Americans are abundant in U.S. sports. Such beliefs have been supported by testimonials from successful black athletes who attribute their fame and wealth to sports. However, the extent to which job opportunities for blacks exist in sports has been greatly overstated. Very little publicity is given to the actual number and proportion of blacks who play sports for a living or make a living working in sport organizations. Also ignored is the fact that sports provide very few career opportunities for black women.

A review of professional spectator sports shows few blacks in any pro sports apart from boxing, basketball, football, baseball, and track. Some of the most lucrative sports for athletes remain almost exclusively white. Tennis, golf, hockey, and auto racing are examples. My best guess is that fewer than 6,000 African Americans, or about 1 in 6,000, are making a good living as professional athletes. In 2002, there were about 42,700 African American physicians, 47,400

> As in society itself, we have a long way to go to achieve equality in sport.
> —Richard Lapchick, founder, Center for the Study of Sport in Society (2002)

lawyers, and 117,000 engineers. Therefore, there were thirty-five times more African Americans working in these three prestigious professions than playing top-level professional sports. Furthermore, physicians, lawyers, and engineers usually have greater *lifetime* earnings than most professional athletes, whose playing careers, on average, last less than 5 years and whose salaries outside top pro leagues rarely exceed $50,000 per year.

Despite the dismal odds of becoming a top professional athlete, young blacks often aspire to reach that goal. Of course, this does not mean that they necessarily ignore other goals as they pursue their sport dreams, but it does suggest a need to remind them regularly that educational goals are important and that there are prestigious and satisfying career opportunities outside of sports (Sailes, 1998). With the powerful sport images that come into the lives of young people every day, sport dreams can be very seductive, especially when other dreams are absent. Unfortunately, some young African Americans see so little hope and justice in the world around them that they focus on televised images of successful black athletes in the NFL and NBA, and those images are very powerful.

Employment Barriers for Black Athletes When sports were first desegregated in the United States, blacks faced **entry barriers:** they had to be outstanding athletes with exemplary personal characteristics before they were given professional contracts (see Kooistra et al., 1993). Prejudices were strong, and team owners assumed that players, coaches, and spectators would not accept blacks unless they made immediate, significant contributions to a team. Black athletes with average skills were passed by. At the same time, white athletes received contracts even when they were not expected to be standout players. The result was that black athletes had performance statistics surpassing those of whites.

Ironically, this reproduced white stereotypes about the physical prowess and intellectual deficits of blacks.

As entry barriers declined between 1960 and the late 1970s, new barriers related to retention took their place. **Retention barriers** were identified by Richard Lapchick (1984) in an analysis of data from the National Basketball Association (NBA). In the early 1980s, Lapchick found that the black NBA players had to maintain higher scoring averages than the white players to be resigned to contracts after five years in the league. In other words, the marginal white players had a much better chance than the marginal black players to be retained and paid by NBA teams. This pattern was also found in the NFL during the early 1990s (Kooistra et al., 1993).

More recent data suggest that these barriers no longer exist in general terms (Leonard, 1995), but it is difficult to conclude that race and skin color have become completely irrelevant in all assessments of the worth of marginal players in certain sports. If race and skin color are relevant, they may influence assessments in very personal, subtle, and selective ways.

There also is little evidence of race-based salary discrimination among players in any of the major team sports. This is probably because it is now relatively easy to measure performance. Objective statistics are kept on nearly every conceivable dimension of an athlete's skill. Agents use these statistics when they represent players in salary negotiations. Agents receive a percentage of players' salaries, so they have a built-in incentive to make sure that discrimination does not affect contracts for any of their players.

Employment Barriers in Coaching and Off-the-Field Jobs In 1987, the longtime director of player personnel for the Los Angeles Dodgers said that blacks are excluded from coaching and administrative jobs in baseball because they "lack the necessities" to handle such jobs. Even though he later apologized for his remark, he caused people to wonder if his beliefs about blacks explained why, during the nearly thirty

years he helped shape the coaching and management staff on the Dodgers, the team never had a black general manager, a black field manager, a black pitching coach at any level, or a black third-base coach (the most influential coach below the head coach on a baseball team).

Of course, the Los Angeles Dodgers were not the only team in recent history with such a record. For example, when the Dallas Cowboys won the Super Bowl in 1994, a press release issued by a national black organization (the NAACP) accused the team of having plantation-like hiring practices. Seventy-five percent of the players on the team were African American, whereas all eleven of the top administrators were white men (Shropshire, 1996). This led Jesse Jackson to form the Rainbow Coalition for Fairness in Athletics, which began to work with the Center for the Study of Sport in Society (CSSS) to put pressure on professional and college sport teams to increase the representation of ethnic minorities and women in administrative and staff positions.

Since 1994, there has been slow progress in most sport organizations. However, football at both the college and professional levels has made no significant changes. Even in 2002, nearly 70 percent of all the NFL players, 28 percent of the assistant coaches, and only 6 percent of the head coaches were black—two out of thirty-two. This led lawyers Johnnie L. Cochran, Jr., and Cyrus Mehri (2002) to submit a report entitled *Black Coaches in the National Football League: Superior Performance, Inferior Opportunities* to the offices of the NFL. The report proposed a "Fair Competition Resolution," which called for systematic changes in the recruitment and hiring process, so that qualified black candidates for head coach positions would be fairly treated. The report noted that, between 1986 and 2001, there was evidence that fairness did not exist. Data were presented to show that

- Black coaches in the NFL during those years averaged 1.1 more wins per season than white coaches.

- Teams coached by blacks went to the playoffs 67 percent of the time, whereas teams coached by whites went only 39 percent of the time.
- During their first season with a team, black coaches won an average of 2.7 more games than their white counterparts during their first seasons.
- In the season prior to being terminated, black coaches won an average of 1.3 more games than their white counterparts won in the season prior to their termination.
- When black coaches were hired, their teams had an average of 7.4 wins per season, and they boosted that record to 9.1 wins during the years they coached.

These data, analyzed by Janice Madden at the University of Pennsylvania supported the observations of a panel of experts assembled by ESPN in connection with its coverage of Super Bowl XXXV (Clayton, 2002). The panel agreed that the lack of minority head coaches was the most serious problem facing the NFL in 2002. Black head coaches outperformed their white counterparts, yet they were hired less often and fired more quickly.

The general pattern in the NFL also characterized big-time college football. This caused Floyd Keith, the executive director of the Black Coaches Association, to issue a report to the NCAA and to begin forming alliances with other civil rights organizations.

As people sought to explain the lack of black head coaches in professional football, *Sports Illustrated* writer Frank Deford said the following:

> Football coaches are executives. . . . [T]he people who hire football coaches probably fail at getting to know young black coaching candidates, there is almost surely some kind of submerged racism, which presumes that, sure, a black man can handle a little basketball club, but a heavy-duty football operation is really too complicated to trust to a minority. (2002, p. 2A)

Explanations for the patterns in big-time college football were slightly different than they were for professional football. Clarence Underwood, a former athletic director at Michigan State University, said that it was "the old boy network that's still alive and well. It's an insidious pattern of racial discrimination." He went on to note that powerful white boosters in college football "want to see someone who looks like them, someone they can rub elbows with at the country club" (in Moran, 2002a, p. 2A). Others agreed. A college football coach must be able to mingle smoothly with powerful alumni and wealthy team supporters. The coach must raise funds, nurture their continued support, play golf with them, and fit into their social settings. It's more than a matter of football knowledge, and black coaches may not be seen by many people as good candidates for such a job (Moran, 2002a, b).

Research in sociology has shown that, when people in positions of power recruit candidates for top management positions, they look for people who think as they do, so that they can work closely together. This is why they often hire fraternity brothers, fellow alumni from college, or people they grew up with. Those who share similar backgrounds are "known quantities"; they are people with whom personal connections can be made or already exist. Thus, if those doing the hiring are white males, they may raise more questions about the job qualifications of those who come from different racial or ethnic backgrounds—backgrounds they may know little about. When candidates have different histories and experiences, those hiring may ask these questions: Can they be trusted? Are they dependable? Will they think the way others do in top management? If there are *any* doubts, conscious or unconscious, those doing the hiring will usually stick with candidates like themselves. This process has been characteristic in sports for many years, and, to the extent that it continues, minority men and all women will remain underrepresented in the power positions in sports.

Opportunities for Ethnic Minorities   The dynamics of ethnic relations in any culture are

Black men and women are seriously underrepresented in coaching jobs at the college and professional levels in U.S. sports. Mike Davis, head basketball coach at Indiana University, is one of a growing number of black male coaches in college basketball and football. Opportunities for black women coaches, however, remain scarce. (NCAA Photos)

unique, and they vary from one ethnic group to another (see chapter 9). Making generalizations about ethnic relations and how they are related to opportunities in sports is difficult. However, it is important to remember that dominant sport forms in any culture tend to reproduce dominant cultural values and the social structures supported by those values. This means two things: (1) members of the dominant culture may

exclude or define as unqualified those who come from different cultural backgrounds, and (2) ethnic minorities often face the challenge of taking on the values and orientations of the dominant culture if they want to become a part of sports and sport organizations.

Of course, some people in sport organizations value cultural diversity and have made space for ethnic minorities in the cultures of those organizations. This has occurred in baseball and soccer as Latinos have been hired for management and administrative jobs. Also, some members of ethnic groups assimilate and willingly accept the "cultural terms" on which dominant sports are based. However, those who give priority to their ethnicity in their identities may not be willing to assign secondary importance to their own cultural values and orientations to play sports or work in sport organizations in which their culture is not valued or even acknowledged by other employees or respected within organizational rules and practices.

People in the United States with Latino, Asian, or Native American backgrounds are underrepresented in many sports and sport organizations. There are many reasons for this, but at least part of this underrepresentation is related to fears of ethnic diversity or a lack of understanding of how ethnic diversity can contribute positive things to the operation and overall culture of an organization. Exceptions to this are found in Major League Baseball and Major League Soccer organizations, where Latinos are relatively well represented in certain job categories. Of course, this primarily is due to the high proportion of Latino players in these leagues (26 percent and 20 percent, respectively in 2002). Neither Asians nor Native Americans fare very well in any U.S. sport organizations, except in a few lower-level staff positions (Lapchick and Mathews, 2002).

In summary, sports are becoming increasingly open and democratic in the provision of economic and career opportunities, but they are far from ideal in this respect. White men have well over 90 percent of the power in sports and sport organizations, and they have used their power to maximize economic returns and opportunities for themselves. With a few exceptions, data show that women, African Americans, and other ethnic minorities have been largely excluded from opportunities at this level of ownership and corporate control. In the case of other career opportunities in sport organizations, there has been more openness in recent years. Women, African Americans, and other ethnic minorities have made their way into staff and middle-management jobs, but they remain seriously underrepresented in head coach and top-level administrative jobs in most sport organizations. Changes in this pattern will occur as the white men who currently hold positions of power in these organizations become more aware of the skills of minority and women candidates, the advantages of ethnic and gender diversity in sport organizations, and the possibility of working effectively with people who are different from them. If this does not occur fast enough, then legal and political pressures will be used to bring about needed changes (Cochran and Mehri, 2002; Moran, 2002a, b; Shropshire, 1996).

SPORT PARTICIPATION AND OCCUPATIONAL CAREERS AMONG FORMER ATHLETES

What happens in the occupational careers of former athletes? Do they have career patterns that are different from the patterns of those who have never played competitive sports? Is sport participation a stepping-stone to future occupational success and upward social mobility? Does playing sports have economic payoffs after active participation is over?

These are difficult questions, and only a few studies have compared former athletes with others on issues related to social class and social mobility. Those studies suggest that, as a group, the young people who had played sports on high school and college teams experienced no more or less occupational success than others from comparable backgrounds. This does not mean that playing sports has never helped anyone in special ways; it means only that there have been no consistent research findings indicating that former athletes have a systematic advantage over comparable peers when it comes to future occupational careers and social class position. Of course, research done a few years ago may not tell us what is happening today, because the meaning and cultural significance of sport participation changes over time, and those changes may be related to career processes in some way.

Research suggests that, *if* playing sports is connected to processes of career success, it occurs in one or more of the following ways:

- Playing sports, under certain circumstances (see the following numbered list), may teach young people interpersonal skills, which carry over into various jobs and enable them to be successful.
- Some people with power and influence may define former athletes as good job prospects and give them opportunities to develop and demonstrate work-related abilities, which serve as the basis for career success.
- Individuals who were very high-profile athletes may be able to use their reputations to obtain and succeed at certain types of jobs.
- Playing sports, under certain circumstances (see the following numbered list), may connect athletes with others who can help them get good jobs after they retire from sports.

After reading this research, my guess is that playing sports is most likely to be positively related to occupational success and upward mobility when it does the following things:

1. Increases opportunities to complete academic degrees, develop job-related skills, and/or extend knowledge about the organization and operation of the world outside of sports

2. Increases support from significant others for *overall* growth and development (not just sport development)
3. Provides opportunities to make friends and develop social contacts with people outside of sports and sport organizations
4. Provides material resources and the guidance needed to use those resources to create or nurture career opportunities
5. Expands experiences fostering the development of identities and abilities unrelated to sports
6. Minimizes risks of serious injuries that restrict physical movement or require extensive and expensive medical treatment

These are not surprising hypotheses. Taken together, they emphasize that playing sports can either constrict or expand a person's overall development (see chapter 4). When expansion occurs, athletes often develop work-related abilities and connections with career opportunities. When constriction occurs, the development of work-related abilities and career opportunities are likely to be limited. For example, in the documentary film *Hoop Dreams*, William Gates, one of the two young men profiled in the film, experienced success partly because his basketball skills led him to be introduced to a wealthy and influential white woman, who served as an advocate in his life. She set him up with summer jobs that expanded his experiences and social contacts, and she paid for him to take the private courses he needed to earn the ACT scores that enabled him to attend a good college on a basketball scholarship. Even though torn knee ligaments kept Gates from reaching the goal of playing in the NBA, he experienced upward social mobility, because playing sports expanded his experiences, relationships, and sense of hope and possibility.

Highly Paid Athletes and Career Success After Playing Sports

Conclusions about the connection among sport participation, career success, and social mobility must be qualified in light of the dramatic increases in the salaries of *some* professional athletes over the past fifteen to twenty-five years (see chapter 11). Before the late 1970s, few athletes made enough money in sports to pave their way into other careers after they retired. However, some top athletes today make enough money in a few years to finance any one of a range of career alternatives after they retire from sports—if they do not throw their money away or hire irresponsible agents to manage their money.

Of course, many professional athletes have short careers or play at levels at which they do not make much money (see figure 10.3). When they retire, they must deal with the challenge of entering another career and making a living. Many experience patterns of success and failure similar to the patterns experienced by comparable others, who did not play sports. Their post-sport careers may not enable them to drive new cars, travel to exciting places, or read their names in newspapers every week, but this does not mean they should be seen as failures or victims of sports.

FIGURE 10.3 Only a small proportion of former athletes are able to cash in on their athletic reputations. The rest must seek opportunities and work just like the rest of us. Those opportunities vary, depending on qualifications, experience, contacts and connections, and a bit of luck.

As noted in chapter 4, retirement from sports is best described as a process rather than a single event, and most athletes don't retire from sports on a moment's notice—they gradually disengage from sports and shift their personal priorities in the process. Although many athletes disengage smoothly from sports, develop other interests, and move into relatively satisfying occupational careers, some do encounter varying degrees of adjustment problems that interfere with occupational success and overall life satisfaction. For example, when sociologist Mike Messner interviewed former elite athletes, he found that those who had been heavily involved in sports since childhood encountered serious adjustment problems as they tried to make the transition out of sports. A former NFL player highlighted these problems with the following explanation:

> [When you retire] you find yourself scrambled. You don't know which way to go. Your light . . . has been turned out. . . . Of course you miss the financial deal, but you miss the camaraderie of the other ballplayers. You miss that—to be an elite, to be one of a kind. . . . The game itself . . . the beating and all that . . . you don't really miss. You miss the camaraderie of the fellas. There's an empty feeling. . . . The one thing that has been the major part of your life is gone. . . . You don't know how people are going to react to you. . . . You wonder and question. (in Messner, 1992, pp. 120–21)

Messner's research led him to suggest that retiring athletes, especially those who had dedicated themselves to playing sports ever since they were children, face two major challenges:

1. Reconstructing their identities in terms of activities, abilities, and relationships unrelated to sport participation
2. Renegotiating relationships with family members and close friends, so that they receive feedback and support for identities having little or nothing to do with playing sports

Messner also noted that young men from low-income families were more likely to have prob-lems when retiring from sports, because they had fewer material resources to aid them in the transition process and because they were more likely to have identities deeply rooted in playing sports. The men from middle-class backgrounds, on the other hand, seemed more likely to benefit from the doors opened by sports and the social connections related to sport participation; they also had greater access to material support and were less likely to have identities exclusively rooted in playing sports.

Studies also have shown that adjustment problems are more likely when an injury forces retirement from sports. Injuries often complicate retirement and tie it to other problems related to self-esteem or health; injuries disrupt life plans by throwing off the timing of retirement and forcing a person into life decisions before they are expected. This is not surprising, and athletes often need career-related assistance when this occurs.

When athletes have problems making the transition out of sports into careers and other activities, it seems that sport organizations have some responsibility to offer assistance, especially in amateur and minor league sports, where athletes earn little or no money for playing sports (Dacyshyn, 1999). Some sport organizations, including universities and national governing bodies, are beginning to do this through various forms of career transition programs. Many of these programs involve workshops dealing with career self-assessments, life skills training, career planning, résumé writing, job search strategies, interviewing skills, career placement contacts, and psychological counseling.

Of course, some organizations do not see the issue of career transition as a high priority, and some do not have the resources to initiate and conduct transition programs or hire others to do so. But there is a growing belief that, after young men and women are expected to train full-time, the organizations that benefit from their dedication have an obligation to help them make a successful transition into life after sports.

Athletic Grants and Occupational Success

Discussions about sports participation and upward social mobility in the United States often include references to athletic scholarships. Most people believe that these scholarships are valuable mobility vehicles for many young people. This belief raises many questions. How many students receive athletic scholarships, as opposed to other forms of financial assistance? How much are athletic scholarships worth to those who receive them? Who receives them and how many recipients would not attend college without them?

Surprisingly, these questions remain unanswered. Colleges and universities do not report the amount of athletic aid that goes to particular student-athletes. Therefore, it is unknown which individual athletes receive scholarships, how much the scholarships are worth, and how important they are in the educational lives of the recipients.

It is known that the actual number of *full* athletic scholarships is often exaggerated. High school students who receive standard recruiting letters from university coaches often tell people they are anticipating *full* scholarships, when, in fact, they may receive only partial aid or no aid at all. College students receiving tuition waivers or other forms of partial athletic aid often lead people to believe they have full scholarships. Athletic scholarships are awarded one year at a time and may not be renewed for certain athletes, who may continue their education while people believe they have scholarships. Finally, many people simply assume that college athletes, especially at big universities, all have scholarships. Of course, such exaggerations are misleading, causing people to think that sport participation has more relevance for upward mobility than it actually does.

According to NCAA data, there were 4.9 million students in NCAA institutions in 2001. Of these, about 111,600 students had some form of athletic aid, although for all three NCAA

AT YOUR FINGERTIPS For more information, about race, ethnicity, and athletic aid, see pages 520–523.

divisions fewer than 23,000 students had full scholarships (room, food, and full tuition). The other 80 percent received aid covering a portion of total expenses. This means that in 1,034 NCAA universities, less than one-half of 1 percent (.46 percent) of all students received full scholarships, and about 2.3 percent of all students received some form of athletic aid. Clearly, far fewer students receive full athletic scholarships than is commonly believed. In fact, academic scholarships are many times more plentiful than athletic scholarships, even though most high school students think otherwise.

Class and racial relations are heavily connected with athletic scholarships. In many universities, black men from middle- and lower-income families play on teams that generate revenues used to fund athletic scholarships for athletes in nonrevenue sports. Athletes in nonrevenue sports often come from wealthier backgrounds, and most are white. Ironically, football and basketball players may be more isolated from campus and community life than athletes in swimming, tennis, soccer, volleyball, rowing, lacrosse, field hockey, and other sports in which white students predominate. If isolation subverts the opportunities that expand experiences and contacts, then playing sports is more likely to contribute to career success for students who already come from successful backgrounds, thereby reproducing existing forms of economic inequality in society. Of course, the few football and basketball players who sign big contracts distract attention away from this more important aspect of class and racial relations.

When athletic aid goes to financially needy young people who focus on learning and earning their degrees, sport participation increases their chances for career success. But how many of

Tens of thousands of college athletes compete on intercollegiate teams without any financial aid related to athletics. Less than 25 percent of all intercollegiate athletes have full athletic scholarships. Many more scholarships are based on academic achievement than on athletic skills. (NCAA Photos)

those athletic scholarships, full and partial, go to young people who could not or would not attend college without them? A portion of those who receive athletic scholarships could and would attend college without them. This does not mean we should do away with athletic grants, but it does mean that links among playing sports, receiving athletic scholarships, achieving career success, and experiencing upward social mobility must be carefully qualified.

SUMMARY

DO MONEY AND POWER MATTER IN SPORTS?

Social class and class relations are integrally involved in sports. Organized sports depend on people with money and economic power. In the process of sponsoring the sports that provide entertainment and participation opportunities, people with money and power fund and promote sport forms that fit their interests and foster ideas supportive of economic arrangements that work to their advantage. This is why the dominant sport forms in the United States and other nations with market economies promote an ideology of competition and achievement emphasizing that "you always get what you deserve, and you always deserve what you get."

This ideology drives a combination of individual achievement and consumption, along with corporate expansion, in society. Using it leads to favorable conclusions about the character and qualifications of those who are wealthy and powerful in society, but it disadvantages those who are poor and powerless. Furthermore, using it leads to the conclusion that economic inequality in society is not only good but also natural.

Class relations also are connected with the ways that wealthy and powerful people around the world have become involved in sport team ownership, event sponsorship and organization, and the media coverage of sports. In fact, sport events seem to be one of the vehicles these people can use to transfer public money into their own hands. As public funds support major forms of sport entertainment in their cities and regions, those with wealth and power receive subsidies and income, which they use to maintain their privilege.

At the same time, class relations have ideological implications in the sense that large segments of the population continue to see sports as enjoyable forms of entertainment brought to them by large corporate sponsors. Although fans do not automatically see sports in the way that sponsors would like them to, most fans raise no critical questions about the ideology of success emphasized in media coverage and conversations about sports.

Sport participation patterns in society and around the world reflect the impact of material resources and social class on the ways in which people live their lives. Organized sports are a luxury that many people around the world cannot afford. Even in wealthy societies, sport participation is most common among those in the middle and upper classes. Patterns of sport participation throughout a society reflect class-based lifestyles, which emerge as people make decisions about how they will use the resources they do have.

Sport participation patterns also reflect the combination of class and gender relations. We see this in the case of lower-income girls and women who have low participation rates, as well as in the case of lower-income men who see sports in terms that have unique identity implications in their lives. Boxing provides an example in which class, gender, and racial relations come together in a powerful combination. The boxing gym provides a safe space, which takes minority men in poor neighborhoods away from the poverty, racism, and despair that spawn violence and desperate behaviors among their peers. The same social forces that lead minority men to choose boxing also give rise to variations of *hoop*

dreams that captivate the attention of young ethnic minorities, especially black males. But even these dreams are now being subverted as public schools in low-income areas are dropping some varsity sport programs.

Patterns of watching sports also are connected with social class and class relations. This is demonstrated by the increased segregation of fans in stadiums and arenas. Luxury suites, club seating, and patterns of season ticket allocations separate people by a combination of wealth and power, so that social class often is reaffirmed when people attend sport events.

Opportunities for careers that hold the hope of upward social mobility do exist for some people in sports. For athletes, these opportunities often are scarce and short-lived, and they reflect patterns of gender and ethnic relations in society. These patterns take various forms in the case of careers in sport organizations. Although opportunities in these jobs have become increasingly open over the past decade, white men still hold most of the top positions in sport organizations. This will change only when the organizational cultures of sport teams and athletic departments become more inclusive and provide new ways for women and ethnic minorities to participate fully in shaping the policies and norms used to determine qualifications in sports and to organize social relations at the workplace.

Research on sport participation and career development generally indicates that, when young people use sport participation to expand their social worlds and personal experiences, they have an advantage when seeking occupational careers. However, when sport participation constricts social worlds and personal experiences, it is likely to have a negative effect on later career success. The existence of these patterns varies by sport. Of course, the extremely high incomes of a few athletes today almost guarantee their future career success and economic security.

Retirement from athletic careers often creates stress and personal challenges, but most athletes move through the retirement process without experiencing *excessive* trauma or difficulty. Those who do experience difficulties are usually those whose identities and relationships have been built exclusively on sports. These people may need outside assistance as they move into the rest of their lives and face the challenge of seeking jobs, maintaining satisfying occupational careers, and nurturing mutually supportive and intimate social relationships.

Athletic scholarships help some young people further their educations and possibly achieve career success, but these scholarships are relatively scarce, compared with other scholarships and forms of financial aid. Furthermore, athletic scholarships do not always change the future career patterns of young people, because many recipients would attend college without sport-related financial assistance.

In conclusion, sports are clearly tied to patterns of class, class relations, and social inequality in society. Money and economic power do matter, and they matter in ways that reproduce economic inequality in society.

 ## SUGGESTED READINGS

Coakley, J., and P. Donnelly, eds. 1999. *Inside sports.* London: Routledge (many chapters contain clear examples of how class intersects with gender and race in everyday sport experiences; articles in part 4 deal with the transitions associated with retirement from high-performance sports).

Eitzen, D. S. 2003. *Fair and foul.* Lanham, MD: Rowman and Littlefield (chapter 9 deals with sports and mobility, and chapter 10 deals with how sports are used to transfer public money into private hands).

Gmelch, G. 2001. *Inside pitch: Life inside professional baseball.* Herndon, VA: Smithsonian Institution Press (an anthropologist travels with players and examines their routines and rituals; also covers issues related to players' wives, fans, and "groupies" and analyzes changes that have occurred in the work lives of players over the past generation).

Gruneau, R. 1999. *Class, sports, and social development.* Champaign, IL: Human Kinetics (analysis of how the meaning, organization, and purpose of sports are closely tied to the struggles between social classes and the processes of domination and subordination in society as a whole; excellent information on theories used to study class and class relations).

McKay, J. 1997. *Managing gender: Affirmative action and organizational power in Australian, Canadian, and New Zealand sport.* Albany: State University of New York Press (data from in-depth interviews and the media coverage of sports are used to show how affirmative action policies are subverted in sport cultures by a combination of class-based and gender relations).

Miracle, A. W., and C. R. Rees. 1994. *Lessons of the locker room: The myth of school sports.* Amherst, NY: Prometheus Books (chapter 6 provides an overview of research findings related to social mobility issues and participation in high school sports in the United States).

Shropshire, K. 1996. *In black and white: Race and sports in America.* New York: New York University Press (focuses on legal processes and issues related to decision-making processes that determine off-the-field positions in professional and college sports; discusses why affirmative action is needed to eliminate historically based, current barriers limiting African Americans' access to management and ownership positions in sports).

Sugden, J., and A. Tomlinson. 2000. Theorizing sport, social class, and status. In *Handbook of sports studies* (pp. 309–21), edited by E. Dunning and J. Coakley. London: Sage (overview of the theoretical perspectives sociologists have used to understand economic inequality and class-based lifestyles in society; describes how the concept of hegemony can be used to understand complex power relations between social classes and other status groups in connection with sports).

WEBSITE RESOURCES

Note: Websites often change. The following URLs were current when this book was printed. Please check our website (www.mhhe.com/coakley8e) for updates and additions.

www.mhhe.com/coakley8e Information on the "Top 25" from the 1996 rankings made by *The Sporting News;* extended discussion of the odds of playing professional sports for people in various racial and ethnic groups; references to films and to how *Hoop Dreams* is related to social class and class relations.

www.sportingnews.com/features/powerful *The Sporting News,* a U.S. weekly, presents annual lists of the 100 most powerful people in sports, often in the first or last issue of the calendar year; the lists are intended to be international, but they focus primarily on power in sports from a U.S. perspective, and they are only one picture of power in the world of sports.

www.finelinefeatures.com/hoop Site for *Hoop Dreams,* a classic documentary film that provides a personalized look at social class and class relations issues in the lives of two young men living in a Chicago neighborhood.

www.eeoc.gov The Equal Employment Opportunity Commission has guidelines for the enforcement of the Equal Pay Act and Title VII as they apply to sex discrimination and compensation for coaches; twenty-three pages of examples and rules, which could be used to make major changes for women who coach in U.S. schools.

www.sportinsociety.org The Center for the Study of Sport in Society often posts its most recent *Race and Gender Report Card;* this provides valuable information about patterns of fairness and discrimination in major sport organizations in the United States.

www.sportinsociety.org/sportscap.html Designed to provide women, people of color, and people with disabilities with improved access to the sporting industry ranging from internships to high-level management, legal, and medical positions.

(Jay Coakley)

Sports and the Economy

What Are the Characteristics of Commercial Sports?

THE POINT OF BIG-TIME sports is, after all, to find new things to sell to sponsors and new ways to get fans to watch.

—**Michael Hiestand, journalist (2000)**

Online Learning Center Resources

Visit *Sports in Society*'s Online Learning Center at **www.mhhe.com/coakley8e** for additional information and study material for this chapter, including

- Self-grading quizzes
- Learning objectives
- Related websites
- Additional readings

A complete outline is available online at
www.mhhe.com/coakley8e.

WHAT CORRUPTS AN ATHLETIC performance . . .
is . . . the presence of an unappreciative, ignorant
audience and the need to divert it with sensations
extrinsic to the performance. It is at this point
that . . . sports . . . degenerate into spectacle.
    —**Christopher Lasch, social critic (1977)**

Sports have been used through history as forms of public entertainment. However, sports never have been so thoroughly commercialized as they are today. Never before have economic factors so totally dominated decisions about sports, and never before have economic organizations and large corporate interests had so much power and control over the meaning, organization, and purpose of sports. The economic stakes for athletes and sponsors have never been higher than they are today. The bottom line has replaced the goal line for many people associated with sports. As an editor at *Financial World* magazine notes, "Sports is not simply another big business. It is one of the fastest-growing industries in the U.S., and it is intertwined with virtually every aspect of the economy. . . . [Sports are] everywhere, accompanied by the sound of a cash register ringing incessantly" (Ozanian, 1995, p. 30).

Sports today are evaluated in terms of gate receipts and revenues from the sale of concessions, licensing fees, merchandise, media rights, and website hits. Games and events are evaluated in terms of market shares, ratings points, and advertising potential. Athletes are evaluated in terms of endorsement potential and media personas; their popularity and celebrity often depend on their ties to corporate names and logos. Stadiums, teams, and athletic events are named after large corporations rather than historical figures and places with local meaning. Corporate interests influence team colors, uniform designs, the scheduling of events, how the media cover events, and even what announcers say during the coverage. In fact, media/entertainment companies own a growing number of sport teams; they sponsor and even own events.

Sports are now corporate enterprises, integrally tied to marketing concerns and processes of global capitalist expansion. The mergers of major corporate conglomerates that began in the 1990s and now continue into the twenty-first century have connected sports teams, sport events, media companies, entertainment industries, and the Internet. The names of transnational corporations have become synonymous with the athletes, events, and sports that provide pleasure in people's lives.

Because of the importance of economic factors in sports, this chapter will focus on the following questions:

1. Under what conditions do commercial sports emerge and prosper?
2. How does commercialization influence the meaning, organization, and purpose of sports?
3. Who are the people who own, sponsor, and promote sports and what are their interests?
4. How much money do athletes make and what is their legal status in various sports?

EMERGENCE AND GROWTH OF COMMERCIAL SPORTS

General Conditions

Commercial sports are organized and played to make money as entertainment events. They depend on a combination of gate receipts, concessions, sponsorships, and the sale of media broadcasting rights. Therefore, commercial sports grow and prosper best under certain social and economic conditions.

First, they are most prevalent in market economies, where material rewards are highly valued by those connected with sports, including athletes, team owners, event sponsors, and spectators.

Second, commercial sports usually exist in societies with large, densely populated cities, because they require large concentrations of potential spectators. Although some forms of commercial sports can be maintained in rural, agricultural societies, revenues in these settings would not support full-time professional athletes or full-time sport promoters.

Third, commercial sports require that people in a society have time, money, transportation, and media connections to attend or to use the media to tune into sport events. Commercial sports are a luxury, and they prosper only in societies where the standard of living is high enough that people can afford to use resources playing and watching events that have no tangible products. Commercial sports require sophisticated transportation and communication systems, so that sponsors can make money. Therefore, they are most commonly found in relatively wealthy, urban, and industrial or postindustrial societies; they are found less often in labor-intensive, poor societies where people focus their energy and resources on staying alive rather than paying to be entertained by athletes.

Fourth, commercial sports require *large amounts of capital* to build and maintain stadiums and arenas in which events can be played and watched. Capital funds can be accumulated in either the public or the private sector, but, in both cases, the willingness to invest in sports depends on anticipated payoffs in the form of publicity, profits, or power. Private investment in sports occurs when investors expect financial profits; public investment people in influential government positions believe that commercial sports will serve their own interests, the interests of "the public," or a combination of both (see chapter 13).

Sports are played in all cultures, but professional sports seldom exist in labor-intensive, poor nations around the world. The Afghan horsemen here are playing buzkashi, a popular sport in their country. But Afghanistan lacks the general conditions needed to sustain buzkashi as a professional sport with paid athletes and paying fans. (Efren Lukatsky; AP/Wide World Photos)

Fifth, commercial sports are most likely to flourish in cultures where lifestyles involve high rates of consumption and emphasize material status symbols. This enables everything associated with sports to be marketed and sold: athletes (including their names, autographs, and images), merchandise, even team names and logos. When people express their identities through possessions such as clothing or equipment, and through associations with visible representatives of the community, they are likely to buy sport tickets and other possessions that associate them with sports, teams, and athletes. Passions and states of mind are sold to audiences, and then audiences are sold to sponsors and the media (Burstyn, 1999).

Class Relations and Commercial Sports

Which sports become commercialized in a society? As noted in chapter 10, priority is usually given to the sports that are followed and watched by people who possess or control economic resources in society. For example, golf has become a major commercial sport, even though it does not lend itself to commercial presentation. It is inconvenient to stage a golf event for a live audience, and it is difficult to cover golf on television. Camera placement and media commentary are difficult to arrange, and live spectators see only a small portion of the action. Golf does not involve vigorous action or head-to-head competition, except in rare cases of match play. Basically, if you don't play golf, you have little or no reason to watch it.

But a high proportion of those who *do* play golf are relatively wealthy and powerful people. These people are important to sponsors and advertisers, because they make consumption decisions for themselves and their families, as well as for their businesses and thousands of employees. They buy luxury cars or computers for themselves, but, more important to advertisers, they buy thousands of company cars and computers for employees. Furthermore,

they make investment decisions involving money from a variety of sources, and they buy high-ticket items that other people can't afford. Golfers as a group have economic clout that goes far beyond their personal and family lives.

This makes golf an attractive sport for advertisers, who sell images and products to consumers with money and influence. This is why auto companies with high-priced cars sponsor and advertise on the PGA, LPGA, and Senior PGA tours. This is also the reason major television companies cover golf tournaments: they can sell commercial time at a high rate per minute, because those watching golf have money to spend—their money *and* the money of the companies, large and small, that they control. The converse of this is also true: sports attracting low- and middle-income audiences often are ignored by television or covered only under special circumstances. If wealthy executives bowled, we would see more bowling on television and more bowling facilities on prime real estate.

Market economies always privilege the interests of those who have the power and resources to influence which sports will be selected for promotion and coverage. Unless people with power and resources are interested in playing, sponsoring, or watching a sport, it is not likely to be commercialized on a large scale. When wealthy and powerful people are interested in a sport, it will be covered, promoted, and presented as if it had cultural significance in society. The sport even may be described as a "national pastime" and come to be associated with the development of ideal personal character, community spirit, civic unity, and political loyalty. Furthermore, it may be supported with public money allocated for the construction of stadiums and arenas, even if this directly subsidizes and benefits wealthy team owners, sponsors, and promoters.

This is one reason football has become "America's game" (Mihoces, 2002). Football celebrates and privileges the values and experiences of the men who control and benefit from corporate wealth and power in North America. This explains why men pay thousands of dollars to buy expensive season tickets to college and professional football games, why male executives use corporate credit cards to buy blocks of "company tickets" to football games, and why corporation presidents write hundred-thousand-dollar checks to pay for luxury suites and club seats for themselves, friends, and clients. Football is entertaining for these spectators, but, more important, it reproduces a way of viewing the world that fosters their interests.

Of course, women who want to be a part of the power structure often discover it is wise to do what the men do. In the United States, seminars on sports are offered to women, so that they can learn the "language of football" and other sports and use it to communicate with the men who control their careers in corporations. If women executives don't go to the next big football game, and take clients with them, they are cut out of the "masculinity loop" that is the core of corporate culture. When going to work on Mondays during the fall, it helps if you "talk football."

The Creation of Spectator Interest in Sports

How do so many people become sport spectators in certain societies? Why do they look to sports for entertainment? These are complex questions with many answers. However, in many societies, spectator interest is related to a general quest for excitement in postindustrial societies, a cultural emphasis on material success, personal experiences in sports, and easy access to sports through the media.

The Quest for Excitement   What happens when social life becomes highly controlled and organized? Can we become stuck in everyday routines to the point that we become emotionally stale and seek activities that offer tension-excitement and emotional arousal? According to figurational sociologists Eric Dunning and

Norbert Elias, historical evidence suggests that this has occurred in modern societies. Sports, they argue, offer contexts in which rules and norms can be defined and interpreted to allow forms of emotional arousal and exciting behaviors that eliminate boredom without disrupting social order (Dunning, 1999; Elias and Dunning, 1986). Sports generally are characterized by a tension between boredom and social disruption. Managing this tension involves a challenge: norms and rules must be loose enough to break boredom, but not so loose that they permit violence or other forms of dangerous or disruptive deviance. When norms and rules become too controlling, sports become boring and people lose interest; when they are too loose, sports become sites for reckless and dangerous behaviors, which can jeopardize health as well as social order. Finding the balance and maintaining it is the trick.

This explanation of spectator interest, based largely on figurational theory, raises other questions. Why do many people give priority to sports over other activities in their quest for excitement? Critical theorists suggest that answers can be found by looking at the connection between ideology and cultural practices. This leads us to consider three other factors.

Success Ideology and Spectator Interest   Many people watch games or read about them now and then, but spectator involvement is highest among those who are committed to the twin ideas that success is always based on hard work and that hard work always leads to success—another way to say that you get what you deserve and you deserve what you get (see chapter 10). These people often use sports as a model for how the social world *should* operate. When sports promote the idea that success is achieved only through hard work and dedication to efficiency, these people have their beliefs and expectations reaffirmed, and they are willing to pay for that reaffirmation. This is why sport media commentators emphasize that athletes and teams make their own breaks and that luck comes to those who work hard. This is why large corporations use the bodies of elite athletes to represent their public relations and marketing images, emphasizing efficiency, power, the use of technology, and the achievement of success (Hoberman, 1994). And this is partly why some high-profile athletes make so much money today—they reaffirm a success ideology, which reproduces privilege among powerful people around the globe.

Youth Sport Programs and Spectator Interest
Spectator interest often is created and nurtured during childhood sport participation. When organized youth sport programs are publicized and made available to many young people in a society, commercial sports have a better chance to grow and prosper. With some exceptions, sport participation during childhood leads to spectator interests during adulthood. Children who learn to value sport skills and emphasize competitive success in their personal experiences generally grow up wanting to watch the "experts" compete with one another. For those who continue to participate actively in sports, watching the experts provides models for improving skills and motives for playing sports as well as they can. For those who no longer play sports, watching the experts maintains connections with the images and experiences of success learned in organized competitive youth sports.

Media Coverage and Spectator Interest The media promote the commercialization of sports (see chapter 12). They provide needed publicity and create and sustain spectator interest among large numbers of people. In the past, newspapers and radio did this job; today television has the greatest effect on spectator involvement; tomorrow it may well be the Internet.

Television has increased spectator access to events and athletes all over the world, and it provides a unique "re-presentation" of sports. It lets viewers see close-up camera shots of the action on the field and the athletes and coaches on the sidelines. It replays crucial plays and shows them in slow motion, helping viewers imagine that even they could do what elite athletes do. It even brings viewers into the locker rooms of championship teams.

On-air commentators serve as fellow spectators for the media audience, including those "interactive" spectators watching television while they are online with sports websites. These commentators heighten identification with athletes and dramatize and embellish the action in an event. They provide inside stories, analyze strategies, describe athletes as personalities, and glorify the event, magnifying its importance.

Television is especially effective in recruiting new spectators. Before they can become faithful spectators, people who have not played a sport themselves must learn the rules and strategies used in a sport. This learning occurs easily through television. No tickets need be purchased, and questions that may sound stupid in front of strangers can be asked without embarrassment in the family living room. In other words, television provides a painless way to become a spectator, and it increases the number of people who will buy tickets, regularly watch televised games, pay for cable and satellite sports programming, and even become pay-per-view customers in the future.

Economic Factors and the Globalization of Commercial Sports

Commercial sports have become global in scope for two reasons. *First*, those who control, sponsor, and promote sports are looking constantly for new ways to expand their markets and maximize profits. *Second*, transnational corporations with production and distribution operations in multiple countries can use sports as vehicles for introducing their products and services all around the world. The following examples illustrate these two reasons (see figure 11.1).

Sport Organizations Look for Global Markets
Sport organizations, like other businesses, wish

"Winning at sports isn't so hard. It's all in the uniform."

FIGURE 11.1 The expansion and growth of commercial sports around the world have little to do with the players' interests. Owners and executives from the media and other corporations are making many of the decisions about sports today.

to expand their operations into as many markets as possible around the world. For example, team and league profits would increase significantly if the U.S.–based NFL and the North American–based NBA, NHL, and Major League Baseball (MLB) were able to sell broadcasting rights to television companies in countries around the world and were able to sell licensed merchandise (hats, shirts, jackets, etc.) to people around the world. This is already occurring, but the continued success of many major sport organizations requires that they create spectator interest outside the boundaries of their home nations.

Success also depends on using the media to export a combination of game knowledge and athlete identification. In this way, sport organizations become exporters of culture as well as products to be consumed. The complex export-import processes that occur in connection with sports were studied by sociologists in the past and have attracted more attention recently (Donnelly, 1996a; Klein, 1991, 1997; Maguire, 1999).

The desire for global expansion was the main reason the NBA was happy to let the so-called

Dream Team play in the Olympics starting in 1992, even though the players risked injury and fatigue, which could have jeopardized their participation in the following NBA season (and did, in a few cases). The worldwide coverage of Olympic basketball provided the NBA with publicity worth many millions of dollars. This publicity has helped market NBA broadcasting rights and official NBA products all over the world. High-profile NBA players have been introduced to hundreds of millions of people, and many of these people have become more interested in seeing these players in action. Therefore, the NBA finals and the NBA All-Star games are now televised in nearly 200 countries every year.

Hockey followed the NBA's lead in entering national "dream teams" in the Olympics. Baseball has even organized The Envoy Program, which sends the best high school and college baseball coaches in North America to work with federations and young players in countries where baseball needs a cultural boost (Johnson, 2000). This program has targeted twenty-nine countries, and now major league baseball merchandise is distributed in nineteen countries outside North America, and nearly one in four players signed to contracts by major league teams were born outside the United States.

The spirit of global expansion has led NFL, NBA, NHL, and MLB teams to play games in Mexico, Japan, England, France, Germany, Australia, and other countries. The NHL always has been a Canadian–U.S. league; MLB and the NBA now have franchises in large Canadian cities; the NFL assisted in the formation of the World Football League and even subsidized the formation of a football league in Europe (Maguire, 1990). Other investors have formed sport organizations to compete for international markets in a range of other sports, the latest being roller hockey.

This spirit of global capitalist expansion is not new; nor is it limited to North American sport organizations. The International Olympic

Committee (IOC) gradually has incorporated national Olympic committees from more than 200 nations and has turned the Olympic games into the most successful and financially lucrative media sport events in history. Soccer's FIFA (Fédération Internationale de Football Association) has a long history of global expansion, which predates the global expansion of any North American sports (Sugden and Tomlinson, 1998, 1999).

When the 1994 Soccer World Cup for men and the 1999 World Cup for women were scheduled in North America, the people in charge of FIFA clearly realized they had much to gain if they could create spectator interest in soccer among Americans. Even though the growth of professional soccer in the United States has been relatively slow since 1994, the media rights fees for televising future World Cup tournaments will increase because of emerging spectator interests in North America. Soccer is second only to basketball in youth participation in the United States, and media companies in the United States have discovered that traditional and new ethnic populations in many U.S. cities are eager to see soccer teams representing their nations of origin or the nations of their parents or grandparents.

Corporations Use Sports as Vehicles for Global Expansion The fact that sports, sporting events, sport teams, and athletes can be used to capture the attention and emotions of millions of people has not gone unnoticed in the world of business. Corporations need symbols of success, excellence, and productivity that they can use to create "marketing handles" for their products and services and to create public good will for their policies and practices. This is why corporations have invested so much money into associating their names and logos with athletes, teams, events, and sport facilities.

People around the world still associate Michael Jordan with the "Air Jordan" trademark copyrighted by Nike. They frequently associate the Olympics with Coca-Cola. In the United States, the crowning Olympic achievement is to have your image on a cereal box. Status among many children depends on wearing expensive shoes and clothing with official logos and other sport images on them.

Companies whose profits depend on the sales of alcohol, tobacco, fast food, and candy are eager to have their products associated with the healthy image of athletes and sports; this enables them to respond to those who would challenge the wholesomeness of their products. After all, if beer, cigarettes, sugar-based soft drinks, beef burgers, deep-fried foods, and candy bars bring us the sports we love, how can they be bad for our health?

Sportswriter Jay Weiner has argued that Michael Jordan has been a key figure in the process of corporations' using sports to boost bottom lines. He explains that Jordan "commercialized his sport and himself, turning both into brands for an emerging legion of sports marketers. . . . In his own way, Jordan did spread an ideology. It was that sports are not just games but tools for advertisers. It was that basketball isn't a playground thing, but a corporate thing" (1999, p. 77).

We now live in an era of the transnational corporation. Of the 100 largest economies in the world in terms of revenues, 51 are corporations and 49 are nations (Anderson and Cavanagh, 2000). General Motors, Wal-Mart, Daimler-Chrysler, Exxon Mobile, Mitsubishi, Mitsui, and Ford Motor Company each has an economy greater than that of over 60 percent of the nations around the world. The 200 largest corporations in the world control over one-third of the economic activity around the globe. The decisions made by executives in these corporations influence the economies of entire nations and even regions of the world: they affect which people have jobs, what they do in those jobs, how much they make, what their working conditions are, what products will be available for purchase, where they will be sold, and how much they will cost.

When these corporations enter the world of sports, they negotiate deals that promote their interests and increase their power in the realm of transnational relations. Their power is largely unchecked; the so-called free trade initiatives of the 1990s, such as the World Trade Organization and the North American Free Trade Agreement, enable many organizations to operate largely outside the laws of any single nation. Capitalist expansion in the past was at least partly regulated, and its negative consequences were partly softened by the laws of nation-states. Today, however, capital flows with few restrictions, often outside the control of nation-states. As corporations and the multibillionaires who own or control them continue to do business around the world, they need to create global images of themselves as positive cultural, political, and economic citizens and leaders.

This is partly why corporations pay billions of dollars every year to sponsor sports and why they spend three times as much sponsoring sports as they do sponsoring the arts, festivals and fairs, and attractions in the United States. For example, General Motors and Coca-Cola together will spend nearly $2 billion to sponsor Olympic sports between 1998 and 2008. Like other transnational corporations, they want to promote the belief that enjoyment and pleasure in people's everyday lives depend on corporations and their products. Their goal is to use this belief as the foundation for *ideological outposts* in the minds of people around the world (see chapter 4). Corporate executives realize that they can use such outposts to defuse opposition to corporate policies, and they can use them as transmission points for delivering a wide range of ideological messages about what is and should be happening in the world. This is an especially useful strategy for global corporations that want to defuse resistance to products that may not be compatible with local cultural values, such as Coca-Cola and Kentucky Fried Chicken in Islamic Pakistan.

For example, when a Coca-Cola executive gave a presentation to IOC officials before the 1996 Olympic Games, he assumed that, after nearly eighty years of sponsoring the Olympics, Coca-Cola had established outposts he could use to transmit messages that the officials would accept, so he told the officials the following:

> Just as sponsors have the responsibility to preserve the integrity of the sport, enhance its image, help grow its prestige and its attendance, so too, do you [in sports] have responsibility and accountability to the sponsor. (in Reid, 1996, p. 4BB)

Of course, in the face of millions of sponsorship dollars, these officials were not likely to oppose the interests of Coca-Cola or to resist the notion that they were responsible for promoting Coca-Cola's interests around the world and would be held accountable for doing so. The fact that drinking cola was not consistent with the nutritional profile of elite athletes or the worldwide health goals of the Olympic Movement no longer mattered to the sports officials. Their

The corporate branding of sport events, facilities, and participants is widespread today. Corporations whose profits come from the sale of alcohol, tobacco, fast food, and candy are especially eager to sponsor sports. They want their products associated with activities defined as healthy or deeply connected with important cultural values, such as those related to the automobile (individualism, power, and speed). (*Colorado Springs Gazette*)

minds had been colonized by Coca-Cola—the outposts were already firmly in place among many of them.

Outposts in Action: Branding Sports   What do ranchers do when they want to prove that they own cattle? They brand them; they sear their logos onto the hide of the animals, so that there is no doubt about ownership or control. Corporations have done the same things with sports (Bellamy, 1998; Klein, 2002).

Sport places have been branded. There are stadiums branded by airlines, such as the Delta Center (Salt Lake), United Center (Chicago), Air Canada Centre (Toronto), Canadian Airlines Saddledome (Calgary), American Airlines Arena (Miami), American Airlines Center (Dallas), Continental Airlines Arena (New Jersey), and America West Center (Phoenix). There are stadiums branded by brewers, such as Coors Field (Denver), Miller Park (Milwaukee), Busch Stadium (St. Louis), and the Molson Centre (Montreal). There are stadiums branded by communications and high-tech corporations, such as the MCI Center (Washington/Baltimore), Qualcomm Stadium (San Diego), Pacific Bell Park (San Francisco), Compaq Center (Houston), Cinergy Field (Cincinnati), and Ericsson Field (Charlotte). There are stadiums branded by auto and oil corporations, such as Ford Stadium (Detroit), General Motors Place (Vancouver), and ARCO Arena (Sacramento). There are dozens of additional stadiums named after other corporations in banking, real estate, and retailing. In fact, North American stadiums without corporate names are becoming rare. Local traditions, used as the basis for naming sport places in the past, are being abandoned, so that taxpayers can pay off debts for new facilities built for the benefit of other corporations that own the teams that use them.[1]

---

[1]Each paragraph in this section could have been extended to a full page of examples of how corporations have branded sports. The examples here are a small sample of what could have been included.

The branding of sport places also exists inside the stadiums, where every available surface is sold to corporate sponsors. Surfaces without corporate messages are now defined as wasted space, even in publicly owned facilities. As corporations brand public spaces, community identities are transformed into brand identities, and the physical embodiments of local traditions and histories are transformed into corporate embodiments of messages to consume and enjoy the place, compliments of corporations that bring pleasure into our lives.

Sport events have been branded. College football fans in the United States watch the Tostitos Fiesta Bowl, the Outback Steakhouse Bowl, the Poulan Weed Eater Independence Bowl, the Federal Express Orange Bowl, the Nokia Bowl, the Insight.com Bowl, and dozens more corporately named events, which change as naming rights contracts expire and new ones are signed.

In U.S. NASCAR auto racing, we watch Winston Cup races, such as the Budweiser Shootout, the Gatorade 125, the Food City 500, the Coca-Cola Racing Family 600, the Pepsi 400, the Tropicana 400, the EA Sports 500, the Mountain Dew Southern 500, and the Pop Secret Microwave Popcorn 400. Furthermore, the cars themselves have been so heavily branded that they are corporate billboards.

Corporate branders have missed very few sports. There are the ESPN XGames, Van's Triple Crown (snowboarding), McDonald's All-American Game (high school basketball), the Sprite Slam Jam Dunk Contest, and the Nike Hoop Summit.

Golfers have recently played in the John Deere Classic, the Advil Western Open, the Nissan Open, the BellSouth Classic, the Master Card Colonial, the LPGA Kraft Nabisco Championship, the ShopRite Classic, and the Longs Drugs Challenge, among many others.

Tennis players in 2002 competed in the RCA Championships, the BMW Open, the Bausch & Lomb Championships, and the Home Depot Championships. The Women's Tennis Association is sponsored by Sanex skin and body products and is called the Sanex WTA. Even equestrian sports have the GTE Directories High Jump.

Corporations brand teams around the world in cycling, soccer, rugby, and most other sports. Teams in Japan are named after corporations, not cities. Players and even referees in most sports wear corporate logos on their uniforms. Soccer teams often are known for their "colors," and corporations have made it a point to incorporate their logos and names onto the jerseys associated with teams. Many soccer teams wear the logo of a sport manufacturer endorsed by the league, along with the logo of the team sponsor. Manchester United, the most famous team in the world, for many years wore the logo of Sharp (electronics) on its uniform, switching to Vodaphone in 2001.

Agents today tell their athletes that they are brands and that their goal is to merge with other commercial entities. We now know "Air Jordan" (Michael Jordan and Nike), "Air Canada" (Vince Carter and Air Canada Airlines), "Shaq Attaq" (Shaquille O'Neal and Reebok), Big Mac (Mark McGwire and McDonald's), and other athletes through their mergers with corporations. We think of them in terms of their endorsement identities as well as their play on the field. These athletes, whose celebrity is so great that it potentially transcends corporate branding, are realizing that they can make more money if they turn themselves into brands than if they simply endorse corporate products.

The Super Bowl, too expensive for even a large corporation to brand on its own, is known as much for its ads as for the game itself. Corporate sponsors of the 2003 Super Bowl paid 2.2 million for thirty-second commercial spots during the telecast of the game. This generated over 140 million in revenues for ABC, the network owning the 2003 television rights. The advertisers paid this amount because they knew their ads would receive much more exposure than the commercial time during the game; the ads also would be previewed, summarized, highlighted, evaluated, and ranked in other sport coverage in the print and electronic media.

Anheuser-Busch (Budweiser) spent over $20 million for its commercial time during the game (not counting its massive expenditures for producing the commercials).

The future of corporate branding is difficult to predict. A cell phone company paid Joseph Chebet to take a portable phone and pretend he was calling long distance to Kenya after he crossed the finish line as the winner of the 1999 "long-distance" Boston Marathon. The call was bogus, but the race and the finish line were branded through a covert strategy. New technologies and strategies are now used as branding strategies. Ads during television coverage are inserted digitally on the field, court, and other surfaces of arenas and stadiums. Virtual advertising projected onto the field of play is becoming more common as people buy video recorders that edit out commercials. Corporations buy brand placement rights, so that their names, logos, and products appear directly in the content of the games and matches. This makes it possible for athletes' uniforms and bodies to be branded and for the brand to be changed whenever a new corporation pays higher rights fees.

Can corporations go too far in their branding of sports? There seems to be little resistance to corporate branding; however, Nike apparently went too far when it attempted to brand the clothing worn by the journalists covering the 1998 Nagano Games. It seems that athletes, teams, events, and places are for sale, but a few of the journalists who report the news about sports are not for sale, yet.

It is obvious that sports are for sale, and corporations are the buyers. Corporate executives realize that sports produce enjoyable and emotional identifications with athletes, teams, events, and places; therefore, corporations have branded them to associate their products and services with sources of pleasure in people's lives. In less than a generation, sports have been so thoroughly branded that many people accept it as inevitable—just the way it is and the way it should be. This is how ideologies are formed and how hegemony occurs in the process (see chapter 4).

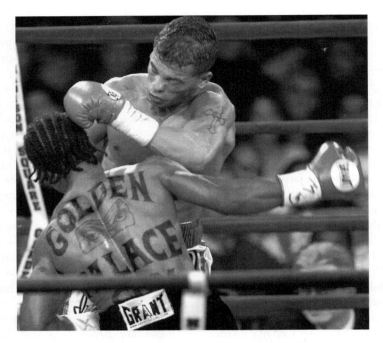

Corporate branding has become pervasive in sports today. We knew it would not be long before bodies came to be branded with corporate logos. People bet on boxing; casinos take bets. Commercial logic would say that this connection should appear on the back of a boxer. Where will corporate branding stop?
(Jeff Zelevansky; AP/Wide World Photos)

The Growth of Commercial Sports

Commercial sports grow and prosper best in urban, industrial societies with relatively efficient transportation and communications systems, combined with a standard of living that allows people the time and money to play and watch sports. Class relations are involved in the process through which sports become commercialized. Spectator interest is grounded in a combination of a quest for excitement, ideologies emphasizing success, the existence of youth sport programs, and media coverage that introduces people to the rules of sports and the athletes who play them. Sport organizations and powerful transnational corporations have fostered the global expansion of commercial sports that can be marketed profitably. This expansion will continue into the foreseeable future as corporations continue to brand athletes, teams, events, and sport places. The next question to ask is whether commercialization changes the games themselves.

COMMERCIALIZATION AND CHANGES IN SPORTS

What happens to sports when they become commercialized and dependent on revenues? Do they change, and, if so, in what ways?

Whenever a sport is converted into commercial entertainment, its success depends on spectator appeal. Although spectators have a variety of motives underlying their attachment to sports, their interest in sport events usually is related to a combination of three factors:

- The uncertainty of an event's outcome ("Is it going to be a close contest?")
- The risk or financial rewards associated with participating in an event ("How much is at stake in the contest?" "How much money, pride, ego, or physical well-being is involved?")
- The anticipated display of excellence, heroics, or dramatic display by the athletes ("Who is playing and how good or entertaining is the person or team?")

When spectators say they saw a "good game," they usually are talking about one in which (1) the outcome was in doubt until the last minutes or seconds, (2) the stakes were so high that the athletes were totally committed to and engrossed in the action, or (3) there were a number of excellent, heroic, or dramatic performances. Games or matches that contain all three factors are remembered and discussed for a long time.

Because uncertainty, high stakes, and excellent/heroic/dramatic performances attract spectators, commercial sports emphasize these things to attract large audiences. To understand the changes associated with commercialization, we must look at three aspects of sports:

1. The structure and goals of sports
2. The orientations of the athletes, coaches, and sponsors
3. The organizations that control sports

Structure and Goals of Sports

Commercialization influences the structure and goals of most newly developed sports, but it has not produced dramatic changes in most long-established sports. Among the new sports developed for commercial purposes, it is clear that rules have been designed to promote on-the-field action that a targeted audience will see as entertaining. Entertainment is *not* the only issue considered in connection with the structure and goals of these sports, but it is a primary issue.

This is apparent in the case of sports such as indoor soccer, arena football, beach volleyball, roller hockey, and certain forms of extreme games. For example, the rules in the XGames are designed to attract the attention of younger viewers who have less interest in football and tennis than in skateboarding, in-line skating, and bicycle jumping; the rules emphasize dangerous and spectacular moves as well as the use of technical equipment manufactured by event sponsors.

Established sports have undergone rule changes to make the action more exciting and understandable for spectators, but the changes have not altered the basic designs and rule structures of the games themselves. For example, the commercialization of the Olympic Games has led to minor rule changes in certain events, but the basic structure of the typical event has remained much as it was before the days of corporate endorsements and the sale of television rights. Of course, some events with little spectator appeal have been dropped from the Olympics, and new sports have been added to attract new viewers, especially younger viewers from wealthy countries, where people have money to spend on sponsors' products. Another example is American football, in which the rules have been changed to protect quarterbacks, to encourage the use of passes in offensive strategy, to discourage strategies that emphasize field goals over touchdowns, and to give teams an extra time-out in connection with a two-minute warning at the end of each half of play. These changes increase entertaining action and provide more time for commercial breaks in the games; however, the basic structure and goals of football have changed little.

Rule development and rule changes associated with commercialization usually are intended to do a combination of five things: (1) speed up the action, so that fans don't become bored; (2) increase scoring to generate excitement; (3) balance competition, so that events will have uncertain outcomes; (4) maximize the dramatic moments in the competition; and (5) provide commercial breaks in the action, so that sponsors can advertise products.

A review of rule changes in many sports shows the importance of these five factors. For example, the designated hitter position in baseball's American League was added to increase scoring opportunities and heighten the dramatic action. Soccer rules were changed to prevent matches from ending in ties. Tennis scoring was changed to meet the time requirements of television schedules. Golf tournaments now involve total stroke counts, rather than match play, so that big-name players will not be eliminated in the early rounds of televised events. Free throws were minimized in basketball to speed up action. Sudden-death overtime periods were added to many sports, so that spectators can determine the winner easily, without having to assess the overall quality of play in an event.

Even though many of these changes have been prompted by commercial concerns, these concerns have not altered the basic structure and goals of most long-established sports. Furthermore, changes also reflect the concerns of athletes, who have more fun when there is more action, more scoring, and a closer contest. Players may object to TV time-outs, but they and their coaches anticipate them and use them in their overall game strategies.

Because sports are social constructions, they change in connection with social relationships and shifts in social conditions and power relations in the society as a whole. Some people regard the structure and goals of sports as sacred and unchangeable, but they overlook the fact that *people* established the rules for all sports, and the orientations of those people were influenced by their relationships and the cultural conditions prevalent at the time the rules were made. Of course, it is important to acknowledge that economic relations and conditions are carefully considered today as changes are discussed and made.

People may voice complaints about changes in the structure and goals of sports when they attend events that have been organized intentionally as

total entertainment experiences, complete with loud rock and rap music, video displays designed to provide entertainment having little to do with sports, paid cheerleaders and mascots who direct crowd behavior, fireworks displays, and on-site announcers who manage spectator emotions with their own excited verbal descriptions of and responses to the action. As dedicated, long-time sports fans sit through this total entertainment experience, in which others do the wave, watch cartoon characters on the video display, and respond to the antics of paid mascots dressed in Disney-type costumes, they complain that the game has changed (see figure 11.2). But, on the field of play, the rules and structure of the game

"Our football league will give the people what they REALLY want—substance-enhanced brutes maiming each other without the restrictions of 'sissy rules.' God bless America."

FIGURE 11.2   When Vince McMahon, majority owner of World Wrestling Entertainment, announced his football league, the XFL, he indicated that the new league would be based on what he learned as he turned pro wrestling into a major entertainment form. NBC liked what he said and signed a TV contract with the league. But the league failed in its first season. Now NBC sponsors Arena Football.

probably have changed little; the biggest changes are in the context surrounding the game and in the orientations of the athletes, coaches, and sponsors.

Orientations of the Athletes, Coaches, and Sponsors

When sports are commercialized, they usually come to be characterized by a "promotional culture" (Gruneau and Whitson, 1993). Like other entertainment industries, commercial sports are geared to selling public performances to audiences and selling audiences to sponsors. Sports are promoted through marketing hype based on myths and images created around players and team identities. Athletes become entertainers, and some even become celebrities. In connection with the promotional culture of commercial sports, the orientations of those connected with the sports tend to emphasize heroic actions in addition to aesthetic actions.

This means that, when sports become entertainment, it is necessary to attract a mass audience to buy tickets or watch events on television. Attracting and entertaining a *mass* audience is not easy. Such an audience consists of many people who lack technical knowledge about the complex physical skills and strategies used by athletes and coaches. Without this technical knowledge, hype and drama become primary sources of entertainment. Hype and drama are easily understood, so these spectators enjoy situations when athletes take risks and face clear physical danger; they are impressed by the dramatic expressions of athletes; and they are entertained by athletes dedicated to the game and to victory, regardless of personal cost.

When people lack technical knowledge about football, they are more likely to be entertained by a running back's end-zone dance after a touchdown than by the lineman's block that enabled the running back to score the touchdown. Those who know little about the technical aspects of ice skating are more entertained by triple and quadruple jumps than by routines carefully choreographed and practiced until they are smooth and flawless. Without dangerous jumps, naïve spectators quickly become bored.

Those who lack technical knowledge about basketball are more likely to talk about a single slam dunk than about the well-coordinated defense that enabled the team to win a game. Karl Malone of the NBA Utah Jazz explains that players know this, and in the NBA they "are more concerned about dunking [than other aspects of the game, because] that's how you get on TV" (in Latimer, 2000, p. 28C). Thus, dunkmania rules, and players are booed if they "just" shoot a layup and ignored if they hit a 15-foot jump shot.

Spectators without technical knowledge about a sport tend to enjoy watching athletes project exciting or controversial personas, and they often rate performances in terms of dramatic expression leading to dramatic results. They are impressed by style as well as skills. They are thrilled by long touchdown passes, not 9-minute touchdown drives made up of 3- to 4-yard runs. They call for home runs, not sacrifice flies. They are more impressed by athletes who collapse as they surpass physical limits than by athletes who know their limits so well they can play for years without going beyond them.

After observing many athletes in all the major sports in the United States, commentator Bob Costas has noted the following:

> The players have caught on to what the cameras want. They know what postures and noises will get them on air. [NBA players] know that cameras are under the basket. So a guy dunks the ball, looks right at the camera and screams. (in Pluto, 1995, p. 275)

Costas knows that the players look at things differently when they are entertainers; in fact, after they do something entertaining, they even look at the replay screens from the field of play to view their own actions as spectators.

Thus, when a sport depends on the entertainment of mass audiences, those who play and coach often revise their ideas about what is important in athletic performances. The danger of movement becomes important in addition to the beauty of movement; style and dramatic expression become important in addition to fundamental skills; pushing beyond personal limits becomes important in addition to exploring limits; and commitment to victory for the team and sponsor becomes important in addition to commitment to participation. When sports become commercialized, most people associated with them develop *heroic orientations* in addition to *aesthetic orientations.*

Figure 11.3 explains these terms and outlines how athletes, coaches, and others associated with a sport might alter how they assess on-the-field performances as a sport becomes increasingly commercialized. It shows that, when there is a need to entertain a mass audience, orientations change. In fact, games or matches may be described as "showtime," and athletes describe themselves as entertainers. This does *not* mean that aesthetic orientations cease to be important or that people are no longer impressed by beauty

and skills in sports, but it does mean that heroic orientations enter into the mix of what constitutes a good sport performance. Heroic actions are what attract a mass audience.

Some athletes, however, realize the dangers associated with heroic orientations and try to limit the emphasis on heroic actions in their sports. For example, some former figure skaters have called for restrictions on the number of triple jumps that can be included in skating programs. These skaters are worried that the commercial success of their sport is coming to rely on the danger, rather than the beauty, of movement. Other skaters, however, seem to be willing to adopt heroic orientations in an effort to please audiences and meet the expectations of many athlete-peers in skating. The dynamics of this process are complex. We explored this in chapter 6, in the discussion of how athletes come to use the norms of the sport ethic to evaluate themselves and others in their sports. Thus, it is not surprising that figure skaters train to hit a long succession of triple jumps, with the hope of landing a quad without breaking bones or

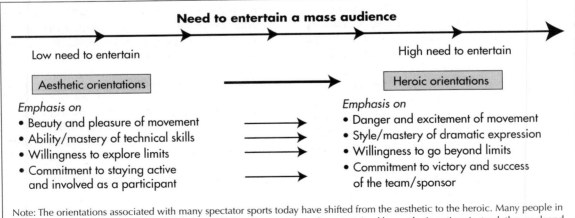

Note: The orientations associated with many spectator sports today have shifted from the aesthetic to the heroic. Many people in a mass audience do not have the technical knowledge about a sport to be entertained by aesthetic action; instead, they seek and focus on heroic action. Therefore, athletes, coaches, and others associated with the game put more emphasis on heroic orientations in their own approaches to action in the game.

FIGURE 11.3   Shifting orientations: what happens when there is a need to entertain a mass audience.

destroying the continuity of their overall skating programs. Heroic orientations are used to define an athlete in figure skating.

As the emphasis on heroic orientations becomes more central in a sport, so does the concern with representing sponsors. According to many observers, this has occurred in NASCAR racing since 2001, when NASCAR signed a 3.2-billion-dollar, eight-year television deal with four major television companies. Veteran driver Kyle Petty says that being a good race car driver and being a good product representative are two different things and that most racing teams today walk a fine line "between performance and promotion." In other words, ability and the mastery of technical skills are different from style and the mastery of dramatic expression. Petty adds that, on NASCAR race tracks today, "There's a lot of good looking guys out there who can walk and talk and chew gum and really sell products but they can't drive a race car" (in Jenkins, 2002a, p. 2A).

Of course, this does not mean that performance is no longer important. But it does mean that performance is increasingly judged in terms of sponsors' interests. If a driver does not win races, but his or her corporate sponsor feels he or she is contributing to product sales, the driver's team and car will stay on the track. If a driver wins consistently and the sponsor's bottom line does not change, the driver may not be on the track in the future. According to one observer, this means that there are racers today "who can't drive a nail," but they remain in the sport "because they're good spokespeople for corporations" (Zengerle, 2002).

Sponsor sales, corporate stock values, and winning usually go hand-in-hand. Logo recognition increases as race-leading cars receive extensive camera coverage during races. Winning drivers show off their logo-laden racing suits as they pop corks on champagne bottles and receive kisses from attractive models in the winner's circle after the race. Winning drivers are interviewed and given opportunities to plug their sponsors as millions of people listen to what they say.

However, the interests of sponsors may be served in other ways. If a team sponsor is selling Excedrin, it may not be as important for a driver to win as to tell fans how much he or she needs Excedrin for the headaches that come with losses. Of course, this is an extreme example, but the point is that driving fast and winning races are not the only ways to promote a sponsor's bottom line. There are many ways to be a "steward of the brand" represented by the logo on the car and the fire suit worn by drivers.

Longtime fans of NASCAR also observed recently that in the FOX television coverage of races, younger drivers are more heavily promoted by announcers in an effort to attract young male viewers (Jenkins, 2002a, b). Darrell Waltrip, a former driver and now a stock car race analyst for FOX, says that car owners today "just need somebody to get in the car that's charismatic, exciting and will drive the wheels off of it" (in Jenkins, 2002a, p. 2A). Older drivers, he says, may be better and faster on the track, but they want more money to race, and they don't receive attention from the demographic segment of the audience that the sponsors hope to attract. Furthermore, many sponsors feel that a new face, unconnected with other products in the past, is the best face to represent their products, so they support younger, attractive drivers and then train those drivers to represent their products without sounding like walking paid commercials, even though they are (Zengerle, 2002).

But what happens to a sport when this orientation is pushed without limits, as Vince McMahon has done with World Wrestling Entertainment and the XFL? This is discussed in the box "*Raw Is War*."

Organizations That Control Sports

Commercialization also leads to changes in the organizations that control sports. When sports

Raw Is War
Commercialization and Heroic Orientations Without Limits

Professional wrestling is commercialization pushed to an extreme. It isolates elements of commercial sports and dramatizes them through parody and caricature (Atkinson, 2002; Rinehart, 1998). In the process, it abandons aesthetic orientations and highlights the heroic.

From the late 1990s through 2001, professional wrestling captured widespread spectator interest and made large amounts of money. It was a smashing commercial success. It turnbuckled, leg locked, and jackhammered its way into popular culture around the globe (Leland, 2000; McShane, 1999).

Events sponsored by the World Wrestling Federation (WWF) and World Championship Wrestling (WCW) sold out stadiums nearly every night in North American cities. *Raw Is War*, a WWF television spectacle, was cable television's highest rated program for 1999 and early 2000. It aired 4 nights a week, with new matches and storylines each night. *SmackDown!*, another WWF event, was the top-rated show on its cable channel during 1999. Pay-per-view events regularly subscribed over half a million viewers at $30 per month and $35–$45 for special events. WWF events were televised in 9 languages in 120 countries. Its videos were the #1-selling "sports videos" in the world, and its action figures outsold all other characters in popular culture. WWF wrestlers Mankind (Rick Foley) and Rock (Dwayne Johnson) had autobiographies that were the #1 and #3 best sellers on the *New York Times* bestseller lists in early 2000. Annual sales for the WWF approached $400 million, and it marketed more than 250 licensed products.

Through 2001, the WCW competed with the WWF for spectators and consumers of its publications and licensed products. Each organization had shows with its own storylines and wrestler-personalities. The WCW highlighted performers such as Goldberg, Sting, and Sid Vicious. Its programs included *Nitro, Mayhem,* and *Thunder*, televised worldwide on Media Mogul Ted Turner's cable stations. *Monday Night Nitro* cut into the audience for both *Monday Night Football* and the *Finals of the NCAA Men's Basketball Tournament;* other WCW and WWF events consistently had higher viewer ratings than NBA games.

The popularity of professional wrestling was grounded in the *heroic orientations* built into the storylines and the personas portrayed in the events. Storylines revolved around hypermasculine, heterosexual, and homophobic strong men with personas that were consistently staged and promoted. These men were either victimized or privileged by the arbitrary and capricious decisions of untrustworthy and greedy corporate bosses. They were either supported or unexpectedly undermined by conniving women, represented as alluring and vulnerable sex objects or exotic and heavily muscled helpmates.

Overall, the events resembled male fantasies about sex and power, as well as male fears about work in a world where they had no control. The audience that was attracted to these events had a clearly identifiable demographic profile and included a disproportionate number of male teens and young adults, a part of the market that many corporations wished to reach. This made their programs valuable commodities.

Everything looked good, but the wave of professional wrestling crested and crashed in 2001. The WCW and the WWF lost many of their headliners. The WCW dissolved, and the WWF changed its name and re-created itself as World Wrestling Entertainment (WWE). Meanwhile, WWE principle owner and president Vince McMahon had long focused his attention on the premier season of the Extreme Football League. The XFL, as it was known, was pro wrestling in pads and helmets. After reasonably successful opening weeks, it fizzled and dissolved at the end of the 2001 season.

Today the XFL is history and the WWE is struggling. It seems that it is difficult to maintain the popularity of events in which the heroic actions and orientations exist without the aesthetic dimensions of physical activity. People may be intrigued by dramatic and melodramatic spectacle, but they will not return week after week if events are unchanging and predictable, or if they do not feel a connection to the players. Without exciting uncertainty or strong identification with players, many people will not see the activity as a sport, at least not enough of a sport to line up for season tickets.

Does the decline of the WWE represent a management and marketing failure, or was the violence parodied in WWE events less entertaining for many people after the terrorist attacks of 9/11/01? Did many wrestling fans just tire of poorly presented storylines, or did the futile struggle for manhood caricatured in the wrestlers' personas no longer resonate with the fans? Did the XFL lose its appeal because the teams had no traditions or widely recognized players, or did fans realize that, in an extreme form, the promotional culture of commercial sports could subvert the joy of watching a game?

Raw (the new name for *Raw Is War*) and *Smack-Down!* continue to appear weekly on cable channels in the United States, but their audience has dwindled. This, combined with the failure of the XFL, raises a question: when do forms of entertainment sports lose their appeal? My sense is that, when sports are organized exclusively around commercial values, they become predictable and boring and, when heroic actions and orientations are the sole attraction, people eventually see events as pointless or exploitive. Too much commercialization destroys the fun. *What do you think?*

Professional wrestling emphasizes extreme heroic orientations with storylines that highlight hypermasculine, heterosexual, and homophobic strong men with personas that are staged in dramatic fashion. These action figures of WWF president Vince McMahon and wrestlers Ken Shamrock and the Undertaker were popular toys for young boys who wanted to "get ready to rumble" during the late 1990s. (Jay Coakley)

depend on the revenues they generate, the control center in sport organizations usually shifts further from the players. In fact, the players in heavily commercialized sports often lose effective control over the conditions of their own sport participation. These conditions come under the control of general managers, team owners, corporate sponsors, advertisers, media personnel, marketing and publicity staff, professional management staff, accountants, and agents. The organizations that control commercial sports are intended to coordinate the interests of all these people, but their primary goal is to maximize revenues. This means that organizational decisions generally reflect the combined economic interests of many people having no direct personal connection with a sport or the athletes involved in it. The power to affect these decisions is grounded in resources that may not be connected with sports. Therefore, athletes in many commercial sports find themselves cut out of decision-making processes, even when the decisions affect their health and the rewards they receive for playing.

As decision making in sport organizations moves further away from athletes, there is a tendency to hire employees, develop policies, and negotiate deals that give a low priority to the interests of athletes. These organizational changes have important implications for what happens in sports. They also make it necessary for athletes to seek new tactics for promoting their own interests, financial and otherwise.

As corporate interests come to dominate sports, athletes often defer to the policy recommendations of team owners, agents, advertising executives, media people, and corporate sponsors. This was vividly illustrated by NBA player Scottie Pippen, who was asked why he was playing in the 1996 Olympics despite a bad ankle, which would interfere with his ability to play for the Chicago Bulls if he didn't rest it. Pippen said, "I made a commitment to a lot of companies, and I'm sticking with it." After he realized he had spoken too truthfully, he added, "But

endorsements aren't the focal point. To play in an Olympics in my own country is something I've always wanted to do" (in Michaelis, 1996, p. 8D). Despite his quick cover-up, it was clear that Pippen had accepted that the interests of his corporate sponsors were primary in his life. He knew he was dependent on corporations, and he answered to them first. Pippen is not alone.

Commercialization has created a situation in which corporations define the conditions of sport participation. This is not especially new in the United States, where people have accepted corporate branding of sports, but this shift is occurring more and more in other countries, where corporate interests promote the use of the U.S. commercial model for their sports, or where transnational corporations take the corporate model wherever they think money or publicity is to be gained by owning and sponsoring sports.

OWNERS, SPONSORS, AND PROMOTERS IN COMMERCIAL SPORTS

Professional Sports in North America

Professional sports are privately owned. The owners of most teams and franchises at all levels of professional sports, from the smallest minor league teams to the top franchises in the NFL, NBA, NHL, and MLB, are individuals or small partnerships. Large corporations, especially entertainment and real estate companies, own a growing proportion of the top teams and franchises (Harvey et al., 2001). Similarly, sponsors and event promoters range from individuals and small businesses to large transnational corporations, depending on the size of the events.

Most people who own the hundreds of minor league teams in North America do not make much money. In fact, most are happy to break even and avoid the losses that are commonplace at this level of professional sports ownership. Also, many teams, leagues, and events have been financial disasters over the past forty years. Four football leagues, a hockey league, a few soccer leagues, a volleyball league, four men's and five women's basketball leagues, a team tennis league, and a number of basketball and soccer teams have all gone out of business, leaving many owners, sponsors, and promoters in debt. This list covers only the United States and doesn't include all those who have lost money on tournaments and special events.

Ownership of the top professional franchises in North America is very different from ownership at other levels of professional sports. Franchise values ranged from about $100 million to over $800 million in early 2003. Owners are large corporations, partnerships of wealthy individuals, or very wealthy individuals who have millions and even billions of dollars in personal assets. Leagues are organized as monopolies, teams often play in publicly subsidized facilities, owners make good to excellent returns on their investments, and support from media companies and corporate sponsors almost guarantees continued financial success at this level of ownership.

Similarly, the large corporations that sponsor particular events, from major golf and tennis tournaments to NASCAR and Grand Prix races, know the costs and benefits associated with the events. Their association with top events not only provides them advertising platforms but also connects them with clearly identified categories of consumers (see figure 11.4). Television companies sponsor events, so that they can control their own programming.

Entertainment companies own teams and sponsor events, so that they can control multiple aspects of the entertainment marketplace and link them together in mutually supportive ways—from Disneyland to ABC television to ESPN to the Anaheim Angels and Mighty Ducks to nationwide promotions at fast-food restaurants, where action figures of sport celebrities can be sold with meals for children. When the Disney-owned Anaheim Angels won the 2002 World Series victory parade was held in

"This is Pepsi McDonald announcing live from L.A.'s Windows 2008 Stadium, where the Microsoft Raiders are set to meet the Boeing Seahawks. Team captains Nike Jones and Budweiser Williams prepare for the Franklin Mint Coin Toss, right after these words from our sponsors."

FIGURE 11.4   Televised versions of commercial sports have become inseparable from the logos and products of corporate sponsors. It is not too far-fetched to imagine this scene in the near future.

the Disneyland, and Mickey Mouse was constantly standing by the coach and the most valuable player.

Sport sponsorships enable companies that sell tobacco, alcohol, and various forms of food with questionable nutritional value to link their products and logos to popular activities. Because people associate sports with physical performance and strong bodies instead of cancer, heart disease, obesity, and other forms of poor health, these companies are eager to be sponsors. It increases their legitimacy in society and defuses resistance to corporate policies, practices, and products.

Investments in sports and sport events are motivated by many factors. In some cases, investors are sports fans with money; they invest to satisfy life-long fantasies, build their egos, or experience vicariously the achievements of athletes. Sports ownership and sport sponsorship gain them more prestige than other business ventures, often making them instant celebrities in their cities; they are famous all over town, from the mayor's office and the Chamber of Commerce to neighborhood bars and local elementary schools. Commercial sports enable these wealthy people to combine business and power brokering with fun.

However, those who invest in sports seldom get so carried away with fun and fantasy that they forget business or what it takes to promote capitalist expansion. They do not enjoy losing money or sharing power. They may look at their athletes as heroes and may even treat them as their children, but they want to control their athletes to maximize returns on their investments. They may be civic boosters and supporters of public projects, but they see the public good in terms that emphasize capitalist expansion and their business interests (Schimmel et al., 1993). Their goals are to generate revenues and establish a firm basis for continued financial success. They may not agree with fellow owners and sponsors on all issues, but they do agree on the need to protect their investments and maximize profits.

> I don't see myself as a hockey team owner. I see myself as a sports/entertainment/media brand manager.
>
> —Ted Lionsis, owner, Washington Capitals (2000)

Team Owners and Sport Leagues as Monopolies

The tendency to think alike has been especially strong among the team owners in the major North American sport leagues. In fact, unity among these owners has led to the formation of some of the most effective monopolies in the history of North American business. Even though each sport franchise in these leagues is a separate business, the franchise owners in each sport have come together to form organizations representing their collective interests. They traditionally have used these organizations to limit the extent to which teams compete against each other for players, fans, media revenues, and sales of licensed merchandise; they also have used the organizations to eliminate competition from those who might try to form other teams and leagues in their sports.

For example, each league (the NBA, the NFL, the NHL, and MLB) has developed a system to force new players to negotiate contracts only with the team that has drafted them; this enables owners to sign new players to contracts without bidding against other teams, which might be willing to pay the players more money. Owners also have agreed to prevent new teams from being added to their leagues without their collective permission; when permission is given, the new team owner is charged an entry fee to become a part of the league. Since the 1960s, when these fees were first assessed, they have escalated from the $600,000 paid by the Dallas Cowboys to join the NFL in 1960 to the $700 million paid by the new Houston Texans, who played their first game in 2002. These are just *entry fees*, divided among the existing owners. They do not include other start-up expenses, player salaries, and operating costs, which amount to $90 million to $140 million per year, depending on the sport. Nor do these fees include "infringement payments" made to existing teams in the same TV markets or the forfeiture of TV revenues during the first year(s) of operation (causing a 5- to 20-million-dollar annual loss, depending on the sport). Furthermore, a new owner can locate only in a city approved by current owners, and no current owner can move a team to another city unless all owners collectively approve of the move.

These policies do two things: (1) they regulate and limit competition between owners, and (2) they prevent new teams from competing with established teams for players, fans, and television rights. Team owners in each league do not allow changes that could threaten their collective interest, their control over the sport, or their ability to make money. This is how monopolies operate (Eitzen, 2000, 2003).

The owners in each sport league also have agreed to sell the national broadcasting rights to their games as a group and then share the revenues from national media contracts. This limits the number of games available to the viewing public, and it even prevents some people from seeing their home teams play in the stadiums built by public money. But it enables team owners to make huge sums of money in their media contracts while forcing people to buy tickets to games. The U.S. Congress has approved this monopolistic method of doing business. This guarantees relatively predictable revenues for team owners and gives them the power to influence television companies and the commentators working for those companies. This is why announcers sound like cheerleaders for the sports their companies pay to broadcast.

Furthermore, team owners have combined their monopolistic media tactics with exclusive-use clauses in their contracts with the stadiums or arenas they use. This has been an effective tool for preventing other leagues from capturing the spectator interest they need to make a profit. Other leagues in each sport have been driven out of business, because existing owners have been allowed to operate as cartels.

Being a part of a legal monopoly has enabled most team owners to make massive sums of money over the past four decades. For example, in the mid-1960s, NFL teams were bought and sold for about $10 million; in 2003, the average franchise value was $531 million. That's an average per team capital gain of $521 million.[2] That amounts to an average *annual* return of over $10 million on an original investment of $10 million. This is what a monopoly does: it limits the supply of teams and drives up the value of existing teams. Of course, team owners do not count capital gains related to rapidly escalating franchise values in their discussions of expenses and revenues, and they usually argue that they must

constantly raise ticket prices to meet expenses. When you are part of a monopoly, you can get away with this (Keating, 2002a).

Even though the NBA, the NFL, the NHL, and MLB are grouped together in this section, these leagues differ from one another in many important ways. These differences are complicated, and they change from year to year as each league encounters new and unique challenges and opportunities. For example, contracts with networks and major cable television companies vary from one league to another. The NHL has been the least successful in negotiating big-money contracts, whereas the NBA and the NFL have been the most successful in recent years (see chapter 12).

Each league also has unique internal agreements regulating how teams can negotiate the sale of *local* broadcasting rights to their games. The NFL does not allow teams to sign independent television contracts for local broadcasts of their games, but MLB does. This has created great disparities in the incomes of baseball teams. For example, the New York Yankees sell their local rights for over $60 million per year, whereas the Montreal Expos sell theirs for about $500,000 per year, 120 times less than rights for the Yankees (Kaplan, 2002). Despite a 2002 labor agreement that enables small-market teams to share a few revenues earned by big-market teams, significant disparities still exist. In fact, the gap between the highest-revenue-generating team (Yankees) in Major League Baseball and the lowest (Montreal) was over $200 million per year in 2002. This is why some teams can hire the best players but others must hire low-cost players unlikely to win a championship.

The biggest differences among the NBA, the NFL, the NHL, and MLB are related to their contractual agreements with players' associations in each league. Although each league traditionally has tried to give athletes as few rights as possible, athletes have fought for nearly forty years to gain control over important parts of their careers and to increase their salaries in the

---

[2]This is an average. Franchise values range from a low of about $80 million for small-market NHL teams to over $800 million for teams such as baseball's New York Yankees and the NFL's Washington Redskins.

process. This will be discussed later in the section, "Legal Status and Incomes of Athletes in Commercial Sports."

Team Owners and Forms of Public Assistance
The belief that cities must have professional sports teams and must provide big sports events in order to be "world-class" has led to many forms of public support for sports owners and sports organizations. The most common form of support is the use of public funds to construct, maintain, and do business in arenas and stadiums. As noted in chapter 10, this type of "stadium socialism" has enabled wealthy and powerful capitalists to use public money for their personal gain. Of course, capitalists are not opposed to welfare when it comes to them.

Owners have justified stadium subsidies and other forms of public support for professional sport teams using five major arguments (Lavoie, 2000):

1. A stadium and a pro team create jobs; those who hold the jobs spend money in the city and pay taxes in the process.
2. Stadium construction infuses money into the local economy; this money is spent over and over as it circulates through the city; and the sales of construction materials generate tax revenues.
3. The team will attract other businesses to the city and will bring visitors from outside the area to spend money in the city.
4. The team will attract regional and national media attention, which will boost tourism, enable local firms to sell their products outside the city, and contribute to overall regional economic development.
5. The team will create positive psychic and social benefits, making people feel better about themselves as individuals and about the city as a whole; pride and social solidarity will be increased in connection with the team's identity.

These arguments sound good, and they often are supported by studies commissioned by team owners and others who want public money to be used to subsidize teams. But dozens of studies done by *independent* economists, both liberal and conservative, do *not* support these arguments (Cagan and deMause, 1998; Hudson, 2001; Noll and Zimbalist, 1997; Rosentraub, 1997). The independent studies generally highlight the following five issues:

1. Teams and stadiums do create jobs; however, apart from highly paid jobs for a handful of athletes, stadium jobs are low-paying and seasonal. Football stadiums are used fewer than fifteen days per year, and the ushers, parking lot attendants, ticket agents, and concessions workers don't make full-time living wages. Furthermore, the vast majority of players' salaries are not spent in the cities where they play. In fact, players may not even live in those cities.
2. Construction materials often are brought in from other locations, as are specialized construction workers. The companies that design and build stadiums are seldom local, and they spend their consulting dollars in other cities.
3. Stadiums do attract other businesses, but these are often restaurant and entertainment franchises with headquarters in other cities. These franchised businesses often drive out locally owned businesses. Spectators do come from out of town, but the vast majority of spectators live close enough to the "homefield" that they do not spend the night in connection with attendance at a game, and they spend a limited amount of money on food and other forms of entertainment outside the stadium.
4. Stadiums and the teams that use them do generate public relations for the city and for tourism, but tourists who visit the city for other reasons may stay away when big sport events are in town or when games are scheduled. Most important is that regional economic development is often limited by a new facility because local people who spend

What defines a world-class city? Powerful local businesspeople and their political allies often believe that sports and sport facilities are needed to stimulate the economy and attract people to their cities. Therefore, they lobby for new stadiums and other sport-related facilities, such as halls of fame. The College Football Hall of Fame is located in South Bend, Indiana, and it has done little to benefit the people of the city, despite large city subsidies. (Jay Coakley)

money at and around the stadium have fewer dollars to spend in their own neighborhoods. A stadium may help businesses in the immediate area, but it often hurts other businesses, because discretionary money is limited in any population (Hudson, 2001). Spending $4,000 on a pair of season tickets to NBA games often means that one will spend less money on going out to dinner and buying entertainment close to home.

5. A pro sport team may make some people feel better, but the macho orientations that accompany the games of most men's pro teams actually may make some people feel uncomfortable. Also, when teams have losing records or lose big games, there is evidence that fans do not feel better about their lives.

These counterarguments are supported by research, but most economists make them with one qualification: whenever a city spends $100–$500 million on a public project, there are bound to be positive benefits. However, the issue is whether the public good could be better served if the money were spent on something other than a stadium used by wealthy owners and players to increase their already sizable assets.

For example, during the 1990s, about $1 billion of mostly public money was spent to build three sport facilities and related infrastructure in Cleveland. Inner-city residents during the same time had to fight the city to fund a drinking fountain in a park in a working-class area of the city, and teachers were holding classes in renovated shower rooms in the public schools. The owners of the sport teams enjoyed profits, because they received a fifty-year exemption on taxes related to their teams and facilities, as well as the equivalent of $120 million in tax abatements on other real estate development in the areas around the stadiums (Bartimole, 1999). This means that, the city loses nearly $50 million in city and county tax revenues each year.

In 1997, Cleveland decided to publicly fund a $280 million football stadium so the city could recruit a new team to replace the Cleveland Browns team that former Browns owner Art Modell had moved to Baltimore in 1995. The state of Maryland had given Modell a rent-free 200-million-dollar stadium, all its revenue-generating potential, and a 50-million-dollar bonus for moving. Maryland spent this money because in 1984 Robert Irsay had moved his Baltimore Colts to Indianapolis because the city had offered him better facilities and more money. When many people in Maryland complained about such a large public subsidy to a wealthy man while schools in Baltimore were rationing toilet paper and chalk and students were wearing coats to class because the schools could not pay their heating bills, Modell responded to the critics by saying the following:

> I feel for the schools. I feel for welfare. But look at the positive effects of pro football on a community, the emotional investment of people at large. You can't equate that with fixing up the schools. (in Brady, 1996, p. 19C)

Meanwhile, back in Cleveland, Richard Jacobs, who had bought the Cleveland Indians

for $45 million in late 1986, saw the value of his team skyrocket, and he sold it for $323 million to Larry Dolan, whose two brothers controlled the massive media company Cablevision. This gave Jacobs capital gains amounting to $21.4 million *per year* for the time he owned the team. The new stadium built by the taxpayers certainly contributed greatly to this gain.

Of course, there are people who object to this form of public stadium subsidy, but they do not have the resources to oppose well-financed, professionally packaged plans developed by experienced political advisors hired by team owners. Furthermore, most of the social activists who might lead the opposition are already busy dealing full-time with problems related to drugs, education, homelessness, poor schools, and the overall shortage of social services in cities. They cannot take leave from these urgent tasks to lobby full-time against the use of public money to benefit billionaire team owners and millionaire celebrity athletes.

This story has been repeated many times in cities around the United States (Eitzen, 2000, 2003; Shropshire, 1999). Team owners enlist the services of large architectural firms, which provide them with lobbyists, political advisors, and public relations people, who make sure the local media cover the campaign for a new stadium from a positive angle. The lobbyists focus on gaining support from politicians and members of committees formed to study the feasibility of building a stadium. Public relations people devise ads that subtly threaten that teams will move unless public money is used in their interest.

The tactic of threatening to move teams unless facilities are built is a form of blackmail used by sport team owners to "encourage" public support. Team owners and advisors try to have votes on bond issues held in political "off years," so that voter turnout will be light. They recommend the formation of stadium taxing districts that encompass white suburbs, where they can count on support at the polls, even if voters in the inner city are opposed to subsidizing the wealthy. They set up "public" support groups, to which they donate large amounts of money, usually 100 times more than opponents can raise, to fund massive advertising campaigns. Meanwhile, sportswriters run supportive stories in major newspapers, sports anchors on the local news talk about the benefits of the new team or new stadium, and sports radio talk show hosts hype the subsidies, even though they are usually supporters of right-wing politics. After all, their media jobs often depend on the vote.

Once a stadium is built, franchises increase in value about 25 percent, and team owners are in a powerful negotiating position to get what they want when it comes to using the stadium for their own benefit. Their success has been so complete that *Financial World* magazine noted that "virtually every stadium is a money pit for taxpayers by any normal measure of return on investment" (Osterland, 1995, p. 107). Of course, the final irony is that many taxpayers cannot afford to buy tickets to see games in the stadiums their money has built.

In addition to facility subsidies, team owners receive other forms of public support. The federal government allows businesses to deduct 50 percent of the cost of game tickets and luxury suite leases as business expenses on their federal tax returns. For example, a company in Denver spends $100,000 on pro sport tickets; $50,000 is deductible; and this saves between $18,000 and $22,000 on company federal and state taxes, so the ticket cost is about $78,000, with indirect government subsidies covering the rest. This is why businesses buy about 75 percent of all season tickets sold by top sport teams. Not only do companies save on taxes while their executives and clients use company tickets to attend games, but they also help teams sell out their seats. This in turn drives up ticket prices for the average fan, whose taxes are paying off the bonds for the stadium. Meanwhile, wealthy people sit in luxury suites and club seats often built with public money and deduct the leases

as business expenses for their corporations. This lowers tax revenues, which could be used for needed public programs.

When thinking about public subsidies to sport teams, it is useful to consider alternative uses of public funds. For example, Colorado Springs used $6 million of public money in 2000 to construct a youth sport complex consisting of 12 baseball, softball, and T-ball fields of various sizes with bleacher seating; 10 soccer/football fields; 6 volleyball courts; an in-line skating rink; a batting cage (for baseball hitting practice); and a number of basketball courts. Meanwhile, nearly $300 million of tax money from Denver and 5 metro area counties was used to build the Denver Broncos and wealthy owner Pat Bowlen a new stadium. Instead of the stadium, the $300 million could have been used to build 600 baseball, softball, and T-ball fields; 500 soccer/football fields; 300 volleyball courts; 50 in-line skating rinks; 50 batting cages; and 250 basketball courts around the metro area. Which of these two alternatives would improve the overall quality of life in the Denver metro area more? The youth facilities would be open 7 days a week to everyone in the community for nominal fees; the new stadium will host 72,000 people 9 times a year at a cost of at least $60 a seat, and people at home will be able to watch the team on TV 9 times a year.

According to urban politics professor Charles Euchner, "Cities have two choices. Forget about major league sports. Or feed the monster" (in Brady and Howlett, 1996, p. 13C). Unfortunately, people in the media and local politics often support feeding the monster, because they benefit from the monster's existence. Do sport reporters make their reputations covering youth sports? Do politicians raise money and attract votes by taking big campaign donors to a local soccer field to watch a pickup game? However, feeding the monster raises serious public policy questions about who should receive public subsidies and what activities and facilities should be supported by public funds.

There are some signs that voters and a few politicians are less likely to approve of feeding the monster in the post-9/11, post-Enron economy in the United States. In 2002, both St. Louis and Minneapolis turned down initiatives that would have allocated public funds for new stadiums. The slogan "Fund the needy, not the greedy" (Simon, 2002) seems to have resonated with voters who have become resentful of CEOs and other superwealthy people engaging in questionable and criminal actions as they amass obscene amounts of personal wealth. This may force more private investments into stadium and arena projects in the future, or there will be more team movement to new cities as team owners seek voters and politicians willing to give them money and tax breaks.

Sources of Income for Team Owners   The owners of top pro teams in the major men's sports make money from the following sources: (1) gate receipts; (2) media revenues, including radio and national, local, cable, and pay-per-view television; (3) stadium revenue, including leases on club seats and luxury suites, concessions and parking, and the sale of stadium advertising and naming rights; and (4) licensing fees and merchandise sales. The amounts and proportions of each of these sources of revenue vary from league to league, and they are difficult to track because team owners try to shelter them, so they will not be counted as part of "league revenues" and included in the total amounts to compute salary caps and player salaries. The majority of revenue for NFL owners comes from television—over 60 percent of all their income—whereas TV revenues for NHL owners are less than 20 percent of their total income. Stadium revenues have become increasingly important in all leagues, and it should be noted that naming rights for some of the newer stadiums and arenas have been sold for as much as $195 million for twenty years (for example, the American Airlines Center in Dallas).

The recent wave of new stadiums is the result of owners' demanding venues that can generate new revenue streams. This is why new stadiums resemble shopping malls with a playing field in the middle. Sociologist George Ritzer (1999) has described them as contemporary "cathedrals of consumption" designed to seamlessly embed continuous consumption opportunities into every aspect of our lives (see figure 11.5). Owners see this as an important means of increasing their profits. They want to capture as much of the entertainment dollar as they can inside the stadium itself and do it with taxpayer money, so that they can avoid debt payments. For example, when Invesco Field at Mile High opened in Denver in 2001, the new revenue stream associated with the stadium netted Denver Broncos owner Pat Bowlen an additional $40 million per year from gate receipts, concessions, and parking, even though there are no more seats in the new stadium than in the old one.

Stadiums are considered to have so much revenue-generating potential that the value of a

FIGURE 11.5   Recently built stadiums resemble shopping malls, and some fans see attendance as a shopping opportunity. They are a captive audience, and team owners want to capture as many of their entertainment dollars as possible. This fan has fallen for the lure of consumption to the point that he is less interested in the game than in buying products to prove he was there.

franchise with a new stadium increases about 25 percent. This means that, if a city builds a 300-million-dollar stadium for a sport team, and the franchise is worth $300 million, the franchise value will increase about $75 million when the stadium is completed. Of course, this increase will go directly into the pocket of the owners when they sell the franchise. In the meantime, the owners can borrow money against the new franchise value to expand their other business investments. This is why team owners often donate a few million dollars to campaigns designed to convince voters that they should build new stadiums with public money.

Of course, owners realize that many people may not feel comfortable with the idea of putting public money into the pockets of the wealthy, so they make sure that, when their teams take the field, court, or ice, announcers describe them as "your" Denver Broncos, Cleveland Cavaliers, Detroit Red Wings, or Seattle Mariners (Sage, 1996). The owners are happy to have people feel as if the teams belong to them, as long as these people let the owners collect all the revenues and keep all the capital gains when they sell the teams.

Amateur Sports in North America

Amateur sports don't have owners, but they do have commercial sponsors and governing bodies, which promote and sanction events and control athletes. Generally, the sponsors are large corporations, which support amateur sports for advertising purposes. The governing bodies of amateur sports operate on a nonprofit basis, although they do use revenues from events to maintain their organizations and their power over amateur sports.

Centralized sport authorities administer amateur sports in most countries. They work with the national governing bodies (NGBs) of individual sports, and together they have control over events, athletes, and revenues. Sport Canada and the Canadian Olympic Association are examples of such centralized authorities; they develop the policies that govern the various national sport organizations in Canada.

In the United States, the organization and control of amateur sports are much less centralized. Policies, rules, fund-raising strategies, and methods of operating all vary from one organization to the next. For example, the major governing body in intercollegiate sports is the National Collegiate Athletic Association (NCAA). For amateur sports not directly connected with universities, the major controlling organization is the United States Olympic Committee (USOC). However, within the USOC, each of more than fifty separate NGBs regulates and controls a particular amateur sport. NGBs raise most of their own funds through corporate and individual sponsors, and each one sets its own policies to supplement the rules and policies of the USOC. The USOC has tried for many years to develop continuity in American amateur sports, but the NGBs and other sport organizations are very protective of their own turf, and they seldom give up their power to regulate their sports; instead, they fight to maintain control over their rules, revenues, and athletes. This has been the basis of many political battles in and among organizations.

All amateur sport organizations share an interest in two things: (1) *power* and (2) the *money* generated through sponsorships and revenue-producing events. Sponsorship patterns in amateur sports also take many forms. Intercollegiate sport programs seek various forms of corporate support. Some universities have, in effect, sold their athletic departments, consisting of all athletic teams and the bodies of athletes, to corporate sponsors in exchange for money, scholarships, and equipment. A growing number of university athletic departments have contracts with major shoe and apparel manufacturers. In the future, others will sign contracts with Pepsi-Cola, Coca-Cola, or MARS. Contracts will require athletes and other students to drink only certain soft drinks or eat certain candy bars on campus or in the locker room at halftime. Of course, this form of sponsorship is a clever way for private corporations to use tax-supported institutions as vehicles for their own profit making, while being hailed on campus as the saviors of sport teams. Corporations and universities enter these agreements outside of any democratic processes, which might involve votes by students, athletes, or the taxpayers whose money funds the universities.

The NGBs of amateur sports long have depended on corporate sponsorship money, and they continue to seek those sponsorships to pay for athlete training, operating expenses, and the staging of events. Designated corporate logos appear on clothing worn and equipment used by amateur athletes. In some cases, individual athletes seek corporate sponsorships on their own, hoping to remain free to train and compete without having their lives completely controlled by NGBs.

As this model of corporate sponsorship is used more and more around the world, the economics of sports increasingly will become tied to the fortunes and fluctuations of market economies and large corporations. Corporations seek out only those sports that will give them the visibility they desire, and economic recessions could mean the end of sponsorships. Future agreements will require athletes and coaches to be spokespersons and cheerleaders for the interests of international corporate capitalism in the world, although this has already happened to a significant degree.

LEGAL STATUS AND INCOMES OF ATHLETES IN COMMERCIAL SPORTS

When sports are commercialized, athletes become entertainers. This is obvious at the professional level, but it is true in other commercial sports, such as big-time college football and basketball. Professional athletes get paid for their efforts, whereas amateur athletes receive rewards within limits set by the organizations that govern their sport participation. This raises two questions: (1) what is the legal status of the athlete-entertainers who work in these sports? and (2) how are athlete-entertainers rewarded for their work?

Many people have a difficult time thinking of athletes as workers, and they hesitate to consider owner-player relations in professional sports as a form of labor relations. This is because people usually associate sports with play in their own lives, and they see sports as fun rather than work. However, when sports are organized to make money, players are workers, even though they may have fun on the job (Zimmer and Zimmer, 2001). Of course, this is not unique; many workers enjoy their jobs and have fun doing them. However, regardless of how much they enjoy their work, issues of legal status and rewards for work are important.

This section will focus on commercial sports in the United States. We will not consider the sports that may collect a few gate receipts but never make enough money to pay for anything beyond basic expenses for the events. Therefore, we will not discuss high school sports, nonrevenue-producing college sports, or other nonprofit local sports in which teams may sell tickets to events.

Professional Athletes

Legal Status: Team Sports   The legal status of athletes always has been the most controversial issue in professional team sports in the United States. Until the mid-1970s, professional athletes in the major sport leagues had little or no legal power to control their own careers. They could play only for the team that drafted and owned them. They could not control when and to whom they might be traded during their careers, even when their contracts expired. To make matters worse, they were obliged to sign standard contracts forcing them to agree to forfeit all rights over their careers to team owners. Basically, they were bought and sold like property and were seldom consulted about their own wishes. They were mercenaries at the mercy of team owners and officials hired by team owners.

In all sports, this system of employee restriction has been called the **reserve system.** Although the dynamics of this system have varied from one league to another, it has enabled team owners to restrict the movement of athlete-employees from one team to another. As long as owners could do this, salaries remained low, and athletes had no power to control the conditions under which they played their sports. Parts of the reserve system continue to exist in professional sports, but various players' associations have challenged the system in court and forced significant changes that increased the labor rights of many professional athletes.

In any other business, a reserve system of this sort would violate antitrust laws. For example, it is illegal for the owners of all computer software firms to form relationships and decide among themselves whom they want to hire next year among all people with degrees in information systems. It also would be illegal for them to agree not to hire graduates who were "reserved" by another company. Such employee restrictions would destroy the freedom of professionals in information systems to choose where and with whom they wanted to work. Furthermore, if these workers could not take jobs with other companies without permission from their current employers, even after their employment contracts had expired, their salaries would be kept low, because companies would not have to compete with each other to hire the people with the best skills. And, if these workers could be sold or traded to other companies without being consulted, they would have no real control over their own careers.

But this type of reserve system has been defined as legal in sports, and owners have used it for many years with minimal interference from any government agency. Team owners justified this form of control over athletes' careers by saying it was needed to maintain a competitive balance among the teams in their leagues. They

argued that, if players were free to work for anyone they wanted to, the wealthiest owners in the biggest cities and TV markets would buy up all the good athletes and prevent teams in smaller cities and TV markets from maintaining competitive teams. The irony of this argument has been that team owners have all been wealthy capitalists who praised the free market, while maintaining that the free market would destroy the business of sports. In other words, these capitalists became "sport socialists" to protect their power and wealth under the umbrella of a monopoly inconsistent with the principles of free enterprise.

Professional athletes always have objected to the reserve system, but they could not mount an effective legal challenge of the system until the 1970s. Then, in 1976, the courts ruled that, under certain conditions, professional athletes had the right to become *free agents*. This right was important, because it allowed players whose contracts had expired to seek contracts with other teams that might bid for their services.

This legal change had a dramatic effect on the salaries of NBA and MLB players beginning in the late 1970s (see table 11.1). For about fifteen years, team owners in the NFL and the NHL avoided much of the effect of this legal change by negotiating restrictions on free agency with players' associations. But, in 1992, after players in both leagues mounted challenges, these restrictions were partially lifted. The hockey players went on a ten-day strike during the Stanley Cup playoffs and forced owners to sign a short-term contract, in which the players obtained slightly more control over their careers. The football players, after challenging the NFL for about five years in a series of court cases, won an antitrust suit, which forced team owners to agree to let NFL players become free agents after being in the league for five years.

It would take many pages to explain the full implications of court decisions and labor negotiations on the legal status and rights of players in each professional team sport. Things change

Table 11.1   Average salaries in major U. S. professional leagues, compared with median family income, 1950–2002[a]

| Year | SPORT LEAGUE | | | | | | Median U.S. Family Income[b] |
	NFL	NBA	WNBA	NHL	MLB	MLS	
1950	15,000	5,100		5,000	13,300	NA	4,000
1960	17,100	13,000		14,100	19,000	NA	5,620
1970	23,000	40,000		25,000	29,300	NA	9,867
1980	79,000	190,000		110,000	143,000	NA	21,023
1990	395,400	824,000		247,000	598,000	NA	35,353
2000	1,116,100	3,600,000	60,000	1,050,000	1,988,034	100,000	50,732
2002	1,316,625	4,500,000	60,000	1,500,000	2,383,300	——	51,500

[a]Data on players' salaries come from many sources. All NFL salaries are from the NFL Players Association (Duberstein, 2002). Average salaries before the mid-1970s are estimates, because players' associations did not exist, and teams were notorious for their inconsistent and creative bookkeeping practices. Average salaries often differ from one source to another, because some are based on rosters at the beginning of the season, whereas others are based on rosters at the end of the season. Differences also reflect whether signing bonuses, prorated portions of those bonuses, and salary deferrals are included with or without interest adjustments.

[b]This represents total family income—parents and children in the same household. Half the families fall above the median, and half fall below. Data are from the U.S. Census; figures for 1950 and 2002 are estimates.

Note: Players' salaries increased slowly from after World War II through the mid-1970s. During those years, pro athletes made from two to four times the median family income in the United States. After free agency was put in place in the 1970s, salaries began to skyrocket. As teams made more revenues from gate receipts and television rights and were forced to compete for players, and as players' unions provided support for players' rights, salaries increased dramatically. In 2002, the ratios between salaries in the major men's professional sports and the median family income were 87:1 for the NBA; 46:1 for MLB; 29:1 for the NHL; 26:1 for the NFL; and 2:1 for the MLS. At the same time, the ratio was 1.2:1 for the WNBA. No wonder so many people identify with the women in the WNBA and why people have so little sympathy for male athletes in labor disputes with team owners, even though many of the owners are billionaires or multibillion-dollar corporations.

every time a new case is resolved or a new labor agreement is made. In part, it was this complexity that kept most players from challenging the restrictions of the reserve system over the years. It was not until the formation of players' associations and unions in the 1970s that they had the support and organization they needed to push for changes. Each players' association used the collective strength of all the players in its league to bargain against the collective strength of all the owners in that league.

Although the players' associations often have been unpopular with many sport fans and detested by team owners and league officials, they have enabled players to gain more and more control over their salaries and working conditions since the late 1970s. Labor negotiations and players' strikes in all professional team sports always have focused on issues of freedom and control over careers, even though money issues have attracted most of the attention in the media coverage. Players always have known that, when they had the freedom to sell their skills to the highest bidder, salaries would increase to the highest level that the owners could afford to pay.

Free agency now exists for veteran players in all leagues. The drafting of rookies still occurs, but the number of rookies reserved through the draft gradually has been cut back, allowing more players to try out with teams they think offer them the best chances of getting contracts. Definitions of who qualifies as a veteran and the amount of freedom enjoyed by free agents vary from league to league.

Although players' organizations and unions have done much to change the legal status of athletes in various professional sports, it has not been easy to keep players organized. Owners don't look kindly on players who have served as representatives in unions or players' associations. Athletes are often hesitant to join any organization that may ask them to strike for an entire season, especially since their careers seldom last more than four to seven years in team sports. Therefore, a season-long strike for the average player means sacrificing 15 to 25 percent of lifetime income as a professional athlete. Strikes are also risky because they alienate fans and because team owners may hire nonunion players. Finally, the highest-paid players in certain leagues are now so wealthy and in such good positions to negotiate contracts on their own that they do not identify with other players, about 15 to 25 percent of whom make the minimum salaries in the leagues, or close to the minimum. Although the unions and players' associations created the conditions for the current good fortune of these superstars, some of them no longer see these organizations as useful to them. The superstars depend on their agents, not on athlete-worker organizations. All these factors make it difficult to keep players organized.

Unlike professional male athletes in top revenue-producing leagues, athletes in most minor leagues and low-revenue sports have few rights and little control over their careers. As one former coach in the Continental Basketball League (CBA) noted, "In this league, [trades are] so easy that teams trade every day. It's like bubble gum cards. I swear, if Michael Jordan were in the CBA, he'd have been traded at least three times" (in Pluto, 1995, p. 280). In the CBA, when a player is injured, he can be cut on the spot, no questions asked. For the pros at this level—who are more numerous than those working at the top levels of professional sports—the pay is low, careers are uncertain, rights are few, and owners have the last word. In fact, the average high school teacher in the United States has a higher salary and more rights as a worker than nearly all pro athletes in minor leagues.

Legal Status: Individual Sports   The legal status of professional athletes in individual sports varies greatly from sport to sport and even from one athlete to another. Although there are important differences among boxing, bowling, golf, tennis, auto racing, rodeo, horse racing, track and field, skiing, biking, and a number of recently professionalized alternative and action sports, a few generalizations are possible.

The legal status of athletes in individual sports largely depends on what athletes must do to train and qualify for competition in their sports. For example, few athletes can afford to pay for all the training needed to develop professional-level skills in a sport. Few athletes are in a position to meet the other requirements associated with official participation in sport competitions, which may include having a recognized agent or manager (as in boxing), being formally recognized by other participants (as in most auto racing), obtaining membership in a professional organization (as in most bowling, golf, and tennis tournaments), or gaining a special invitation through an official selection group (as in pro track and field meets).

Whenever athletes need sponsors to pay for their training and whenever contractual arrangements with other persons or groups are required for their participation, the legal status of athletes is shaped by their agreements with sponsors and sanctioning groups. This is why the legal status of athletes in individual sports varies so much. Let's use boxing as an example. Because many boxers come from low-income backgrounds, they cannot develop on their own the skills they need to become recognized competitors. They need trainers, managers, and sponsors of their training. After their skills are developed, it takes money and carefully nurtured business connections to arrange and promote bouts.

Relationships with trainers, managers, and sponsors come with conditions attached for the boxers. These conditions may be written in formal contracts or based in informal agreements. In either case, they require the boxers to forfeit control of their lives and a portion of the rewards they may earn in bouts in return for the help they need to become professionals. Unless boxers have good legal experience or win a few big-money fights, they seldom have control over their careers. They are forced to trade control over their bodies and careers for the opportunity to continue boxing. This is a classic example of how class relations operate in sports: when people lack resources, they cannot negotiate the conditions under which their sport careers develop.

The legal status of athletes in individual sports is defined in the bylaws of some professional organizations, such as the Professional Golf Association (PGA), the Ladies' Professional Golf Association (LPGA), the Association of Tennis Professionals (ATP), and the Professional Rodeo Cowboys Association (PRCA). Because athletes control many of these organizations, their policies support athletes' rights and enable athletes to control the conditions under which they compete. Without these organizations, athletes in these sports would have few guaranteed rights.

Income: Team Sports Despite the publicity given to the supercontracts of some athletes in the NBA, the NFL, the NHL, MLB, and premier soccer leagues in Europe, salaries vary widely across the levels and divisions in professional team sports. For example, many players at the minor league level in baseball, hockey, and other team sports make less than social workers, teachers, and other nonsport workers. According to U.S. Census data on income by occupation, the median salary for professional athletes in 2000 was $32,700; half of all pro athletes made less than this amount, and half made more.

Salaries for about 100 players in the National Basketball Developmental League average about $30,000 per year. In the new NBA Rookie League, they are $25,000 per year. Salaries for more than 3,000 players on 160 minor league baseball teams and a similar number of minor league hockey players range from $100 a game, at the lowest levels, to a high of about $60,000 per year at the top minor league level (Renck, 2002). These are seasonal jobs with few benefits. However, we hear only about salaries among top players in the top leagues (see figure 11.6).

To understand the range of income in pro sports, consider that, during the 2002 baseball season, 10 percent of the players made 40 percent of all the salary money paid to Major League Baseball players. Collectively, this top 10 percent made $70 million more during the season than all the salary money paid to 80 percent of all major league players (Kaplan, 2002). This is why the average (i.e., mean) salary in Major League Baseball is about $2.4 million per year, whereas the median salary is less than $900,000 per year. The big salaries for a few players drive up the

SIDELINES

©1982 M.T.F.-T.W.S.-Lakewood. CO

"I make $16 million a year, and I don't feel guilty!"

FIGURE 11.6 Most athletes generate revenues that match their salaries or prize money. Like other entertainers, a few of them have benefited from national and international media exposure. Sport events are now marketed in connection with the celebrity status and lifestyles of high-profile athlete-entertainers.

average for the entire league. This is true in all the major men's professional leagues.

Putting the growing salary inequality in sports into more personal terms, consider that the $23.6 million earned by Shaquille O'Neal during the 2002–2003 basketball season was nearly $5 million more than all 200 WNBA players made during their 2001 and 2002 seasons. O'Neal's salary will surpass $32 million for the 2005–2006 season, according to his current contract. Meanwhile, half of all NBA players make less than $2 million annually, and many make between $350,000 and $400,000 per year. O'Neal makes more than the combined salaries for the 70 lowest-paid players in the NBA.

As top stars make salaries that are increasing at rapid rates, most of the hockey and baseball players on more than 300 minor league teams across North America would love to make $30,000 per season, and they only dream of making the $400,000 minimum salary in the NHL or the $300,000 minimum in Major League Baseball.

It's also important to remember that megasalaries are quite new in professional team sports; they did not exist before 1980. For example, when I graduated from college in 1966 with a degree in sociology, I had a job offer from a public agency, which would have paid me about 60 percent of the average salary of NBA players that year. Today, a new graduate with a bachelor's degree would be lucky to find a job paying more than 1 percent of the average NBA salary.

The data in table 11.1 indicated that players' average salaries have grown far beyond median family income in the United States. For example, players in 1950 made average salaries that were not much different from the median family income. In 2002, players' salaries were up to forty-four times greater than the median family income. This disparity between players' salaries and general family income is the reason so many fans no longer see the players as "workers" and why they do not side with the players during strikes and lockouts. Of course, siding with owners is also difficult, because most of them make more than even the highest-paid players when you add their salaries and capital gains on franchise values. It is important to remember that, as of 2002, the estimated percentage of league revenues received by players ranged from 52 percent to about 70 percent. The owners used the rest of the annual revenue to cover other expenses and to pay themselves. Each league, except the NHL, has a team salary cap, and owners pay athletes only what they must to sign them to contracts. Contract amounts are shaped by the economics of the league and the labor agreements that players' associations have with leagues.

The dramatic increase in salary at the top level of pro sports since 1980 is due to two factors: (1) changes in the legal status and rights of players, which have led to free agency and the use of a salary arbitration process, and (2) increased revenues flowing to leagues and owners. Salaries for every year in each major team sport since 1970 show that large increases in salary levels have corresponded closely to court decisions and other events changing the legal status of athletes and giving them bargaining power in their contract negotiations with team owners. Unions and lawsuits have worked for some athletes, as they have for many workers in other industries.

Income: Individual Sports As with team sports, publicity is given to the highest-paid athletes in individual sports. However, not all players in these sports make enough money from tournament winnings to support themselves comfortably. In fact, many golfers, tennis players, bowlers, track and field athletes, auto and motorcycle racers, rodeo riders, figure skaters, and others must carefully manage their money, so that they do not spend more than they win as they travel from event to event. When tournament winnings are listed in the newspaper, nothing is said about the expenses for airfares, hotels, food, and transportation or about other expenses for coaches, agents, managers, and various support people. The top money winners don't worry too much about these expenses, but most athletes in individual sports are not big money winners.

In recent years, the disparity between the top money winners and others has increased considerably on the men's and women's golf and tennis tours. Many people are surprised to learn that 90 percent of the 1,921 players registered on the Sanex Women's Tennis Association Tour made less than $40,000 in prize money during the 2002 season, and over half made less than $1,000 for the year. This pales in comparison with the nearly $6 million won by Venus and Serena Williams in the same year.

The vast majority of the men and women playing professional tennis, golf, and other individual sports do not make enough money to pay their competition expenses each year, although a lucky few have sponsors who pick up training and travel expenses. But some athletes in individual sports may be under contract to share their winnings with the investors who sponsor them. The investors cover expenses during the lean years but then take a percentage of winnings when the athletes win matches or tournaments. For example, boxers traditionally have received very little of the prize money from their bouts; even today, much goes to promoters, managers, trainers, and sponsors. Only a few boxers avoid this situation or make so much that it is not important; most others face bankruptcy or a working-class lifestyle soon after their careers are over. But these boxers are ignored as attention is focused on the multimillion-dollar purses in the highly publicized heavyweight bouts covered on pay-per-view television. People read that Mike Tyson made $75 million for just over fifty minutes of prize fighting in 1996, and they talk about that instead of all those who never covered expenses. But journalist Jack Newfield (2001) reminds us that boxers "have no pension, no union, no health insurance, no voice. For every George Foreman who gets rich, there are 1000 you never hear of who end up with slurred speech, failing memory

and an empty bank account" (p. 14). To make matters worse in the case of boxing, about fifty boxers died in the ring between 1970 and 2001.

Sponsorship agreements sometimes cause problems for professional athletes in other individual sports as well. Being contractually tied, for example, to an equipment manufacturer or another sponsor often puts athletes in a state of dependency. They may not have the freedom to choose when or how often they will compete, and sponsors may require them to attend social functions, at which they talk with fan-consumers, sign autographs, and promote products.

The money is very good for a few athletes in individual sports, whereas most others struggle to cover expenses. Only when sport events are broadcast on television can athletes expect to compete for major prize money and earn large incomes.

Amateur Athletes in Commercial Sports

Legal Status of Amateur Athletes   The primary goals of amateur athletes always have been simple: to train and to compete. However, the achievement of those goals has not always been easy, because amateur athletes have not had significant control over the conditions of their sport participation. Instead, control has rested in the hands of amateur sport organizations, each setting rules that specify the conditions under which training and competition can occur. Although these rules usually are intended to ensure fairness in competition, they sometimes have been used to protect the power and interests of the organizations, rather than the athletes they are supposed to serve. When this has happened, amateur athletes have not been able to participate when and where they would prefer to.

The total powerlessness of amateur athletes in the United States led to the formation of the U.S. President's Commission on Olympic Sports in 1975. The commission's report was instrumental in the passage of the Amateur Sports Act of 1978.

The Amateur Sports Act did not guarantee amateur athletes any rights, but it did create the USOC, and it clarified the relationships among various sports organizations, so that organization officials would be less likely to interfere with participation opportunities for athletes. Interference continues today, but it is less disruptive of training and competition than in the past.

The continued lack of power among amateur athletes is especially evident in U.S. intercollegiate sports. Even in revenue-producing intercollegiate sports, athletes have few rights and no formal means of filing complaints when they have been treated unfairly or denied the right to play their sports. The athletes are not allowed to share the revenues they generate and no control over how their skills, names, and images can be used by the university or the NCAA. For example, when college athletes become local or national celebrities, they have no "right of publicity" enabling them to benefit from their celebrity status. They cannot endorse products or be paid when universities use their identities and images to promote events or sell merchandise.

Although many amateur athletes recognize the problems associated with their lack of rights, it has been difficult for them to lobby for changes. Challenging the university and the NCAA in court is expensive and would take years of a young person's life. Forming an athletes' organization would make it possible to bargain for rights, but bringing together athletes from various campuses would require many resources, and convincing athletes, many of whom have adjusted to their dependency and powerlessness, to take assertive and progressive action would be a major challenge. Furthermore, the prospect of college athletes' engaging in collective bargaining to gain rights and benefits would be seen as a serious threat to the whole structure of big-time college sports. Athletes may be treated as employees by coaches and athletic departments, but there is a fear that, if they were legally defined as employees, they would be eligible for the same

considerations granted to other workers in the United States. This makes everyone from coaches to university presidents nervous.

Although recent changes have called for the appointment of varsity athletes to certain NCAA committees, the likelihood of significantly increasing athletes' rights is not great. Athlete advisory committees now exist at the NCAA, conference, and campus levels, but there are no formal structures for effectively gaining more control over the conditions of training and competition. In the meantime, athlete advocacy groups outside the university are needed; athletes need support in gaining at least some control over their sport lives and the revenues created by their skills.

Amateur athletes in Olympic sports have made some strides to gain control over their training and competition, but it has been difficult for them to make an impact on the organizations that control their sports. In fact, as sports become more commercialized, the centers of power in sports move further and further away from athletes. Now that athletes are included on advisory boards for NGBs, sponsors and media people who operate outside the NGBs are making many of the decisions about training and competition. The paradox for athletes is that, as they gain more resources to train and compete, the control of their training and competition moves further away from them. The exceptions, of course, are those athletes with national visibility and the individual power to negotiate support that meets their interests.

Income of Amateur Athletes   Amateur athletes in commercial sports face another paradox: they generate money through their performances, but they often face limitations in sharing that money with sponsors and sport organizations. Although American college athletes may receive limited athletic aid and U.S. and Canadian national team athletes may receive stipends for living expenses while they train, many amateur athletes receive no compensation at all for their involvement in events generating gate receipts and media rights payments.

Intercollegiate athletes playing big-time college football and basketball may generate millions of dollars for their universities, but NCAA rules prohibit them from receiving anything more than renewable one-year scholarships, and those scholarships may not cover more than tuition, room, meals, and books. This means that a football or basketball player from a low-income family can bring fame and fortune to a school for three or four years and never legally receive a penny for college expenses outside the classroom—no money for clothes, a personal computer, academic photocopying, school supplies, laundry, transportation around town, dates, travel home for vacations, non-sport-related medical or dental bills, phone calls home, and so on.

It is the unfairness of this situation that has led to many of the under-the-table cash payments to college athletes. These payments and other illegal gifts have become so commonplace that many leaders in college sports have suggested that the NCAA revise its policies on

The NCAA strictly limits the sport-related incomes of college athletes, even though the athletes may generate millions of dollars of income for their universities and the NCAA. Tickets to this Notre Dame football game cost the same as tickets to an NFL game, and television rights fees paid to Notre Dame are exceptionally high. However, the college athletes receive rewards that are a small fraction of the salaries received by NFL players. (Jay Coakley)

compensation for athletes. However, it is not easy to develop a fair method of compensation. Therefore, some top-level college athletes leave college long before graduation as they attempt to play professional sports.

Other amateur athletes in both college and Olympic sports face similar difficulties in capitalizing on their commercial value. However, changes in eligibility rules now permit some athletes to earn money without jeopardizing their participation status in amateur sports. Rules are less restrictive than they have been in the past. However, many athletes still cannot make money *beyond* an approved basic cost-of-living stipend and travel expenses related to training and competition in their sport. Therefore, if a sixteen-year-old gymnast on the U.S. national team takes money to be a part of an exhibition tour after the Olympics, she is not eligible to participate in NCAA college gymnastics. This also means she may not receive an athletic grant to attend college. Furthermore, if an Olympic figure skater participates in a professional skating competition, her amateur status may be revoked.

Even though some of the restrictions of amateurism have been lifted in Olympic-type sports, many athletes do not share in the revenues generated by the events in which they participate. For example, the Olympic Games generate hundreds of millions of dollars in gate receipts and sponsorships, but the athletes who make the games possible receive none of that money, apart from training support through the sport organizations they are affiliated with and the cash awards medal winners *sometimes* receive from those organizations.

Questions about the fairness of this situation have been raised by an increasing number of athletes. University of Ottawa economist Mark Lavoie (2000) has noted that "the day cannot be too far off when the so-called amateur athletes will threaten to go on strike in order to get their share of the huge revenues generated by worldwide mega-events such as the Olympic Games" (p. 167).

SUMMARY

WHAT ARE THE CHARACTERISTICS OF COMMERCIAL SPORTS?

Commercial sports are visible parts of many contemporary societies. Their growth is associated with urbanization, industrialization, improvements in transportation and communications technology, the availability of capital resources, and class relations.

People's interest in paying to watch sports is encouraged by a quest for excitement in highly organized and controlled societies, a cultural emphasis on individual success, widely available youth sport programs, and extensive media coverage of sports.

The recent expansion of commercial sports also has been fueled by sport organizations seeking global markets, as well as transnational corporations using sports as vehicles for global expansion. The global expansion of commercial sports will continue as long as it serves the interests of transnational corporations.

Commercialization has influenced changes in the structure and goals of certain sports, the orientations of people involved in sports, and the organizations that control sports. Those connected with commercial sports tend to emphasize heroic orientations over aesthetic orientations. Style and dramatic expression impress mass audiences, whereas fine distinctions in ability often are overlooked, except by those who have deep knowledge about a particular sport. Overall, commercial sports have been packaged as total entertainment experiences for spectators, even spectators who know little about the games or events they are watching.

Commercial sports are unique businesses. At the minor league level, most of them do not generate substantial revenues for owners and sponsors; in fact, they are risky businesses. However, team owners at the top levels of professional sports have worked together to make their leagues into effective entertainment monopolies.

Along with event sponsors and promoters, these owners are involved with commercial sports to make money while having fun and establishing good public images for themselves or their corporations and its products, policies, and practices.

Owners in the major team sports have used monopolistic business practices to keep costs down and revenues up, especially through their collective sale of broadcasting rights to media companies. Profits also have been enhanced by public support and subsidies, often associated with the construction and operation of stadiums and arenas.

It is ironic that North American professional sports often are used as models of democracy and free enterprise, when, in fact, they have been built through a system of autocratic control and monopolistic organization. As NFL team owner Art Modell once said about himself and his fellow owners in the NFL, "We're twenty-eight Republicans who vote socialist." What he meant was that NFL owners are conservative individuals and corporations that have eliminated much free market competition in their sport businesses and have used public money and facilities to increase their wealth and power.

The administration and control of amateur commercial sports rest in the hands of numerous sport organizations. Although these organizations exist to support amateur athletes as they train and compete, major goals within the organizations have been to maintain power and control and to maximize revenue generation. Those with the most money and influence usually win the power struggles in amateur sports, and athletes seldom have had the resources to promote their own interests in these struggles. Corporate sponsors have become a major force in amateur sports, and their interests have a major impact on what happens in these sports.

Commercialization has made athletes entertainers. Athletes generate revenues through their performances. Therefore, issues related to players' rights and the sharing of the revenues generated by their performances have become very important. As rights and revenues have increased, so have players' incomes. Media money has been key in this process.

Not all athletes in professional sports make vast sums of money. Players outside the top men's sports, and golf and tennis for women, have incomes that are surprisingly low. Income among amateur athletes is limited by rules set by governing bodies in particular sports. Intercollegiate athletes in the United States have what amounts to a maximum wage in the form of athletic scholarships. This has led to illegal under-the-table payments to some college athletes, especially those from low-income backgrounds. In other amateur sports, athletes may receive direct cash payments for performances and endorsements, and some receive support from the organizations to which they belong, but relatively few make large amounts of money.

The structure and dynamics of commercial sports vary from nation to nation. Commercial sports in most of the world have not generated the massive amounts of revenues associated with a few high-profile, heavily televised sports in North America, Japan, and Western Europe. Profits for owners and promoters around the world increasingly depend on supportive relationships with the media, governments, and large corporations. These arrangements have done much to shape the character of all sports in North America, professional and amateur.

Of course, the commercial model of sports is not the only one that might provide athletes and spectators with enjoyable and satisfying experiences. However, because most people are unaware of alternative models, they simply continue to express a desire for what they get, and their desires are based on limited information influenced by people with commercial and corporate interests (Sewart, 1987). Therefore, changes will occur only when people connected with sports are able to develop visions for what sports could and should look like if they were not shaped so overwhelmingly by economic factors.

SUGGESTED READINGS

Cagan, J., and N. deMause. 1998. *Field of schemes: How the great stadium swindle turns public money into private profit*. Monroe, ME: Common Courage Press (journalists describe how professional team owners in the United States use public money to establish and promote their business operations; discussion of how these strategies might be undermined or resisted).

Danielson, M. N. 1998. *Home team: Professional sports and the American metropolis*. Princeton, NJ: Princeton University Press (an economist analyzes the connections between pro sport teams in North America and the places where teams play; focuses on relationships between teams and city governments).

Lavoie, M. 2000. Economics and sport. In *Handbook of sports studies* (pp. 157–70), edited by J. Coakley and E. Dunning. London: Sage (overview of research on labor economics and the economics of professional sports; special attention is given to salary determination, free agency, salary caps, profit maximization, and franchise location).

Sage, G. H. 1998. *Power and ideology in American sport: A critical perspective*. 2d ed. Champaign, IL: Human Kinetics (chapters 6–9 analyze commercialization and the political economy of sports in the United States).

Wetzel, D., and D. Yaeger. 2000. *Sole influence: Basketball, corporate greed, and the corruption of America's youth*. New York: Warner Books (journalists describe how sneaker companies develop connections and brand loyalty among young athletes; shows how black market professionalism exists among high school and college athletes and how young athletes are misled and exploited by large corporations).

Wilson, J. 1994. *Playing by the rules: Sport, society, and the state*. Detroit: Wayne State University Press (social political analysis of how the relationship between sports and the state in the United States has developed to enable the commercialization of sports to occur; deals with economic issues as they are connected with public policy and law through recent history and with emerging global issues).

WEBSITE RESOURCES

Note: Websites often change. The following URLs were current when this book was printed. Please check our website (www.mhhe.com/coakley8e) for updates and additions.

www.mhhe.com/coakley8e Information on "outposts in action" and financial data on escalating franchise fees and franchise values; discussions of top athletes' salaries, endorsements, and why ticket prices to top events are increasing so rapidly.

www.fieldofschemes.com Representing the book of the same name by Joanna Cagan and Neil deMause; site contains information from the book as well as key links to recent articles and related sites.

www.sportslaw.org/slapubs.htm The Sports Lawyers Association publishes the *Sports Lawyers Journal*; this site lists articles, many of which are devoted to the legal issues associated with the special legal context in which professional sport teams operate.

www.HockeyZonePlus.com Data on the business and economics of hockey in Canada and around the world; salary information for teams, NHL players, and players in nine leagues around the world, including the professional hockey league in Russia; information on the values of franchises, team ownership, attendance, and coaches' salaries, as well as much additional financial information.

www.nfl.com Any of the sites for professional sport leagues provide a picture of how they present themselves for commercial purposes; don't expect to find any critical information at these sites.

www.wwe.com Illustrates extreme example of "entertainment sport."

chapter 12

(Jay Coakley)

Sports and the Media

Could They Survive Without Each Other?

IGNORING MEDIASPORT today would be like ignoring the role of the church in the Middle Ages or ignoring the role of art in the Renaissance; large parts of society are immersed in media sports today and virtually no aspect of life is untouched by it.

—**Michael Real, media scholar (1998)**

Online Learning Center Resources

Visit *Sports in Society*'s Online Learning Center at **www.mhhe.com/coakley8e** for additional information and study material for this chapter, including

• Self-grading quizzes
• Learning objectives
• Related websites
• Additional readings

A complete outline is available online at
www.mhhe.com/coakley8e.

OF THE MILLIONS [of dollars] that circulate in the media sport industry, only a small proportion is ever used to nurture grassroots sport. . . . [Elite] sport is now, more than ever, the playground of corporate capitalism.

—**Gary Whannel, media scholar (2002)**

IF [TEAMS AND TICKET PRICES] are chasing people out of the arena and onto their couches, it doesn't matter as long as those people are watching sports on television. Television is where corporate America makes its money.

—**David Carter, sports marketing consultant (2002)**

SPORT AND THE MEDIA must surely be the most potent combination of forces amongst the key factors in the globalization game. They have a unique synergy.

—**Robert Davies, chief executive, International Business Leaders Forum (2002)**

The media, including newspapers, magazines, books, movies, radio, television, video games, and the Internet, pervade culture. Although each of us incorporates the media into our lives in different ways, the things we read, hear, and see in the media are important parts of our experience. They frame and influence how we think about the world.

We use media images and messages as we evaluate social events and envision the future. We also use them as we form ideas about everything from personal relationships and consumer products to political candidates and international affairs. This does not mean that we are slaves to the media or that we are passive dupes of those who control the media. The media don't tell us what to think, but they greatly influence what we think about. Our lives and our social worlds are clearly informed by media content, and, if the media didn't exist, our lives would be different.

Sports and the media are interconnected parts of our lives. Sports programming is an important segment of media content, and many sports depend on the media for publicity and revenues. In light of these interconnections, five general questions are considered in this chapter:

1. What are the characteristics of the media?
2. How are sports and the media interconnected?
3. What images and messages are emphasized in the media coverage of sports in North America?
4. Do the media influence sport-related choices and actions?
5. What are the characteristics of sports journalism?

CHARACTERISTICS OF THE MEDIA

Revolutionary changes are occurring in the media. The personal computer and the emergence of the Internet have propelled us into a transition from an era of sponsored and pro-grammed media for mass consumption into an era of personally generated and constructed media content and experiences. The pace and specific implications of this transition are unknown, but college students are among those whose experiences are on the cutting edge of this media revolution. Although it is important to discuss new trends associated with this transition, and to develop frameworks for describing and explaining what is now and will be in the future, it is also important to understand the traditional media and their connections with sports.

In this chapter, I distinguish between print media and electronic media. **Print media** include newspapers, magazines and fanzines, books, catalogues, event programs, and even trading cards: words and images printed on paper and available to many readers. **Electronic media** include radio, television, film, video games, the Internet, and online publications of many types: words, commentary, and images we receive in audio and video forms. Computers and the Internet have blurred traditional lines separating print media from electronic media, because they present virtually unlimited online combinations of the printed word and audio/video content.

Taken together, the media provide *information*, *interpretation*, and *entertainment*. Sometimes they provide two or all three of these things simultaneously. However, entertainment goals are likely to be given a higher priority than information and interpretation in commercial media.

The media connect us with parts of the world and enable us to construct a version of that world. They bring us information, experiences, people, images, and ideas that would not otherwise be part of our everyday lives. However, they connect us with *selected* information experiences, people, images, and ideas, and we construct our sense of reality in the process.

Media content—what we do and do not read, hear, and see—is edited and "re-presented" by others: the producers, editors, program directors, technicians, programmers, camerapersons, writers, commentators, sponsors, and Internet site providers. These people provide information, interpretation, and entertainment based on their interest in one or more of five goals. (1) making profits, (2) shaping values, (3) providing a public service, (4) building their own reputations, and (5) expressing themselves in technical, artistic, or personal ways.

In nations where most of the media are privately owned and operated, the dominant interest is profit making. This is not the only interest, but often it is the most influential. For example, media expert Michael Real explains that there has been no greater force in the construction of media sport reality around the world than "commercial television and its institutionalized value system [emphasizing] profit making, sponsorship, expanded markets, commodification, and competition" (1998, p. 17). The Internet will be the major force influencing media reality in the future, and commercial interests are currently using their resources to influence the value systems that underlie the content of online material.

In nations where the popular media are controlled and operated by the state, the dominant interests are shaping values and providing a public service. However, state control of the media has steadily declined as television and newspapers have become privatized and as more people seek online access to information, interpretation, and entertainment.

Power relations in society also influence the priority given to the five goals that drive media content. Those who make decisions about content and programming act as filters as they select and create the images and messages represented in the media. In the filtering, and representation process, these people usually emphasize images and messages consistent with dominant ideologies in society as a whole. Thus, the media often serve the interests of those who have power and wealth in society. As corporate control of the media has increased and the media have become hypercom-mercialized, media content has emphasized consumerism, individualism, competition, and class inequality as natural and necessary in society, while it marginalizes any emphasis on civic values, anticommercial activities, and political activity (McChesney, 1999).

Of course, there are exceptions to this pattern of promoting corporate interests, but, whenever people use the media to challenge dominant ideologies, they may risk their reputations and careers. This discourages particular types of programming or leads to self-censorship that defers to the interests of those with power and money.

Even when there is legal protection for freedom of speech, as in the United States, those who work in the media often think carefully before presenting images and messages that challenge the interests of those who have power and influence in society, especially when those powerful people own the media and sign the paychecks of those who work for them.

This does not mean that those who control the media ignore what we think or that we in media audiences are forced to read, hear, and see things unrelated to our interests. But it does mean that, apart from e-mail and the websites we create, we seldom have direct control over the content of what we read, listen to, and see in the media. The media re-present to us edited versions of information, interpretation, and entertainment—versions that people who control the media think we want to consume (see figure 12.1).

In the case of sports, those who control the media not only select which sports and events will be covered but also decide what kinds of images and commentary will be emphasized in the coverage (Kinkema and Harris, 1998; Rowe, 1999). When they do this, they play an important role in constructing the overall frameworks that we in media audiences use to define and incorporate sports in our lives.

Those of us who have grown up with television seldom think about media content in this way. For example, when we watch sports on

"Quick! Over here—I think we've got our next "Up Close and Personal" segment for our prime-time program!"

FIGURE 12.1   Media representations of sports are carefully selected and edited. Commentary and images tend to highlight dramatic action, even when it is a minor part of an overall event. Some media people are quite effective in seeking out pain and tragedy.

television, we don't often notice that the images and messages we see and hear have been carefully designed to heighten the dramatic content of the event and emphasize dominant ideologies in the society as a whole. The pregame analysis, the camera coverage, the camera angles, the close-ups, the slow-motion shots, the attention given to particular athletes, the announcer's play-by-play descriptions, the color commentary, the quotes from athletes, and the postgame summary and analysis are all presented to entertain media audiences and keep sponsors happy.

Television commentary and images tend to highlight action, competition, aggression, hard work, individual heroism and achievement, playing with pain, teamwork, and competitive outcomes. Television coverage has become so seamless in its representations of sports that we often

define televised games as "real" games, more real even than the games seen in person at the stadium. Magazine editor Kerry Temple explains:

> It's not just games you're watching. It's soap operas, complete with story lines and plots and plot twists. And good guys and villains, heroes and underdogs. And all this gets scripted into cliffhanger morality plays. . . . And you get all caught up in this until you begin to believe it really matters. (1992, p. 29)

Even though the media coverage of sports is carefully edited and re-presented in total entertainment packages, most of us believe that, when we see a sport event on television, we are seeing it "the way it is." We also think that, when we hear the commentary or read the report on the event, the commentators and journalists are "telling it like it is." We don't usually think that what we are seeing, hearing, and reading is a series of commentaries and images selected for particular reasons and grounded in the social worlds and interests of those producing the event, controlling the images, and delivering the commentary. After all, television coverage gives us only *one* of *many* possible sets of images and messages related to a sport event, and there is a wide array of images and messages that we do *not* get. For example, if we were to go to the event in person, we would see something quite different from the images re-presented on television, and we would come up with our own descriptions and interpretations, which might be completely unrelated to those provided by media commentators.

This point was clearly illustrated in the NBC coverage of the 1996 Olympics in Atlanta. NBC strategically created entertaining drama by re-presenting what media analysts have described as "plausible reality" in their broadcasts; to do this, they deliberately withheld information, so that they could frame events in their terms, even though they knew those terms to be contrary to what was expressed by the athletes and others involved. They gave priority to entertainment over news and information. Former Olympic swimmer Diana Nyad, who was in Atlanta for the event, observed, "Compared to the TV audience, the people in Atlanta have seen a completely different Olympics" (National Public Radio, 1996). She also noted that television and other media coverage revolves around a focus on gold medals, which is a distortion of what the live events involve for most of the athletes and spectators.

According to *New York Times* writer Robert Lipsyte (1996), televised sports have become a form of "sportainment," which is the equivalent of a TV movie that purports to be based on a true story. In other words, television constructs sports and viewer experiences in important ways. And it happens so smoothly that most people think that when they watch a game on television they are experiencing sports in a natural form.

To illustrate this point, think about this question: What if all television documentaries were sponsored by environmental organizations, by women's organizations, or by labor organizations? They would probably raise questions about the content of the programs, the interpretations of the announcers, and the political biases built into the images and commentary. They would look for ways in which the interests of the environmentalists, feminists, or labor organizers shaped the images and messages and influenced the overall information, interpretation, and entertainment in the documentaries.

We know that over 99 percent of all sports programming in the media are sponsored by capitalist corporations, which succeed or fail depending on their ability to generate profits, so why do we not ask more questions about what this means? Why do we spend so little time thinking about *why* we see what we see in sports coverage, *why* we hear the things commentators say during the coverage, and *what* we do *not* read, see, and hear as we consume media sports?

Whether we are aware of it or not, our experiences as spectators are heavily influenced by the decisions of those who control the media,

The XGames were created by ESPN. ESPN is owned by ABC. ABC is owned by the Walt Disney Company. Disney owns the Anaheim Angels, a Major League Baseball team, and the Mighty Ducks, a team in the National Hockey League. These connections influence what we see, hear, and read in connection with media sports. No wonder champion athletes who play on games televised by ABC often say they are going to Disneyland. (Becky Beal)

and their decisions are influenced by social, political, and economic factors—including dominant ideologies related to gender, race, and class (see chapters 8 through 10). We will explore this issue in the section on "Themes Underlying Media Images and Commentary."

Characteristics of the Internet

The Internet extends and radically changes our media connections with the rest of the world, because it gives us virtual access to potentially unlimited and individually created and chosen information, interpretation, and entertainment. A simple way to explain this is to say that being online is partly like having open voice, video, and text connections with everyone in the world who also is online. Some of these connections permit real-time interaction, whereas others provide posted text and images, which we can access on our own terms and in our own time frame. For example, we can interact with fellow fans in chat rooms; ask questions of players and coaches; locate scores, statistics, and various sport-related materials that others have displayed online; and we can play online games associated with sport events around the world.

Unlike television, the Internet is not limited to sequential programming. Television may offer dozens and even hundreds of channels, but we are forced to watch programs on schedules set by television companies, although we can record them and watch them on our own time as the television companies have presented them.

The Internet is unique in that it offers the possibility of accessing variously created media content on our own time at our own pace. In fact, we can even create media content to match our interests and the interests of our friends. This gives us a form of control that radically alters media experiences and mediated realities.

In the case of sports, most people use the Internet as an extension of the existing media. They may link to team sites and listen to live game audio because local radio and television does not cover all games. However, the audio is from television broadcasts of games televised in other regions.

People may go online to order tickets or make reservations for tee-times instead of using the phone to do the same thing. They may go to a team's chat room for postgame discussions instead of joining game-related conversations on talk radio or initiating them by calling friends on the phone. They may use online sites to track game statistics and read posted commentary to complement the commentary and images in the games they watch on television or read about in the print media. They may join online fantasy leagues and use the data summaries provided by an Internet site, so that they don't have to use newspapers' box scores as sources of information about the performance statistics of the players they have selected for their fantasy teams. They may place bets and check scores online instead of calling bookies and watching television to find scores.

The fact that heavily used Internet sites are sponsored and maintained by existing media companies means that the Internet, in some ways, extends the reach, influence, and power of existing media organizations. However, the Internet also provides virtual access to nearly unlimited information around the world and potentially frees people of the control of large media companies.

If we want real-time scores of major spectator sports played anywhere in the world, we can obtain them through many online news sites. Of course, many of us also have access to numerous television channels and may obtain real-time scores through them. However, if we are online, we can go immediately to the sport and the score we are looking for without waiting for a commentator or television channel to provide information about the event.

If we want sports stories by journalists, we now have virtual access to stories written by newspaper, magazine, and online journalists around the world.[1] The material that many people write is not immediately accessible online,

---

[1] Internet sports reporters often have difficulties obtaining "press passes and privileges" at traditional sport events. Although events such as the XGames issue over one-third of their press credentials to "dot.com" reporters, Internet sites were denied credentials at the 2000 NCAA Men's Final Four games. The site representatives argued with the NCAA, saying that they have ten times the readers that an average city daily newspaper has.

but we are moving in that direction. We already know that certain sources require subscriptions for access. There are registrations and subscriber fees, and we make choices, just as we do with our newspaper and magazine subscriptions. The difference is that with online material we are not forced to wait for our newspapers or magazines to be delivered by carriers or surface mail, and we have free sites offering many of the same things as the sites that require fees.

Information, interpretation, and entertainment from numerous sources continue to be available to us. It will remain that way as long as the Internet remains open to all and people are committed to public access to information and ideas. However, large corporations, especially media and entertainment companies, are working hard and investing massive amounts of money to frame and shape the Internet in terms that fit their interests. This means that the Internet is contested terrain, and there will be important struggles over issues of access, ownership, and the rights of users to share information and ideas. Through 2003, these struggles have revolved around sharing music files. But in the longer term they have important implications for the future of democracy and the dynamics of social life as a whole. If large media corporations suppress policies that guarantee a free and open Internet, they will undermine a key opportunity to revolutionize the media.

Will the Internet primarily be a vehicle for democratizing social life and freely sharing ideas and information without constraints set by private interests? Or will the Internet primarily be a means of expanding capital, increasing productivity and consumption, reproducing the values that drive market economies, and maintaining the notion that corporations are the source of pleasure and excitement in our lives? The answers to these questions will emerge as we struggle over how the Internet will be incorporated into our lives.

As more of us experience sports online, buy the software needed for coordinated audio/video/data streaming, and gain access to broadband Internet connections, we will have more control over the conditions of media sport consumption. Theoretically, the Internet can provide each of us with the ability to create our own spectator sport realities and experiences.

People today can have interactive experiences through online connections during a game. In the future, they will use the Internet to make choices about camera angles during a game, follow athletes into locker rooms, listen to what coaches and players say, pull up data they wish to see during the game, and even select audio commentary or interactive commentary as they watch. If they subscribe to certain sites, they will watch players' home lives. This, of course, will bring spectators closer and closer to the people, emotions, and actions in events.

As this occurs, being a spectator will become a more active and creative experience, and spectators will participate directly in the construction of media reality. In a sense, they will assume positions similar to those of journalists and announcers and will become part of the construction of events. How this will change the reality of mediated sports and our experience of them remains to be seen.

The future is difficult to predict. Will people choose 500-channel high-definition digital television over the medium of the Internet? Will WebTV become widespread, so that people can have both? Will the economics of technology and the "digital divide" between technology haves and have-nots segregate spectators even further by social class? Will the culture of the Internet favor some people over others, or will it enable all spectators to create realities that fit interests related to gender, race and ethnicity, and social class? Answers to these questions will depend on forces shaping the future of the Internet. Commercial forces guarantee that the first people to enjoy new spectator experiences and realities will be those with the money or organizational connections to buy or gain access to the hardware, software, and bandwidth to move around the Internet as fast as they wish and to as many sites as they wish. Class relations will influence future Internet spectator experiences, but, depending on public policies and programs, the Internet could also blur class differences when it comes to future access to information, interpretation, and entertainment.

Characteristics of Video Games and Virtual Sports

Sports also come into our lives through video games and virtual experiences. Sport video games are popular in wealthy nations, and some people have even participated in virtual sports of various types, although most virtual sports are experimental and not available for general participation.

The images in video games have become increasingly lifelike, and those who play the games have uniquely active spectator experiences. Social science research on video games has focused on violence and gender issues in action games generally. It has not focused on games modeled after "real" sports.

It is clear that people who play sport video games have different experiences than those who watch televised sport events. Golf fans may now match their video golf skills with the physical skills of pro golfers by going online and golfing on the same course as Tiger Woods or other high-profile players whose shots have been represented and archived through digitized images. This changes watching a tournament into a participatory experience, unlike spectator experiences in the past. Research is needed to document, describe, and analyze these differences and the character of the experiences and realities of those who select video games, choose challenges, control action, and compete against other players or standards programmed into the game.

Those who play video sports games are usually regular consumers of standard sport media events. Their interest in and enjoyment of the video games is tied to their knowledge about a sport, sport teams, and athletes. This knowledge continues to be gained primarily through social relationships and traditional media. The experience of playing and watching video games will change as more people play each other on the Internet in worldwide leagues while others watch. It is unknown whether such games will actually replace other forms of sports media consumption or extend them. This and related issues are discussed in the box "No Refs. No Rules. No Mercy."

The experiences of video game players are influenced by the ethos that underlies the programmed images and actions in the games. Game players have choices, but those choices are not unlimited, nor are they ideologically neutral. The games clearly express the elements of traditional masculinity and other values associated with major media sports, although research is needed on what this means for the experiences of those who play the games.

Virtual sports have not been discussed among those who study sports in society. As the technology of virtual reality evolves, people will be able to become immersed in new ways in the action of an activity. What this will mean is unknown at this time.

Many people in the future may prefer virtual sports to what we define as sports today. In fact, a book on sports in society written fifty years from now may focus almost exclusively on the experiences and realities of a wide variety of virtual sports and the athletes who participate in them. In the meantime, it is important to understand the relationship between sports and the media in the early twenty-first century and to know how each has influenced the other.

SPORTS AND THE MEDIA: A TWO-WAY RELATIONSHIP

The media and the commercialization of sports are closely related topics in the sociology of sport. In fact, the media intensify and extend the process and consequences of commercialization. For this reason, much attention has been given to how sports have been influenced by the media, whereas less attention has been given to how the media have been influenced by sports. We do know that there is a reciprocal relationship between these two important spheres of life: each has influenced the other, and each has grown to depend on the other for its popularity and commercial success.

Sports Depend on the Media

The existence and success of commercial sports and sport organizations depend heavily on the media, but this statement must be qualified. People played sports long before the media began to cover and re-present the events. Even now, people participate in a variety of sports that receive no media coverage. When sports exist just for the participants, there is no urgent need to advertise games, report on the action, publish results, and interpret what happened. The players already know these things, and they are the only ones who matter. There is no need to attract and entertain ticket-buying spectators. It is only when sports become commercial entertainment that they depend on the media.

Sports are unique forms of entertainment. They require the media to provide a combination of coverage *and* news. People attend plays and concerts, and engage in many leisure activities without needing regular media coverage to enhance enjoyment. However, with sports, this coverage is very important. When a stage play is over, it's over—except for a review after opening night and the personal conversations of those who attended the play. When a sport event is over, many people wish to discuss statistics, important plays, records, standings, the overall performances of the players and teams, upcoming games or matches, the importance of the game or match in terms of the season as a whole, the postseason, the next season, and so on. The media are important vehicles for these discussions.

Without media coverage, the popularity and revenue-generating potential of commercial spectator sports would be seriously limited. Information about events generates interest, and interest generates revenues from the sale of tickets, luxury suites, club seats, concessions, parking, team logo merchandise, and licensing rights. After games or matches have been played, the scores become news items, and the interpretations of the action become entertainment for fans, regardless of whether they attended the event in person or not. This seems to be the case globally—for bullfights in Mexico, hockey games in Canada, soccer matches in Brazil, and sumo wrestling bouts in Japan.

Sports promoters and team owners are well aware of the need for the media coverage of sports. Therefore, they often go out of their way to accommodate reporters, commentators, and photographers (Koppett, 1994). Approved media personnel are given comfortable seats in press boxes, access to the fields of play and the players' locker rooms, summaries of statistics and player information, and play-by-play information on what is happening during events. Providing these services costs money, but it guarantees media coverage, and it encourages those covering the events to be supportive and sympathetic in what they show, write, and say.

Although all commercial spectator sports depend on the media, some of them have a special dependence on television. Television is different from the other media in that television companies pay considerable amounts of money for broadcasting rights. As shown in table 12.1 and figure 12.2, rights fees provide sports with predictable sources of income. Once contracts are signed, television money can be counted on, regardless of bad weather, injuries to key players, and the other factors that interfere with ticket sales and with other on-site revenue streams. Without television contracts, commercial success is unlikely for most spectator sports.

Television revenues also have much greater growth potential than do revenues from gate

Table 12.1   Escalating annual media rights fees for major commercial sports in the United States (in millions of dollars)[a]

Sport	1986	1991	1996	2001	2005
NFL	400	900	1,100	2,200	2,200
MLB[b]	183	365	420	417	558
NBA	30	219	275	660	767
NHL[c]	22	38	77	120	120
NASCAR	3	NA	NA	412	
NCAA Men's Basketball Tournament	31	143	216	216	550[d]
NCAA (all women's championships)	NA	NA	NA	NA	18.5
WNBA	NA	NA	NA	0	0[e]

[a]These amounts are not inflation-adjusted. Most data come from *USA Today*.
[b]Amounts for baseball do not include local television or radio rights fees negotiated by individual teams or national radio rights fees; amount for 1996 includes national radio rights.
[c]Includes U.S. and Canadian rights; only U.S. rights for 2001.
[d]Will gradually increase to $764 million in 2013; these amounts include rights to broadcast on television, radio, and the Internet the men's basketball tournament and other championship events, excluding football.
[e]This could change if contracts expiring in 2003 are negotiated with new terms.

receipts. Only so many tickets can be sold to an event, and tickets can cost only so much without turning people off. But television audiences can include literally billions of viewers, now that satellite technology transmits signals to most locations around the globe. For example, Australian Olympic scholars Kristine Toohey and Anthony Veal (2000) estimate that a cumulative audience of over 25 billion viewers in over 200 countries watched television coverage of the 2000 Olympic Games in Sydney, Australia. The audience was attracted by 3200 hours of coverage supplied by 180 broadcasting organizations that paid over $800 million of rights fees to the International Olympic Committee. These organizations covered 290 events with over 10,000 personnel, 700 cameras, 400 video tape machines, and fifty trailers of equipment. The goal was to turn the entire world into an audience for sports. More recently 1.1 billion people watched Brazil's men's team defeat Germany in the finals of the 2002 World Cup. The cumulative audience for the sixty-four games during the Cup tournament was over 31 billion people. This makes it the most viewed event in television history.

The size of the potential TV audience and the deregulation of the television industry are the two main reasons television rights have increased in value at phenomenal rates since the early 1970s (Bellamy, 1998). Television rights fees not only have made commercial sports more

The media enable some athletes to become global celebrities and benefit from windfall income related to their popularity. They know that their celebrity depends on using and maintaining close connections with the media. Michael Jordan has been an expert at doing this. (Darron Cummings; AP/Wide World Photos)

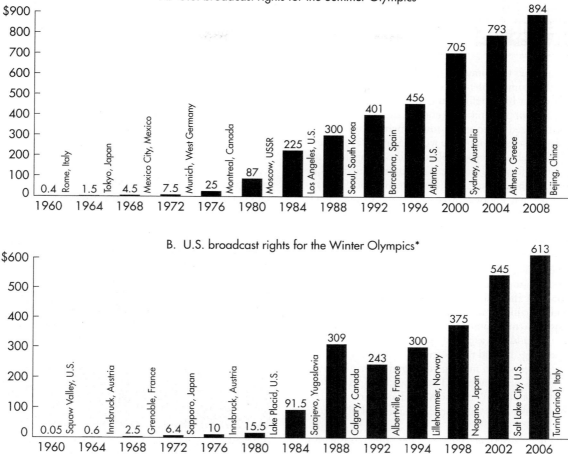

A. U.S. broadcast rights for the Summer Olympics*

B. U.S. broadcast rights for the Winter Olympics*

*The IOC also receives rights fees from other television companies around the world. Europe, Japan, and continental Asia are paying increasingly higher fees. NBC paid about $250 million more for the Sydney Games than for the Atlanta Games because it televised 276 hours of coverage on its cable channels, CNBC and MSNBC. This was in addition to the 161 hours it televised on NBC. Its goal of using the Olympics to boost global legitimacy and viewer ratings for its cable stations was successful; plus, the network made a 50-million-dollar profit on the games themselves.

FIGURE 12.2   Escalating media rights fees for the Olympics (in millions of dollars).

profitable for promoters and team owners but also have increased the attractiveness of sports as vehicles for advertising products nationally and internationally (Whitson, 1998). This enables athletes to demand higher salaries and turns some of the athletes into national and international celebrities, who then use their celebrity status to endorse products sold around the world.

For example, Tiger Woods' global popularity is due as much to the invention of the satellite dish as to his golf skills or the clubs he uses.

As it becomes realistic to broadcast games and events on the Internet, there will be interesting changes in how media rights are negotiated. The global reach of the Internet creates new possibilities for big companies, which want

REFLECT ON SPORTS

"No Refs. No Rules. No Mercy."*
Video Games as Simulated Sports

Video games that simulate sports have become so realistic that some athletes even use them to train. The games offer high-definition graphics, intense interactivity, and opportunities to control the action.

Organized video game tournaments attract thousands of players around the world. Some players identify themselves as cyberathletes and participate in the Cyber Professional League. They train regularly; they have fans and agents; and, if they are high-profile players, they may endorse products related to the games. Prizes for the big tournaments may be cash—up to $50,000—or cars. *Game Now* magazine enables players to keep up with the latest news and developments.

John Madden, known to football fans over the age of thirty as a former NFL coach and longtime NFL commentator (recently on *Monday Night Football*), is known to the under-thirty-year-old game player as a video game brand. His *Madden NFL* games are among the most popular video games on the market. When Madden was asked to comment on the video game craze, he said that software developers have become successful in making video games that look like the games on television. They have been so successful, he noted, that television producers are now trying to make the games on television look like video games.

When developers create games, they consult top athletes to make sure that game situations and players' movements are portrayed accurately. Most top players take a special interest in this process because they want their moves and actions in the game to match their moves and actions on the playing field. Even their unique mannerisms are filmed, so that they can be portrayed in the video games.

Some of the games have become so popular with the athletes themselves that coaches worry that they are distracting players from real games. In fact, according to an ESPN report on video games, some NFL and NBA players would rather play video games of their sports than watch televised real-time games.

Some race car drivers work with software developers to make sure that the tracks simulated in racing games match the tracks on which real races are held. This enables them to use the games to quicken their reflexes and improve eye-hand coordination and steering

This image from EA Sports™ *Madden NFL 2003*, a popular video game, shows that graphics in these games are very similar to televised images from real-time games. As television producers use filters to make real-time games appear more like video games, we see an interesting blurring of image and reality. (© 2002 Electronic Arts, Inc.; © 2002 NFL Players; reproduced with permission)

to reach relatively wealthy people worldwide; however, it also creates challenges, because it cuts into the television rights that have been negotiated within various regions around the world. This challenge has, for example, pre-

vented the International Olympic Committee (IOC) from selling Internet rights to the Olympics. After all, what would NBC television say if AOL Time Warner or Fox Sports Online were to present the Olympics on the Internet wheel responses at the same time that they encounter precisely simulated track designs. Some drivers claim that playing the games helps them visualize the characteristics and designs of the tracks on which they race.

A goal of software designers is to develop games that match the audio, visual, and emotional experiences of the players themselves. Some designers dream about creating a game that actually offers a wider range of emotional experiences than players have in real-time games. These goals and the financial stakes associated with them push game designers to refine graphics, action, and game possibilities.

Meanwhile, more and more children are being introduced to sports through video games. They learn rules and game strategies as they play. They are introduced to the moves involved in a sport, and their initial emotional experiences in certain sports are felt in front of their televisions rather than on playing fields.

Adult game players outnumber the children who play. Many college students, most of them young men, are avid game players. Status among dorm residents may even reflect prowess in simulated sports. Playing games provides regular social occasions similar to those provided by regular sport events.

As high-speed Internet connections become more common, cybersports are bound to become more popular. Technology will enable players to compete with opponents around the world and even form teams with rosters of players who have never met each other in person. Spectators will be able to watch games online and even listen to the voices of the players as they compete. I would be surprised if bookies did not provide opportunities for players and spectators to place bets on sport video game outcomes.

These developments raise numerous sociological questions and issues. Studies of simulated sports and video games are rare. We know little about the experiences of players, the social settings created around the games, and what players learn about themselves and others during their experiences.

Will playing video games influence how people play real-time sports? Will the norms in real-time sports be influenced by players' experiences in simulated sports? Will children be introduced to sports through video games rather than informal games? If so, will video game experiences influence what they will expect in real-time games?

After playing video sports for two years, will six-year-olds be willing to listen to whistle-blowing coaches when they are accustomed to controlling players, game strategies, and game conditions on their own? Will children bring new forms of game knowledge to the playing fields where they create and play informal and formally organized games? How will that knowledge influence the games they play?

Will some children simply stay home in front of their monitors and televisions as they control their own games without accommodating the wishes of teammates or obeying the commands of coaches? Will they know that, when they do this, they are submitting themselves to the ideas and boundaries set by the software designers and game producers? To whom are those designers and producers accountable? *What do you think?*

---

*Sales logo of the game *NFL Blitz*. For more information on this topic, see ESPN's *Outside the Lines* primetime special, *Simulating Sports: The Video Game Craze*.

· ·

and cut into NBC's audience in the United States and around the world on its cable stations, CNBC and MSNBC? The answer: NBC and every other company that had bought television rights would sue the IOC.

Have Commercial Sports Sold Out to the Media?   There is no question that some sports have become dependent on television for revenues and publicity. The NFL, for example, brings in about 60 percent of its revenues from television contracts. However, television money comes with strings attached.

Accommodating the interests of commercial television has required numerous changes in the ways sports are organized, packaged, scheduled, and presented. Some of these changes include the following:

- The schedules and starting times for many sport events have been altered to fit television's programming needs.
- Halftime periods in certain sports have been shortened, so that television audiences will be more likely to stay tuned to events.
- Prearranged schedules of time-outs have been added to football, basketball, and hockey games to make time for more commercials.
- Teams, leagues, and tournaments have been formed or realigned to take advantage of regional media markets and to build national and even international fan bases for sports, leagues, and teams.

Many other changes associated with television coverage are not entirely due to the influence of television. For example, college football teams added an eleventh game to their schedules, and professional teams extended their seasons and the number of games played. But these changes would have occurred even without television. Commercial sports would have added extra games simply to increase gate receipts. Extra games do make television contracts more lucrative, but the economic reasons for adding games include more than just the sale of television rights. The same is true for the additions of sudden death overtime periods in some sports, the tiebreaker scoring method in tennis, the addition of medal play in golf, and the three-point shot in basketball. Each of these changes is grounded in general commercial interests that exist apart from television coverage. However, *television adds to the urgency and importance of these changes.*

Television *expands and intensifies* the commercial interests that are already an important part of spectator sports in many societies (Bellamy, 1998). Although some changes in sports result from the requirements of television coverage, the real reason for most changes over the past three decades has been the desire to produce more marketable entertainment for all spectators and a more attractive commercial package for sponsors and advertisers.

These changes have been made willingly in most cases. The trade-offs usually have been attractive for both players and sponsors. In fact, many of the sports and athletes not currently receiving television coverage gladly would make changes in the way their events are packaged, scheduled, and presented if they could reap the attention and money associated with television contracts. Are there limits to what they would change for television coverage? In many cases, yes; in a few cases, no. Selling out is not so much a matter of making changes. It is a matter of sharing control over the conditions of sports participation.

Have the Media Corrupted Sports? When people discuss sports and the media, many voice the concern that dependence on the media, especially dependence on television, might corrupt sports. However, the notion that television is the root of all evil in sports fails to take into account two factors:

1. *Sports are not shaped primarily by the media in general or by television in particular.* The idea that television by itself has somehow transformed sports does not hold up under careful examination. Sports are social constructions. As such, they are created over time through interactions among athletes, facility directors, sport team owners, event promoters, media representatives, sponsors, advertisers, agents, and spectators—all of whom have diverse interests. The dynamics of these interactions are grounded in power relations and shaped by the resources held by different people at different times. Although

not everyone has equal influence over changes occurring in sports, media interests are not the only factors producing changes in sports or in the relationship between sports and the media. It is unrealistic to think that those who control the media determine sports to fit their interests alone. But it is equally unrealistic to ignore their power.

2. *The media, including television, do not operate in a political and economic vacuum.* The concerns of those connected with sports and the relationships they have with one another are heavily influenced by the social, political, and economic contexts in which they live. The media in most countries are regulated by government agencies and policies. Although these regulations have been loosened or lifted in recent years, the media must negotiate contracts with teams and leagues under legal constraints. Economic factors also constrain the media by setting limits on the value of sponsorships and advertising time and by shaping the climate in which types of programming, such as pay-per-view sports and cable and satellite subscriptions, might be profitable. Finally, the media also are constrained by social factors, which inform people's decisions on whether they will read about, listen to, or watch sports.

These two factors raise serious questions about whether sports have been corrupted by the media. There are certainly important connections between these two spheres of life, but those connections are grounded in complex sets of social, economic, and political relationships, which change over time and vary from culture to culture. It is these relationships that we must understand if we wish to study the media's impact on sports. In other words, the conclusion that the media corrupt sports is based on an incomplete understanding of how the social world works and how sports are connected with social relations in society.

With that said, it is also important to remember that nearly all of the most powerful people in sports around the world are CEOs or owners of major, global corporations. Nearly all of them are white men from English-speaking nations, and each wants to offer programming that people around the globe will watch and that transnational corporations will sponsor and use as advertising vehicles. The sports selected for national and global coverage have been and will continue to be dependent on the media for their commercial success, and the salaries and endorsement income of many top athletes also have been and will continue to be dependent on the media. However, there are two sides to this process. This brings us to the next issue.

The Media Depend on Sports

There is much more to the media than sports coverage. This is especially true for magazines, books, radio, movies, and the Internet, although it is less true for newspapers and television. The Internet does not depend on sports, but certain online services may make money on sports fans who use the Internet to get up-to-the-minute scores, to obtain information about particular events, to place bets with off-shore bookies, and to enter online discussions about athletes, teams, and events.

Neither the book publishing nor the movie industry depends on sports. Until recently, there have been very few successful books and movies about sports. The urgency and uncertainty that are so compelling in live sports are difficult to capture in these media. However, since the late 1980s, both publishers and movie studios have produced projects with tragic, inspiring, and outrageous stories about sports figures.

Most radio stations give coverage to sports only in their news segments, although local football, baseball, and men's basketball games often are broadcast live on local radio stations. Some communities have talk radio stations that feature sports talk programs that attract large audiences.

These audiences also have clear demographics: most listeners are young men with higher than average incomes. This, of course, helps radio stations sell advertising.

Most magazines devote little or no attention to sports coverage, although the number of general and special interest sport magazines and fanzines in the United States and other countries is increasing. A quick study of any local magazine rack shows that people who are interested in skiing, skateboarding, snowboarding, biking, motocross, car racing, and dozens of other sports now have magazines devoted to their interests.

The media most dependent on sports are newspapers and television. The companies that control these media are at least partially dependent on sports for their commercial success. This is especially true in the United States.

Newspapers Newspapers at the beginning of the twentieth century had a sports page, which consisted of a few notices about upcoming activities, a short story or two about races or college games, and possibly some scores of local games. By the late 1920s, the sports page had grown into the sports "section," which resembled the sports sections of today's newspapers. As sports have become highly visible everyday life activities in many postindustrial societies, special daily and weekly sports newspapers have emerged, which are completely dependent on sports. Furthermore, sports coverage has gradually grown to account for 25 percent or more of the content of major newspapers in most cities.

In most major North American newspapers, more daily coverage is given to sports than to any other single topic of interest, including business or politics. The sports section is the most widely read section of the paper. It accounts for at least one-third of the total circulation and a significant amount of the advertising revenues for big-city newspapers. It attracts advertisers who might not put ads in other sections of the paper. Advertisers know that, if they want to reach young to middle-aged males with average or above-average incomes, they should place ads in the sports section. This is an attractive prospect for businesses that sell tires, automobile supplies, new cars, car leases, airline tickets for business travelers, alcoholic beverages, power tools, building supplies, sporting goods, hair growth products, and even steroids. Other advertisers are clinics and doctors specializing in treating impotence, selling Viagra, or providing testosterone and other hormone therapies. Additionally, there are bars or clubs providing naked or near-naked female models and dancers and organizations offering gambling advice and opportunities (see a sample of major-city newspapers to confirm this). Ads for all these products and services generate considerable revenues for newspapers.

The future of newspapers' dependence on sports is difficult to predict. If the Internet becomes the main source of information about big-time sports nationally and around the world, then newspapers may return to emphasizing information and the interpretation of local sports, including high school varsity teams, small college teams, and even youth sports. This can already be seen as more major-city newspapers publish "prep sections" on a weekly basis and highlight local athletes. They know that, if people in Seattle use the Internet to read about the Seahawks, they will still have to buy the local paper to read about Newport High School's football and volleyball teams.

Television Some television companies in North America also have developed a dependence on sports for programming content and advertising revenues. For example, sport events are a major part of the programming schedules of national network stations in the United States and many cable and satellite-based stations. Some television companies even sponsor events, which they then promote and televise, such as ESPN's ownership and presentation of the XGames.

Sports account for a growing proportion of income made on the sales of commercial time by television companies. Many cable and satellite companies have used sport programs to attract subscribers from particular segments of the viewing public, and then they have sold audiences to advertisers. In 2003, ESPN's three channels transmitted sports coverage to more than 150 countries in more than a dozen languages. Fox Sports channels also televise a range of sports coverage around the world. People in the United States and some other parts of the world can watch sport programs nearly 24 hours a day, if they have the time and interest and pay for the cable or satellite connections and sports events channel packages. In fact, over the next few years, we can expect to see a half dozen cable channels dedicated exclusively to particular sports, such as the National College Sports Network, the Tennis Channel, Blackbelt TV, NBA TV, The Football Network, and others.

An attractive feature of sport programs for the major U.S. media companies is that events often are scheduled on Saturday and Sunday afternoons—the slowest time periods of the week for general television viewing. Sport events are the most popular weekend programs, especially among male viewers who may not watch much television at other times during the week. This means the networks are able to sell advertising time at relatively high rates during what normally would be dead time for programming.

Media corporations also use sport programs to attract commercial sponsors that might take their advertising dollars elsewhere if television stations did not cover certain sports. For example, games in major men's team sports are ideal for promoting the sales of beer, life insurance, trucks and cars, computers, investment services, credit cards, and air travel. The people in the advertising departments of major corporations realize that sports attract male viewers. They also realize that most business travelers are men and that many men make family decisions on the purchases of beer, cars, computers, investments, and life insurance. Finally, advertisers also may be interested in associating their product or service with the culturally positive image

NBC Sports pays the University of Notre Dame about $9.2 million per year to televise its football games. The games are televised on Saturday afternoons, usually a slow time for network programming. The games attract a relatively high-status male audience, which NBC can deliver to sponsors, who will pay large fees to deliver their messages to that audience. (Jay Coakley)

of sports. This is especially important for a product such as beer, which may be a target for neo-prohibitionists, or tobacco, which is a frequent target of health advocates, among others.

Golf and tennis are special cases for television programming. These sports attract few viewers, and the ratings are exceptionally low. However, the audience for these sports is attractive to certain advertisers. It is made up of people from the highest income groups in the United States, including many professionals and business executives. This is why television coverage of golf and tennis is sponsored by companies selling luxury cars and high-priced sports cars, business and personal computers, imported beers, investment opportunities with brokers and consultants, and trips to exclusive vacation areas. This is also why the networks continue to carry these programs despite low ratings. Advertisers are willing to pay high fees to reach high-income consumers and those executives who make decisions to buy thousands of "company cars," and computers at the same time that they invest millions of dollars for employee pension plans.

With such viewers, these programs don't need high ratings to stay on the air.

In the mid-1990s, television executives "discovered" women viewers of sports and women's sports. Data since the late 1980s have indicated that women have made up more than half the viewing audiences for both Winter and Summer Olympic Games. This has led NBC to hype women's sports, to appeal to women viewers during subsequent telecasts of the games, and to emphasize gender equity in scripted studio commentary, although the actual on-site coverage of events has favored men, as it has in past games (Eastman and Billings, 1999).

Other women's sports have also attracted television coverage, although the coverage they receive pales in comparison with the coverage received by men's sports. Women's events don't receive more coverage partly because women viewers of women's games have not been identified as a target audience by advertisers. Furthermore, men make up over half of the viewing audience for most women's sports. Because those men also watch men's sports, sponsors have already reached them during the coverage of men's events.

Cable and satellite television companies also have found they can attract advertising money by televising sports that appeal to clearly identified segments of consumers. For example, the XGames, which consist of sports appealing to young people, especially young males between twelve and twenty-five years old, attract advertisers selling soft drinks, beer, telecommunications products, and sports equipment such as helmets, shoes, and skateboards.

Over the past two decades, television companies have paid rapidly increasing amounts of money for the rights to televise certain sports. This was shown previously in the data in table 12.1 and figure 12.2. The contracts for these rights are negotiated every few years; some may be negotiated annually. In the case of the major men's spectator sports in the United States and around the world, contracts may involve hundreds of millions of dollars, and more than a billion dollars, in the cases of the Olympics, the NFL, the NBA, the NCAA Men's College Basketball Tournament, soccer's World Cup, and premier-level soccer in England.

Figure 12.3 and table 12.1 illustrate the increases in television rights fees paid by U.S.

Table 12.2 The top twenty-five U.S. network telecasts ranked by household projections (1961–2002)

Program	Date	Average U.S. Audience (in Millions)[a]
1. *M*A*S*H** (special)	2/28/83	50.2
2. Winter Olympics	2/23/94[b]	45.7
3. Super Bowl XXX	1/28/96	44.2
4. Super Bowl XXXII	1/25/98	43.6
5. Super Bowl XXXIV	1/30/00	43.6
6. Super Bowl XXVIII	1/30/94	42.9
7. Super Bowl XXXVI	2/3/02	42.6
8. *Cheers*	1/20/93	42.4
9. Super Bowl XXXI	1/26/97	42.0
10. Super Bowl XXVII	1/31/93	42.0
11. Winter Olympics	2/25/94[b]	41.5
12. Super Bowl XX	1/26/86	41.5
13. *Dallas*	11/21/80	41.5
14. Super Bowl XXXV	1/28/01	41.3
15. *Seinfeld*	5/14/98	40.5
16. Super Bowl XVII	1/30/83	40.5
17. Super Bowl XXI	1/25/87	40.0
18. Super Bowl XVI	1/24/84	40.0
19. Super Bowl XXXIII	1/31/99	39.9
20. Super Bowl XXIX	1/29/95	39.4
21. Super Bowl XIX	1/20/85	39.4
22. Super Bowl XXIII	1/22/89	39.4
23. Super Bowl XXV	1/27/91	39.0
24. Super Bowl XVIII	1/22/84	38.9
25. *NBC Sunday Night Movie* (*The Day After*)	11/20/83	38.6

Source: Based on data from A.C. Nielson as of September 2002.
[a]Numbers refer to the average audience for the duration of the telecast; average telecast for a Super Bowl game is about 210 minutes.
[b]Telecasts on these days featured women's figure skating—specifically, the programs skated by Nancy Kerrigan and Tonya Harding.

FIGURE 12.3 A handful of powerful global media companies control media representations of sports around the world. This has serious implications for what sports we see or don't see, especially in developing nations. Some people wonder what this will mean in the long run, whereas others don't give it much thought as they watch what the media re-present.

media companies for the Olympic Games and major men's professional team sports. These data indicate that television executives want sports in their programming, and they think that sports will increase their profits. They realize that the Olympics have become the biggest world television event in history, that eighteen of the top twenty-five television programs in U.S. history have been Super Bowls (see table 12.2), that the cost of advertising on the *top* sport events is generally much higher than it is for other types of programs ($2.2 million for a thirty-second slot during the 2003 Super Bowl), that sports events involve minimal production costs, and that they have relatively predictable ratings. Even though there have been cases in which television companies have lost money on sports, profits are generally good, and sport programs can be used as a platform to promote other programs and attract hard-to-reach viewers.

Another trend is that, as televised sport events have increased, the ratings for many particular events have gone down. As people have more choices, the viewing audience becomes frag-

mented. More people are watching television sports, but there are more choices than ever before. This means that rights fees for the very large events will continue to increase, but fees for other events, including some "special interest" events (such as bowling, in-line skating championships, and international skiing races) will be limited. When interest among particular viewers is especially strong, as for championship boxing and certain other sport events, pay-per-view (PPV) sports programming will push rights fees to high levels. Television companies know that PPV sports can generate massive revenues, but they also know that pay-per-view events must be introduced cautiously and selectively. Many viewers are not willing to pay upfront to see an event on television; nor are they accustomed to doing so. In the meantime, pay-TV has become an accepted part of people's lives in the form of subscription fees for cable and satellite sports channels. In fact, subscription fees in the United States increased nearly 400 percent between 1985 and 2003, and part of the increase was due to rights fees paid by cable companies to televise sports.

The fragmentation of television sports audiences will continue. New technology brings as many as 500 channels into some people's homes. Some of these channels will provide sports coverage and will come to depend on sports for their income. As new digital television technology is sold to consumers around the world, it is certain that television companies will use sport events strategically to encourage consumers to invest in the switch from their old analog televisions to digital sets.

Regular sports programming provides opportunities for major television companies to promote their other programs and boost ratings during the rest of the week. It also serves a public relations function, by enhancing the image and legitimacy of television among people who may watch very few programs other than sports.

In 1994, Rupert Murdoch, owner of the Fox Television Network in the United States, paid the NFL $1.58 billion and the NHL $155 million in an attempt to use pro football and hockey coverage between 1995 and 1999 as the centerpiece of a global corporate expansion strategy. Murdoch's idea was to use "Fox-televised athletes as a sort of human growth hormone for the network's other programming" (Knisley, 1996). He knew that North American television viewers were dedicated to watching NFL football and NHL hockey, and he used that knowledge to leverage his plan to acquire local television affiliates around the United States and thereby compete with the major television networks. Murdoch also planned to use sports coverage as part of a global expansion through his other media companies around the world. He even bought the Los Angeles Dodgers in 1998 for $311 million (a record payment for a baseball franchise at the time) and tried to purchase the Manchester United Football Club in England in 1999 for $1 billion. Manchester United is the largest and most highly valued soccer club in the world, and the British government disallowed his takeover bid because it would have given him too much control over sports. However, his overall strategy of acquiring sport teams and television rights to cover sports has worked, and his News Corp conglomerate is among the most powerful media organizations in the world. In late 1997, Fox Television, owned by Murdoch, was able to pay $4.4 billion for the rights to televise selected NFL games through 2005.

Other corporations have also used this strategy as they have initiated a series of vertical and horizontal mergers and acquisitions in the entertainment, news, sports, television, and Internet industries. As the twenty-first century began, there were eight major global corporate conglomerates controlling most of what we do and don't read, see, and hear in the media (McChesney, 1999).

When America Online (AOL) bought Time Warner, the world's biggest media company and all of its sports holdings (including the CNN/*Sports Illustrated* combination), the centralization of print and electronic media power continued and embraced the Internet in the process. Of course, this has serious implications for the types of sports programs we see and don't see, what we hear and don't hear in commentary, the sites we visit on the Internet, and the corporate messages that are presented in connection with athletes, teams, events, and sport places (see figure 12.3). More important, it has serious implications for the viability of democracy around the world, because democracy depends on the free flow of information from diverse sources.

Sports and the Media: A Relationship Fueled by Economics and Ideology

There is no question that commercial spectator sports depend heavily on the media, although noncommercial sports continue to exist and often thrive without media coverage. Similarly, some media companies that publish daily newspapers in the United States and produce television programs depend on sports to generate circulation and viewer ratings.

When media are privatized and run as for-profit businesses, the interdependence of sports and the media is grounded primarily in concerns about money and profits. Sports can sell newspapers and attract television viewers. This helps sell advertising space and advertising time. In turn, the media generate revenues for sport organizations and create sport-related images, which can be sold in connection with everything from coffee mugs and jackets to shoes and baseball gloves. Sports and the media clearly have a relationship in which each depends on the other for its commercial success and its prominent place in popular culture in many societies around the world.

Since the 1970s, global economic factors have intensified the relationship between sports and the media. Major transnational corporations have needed vehicles for developing global name recognition, cultural legitimacy, and product familiarity. They also have been eager to find ways to promote ideological support for a way of life based on consumption, competition, individual achievement, and comparisons of status and material possessions. Media sports clearly have offered global corporations a means of meeting these needs: certain sport events attract worldwide attention; satellite technology takes television signals around the world; sport images are associated with recognizable symbols and pleasurable experiences by billions of people; and sports and athletes usually can be presented in politically safe ways by linking them with local identities and then using them to market products, values, and lifestyles that are related to local cultures or to accepted forms of global culture. Therefore, powerful transnational corporations have underwritten or sponsored the media coverage of sports, especially on television.

An important source of corporate sponsorship money for sports comes from the alcohol and tobacco industries. For them, the sports media are key vehicles for presenting and promoting their products in connection with activities defined as healthy by most people around the world. This enables them to present positive corporate and brand images, which they hope will counteract negative images about their products. We find these images most frequently in print media and stadium signage. They regularly appear in the prime advertising space of sports magazines and on the surfaces of stadiums and other facilities that host car, dog, and horse races. This is important to tobacco and alcohol companies, because their advertising has been banned on television in some nations. The fact that sports magazines receiving large amounts of advertising money from these companies do not publish critical articles about sports and smoking and drinking is an important side benefit for the companies (Crompton, 1993).

Finally, it is important to remember that the male executives of large media corporations love sports on a personal level. They use sports metaphors in their everyday business language, they like to be around sports figures, and they pay high-profile coaches up to $50,000 for a one-hour speech to boost the morale and competitive orientations of their employees (Horovitz, 2000). Masculine culture is deeply embedded in large media corporations, and sports are a top priority among powerful corporate executives. Few of these male executives take time to attend cast parties for a soap opera series, but many of them rush to attend the Super Bowl, the Masters (golf tournament), and other high-profile sport events. In fact, they use their sponsorship money to get close to the athletes, and they spend millions entertaining their clients and fellow executives during trips paid for with company credit cards. This combination of masculine ideology and government supported tax deductions for sport entertainment is a key factor in media dependence on sports.

It is clear that the marriage of sports and the media has been held together and strengthened by the vast amounts of money coming from corporations whose executives see sports as tools for promoting profits and ideologies consistent with their interests—both personal and corporate. When profits are low, their shared interest in promoting ideologies supportive of general capitalist expansion keeps the partners together.

Ideology is a key factor holding the sport-media marriage together. This is not a marriage based solely on money. This "married couple" also wishes to produce a generation that will accept capitalist expansion as normal and become obsessive consumers in the process. This will enable the sport-media couple to maintain its power and wealth long into the future.

IMAGES AND NARRATIVES IN MEDIA SPORTS

To say that sports are "mediated" is to say that they are re-presented to readers, listeners, and viewers through selected images and/or narratives. A growing number of people who study sports in society do research that involves digging into these selected images and narratives to identify the ideas or themes on which they are based. As they do their digging, they assume that media sports are symbolic constructions, much like Hollywood action films, television soap operas, and Disney cartoons (Andrews and Jackson, 2001; Rowe, 1999; Wenner, 1998; Whannel, 2002). In other words, a telecast of an American football game is a representation of certain people's ideas about football, social life, human beings, what is important in the world, and what the viewing audience wants to see and hear. Although different people interpret media images and narratives in different ways, many people use mediated sports as reference points as they form, revise, and extend their ideas about sports, social life, and social relations.

Because media sports are part of everyday experience in today's societies, it is important to consider the following questions:

1. How are sports constructed in and through the media?
2. What general ideas or themes underlie the images and narratives re-presented in media sports?

3. Does consuming media sports have an effect on our choices and actions in our everyday lives?

How the Media Construct Sports

When media are privately owned and dependent on financial profits, sports are selected for coverage on the basis of their entertainment value and revenue-generating potential. The images and narratives are presented to provide as much of the event as possible and to fit the perceived interests of both the audience and the sponsors. Sports that are difficult to cover and present as a profitable entertainment package usually are ignored by the media, or they are covered only in terms of occasional highlights, emphasizing spectacular and heroic injuries or achievements.

The sports pages of most major newspapers and articles in sports magazines provide scores, statistics, accounts of big plays and individual heroics, and behind-the-scenes stories; they use photos to depict action. Television coverage focuses on the ball (puck, etc.) and individual athletes, especially those who are currently winning the game, match, meet, or race. Television announcers provide play-by-play analysis and narratives designed to entertain a mass audience. The major differences in how the traditional print media and electronic or broadcast media construct sports are summarized in table 12.3.

The sports media in general present images and commentary that "hype" sports by exaggerating the spectacular, inventing and focusing on rivalries, and manufacturing reasons that events are important and should be read about, listened to, or viewed. They also emphasize elite sport competition (Lowes, 1999). For example, U.S. newspapers and television increased their coverage of professional sports through the twentieth century and decreased coverage of amateur sports, except for big-time college football and men's basketball. This shift was accompanied by a growing emphasis on the importance of winning and heroic actions instead of other factors

Table 12.3   Differences between newspaper/magazine and radio/television coverage of sports

Newspaper/Magazine Coverage	Radio/Television Coverage
• Emphasizes news and information	• Emphasizes entertainment
• Offers summaries of past events	• Offers play-by-play images and narratives
• Provides concrete information and data	• Provides real-time representations of action
• Bases success on maintaining credibility	• Bases success on generating hype
• Highlights behind-the-scenes stories	• Highlights action and heroic plays
• Is more likely to provide criticism of sports and sport personalities	• Is more likely to provide support for sports and sport personalities

Source: Based on material in Koppett, 1994.

associated with sports and sport participation. The result is that media audiences consume carefully "selected" versions of sports. These versions represent what corporate sponsors will fund with their advertising money and what media people think audiences want to consume.

It is important to study this "construction process" because popular ideas about sports are heavily informed by the images and narratives re-presented in media sports. Furthermore, the themes underlying these images and messages influence our ideas about social relations and social life in general. In other words, cultural ideology is embedded in media coverage.

Themes Underlying Media Images and Narratives

Success Themes   The images and narratives re-presented in mediated sports emphasize themes that identify important issues and particular ways of looking at and interpreting the world. For example, television broadcasts of sports in the United States emphasize success through competition, hard work, assertiveness, domination over others, obedience to authority, and big plays such as home runs, long touchdown passes, and single-handed goals. The idea that success also can be based on empathy, support for others, the sharing of resources, autonomy, intrinsic satisfaction, personal growth, compromise, incremental changes, or the achievement of equality gets little or no attention.

Media representations of sports exaggerate the importance of competitive rivalries and winning and losing in athletes' lives. For example, ESPN has organized its coverage of the XGames around the competitive quest for medals, when, in fact, many of the athletes and the spectators at the events are not very concerned about competition or medals (Crissey, 1999; Florey, 1998). The athletes enjoy the external rewards that come with winning and they certainly want to demonstrate their competence, but they also emphasize expression and creativity apart from scores and competitive outcomes. Furthermore, they see friendships with other competitors as more important than media-hyped rivalries. However, media coverage highlights competitive success, because it is valued in the culture as a whole, and it is easy to use to attract sponsors and consumers.

The success theme underlying images and narratives in U.S. media sports is less apparent in media sports in other cultures. Televised sports in the United States emphasize winners, losers, and final scores. Even silver medals are defined as consolation prizes at best; bronze medals seldom are discussed; and games for third place are seldom played anymore, much less covered by the media.

Writers and announcers focus on "shootouts" and sudden death playoffs instead of ties, they define *success* in terms of dominating others, and they praise those who make big plays or big hits and sacrifice their bodies for the sake of a win. Rare are references to learning, enjoyment, and competing *with* others, even when players see their participation in these terms, and many do. Thus, the media don't "tell it like it is." Rather, they tell it in a way that supports the interests of those who benefit from cultural commitments to competition, productivity, and material success.

Of course, this does not mean that most people do not enjoy media sports. Enjoyment is central, and it drives media sport consumption. However, there are many ways to enjoy sports, and the media highlight the ways that fit popular and corporate interests simultaneously. Discovering other ways to enjoy sports is left to individuals and groups, who actively seek alternatives to commercialized media sports.

Masculinity and Femininity Themes   There are both gender equity issues and ideological issues in the media coverage of sports. Even in the twenty-first century, men's sports receive well over 80 percent of the coverage in all the media, and the images and narratives about gender tend to reproduce traditional gender ideology (Duncan and Messner, 1998).

Coverage of women's sports is not a priority in the media, except in the Olympics, figure skating events, major tennis and golf tournaments, and some pro and college basketball games. Soccer received a wave of attention at the end of the twentieth century as the U.S. Women's World Cup champions were described as the "(middle-class, white) girls next door" and "babe city" and as people wondered about the "real" meaning of Brandi Chastain's spontaneous removal of her jersey after scoring the winning goal in the World Cup.

Overall, the coverage of women's sports in big-city newspapers has increased since the mid-1990s, but it remains less than 15 percent of the sports section of U.S. newspapers and even less in most other countries. Sports magazines have been notoriously slow to cover women athletes and women's sports, although they frequently have images of women as sex objects in ads for cigarettes, liquor, and other products. This pattern of underrepresentation of women's sports in the media exists around the world (see Urquhart and Crossman, 1999).

Progress has occurred in the case of some coverage. For example, *USA Today* now publishes a multipage section on the NCAA basketball tournament, with nearly 25 percent of the space devoted to the women's tournament and women athletes and coaches. Men receive nearly 50 percent of the space, and the remaining 30 percent consists of advertising. However, this is an exception to everyday patterns. Women receive this much coverage only in the case of special events. More typical of everyday coverage patterns was national television coverage of 270 regular season men's college basketball games and only 29 women's games during the 1999–2000 NCAA season.

Everyday coverage of women's sports continues to make up about 10 to 15 percent of total sports coverage at best. *SportsCenter*, ESPN's popular sports news program, devotes about 3 percent of its daily coverage to women athletes, and about 1 percent of the day-to-day coverage of "alternative/extreme" sports focuses on women athletes (Messner et al., 1999).

Women's sports are televised more than they were in the early 1990s, especially on certain cable stations, but the coverage given to women's sports is not much more than 15 percent of all television sports programming. The women's sports that have been covered regularly in the media are those emphasizing grace, balance, and aesthetics—attributes consistent with traditional gender ideology and images of femininity (Duncan and Messner, 1998; Jones et al., 1999).

Olympic media coverage in the United States highlights women gymnasts, swimmers, and divers in the Summer Games and women figure skaters and skiers in the Winter Games. Individual sports are given priority over team sports in the coverage (Tuggle and Owen, 1999), and women's figure skating is the most frequently televised women's sport event. The men's sports most often covered emphasize height, physical strength, speed, and the use of physical force and intimidation to dominate opponents—all qualities consistent with traditional images of masculinity. For example, football is by far the most popular televised men's sport in the United States, and television coverage emphasizes traditional notions of masculinity (Mihoces, 2002; Weisman, 2000).

Coverage of women's sports through the 1980s and most of the 1990s contained commentaries that often highlighted the personal characteristics of the athletes, such as their attractiveness, their spouses and children, their domestic interests and skills, and their vulnerabilities and weaknesses (Eastman and Billings, 1999; Weiler and Higgs, 1999). Television commentators for

women's sports have in the past referred to women athletes by their first names and as "girls" or "ladies," although this pattern has changed as researchers have called attention to its sexist implications. Commentators for men's sports have seldom referred to men athletes by their first names and almost never call them "boys" or "gentlemen." It is assumed that playing sports turns boys into men. Similarly, references to physical strength have been much more common in commentaries about men athletes, even though women clearly demonstrate strength and power, even in sports such as figure skating, golf, and tennis (Weiler and Higgs, 1999). A recent exception to this has been the coverage given to Venus and Serena Williams. After the media were able to look beyond the beads in their hair and the fact that they did not present themselves as if they

Football is the most popular televised sport event in the United States. The television coverage of football tends to reproduce the traditional gender values that are important to many people in the culture. (University of Colorado Media Relations)

were raised in country club settings, they began to refer to their strength, power, and speed. Similar comments have been made about Jennifer Caprioti, although the acknowledgment of the physical characteristics of the Williams sisters is unprecedented in tennis coverage.

Men's sport events often are promoted or described as if they had special historical importance, whereas women's sports events usually are promoted in a lighter, less serious manner (Duncan and Messner, 1998). Men's events are unmarked by references to gender and represented as *the* events, whereas women's events almost always are referred to as *women's* events. For example, there has always been "The World Cup" and "The Women's World Cup" in soccer coverage of the men's and women's tournaments around the world.

Women's sport events and women athletes receive few major headlines in newspaper sports sections and few lead stories in television sports news. Over the years, men have been featured on about 90 percent of the covers of *Sports Illustrated (SI)*, and half of the women featured on *SI* covers have not even been athletes. This is slowly beginning to change, although many people feel that the annual "swimsuit edition" negates any progressive change that has occurred in the rest of *SI*'s editorial policy (see Davis, 1997). *Women's Sports and Fitness* and other magazines that cover women's sports focus more on issues of fitness and appearance than on achievements in sports.

ERASING HOMOSEXUALITY Homosexuality is ignored in nearly all media coverage, whereas heterosexuality is acknowledged directly and indirectly among men and women in sports (Duncan and Messner, 1998; Kane and Lenskyj, 1998; Sabo and Jansen, 1998). Lesbian images are carefully erased from coverage, even though the partners of players and coaches are known and visible among spectators. Men's physical connections with each other are noted when they hold hands in a huddle or pat one another on the buttocks, but similar connections among women athletes are ignored for fear that lesbian images might offend media audiences. It seems that people seldom raise questions about the assumed heterosexuality of male athletes, no matter what men do on the field. At the same time, some people raise questions about female athletes at the slightest sign that heterosexuality may be in doubt. This is another way that gender ideology influences what people see in the world around them.

Lesbian athletes in golf, tennis, and basketball are never profiled in ways that acknowledge partners or certain aspects of their lifestyles—those parts of their personal stories are not told. In media-constructed sport reality, lesbians and gay men in sports generally are invisible unless they publicly come "out" as gay. Even then, they are marginalized in coverage. As media studies scholar Pam Creedon notes, "Homosexuality doesn't sell" (1998, p. 96). Meanwhile, heterosexual athletes and their partners are discussed and pictured in everything from the *Sports Illustrated* swimsuit edition to the television coverage of postgame victory celebrations, and nobody accuses these heterosexual athletes of pushing their values and agendas on others.

MEDIA ORGANIZATIONS ARE GENDERED The patterns associated with gender have been slow to change, partly because sports media organizations in all societies are "gendered institutions" (Creedon, 1998). Most of these organizations have been structured and scheduled around men's sports. Reporters' work schedules have been established around the coverage of men's sports to such an extent that covering of women's sports often requires changes in institutionalized patterns of sports media work. Furthermore, the *vast* majority of sports media personnel are men, and the highest-status assignments in sports media are those that deal with men's sports.

Even women reporters and announcers know that their upward mobility in the sports media industry demands that they cover men's events in much the same ways that men cover them. If they insist on covering only women's events, or if they are assigned only to women's events, they will not advance up the corporate ladder in media organizations. Advancement also may be limited if they insist on covering men's sports in new ways that don't reaffirm the "correctness" of the coverage patterns and styles developed by men.

Although women in the print media regularly cover men's sports, few women ever have done regular commentary for men's sports in the electronic media apart from occasional "sideline reports." Women reporters who cover men's sports are more readily accepted in the locker rooms of men's teams than they were in the past, although male athletes and coaches have been very protective of this masculinized space. Changes have occurred partly because men have discovered clever ways to maintain privacy, such as using towels and robes and having designated interview times—just as women athletes have always done when male reporters cover their events. However, it took the men nearly two decades to make these discoveries, because deeply rooted gender ideology often impedes one's ability to be creative and flexible.

When it comes to issues of masculinity, most sports coverage uses images and narratives that reproduce dominant ideas about manhood. Most television sports can be characterized as soap operas for men. The serialized nature of the broadcasts and the storylines they represent facilitate the construction of a symbolic and an actual community of sport spectators that is as masculine as the culture represented by the players on the field (Rose and Friedman, 1997).

Michael Messner and his colleagues (1999) report that the sports coverage most often consumed by boys in the United States depicts aggression and violence as normal and exciting behavior, portrays athletes who play in pain as heroes, uses military metaphors and terminology related to war and weapons, and highlights conflict between individuals and teams. Furthermore, women are seldom seen in the sport programs that boys watch most often, and, when

women do appear, they often are portrayed as sex objects, cheerleaders, spectators, and supportive spouses and mothers on the sidelines of the action. In the case of pro wrestling, one of the most popular "sport" programs watched by boys in recent years, women also appear as "arm jewelry" and "trophy-partners" for male wrestlers and as leather-clad strong women with breast implants.

Overall, gender themes related to masculinity and femininity remain central in media representations of sports. This is highlighted in the box "Meet the Press." However, it is important to note that few of us accept media representations at face value. We make sense of representations in our own terms. When we have special knowledge or personal connections with a sport or the athletes involved, we often ignore or become critical of media representations (Bruce, 1998).

Race and Ethnicity Themes   Just as media coverage of sports can influence ideas about gender and gender relations, it also can influence ideas about race and ethnicity and racial and ethnic relations. However, patterns related to the media representations of race and ethnicity in sports have not been as clear as they have been for gender.

Racial stereotypes have influenced coverage in the past, but more recently those who produce media representations of sports in the United States seem to be sensitive to many racial issues and the general issue of cultural diversity (Sabo and Jensen, 1998). Journalists are less likely to use descriptions of white or black athletes that reproduce traditional, racist stereotypes. However, interviews with black sports journalists and announcers indicate that they remain wary of what they see as a disproportionate number of "poor boy makes good" stories written about black athletes and of coverage highlighting the material possessions of black athletes who have large pro contracts. They feel that, because successful black athletes have lifestyles that don't fit white stereotypes, many white people who produce and consume media content define this as

REFLECT ON SPORTS

Meet the Press
It's Not Always Easy for Women Athletes

Johnny Miller is a former pro golfer. In July 2002, he was the NBC analyst covering the U.S. Women's Open. Julie Inkster, a forty-two-year-old veteran of the women's tour and winner of many tournaments, had just won the Open, the most prestigious event of the season. Miller met her as she was declared the winner and said excitedly, "It's big stuff when you win at 42. You're supposed to be home cooking meals at 42—you'd think, for most women." Apparently, when Miller looked at this champion golfer, he saw a mother and wife, standing in the kitchen preparing meals for her two children and husband. His vision was blurred by an ideology that distracted him as he interviewed a champion golfer who had just won the biggest tournament of the year.

Miller knew he'd made a mistake, but ideology is powerful, especially when you talk or act spontaneously. Inkster was gracious in her response, saying that she had achieved balance in her life by being able to coordinate her career with her family life. She was tactful as she dealt with Miller's gendered view of her, and she focused on her excitement about playing better golf than any woman in the world during the previous three days.

A few months before Miller interviewed Inkster, Tiffany Milbrett, the best soccer player in the United States during the 2002 professional Women's United Soccer Association season was being photographed for a magazine story about her. During the photo shoot, the photographer asked her to remove her bra. Milbrett was shocked at the request. Without hesitating, she reminded those at the shoot.

> I'm not a model. I'm an athlete. I only want to make money doing my trade. The rest I don't really care for. I don't give a rat's ass about being sexy. (in Adelson, 2002, p. 76)

Like Milbrett, many young women athletes face a dilemma when they meet people in the media who insist on sexualizing them. They must decide if they should just play sports and hope that they will be rewarded as athletes or if they should also present their bodies in sexualized terms to attract attention, sponsors, and media support. Milbrett decided against allowing her body to be represented in sexualized terms in the media, but other women athletes either conform to or exploit expectations based on traditional ideas about what women should be.

• •

newsworthy. Wealthy blacks then become "news," whereas wealthy whites are just wealthy people.

IMAGES OF "ANGRY, VIOLENT" BLACK MEN Another issue that remains contentious is that representations of black men in newspapers and television coverage appear almost exclusively in stories and programs related to sports, entertainment, and crime (Hawkins, 1998). Furthermore, when black male athletes are represented in magazine and television ads, they often are depicted as fearsome, angry, and potentially violent characters (Dufur, 1998). Of course, white male athletes also are depicted in this way, but the implications of these depictions must be viewed in the context of U.S. culture, where skin color often influences the perception of certain types of images.

Research is needed on this issue, but there is a chance that more white people perceive individual black male athletes presented as fearsome, angry, and potentially violent as representative of all black men than perceive fearsome, angry, and potentially violent white male athletes as representative of all white men. For example, when white people see images of white males who are aggressive or violent, most of them do not cross the street to avoid encounters with white men.

When Anita Marks, the quarterback for the Miami Fury in the Independent Women's Football League, explained her appearance in *Playboy* magazine in late 2002, she said,

> Women in sport need to have two personas. What they believe is right is not going to make them money. It isn't going to make you famous. (in Adelson, 2002, p. 76)

Marks let the photographers call the shots, although she chose from a limited set of alternatives to do what she hoped would make her famous.

A different approach was taken by Brandi Chastain when she posed nude in *Gear* magazine. She pointed out that she had "worked her ass off" to get her body in shape and was proud to have her physical strength and beauty represented in the media. Some women athletes agree with Chastain, others do not.

As we think about the media and gender, many of us have difficulty analyzing these issues. In the case of Miller's interview with Inkster, is it always a problem when people in the media view athletic achievements in connection with other important identities, relationships, and activities in an athlete's life? Are there ways to interview athletes and talk about their lives without letting questions and comments be shaped by ideologies that have disadvantaged entire categories of people in society?

In the case of Milbrett, Marks, Chastain and other women athletes, what are the guidelines and limits for media representations of athletes' bodies? More to the point, who should determine those guidelines and limits and what can be done to increase the chances that those determinations will be based on critically informed choices? Tiffany Milbrett "doesn't give a rat's ass" about being sexy, at least in front of a camera under conditions that she had not chosen. But, if other athletes choose to be represented as sexy in the media, should they be targets of criticism?

These questions are best answered if we consider issues of power combined with our awareness of ideology. If women athletes have control over how they are represented in the media, and they critically understand the importance of media images in our culture, it would be much easier for them to meet the press. But that leaves the toughest question unanswered: how do women gain that control? *What do you think?*

- -

Their responses to black men, however, are more likely to be based on generalizations formed in connection with media representations.

Similarly, when the media covered the two killers at Columbine High School after the 1999 shootings, their whiteness was never an issue, and most people did not generalize violent tendencies to all white teens; the coverage and audience responses probably would have been very different had the two killers been young black men.

The erasure of skin color does not occur in the same way for black men and women as it does for whites. A 400-year legacy of racism, and the racial images associated with that legacy, remains in U.S. culture. Does this legacy influence how people make sense of the images represented in the media? Do some people see physically talented or angry black male athletes in different terms than physically talented or angry white male athletes? If they do, then media representations influence people in racial ways, even when media producers are sensitive to racial issues and do their best to avoid stereotypes. However, equal coverage sometimes does not lead to equal perceptions. This is a crucial and puzzling point, which must be considered when we discuss racial themes in media sports coverage.

DIFFERENT WAYS TO SEE "COLOR ADJUSTMENTS" Equally important and sometimes puzzling is the fact that, when media coverage avoids stereotypes and represents successful images of black athletes, some whites conclude that racism is no longer a problem in society. This is because the media do not represent a full range of racial issues and perspectives in their content, and sports fans may not have enough information to put images of successful black athletes into a fully realistic context. Of course, this is frustrating to those in the media who have made successful efforts to avoid stereotypes in their coverage, but it reminds us that simple "color adjustments" (Riggs, 1991) in the media do not change the context in which people make sense of what they see, hear, and read in the media.

Along these lines, research shows that media coverage of sports can influence the aspirations and choices of African American children, especially boys. If African American children watch television and see black athletes excelling in a few sports, and if they think their personal and cultural destiny is to achieve great things in sports, these children may dedicate themselves to becoming athletes. If this choice leads them to give lower priority to pursuing educational and other occupational goals, then racial inequalities will be reproduced in the process. However, if this choice leads other people to take them seriously as human beings and to become advocates for their interests on and off the playing field, then positive changes will occur.

ETHNICITY AND NATIONALITY Themes related to ethnicity and nationality also have existed in sports media coverage. Although media personnel in some nations have been alerted to how ethnic and national stereotypes may influence their representations of athletes and teams, evidence suggests that subtle stereotypes occasionally are used in media sports coverage (Mayeda, 1999; Sabo and Jensen, 1998; Sabo et al., 1996). For example, commentators have occasionally portrayed Asian athletes as methodical, mechanical, machinelike, mysterious, industrious, self-disciplined, and intelligent. The achievements of Asian athletes may be attributed more to cognitive rather than physical abilities, and stereotypes about height and other physiological characteristics are sometimes used to explain success or failure in sports. Latinos occasionally have been described as flamboyant, exotic, emotional, passionate, moody, and hot-blooded (Blain et al., 1993). Of course, it is important to acknowledge the existence and influence of cultural factors in sports, but it also is important for journalists to know enough about ethnicity and ethnic relations that they don't inadvertently use stereotypes instead of learning about the experiences and characteristics of the people they describe and discuss.

Of course, stereotypes of people from different nations and cultures vary around the world. International political and economic relationships often influence stereotypes and how they are applied in the media coverage of sports. The sports journalists most likely to avoid the use of stereotypes are the ones that understand the history of those relationships and their implications for ethnic relations.

Finally, it also is important to study what the media do not cover when it comes ethnicity and ethnic relations. For example, media coverage of U.S. sports generally has ignored spectators who use chants and gestures grounded in long-held, Hollywood-generated stereotypes of Native Americans. The twenty-five-year-long protest by Native Americans of the misuse of team names, logos, and mascots has received little attention by the media. Although some newspapers have refused to use "Redskins" as the name of the NFL team in Washington, DC, journalists and announcers have not hesitated to use names and display logos based on racist caricatures. When coverage ignores important racial and ethnic issues, this becomes important in studies of the media.

MAKING CHANGES One way to reduce covert racial bias in the media is to hire more black and other ethnic minority reporters, editors, photographers, writers, producers, directors, camerapersons, and commentators (Rowe, 1999). Lip service has been paid to this goal, and progress has been made in certain media, but members of racial and ethnic minorities are still underrepresented in many sports newsrooms, press boxes, broadcast booths, and media executive offices. This is unfortunate, because we can learn from colleagues whose backgrounds are different from our backgrounds. When we do not have the advantage of working in racially and ethnically diverse settings, another way to increase racial awareness is to provide all personnel with regular training workshops on racial ideology and racial and ethnic relations. When this has been done, it has been effective (Thomas, 1996).

Other Ideological Themes in Media Sports It is not easy to identify themes underlying the images and narratives in media sports. Analyses using critical theories have focused on the extent to which images and narratives in media sports represent dominant ideas about social life and social relations in society as a whole. These studies have identified the three themes we have already discussed (success, gender, and race and ethnicity), as well as themes related to nationalism, competitive individualism, teamwork, aggression, and consumerism (Andrews and Jackson, 2001; Kinkema and Harris, 1998; Real, 1998; Rowe et al., 1998).

These themes should not surprise anyone who has read about, listened to, and viewed sports in the United States. The images and narratives in media sports clearly emphasize *nationalism and national unity* grounded in traditional American loyalty and patriotism. In fact, the sports that were "invented" in the United States—football, basketball, and baseball—are the most widely televised sports in the country. Other sports may get covered, but, if they don't

fit with traditional ideas about what it means to be an American, they don't receive priority coverage. When teams and athletes from the United States are competing against teams and athletes from other countries, the sport events are usually framed in an "us versus them" format. When American teams or athletes win, media commentators declare proudly, "*We* won" (see chapter 13).

Media images and narratives also emphasize *individual efforts* to achieve competitive victories, even in the coverage of team sports. Games are promoted with announcements such as these: "Brett Favre and his Packers are looking for blood against Kurt Warner and the St. Louis Cardinals" or "It's Chris Webber versus Shaquille O'Neil as the Kings face the Lakers." These promos emphasize the idea that individuals must take responsibility for what happens in their lives and that team failures can be traced to individual failures and flaws. This idea is central to the ideology of American individualism, which influences everything from the structure of our welfare system to the ways employees are evaluated and rewarded in the economy.

Apart from emphasizing individualism, media images and narratives also stress *teamwork*, in the form of obedience to authority, group loyalty, and the willingness to sacrifice for the good of the group (Kinkema and Harris, 1998). Media coverage clearly identifies coaches as the organizers and controllers of teams. Commentators praise athletes for being team players and praise coaches for their ability to fit players into team roles that lead to victories. This teamwork theme clearly fits with the ideology underlying the American market economy and most American business organizations: teamwork means loyalty and productivity under the direction of a leader-coach.

The importance of *mental and physical aggression* is another theme underlying the images and narratives in media sports. Rough, aggressive play is described as a sign of commitment and skill and players are praised as "warriors" (Messner et al.,

1999). Tackles in football are described as bone-crushing hits, hard fouls in basketball are described as warnings to the opposition, and brush-back pitches in baseball are said to keep batters on their heels.

Even the scores on the late-night news are full of violent images: the Heat *annihilated* the Knicks, the Jets *destroyed* the Dolphins, the Blackhawks *scalped* the Bruins, Hingis *blew away* Davenport, and on and on. The scores sound like the results of military operations in a war. In fact, the language of media sports in the United States is a language of violence and warfare (see figure 12.4). Aggression is celebrated, whereas kindness and sensitivity are dismissed as indications of weakness.

"Yes, I KNOW I let you watch NYPD Blue and Alias with me, but I'm afraid this hockey game is MUCH too violent for children."

FIGURE 12.4 This father has distinguished between fictional violence and real-life violence on television. Does watching real-life violence in certain sports have an impact on viewers? If video games are rated for violent content, why isn't the same done for sport events in which the violence is real and has real consequences for players and their families?

This content clearly fits with the ideology many Americans use to determine strategies in interpersonal, business, and international relations: "kicking ass" is a celebrated goal, and failing to punish the opposition is a sign of weakness. Presenting games as personal confrontations and mean-spirited turf wars has long been a strategy in media sports. As professional wrestling took this strategy and pushed it to an extreme, people wondered what it says to viewers. However, pro wrestling only extended and amplified the hype the media have used to promote mainstream sports for many years.

Finally, the emphasis on *consumerism* is clear in the media coverage of sports: over 15 percent of televised sports consists of commercial time, ads fill newspapers and magazines, and Internet sites use multiple strategies to attract attention to ads located on screens containing scores, commentary, and links. "TV time-outs" are a standard feature of televised football and basketball games, and announcers remind media spectators, "This game is being brought to you by (corporate name)." Super Bowl commercials are even the subject of special analyses, and media audiences are polled to see which Super Bowl commercials they liked and did not like.

The audiences for media sports are encouraged to express their connections to teams and athletes by purchasing shirts, shoes, jackets, official NFL hats, official NBA sweatpants, and Notre Dame coffee cups, among literally thousands of other branded products. This is clearly consistent with consumer ideology in American society. "You are what you buy" is one of the tenets of a market economy.

Themes in Media Images and Commentary
Overall, the images and narratives in the media coverage of sports in the United States stress themes representing conventional ideology and widespread ideas about how the world does and should work:

• Order, control, and tough discipline are essential.

- Gender differences are grounded in nature, not culture.
- The primacy of the nation must be preserved, unless capital expansion requires a blurring of national boundaries.
- Individuals must be accountable, work in teams, and outproduce others.
- Consumption is essential to happiness and is the basis for identity.
- Race and ethnicity are most likely to be recognized when athletes are not whites from European backgrounds.

These themes run through media sports. This is the reason media coverage of sports is heavily sponsored by people and corporations with power and influence in society—they favor these themes, and they sponsor images and narratives that inject them into the public consciousness.

Media Impact on Sports-Related Behaviors

Active Participation in Sports Do the media cause people to be more active sport participants, or do they turn people into couch potatoes? This is an important issue, especially in the United States. More people watch sports on television than ever before, and obesity rates are the highest in U.S. history. This is not to say that watching sports on television causes obesity and the health problems associated with obesity, but it suggests that we should do research to explore possible connections between these two factors.

When children watch sports on television, some copy what they see, if they have or can make opportunities to do so. Children are great imitators with active imaginations, so, when they see and identify with athletes, they may create informal activities or seek to join youth sport programs to pursue television-inspired dreams. Participation grounded in these dreams does not last long, especially after the young people and their parents discover that noteworthy accomplishments require years of dedication and expense. However, other motives may develop in

the process and inspire healthy participation patterns.

Many adults who watch sports on television do not play anything they watch, whereas many others are active participants in one or more sports (Wenner and Gantz, 1998). However, it is important to remember that, as the television coverage of sports has increased since the early 1970s in the United States, so, too, have obesity and inactivity. It is not known if there is a connection, but there is a need to study cultural changes as they are related to the use of the media in people's lives. The safest conclusion is that the media probably have no major *net* effect one way or the other on active participation in sports and other physical activities.

Attendance at Sport Events

Game attendance is related to many factors, and its relationship to the media is complex. On the one hand, the owners of many professional teams enforce a television blackout rule based on the belief that television coverage hurts game attendance and ticket sales. In support of this belief, many people say that they would rather watch certain sport events on television than attend them in person. On the other hand, it is clear that the media publicize sports, promote interest in them, and provide the information people need to identify with athletes and teams and to become committed fans—and, therefore, potential game attenders (Wann, 2000; Weiss, 1996; Zhang et al., 1997).

The most logical conclusion is that the media and game attendance are positively related: people who watch more games on TV also attend more games (Zhang et al., 1996a). However, we must qualify this conclusion. First, as ticket prices increase, and as the numbers of local elite games increase across various sports, more people may limit attendance when there is the option of watching a local game on television. Second, because the media focus attention on elite sports, such as NBA basketball, they may

The media focus on elite sports, and they usually attract spectators to high-profile events, such as this NBA playoff game in Seattle. Does this undermine attendance at less elite events, such as minor league and high school games? (Dennis Coakley)

undermine attendance at less *elite events, such* as local high school games. Thus, the media may be positively related to attendance at the top levels of competition but negatively related to attendance at lower levels of competition (Zhang et al., 1996b). Research is needed to explore this issue in more depth.

Gambling on Sports

Betting on sports is widespread, especially among college students who have access to the Internet and all the gambling opportunities available through the Internet (Brown, 2000;

Crist, 1998; Jenkins, 2000; Layden, 1995a, b, c), but the only certain link between gambling and the media is an indirect one. The media, especially newspapers, television, and the Internet, make people aware of *point spreads* and *betting odds* for various events. Point spreads and betting odds are determined by bookies, who want to make sure they don't go broke by taking too many bets on a particular outcome in a sport event. When the media publicize point spreads and odds, and when bets can be placed online, the media certainly make it easier for people to bet on sports. However, it is difficult to defend the conclusion that the media or the Internet *causes* gambling.

Relatively few people see betting on sports as an important legal or moral issue, despite its destructive consequences for those who become dependent on the excitement of betting money on a game. Many people are accustomed to buying lottery tickets and participating in state-sponsored gambling activities, so it is difficult to convince them to take seriously restrictions that limit or ban betting on sports. Gambling is also encouraged by a cultural emphasis on striking it rich and getting something for nothing. In the meantime, people use the media as vehicles to gain the information they need in the gambling process and, in some cases, to place their bets. However, to say that the media cause or even encourage gambling is to ignore the social and cultural contexts in which people choose to place bets on sports.

Audience Experiences with Media Sports

Media sports provide topics of conversation, sources of identity, feelings of success when favorite teams win, opportunities to express emotions, occasions for getting together with others, and a focus for those who are passing time alone (Wenner and Gantz, 1998).

A summary of audience research done by media studies experts Lawrence Wenner and Walter Gantz (1998) indicates that U.S. adults integrate media sports into their lives in a variety of ways. Although studies have identified some adults, more men than women, who focus considerable attention on watching sports, overall patterns indicate that watching television sports is not a major activity in the lives of most adults.

Studies summarized by Wenner and Gantz also have found that men and women who live together often share time watching sports and that this usually is a positive activity in their relationships. In other words, "stay-at-home armchair quarterbacks" and "football widows" are not as common as many people believe. Men do watch sports more than women watch, and men are more likely to be committed fans. However, when men and women are highly committed fans, they watch and respond to sports on television in very similar ways. In fact, data suggest that "fanship" is more important than gender or any other factor when it comes to people's viewing experiences. Scheduling and viewing conflicts occur for some couples, but most couples resolve conflicts without negative effects on their relationships. Partners usually learn to accommodate each other's viewing habits over time as they live together. When differences in viewing habits and fanship are associated with problems, there usually is a history of relationship problems, and many factors other than watching sports on television are the causes of those problems.

Future studies along these lines will tell us more about how media sport experiences are integrated into our lives and how they become activities around which social life occurs. The use of the Internet and video games should be included in these studies.

THE PROFESSION OF SPORT JOURNALISM

Leonard Koppett, a well-known and respected sportswriter, has said that one of the goals of sport journalism is "the generation of more and more entertaining material about something that doesn't *really* matter too much" (1994, pp. 162–63). However, sports do matter—not because they produce a tangible product or make an essential contribution to our survival but because they represent ideas about how the world works and what is important in life. Therefore, sports journalists do things that matter very much when it comes to cultural ideology and the public consciousness.

In addition to constructing the meanings associated with people's experiences of sports, journalists also help people enjoy and understand sports. Furthermore, media coverage often has an impact on sports and the athletes who are covered. As used in this section, the term *journalists* includes writers in the print media and announcers in the electronic media.

Journalists on the Job: Relationships with Athletes

As the television coverage of sports has expanded, sportswriters for newspapers and magazines have had to come up with stories that go beyond the action and scores in sports. This has forced them to seek information about the personal lives of the athletes whom fans have watched on television. As journalists have sought this information, the athletes have discovered that they can no longer trust writers to hold information in confidence, even if it is disclosed in the privacy of the locker room: if sportswriters hear an athlete say something that might attract readers' attention, the statement is likely to be printed. This has prevented many athletes from saying the spontaneous things that would make good material for reporters, and it has created tension between players and sportswriters.

This tension between players and sportswriters has intensified as differences in their salaries and backgrounds have become more pronounced. For example, wealthy black and Latino athletes without college degrees have little in common with middle-class, college-educated,

Euro-American writers. In the face of these differences, journalists in the print media have felt less compelled to protect or glorify athletes in their stories, and athletes have become increasingly protective of their wealth and status and wary of the motives of writers.

One of the outcomes of this situation is that team owners and athletic departments in U.S. universities have found it necessary to offer players training sessions on how to handle interviews without saying things that sound bad or can be misinterpreted. However, tensions remain and, in some cases, have been so strong that players have threatened writers, and writers have quit their jobs in search of less stressful occupations.

Tensions also have called attention to ethical issues in sports journalism. Responsible journalists, including writers and announcers, have become sensitive to the fact that they should not jeopardize people's reputations simply for the sake of entertainment. This does not mean that journalists should avoid criticism that might hurt

someone, but it does mean that they should never hurt someone unintentionally or without good reason (Koppett, 1994). Otherwise, they are engaging in destructive, self-serving sensationalism, which raises ethical concerns about the invasion of privacy. Unfortunately, journalists constantly face gray areas in which ethical guidelines are not clear, and the need to present attractive stories often encourages them to push ethical limits.

Sportswriters and Sports Announcers: A Comparison

Not everyone who covers sports for the media has the same focus. In the print media, the focus is on entertaining people with information and in-depth analysis, whereas radio and television announcers entertain people with images and commentary, which create on-the-spot urgency. The implications of these differences are summarized in table 12.4.

Table 12.4   Sportswriters and sports announcers: a comparison of roles

Role Characteristics	Sportswriters[a]	Sports Announcers[b]
• Job security	High	Low
• Salary	Low	High
• Popularity/public recognition	Low	High
• Freedom of expression in job	Moderate to high	Low; heavily restricted
• Purpose of role	To give information about sport events	To "sell" sport events; to entertain
• Role expectations	To be objective investigators	To be personable entertainers
• Opportunities to do investigative reporting	Sometimes	Very rare
• On-the-job contacts	Copy desk editors and subeditors	Broadcast executives, team management, sponsors, advertising people
• Relationships with players	Often tense and antagonistic	Friendly and supportive
• Level of response evoked from public	Low to moderate	Moderate to high

Source: Adapted from Koppett, 1994.
[a]The primary focus here is on newspaper reporters. Magazine writers have similar jobs, but they are different in that they often cover issues and topics in greater depth.
[b]The primary focus here is on television announcers. Radio announcers have similar jobs, but they are different in that they must focus more on description in their commentary and less on interpretation.

According to sports journalist Leonard Koppett (1994), the main difference between sports coverage in the print media and sports coverage in radio or television broadcasts is this: the print media woo readers with reliable and thorough stories, whereas radio and television broadcasts try to dazzle and fascinate audiences enough to keep them glued to their sets. Therefore, the print media hire writers who can tell reliable and thorough stories, whereas broadcast companies hire announcers who can excite and entertain an audience with rapid commentary (see figure 12.5). This is why newspaper and magazine writers (especially the latter) do the most thorough investigative reporting and why the most popular media personalities sit in television broadcasting booths and talk with a sense of urgency about whatever is occurring in an event.

While considering these differences and reviewing table 12.4, remember that there are exceptions to these role descriptions. Some writers go beyond information and analysis and write to be provocative or to shock and entertain. The successful ones have relatively high salaries and a reasonable amount of job security, especially those who are provocative. On the other hand, some television announcers do investigative reporting in which information and analysis take priority over entertainment. Given these exceptions, the major differences between sportswriters and sports announcers are accurately represented in table 12.4.

The efforts of television companies to provide a combination of play-by-play commentary and entertainment lead them to hire popular retired athletes and coaches to be announcers. Media companies cover sports as infotainment rather than news, and those who announce the games must be entertainers. Of course, the announcers also must be perceived to take the events seriously so that people in the media audience will identify with them and define them as credible when it comes to analyzing game situations. When spectators hear commentary from former athletes and coaches, they often feel that they have an inside source for what is happening in the event.

Regardless of the specific characteristics of announcers and commentators, the content of their narrative stays within parameters set by teams and television companies. Popular radio and television announcer Chip Caray, who has worked on broadcasts for the Atlanta Braves, the Seattle Mariners, and the Chicago Cubs, explains, "Our bosses expect us to broadcast a certain way. No one has ever told me how to broadcast. But I draw my paycheck from the same place as the players" (in Russo, 1999, p. 7D). This is why announcers seldom stray from a fairly standard entertainment approach and why we should never expect to hear critical comments about

"I may be just a rookie anchorman, but I know how to report violence, drug abuse, and corporate corruption—I used to do the sports."

FIGURE 12.5 "If it bleeds, it leads." This is one of the guidelines used in the media coverage of sports and the local news. As critical media consumers, we know that such representations are not accurate indicators of what generally happens in sports or our communities.

sports as social phenomena as we watch sports on television.

SUMMARY

COULD SPORTS AND THE MEDIA SURVIVE WITHOUT EACH OTHER?

It is difficult to understand social life today without giving serious attention to the media and media experiences. This is why we study the relationship between sports and the media.

Media sports, like other parts of culture, are social constructions. This means they are created, organized, and controlled by human beings, whose ideas are grounded in their social worlds, experiences, and ideologies. The media do not *reflect* reality as much as they provide *representations* of selected versions of reality. These selected representations are grounded in power relations in society. Therefore, the images and messages contained in the media often represent dominant ideas and ideologies and promote the interests of those who benefit most from those ideas and ideologies. The possible exception to this is the Internet, a medium that offers revolutionary potential in that it enables people to create their own media content.

Sports and the media have grown to depend on each other as both have become more important parts of cultures in many societies. They could survive without each other, but they would both be different than they are now. Without the media, commercial sports would not be so widespread, and there would be less emphasis on elitist forms of competitive sports, although active participation in sports would not automatically increase. Without exposure to sports through the media, people would probably give lower priority to organized competitive sports in their everyday lives.

The media also could survive without sports. But they, too, especially newspapers and television, would be different. Without sports, newspaper circulation probably would decrease, and television programming on weekends and holidays would be different and less profitable for television companies.

The strong symbiotic relationship between sports and the media suggests that none of us will live to see organized sports without media coverage or the media without sports content and programming. However, history also shows that this relationship has developed within a larger cultural context, one in which high priority is given to commercial profits and the creation of attractive media events. Furthermore, the relationship between sports and the media has been created through the ever changing interactions among athletes, agents, coaches, administrators, sport team owners, sponsors, advertisers, media representatives, and a diverse collection of spectators. Each group has tried to influence the relationship, and each has had a different amount of resources to use in the process.

Sports coverage in the electronic media is represented to audiences with dramatic, exciting, and stylized images and narratives designed to be entertaining for audiences and attractive to sponsors. The influence of these media sports on each of us depends on how we experience sports in our everyday lives. Direct experiences with sports influence how we interpret and use what we read, listen to, and view in the media. If we have little direct experience in and with sports, the media play a more central role in creating our sport realities and in influencing how those realities are integrated into the rest of our lives.

Research suggests that dominant ideologies related to success, gender, race and ethnicity, nationalism, competition, individualism, teamwork, violence, and consumerism are perpetuated through the images and commentaries contained in the media coverage of sports in the United States. Future research will tell us more about how people use media content as they form ideas about sports, their social relationships, and the social world.

Especially important in the future will be research on how people use the Internet and video games as sites for constructing their experiences in and with sports. There are thirteen-year-olds who would much rather play sport video games than watch games on television. In the future, many of them will do both at the same time. And there are twenty-five-year-olds who enjoy the sport-related interactive experiences they have on the Internet more than the games themselves. Media sports and the experiences associated with them are changing rapidly, and it is important that we study them in ways that promote critical media literacy rather than the uncritical celebration of media culture (Kellner, 1995).

SUGGESTED READINGS

Andrews, D. L., and S. J. Jackson. 2001. *Sport stars: The cultural politics of sporting celebrity.* London/New York: Routledge (sixteen articles focusing on the cultural, political, economic, and technological factors that influence sport celebrity and how sport celebrities influence the everyday lives of people).

Brookes, R. 2002. *Representing sport.* London: Arnold (focuses on how global and commercial forces influence the relationship between sports and the media; uses international examples to show how media sports influence identity and ideas about nation, gender, and race around the world).

Messner, M., et al. 1999. *Boys to men: Sports media.* Oakland, CA: Children Now (www.children@childrennow.org) (analysis of messages about masculinity contained in sports programming and commercials during sport programs; based on a national U.S. poll of children, focus groups, and analysis of sport programs and commercials).

Rowe, D. 1999. *Sport, culture, and the media: The unholy trinity.* Buckingham and Philadelphia: Open University Press (analyses of the processes of "making media sports" and how media studies can be used to "unmake" and understand sports commentating, writing, photography, filming, and Internet sites).

Wenner, L., ed. 1998. *MediaSport.* London/New York: Routledge (seventeen chapters written by experts on the media and sports; emphasizes critical cultural studies approaches to research on media production, institutions, texts, and audiences; chapters emphasize issues related to gender, race and ethnicity, celebrity, globalization, and corporate influence).

Whannel, G. 2000. Sports and the media. In *Handbook of sports studies* (pp. 291–308), edited by J. Coakley and E. Dunning. London: Sage (overview of the sports-media relationship and its implications for global social processes).

Whannel, G. 2002. *Media sport stars: Masculinities and moralities.* London/New York: Routledge (analysis of how the media have created sport stars around particular ideological themes—in this case, around prevailing notions of masculinity, goodness, and the importance of consumption in society).

WEBSITE RESOURCES

Note: Websites often change. The following URLs were current when this book was printed. Please check our website (www.mhhe.com/coakley8e) for updates and additions.

www.mhhe.com/coakley8e Essays on the ideology underlying media sports, the interdependence of the Olympics and the media, and the impact of watching violent sports on behavior.

www.aafla.org Amateur Athletic Foundation site; go to "AAF Research Reports" for sports media studies on children and sports media, gender issues, race and ethnicity issues.

www.real-sports.com Site for the magazine *real SPORTS*, dedicated to the coverage of women in sports; no ads for beauty products, as in "fitness and sports" magazines for women.

www.nfl.com/fans/forher/index.html Site designed to recruit women to watch NFL games and become NFL fans.

(Victoria Arocho, AP/Wide World Photo)

Sports and Politics

How Do Governments and Globalization Influence Sports?

NO PERSON SHALL roller-skate, skateboard or operate a bicycle in violation of the limitations set forth on regulatory signs posted pursuant to this section.

—**Los Angeles Municipal Code,
sec. 85.07 (2002)**

 **Online Learning Center Resources**

Visit *Sports in Society*'s Online Learning Center at **www.mhhe.com/coakley8e** for additional information and study material for this chapter, including

- Self-grading quizzes
- Learning objectives
- Related websites
- Additional readings

A complete outline is available online at www.mhhe.com/coakley8e.

WE HAVE WAGED a lengthy and tireless battle to create a [revolutionary] sports culture. . . . This is what has allowed our country to reach a place of honor in sports . . . recognized by the entire world.

—Fidel Castro, president of Cuba (2001)

I AM PERSONALLY asking the U.S. World Cup team . . . to insist that the next game they play, they play with soccer balls that are certified "not made with child labor."

—Tom Harkin, U.S. senator from Iowa (2002)

Organized competitive sports long have been connected with politics, government, and the nation-state. **Politics** refers to power and how it is gained and used in social life, and **government** refers to formal organizations and agencies that have the authority to make rules regulating people's behavior. Politics is involved in all social relationships and organizations, including those related to sports.

Governments operate in connection with nation-states, and they influence sports in many ways. **Globalization** consists of the long-term processes of social change that involve relationships between nation-states and the use of power on an international level.

This chapter deals with sports and politics. The goal is to explain how sports are involved in politics on many levels and how politics are involved in sports. Chapter content focuses on four major issues:

1. The reasons governments become involved in sponsoring and controlling sports
2. How sports are connected with important political processes, especially at the global level
3. The role of the Olympic Games in global politics and global culture
4. The political processes that occur in sports and sport organizations

When reading this chapter, remember that *power* is the key concept in politics. As used in this chapter, the term **power** refers to an ability to influence others and achieve goals, even in the face of opposition from others (Weber, 1968/1922). **Authority** is a form of power that comes with a recognized and legitimate status or office in an organization or set of relationships. For example, a large corporation has *power* if it can influence how people think about and play sports and if it can use sports to meet its corporate goals. Sport organizations such as the IOC, FIFA, the NCAA, and a local parks department

have *authority* over the sports they administer, as long as people associated with those sports accept the organizations as legitimate sources of control. This example alerts us to the fact that, in this chapter, *politics* refers to more than issues concerning formal sport governing bodies; instead, it refers to all forms of power relations in sports.

THE SPORTS-GOVERNMENT CONNECTION

When sports become popular community activities, government involvement often increases. Many sports require sponsorship, organization, and facilities—all of which depend on resources that few individuals possess on their own. Sport facilities are often so expensive that regional and national governments may be the only community entities with the power and money to build and maintain them. Therefore, many people see government involvement in sports as a necessity.

Government involvement also is tied to the belief that sport participation, sport organizations, and the people associated with sports often need to be regulated and controlled by an independent agency that represents the interests of all people in a community or society.

The nature and extent of government involvement in sports vary from one community and society to the next, and government involvement occurs for one or more of the following seven reasons (Houlihan, 1994, 1997, 2000):

1. To safeguard the public order
2. To maintain health and fitness among citizens
3. To promote the prestige and power of a group, community, or nation
4. To promote a sense of identity, belonging, and unity among citizens
5. To reproduce values consistent with dominant ideology in a community or society

6. To increase support for political leaders and government
7. To promote economic development in a community or society

Safeguarding the Public Order

Governments often make rules about what sports are legal or illegal, how sports must be organized, who should have opportunities to play sports, where certain sports may be played, and who can use public sport facilities at certain times. Ideally, these rules protect individuals and groups as they pursue interests that may conflict with the interests of other individuals or groups. This is why a government might officially ban sports such as bullfighting, bare-fisted boxing, or even bungee jumping. In the case of commercial sports, governments may regulate the rights and duties of team owners, sponsors, promoters, and athletes.

Local governments may try to eliminate conflicts by requiring permits to use public facilities and playing fields. They may pass rules prohibiting potentially dangerous sport activities in public places. For example, skateboarding, in-line skating, and bicycling may be banned on city sidewalks or in certain public parks, or they may be confined to certain areas, so that pedestrians will feel safe. Likewise, local officials may close streets or parks to the general public, so that sport events can be held under controlled and safe conditions. For example, marathons in such places as New York City and London require the involvement of the government and government agencies, such as the city police.

Governments may pass laws or establish policies that safeguard the public order by guaranteeing that participation in publicly funded sports is open to everyone. Title IX in the United States is a classic example of a federal government regulation intended to promote gender fairness in school programs. Sport Canada, the national organization that oversees high-performance sports in Canada, has established a nationwide

AT YOUR FINGERTIPS   For more information on Title IX, see pages 238–242.

policy on women in sport. This policy outlines equity strategies that safeguard the notion of fairness throughout the country. Governments around the world are enacting or considering similar laws to establish fairness in sport participation opportunities for people with disabilities.

Similarly, the U.S. Congress passed the Amateur Sports Act in 1978 and created the

Local governments often regulate where and when certain sports may be played. These boys feel their interests have not been fairly represented by government decisions about where they can skateboard. For that reason, they regularly challenge the regulations. (Jay Coakley)

USOC, the official nongovernmental body designated to organize sports for amateur athletes and to protect athletes from exploitation at the hands of numerous unconnected and self-interested sport governing bodies around the nation. In 1998, the act was revised to require the USOC to support and fund Paralympic athletes, because people with disabilities were not being given sufficient opportunities to participate in elite amateur sports. This change has caused considerable debate and a few lawsuits in the United States, as people with disabilities demand the support and funding they deserve.

Safeguarding the public order also involves policing sport events. Local police or even military forces may be called on to control crowds and individuals who threaten the safety of others. During the Olympics, for example, the host city and nation provide thousands of military and law enforcement officials to safeguard the public order—more than 15,000 in Atlanta (1996) and Sydney (2000). In the face of new terrorist threats, government involvement to maintain security is expected by most people.

Some governments have attempted to safeguard the public order by sponsoring sport events and programs for at-risk youth. Sports, it is argued, can be used to keep them off the streets and thereby control crime rates, vandalism, loneliness, and alienation. However, many of these programs fail, because they do not deal with the deprivation, racism, poverty, dislocation, community disintegration, and political powerlessness that cause social problems in communities and societies.

Finally, sports often have been used in military and police training, so that the soldiers and police will be more effective protectors of the public order. For example, military academies in the United States and other countries traditionally have sponsored numerous sports for their cadets, and the World Police and Fire Games are held every two years because people believe that sport participation keeps law enforcement officials and firefighters prepared to safeguard the public order.

Maintaining Health and Fitness

Governments also have become involved in sports to promote health and fitness among citizens. For example, nations with government-funded health insurance programs often promote and sponsor sports to improve physical health in the general population and thereby reduce the cost of health services.

Similar motives have led to government sponsorship and organization of fitness and sport programs in other nations. Many people believe that sport participation improves fitness, fitness improves health, and good health reduces medical costs. This belief persists in the face of the following factors (Howell and Ingham, 2001; Howell et al., 2002; Nixon, 2000; Waddington, 2000):

- Many of the illnesses that increase health-care costs are caused by environmental factors and living conditions, and they cannot be changed through any sport or fitness program.
- Certain forms of sport participation do not lead to overall physical fitness or identifiable health benefits.
- The win-at-all-costs orientation, which sometimes develops in connection with sports, may actually contribute to injuries and increased health-care costs (for example, more than 40,000 knee injuries in American football every year require costly care, surgery, and rehabilitation).
- The demand for health care sometimes increases when people become more concerned with fitness and the physical condition and appearance of their bodies. This is because people who participate in competitive sports can become so concerned with performance that they seek specialized medical care for training and rapid rehabilitation from sport injuries.

Because of these factors, governments are cautious and selective in their sponsorship of sports for health purposes. Today, governments are more likely to emphasize noncompetitive physical activities and exercise with clear aerobic benefits and less likely to sponsor highly competitive sports involving physical contact and norms promoting the physical domination of opponents. The former promote health, whereas the latter often damage health.

In the past, government involvement in sports also was grounded in the belief that fitness and physical abilities are related to economic productivity. Although this relationship is hard to prove, some private corporations fund their own fitness centers and sport programs, thinking that it will make their employees more productive while improving employee health and controlling insurance costs. However, many companies have learned that productivity and worker satisfaction are related to the overall quality of working conditions and workers' autonomy, not to employee fitness or opportunities to participate in sports. This is not to say that neither governments nor corporations should provide sport participation opportunities for people. Instead, it emphasizes that sport provision does not replace the need to provide overall working conditions that are safe, fair, and responsive to the lives of workers.

Finally, the relationship between sport participation and overall health and fitness is a complex one. Certainly, engaging in rigorous physical activities does have health benefits. There are many studies that document this. However, when we discuss health issues it is important to distinguish general physical activities and systematic exercise from competitive sports. Competitive sports can promote overall health if they do not involve forms of participation in which performance is valued over physical well-being. Playing sports is beneficial when it enables us to understand our bodies and maintain our physical well-being; it is not beneficial when it involves the overuse of our bodies, the use of our bodies as weapons, and overconformity to the norms of the sport ethic, as explained in chapter 6. This is why health professionals sometimes disagree when it comes to recommending government involvement in sports to promote health and fitness.

> Winning medals is a platform for us. It provides us the foundation, the basis, the significance to influence society. We influence society by winning medals and hearts and minds.
>
> —Lloyd Ward, former CEO, U.S. Olympic Committee (2002)

Promoting the Prestige and Power of a Group, Community, or Nation

Government involvement in sports frequently is motivated by a quest for recognition and prestige. This occurs on local, national, and even global levels. For example, a spokesperson for the South Korean government said that its sponsorship of the 1988 Summer Olympic Games was an announcement to the world of its emergence as a developed nation with a strong economy. The 1996 Summer Games provided an occasion for local boosters to present Atlanta as a world-class city symbolizing the "new South," now open to all people regardless of race or national background. Sydney, the host of the 2000 Summer Games, was presented to the world as a city with clean air in a country with a pleasant climate and vital business connections with emerging nations in Asia. Salt Lake City used the 2002 Winter Olympics to present itself as an economically progressive area and an attractive tourist destination.

This quest for recognition and prestige also underlies government subsidies for national teams across a wide range of sports, usually those designated as Olympic sports. Government officials use international sports to establish their nation's legitimacy in the international sphere, and they believe that, when athletes from their nation win medals, their national image is enhanced around the world.

This belief is so strong that many governments now offer their athletes financial rewards for winning medals in the Olympics. The importance of national success in sports is not new. Even back in 1958, when Brazil won its first World Cup in soccer, there was a strong feeling among most Brazilians that they could now stand tall in the international arena and that their way of life was equal to or perhaps even better than those of the nations of Europe. They felt that Brazil now had to be recognized and dealt with as an equal in international relations (Humphrey, 1986). Similar feelings have been expressed more recently in connection with World Cup performances by soccer teams from such African nations as Cameroon and Nigeria.

In a similar manner, many people believe that a nation's failures in international sport events cause a loss of prestige in the global political arena. During the late-twentieth century when national teams from England lost in major international competitions to teams from countries that had learned to play sports invented in England, some people in England worried that the losses were symptoms of their nation's general decline in world affairs (Maguire, 1994, 1999). In response, the British government increased funding to support the development of elite athletes.

Attempts to gain recognition and prestige also underlie local government involvement in sports. Cities may fund sport clubs and teams and then use those teams to promote themselves as good places to live, work, locate a business, or spend a vacation. In fact, some people in North America feel that, if their city does not have one or more major professional sport team franchises, it cannot claim world-class status (see Whitson and Macintosh, 1996). Even small towns use road signs to announce the success of local high school teams to everyone driving into the town: "You are now entering the home of the state champions" in this or that sport. State governments in the United States traditionally have subsidized sport programs at their colleges

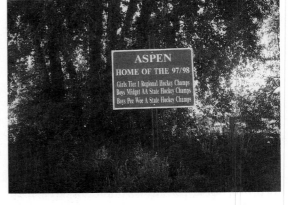

Local government combines with private funding to support hockey programs in Aspen, Colorado. In recent years, the city announces its competitive success on a road sign that greets thousands of tourists every year. (Jay Coakley)

and universities for similar reasons: competitive success is believed to bring prestige to the entire state, as well as to the school represented by the athletes and teams; prestige attracts students, students pay tuition, and tuition pays for educational programs.

Promoting a Sense of Identity, Belonging, and Unity

Groups, organizations, towns, cities, and nations have used sports to express collective sentiments about themselves (Allison, 2000; Bairner, 2001; J. M. Bradley, 2002; Houlihan, 2000; Jutel, 2002; Maguire, 2000; Maguire et al., 2002; Nauright, 1998; Van Bottenburg, 2001). Any team or athlete representing a specific group has the potential to bring people together and to create emotional unity among group members.

When a nation's soccer team plays in the World Cup, people across the nation are united, regardless of differences in race, religion, language, education, occupation, and income. This unity may be connected with their feelings of attachment to the nation as a whole and their convictions about the nation's history and traditions, even about its destiny in the world order.

However, it is important to ask critical questions about the long-term consequences of this emotional unity and about whose interests are served by the images, traditions, and memories around which identities are expressed. When government involvement and sponsorship of a sport are designed to promote a sense of identity and unity among a collection of people, it is important to understand how that identity and unity are connected with patterns of power and social relations. For example, when men's sports are sponsored and women's sports are ignored, what does that say about a group's identity and the values around which the identity is created? What if the sport involves participants from only one ethnic group or from a particular social class? These questions show that identity itself is political, in the sense that it can be constructed around various ideas of what is important in a group.

> Sport is an important tool for "imagining" nationhood. It is a perfect forum for constructing identity.
>
> —Annemarie Jutel, Physical
>   Educator (2002)

Furthermore, the unity created by sports does not change the important social, political, and economic realities of life in any way. In fact, after games end, social distinctions quickly are reaffirmed as people go about their everyday lives (Arbena, 1988). Of course, the emotional unity that sports sometimes create feels good, and it even may be associated with a spirit of possibility, but it can gloss over the need for social transformation, rather than inspiring collective action that might transform society and make it more fair and just.

Local government involvement in sports is also motivated by concerns to promote and express particular forms of identity. Club soccer teams in Europe often receive support from local governments, because the teams are major focal points for community attention and involvement. The teams not only reaffirm community identity among local citizens but also bring large numbers of community people together when games are played. In fact, the games often become important social occasions within towns or regions and provide opportunities for meeting new people, renewing old acquaintances, and maintaining a personal sense of belonging to a group. In this context, we can consider sports to be *invented traditions* used to remind people of what they share and how they are connected with one another.

When the population of a community or society is very diverse, or when social change is rapid and widespread, governments are even more likely to intervene in sports for the purpose of promoting a sense of identity and unity (Maguire and Stead, 1996). For example, as national boundaries have become less and less visible and relevant in people's lives, many national governments around the world have used sports to promote a sense of national identity (Houlihan, 1994; Maguire, 1999). Even though the long-term effectiveness of this strategy is difficult to assess, many government officials are convinced that sports create more than temporary good feelings of togetherness. Of course, it is important to remember that nearly all of these officials are men, and the sports they support often are tied to traditions that have privileged men in the past. As always, there are several layers to the politics associated with sports.

Reproducing Values Consistent with Dominant Ideology

Governments also become involved in sports to promote certain values and ideas among citizens. For example, governments generally have strong vested interests in maintaining the idea that success is based on discipline, loyalty, determination, and the ability to keep working in the face of hardship and bad times. Sports, especially world-class and elite competitive sports, have been used in many nations to promote these values and to foster particular interpretations of how social life does and should work.

This was a major motive for the government sponsorship of sports in the former Soviet Union, as articulated by a prominent Soviet sociologist:

> Physical culture is an important means to educate . . . an active fighter for communism, and it is an effective social factor in the ideological education of the public. . . . When people engage in physical exercise their ideology and moral consciousness are shaped through acquiring information on sports ethics and its manifestation in the activities of Soviet athletes; this is assimilated through the practical mastery of communist standards of behavior during training and competition. (Ponomaryov, 1981, pp. 117–18)

However, because most people in the Soviet Union did not accept government-sponsored ideas, they attached their own meanings to Soviet sports. Instead of associating them with collectivism and comradeship, they saw them as symbols of government coercion, exploitation, and distorted national priorities (Riordan, 1993). Sports could not rescue the political ideology of Soviet communism.

In nations with market economies—such as the United States and Canada—sports often are associated with success and hard work, so, instead of references to collectivism and the common good, there are references to competition and individual achievement. Instead of an emphasis on comradeship, there are stories showing how individuals have reached personal goals and experienced self-fulfillment through sports. An emphasis on competition, personal achievement, and individual fulfillment pervades the media coverage of sports in nations with market economies. Although it is not known whether such an emphasis actually strengthens a popular commitment to dominant cultural ideology, it clearly provides people with a vocabulary and real-life examples that are consistent with dominant ideology. In a sense, the vocabulary and stories that accompany sports in market economies

tend to emphasize that using competition to achieve personal success and to allocate rewards to people is natural and normal, whereas alternative approaches to success and allocating rewards are inappropriate.

A classic example of a government's use of sport to promote its own political ideology occurred in Nazi Germany in 1936. Most countries hosting the Olympic Games have used the occasion to present themselves favorably to their own citizens and the rest of the world. However, Adolf Hitler was especially interested in using the games to promote the Nazi ideology of "Nordic supremacy" through the Berlin Games, which preceded World War II. The Nazi government devoted considerable resources to the training of German athletes, and those athletes won eighty-nine medals: twenty-three more than U.S. athletes won and over four times as many as any other country won during the Berlin Games. This is why the performance of Jesse Owens, an African American, was so important to countries not aligned with Germany at that point in history. Owens' four gold medals and world records challenged Hitler's ideology of Nordic supremacy, although it did not deter Nazi commitment to a destructive political and cultural ideology.

The Cold War era following World War II was also full of incidents in which countries, especially the United States, the USSR, and East Germany, used the Olympics and other international sport competitions to make claims about the superiority of their political and economic systems. Today, such claims are less apt to be associated with international sports; instead, there is a growing emphasis on the logos and products of corporate capitalism.

Increasing Support for Political Leaders and Government

Government authority rests ultimately in legitimacy. If people do not perceive political leaders and the government as legitimate, trouble is inevitable. In the quest to maintain legitimacy, political officials and ruling government parties

President George W. Bush, like other U.S. presidents, used sports for political advantage. He seldom missed opportunities to be seen or to be connected with highly visible championship teams and successful athletes. Politicians in other societies have done the same thing, although few have used sports as much as politicians in the United States have. (Jerry Lampen, AP/Wide World Photos)

may use sports. They assume that sponsoring or promoting sports that people value and enjoy increases their perceived *legitimacy* in the eyes of citizens. This is why many political figures present themselves as friends of sport, even as faithful fans. They may make it a point to attend highly publicized sport events and associate themselves with high-profile athletes or teams that win major competitions. U.S. presidents traditionally have associated themselves with successful athletes and teams, and have invited champions to the White House for photo opportunities. Of course, U.S. politicians are not the only ones to do this. There are similar examples from other countries. When taken together, these examples provide strong support for the idea that governments and government officials use sports to promote themselves.

Some male former athletes and coaches in the United States have even been able to use their celebrity status from sports to gain popular support for their political candidacy. The most publicized example of this is Jesse Ventura, a former professional wrestler, who was elected governor of Minnesota in 1998 and flirted with the idea of running for president in 2000. Other former athletes and coaches have been elected to state legislatures and to the U.S. Congress and Senate, using their status from sports to increase their legitimacy as candidates.

Promoting Economic Development

Since the early 1980s, government involvement in sports often has been motivated and justified for the purpose of promoting economic development (Schimmel, 2000, 2002). Cities may spend large amounts of money to assemble and submit bids to host the Olympic Games, World Cup tournaments, world or national championships, Super Bowls, All-Star Games, high-profile auto races, golf tournaments, and track and field meets. Although some of these sport events do not show a profit for themselves, they may increase profits for other powerful economic interests in communities.

Governments are also interested in the long-term economic benefits of hosting events. Officials even may use the events as occasions for making contacts with corporations looking for new sites to locate their offices and operations. Or officials may use the events to highlight and promote products made by local businesses. In many cases, hosting a sport event now combines the interests of civic boosters and government officials in a general effort to enhance the local economy (Huey, 1996).

The use of sports in promoting economic development is controversial. Some government officials in cities around the world have doubts about the impact of publicly funded sports facilities, events, and programs on general economic development (Lenskyj, 2000; Schimmel, 2002). Much recent evidence suggests that the forms of economic development associated with sports often benefit relatively few people, usually those who are already wealthy and powerful (see chapters 10 and 11). Of course, those people often try to encourage those forms of government involvement in sports that benefit them.

Conclusion and Qualification: Critical Issues and Government Involvement in Sports

It is important to raise questions about government involvement in sports and the "public good." Of course, it would be ideal if all governments promoted equally the interests of all citizens, but differences between individuals and groups make this impossible. This means that government involvement in sports usually reflects the interests of some people more than others. Those who benefit most tend to be people capable of influencing policymakers. This does not mean that government policies only reflect the interests of wealthy and powerful people, but it does mean that policies are influenced by power struggles among groups within a society.

History shows that, when government intervention occurs, priority is often given to elite sport programs, rather than to general sport participation. Of course, there are exceptions to this, but seldom are elite programs ignored or given a low priority. Those who represent elite sports often are organized, generally have strong backing from other organized groups, and can base their requests for support on visible accomplishments achieved in the name of the entire country, community, or school. Those who would benefit from mass participation programs are less likely to be politically organized or backed by other organized groups, and they are less able to give precise statements of their goals and the political significance of their programs. This does not mean that mass participation is ignored by government decision makers, but it does mean that it usually has lower priority for funding and support.

Opposition to the priorities that guide government involvement often is defused by the myth that there is no connection between sports and politics. Those who believe this myth seldom have their interests reflected when government involvement occurs. Those who realize that sports have political implications and that governments are not politically neutral arbitrators of differences within societies are likely to benefit the most when government intervention occurs. Sports are connected with power relations in society as a whole; therefore, sports and politics cannot be separated.

SPORTS AND GLOBAL POLITICAL PROCESSES

International Sports: Ideals Versus Realities

Achieving peace and friendship among nations has been a longstanding ideal underlying international sports. It was emphasized by Baron Pierre de Coubertin, the founder of the modern Olympic Games in 1896, and by many others since then. The hope has been that sports would do the following things:

- Open communication lines between people and leaders from many countries
- Highlight shared interests among people from different cultures and nations
- Demonstrate that friendly international relationships are possible
- Foster the cultural understanding needed to eliminate the use of national stereotypes
- Create a model for cultural, economic, and political relationships across national boundaries
- Establish working relationships that develop leaders in emerging nations and that can be used in efforts to close the gap between wealthy nations and poorer nations

During the past century, these ideals have been achieved to some degree on some occasions. International sports have had little impact in the realm of **serious diplomacy,** although they have promoted varying degrees of **public diplomacy.** In other words, when it comes to *serious issues of vital national interest,* sports have had no political impact; government officials do not use sports in their negotiations about crucial national and international policies. However, when it comes to *public expressions of togetherness,* such as cultural exchanges and general communication among officials from various nations, sports have been useful on many occasions.

International sports have provided opportunities for officials from various countries to meet and talk, even though sports don't influence what is discussed or the outcomes of the discussions. Furthermore, these sports have brought together athletes, who learn from and about one another; however, athletes have no influence on political decisions, and relationships between athletes have no political significance.

These points were illustrated clearly in 1999, when the Cuban National Baseball Team played the Baltimore Orioles in Cuba and then again in Baltimore. Public discourse was affected, but the games had no discernable impact on political relations between the two countries (Pettavino and Brenner, 1999).

Apart from times when sports are associated with public diplomacy, history shows that most nations have used sports and sport events, especially the Olympic Games, to pursue their own interests, rather than the collective goals of international communication, understanding, friendship, and peace. Nationalist themes have been clearly evident in many events, and most nations have used sport events regularly to promote their own military, economic, political, and cultural goals. This was particularly apparent during the Cold War era following World War II and extending into the early 1990s. In fact, the Olympics often were presented as extensions of so-called superpower politics.

The connection between international sports and politics was so widely recognized in the early 1980s that Peter Ueberroth, president of the Los Angeles Olympic Organizing Committee, said that "we now have to face the reality that the Olympics constitute not only an athletic event but a political event" (*U.S. News & World Report,* 1983). Ueberroth was not being prophetic when he made this statement; he was simply summarizing his observations of Olympic history. From his perspective in 1983, it was clear that nations seldom put international friendship and world peace ahead of their own interests in connection with the Olympics. The demonstration of national superiority through sports was the major focus for the so-called world powers.

Wealthy and powerful nations have not been the only ones to use international sports to promote political interests. For example, many nations lacking international political and economic power have used sports in their overall quest for international recognition and legitimacy. For them, the Olympics and other international sports have been stages for showing that their athletes and teams can stand up to and sometimes defeat athletes and teams from wealthy and powerful nations. For example, the

Wealthy and powerful nations have always had a major share of power in international sports. The games and sports of these nations form the foundation of the Olympic Games. In this historic photo of the 1936 Olympic Games in Berlin, the U.S. team salutes as it represents U.S. interests in pre–World War II Europe. The Nazi flag (far right) is prominently displayed by the host nation. Adolf Hitler used the Games to promote Nazi ideology. (USOC Archives)

ability of athletes and teams from the West Indies and India to do well in important cricket competitions against teams from England has been seen by West Indian and Indian people as a symbol of their emerging independence and autonomy in relation to one of the countries that colonized their homelands in the past.

National leaders also have realized that hosting the Olympics is a special opportunity to generate international recognition, display national power and resources to a global audience, and invite investments into their economies. This is one of the reasons that bid committees from prospective host cities and nations sometimes have used gifts, bribes, and financial incentives

to have IOC members vote for them in the bid selection process (see pages 473–476).

The political goals of the nations hosting major international events have been highlighted when other nations have boycotted those events. For example, the 1980 Moscow Games were boycotted by the United States, Canada, and their political allies to protest Soviet military actions in Afghanistan. The USSR and its allies then boycotted the 1984 Los Angeles Games to protest the commercialization of the games and to avoid potentially threatening behavior by what they expected to be jingoistic U.S. spectators. However, each of these Olympic games was held despite the boycotts, and each host nation unashamedly displayed its power and resources to other participant nations. Furthermore, the boycotts had no major effect on national policies in any of the countries involved.

Global media coverage has intensified and added new dimensions to the connection between sports and politics. For example, television companies, especially the American networks, traditionally attracted viewers to their Olympic coverage by stressing political controversies along with national interests and symbols. The theme of their coverage between 1960 and 1988 was less focused on international friendship than on "us versus them" and "this nation versus that nation." The networks justified this coverage by claiming that U.S. viewers preferred nationalistic themes that extolled U.S. values and that claimed U.S. global political superiority.

Although past media coverage of the Olympics and other international sports encouraged ethnocentrism and a militaristic approach to international relations, more recent coverage has reflected the end of the Cold War and the emerging global marketplace. Nationalist themes still exist, but they are not as important as the themes of material consumption and global capitalist expansion. The need to do something about this is highlighted in the box "Olympism and the Olympic Games."

Nation-States, Sports, and Cultural Ideology

Sports have been used to promote ideas and orientations that fit the interests of the most powerful and wealthiest nations in the world. Participation in major international sport events often has meant that less powerful nations must look to the so-called superpowers for guidance and resources. This has encouraged people in relatively poor nations to deemphasize their traditional folk games and focus their attention on sports that are largely unrelated to their own values and experiences. Furthermore, it has led them to be involved in events over which they

have little control. Generally, if they want to play, they must go along with the conditions determined by people in powerful nations.

When this occurs, people in poorer nations find that they buy, beg, or borrow everything from equipment to technical assistance from people in wealthy nations. This often promotes dependency on economically powerful nations, and sports become vehicles through which powerful nations extend their control over important forms of popular culture around the world.

When people in poorer nations are committed to maintaining traditional cultural practices, including their native games, they resist the ideological influence associated with this type of "cultural imperialism," but resistance can be difficult when the rules and organization of popular international sports are so closely tied to the ideologies of powerful nations. For example, when an American sport such as football is introduced to another country, it comes with an emphasis on ideas about individual achievement, competition, winning, hierarchical authority structures, and the use of technology to shape bodies into efficient machines. These ideas may not be completely accepted by those learning to play and understand football, but they do encourage orientations that work to the advantage of the United States, as well as to the long-term disadvantage of the less powerful nations. As a writer at *Newsweek* noted in a summary of the twentieth century, "Sports may be America's most successful export to the world. . . . Our most visible symbol has evolved from the Stars and Stripes to Coke and the Nike Swoosh" (Starr, 1999, p. 44).

Ideally, sports can be vehicles for cultural exchanges through which people from various nations *share* information and develop *mutual* cultural understanding. But true fifty-fifty sharing and mutual understanding are rare when two nations have unequal power and resources. This means that sports often become cultural exports from wealthy nations incorporated into the everyday lives of people in other nations. Of course, these imported sports may be revised and

REFLECT ON SPORTS

Olympism and the Olympic Games
Are They Special?

Are the Olympics just another international sport event, or are they special? To answer this question, we can consult the The Olympic Charter, the official statement of the philosophy, goals, and rules for the Olympic Games. Paragraph 2 of the *Fundamental Principles* in the charter states the following:

> Olympism is a philosophy of life, exalting and combining in a balanced whole the qualities of body, will and mind. Blending sport with culture and education, Olympism seeks to create a way of life based on the joy found in effort, the educational value of good example and respect for universal fundamental ethical principles.

The fundamentals of The Olympic Charter are simple and straightforward. They emphasize that the Olympics should involve opportunities for people to learn about and connect with others from different nations and cultural backgrounds. These ideals are important, because our future on this planet depends on our working together as global citizens.

The goal of Olympism is not to inspire everyone to think alike or believe that all human beings are basically the same. Instead, it is to establish processes through which we learn to understand and appreciate our differences and work together to sustain healthy and safe lifestyles for people around the world. If the Olympic Games can be organized and played to promote these goals, they are, indeed, special.

Unfortunately, the Olympic Games clearly fall short of meeting these ideals. Nationalism and commercialism exert so much influence on how the Olympic Games are planned, promoted, presented, and played that the goal of global understanding and togetherness receives only token attention.

According to Michael Real (1996), a professor of communication who has studied the Olympics as a media spectacle, the current method of selling media broadcasting rights tends to subvert Olympic ideals. Television companies buy the rights to take the video images they want from the Olympics and combine them with their own commentaries for audiences in their countries. Thus, instead of bringing the world together around a single experience, the coverage presents heavily nationalized and commercialized versions of the Olympic Games. It is, of course, possible for these consumers to impose their own meanings on this coverage, but the coverage itself serves as the starting point for how they think about and make sense of the Olympics.

Viewers who wish to use the Olympics to visualize global community constructed around cultural differences and mutual understanding can do so, but current TV coverage provides little assistance in this quest. Instead, it highlights the association between large corporate sponsors and human achievement. In the process, many people come to believe that corporations really do make the Olympics possible. As they watch the events, about 20 percent of television time presents messages from those corporations, the companies that, in the words of the announcers, "bring you the Olympics."

People don't accept these messages in literal terms, but corporate sponsors bet hundreds of millions of dollars every two years that the association between their logos and the Olympic Rings discourages criticism of their products and encourages people to consume those products regularly.

The overt commercialism in the Olympics has led many people, including officials and athletes, to raise questions about the meaning of the Olympics. Shirley Babashoff, a swimmer who won two gold and six silver Olympic medals in 1972 and 1976, watched the 1996 games and said this:

> The Olympics is not about sports any more. It's about who can win the most money. It's like going to Disneyland. (in Reid, 1996, p. 4BB)

A high-ranking Olympic official came to this conclusion:

> I'm on the verge of joining those who think it's time for the Olympics, in their present context, to die. And they need to die for the same reason the ancient Olympic Games died—greed and corruption. And they're just about at the point now. (in Reid, 1996, p. 4BB)

Charles Barkley, an outspoken member of the U.S. men's basketball "Dream Team," noted in 1992 that the purpose of the games had little to do with Olympic ideals. He said,

> I know why we're here. We're here to spread basketball internationally and make more money for somebody. . . . We're going to win the gold medal, but there won't be any life changing decisions made because of it. . . . [P]oor people will still be poor and racism and sexism will still exist. (in DuPree, 1992, p. 7E)

These quotes support the need to make changes. The IOC issues regular press releases full of rhetoric about friendship and peace, but it has made no concerted effort to take that rhetoric seriously. It has not constructed programs and processes making it clear to athletes and spectators that the games are about cultural understanding and working together in socially responsible ways. This point has been made by Bruce Kidd, a former Olympian who is now a physical and health educator at the University of Toronto. Kidd (1996a) argues that the time is right to make the Olympic Games special by using them to highlight cultural and social issues and to promote social responsibility around the globe.

Kidd suggests that athletes be selected to participate in the Olympics on the basis of their actions as global citizens, as well as their athletic accomplishments. There also should be a curriculum enabling athletes to learn about fellow competitors and their cultures. The games should involve formal, televised opportunities for intercultural exchanges, and athletes should be ready to discuss their ideas about world peace and social responsibility during media interviews. The IOC should sponsor projects so that citizen-athletes have opportunities to build on their Olympic experiences through service to others around the world. A proportion of TV rights fees could be used to make this happen. IOC members then could talk about real examples of social responsibility connected with sports. The personal stories that television companies present during coverage of the games could then highlight the ways that athletes are socially responsible, rather than focusing on soap-opera-like personal tragedies and experiences. TV viewers may

find stories about how the Olympics make the world a better place as entertaining and inspiring as tabloid-like coverage of heartbreaking stories about beating the odds to win medals.

Additionally, the IOC should control both nationalism and commercialism more carefully as it organizes the games and sells broadcasting rights. I offer the following suggestions:

- *Do away with national uniforms for athletes.* Let athletes choose from uniforms designed by artists from various countries to express various cultural themes from around the world. This would minimize nationalism and inspire forms of expression that promote cultural understanding.
- *Revise the opening ceremonies, so that athletes enter the arena with others in their events.* The emphasis would be on unity and fellowship, not on the political and economic systems in which the athletes were born through no choice of their own. Artists from around the world would be commissioned to design flags for various sports. National flags would be displayed collectively in the middle of the field to emphasize unity amid difference.
- *Eliminate national anthems and flags during the award ceremonies.* Present medals in the stadium at the end of each day of competition in such a way that the emphasis during awards ceremonies is on the athletes as representatives of all humanity, rather than of nations.
- *Eliminate medal counts for nations.* National medal counts are contrary to the spirit of the Olympic Movement. They foster chauvinism, intensify existing political conflicts, and distract attention from the achievements of athletes.
- *Eliminate or revise team sports.* Team sports, as they are now structured, automatically focus attention on national affiliations. They encourage players and spectators to perceive games in terms of national honor and pride. If team sports are not eliminated, then develop a method of choosing

Olympism and the Olympic Games (continued)
Are They Special?

teams so that athletes from different countries play on the same teams and athletes from any one nation play on different teams. Then "dream teams" would emphasize international unity, rather than a nationalist and commercial approach to sports.

- *Add to each game "demonstration sports" native to the cultural regions where the games are held.* Because television influences how sports are imagined, created, and played around the world, mandate television coverage of these native games, so viewers have expanded notions of physical activities, which may inspire creative changes in their sport participation.
- *Use multiple sites for each Olympic Games.* This would enable nations without massive economic resources to be hosts. Poorer nations that host only a portion of the events would benefit economically, and multiple sites would enable media spectators to see a wider range of cultural settings while still seeing all the events in the games. Furthermore, even when wealthy nations host the entire games, they are forced to build too many massive facilities that will never be used to full capacity in the future. This usually involves a waste of already limited public funds.
- *Emphasize global responsibility in media coverage and commercials.* Television contracts could mandate an emphasis on global responsibility. Expressions of this theme could be developed by athlete committees' working with committees from the

Olympic Academy, which includes scholars committed to the spirit of Olympism. This would link corporate sponsors to the special meaning of the Olympics and provide support for athletes as global citizens.

- *Provide television time for nonprofit human rights groups that work with athletes and sport organizations to promote social justice.* This would give the viewers of the Olympics an opportunity to hear messages that are not created or censored by corporations and market forces. The commercial media would resist this, but it could be made a condition of receiving the rights to cover the games, and the nonprofit groups to receive time could be identified by athletes involved in human rights and social justice work.

Many people will say that these suggestions are idealistic and that they do not match how they view the Olympics. However, the Olympic Movement was founded on idealism and was meant to inspire visions of what our world could be. Just because many of us have learned to define the Olympic Games in other ways does not mean that we should not discuss what they have come to be and then consider changing them to achieve in more direct ways the ideals on which they were founded.

Because the Olympic Games capture the attention of one-third of the world's population, they should be used as something other than global marketing

reshaped to reaffirm local values and lifestyles. However, even when that occurs, it is likely that the people in traditional cultures become increasingly open to the possibility of importing and consuming other goods, services, and ideas from the wealthy nations. Unless political power and economic resources are developed in connection with this process, poorer nations become increasingly dependent on wealthy nations. Of

course, this is a complex process, involving many issues in addition to those related to sports.

New Political Realities in an Era of Transnational Corporations

Today, international sports are less likely to be scenes for nationalistic displays than scenes for commercial displays by large and powerful opportunities for transnational corporations and political stages for wealthy nations, which can afford to produce medal-winning athletes. The present is a good time for the Olympics to put into practice the ideals of The Olympic Charter. As this is done, the Olympics should formulate a new motto, one that goes beyond "Citius, Altius, Fortius" ("faster, higher, stronger"), one that takes the Olympics beyond nationalism and commercialism. What about "Excellence for Humanity"? *What do you think?*

Corporate sponsors pay millions of dollars to have their logos and products associated with the USOC. The USOC gives a prominent place to this display at its training center complex in Colorado Springs. One of the issues of concern in the sociology of sport is the extent to which the meanings and images associated with the Olympics are used to promote capitalist expansion rather than the goals of Olympism. (Jay Coakley)

transnational corporations. This was clearly evident in Atlanta (1996), Nagano (1998), Sydney (2000), and Salt Lake City (2002), and it will be evident in future locations.

Global politics have changed dramatically over the past decade. Nation-states have been joined by powerful transnational organizations in global power relations. As noted in chapter 11, about half of the largest economies in the world are corporations, *not* nation-states. As nation-states have lifted trade restrictions, decreased tariffs, and loosened their internal regulations to promote their own capitalist expansion, transnational corporations have become increasingly powerful players in global politics. Many of them are now more powerful in economic terms than the nations in which their products are manufactured. This, of course, gives them political power as well.

Therefore, instead of focusing just on international relations when we study sports and political processes, we must broaden our focus to consider *transnational relations*. This enables us to acknowledge that nation-states are now joined by major corporations and other powerful transnational organizations as global political players.

Nationalism still exists in connection with international sports, especially those played in regions where political and economic issues call attention to national differences and interests. However, in the case of many sport events, the differences between national interests and identities and corporate interests and identities are becoming increasingly blurred. This was highlighted by Phil Knight, the CEO of the U.S.–based Nike Corporation, as he explained the basis for his team loyalty during the 1994 World Cup:

> We see a natural evolution . . . dividing the world into their athletes and ours. And we glory ours. When the U.S. played Brazil in the World Cup, I rooted for Brazil because it was a Nike team. America was Adidas. (in Lipsyte, 1996b, p. 9)

Knight's point was that he identified teams and athletes in terms of corporate logos, not nationalities. He knew that Nike's markets were not limited to the United States. They were and continue to be worldwide, and this was why Nike gave Brazil's national sport teams $200 million for the right to use the Brazilian soccer team to market Nike products around the world through the year 2005. Knight sees logo loyalty as more important than national loyalty when it comes to international sports; he sees consumerism replacing patriotism when it comes to identifying athletes and teams; he sees international sport events as sites for Nike and other corporate sponsors to deliver advertising messages promoting their companies' interests, and promoting general global capitalist expansion. Furthermore, he and fellow executives from other powerful corporations see this as good for the people of the world. Their conclusion would be similar to conclusions made by those using functionalist theory: sport contributes to economic expansion, and this is good for everyone in the world.

To the extent that corporate sponsors influence sport events and media coverage, international sports televised around the world are used as vehicles for presenting to massive audiences a range of messages promoting the interests of corporate capitalism (Donnelly, 1996a). These messages are directed to spectator-consumers, not spectator-citizens (see figure 13.1). Instead of focusing on patriotism or nationalism, the messages that come with international sports now focus on status consciousness and individual consumption. Sports that don't enable corporations to deliver their messages to consumers with purchasing power are not sponsored. If spectators and media audiences are not potential consumers, corporations see little reason to sponsor events, so, unless the media are publicly owned, they are not likely to cover events viewed by those who have little purchasing power.

Of course, the power of corporations is not unlimited or uncontested, as conflict theorists would have us conclude. Figurational research has identified cases in which local populations use their own cultural perspectives to interpret and apply the images and discourses that come with global sports and global advertising (Maguire, 1999; Maguire and Pearton, 1999). However, those who use critical theories note that global media sports and the commercial messages that accompany them often cleverly fuse the global and the local through thoughtfully and carefully edited images of local traditions, sport action, and consumer products (Andrews and Silk, 1999; Carrington and Sugden, 1999; Jackson and Hokowhitu, 2002; Jackson and Scherer, 2002; Silk, 1999). They argue that these fused images tend to "detraditionalize" local cultures by presenting local symbols and lifestyles in connection with consumer products.

Nike has been especially clever in this regard. As cultural theorist David Andrews points out,

"Well, at least nobody can accuse the Olympics of producing NATIONALISM anymore."

FIGURE 13.1   Nationalism continues to exist in connection with the Olympic Games, but powerful transnational corporations have been successful in combining national identities and the Olympics with an ideology that promotes consumption, competition, and individualism. Corporate logos now are as visible as national flags at most international sport events.

Nike commercials that aired in connection with global sport events during the late 1990s masterfully presented images from numerous localities around the world. These local images were "reassembled" and situated in connection with Nike products, such as soccer apparel worn by players from many nations as they kicked a soccer ball in numerous locations around the globe. Andrews argues that Nike captures local traditions and wraps its branded jerseys around them until there is little else to be seen or discussed. This has now become a common advertising strategy.

The conclusions made by critical theories have not been explored sufficiently in research, but it is clear that, as corporations join or replace nation-states as sponsors of athletes and teams around the world, sports do become framed in new political terms. According to John Horan, the publisher of *Sporting Goods Intelligence*, "It's not the Free World versus Communism anymore. Now

you take sides with sneaker companies. Now everybody looks at the Olympics as Nike versus Reebok" (in Reid, 1996, p. 4BB). Horan's conclusion is probably distorted by his hope that global sports are perceived in this way. However, despite some distortion and exaggeration, Horan expresses the intent of transnational corporations as they spend billions of dollars to sponsor sports around the world.

The late Roone Arledge, former president of ABC News and director of ABC Sports, noted that this intent was becoming a reality in connection with sport events. He observed that the Olympic Games are "basically a commercial enterprise that tries every four years to make as much money as it possibly can," and the games don't have "much to do with the heroic words that we use to describe them" (in Reid, 1996, p. 4BB). Reaffirming Arledge's conclusion, Dick Ebersol, president of NBC Sports, explained that NBC paid over $3.5 billion for the U.S. rights to televise all Olympic Games from 2000 to 2008, because the Olympics "has this amazing ability to put the whole family in front of the television together, which is what advertisers are grabbing at" (in Steinbreder, 1996, p. 38).

These statements, made only thirteen years after Peter Ueberroth, president of the Los Angeles Olympic Organizing Committee, described the Olympics as an athletic-*political* event, illustrate the power of corporate capitalism. In just over a decade, the characterization of the largest sport event in the world changed from athletic-*political* to athletic-*economic*.

Representatives from many major corporations around the world have come to see the potential of sports to establish new commercial markets and to promote the ideology of consumerism, which drives those markets. Although the sponsorship money coming from these corporations is welcomed by those who benefit from it, the primary goal of those who own and control the corporations is to make profits.

Coca-Cola may sponsor the Olympics because it wants to bring people together, but it is primarily interested in selling as many Cokes as possible to 6.3 billion people around the world. This is also why the MARS candy company pays millions to be the official snack food of the Olympics and why McDonald's uses the Olympics and nearly fat-free athletes' bodies to market hamburgers and fries around the world.

According to Sut Jhally, a noted communications professor from the University of Massachusetts, transnational corporations pay billions of dollars to sponsor global sports in an effort to become "global cultural commissars." Jhally says that, if you listen closely and critically to the advertisements of these sponsors, you'll discover that, in addition to their products, they are selling a way of life based on consumption. They use sports to present images and messages emphasizing individual success through competition, production, and consumption. They know that elite competitive sports are ideal vehicles for presenting these images and messages, because

such sports have become primary sources of entertainment around the world. When people are being entertained while watching these sports in person or on television, they are emotionally primed to hear what the sponsors have to say.

Of course, many people ignore the images and messages emphasized by sponsors, or they redefine them to fit local and personal circumstances. But this does not prevent large corporations from spending billions to deliver them. Advertisers understand that sooner or later the images and messages associated with sources of pleasure and entertainment in people's lives will in some form enter the imaginations and conversations of a proportion of those who see and hear them. Commercial images and messages do not dictate what people think, but they certainly influence what people think about, and, in this way, they become a part of the overall discourse that occurs in cultures around the globe.

We should not interpret this description of the new politics of sports to mean that sports around the world somehow have fallen victim to a global conspiracy hatched by transnational corporations. It means only that transnational organizations have joined nation-states in the global political context in which sports are defined, organized, planned, promoted, played, and presented, and given meaning around the world (Jackson and Scherer, 2002; Silk, 1999).

Other Global Political Issues

As sports have become increasingly commercialized, and as national boundaries have become less relevant in sports, an increasing number of athletes have become global migrant workers. They go where their sports are played, where they can be supported or earn money while they play, or where they can have the cultural experiences they seek. This global migration of athletes has raised new political issues in connection with sports.

Another global political issue is related to the production of sporting goods. As the demand for sports equipment and clothing has increased in wealthy nations, transnational corporations have cut costs for those products by manufacturing them in labor-intensive poor countries, where wage costs are extremely low. The result has been a clear split between the world's haves and have-nots when it comes to sports: those born into privilege in wealthy nations consume the products made by those born into disadvantaged circumstances in poor nations. This is not a new issue, but it ties sports to global politics in yet another way.

Athletes as Global Migrant Workers Human history is full of examples of labor migration, both forced and voluntary. Industrial societies, in particular, have depended on mobile labor forces responsive to the needs of production. Now that economies have become more global, the pervasiveness and diversity of labor migration patterns have increased. This is true in sports as well as other occupational categories (Maguire, 1999; Maguire et al., 2002; Stead and Maguire, 2000). Athletes frequently move from their hometowns when they are recruited to play elite sports, and then they may move many times after that, as they are traded from team to team or seek continuing opportunities to play their sports.

As geographer John Bale and sociologist Joe Maguire have noted in a book on athletic talent migration (1994), athletes move from state to state and region to region within nations, as well as from nation to nation within and between continents. They have noted also that each of these moves raises issues related to the following: (1) the personal adjustment of migrating athletes, (2) the rights of athletes as workers in various nations, (3) the impact of talent migration on the nations from and to which athletes migrate, and (4) the impact of athlete migration on patterns of personal, cultural, and national identity formation.

Some migration patterns are seasonal, involving temporary moves as athletes travel from one climate area to another to play their sports. Patterns may follow annual tour schedules, as athletes travel from tournament to tournament around a region or the world, or they may involve long-term or permanent moves from one region or nation to another.

The range of personal experiences among migrating athletes is great. They vary from major forms of culture shock and chronic loneliness to minor homesickness and lifestyle adjustments. Some athletes are exploited by teams or clubs, whereas others make great amounts of money and receive a hero's welcome when they return home in the off-season. Some encounter prejudice against foreigners or various forms of racial and ethnic bigotry, whereas others are socially accepted and make good friends. Some cling to their national identities and socialize with fellow athletes from their homelands, whereas others develop more global identities unrelated to one national or cultural background. In some cases, teams and clubs expect foreign athletes to adjust on their own, whereas others provide support for those who need to learn a new language or become familiar with new cultural settings (Klein, 1991).

Athletic talent migration also has an impact on the nations involved. For example, many Latin American nations have their best baseball players recruited by Major League teams in the United States. This not only depletes the talent the Latin American nations need to maintain professional baseball in their local economies but also forces them to depend on U.S.-based satellite television companies even to watch the players from their nations. As Major League Baseball teams in North America recruit stars from professional teams in Japan, some Japanese people worry that this trend could destroy professional baseball in their country. At the same time, they are proud that Japanese players excel on Major League teams. As they watch Major League games on satellite television, attendance and television ratings for Japanese baseball decline.

Furthermore, as people in other countries and continents watch sports based in the United States and Canada, they often are exposed to images and messages consistent with the advertising interests of corporations headquartered in the United States. Similar patterns exist in connection with European soccer teams that recruit players from around the world. In fact, soccer has higher rates of talent migration than other sports, although hockey, track and field, and basketball have high rates as well. The impact of this migration on national talent pools and on the ability of local clubs and teams to maintain economically viable sport programs is complex. Talent migration usually benefits the nation to which athletes move more than it benefits the nation from which athletes come, but this is not always the case.

The impact of global migration by athletes on how people think about and identify themselves in connection with nation-states is something we know little about. Many people appreciate athletic talent regardless of the athlete's nationality. At the same time, many people have special affections for athletes and teams representing their nations of citizenship or their nations of origin. Leagues such as the NHL are open to athletes from all nations. In fact, even though most of the teams are located in U.S. cities, less than 20 percent of the players are U.S.-born; about 60 percent are from Canada, and nearly 30 percent are from European nations. In Major League Baseball, over one-fourth of the players on Major League teams and over 40 percent of the players at all levels of professional baseball in North America were not born in the United States. Among the 416 players on 29 NBA teams at the start of the 2002–2003 season, 67, or 16 percent, were born outside the United States.

These trends have been worrisome to some people. This is why some leagues have quotas that limit the number of foreign-born or foreign-nationality players that teams may sign to contracts. For example, in the early 1990s, Japan banned U.S. women basketball players from its professional league. At the same time, professional leagues in Italy, Spain, and France allowed their teams to have up to two foreign players, many of whom were from the United States. In 1996, England lifted all quotas for both men's and

In 2003, about 67 of the 416 players in the NBA were born outside the United States. Mark Cuban, owner of the Dallas-Mavericks, has assertively recruited players globally and marketed his team in the countries from where his players come. Eduardo Najera (#14) is from Mexico. Standout player Yao Ming (#11) of the Houston Rockets is from China and has created interest in the NBA among millions of people from his native country. (LM Otero; AP/Wide World Photos)

women's pro basketball teams; during the same year, the new MLS (Major League Soccer) in the United States limited the number of non–U.S. players to four per team. Currently, some people in the United States are calling for limits on the number of foreign athletes who can play on intercollegiate teams. At the same time, many athletic departments are recruiting more athletes from outside the United States.

As commercial sport organizations expand their franchise locations across national borders, and as they recruit athletes regardless of nationality, talent migration will increase in the future. The social implications of this trend will be important to study and understand.

Global Politics and the Production of Sports Equipment and Apparel

Free trade agreements (for example, GATT and NAFTA), signed by many nations in the mid-1990s, have created a new global economic environment. In this environment, it is cost-effective for large corporations selling vast amounts of goods to people in wealthy nations to locate production facilities in labor-intensive poor nations. These corporations are taxed at much lower rates when they move products from nation to nation, so they can make products in nations where labor is cheap and regulations are scarce and then sell them in wealthy nations, where people can afford to buy them.

These political-economic changes mean that, through the 1990s, most athletic shoes costing well over $100 a pair in the United States were cut and sewn by workers making less than 25 cents per hour in China and Indonesia, less than 75 cents per hour in Thailand, and less than $2.25 per hour in South Korea (Enloe, 1995; Kidd and Donnelly, 2000; Sage, 1999).

Similar patterns existed in connection with the production of clothes bearing patriotic-looking red, white, and blue NFL and NBA logos sold in the United States (Sage, 1996). Soccer balls sanctioned by FIFA, the international soccer federation, often were hand-sewn by child laborers making far less than poverty-level wages in poor nations, where people were desperate for any kind of work. And, while Nike athletes were making millions of dollars on their shoe endorsements, Nike shoes were being made mostly by young women in Southeast Asia working ten to thirteen hours a day, six days a week under oppressive conditions for 13–20 cents per hour (U.S. dollar)—far below a living wage in China, Vietnam, and Indonesia.

This exploitation attracted worldwide attention among religious, human rights, and labor organizations, as well as other activist groups. Sport sociologist George Sage (1999) has described the international Nike transnational advocacy network, which emerged during the mid-1990s. This network of dozens of organizations from many countries gradually mobilized consciousness and various forms of political action, which influenced various government policies on labor and human rights issues and Nike's relationship with production contractors in Southeast Asia. The network was so effective that the Nike logo became associated with sweatshops and unfair labor practices in the minds of many consumers. Nike's earnings declined, and its executives began to take responsibility for making changes in its production facilities; they even downsized the swoosh logo and converted the print logo to *nike* with a small *n* because they wanted to understate their presence and avoid negative attention among potential consumers.

Sage's case study of the Nike transnational advocacy network is heartening, because it documents the power of people to make change. The Internet and other global communications technologies make it possible for people around the world to mobilize in response to human rights violations and other important social issues. Of course, many factors influence the formation of a transnational advocacy network, but, when issues resonate across many groups of people, a network of organizations and individuals can organize, take action, and have an impact on global political processes. If this were not possible, what would stop transnational corporations, which are accountable to nothing but a generally underregulated global marketplace, from pursuing their interests in whatever ways they wish?

In November 2001, the University of North Carolina signed a contract with Nike, contingent on the sporting goods company following an antisweatshop code for all equipment and apparel provided to university teams. For the university, a primary goal of this $28 million contract was to force Nike to end its exploitive child labor practices. Representatives of the campus

Since the late 1990s, there has been a growing awareness of exploitive labor practices to produce sports equipment and apparel. These photos, provided by The Global March Against Child Labour, show a twelve-year-old girl in India sewing a soccer ball. The ball is stamped with the claim that it is made with "Child Free Labor." It should read "Made by Underpaid and Exploited Children."

saw this as one step in dealing with the general exploitation of labor in poor nations where there are few or no laws protecting workers or regulating the conditions under which they work.

Other universities have considered taking or have taken similar steps (Sage, 1999). In the case of Nike, this type of action can be effective because it has contracts with 200 college and university athletic departments. But exploitation continues to exist as corporations seek the cheapest labor they can find to manufacture their products. This exploitation will end only when consumers in wealthy nations take collective social actions that demand changes in public and corporate policies around the world. Human rights and social justice groups have fought these battles for many years, but they need help.

Making Sense of Today's Political Realities

It's not easy to explain all the changes discussed in this chapter. Are sports simply a part of general globalization processes through which various sport forms come together in many combinations? Are we witnessing the modernization of sports? Are sports being Americanized? Europeanized? Asianized?

Are we seeing sports simply being diffused throughout the world, with people in some countries emulating the sports played in other countries, or are sports being used in connection with new forms of cultural imperialism and colonization?

Are sports tools for making poorer nations dependent on wealthier ones, or are they tools for establishing cultural independence and autonomy in emerging nations?

Is it accurate to say that sports are becoming commercialized, or should we say that corporations are appropriating sports for the purpose of global capitalist expansion?

Are traditional and folk sports around the world being destroyed by heavily publicized sports based in wealthy nations, or do people take sport forms from other cultures and creatively adapt them to their own circumstances?

Are sports becoming more democratic, or have new forms of sponsorship actually restricted people's choices about when and how they will play sports?

Those who study sports as social phenomena now are devoting more of their attention to these questions. The best work on these issues involves data collected at global *and* local levels (Donnelly, 1996a; Guttmann, 1994; Harvey et al., 1996; Maguire, 1999). This work calls attention to the fact that powerful people do not simply impose certain sport forms on less powerful people around the world. Even when sports from powerful nations are played in other parts of the world, the meanings associated with them often are grounded in the local cultures in which they are played. It is important to understand global trends, but it is also important to understand the local expressions of and responses to those trends. Power is a process, not a thing; it is always exercised through social relations, so the study of power must focus on how people agree and disagree with one another as they attempt to live their lives in meaningful terms. This is true in connection with sports, as it is in other dimensions of social life.

POLITICS IN SPORTS

The term *politics* usually is associated with formal government entities in the public sphere. However, politics include all processes of governing people and administering policies, at all levels of organization, public and private. Therefore, politics are an integral part of sports, and many local, national, and international sport organizations are referred to as "governing bodies."

Sport organizations do many things, but most are concerned with providing and regulating sport participation opportunities, establishing and enforcing policies, controlling and standardizing competitions, and acknowledging the accomplishments of athletes. This sounds like a straightforward set of tasks. However, they seldom are accomplished without opposition, debate, and compromise. Members of sport organizations may agree on many things, but they also have different interests and orientations. In fact, conflicts often arise as people deal with the following questions surrounding sports and sport participation:

1. What qualifies as a sport?
2. What are the rules of a sport?
3. Who makes and enforces the rules in sports?
4. Who organizes and controls games, meets, matches, and tournaments?
5. Where do sport events take place?
6. Who is eligible to participate in a sport?
7. How are rewards distributed to athletes and other organization members?

Because some people mistakenly assume that sports are pure activities and should be separate from the everyday world, they are sometimes shocked and disappointed when they hear that sports involve politics. However, just as sports are connected with political processes in the larger social world, sport events and organizations involve politics of their own. These politics affect everyone involved, from athletes, coaches, and administrators in sport organizations to promoters, sponsors, and spectators. The following seven sections discuss examples of politics in sports as they are related to the questions above.

What Qualifies as a Sport?

As noted in chapter 1, there is no universal agreement on the definition of *sports*. What is considered a sport in a society or in a particular event, such as the Olympics, is determined through political processes (Donnelly, 1996b).

The criteria used to identify sports reflect the ideas and interests of some people more than others. In the Olympics, for example, a competitive activity or game for men is not considered for recognition as a sport unless it is played in at least seventy-five countries on four continents;

an activity or a game for women must be played in at least forty countries on three continents. It also must have an officially designated international governing body, a requisite number of national governing bodies, and a history of international championships before the IOC will consider recognizing it as an Olympic sport.

In these days of multibillion-dollar media contracts, an activity or a game is more likely to be recognized as a sport if it is attractive to television and if it attracts the interest of younger viewers, who in turn attract new advertisers and corporate sponsors to the Olympics. It also helps if women play the activity, because more women than men watch the Olympics and because the IOC is concerned that its failure to reach gender equity might create bad publicity for the Olympics as a whole.

Of course, this way of defining *sports* favors the nations that historically have emphasized competitive games and have had the resources to export their games around the world. Former colonial powers are especially favored, because they used their national games to introduce their cultural values and traditions to colonized peoples around the world. Wealthy and powerful nations today not only have their national sports broadcast on satellite channels around the world but also have the resources to subsidize the development of these sports, so that they are played in many countries. Therefore, when it comes time for IOC recognition, the sports from wealthy nations are at the top of the list. When these sports are recognized, the cultural values and traditions of wealthy and powerful nations are reaffirmed. In this way, the games of wealthy and powerful nations become the sports of the world.

This is also the reason native games in traditional cultures are not a part of the Olympic Games. Games played in limited regions of the world don't qualify for recognition as sports. Thus, if people from nations with traditional cultures want to participate in the Olympics, they must learn to play activities and games popular in wealthy nations. Since people in

Kato is an Asian game, played here at the twenty-second annual Minnesota Hmong Sports Event in St. Paul, Minnesota. The large Hmong population in the upper Midwest of the United States uses traditional sports to reaffirm their cultural heritage. However, it is unlikely that Kato or other traditional Asian or African games will be added to the list of Olympic sports. The definition of an Olympic sport favors sports developed and played in Western Europe and North America. (Eric Miller; AP/Wide World Photos)

traditional cultures lack access to the equipment and facilities needed to train in their homelands, they must depend on support from people and organizations in wealthy nations to become international athletes in recognized sports. In this way, sports become vehicles through which people and organizations in wealthy nations can gain a foothold in traditional cultures and influence social change processes to their own advantage.

This type of political process also occurs in other contexts. For example, for well over 100 years, the men who have controlled athletic departments in North American high schools and colleges have used a power and performance model to designate certain activities as varsity sports. Then they have organized these sports to emphasize competition and dominance, so that the sports fit their notions of character and excellence. Over the years, this way of defining and organizing sports seldom has been questioned, but, because gender equity has become an issue,

some people now argue that full equity never will be achieved unless such questions are raised. If power and performance sports attract far fewer girls and women than boys and men, it may be time to ask questions about what gets to count as a varsity sport and why. When we ask these questions, we immediately notice the existence of politics in sports.

The development of criteria underlying the meaning and organization of sports also occurs on a global scale. Sociologist Peter Donnelly (1996b) illustrates this in his analysis of the way the ideologies of Olympism and professionalism are being combined to form a global sport monoculture, which he calls "prolympism." Prolympism is quickly becoming the model for determining what activities count and get funded as sports in nations around the world, even in nations where traditional games are clearly inconsistent with professionalism in any form, so the politics of defining *sports* are both local and global in impact.

What Are the Rules of a Sport?

Sports are social constructions. This means that people create them as they interact with one another and identify physical challenges within the constraints of environment and culture. The rules that govern sports are also social constructions and, as such, are determined through political processes. Why should first base be 90 feet from home plate in Major League Baseball? Why should a basketball rim be 10 feet above the ground? Why should the top of volleyball nets be 88 1/8 inches off the ground in international women's volleyball? Why can't pole-vaulters use any type of pole they want? Why can't tournament golfers use any type of golf club or golf ball they want? Why is 6 centimeters the maximum height for the sides of bikini bottoms worn by women in beach volleyball? This list of questions could go on and on. The point is that the rules of sports can be based on many concerns, and this makes them political. Because sports have more rules than most human activities, they are more political than most things we participate in during our lives.

Who Makes and Enforces the Rules in Sports?

The rules of an "official" sport are determined by a governing body that is recognized as the official source of information and regulation for those who play the sport. The process of becoming recognized as the *sole* governing body of a sport clearly involves politics (Sugden and Tomlinson, 1998, 1999). Governing bodies have power, status, and control over resources, so it is common for more than one group to claim that it is the rightful rule-making body. The simultaneous existence of various governing bodies can create confusion for athletes and spectators in a sport. Professional boxing, for example, has at least four governing bodies (the WBO, the WBU, the WBF, and the IBO), each with its own weight categories and championships and each claiming to be the official rule-making body for boxing. Such sports as skateboarding and in-line skating have had at least two organizations vying to be official governing bodies. As these organizations seek to establish power over these sports and the athletes who participate in them, they battle each other to recruit dues-paying members and to sponsor competitive events, especially national and international championships. In the process, their policies confuse athletes and limit participation opportunities. When this occurs, people clearly see the politics in sports.

When rules exist, there is also a need for rule enforcement. This adds another political dimension to sports. Anyone who has ever refereed or officiated a game or match will tell you that rule violations are seldom clear-cut, that identifying violations is difficult, and that few people see violations the same way. Rule violations occur on a regular basis in many sports, but the best referees have learned when to call fouls or penalties in connection with these violations. In fact, referees and officials discuss when they should or should not call fouls during games and matches. Making sports appear to be fair to both athletes and spectators is a political challenge.

Dealing effectively with off-the-field rule violations is also a political challenge. What happens to a player's status on a team when he or she has violated a team rule related to off-the-field conduct? The process of investigating rule violations, determining innocence or guilt, and punishing rule violators involves determinations of what is good and bad for sports, sport organizations, and various people connected with sports. These determinations may be grounded in ideas about fairness, moral principles, economic interests, personal reputations, organizational prestige, or other factors. How these factors are defined and which ones prevail in the rule enforcement process are matters for discussion, debate, and compromise.

We also see the politics of rule enforcement in the policies of sport organizations. For example, the NCAA, the primary governing body for intercollegiate sports in the United States, is made up of representatives of member universities located all around the United States. Because college sports mean different things from one region of the country to another, these representatives often have contradictory ideas about what is legitimate conduct and what is not (Baxter et al., 1996). Developing a set of rules and enforcement procedures under these conditions involves intensely political processes. Rule enforcement inevitably creates dissent among the members whose ideas about legitimate conduct are not consistent with what the NCAA has determined to be "right and official." When this occurs, political processes become heated, and it occurs often.

Who Organizes and Controls Games, Meets, Matches, and Tournaments?

Representatives of official governing bodies usually are responsible for the organization and control of sport events. Standards emerge when the governing body is stable, but standards never are established once and for all time. For example, even though officials from governing bodies have devised formal standards for judging performances in sports such as figure skating, diving, and gymnastics, research shows that judges' votes are influenced by political loyalties, personal connections, coercion by people in positions of power, and even bribes (Jennings, 1996a; Jennings and Sambrook, 2000; Seltzer and Glass, 1991). This has been a serious issue in many Olympic Games, but it became widely publicized in 2002, when a judge for the figure skating pairs competition allegedly favored a Russian couple over a Canadian couple. Her scores determined who received the gold and silver medals, respectively. The complexity and intrigue of this case were covered in many popular sources (Michaelis, 2002). The public outcry was massive. After much debate, the International Skating Union (ISU) awarded the Canadian couple a gold medal without taking the gold medal away from the Russian couple. Then the ISU changed its rules to discourage unfair judging in the future. Skaters, however, objected strongly

to the new judging procedures, and the politics in the ISU remain contentious.

The process of trying to guarantee fair judging remains an issue in figure skating, as well as in other sports. When international politics influence judges, it is disheartening to athletes, but it should be no more disheartening than the knowledge that "cuteness," "hairstyles," "body build," and "eye color" can also influence judges when it comes to women athletes in certain events. This is a form of cultural politics that lead some athletes to spend thousands of dollars on everything from braces for their teeth to plastic surgery for their jaws and noses. Politics come in many forms.

Now that sports have become commercialized, the organization and control of events may be shared by official governing bodies and a combination of corporate sponsors and media production people. The location and timing of events, event schedules, the choice of people to be given press passes to cover events, the choice of which television company will have the rights to broadcast the events, the choice of which corporate logos will be associated with the events, and other issues are resolved through political processes. The participants in those processes and their interests change from one event to the next; this means that the politics in sports never end.

Where Do Sport Events Take Place?

The politics of place are an integral part of sports. Site selection decisions are contentious as sports, teams, and events use and are used by towns, cities, and nations for economic purposes.

Certainly, the selection of Olympic sites is a political process, as seen during and after the site selection vote-buying scandal involving the IOC and the Salt Lake Olympic Organizing Committee during the 1990s. When people around the world learned that cities can make profits as hosts of the Games, bid committees became involved in wining, dining, bribing, and pressuring the IOC members, whose votes determine which cities host the games. As investigative journalist

How are athletes judged during competitions? This political issue has caused serious controversy in many sports. This photo shows the Canadian couple (right) that thought they had won the pairs event in Salt Lake City during the 2002 Olympic Games and the Russian couple (left) that was awarded the gold medal. When it was discovered that a judge had submitted scores intentionally favoring the Russian couple, there was a massive investigation involving the FBI and many sport organizations. It led to changes in how judging occurs, but it did not end the controversy. (Lionel Cironneau; AP/ Wide World Photos)

Andrew Jennings wrote and talked about the scope of this process and the amounts of money involved, most people thought he was given to exaggeration (Jennings, 1996a; Jennings and Sambrook, 2000; Simson and Jennings, 1992). However, subsequent information has shown that his accusations of corruption and criminal activity were accurate (see figure 13.2).

The politics of site selection also operate in other ways. For example, Atlanta's bid for the 1996 Games was influenced by everything from the television rights fees anticipated from U.S.–based television companies to the location of the international headquarters of Coca-Cola, the largest corporate Olympic sponsor in the world, in Atlanta. The red-and-white Coke logo

was so evident around Atlanta and in Olympic venues that many observers described the games as the "Coca-Colympics."

The selection of Beijing, China, for the 2008 Summer Olympic Games involved both political considerations and complex political processes. China was desperate to host the games because it wanted to showcase its culture, encourage tourism, court business investments, and claim political legitimacy as a global power. The members of the IOC selection committee were influenced by many considerations: China was home to nearly 20 percent of the world's population, it had never hosted an Olympic Games, bringing Olympism to China would strengthen the Olympic Movement, and the potential economic

"I prefer to think of it as my personal 'opening ceremonies.'"

FIGURE 13.2 The scandals related to the Olympic site bidding process after 1985 raised serious questions about the too often assumed "purity" of the Olympic Games. The publicity associated with these scandals and the illegal and unethical actions of members of the Salt Lake Olympic Organizing Committee during the 1990s has led to reforms of the Olympic bid process. The goal of these reforms is to eliminate scenes like this from future bid processes.

benefits of awarding the games to China were very high because corporate sponsors would see China as a prime site for capitalist expansion.

NBC, the U.S. network with the rights to televise the 2008 Games, saw China as an attractive site for marketing its coverage. NBC knew that, by 2008, many Americans would be very interested in China because of its size, power, and culture. NBC also knew it could use that interest to boost its ratings and sell expensive advertising to sponsors.

At the same time, many people objected to awarding the games to China because of its questionable human rights record, its history of communism, and its policies related to population control, among other things. Overall, the global politics related to the Beijing selection were complex.

Site bids for events such as Super Bowls, All-Star games, the NCAA men's and women's basketball tournaments, and other international events may not cost as much as bids to host the Olympics, but they are just as political.

Sports and the politics of place in many parts of the world also reflect environmental issues. For example, the use of open space or agricultural land for golf courses is being contested in Europe, Japan, and even North America. The Global AntiGolf Movement has developed in connection with widespread objections to the use of chemical fertilizers and massive water resources to keep grass soft and green for golfers representing the economic elite in societies. This organization has 250 member lobbying groups in 15 countries, and it has coordinated protests and other antigolf campaigns around the world.

Ski resort expansion in North America, Europe, and Japan also has been resisted for environmental reasons. The organizers of the 2000 Sydney Games faced severe criticism when they failed in important ways to live up to the environmental principles developed by the original bid committee (Lenskyj, 1998). Such examples highlight the fact that the politics of place in sports often involve local opposition to the hosting of events and the building of facilities.

Who Is Eligible to Participate in a Sport?

Who plays and who doesn't play is often a hotly contested issue in sports. People in various governing bodies make determinations about participation eligibility. They may use factors such as gender, age, weight, height, ability (and disability), place of residence, citizenship, educational affiliation, grade in school, social status, income, or even race and ethnicity to determine participation eligibility. Although eligibility policies often are presented as if they were based on unchanging truths about human beings and sports, they are grounded in standards debated and agreed upon by groups of officials. These agreements are forged through political processes.

People often debate the seeming arbitrariness of eligibility rules. For example, NCAA eligibility rules are so complex that the organization publishes brochures and supplements explaining who may and may not play under various conditions. Lawsuits may be filed when people feel they have been excluded unfairly from participation. High school students have also challenged eligibility rules when their families have moved from one school district to another and discovered they were ineligible to play varsity sports. The "no pass, no play" rules in U.S. high school sports have been the subject of political debates in many states. Even in youth sports, there are frequent debates about the age and weight rules used to determine eligibility. Athletes with disabilities regularly challenge rules prohibiting their participation in certain sports. Within events such as the Paralym-

pics, for athletes with disabilities, there are frequent debates about disability classifications and eligibility.

There are literally hundreds of other noteworthy cases of eligibility politics in amateur and professional sports. As globalization increases, the debates about eligibility as it is related to citizenship, nationality, and place of residence will be debated more often. Amateur sports have been the scene of longstanding debates over the meaning of *amateur* and qualifications for amateur status. Because these meanings are socially determined, they change over time. This will always be the case, and this is why politics will always be a part of sports.

How Are Rewards Distributed to Athletes and Others?

The distribution of rewards is an issue at all levels of sport participation. Coaches, league administrators, and parents often must decide who will receive special commendations, certificates of accomplishment, and trophies. "Who gets what?" is a political question, and the answers are not always clear-cut. People discuss, debate, and sometimes argue heatedly over the issue of rewards. As the level of competition increases, so do the stakes associated with participation. At the highest levels of competition, the politics of rewards can involve massive amounts of money and status.

With the increased commercialization of sports, there have been longstanding, heated debates about how revenues should be distributed among sport organizations, organization officials, owners and promoters, athletes, and others connected with sports. As noted in chapter 11, the political processes associated with the distribution of revenues in commercial sports are complex and never-ending. Of course, these processes take various forms and come to different resolutions in different countries and in different sports.

A major "who gets what?" issue debated regularly in U.S. sports concerns pay for intercollegiate athletes. Why should a talented intercollegiate football player who risks his health and endures pain and injury while generating millions of dollars for his university be limited to receiving an athletic grant-in-aid that is worth only a fraction of what NFL players are paid? Why is this player not allowed to make money selling his own image on shirts or coffee mugs, while the university uses his image to market everything from the school itself to merchandise with the university logo on it? Athletes in revenue-producing sports say this is unfair; university spokespeople say that there is no fair way to pay all athletes who play on varsity teams, and there is no way to determine the dollar value of

the contributions made by athletes in revenue-producing sports. And the debate continues.

Other debates revolve around questions such as these: Why should professional sport team owners make more money than the best players on their teams? What percentage should agents receive when they negotiate player contracts? Why should prize money in a NASCAR race reflect how many times a driver and team have raced in the past in addition to how they finished the race? Why should Olympic athletes not be paid for their participation when they collectively generate over a billion dollars during a

Why should the USOC receive a portion of the television rights fees paid to the IOC by U.S. television companies? This policy perpetuates the inequalities between the training facilities in wealthy nations and the facilities in poorer nations. It is difficult to separate the joy of sport participation, as shown in this sculpture at the USOC Training Center in Colorado Springs, from the joy of having access to state-of-the-art training opportunities. (Jay Coakley)

Summer Olympics? Why should the IOC receive 33 percent of the revenues for the Olympic Games, when it does little other than award the games to a particular city while its members are wined and dined in lavish style in the process? Why should the USOC receive 12.75 percent of the money paid by U.S. television companies for the rights to broadcast the Olympics? Why should professional athletes who receive medals not be allowed during the medal ceremonies to wear warm-up suits made by the companies who pay them endorsement fees? Should athletes receive compensation when companies use their images and uniform numbers in expensive video games that sell million of copies? Who owns the surfaces of athletes' bodies and who may use them for commercial purposes? If athletes' bodies are used in video games, how should the revenues from those games be allocated? These and hundreds of similar questions show that the "politics of rewards" are an integral part of sports.

Sometimes rewards involve status or prestige, rather than money. For example, in 1992, there was considerable debate in Japan over whether Akebono (formerly named Chad Rowan), an American sumo wrestler from Hawaii, should be voted into the rank of *yokozuna*, or grand champion, by the Yokozuna Promotion Council. Many Japanese people warned the council that, if such a prized honor were not reserved for native Japanese, Japan might lose control of a celebrated part of its own culture. When the council voted to name Akebono as the sixty-fourth *yokozuna* in over 300 years of sumo wrestling, many people voiced objections.

Similar political debates over status occur in connection with the selection of American professional athletes for Halls of Fame and All-Star games. Even Little League teams have "politics of status" connected with "the most improved player of the year," "the most valuable player," "the most dedicated player," and so on. When people agree on the players who should receive such awards and special status, they tend to forget that the selection process is political. It is

only when they don't agree with the selection that they talk about politics in sports.

SUMMARY

HOW DO GOVERNMENTS AND GLOBALIZATION INFLUENCE SPORTS?

Sports and politics are inseparable. Sports do not exist in a cultural vacuum. They are integral parts of society and culture. Therefore, they influence and are influenced by political forces. Government involvement in sports is related to the need for sponsorship, organization, and facilities. The fact that sports are important parts of people's lives and that sports can be the scene for problems often leads to government regulations and controls. The forms of government involvement in sports vary by society, but they generally occur to (1) safeguard the public order, (2) maintain health and fitness among citizens, (3) promote the prestige and power of a group, community, or nation, (4) promote a sense of identity, belonging, and unity among citizens, (5) reproduce values consistent with dominant ideology, (6) increase support for political leaders and government structures, and (7) promote economic development.

The rules, policies, and funding priorities set by government officials and agencies reflect the political struggles among groups within any society. This does not mean that the same people always benefit when government involvement occurs, but it does mean that involvement seldom results in equal benefits for everyone. For example, when funds are given to elite sport programs and the development and training of elite athletes, fewer funds are available for general-participation programs. Of course, funding priorities could favor mass participation instead of elite sports, but the point is that the priorities themselves are subject to debate and negotiation. This political process is an inevitable part of sports.

History shows that groups with the greatest resources, organization, and outside support and with goals that fit most closely with the political positions of public officials are most likely to be favored when government involvement in sports occurs. The groups least likely to be favored are those that fail to understand the connection between sports and politics or that lack the resources to influence political processes effectively. When people believe the myth that sports and politics are unrelated, they remain at a disadvantage when rules and policies are made and funds are allocated.

The connection between sports and global political processes is complex. Ideally, sports bring nations together in contexts supportive of peace and friendship. Although this has occurred, the reality is that most nations have used sports to foster their own interests. In fact, displays of nationalism have been common at international events. The Olympic Games are a good case in point. The major emphasis among many of those who promote and watch the Olympics is on national medal counts and expressions of national status or superiority.

Powerful transnational corporations have joined nation-states as major participants in global politics. As a result, sports have been used increasingly for economic as well as political purposes. Nationalism and the promotion of national interests remain a part of global sports, but consumerism and the promotion of capitalist expansion have become more important since 1991 and the end of the Cold War. Within the context of transnational relations, athletes and teams now are associated with corporate logos as well as nation-states. Global sport events are now political *and* economic. They serve as settings for presenting numerous images and messages associated with the interests of nation-states and corporate sponsors. The dominant images and messages are consistent with the interests of the major corporate sponsors, and they tend to promote an ideology infused with the capitalist values of individualism, competition, production, and consumption.

Global political processes also are associated with other aspects of sports, such as the migration patterns of elite athletes and the production of sporting goods. Political issues are raised when athletes cross national borders to play their sports, as well as when transnational corporations produce sports equipment and clothing in labor-intensive poor nations and then sell those items in wealthy nations. We can understand these and other issues associated with global political processes only if we study sports on both global and local levels. This enables us to determine when sports involve reciprocal cultural exchanges leading to mutual understanding among people from different parts of the world and when they involve processes through which powerful nations and corporations exercise subtle influence over social life and political events in less powerful nations around the world. Research on this topic suggests that the role of sports in global political processes is very complex.

Politics are also part of the very structure and organization of sports. Political processes exist because people in sport organizations must answer questions about what qualifies as a sport, what the rules of a sport should be and how they should be enforced, who should organize and control sport events, where sport events should occur, who is eligible to participate, and how rewards will be distributed. This is why many sport organizations are described as governing bodies: they are responsible for making decisions that affect everyone connected with sports.

Overall, research on the connections between sports and social relations in local, national, and international contexts clearly shows that sports are inseparable from politics and political processes.

SUGGESTED READINGS

Bairner, A. 2001. *Sport, nationalism, and globalization: European and North American perspectives.* Albany: State University of New York Press (analysis of sports and national identity in the context of globalization; analyzes how people in Ireland, Scotland, Sweden, the United States, and Canada have dealt with global forces in connection with sports).

Houlihan, B. 1997. *Sport, policy, and politics: A comparative analysis*. London: Routledge (written from a public policy perspective; focuses on the motives and processes behind sport policies in Australia, Canada, Ireland, the United Kingdom, and the United States).

Jennings, A., and C. Sambrook. 2000. *The great Olympic swindle: When the world wanted its games back*. London: Simon and Schuster (the investigative journalist who wrote *The Lords of the Rings* in 1992 and *The New Lords of the Rings* in 1996 teams up with a financial writer to outline the operations of the IOC and describe the corruption and criminal actions of those who control Olympic sports; controversial and painstakingly researched).

Kruger, A., and J. Riordan, eds. 1996. *The story of worker sport*. Champaign, IL: Human Kinetics (unique collection of papers highlighting the ways in which sports have been used for explicitly political purposes by workers in Europe, the former USSR, and Canada; the papers show how sports can be used to inspire a collective consciousness among people at various levels of social organization).

Lafeber, W. 2000. *Michael Jordan and the new global capitalism*. New York: W. W. Norton (critical look at how Michael Jordan's product endorsements have been used to export U.S. products to over 100 countries around the world and, in the process, influence consumption patterns and cultures).

Lenskyj, H. J. 2000. *Inside the Olympic industry: Power, politics, and activism*. Albany: State University of New York Press (critical analysis of the Olympics as a social phenomenon; emphasis on the internal politics of the games and the impact of the games on the cities and countries that host them).

Maguire, J. 1999. *Global sport: Identities, societies, civilizations*. Cambridge, England: Polity Press (detailed analyses of the complex global processes associated with sports; pulls together over a decade of the author's research on theoretical issues, athletes as global workers, the global sports industry, the global media-sport complex, and globalization and national identity issues).

Miller, T., ed. 2001. *Globalization and sport: Playing the world*. London: Sage (articles focus on how sports

are implicated in general processes of cultural production and how sports play a central role in processes of globalization).

Schaffer, K., and S. Smith, eds. 2000. *The Olympics at the millennium: Power, politics, and the Games*. New Brunswick, NJ: Rutgers University Press (eighteen articles covering many social and cultural issues related to international sports; articles are written primarily from critical perspectives).

Senn, A. E. 1999. *Power, politics, and the Olympic Games: A history of the power brokers, events, and controversies that shaped the games*. Champaign, IL: Human Kinetics (historical account of politics in the Olympics and how powerful individuals and nation-states have used the Olympic Movement and the Olympic Games for their political purposes).

Toohey, K., and A. J. Veal. 2000. *The Olympic Games: A social science perspective*. New York: CABI (broad, accessible overview of the cultural and economic significance of the Olympic Games from their origins in ancient Greece through the formation of the modern games and up to the Summer Games in Sydney; chapters deal with politics and nationalism, economics, mass media, drugs, gender, and the future of the Olympic Games).

Van Bottenburg, M. 2001. *Global games* (translated by Beverley Jackson). Urbana: University of Illinois Press (using history, sociology, and social psychology, the author provides an answer to the question of why certain sports have become popular in certain countries; describes the social significance and politics of sports around the globe).

WEBSITE RESOURCES

Note: Websites often change. The following URLs were current when this book was printed. Please check our website (www.mhhe.com/coakley8e) for updates and additions.

www.mhhe.com/coakley8e Click on chapter 13 for information on sports and international relations, gift giving and the Olympic scandal, and politics and the Paralympic movement.

www.ucalgary.ca/library/ssportsite/ Start at this site to find information on "National Sport Structures and Organizations"; links to nearly every established organization in the world that has a website, including National Olympic Committees, government sport organizations around the world, and International Sport Federations.

www.olympic.org International Olympic Committee; links to National Olympic committees around the world and information about the IOC and its programs.

europa.eu.int/comm/sport/index en.html The site of *Sport and European Union* covers issues related to the development of sport through the European Union; contains information about the politics of coordinating national sport governing bodies with this international governing body.

www.usoc.org United States Olympic Committee site with links to thirty-five national governing bodies for Olympic sports, five governing bodies for Pan American sports, seven organizations for the disabled in sports, and other education-based and community-based multisport organizations.

www.iwg-gti.org International Working Group on Women and Sport; contains information on programs, policy issues, and problems faced by girls and women in nearly 100 countries; information reveals different patterns of government involvement, as well as the cultural issues that influence programs, policies, and problems; key links to other international sport organizations.

www.ajennings.8m.com Andrew Jennings, an investigative journalist, has studied the IOC and various national Olympic committees for over a dozen years; this site highlights his work and the work of others who have written articles on the politics and corruption in elite international sports.

www.aafla.com The Amateur Athletic Foundation in the United States has an outstanding collection of historical and political information about sports, especially international sports; go to "Sports Library."

http://globalmarch.org/index.html Site for The Global March Against Child Labour, an international movement based in India and focused on eliminating exploitive work that condemns millions of children to lives of servitude and suffering; link to its 2002 World Cup project and photos of children in India and Pakistan sewing soccer balls, some with "Child Free Labor" labels on them.

www.nikewages.org Site of *Educating for Justice* formed by former college students who began a grass-roots campaign to end social injustice; its *Nike Corporate Accountability Campaign* is explained at this site.

chapter 14

(H. Armstrong Roberts)

Sports in High School and College

Do Varsity Sport Programs Contribute to Education?

IN AMERICA, ESPECIALLY in suburban communities, having a good football team or a basketball team is synonymous with being a good school.

—Gerald Tirozzi, executive director, National
Association of High School Principals (1999)

 Online Learning Center Resources

Visit *Sports in Society*'s Online Learning Center at **www.mhhe.com/coakley8e** for additional information and study material for this chapter, including

- Self-grading quizzes
- Learning objectives
- Related websites
- Additional readings

A complete outline is available online at www.mhhe.com/coakley8e.

THE CURRENT COLLEGE sports landscape is meaner than ever, more overtly commercial, more winner-take-all. And just as in the rest of the economy, the gap between rich and poor is widening.

—**Michael Sokolove, journalist (2002)**

AMERICAN STUDENTS ENCOUNTER two distractions in high school that other nations minimize—part-time work and sports. . . . Part-time work may capture students' time. Sports captures their hearts.

—**Tom Loveless, *The 2002 Brown Center Report on American Education***

483

The emergence of modern organized sports is closely tied to education in both England and North America. However, few schools outside North America and parts of Japan sponsor and fund interschool varsity sport programs. Organized sports for adolescents and young adults in most countries are tied to community-based athletic clubs funded by members or a combination of public and private sources.

Interscholastic sports have become an accepted and important part of U.S. high schools and colleges, and they are becoming increasingly important in Canadian and Japanese schools. When the emphasis on varsity sports dominates the public profiles and symbols associated with schools, many people become concerned about their impact on the achievement of the overall educational mission of high schools and colleges.

This chapter explores issues related to interscholastic sports. It is organized around four major questions:

1. What are the arguments for and against varsity sports?
2. How are interscholastic sport programs related to the educational experiences of athletes and other students in high schools and colleges?
3. What effects do interscholastic programs have for high schools and colleges as educational organizations?
4. What are the major problems associated with high school and college sport programs and how might they be solved?

ARGUMENTS FOR AND AGAINST INTERSCHOLASTIC SPORTS

Most people in the United States take interscholastic sports for granted. The programs are simply an expected part of life at school. However, budget cutbacks and highly publicized problems in certain high school and college programs have raised questions about how sports are related to educational goals and the development of young people. Similar questions are being raised about interscholastic sports in Canadian schools. Responses to these questions are varied. Program supporters claim that interscholastic sports support the educational mission of schools, whereas critics claim that they interfere with that mission. The main points made on both sides of this debate are summarized in table 14.1.

When people enter this debate, they often exaggerate the benefits or the problems associated with varsity sport programs. Supporters emphasize glowing success stories, and critics emphasize shocking cases of excess and abuse, but the most accurate descriptions probably lie somewhere in between. Nonetheless, both the supporters and the critics call attention to many of the important issues in the relationship between sports and education. This chapter will focus on many of those issues.

INTERSCHOLASTIC SPORTS AND THE EXPERIENCES OF HIGH SCHOOL STUDENTS

Do varsity sport programs affect the educational and developmental experiences of high school students? This question is difficult to answer. Education and development occur in connection with many activities and relationships. Even though varsity sport programs are very important in some schools and for some students, they constitute only one of many potentially influential experiences. Quantitative research on this issue, usually based on functionalist theory, has focused primarily on the characteristics of varsity athletes and how they compare with the characteristics of other students. Qualitative research, often guided by interactionist and critical theories, has focused on how interscholastic sports are connected with the overall school-based culture that exists among high school students.

Table 14.1   Popular arguments for and against interscholastic sports

Arguments For	Arguments Against
1. They involve students in school activities and increase interest in academic activities.	1. They distract students' attention from academic activities.
2. They build the self-esteem, responsibility, achievement orientation, and teamwork skills required for occupational success.	2. They perpetuate dependence, conformity, and a power and performance orientation that is no longer appropriate in postindustrial society.
3. They provide fitness training and stimulate interest in physical activities among all students in the school.	3. They turn most students into spectators and cause too many serious injuries to athletes.
4. They generate the spirit and unity necessary to maintain the school as a viable organization.	4. They create a superficial, transitory spirit, which has nothing to do with educational goals.
5. They promote parental, alumni, and community support for all school programs.	5. They deprive educational programs of resources, facilities, staff, and community support.
6. They give students opportunities to develop and display skills in activities valued in the society at large and to be recognized for their athletic skills.	6. They create strong pressure on athletes and support a hierarchical status system in which athletes are given excessive privilege, which may be used to assert dominance over other students.

High School Athletes[1]

Studies have shown consistently that, when compared with students who do not play varsity sports, high school athletes, *as a group*, generally have better grade point averages, more positive attitudes toward school, more interest in continuing their education after graduation, and a slightly better educational achievement rate (see Miracle and Rees, 1994; Rees and Miracle, 2000). These differences usually have been modest, and it has been difficult for researchers to separate the effects of sport participation from the effects of social class, family background,

support from friends, and other factors related to educational attitudes, performance, and grades. However, membership on a varsity team is a valued source of status in most U.S. schools, and it seems to go hand in hand with positive educational experiences for some students, reduced dropout rates, and increased identification with the school (Marsh, 1993; McNeal, 1995). However, research has not told us what it is about sport participation that causes these positive experiences.

Of course, the most logical explanation for differences between varsity athletes and other students is that interscholastic sports, like other extracurricular activities, attract students who already have the characteristics associated with academic and social success in high school. Most studies have not been able to test this explanation, because the researchers don't actually follow students during their high school careers to keep track of how and why changes occur in their lives. Usually, the studies simply report information collected from students at one point in time and then compare students who play on

---

[1]The term *student-athlete* is not used in this edition of *Sports in Society*. All varsity athletes in high schools and colleges are students, just like band members and debaters. Using *student* to refer to them is redundant. Furthermore, the NCAA has fostered the use of *student-athlete* to routinely deflect the criticism that academic matters are a low priority in big-time athletic programs. In light of the need for real reforms in college sports, I find this strategy to be superficial, which is another reason I do not use the term (see www.thedrakegroup.org/02props.html)

sport teams with students who do not. This makes it impossible for researchers to say whether playing varsity sports really changes people or whether students who try out for teams, are selected by coaches, and choose to remain on teams are simply different from other students *before* they become varsity athletes.

The mere fact that young people grow and develop during the same years that they play on varsity teams does not mean that sport participation *causes* the growth and development. After all, fourteen- to eighteen-year-olds grow and develop in many ways whether they play varsity

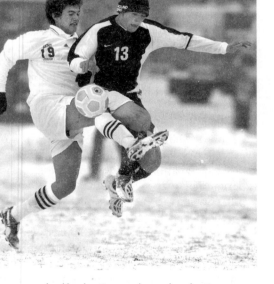

Processes of self-selection and coach selection ensure that students who become high school athletes often have different characteristics than other students before they play varsity sports. They may learn things in sports, but it is difficult to separate these things from what occurs in general developmental processes unrelated to sport participation. (Marc Piscotty; Rocky Mountain News)

sports or do other things. Most studies do not distinguish among all the activities and experiences that might explain growth and development among students.

Fortunately, some quantitative studies have followed students over time and have measured changes in their lives. These studies suggest that young people who play on varsity sport teams are more likely to come from *economically privileged* backgrounds and have *above-average* cognitive abilities, self-esteem, and academic performance records, including grades and test scores (Fejgin, 1994; Melnick et al., 1988; Rees et al., 1990; Spreitzer, 1995). In other words, students who try out for teams, make teams, and stay on teams often are different in certain ways from other students *before* they become high school athletes.

This type of *selection-in process* is common in most extracurricular activities, not just varsity sports. Students who choose to participate in official, school-sponsored activities tend to be slightly different from other students. These differences are greatest in activities in which student self-selection is combined with formal tryouts, in which teachers or coaches select students for participation. In the case of varsity sports, this self-selection and selection by coach process is especially powerful, because it is an extension of a long-term selection-in process, which begins in youth sports and continues through junior high school.

Research also suggests that students who play varsity sports for three years during high school are different from those who are cut from or quit teams. Those who are cut or quit are more likely to come from *less advantaged* economic backgrounds and have *lower* cognitive abilities, *lower* self-esteem, and *lower* grade point averages than those who remain on teams (Spreitzer, 1995). Furthermore, athletes who have failing grades are usually declared ineligible and then become nonathletes. This guarantees that nonathletes have lower grades when researchers do studies in high schools and compare the grades of athletes and nonathletes!

Overall, these findings suggest that, in addition to a *selection-in process*, there also is a complex *filtering-out process* that occurs in interscholastic sports. These processes combine to influence who does and who does not play varsity sports.

Further complicating our efforts to learn about the effects of playing high school sports is the fact that many students on varsity teams also participate in other extracurricular activities. Determining whether changes in their lives are due to playing sports or to participating in other activities, such as working on the yearbook, being in a student club or student government, or doing community service, is nearly impossible.

Tracking the influence of sport participation in a person's adult life and occupational career is even more challenging. The meanings people give to participation change over time and vary with social and cultural forces related to gender, race and ethnicity, and social class. For example, information about how many CEOs of Fortune 500 companies played one or more high school sports tells us nothing about the effects of sport participation. The occupational success of these people, most of whom are white men, is related strongly to their family backgrounds, social networks, and the gender and ethnic relations, which have existed in post-industrial societies during the past fifty years. Of course, this does not mean that these men have not worked hard or that sport participation is irrelevant to who they are and what they do, but the importance of playing varsity sports cannot be understood apart from other social factors.

The operation of social and cultural forces has also been illustrated in data on the sexual behavior of high school students. Interviews with 611 15- to 18-year-old students in New York State indicated that the young women who played varsity sports had *lower* rates of sexual activity (fewer sex partners, lower frequency of intercourse, and later initiation of sexual activity) than their female counterparts who did not play sports (Miller et al., 1998, 1999). However, the young men who played sports had *higher* rates of sexual activity than their male counterparts who did not play sports. The authors suggest that playing on varsity teams enhances the social status of both young women and men. This gives them more control over the dynamics of their relationships and enables them to regulate sexual activity on their own terms. To the extent that there are control issues that favor males in adolescent sexual relationships, young women may use increased control to resist sexual relationships that may be exploitive, whereas young men may use their control to gain sexual favors from young women (Risman and Schwartz, 2002). Therefore, sport participation may affect behaviors and relationships, but we must understand cultural issues and the dynamics of social relations in order to explain how this occurs. Sport participation cannot be understood apart from social meaning, and social meaning is created in a real world, where perceptions of gender, skin color, sexuality, social class, and other factors have consequences in people's lives (Godley, 1999a; Hanson and Kraus, 1999).

What Research Tells Us

What does research tell us about interscholastic sports and the experiences of young people? Studies done over the past thirty years suggest the following:

1. We should be careful when generalizing about the educational value of interscholastic sports. Playing varsity sports does not produce systematic negative effects, but neither does it automatically change high school students in positive ways, making them significantly different from other high school students. Usually, those who try out for teams, are selected by coaches, and stay on teams for more than one year are somewhat different from other students before they put on their uniforms. Therefore, one-time statistical comparisons between so-called athletes and nonathletes

REFLECT ON SPORTS

Status and Privilege in Student Culture
Do Athletes Rule U.S. High Schools?

After the shootings that killed fourteen students and a teacher/coach at Columbine High School in Littleton, Colorado in 1999, some people raised questions about interscholastic sports and the dynamics of status and privilege in student culture. Among other things, they wondered if some varsity athletes are accorded forms of privilege that other students perceive to be unfair and that some varsity athletes use to assert physical and social dominance over others whom they identify as "deviant" or unworthy of respect for some reason.

At the same time, a number of "anti-jock" webzines and personal websites emerged and served as vehicles for current and former students to express resentment of high school cultures in which people associated with sports were privileged whereas others were marginalized (Wilson, 2002).

This is a controversial issue, but it is important to think about and study. Most high schools have complex status systems and multiple popularity criteria. Students identify and differentiate each other in many ways, depending on what they define as socially important in their social lives. These definitions vary from one school to another and from group to group in the same school, but this process of identification and differentiation occurs in all social groups. However, when differences are used for ranking one another in terms of superiority and inferiority and then identifying particular students as targets for harassment or intimidation, there is cause for concern. If students, teachers, and administrators ignore systematic and chronic harassment and intimidation, problems may become serious and volatile.

Data on how varsity sport participation is involved in this issue are scarce. Interscholastic sports are associated with the status hierarchies in many U.S. high schools, but seldom have critical questions been asked about how sport-related status might be connected with patterns of harassment and intimidation in student culture.

When ESPN, a major U.S.–based media organization, did a random telephone survey of 800 high

tell us little about the actual experiences of playing sports and how they affect the lives of young people.

2. If we want to learn about the effect of interscholastic sports in the lives of high school students, we must do long-term studies of the overall lives of students, not just their sport lives. Growth and development occur in connection with many experiences—some inside the school and some outside. Unless we know about young people's lives in general, we can't claim that varsity sport participation is more influential than working at a part-time job, joining the debate team, writing for the school newspaper, or caring for younger brothers and sisters when it comes to overall growth and development.

3. We should examine how the educational lives of varsity athletes might be different from the lives of other students. Do those who play sports receive more academic support and encouragement from family, friends, and teachers? Do teachers evaluate them differently? Do they make different academic decisions than other students do? How does the issue of eligibility affect those decisions? Do those who play sports receive privileges that change how they view their schools and their educations? Does everyone who plays sports receive similar favorable treatment? If a student plays a sport outside of school, such as motocross racing or figure skating, does that have the same consequences as playing on a high-profile varsity basketball team?

school students about a month after the Columbine shootings, about one-third of the students said that some or a lot of tension existed between athletes and nonathletes in their high schools (ESPN, 1999). About half of the students were aware of athletes who had physically mistreated nonathletes, and about 70 percent were aware of athletes who verbally mistreated nonathletes. Seventy percent identified football players as the athletes who most often mistreated nonathletes, 10 percent identified male basketball players, 2 percent identified wrestlers, and 1 percent identified female basketball players. Nearly 80 percent said that athletes sometimes or often received special treatment from teachers or administrators.

Even though these data are sketchy, they indicate that there is a potential problem in need of research, that some athletes bully other students, and that these athletes are nearly always males and most often play high-profile sports in the school.

Systematic and chronic bullying is probably most likely in schools where there is little social, ethnic, and social class diversity and where conformity to "straight norms" is highly valued. It is in these schools that difference may come to be defined as deviance in the minds of some students in higher-status groups. If high-status students feel that they have the physical power to become informal enforcers of straight norms and have the social power to play this role without being questioned by school authorities, they may pick on the students they define as deviating from certain norms related to appearance and behavior.

These student bullies are *not* always in the so-called jock clique in the school. However, male athletes from certain sports are involved frequently enough for us to examine critically (1) the impact of interscholastic sports on the lives of *all* students, (2) the forms of status and privilege enjoyed by athletes, and (3) the ways athletes use their status and privilege in the social life of their schools. *What do you think?*

4. We should study the effect of varsity sports on the larger student culture that exists in high schools. It may be that the social importance of sports rests in how they are connected with the dynamics of social relations in an entire school. It would seem to be a higher priority to study this possibility than to focus only on the students who try out for and make teams. Varsity sports probably affect more than just athletes.

Student Culture in High Schools

Sociologists long have recognized that varsity sports are among the most important social activities sponsored by high schools (Rees and Miracle, 2000). Being a varsity athlete usually brings a student prestige among many peers, formal rewards in the school, and recognition from teachers, administrators, and even people in the community. Athletes, especially males in high-profile sports, usually are accorded recognition that enhances their popularity in student culture. Pep rallies, homecomings, and other special sport events traditionally have been scheduled and promoted as major social occasions on school calendars. These social occasions often are important for students because they provide opportunities for social interaction—especially male-female interaction—outside the classroom. Furthermore, parents, even strict, controlling parents, usually define school-sponsored sport events as approved social activities for their sons and daughters. Parents often permit their children to attend these events while forbidding them to go other places.

From a sociological perspective, it is important to ask what varsity sports contribute to student culture in a high school. Because these sports and sport events are socially significant activities in the lives of many students, they have the potential to influence students' values and behaviors. For example, do they influence how students evaluate one another or how they think about social life and social relations? The serious implications of these questions are discussed in the box "Status and Privilege in Student Culture."

Sports and Popularity   For many years, student culture was studied simply in terms of the factors that high school students use to determine popularity. Research usually found that male students wished they could be remembered as "athletic stars" in high school, whereas female students wished to be remembered as "brilliant students" *or* "the most popular." More recent

Sport participation often gives young women opportunities to establish personal and social identities based on skills respected by peers and the community at large. However, playing sports usually does not bring as much popularity to girls as it does to boys in U.S. high schools. (Tini Campbell)

research indicates that many young men in high school prefer to be known as "scholar-athletes," whereas young women prefer to be known as "scholars" *and* "members of the leading social group" (Chandler and Goldberg, 1990). Therefore, the link between being popular and being an athlete has traditionally been stronger for male students than for female students. When it comes to popularity for high school women, being in the in-group is crucial, and being an athlete does not by itself put a female student in the in-group.

What do these research findings mean? Are young men more concerned with being athletes than with being scholars? Are young women unconcerned about sports? The answer to both these questions is no. In fact, most high school students *are* concerned with academic achievement. They are aware of the importance of going to college, and their parents usually remind them regularly of how important school should be in their lives.

In addition to academic achievement, high school students are concerned with four things: (1) social acceptance, (2) personal autonomy, (3) sexual identity, and (4) growth into adults. They want to be popular enough to fit in with peers and have friends they can depend on; they want opportunities to control their lives; they strive to feel secure about their own sexual identity; and they want to show others that they are mature enough to be taken seriously.

This means that the *social* lives of adolescents revolve around a wide range of important factors. Because males and females in North America are still treated and evaluated in different ways, adolescents use different strategies for seeking acceptance, autonomy, sexual development, and recognition as young adults. As things are now, sport participation is an important basis for popularity for young men, as long as they don't completely neglect their academic lives. In fact, young men who don't act tough may be marginalized in student culture, so they put a premium on playing sports, especially contact sports (Eder, 1995).

Sport participation is also important for young women, but being an athlete usually must be combined with other things for a young woman to be popular in the student cultures of most high schools. Young women don't have to be traditionally feminine to be popular, but they usually must show they are something other than tough, competitive athletes. Physical attractiveness remains a key factor for young women's popularity in student culture, whether they play sports or not (Eder, 1995). Thus, it seems that the visibility and status gained by high school athletes have different implications for young men than for young women in high school student culture.

Sports and Ideology   Interscholastic sport programs do more than simply affect the status structures of high school students. When Pulitzer Prize–winning author H. G. Bissinger wrote about a high school football team in Odessa, Texas, he observed that football "stood at the very core of what the town was about. . . . It had nothing to do with entertainment and everything to do with how people felt about themselves" (1990: 237).

Bissinger noted that football in Odessa and many other towns across the United States was important because it celebrated a male cult of toughness and sacrifice and a female cult of nurturance and servitude. Team losses were blamed on coaches' not being tough enough and players' not being disciplined and aggressive. Women stayed on the sidelines and faithfully tried to support and please the men who battled on behalf of the school and town. Attending football games enabled students and townspeople to reaffirm their ideas about "natural differences" between men and women. Young men who couldn't hit hard, physically intimidate opponents, or play with pain were described as "pussies." Some athletes considered "gay bashing" an approved weekend social activity, and a player's willingness

to sacrifice his body for the team was taken as a sign of commitment and character.

Bissinger also noted that high school sports were closely tied to a long history of racism in the town, and football itself was organized and played in ways that reaffirmed traditional racial ideology among whites and produced racial resentment among African Americans. Many white townspeople in 1988 still referred to blacks as "niggers," and they blamed blacks and Mexicans for most of the town's problems. Furthermore, white people generally used physical explanations based on traditional racist ideology to explain the abilities or lack of abilities of black players: when these players succeeded, it was due to their "natural physical abilities," and, when they failed, it was due to a lack of character or intelligence.

Unfortunately, Bissinger did not write about the students who didn't participate in sports or those who didn't agree with the values and experiences celebrated through football. His account provides only a partial picture of sports and student culture. However, a study by anthropologist Doug Foley (1990a, 1999b) provides a more complete description and analysis of student culture.

Foley studied a small Texas town and focused much of his attention on students in the local high school. He paid special attention to the school's football team and how the team and its games were incorporated into the overall social life of the school and the community. He also studied the social and academic activities of a wide range of students, including those who ignored or deliberately avoided sports.

Foley's findings revealed that student culture "was varied, changing, and inherently full of contradictions" (1990a, p. 100). Football and other sports provided important social occasions for getting together with friends, flirting, and defusing the anxiety associated with tests and overcontrolling teachers, but sports were only one part of the lives of adolescents at the school. Students used their status as athletes in their "identity performances" with other students and with adults, but, for most students, identity was grounded more deeply in gender, class, and ethnicity than in sport participation.

Foley concluded that sports were important to the extent that they presented students with a vocabulary they could use to identify important values and interpret their experiences. For example, most sports came with a vocabulary that extolled individualism, competition, and differences based on gender, skin color, ethnicity, and social class and then treated these values and differences as natural aspects of human life. As students adopted and used this vocabulary, they perpetuated the status quo in the school and in their town. In this way, traditional ide-

ologies related to gender, race, and class continued to influence social relations in the town's culture.

Research suggests that the most important social consequences of interscholastic sports may be their effects on ideas about social life and social relations in society as a whole, rather than their effects on athletes' grade point averages, attitudes toward school, and popularity.

Additional Effects of High School Sports

Being Noticed and Rewarded   Research on interscholastic sports indicates that, in and of

Ideology is learned in many ways through sports. When students from this school in Wisconsin built a mock grave containing "dead Indians" and put up a sign "11 little tiny INDIAN BOYS REST IN PEACE," they were reaffirming historical stereotypes about Native Peoples. Many of them learned how to count backwards with a "10 little Indians" song, and they integrated that vocabulary into their sport-related rituals. (Kristie Ebert)

themselves, sports are not educational. However, if sports are organized and played in certain ways, they do support educational goals.

When varsity sports are organized so that young people are taken seriously as human beings and valued by those who are important in their lives, sport participation can contribute to their educational development (Mahiri, 1998). However, if varsity sports are organized in ways that lead young people to think that adults are controlling them for their own purposes, interscholastic programs often become developmental dead ends, and students, become cynical about school and society.

Positive adolescent development is most likely when students (1) are active participants in their schools, (2) when they have a range of opportunities to develop and display competence in settings where they are noticed and rewarded, and (3) when they have chances to prove they are becoming valued adults in their communities. If interscholastic sports and other school activities are organized to do these three things, they will contribute to education and development, because students will be noticed in positive ways and will be more likely to identify with the school and its educational mission.

Attracting Adult Advocates   Interscholastic sports also can be valuable if they provide young people with opportunities to meet adults who can be advocates in their lives. This is especially important in schools located in low-income and impoverished areas, where young people are in serious need of adult advocates with the resources to facilitate overall development. Sports can give these young people chances to be noticed for something good, rather than for how "bad" they are in the school hallways or on the streets. When adult advocates are scarce in the local neighborhood, sports can provide these young people with the "hook-ups" they need to gain access to opportunities that other young people take for granted.

Providing Occasions for Learning   Sports also can be valuable educationally if teachers and coaches take them seriously as learning experiences (Mahiri, 1998). For example, Jomills Braddock and his colleagues (1991) have studied the importance of sports to young black males and have argued that sports in middle schools could be used to spark a commitment to education among many young people ready to give up on classroom learning by the time they are seventh- or eighth-graders. They have suggested the following:

> Both players and nonplayers . . . could write or contribute to sport columns in school or local newspapers, thereby enhancing student writing and language skills. Students could collect and generate team and player statistics for a variety of school and local sport activities, utilizing . . . crucial . . . mathematical skills. . . . [Students] could organize the sport sections of school yearbooks, participate on a sports debate team, or perhaps start a sports enthusiast club. (Braddock et al. 1991, p. 129)

The point of these suggestions is to use sports as part of a larger process of giving students responsibility, including them in activities that will help them develop skills, rewarding them for their competence, and connecting them with adults who can exert positive influence in their lives.

This notion of deliberately designing sports to give students responsibility has been emphasized in applied research on moral and social development (Martinek and Hellison, 1997; Shields and Bredemeier, 1995). This research also suggests that, unless adult leaders take care, sport participation may take forms that actually subvert moral development and responsibility among young people. For example, some high school student-athletes may feel that playing sports is more important than anything they do and that they actually deserve special treatment, even if they are not responsible about their schoolwork and even if they fail to follow rules that other students are expected to follow. When

Most discussions of college sports focus on big-time Division I NCAA athletes and teams. Division II and Division III athletes and sports receive little attention. We need more research on the everyday experiences of athletes in these programs and how they integrate college sports into their lives. (Hal Stoelzle; *Rocky Mountain News*)

this occurs, sports do not provide occasions for learning anything of value.

INTERCOLLEGIATE SPORTS AND THE EXPERIENCES OF COLLEGE STUDENTS

Does varsity sport participation affect the educational and developmental experiences of college athletes?[2] This question is asked every time media stories tell about the academic failures of college athletes and the failures of colleges and universities to take the education of athletes seriously. Research on these issues is limited.

---

[2]This chapter focuses on four-year institutions. Junior colleges and two-year community colleges are not discussed. Research is needed on similarities and differences between the sport programs in two- and four-year institutions.

As we discuss intercollegiate sports in the United States, it is important to understand that college sport programs are very diverse. If we assume that all programs are like the ones we read and hear about in the media, we are bound to get a distorted view of athletes, coaches, and athletic programs.

Intercollegiate Sports Are *Not* All the Same

The amount of money spent every year on intercollegiate sports varies from less than $400,000 at some small colleges to over $60 million at a few large universities. Large universities may sponsor ten to eighteen varsity sports for men and a similar number for women, whereas small colleges may have only a handful of varsity sports and a number of club sport teams. In small colleges, coaches often teach academic classes, and one person may coach two or more teams and teach courses as well. Larger universities have multiple coaches for most sports. Few of the coaches teach courses, and most have no formal connection with the academic programs of the school.

Schools with intercollegiate sports are generally affiliated with one of two national associations: the National Collegiate Athletic Association (NCAA) or the National Association of Intercollegiate Athletics (NAIA). With over a thousand member schools, the NCAA is the largest and most powerful association. Its member institutions are divided into 5 major divisions, reflecting program size, level of competition, and the types of rules that govern sport programs. *Division I* includes (in early 2003) 325 schools with "big-time" programs. This division contains three subdivisions: 117 schools with big-time football teams (I-A), 123 schools with smaller football programs based on stadium size and average paid attendance (I-AA), and eighty-five schools without football teams (I-AAA). *Division II* and *Division III* contain 270 and 410 schools, respectively. These schools have smaller programs and compete at less than a big-time level, although competition is often intense.

Schools with *big-time programs* usually emphasize either football or men's basketball, because these sports have the best potential to generate revenue. Football has the greatest potential to make money. It brings large profits to about sixty to seventy of the largest universities, but it regularly loses money in the other 170 Division I universities (Fulks, 2002; Zimbalist, 1999). Men's basketball seldom generates as much money as football, but it costs less and the risk of large losses is lower. Although hockey and women's basketball make money in a few schools, no other sports make enough money to pay their own expenses, so "big-time" does not necessarily mean big profits or even big revenues.

The general level of athletic talent is higher in NCAA Division I schools than it is in Division II or III or the NAIA. Athletes in Division I schools are more likely to have athletic grants-in-aid and access to academic support programs sponsored by athletic departments.[3] In addition, the amount of team travel in Division I schools is greater, the national and regional media coverage is more extensive, and the stakes associated with winning and losing are greater.

Not all schools maintain membership in the NCAA. Some choose to affiliate with the NAIA. NAIA schools also have teams in up to twelve sports for men and eleven for women. Athletic grants-in-aid may or may not be given, and most programs and teams are not considered big-time. The NAIA listed 309 colleges and universities as members in 2002, about 113 fewer members than in 1993. The NAIA currently has a difficult time maintaining its membership in the face of the growing power and influence of the NCAA, which has nearly complete monopoly control over intercollegiate sports. The budget of the NCAA dwarfs the budget of the NAIA.

Christian colleges and Bible schools also have sport programs. One hundred twelve of these are affiliated with the National Christian College Athletic Association (NCCAA), although nearly half maintain dual memberships in the NCCAA and either the NAIA or NCAA Division III.

Even though the vast majority of intercollegiate sport teams are not considered big-time, people often think that what they see and read in the media represents all college sports. However, this is *not* the case. Most sports at most schools do not resemble the big-time revenue-producing, high-profile sports that capture so much popular attention.

It is important to study big-time programs and high-profile sports, because they occupy a socially prominent place on major college campuses

---

[3]Universities do not report the types and amount of athletic aid they award to students. According to researchers at the NCAA, only about 20 percent of students who receive athletic aid receive full scholarships; therefore, about 80 percent of student-athletes at the 325 Division I NCAA universities receive no athletic aid or partial aid, such as tuition waivers, housing, or meal tickets. However, this amounts to about $975 million of scholarships each year.

that have large student enrollments. However, when we focus only on those programs and sports, we develop distorted views of intercollegiate athletic programs and student-athletes.

Athletes in Big-Time Programs

Being an athlete in a big-time intercollegiate program is not always compatible with being a good student. This is especially true for those who play on *entertainment-oriented* sport teams—the teams that attempt to attract significant revenues. Athletes in big-time programs often have some form of scholarship aid, and they are expected to commit much time and energy to their sports. Not surprisingly, these commitments interfere with academic work or make it unimportant when a person becomes exclusively focused on his or her sport.

Research done by sociologists Patti and Peter Adler (1991, 1999) provides systematic information about the everyday lives of young men in a big-time intercollegiate program and how they make choices related to sports, school, and social life. After spending eight years observing, interviewing, traveling with, and hanging out with athletes and coaches, the Adlers concluded that playing in a big-time basketball program and being seriously involved in academics seldom go hand in hand. The young men they studied usually began their first year of coursework in college with optimism and idealism, because they expected their academic experiences to contribute to their future occupational success. However, after one or two semesters, the demands of playing basketball, the social isolation that goes along with being an athlete, and the powerful influence of the athletic subculture in a big-time program drew them away from academic life.

The men discovered that it was necessary to select easy courses and the least challenging majors if they were to meet the coaches' expectations on the basketball court. Fatigue, the pressures of games, and limited time kept them from

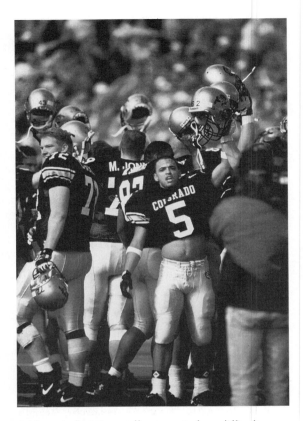

Athletes in big-time college sports face difficult choices when it comes to allocating time and energy to academic work, sport participation, and social activities. When academic work is given a low priority, questions about the educational relevance of intercollegiate sports are raised. (Brian Lewis, University of Colorado Media Relations)

becoming seriously involved in academic life. Furthermore, nobody ever asked these athletes about their academic lives. Attention always was focused on basketball, and few people really expected these young men to identify themselves as students or to give priority to coursework. The fact that many of these young men were black accentuated this social dynamic—many people assumed that young black men in a sport such as basketball had no interests or abilities other than running and jumping. This is racial ideology in action on college campuses.

When these young men received positive feedback, it was for athletic, not academic, performances. Difficulties in their courses often led the athletes to view academic life with pragmatic detachment. Thus, they became very practical in how they chose classes and arranged course schedules. They knew what they had to do to stay eligible, and coaches would make sure their course schedules were arranged so they could devote their time and energy to basketball. After taking a series of easy but uninteresting courses, and having a tough time in other courses, they gradually detached themselves from academic life on the campus.

This entire process of academic detachment was encouraged by the peer subculture that developed among the athletes. These young men were with one another constantly—in the dorms, at meals, during practices, on trips to away games, in the weight room, and on nights when there were no games. During these times, they seldom talked about academic or intellectual topics. If they did talk about the courses they were taking, it was in negative terms. They encouraged cutting classes rather than attending regularly, and they joked about each other's bad tests and failing papers. They provided each other with needed social support, but it was support only for their athletic identities. Therefore, many came to see themselves as athletes registered for courses, not as *students*.

Not all the athletes the Adlers studied experienced academic detachment. Some managed to strike a balance between their athletic and academic lives. This was most common among those who had entered college with realistic ideas about academic demands and those whose parents and peers actively supported academic achievements. However, striking this balance was never easy. It required solid high school preparation, combined with an ability or luck in developing relationships with faculty and other students. These relationships with people outside of sports were important, because they emphasized academic achievement and provided day-to-day support for academic identities.

The Adlers also found that the structure of big-time intercollegiate sports worked against maintaining a balance between athletics and academics. For example, as high-profile people on campus, these young men had many social opportunities, and it was difficult for them to pass up those opportunities to focus on coursework. Road trips to away games and tournaments took them away from classes for extended periods. They missed lectures, study groups, and tests. Their tight connections with fellow athletes isolated them from the general social and academic life of the university.

Of course, these young men generated revenue and publicity for coaches, athletic department administrators, and the university itself. Academic detachment was not a problem for the school, as long as the young men did not get caught doing something illegal and as long as the coach was able to control them on and off the court. Academic detachment was only a problem for the young men after their eligibility was gone and they wondered what life would be like after big-time college basketball. Meanwhile, the university had already recruited another collection of eager young men, who would attract fans, boosters, and the media with their exceptional basketball skills.

The Diversity of Athlete Experiences

Many entertainment-oriented intercollegiate sport teams are characterized by chronic problems, shamefully low graduation rates, and hypocrisy when it comes to education. However, there are many other teams in a variety of sports that are organized in ways that allow athletes to combine sport participation with academic and social development. This combination is most likely when athletes enter college with positive attitudes about school and the value of a college education and then receive support for academic involvement and the formation of academic identities (Meyer, 1988, 1990; Shulman and Bowen, 2001).

Athletes in sports that support academic involvement may train very hard and define athletic success as important, but most of them also give priority to academic work and other opportunities apart from training and competition. This awareness usually is grounded in a combination of factors, including (1) past experiences that consistently reaffirmed the importance of education in their lives, (2) social support systems that foster the formation of academic identities, (3) perceived access to career opportunities following graduation, and (4) social contacts and experiences that expand confidence and skills apart from sports.

Many coaches in programs that actively support academic success may schedule practices and games that do not interfere with coursework. Athletes may miss games and meets because they must study for or take tests, write papers, or give presentations. Team members may discuss academic issues with one another and support each other when it comes to academic performance. In other words, there *are* sport programs and teams that do not subvert the educational mission of higher education. These programs generally include the following: (1) many teams in Division II and the NAIA; (2) many men's teams in sports where the emphasis is not on supplying entertainment, producing revenue, or becoming a professional athlete; (3) most women's teams; and (4) most teams in Division III.

Grades and Graduation Rates: Athletes in Big-Time College Sports

Unlike athletes in high schools and participation-oriented, lower-profile intercollegiate programs, many athletes in big-time university programs differ from other students on campuses. Although their characteristics vary from one sport to another, they tend to come from more diversified socioeconomic backgrounds than other students, and they often choose different courses and majors. This makes it difficult to compare their academic achievements with the achievements of other students. Comparisons are also difficult because grade point averages (GPAs) have different meanings from one university to another and from department to department within a single university. It is even difficult to use graduation rates as indicators of academic experiences across schools, because academic standards and requirements vary between schools and from program to program within schools.

Research findings on grades are confusing. Some studies show athletes earning higher grades than students who do not play on varsity teams; others show the exact opposite. Some studies show athletes attending graduate school more often than nonathletes, and others show athletes taking an abundance of courses requiring little or no intellectual effort. Any interpretation of information on grades must take into account the following possibilities:

> The growing gap between college athletics and educational values is a major, unavoidable issue.
> —James Shulman and William Bowen, *The Game of Life* (2001)

1. Athletes in certain sports sometimes are overrepresented in specific courses and majors. This phenomenon is known as *clustering*, and it seems to happen most often on teams emphasizing eligibility over academic achievement and intellectual development. Therefore, we should not lump together all intercollegiate athletes when we discuss grades and graduation rates. Clustering does not occur among athletes in all sports; when it does occur, it may be due partly to the need to schedule courses around the time demands of sports. Experiences from sport to sport vary according to many factors.

2. Athletes in entertainment-oriented sports often go to college with lower high school GPAs and lower ACT and SAT scores than other students, including most other athletes, at their universities. Sometimes their academic goals are quite different from the goals of other students. Their academic choices and their grades are affected strongly by their goals.

Prior to 1989, data on graduation rates were confusing, because they were computed in many different ways. However, because the rates for many highly visible teams were shamefully low in many universities, and because the federal government threatened to force universities to disclose graduation rates, the NCAA began in 1992 to publish systematic records of "six-year graduation rates" for all member institutions and for each major division. This forced most institutions, especially those with big-time sport programs, to devote more attention to the educational lives of athletes. The results of their efforts have been mixed. There has been some progress, but many problems remain. We no longer hear of college athletes who cannot read, as we did in the 1980s. But there are cases in which academic integrity is seriously compromised in efforts to recruit and keep star athletes eligible. This is most likely to occur when athletes can help schools make millions of dollars in TV rights money for bowl games and the men's NCAA postseason basketball tournament.

According to 2002 data on graduation rates at NCAA Division I universities, we can draw the following conclusions (the "NCAA Division I Graduation Rates Report" is published annually):

• College athletes with scholarships graduate at about the same rate and in the same length of time as other students do. Fifty-eight percent of the students who entered Division I universities as first-year students during the 1994–1995 academic year had graduated by the spring of 2002, whereas the rate for all

athletes over the same time period was 60 percent. Athletes in the report included all those who received athletic grants-in-aid. For purposes of comparison, I exclude data on athletes who transferred into schools during their third year of college.

• The graduation rate for female athletes continues to be higher than the rate for male athletes. Female athletes in 2002 had a 69 percent graduation rate (compared with

The graduation rates for women athletes are higher than for men who play college sports. However, as women's teams have become entertainment-oriented, graduation rates have declined. This may be due to a shift in priorities or to the tendency of some athletes to leave school early or transfer to other schools when they see better sport opportunities. Research is needed on this issue in men's and women's sports. (NCAA Photo)

a rate of 61 percent for females in the general student body), whereas male athletes had a 54 percent graduation rate (compared with a rate of 56 percent for the males in the general student body). Graduation rates at schools where women's teams have become more entertainment-oriented declined slightly beginning in the mid-1990s. For example, the rates for women's basketball fell from 65 percent in 1996 to 59 percent in 2002; for black women basketball players who entered universities as first-year students, rates fell from 69 percent in 1996 to 59 percent in 2002. This suggests that "going big-time" does not contribute to educational improvement.

- Graduation rates are lowest in the revenue-producing sports, especially men's basketball (43 percent) and football (52 percent); these rates are below the rates for athletes in other sports (60 percent) and for the general student body (58 percent).

- Schools ranked in the "top twenty" in football and men's and women's basketball have lower graduation rates among athletes in those sports than the rates at less highly ranked schools; basketball teams that go to NCAA postseason tournaments and football teams that go to bowl games have lower graduation rates than basketball and football teams at other schools (Jackson, 2000, 2001; Lapchick, 2002).

- The graduation rates for black male athletes (43 percent) are lower than rates for other male athletes (59 percent), but they are higher than the rates for black males in the general student body (34 percent). Also, graduation rates for black males have increased since 1986, when minimum academic standards for scholarship athletes were established for all Division I universities. However, about one-fourth of all Division I universities have graduation rates of less than 25 percent for minority males, most of whom are black.

What do these patterns mean? With whom should we compare athletes when we assess the academic integrity of big-time sports? Should athletes be compared with regular full-time students who work thirty or more hours per week, because athletes often devote at least that many hours to their sports? Should athletes be compared with other students who have scholarships, or with those who enter college with similar ACT or SAT test scores and high school grades, or with those who enter college with similar academic goals and socioeconomic backgrounds? Should we compare the rates of athletes in sports that recruit high percentages of blacks with rates for the general student body in universities that are predominantly white?

My conclusion is that there is no single ideal comparison. We must make many comparisons to get a comprehensive and fair idea of whether sport teams, athletic departments, and universities are living up to the spirit of higher education. There are some teams in some universities that clearly give higher priority to athletic success than they give to academic success. Although we should not use those teams to make generalizations about all teams at all universities, neither should we ignore them and their exploitive and hypocritical practices. Furthermore, we should not ignore all the "wannabe" teams in Divisions I-AA, I-AAA, and II in which athletes, coaches, and administrators aspire to be big-time, even if it means compromising academic integrity.

Finally, even though graduation is an important educational goal, it should not be the only criterion used to judge academic success. Degrees are important, but they may not mean much unless those who receive them have learned something while in college. It is difficult to measure learning or increased intelligence in a survey of athletes, but it is possible to examine whether athletic departments operate in academically responsible ways. This could be done in connection with the periodic academic certification process that all universities undergo, but, until this occurs, we must depend on grades and graduation rates to examine what is going on. Rates and statistics don't identify all the problems or what should be done to correct them, but they alert us to *possible* problems and the need for investigation and action, and there are plenty of problems.

The Challenge of Achieving Academic Goals

During the 1980s and early 1990s, much publicity was given to evidence that many big-time, entertainment-oriented athletic departments were systematically ignoring the educational experiences of athletes (see figure 14.1). Information about how some athletic departments recruited, used, and abandoned young men in their quest to win games and make money became so widespread that the integrity of the universities themselves was questioned.

Since 1982, when the NCAA first enforced rules (Proposition 48) that set minimum standards for a first-year athlete to be eligible to play on Division I college teams, there have been

"I like your new recruit, coach, an excellent example of higher education!"

FIGURE 14.1 In big-time intercollegiate sports, coaches and university presidents have been known to distort the meaning of higher education.

many attempts to make intercollegiate programs more educationally responsible. The fact that graduation rates among athletes have increased as rules have become more strict, led the NCAA, in late 2002, to draft even stricter rules for eligibility. As of fall 2003, athletes are not eligible unless they complete 40 percent of their graduation requirements with a GPA of at least 1.8 by the end of their second year (up from 25 percent in 2002); 60 percent of requirements must be completed with a GPA of 2.0 by the end of their third year (up from 50 percent and 1.8), and 80 percent must be completed with a GPA of 2.0 by the end of their fourth year (up from 75 percent and 1.9). Eligibility among first-year athletes requires completion of fourteen English, math, science, and other core high school courses (up from thirteen).

Additionally, first-year athletes must meet minimum requirements on a sliding scale that combines high school GPAs and ACT/SAT scores. This scale was revised so that higher GPAs could be used to offset low standardized test scores. This was done to defuse objections based on research showing that social class and ethnicity are strongly related to scores on standardized tests and that the scores are not valid predictors of academic success among students from certain backgrounds.

As of early 2003, the NCAA was also considering regulations that would prevent schools from participating in postseason play, such as bowl games and the NCAA basketball tournament, if graduation rates among athletes fell below a certain percentage. This was recommended in a 2001 report by the prestigious Knight Foundation Commission on Intercollegiate Athletics. Such a rule is controversial because it will prevent some schools from making millions of dollars in postseason bowl games and tournament games. People are concerned that many of the teams with the best records in football and men's basketball have graduation rates that fall below the suggested thresholds. If these rules had been in effect for the 2001 football season and 2002 men's basketball season, well over half the teams playing bowl games and receiving tournament bids would have been ineligible to play.

Changes in NCAA eligibility rules have been designed to do three things: (1) send messages to high schools and high school athletes that a commitment to academic achievement is required to play big-time college sports, (2) set new guidelines for schools that had ignored their academic mission in connection with their sport programs, and (3) encourage schools to provide college athletes the support they need to meet academic requirements and achieve academic goals.

Progress has occurred, but it has varied widely from one university to another, and many people feel that reforms have fallen far short of what needs to be done to restore academic integrity to many intercollegiate programs (Shulman and Bowen, 2001; Sperber, 2000). In fact, experience clearly shows that big-time sport programs— especially entertainment-oriented programs— are *very* difficult to change. Teams in those programs are tied to many interests having nothing to do with education. Some young people on those teams are in school only to receive the coaching they need to stay competitive in amateur Olympic sports or to be noticed as they strive to enter professional sports. Coaches for those teams often view sports as businesses, and they are hired and fired on the basis of how much revenue they can attract to the athletic program. Even some academic administrators, including college presidents, use the programs for public relations and fund-raising tools instead of focusing on them as programs that directly serve educational purposes for athletes and the campus as a whole.

Major corporations sponsor the media coverage of intercollegiate sports and support teams for advertising purposes, *not* educational purposes. These corporations have little or no interest in the academic development of athletes. When a shoe company pays a coach or school to put its shoes on athletes' feet, or when a soft drink company buys an expensive scoreboard with its logo on it, company executives don't care if athletes are learning in their courses, as long as they attract positive attention to the company's products. Similarly, the local businesses that make money when the home team attracts fans are not concerned about GPAs and graduation rates as long as athletes bring to town masses of money-spending spectators for every home game.

In addition to the commercial interests of sponsors and boosters, as well as the often distorted, nonacademic orientations of some young people who attend college to play sports, there are other factors that interfere with establishing the academic integrity of intercollegiate programs. An examination of academic support services for athletes highlights some of those factors.

Academic Support Programs Through the late 1980s and the 1990s, nearly every athletic department with big-time sport programs developed or expanded its athlete academic support services. The stated goals of these support centers was to assist athletes in the pursuit of educational achievement.

According to Jack Rivas, president of the National Association of Academic Advisors for Athletics, the counselors and staff in these centers help "student-athletes get the full college experience." He explains that he and other counselors "are not eligibility checkers. We do not do the work. We are there to help student-athletes navigate the system" (Brady, 1999a, p. 3c). However, most academic support service programs are administered by and located in the athletic departments of universities. This not only further separates athletes from academic life on the campus but also locates support where the likelihood of compromising academic goals is higher than it would be if support were provided by a faculty-controlled program with no connection to the athletic department.

Research suggests that academic support services may not increase graduation rates among athletes (Sellers and Keiper, 1998), although they do keep more athletes eligible to play sports. Furthermore, a few highly publicized cases involving counselors who wrote numerous papers for athletes have raised additional questions about whether some of these support centers focus on eligibility more than academic development and achievement. The fact that top-ranked academic institutions have been involved in these cases raises serious questions about what occurs in academic support services in the athletic departments at other universities (Wertheim and Yaeger, 1999).

If faculty members administered academic support services for athletes, things would be better, but problems would remain. Lynn Lashbrook, the former president of the National Association of Academic Advisors for Athletics, explains that even some faculty members are willing to bend principles when it comes to dealing with varsity athletes. The counselors in the academic support service programs call them "friendly faculty." Lashbrook says that "every school has them, and every athletic department knows who they are" (Wertheim and Yaeger, 1999, p. 92). Even faculty members who are not "friendly" with the athletic department sometimes feel pressure to give special consideration to athletes. As one professor at the University of Minnesota noted, "who wants to be the guy who costs us the star basketball player?" Lashbrook adds that the stakes for faculty and staff at some universities are high. She says,

> If you're viewed as somebody against athletics, it could affect your career climb on that campus and even your job placement somewhere else because athletics is so powerful. (Wertheim and Yaeger, 1999, p. 96)

When athletes are expected to be ready to play in games that have multimillion-dollar stakes, it is not always easy to put education first. If it is not easy for a professor, how difficult must it be for a first-year teaching assistant who grades tests in a course taken by key members of a revenue-producing team scheduled to play on national television and maybe go to a bowl game, which would bring the university $15 million?

Despite new rules for NCAA schools, there also have been cases in which people have used junior colleges and private high schools and colleges to "create" academic records for athletes, which have enabled them to meet qualifying rules without academic benefit. In fact, many coaches have used community and junior colleges to circumvent rules on their campuses. Even today, after two years in good standing at a community college, an athlete can enter a major university without meeting the admissions standards that an entering first-year athlete must meet. After coming from a community college, athletes may be registered for relatively easy courses, which keep them eligible without giving them the credits they need to graduate in a timely manner. Rules are supposed to keep this from occurring, but clever people who ignore educational issues often find ways around those rules.

Prospects for Change   The challenge of achieving academic goals remains difficult. According to Terry Holland, a former coach and current athletics director emeritus at the University of Virginia, "We need clear and consistent action, not just words, to demonstrate to our athletes that classroom performance is our No. 1 priority" (2002, online). Alexander Wolff, a journalist who covers educational issues for *Sports Illustrated* says that, "if the NCAA were serious about reform, it would abolish freshman eligibility and dock schools one scholarship for every player they fail to graduate" (2002a, p. 29). Hundreds of other suggestions have been made by others (Knight Foundation, 2001). In the meantime, Patricia Viverito, commissioner of the Gateway Football Conference offers this suggestion:

> I think we're at a real crossroads, I keep being hopeful that presidents will sort of see the big picture and recognize that we are migrating further and further away from an educational

Division I basketball and football generate many millions of dollars in revenue, not just for universities and the NCAA but also for corporate sponsors and other businesses that depend on money and publicity related to games. This has made big-time college sports very difficult to change. Many people, including college presidents, have a vested interest in maintaining them as they are. (NCAA Photos)

model, and that someone is going to right that course and force us to do things in a more reasonable fashion. (in Suggs, 2002, online)

Unfortunately, presidents have been slow to take assertive and effective actions in the past.

DO SCHOOLS BENEFIT FROM VARSITY SPORTS?

The influence of high school and college varsity sport programs extends well beyond the athletes who play on teams. In this section, we will look at the effect of these programs on schools as organizations. In particular, we will examine school spirit and school budgets.

School Spirit

Anyone who has attended a well-staged student pep rally or watched the student cheering section at a well-attended high school or college game realizes that sports can generate impres-

sive displays of energy and spirit. Of course, this does *not* happen with all sport teams in a school, nor does it happen in all schools. Teams in low-profile sports usually play games without student spectators. Teams with long histories of losing records seldom create a spirited response among more than a few students. Many students could not care less about school teams, and some students are clearly hostile to varsity sports and the attention received by some teams and athletes. However, in many cases, varsity sport events do provide the basis for spirited social occasions, and some students use those occasions to express their feelings about themselves, their teams, and their schools.

Proponents of varsity sports say that displays of school spirit at sport events strengthen student identification with their schools and create the feelings of togetherness needed to achieve educational goals. Critics say the spirit created by sports is temporary, superficial, and unrelated to the achievement of educational goals. A football coach at a high school in Florida notes, "[Students] all yell and scream at the pep rally and only a few hundred kids will show up at the game. On Monday morning 70% of them won't know whether we won or lost" (in Wahl, 1998, p. 100).

Being a part of any group or organization is more enjoyable when feelings of togetherness accompany the achievement of goals. In the United States—and to an increasing extent in Canada and Japan—sports are one of the ways these feelings of togetherness are created in schools (Rees and Miracle, 2000). However, there is nothing magical about sports. Schools in other countries have used other methods to bring students together and provide enjoyable, educational experiences revolving around recreation and community service.

People outside the United States often see varsity sports in U.S. schools as elitist activities that involve most students in the passive role of spectator, which produces little in the way of educational experiences. They note that the resources devoted to sports might be used to fund other integrative activities that would involve more than cheering for teams, while providing experiences that actually make young people feel they are valued as contributing members of their communities. In response to the belief that sports "keep kids off the streets," they say that, instead of varsity sports, there should be programs through which young people can make the streets better places to be.

The spirit associated with high-profile intercollegiate sports is exciting for some students, but only a proportion of the student body attends most big-time intercollegiate games. Either the students are not interested in attending the games or the athletic department limits student tickets because they can sell seats at a higher price to nonstudents. There is no doubt that the games of big-time sport teams often are major social occasions on university campuses. They inspire displays of spirit, but there are questions about whether this spirit serves educational functions or simply provides entertaining social occasions for students bored with or stressed out by academic work. If it is the latter, then many universities may be missing opportunities to critically assess their academic programs rather than having sports somehow promote the programs by obscuring problems.

In summary, varsity sports often create school spirit. However, for that spirit to have educational significance, it must be part of an overall school program in which students are treated as valued participants and given a sense of ownership in the school and its programs. Unless students are actively involved in what happens every day at school, their cheering at weekly games is simply a superficial display of youthful energy having nothing much to do with education.

School Budgets

High Schools What are the financial consequences of interscholastic sport programs? Most high school programs are funded through school district appropriations. Seldom does the money spent directly on varsity teams exceed 3 percent of the budget for any school. In fact, in most cases, expenditures for interscholastic sports account for less than 1 percent of school budgets. When certain sports enjoy big budgets, much of the money comes from gate receipts and donations from booster clubs. This sometimes happens in towns where people are focused on a high-profile high school team and where there are large stadiums or arenas.

Usually, interscholastic sports do not cut into the resources used for basic educational programs, but neither do they add to those resources. In cases in which classroom teachers try to do their jobs without adequate funds for educational supplies, they and others may look to varsity sport programs as a place to make budget cuts. In the face of recent budget problems, this continues to happen in many schools and districts. This has given rise to a search for funds through a combination of sport participation fees and corporate sponsorships. Both these alternatives create problems.

Participation fees make sport participation less accessible to students from low-income families and add to the elitist profile that high school sports already have.

Corporate sponsorships connect the future of sport programs with the advertising budgets and revenue streams of private corporations. This creates serious problems when advertising budgets

> The U.S. permits sports a place in the life of high schools that other countries avoid. Team sports abroad are often organized by clubs outside the school.
>
> —Tom Loveless, Director, Brown Center on Education Policy (2002)

are cut or when sponsorships are not generating enough profits to satisfy stockholders and corporate executives. Corporations may then withdraw their support, and programs are left with no funds.

Other problems occur when the interests of corporate sponsors do not match the educational goals of schools and school sports. Promoting the consumption of candy, soft drinks, and fast foods through ads and logos on gym walls and team buses often directly contradicts the health and nutrition principles taught in high school courses. This clearly subverts education and makes students cynical about learning and education. This possibility has led many people to question the educational wisdom of funding sports by selling the student body to corporations. This has intensified debates about how varsity sports should be funded by high schools and whether they are worth the expense.

Colleges and Universities   The relationship between varsity sports and school budgets is much more complex on the college level. Intercollegiate sports at small colleges are usually low-budget activities funded through a combination of student fees and money from the general fund controlled by the school president. Of the nearly 1,200 universities and colleges in NCAA Divisions I and II, the NAIA, and the NCCAA, only about fifty make a profit in their sport programs. During the late 1990s, Division II institutions with football teams had average deficits of about $500,000, whereas those without football teams lost about $400,000 per year (NCAA N, 1998) At the 325 NCAA Division I universities, vast sums of money often are spent on intercollegiate sport programs. This money comes from gate receipts, the sale of media rights, student fees, the general fund controlled by the university president, the boosters, concessions, logo license fees, corporate sponsors, and government subsidies.

Big-time athletic departments are run as businesses that pay no taxes (Sack and Staurowsky, 1998; Zimbalist, 1999). They try to be self-supporting, if not profit making. Today, there are a handful of haves and a large barrel full of have-nots when it comes to wealth among intercollegiate athletic departments. Comparing athletic programs at different schools is difficult, because each uses a different accounting method, many of which hide expenses and make it difficult to identify all revenue sources. It takes a financial wizard to determine the expense categories for the dozens of major new stadiums and arenas being built by universities, and it is safe to assume that a portion of those expenses, sometimes a large portion, is not billed to athletic departments. A luxury weight-training facility may be billed to the campus health and fitness budget, a luxury reception room may be billed to the president's entertainment fund, and so on. Furthermore, because the athletic department claims that intercollegiate football and basketball are educational rather than commercial activities, they build facilities with money from tax-free bonds, which force taxpayers in the state to subsidize the football and basketball programs (Sack and Staurowsky, 1998; Zimbalist, 1999).

Big-time teams sometimes claim to be making money when they are shuffling many of their expenses for facility maintenance, academic support, utilities, insurance, medical care, films and videos, and advertising to university accounts outside the athletic department. Ironically, on a cash flow basis, men's sports do better than women's sports only in Divisions I-A and I-AAA. Women's sports in Divisions I-AA, II, and III have smaller deficits than men's sports. This means that, in many NCAA schools, women's teams do better financially than men's teams—that is, they have fewer losses.

When profits are made by a team, they usually are kept in the athletic department and used to support other sports or to expand team budgets. Sometimes profits made by a team are used to increase that team's budget. There have been only a few cases in which money made by sport teams has been used to support nonsport programs in the university. Most often, money from the university's general fund is used to support sport teams, not the reverse.

As of 2002, only fifteen Division I-A universities spent more on all of their women's sport teams than they did on football alone. In most NCAA schools, women's sport programs have smaller financial deficits than men's sports. This means that men's sports have a higher net cost than women's sports have in most schools. (NCAA Photos)

Attempts to contain spiraling costs in intercollegiate programs generally have failed. Big-time programs that make large amounts of money in their revenue-producing sports and have successful fund-raising programs do not want to forfeit this competitive advantage. They can outspend their competitors and win games in the process, even though they may obscure the educational foundations of intercollegiate sports.

When big-time sport programs lose large amounts of money, why do universities continue to support them? There are three reasons. *First*, many people believe the programs have *indirect* financial benefits. *Second*, many people think the losses are justified in light of the values cele-brated by sports, especially men's football. *Third*, many people dream that someday, if everything goes right, they will have a program like that of the University of Michigan, Notre Dame, or Florida State University.

Indirect Benefits of Intercollegiate Programs

When supporters of big-time sports talk about "indirect benefits," they mean two things: (1) increased donations to the university endowment and (2) increased publicity, which in turn increases student applications, which in turn raise the academic qualifications of the student body, which in turn make the school a better academic institution. However, research suggests that neither of these benefits exists (Shulman and Bowen, 2001; Sperber, 2000; Zimbalist, 1999).

Benefits for the general endowment are rare, because big donors whose giving is inspired by sports are usually more interested in bowl games than Nobel prizes, and they donate to the athletic department, rather than the general endowment. When average alumni give to the athletic department, they sometimes decrease the amount they give to the endowment, and, when athletic departments do things that tarnish the image of the university, many people may withhold donations (Sheehan, 1996).

In the case of student applications, few students actually choose a college on the basis of the records of its sport teams. The students who do make such a choice are not usually the best students in the applicant pool (Zimbalist, 1999). In general, the choice of a college depends more on the quality and availability of academic programs, tuition costs, housing arrangements, parents' wishes, the enrollment decisions of close friends, and the location of the school, rather than the win-loss records of big-time sport teams (see figure 14.2).

It is true that sport programs are used in fund-raising efforts. University presidents and development officers often use sport events as social occasions to bring wealthy and influential people

"I told you we sent our daughter to a top-notch school! Her bas-ketball team just beat Duke University."

FIGURE 14.2   Do people equate academic quality with athletic success? Do students choose a school because of its athletic teams? Data on these questions are sometimes confusing, but most research indicates that winning athletic teams have little impact on fund-raising and no impact on educational quality.

to their campuses. They know these people will not donate new buildings simply because the football team plays in a bowl game. They also know that pouring money into expensive sport teams is not the way to solve money problems at their schools. However, this does not stop them from using the publicity created by high-profile teams to call attention to the academic reputation and potential of their universities.

When sport events are used in connection with fund-raising, university leaders must be careful not to create an image of the school as a "sports factory." This can cause prospective donors to question the quality of academic programs, and it can backfire if the athletic programs are perceived as lacking integrity and honesty.

It must be acknowledged that, when sports have been used to create a university's public relations image, varsity teams cannot be dropped suddenly without causing some problems. However, if there are good reasons for dropping sport

programs, most alumni and other donors respect the decision to do so. Furthermore, many colleges and universities have not used sports to create public relations images, and some of these institutions have been very successful at fundraising. They highlight academic and research programs, rather than coaches and quarterbacks. When their programs are good, their donations are as high as those to schools with publicized sport programs.

Indirect Costs of Intercollegiate Programs
In 2001, James Shulman and William Bowen, respected experts on higher education, published *The Game of Life*. In this book, they analyzed data from 1951 through the 1990s for thirty colleges and universities that have highly selective admissions policies. The schools in their sample included public and private Division I universities, Division IAA Ivy League universities, and Division III colleges and universities. Their findings cannot be generalized to all colleges and universities, but they identify potential institutional costs associated with current intercollegiate athletic programs. Shulman and Bowen noted the following:

- Students recruited as athletes have enjoyed a substantial advantage in the admissions processes at most colleges and universities. In the early 1990s athletes had a 50 percent better chance than other students of being admitted, relatives of alumni had a 25 percent better chance, and minorities had a 19 percent better chance. This advantage for athletes has become even more pronounced in recent years.
- The ACT/SAT differences between athletes and other students have grown consistently since the late 1980s. Athletes admitted to schools now score considerably lower on these standardized tests than other students admitted to the same schools, and this lowers the general academic qualifications of students as a whole.

- Since the late 1980s the academic performance of athletes has been consistently lower than would have been expected on the basis of their test scores and other factors considered in the admissions process. This has been especially true when athletes have been on teams with a heavy "sport focus" and when they identified coaches as their primary mentors. Because other students in time-intensive extracurricular activities excelled beyond academic expectations, underperformance among athletes has not been so much due to time issues as to a "culture of sport" in which academic performance has been given a lower priority than athletic excellence.

- The lives of athletes on college campuses have become increasingly different and separate from the lives of other students. This has occurred because athletes now experience more pressure to focus on their sports than ever before, whereas other students experience more pressure to focus on their academic work than ever before. As differences in values and experiences have become greater between athletes and other students, athletes have tended to band together in their social and academic lives, and other students have to seen athletes as privileged and distinct from the student body as a whole. In some cases, this has led to a general decline in student attendance at athletic events, and it has strengthened the social foundations of a separate "athletic culture" on campuses.

- The emphasis on athletics and the funding for sports has detracted from an emphasis on other extracurricular activities, such as publishing a school paper, staging plays, debating, and other activities, none of which has paid coaches or well-established infrastructures that can be used to recruit and train students. Per-student funding for sports often was two to three times higher than the combined expenses for all other extracurricular activities on campuses during the late 1990s.

Overall, Shulman and Bowen found a growing divide between athletic and academic programs and increasing tension between core educational values and processes of decision making and resource allocation on college campuses.

This tension has been building since the 1980s, and there is a growing resentment of athletic programs among some faculty and a growing sense among financial supporters that, when colleges and universities put too much emphasis on intercollegiate sports, academic life suffers. This means that it is crucial for this athletic-academic gap to be addressed.

To reduce these academic costs, it is necessary for groups of colleges and universities to work together. If one school acts alone, its teams are put in a bad position and campus morale can be damaged. As changes are discussed, Title IX compliance provides an opportunity to reconsider the role and organization of college sports in the university and in higher education as a whole. Instead of replicating men's programs to achieve equity, it may be wiser to restructure intercollegiate athletics, so that their indirect costs are controlled and academic goals are supported. Other suggestions are offered in the section, "Intercollegiate Programs: Problems and Recommendations."

VARSITY HIGH SCHOOL SPORTS: PROBLEMS AND RECOMMENDATIONS

High school sport programs generally enjoy widespread support, and many people have vested interests in keeping them the way they are. Many high school sport programs are doing a good job of providing students opportunities to develop and display physical skills in ways that have educational relevance. Other sport programs have not only lost direct connections with education but also have subverted the educational process for some students. Problems vary from one high school program to the next, but the most serious problems include the following: (1) an overemphasis on "sports development" and big-time program models, (2) limited participation access for students, and (3) an emphasis on varsity sports that distorts the status system among students.

Overemphasis on "Sports Development" and Big-Time Program Models

The Problem Some high school administrators, athletic directors, and coaches seem to think that the best way to organize high school sports is to model them after big-time intercollegiate programs. When this happens, people involved with varsity sports become overconcerned with winning records and the presentation of tightly organized, high-profile programs to the community at large. These programs often highlight football or boys' basketball, but other teams can be highlighted, depending on local traditions. In the process of trying to build high-profile sport programs, teachers, coaches, and administrators may overlook the educational needs of all the students. They can be caught up in the effort to be "ranked," rather than to respond to the needs of all students.

People who focus on sports development often give lip service to the idea that sports must be kept in proper perspective, but many forget their own words when it comes to the programs at their schools. In fact, they may even encourage students to specialize in a single sport for twelve months a year, instead of encouraging them to develop a wide range of skills in various sports (Wolff, 2002c). They set up sport camps or identify camps that they strongly encourage "their athletes" to attend during summer break. They sometimes forbid their athletes to play other sports and then recommend that they join community clubs, where they can continue playing through the off-season. They continually tell students that they must sacrifice to achieve excellence in the future. This, of course, turns off many students who want to have

fun with a sport right now and who want to enjoy participation, even if they do not plan on being All-American athletes in the future. When young athletes focus on sport development, they may overconform so much to the sport ethic (see chapter 6) that they jeopardize other important developmental activities and relationships in their lives.

When people adhere to a sports development model, they hire and fire coaches on the basis of win-loss records rather than teaching abilities. They even may describe coaches as good teachers when teams have winning records and as bad teachers when teams lose. Their goal is to build a winning tradition without ever critically examining how such a tradition is connected to the education of students. They just assume that winning is educational. This orientation has led an increasing number of high schools to recruit seventh- and eighth-grade athletes in certain sports to build big-time teams that will be highly ranked on the national or state level. They want to use the public relations generated by popular spectator sports to increase their visibility and status. Private schools want to use the public relations to recruit more tuition-paying students (Ruibal, 2002). Corporations that sell sports apparel and equipment often intensify this orientation and even facilitate recruiting and transfer practices that have no real educational relevance in the lives of young students.

These big-time sport programs have created an atmosphere in which many high school students mistakenly believe that athletics are a better route to rewards and college scholarships than academics are. This is just one of the ways that some varsity sport programs can subvert the achievement of educational goals.

Recommendations for Change Varsity sport programs ought to be critically assessed on a regular basis. Coaches should be provided with opportunities to learn more about the ways sports can be made into educationally relevant activities. Coaches also should be given access to coaching education programs and other professional development opportunities that emphasize student development rather than sports development, if such programs exist today.

The educational value of state and national rankings should be assessed. Is there a need to crown national high school championship teams and state championship teams? Are there alternative ways to define and seek excellence other than through such a system? Why not give higher priority to sports involving active participation rather than those that are supposed to attract spectators?

There could be more combined male/female teams in sports such as long-distance running, doubles tennis and badminton, bowling, golf, cycling and tandem cycling, soccer, hacky sack, wall climbing, archery and shooting, volleyball, swimming, racquetball, and billiards. If a person's high school years are a time for social development, playing these sports should be more valuable than watching spectator sports based on entertainment models. Scoring and handicap systems could be designed to accommodate skill differences and promote physical and social development, rather than sports development.

Limited Participation Access

The Problem   The major advantage of interscholastic sports is that they provide students with opportunities to develop and test their skills, especially physical skills, outside the classroom. However, when high school programs emphasize power and performance sports, they discourage participation by some males and many females who prefer sports emphasizing pleasure and participation. In fact, this may be the major factor that prevents schools from meeting their gender equity goals, despite persistent attempts to make sure opportunities are available for females: females may not be as eager to play sports that are built around the idea of "proving who the better man is." At any rate, most high schools have not achieved gender equity when it comes to sport participation.

Budget cuts also have interfered with changing or expanding programs in creative ways. One of the biggest threats to more open participation in varsity sports is the use of participation fees. Another threat is the use of private booster organizations to fund football or boys' basketball in ways that skirt or violate laws about gender equity and certainly subvert any notion of democratic participation in the student body as a whole (Fish and Milliron, 1999).

Recommendations for Change   Not everyone is physically able or motivated to participate in interscholastic sports based on a power and performance model. Those who do not measure up to their bigger, faster, taller, and stronger classmates need participation alternatives. There is no reason only one team should represent a school in varsity competition. Why not have two or more teams? Why not have a football league with players under 140 pounds, a basketball league with all players under 5'8" tall, or track meets with height and weight breakdowns for certain events? Where this has been tried, it has been successful.

There should be efforts to develop new interscholastic sports in which size and strength are not crucial for success. Too often, the focus is on football and basketball rather than a variety of sports suited for a variety of participants. Why not have teams in Frisbee, racquetball, flag football, softball, in-line skating, or any other sport for which there is enough local interest to get people to try out? With a little guidance, the students themselves could administer and coach these teams and coordinate meets and games with opponents at other schools. If responsibility builds autonomy and decision-making skills, why not let students direct their own teams, so that more of them have opportunities to participate? This has been done with success in many countries, and it costs almost nothing.

Students with disabilities have been almost totally ignored by varsity sport programs. Schools should develop sport participation opportunities for these students. This could occur in a combination of specially designed programs or by including athletes with disabilities on existing high school teams. This would not work in all sports, but there are certain sports in which competitors with disabilities could be included in games, meets, and matches. If there are not enough athletes with disabilities in one school, then combine schools or have one team from an entire conference.

Girls' sports still do not have the support that boys' sports enjoy. Of course, this problem has a history that goes far beyond high school. But the result is that girls still participate at lower rates than boys (see figure 14.3). In some areas, there is still an emphasis on boys' teams as the most important teams in the school. Gender equity in varsity programs could be achieved in some schools through such gender-mixed sports as those recommended in the section "Recommendations for Change" on page 511.

More schools are now using participation fees to save interscholastic sports. This strategy may work, but it may also limit participation among students from low-income families, even when fee waivers are available. If fees are necessary to save programs, all students should work for the money to cover program expenses, or there should be public organizations that establish scholarship funds to pay fees for students in need of assistance.

Emphasis on Varsity Sports That Distorts the Status System Among Students

The Problem   This issue was raised in "Reflect on Sports" on page 488. I include it here because the growing emphasis on sports in North American culture will continue to carry over into high school culture. This means that administrators, teachers, and coaches must be very careful

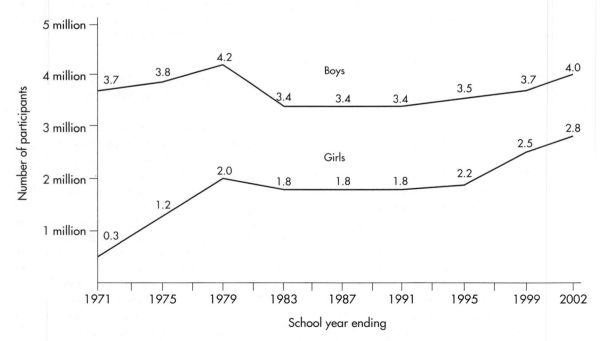

FIGURE 14.3   Boys and girls participating in interscholastic athletics, 1971 to 2002. (*Source:* National Federation of State High School Associations, 2002.)

not to unintentionally encourage the formation of a status system in which athletes are privileged in ways that contribute to feelings of animosity among other students and to patterns of harassment and exploitation engaged in by some athletes.

Leon Botstein, education critic and president of Bard College, has noted that today's high schools must be reformed because they "trap [adolescents] in a world of jock values and anti-intellectualism, like trying to cram a large person into a small, childish uniform." These are harsh words, but they should inspire critical assessments of school cultures in which the most revered students are those who can "kick ass" on a football field or hit 20-foot jumpers at the buzzer. Bernard Lefkowitz, author of *Our Guys* (1997), a book on a gang rape by high school athletes in New Jersey, has observed that tensions between athletes and nonathletes in high schools can be intense when students who aren't on varsity teams feel that, in comparison with athletes, they do not receive recognition for their qualities and contributions at school (ESPN, 1999). When varsity sports are overemphasized in the overall organization of school activities, some students are unintentionally marginalized and cut off from the connections they need to feel valued. This subverts education.

Recommendations for Change   It is a cliché to say that sports must be put into proper perspective. However, adults who control high schools should take the message of this cliché to heart. They must carefully assess how systems of privilege operate in schools. This is not an easy task, because expressions of privilege often are difficult to identify when adults are not personally familiar with the subtleties of student behavior in classrooms, hallways, cafeterias, parking lots, and other common spaces in and around the schools (even the restrooms). The challenge, of course, is to become aware without engaging in surveillance strategies, which invade students' privacy and turn the school into a mini police state.

The best strategy is to bring students together in policy-assessing and policymaking groups in settings where students with different interests and attributes can learn to treat each other in civil and respectful ways. Friendship groups are important in the development of adolescents, so it is important to accept the selective interaction patterns that young people find comfortable and reaffirming, but at the same time it is important to ensure that systems of privilege do not pit these friendship groups against one another in the school.

Another strategy is to give equal attention and recognition to students' accomplishments in activities other than sports. Also, it is important to encourage local media to do the same. As Jay Weiner, a sportswriter at the *Minneapolis Star Tribune*, asks, "Why should local news coverage of high school sports exceed coverage given to the band, debating society, or science fair?" He points out that, when "sports stars are introduced to the culture of athletic privilege at a very young age," perspectives will be distorted in schools (Weiner, 2000, p. 50).

INTERCOLLEGIATE SPORTS: PROBLEMS AND RECOMMENDATIONS

Problems are not new to intercollegiate sports. Even in the late nineteenth century, college teams were accused of being too commercial and professional. In the mid-1920s, the Carnegie Corporation commissioned a study that found intercollegiate programs to have problems related to commercialism, professionalization, and the neglect of educational issues (Savage, 1929).

These problems continued to grow along with the size, popularity, and scope of intercollegiate sports. Television created new sources of revenue, attracted new fans, and took sports further away from educational concerns. Then, in the light of the civil rights and women's movements, people realized that intercollegiate programs were racist, sexist, and unresponsive to the

At the height of the civil rights movement in 1966, the NCAA men's basketball finals involved an all-white University of Kentucky team playing a University of Texas, El Paso, team that started five black players. This game forced people to acknowledge the racial segregation that had been taken for granted in major college sports. (NCAA Photos)

participation needs of minority and women students. These and other issues, such as recruiting abuses and economic problems, led the American Council on Education to sponsor another investigation in 1973. It was not surprising that this study discovered the same problems found in past studies (Hanford, 1974, 1979).

In 1991, 1992, and 1993, the Knight Foundation Commission on Intercollegiate Athletics issued three influential reports in which it noted that big-time intercollegiate sports remained in need of drastic reforms.

In 2001, the Knight Foundation Commission saw fit to issue a fourth report, *A Call to Action: Reconnecting College Sports and Higher Education.* It made further recommendations for eliminating what it defined as the continuing excesses of college sports.

These reports, combined with other research, indicate that the major problems confronting college sports today are the following: (1) an emphasis on entertainment and commercial values, (2) a lack of athletes' rights, (3) gender inequities, and (4) distorted priorities related to racial relations and education.

Emphasis on Entertainment and Commercial Values

The Problem   Big-time intercollegiate athletics has become a major commercial entertainment industry, with goals and operating methods that are separate from and often directly opposed to the educational mission of U.S. universities (Sperber, 1990).

Evidence shows that, when sport programs become big businesses, financial concerns take priority over educational concerns. When media rights to games are sold, the academic progress of the college players often becomes less important than television ratings and network profits. Corporate sponsors are not concerned with educational issues when they sponsor sports—their survival depends on profits, not the academic progress of athletes. Educational concerns may not be given top priority when people having nothing to do with higher education are making many of the decisions affecting intercollegiate sports.

What happens when experts in marketing, the media, and large corporations produce and present intercollegiate sports under their logos for their interests? Corporate sponsorships have brought needed revenues to *some* sports in *some* programs, but they also have intensified the emphasis on entertainment and have marginalized the sports that do not attract spectators. This has seriously compromised, if not eliminated, the educational relevance of college sports.

Entertainment goals have also intensified the hypocrisy underlying descriptions of programs as amateur sports that benefit the participants. As ESPN's Tony Kornheiser notes,

> College basketball players watch the coach roaming the sidelines in his $1500 custom-made suit. They read about his $500,000 salary and $250,000 perk from some sneaker deal. They watch the schools sell jerseys [and T-shirts] with the players' numbers on them. They see the athletic director getting rich and the college president getting rich and NCAA officials getting rich and the coach's dog getting rich. And you wonder why they might ask, "Hey where's my share? What am I, a pack mule?" (1999, p. 46)

This hypocrisy intensifies the expectation of privilege among many athletes. When they act on those expectations, they may do foolish or deviant things. Then they are sanctioned and condemned for bringing down the system. Meanwhile, others in this distorted and unfair system continue to make money and blame problems on a few athletes who are said to lack discipline and character.

Recommendations for Change   At least three recommendations have been offered as solutions to the problem of commercialization:

1. Separate big-time teams from universities and let them continue to operate as businesses and as "minor leagues" for pro sports.
2. Pay athletes a living wage and provide other employee benefits.
3. Impose cost-containment measures on athletic departments and particular sport teams and regulate corporate involvement in intercollegiate sports.

The first recommendation is probably very unrealistic. It avoids the challenge of making

intercollegiate sports educationally relevant. The second recommendation is unworkable. Athletic departments, even the most profitable, cannot afford to pay all athletes. Paying only the athletes who play on teams that take in revenues would violate Title IX law. Also, how would the athletes' market value be determined, especially on teams that record losses or low profits when they don't go to bowl games or postseason tournaments? The third recommendation is the only one that faces the challenge of restoring educational relevance to intercollegiate sports. If serious, enforceable cost-containment measures and team spending limits were implemented, and if television revenues were more equally shared in all three NCAA divisions, the financial spending race could be controlled.

Corporate support also can be regulated, so that sport programs are not dependent on the advertising and profit needs of private companies. Telling athletes what logos they must wear is hardly consistent with what students should learn in an open educational environment. Classroom teachers are not allowed to sell their students to corporations. This is a good policy, and it should apply to the athletic department as well as to academic departments. Corporate sponsorships should be negotiated under conditions that demand open and critical education and student freedom and autonomy.

Cost containment, spending limits, revenue sharing, and sponsorship restrictions must also be combined with regular evaluation of athletic departments in educational terms. In fact, the academic accreditation of universities should involve an assessment of the educational relevance of athletic programs.

If these recommendations cannot be implemented, all varsity sports should be replaced by student-controlled club and intramural sports. This is an extreme suggestion, but the chronic problems and glaring hypocrisy of existing entertainment-professional-commercial programs call for extreme measures. Furthermore, it would make sense if student fees and state money were used to benefit all students instead of the elite few.

Lack of Athletes' Rights

The Problem   Athletes in big-time intercollegiate programs receive intrinsic rewards, and some receive extrinsic rewards in the form of prestige and grants-in-aid. However, much of their lives are lived under the control of others. Additionally, athletes in the major revenue-producing sports have lives that are more separate from the general student body than ever before.

Sociologist Stan Eitzen notes that athletes face a situation very similar to the one faced by people in nations ruled by dictators: they have no free speech and no basis for challenging the system that controls them. Athletes with a grievance against a coach or an athletic department are on their own and risk losing their scholarships and eligibility if they speak out. This is because "they have no union, no arbitration board, and rarely do they have representation on campus athletic committees" (Eitzen, 1999, p. 98).

Some athletes generate millions of dollars for their coaches and athletic departments but are limited in what they can receive from schools. They must make four-year commitments to schools, but schools make only year-to-year scholarship commitments to athletes. Coaches and representatives of the athletic department may invade athletes' privacy, whereas athletes must accept all rules imposed by coaches, athletic departments, and the NCAA without any voice in the formation of those rules. Athletes seldom have any mechanism through which they can safely object to abusive and oppressive actions by coaches or athletic department officials (Moye and Harrison, 2002).

How can we describe sports as educational when they are organized as an antithesis of democracy? How can we organize college sports as capitalist enterprises and then deny the athletes in those programs opportunities to make money from their own names and reputations outside the university?

Recommendations for Change   Athletes should be represented as voting members on university athletic committees and in the NCAA. Athletes should be able to register complaints and have them investigated in ways that do not jeopardize their scholarships or status on teams. Athletes should be formally involved in the evaluation of coaches and team programs, and all teams should be required to have athlete advisory/disciplinary committees that handle team issues. Furthermore, every university should have an independent ombudsperson (an appointed official who investigates situations in which individuals' rights may have been violated) whom athletes can contact when they need an advocate to help them deal with the athletic department, team, or coach on issues related to their rights.

Unless sport participation is clearly part of an open and democratic educational experience, big-time sports should be treated as businesses, with employees who have a right to be paid for their work. As they now exist, many sport programs are the only major form of show business in society in which the entertainers receive no money (Kornheiser, 1999).

As the NCAA receives $6 billion for selling television rights to the men's basketball tournament and as schools and conferences cash checks for well over $10 million for single bowl game appearances, big-time sports look very much like gilded plantations, where people are used as workers and given basic necessities but do not share in the fruits of their labor. If it is not practical to pay all athletes, then at least let them make money and form economic relationships outside the university. In other words, drop the myth of amateurism and quit hiding the hypocrisy of programs behind outdated notions of what sport has become in the United States (Sack and Staurowsky, 1998).

Gender Inequities

The Problem   Women students outnumber men students in most universities. All students

FIGURE 14.4 After having all the toys in the school, rules about sharing half of them with the girls may be strongly resisted. Many of the men who administer athletic programs in high schools and colleges grew up with the idea that males deserve more than females when it comes to sport programs.

pay student fees, and these fees are used to support intercollegiate sports. This was true even before there were women's teams at many universities. This means that for many years women students subsidized athletic programs that offered opportunities only to men. Men became accustomed to this sexist support system, and, when Title IX became law in 1972, many of them resisted the notion of sharing resources: they said sharing would hurt the men, who had had nearly all the opportunities and resources for the previous eighty years (see figure 14.4). However, the law demanded that women and men have equal opportunities to play sports and fair shares of resources in any organization that receives money from the federal government (see chapter 8 for an explanation of this law).

Even though Title IX was passed over thirty years ago, gender equity has not been achieved in most intercollegiate athletic programs. As the twentieth century closed, data on gender equity for the 1999–2000 academic year showed that women made up 53 percent of the student body and 43 percent of the varsity athletes in 325 Division I universities, and they received 44 percent of the scholarships, 34 percent of the coaching salary budgets, 32 percent of the recruiting budget, and 34 percent of the total operating budget (see figure 14.5).

As of 2002, 42 percent of the athletes at all three NCAA Division levels were women (150,186), and 58 percent were men (210,989). At the same time, 55 percent of all undergraduate students at those schools were women, and 45 percent were men. Although proportionality may not be the best way to measure equity, current patterns of opportunities and financial support strongly suggest that inequities continue to exist.

Of course, a sizable portion of these differences are due to the expenses for football and men's basketball, each of which have skyrocketing salaries for coaches and sizable expenses for recruiting and other operational expenses. Football also uses a large share of the scholarship dollars. In the sixty-seven universities in the top six intercollegiate conferences (The Atlantic Coast,

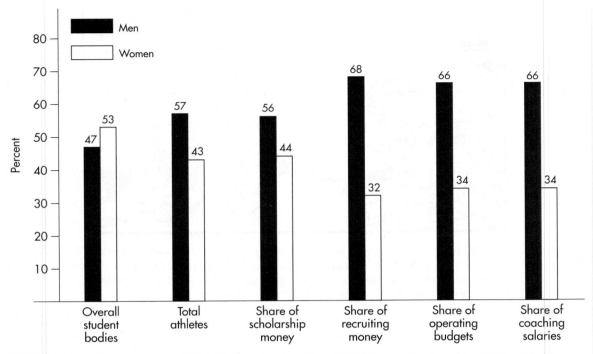

FIGURE 14.5   Gender equity in NCAA Division I universities, 2002. (*Source: The Chronicle of Higher Education* survey of 321 NCAA Division I universities (Suggs, 2003)

Big East, Big Ten, Big 12, Pacific-10, and Southeastern), football and men's basketball now make enough money, due to massive increases in television rights fees, to boost the overall budgets for women's sports. However, at the same time, the expenses for football and men's basketball have increased. Therefore, women's programs at these universities have grown significantly and opportunities for women to play sports and receive scholarships have increased, although women's programs still operate on about half the dollars that are spent on men's programs.

The schools with the largest gender inequities are the approximately 170 universities in Division I-A and I-AA that maintain football programs but do not share the recent windfall television revenues enjoyed by the sixty-seven universities in the wealthy conferences. When money is spent on costly football programs that do not make profits, it is difficult to fund women's sports at higher or equitable levels.

Overall, only a few universities have achieved gender equity, but certain forms of progress toward equity have been helped by football in about seventy of the largest universities in the United States and hindered by football in about 175 large and mid-sized universities. However, many of the men who administer about 80 percent of all intercollegiate sport programs are former football coaches, and they are not inclined to cut scholarships and other expenses for football. Instead they cut "minor" men's sports and blame it on Title IX. The men who are victims of these cuts attack Title IX and see women's sports, rather than football, as the problem. The hegemony of football and the men's fears of aligning themselves with women have clouded their analysis of the situation.

Meanwhile, supporters of intercollegiate football face a glaring contradiction. As Andrew Zimbalist (1999) notes, when the NCAA and athletic departments want to avoid issues such as paying athletes, paying taxes on profits, complying with antitrust regulations, raising money without their tax-exempt bonding status (for stadiums and arenas), they claim that football is part of education and must be treated as a nonprofit, educational enterprise. However, when women say they should share equally in the educational opportunities offered by sports, the same people say that big-time intercollegiate sports are a business and that the market is biased in favor of men in ways that cannot be controlled. They also say that, if women want more resources, big-time football is the best way to generate revenues for everyone, even though 70 percent of all football programs lose money.

This is why Title IX is still controversial in the twenty-first century—it exposes the ultimate educational hypocrisy and contradictions of big-time intercollegiate sports. This makes people angry or defensive, depending primarily on how they feel about football.

> **Football is the S.U.V. of the college campus: aggressively big, resource-guzzling, lots and lots of fun and potentially destructive of everything around it.**
> —Michael Sokolove,
> journalist (2002)

Recommendations for Change Many gender equity recommendations have been made since 1972, when Title IX became law. The main problem has been eliciting compliance from athletic departments. Athletic department leaders claim that equity is not possible unless there are major changes in how football is organized and played and that changes would jeopardize revenues.

This is a serious dilemma, and there is no way around it. My recommendation is that universities cut football expenses through cost-containment measures established at each NCAA division level, cut the size of football teams, and build a few women's sports into

revenue producers. If all men's football teams were to operate with similar resources, we would see who the best coaches and teams are, rather than seeing teams with fat budgets win year after year—at least in the years they are not on probation for breaking NCAA rules.

When revenue-production issues are discussed, it is also important to remember that it took about 100 years to build intercollegiate football and men's basketball into products that could make money for a few schools. Shouldn't women be given as much time to build their programs and make women's sports an important and visible part of the culture on university campuses? If not, maybe universities should abandon spectator sports and return to student-based sport programs with clear educational relevance.

Distorted Priorities Related to Racial Relations and Education

The Problem NCAA data in 2002 indicated that, although blacks made up about 10 percent of the student bodies at Division I universities, they accounted for 21 percent of the athletes, 46 percent of the football players, and 55 percent of the men's and 34 percent of the women's basketball players with athletic aid. About 82 percent of all black male athletes played in two sports—football and basketball—the only two sports that produce revenues and the sports with the lowest graduation rates.

This means that, in some programs, black males with low graduation rates generated revenues that funded the programs and scholarships of white men and women athletes in other sports and paid for their coaches, nearly all of whom were white. Black athletes are keenly aware of this and become very frustrated when whites accuse them of having it easy (C. K. Harrison, 1995).

Do black athletes feel that they should be accorded special privileges because of their contributions? Does this create tensions on campus, and is it related to some of the behavior problems among black athletes? There are no data on this, but these are important research questions.

Overall, 10 percent of all black male students (1 in 10) in Division I universities are athletes. This is the case for just over 2 percent of white male students (1 in 44), 2 percent of black female students (1 in 43), and just under 2 percent of white female students (1 in 52). Nearly 16,700 black athletes, first-year through seniors, received some form of athletic aid in Division I universities during 2002, and I estimate that

about 13,000 of them received what might be called *full* scholarships. This constitutes about 1 in 2,308 blacks between eighteen and twenty-two years old in the U.S. population. In other words 99.6 percent of college-age blacks *do not have* athletic aid. However, the image in the minds of many people is that black males are superathletes who use their physical skills to go to college. This misperception is grounded in the skin color profiles that people observe when they watch the big-time revenue-producing college sports on television. Figure 14.6 highlights the data on which this misperception is based.

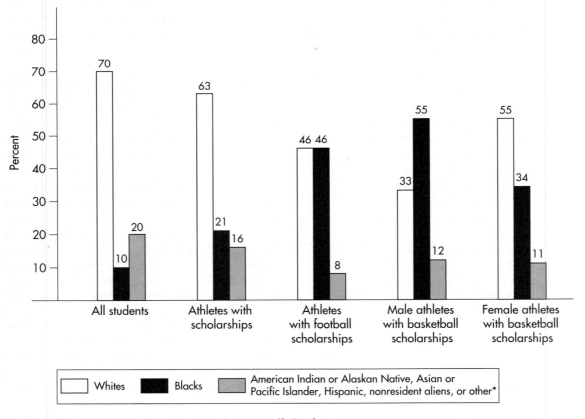

FIGURE 14.6 Percentages of students and athletes in NCAA Division I universities by skin color and ethnicity, 2002. (*Source:* 2002 NCAA Division I Graduation-Rates Report.)

The images represented in these data reinforce dangerous racial stereotypes, and these stereotypes demoralize thousands of black students struggling to use education rather than sports in their pursuit of opportunities. The message in these data is described by former NBA player Charles Barkley, when he observed that, as an African American, if "you make 20 points, you get 10 rebounds, [universities will] find you. But you make straight A's in the same school, they don't even know you're there. And that's sad. That's very sad about this country (in Romano, 1995, p. C3)."

Of course, many young black men and a growing number of black women benefit from athletic scholarships. This is not the problem. The problem is that universities have capitalized on the racist myth that blacks can use sports to improve their lives, while at the same time they have not devoted enough resources for recruiting black students and changing racial relations on the campus as a whole.

Meanwhile, many black athletes feel isolated on campuses where there are few black students, faculty, and administrators. This isolation is intensified by many factors (Fudzie and Hayes, 1995; Hawkins, 2000):

1. Racial and athletic stereotypes used by some people on campus
2. The amount of time athletes must devote to their sports
3. Barriers interfering with in-class, academic networking connecting black athletes to other students
4. A lack of campus activities related to the interests and experiences of black students in general
5. A lack of social self-confidence among black athletes who find campus life unrelated to their experiences
6. Cultural differences between black athletes and many other students
7. Feelings of jealousy among white students who mistakenly conclude that all black athletes have it made and don't have to work hard

The isolation is especially intense if black athletes come from working-class or low-income backgrounds and white students come from upper-middle-income backgrounds. This provides a combination of ethnic and socioeconomic differences that create problems unless the administration, faculty, and professional staff make a concerted effort to promote understanding and connections between students from different backgrounds. Putting athletes in their own dorm wings, creating special academic support programs, and giving them athlete centers where they can recreate and hang out with other athletes in their sports may obscure the problems and keep them out of sight, but they do not deal with them (Hawkins, 2000).

Although most research has focused on black men, black women face similar situations in predominantly white institutions (Bruening et al., 2002; Corbett and Johnson, 2000; Daniels, 2000; Smith, 1999; Stratta, 1995, 1997; Suggs, 2001; Winlock, 2000). However, black women also deal with gender inequities, so they face the dual challenge of dealing with racism *and* sexism. They see not only a lack of blacks in positions of power and authority within their schools and athletic departments but also a lack of women, especially women of color. Because black women face slightly different challenges than those faced by black men in U.S. society, and because women's athletics often are defined differently than men's athletics, black women athletes have slightly different experiences than black male athletes have. These differences are poorly understood, and more research is needed.

Another issue facing black women is that, apart from basketball and track, less than 3 percent of the women who receive scholarships in all other Division I women's sports are black; 73 percent of all black women athletes are in basketball and track.

African American women face many challenges when they play sports at predominantly white institutions. Apart from basketball and track, black women receive only 3 percent of the scholarships in NCAA sports. Many of these athletes, such as this gymnast on UCLA's 2001 championship team, may be the only black women on their teams. In terms of consequences, Title IX has created more benefits for white women than for black women. (NCAA Photos)

As soccer, rowing, golf, and lacrosse have expanded with efforts to comply with Title IX, black women have seldom benefited. These sports have rosters that are mostly white. The main problem is one of access: black girls do not have opportunities to play most of these high-growth sports in settings where they can develop top-level skills. When black women do play these sports, they often find their experiences to be socially isolating (Bruening et al., 2002). Tina Sloan Green of the Black Women in Sport Foundation has made the case that "Title IX was for white women" and that black women have not been a priority when most whites think about expanding sport opportunities for girls and women (Suggs, 2001). This is a serious issue, which most people have ignored.

Recommendations for Change Universities must be more aggressive in recruiting and supporting minority students who are not athletes, as well as in recruiting minority coaches and faculty. It is not fair to bring black or other ethnic minority athletes to campuses where they have little social support and little they can identify with. Furthermore, white students and faculty must be made aware that not all blacks play sports or are even interested in sports. If universities would make more concerted efforts to incorporate racial and cultural diversity into all spheres of campus life, recruiting black athletes would not be defined as part of a distorted set of priorities.

We need more visible models of campus cultures in which students, staff, faculty, and administration appreciate cultural differences and use them as a basis for expanding their knowledge and understanding of the diverse world in which we all live. This should be one of the core organizing principles on all college campuses today. When universities present to the world an image of physically talented black athletes and intellectually talented white scientists, racism is perpetuated, intended or not. Universities somehow must present to young black men and women the message that they will be recruited primarily for their intellectual skills.

The message to white men and women must be that the university is a setting in which people from diverse backgrounds meet and use their differences to create a wide range of learning experiences. Sports can be a part of this process, but only when black students constitute about the same percentage of the student body as they do of the athletic department.

SUMMARY

ARE VARSITY SPORTS EDUCATIONAL?

It is difficult to generalize about high school and college sport programs. They differ from one another in numerous ways. However, varsity sports have no place in high schools or colleges unless they are legitimate parts of educational programs and unless they receive their direction from educational purpose. At a minimum, if the programs do not benefit athletes educationally, they cannot be justified as school-sponsored activities.

There is no consistent evidence that high school sports produce negative consequences for those who participate in them. Of course, some

schools, coaches, parents, and athletes lose sight of educational goals in their pursuit of competitive success. Sports can be seductive, and people connected with high school teams sometimes require guidance to keep their programs in balance with the academic curriculum. It is up to school superintendents and principals to oversee what happens in their districts and schools. Parents also should be sensitive to the potential of sports to subvert educational goals. When sport participation interferes with educational achievement, steps must be taken to restore sports to their proper place.

A main theme in this book is that sports are social constructions. That is, sports can be organized and played in many ways, and people can creatively influence the meanings associated with sports to meet specific goals. However, most people associated with interscholastic sports simply have assumed that sports and sport participation *automatically* produce positive results, so they have not taken the time to critically examine sports in student culture as a whole.

The possibility that sport participation might interfere with the educational progress of athletes is greatest in big-time intercollegiate programs. The attractiveness of being an athlete in a big-time program is often enough to distract students from academic work. In fact, it can make coursework nearly irrelevant in the lives of impressionable young people, especially young men who see their destinies being shaped by sport achievements, not academic achievements.

Interscholastic sport programs usually create school spirit. But it is not known if that spirit contributes to the achievement of educational goals. Although it is certain that other school activities could be used to bring students together, sports do provide students with high-profile social activities that make schools more interesting places to be. Although they occupy the everyday attention of a considerable number of students, it is unknown whether they systematically distract attention from academic matters or the conditions under which they are most likely to do so.

It is doubtful that high school sport programs seriously cut into budgets for academic programs. The money they require is well spent if they provide students opportunities to explore their physical selves and meet challenges outside the classroom. On the intercollegiate level, the funding situation is complex and confusing. However, it is clear that most programs are not self-supporting and that they do not generate revenues for their schools' general funds. What is not clear is the extent to which the athletic programs divert money from academic programs or contribute to them in indirect ways.

High school programs subvert the achievement of educational goals when they overemphasize sports development, limit access to participation, and distort the status system among students. Similarly, intercollegiate programs are counterproductive to the reputation and mission of higher education when they are characterized by commercialism, a lack of rights for athletes, gender inequities, and distorted priorities related to racial issues and education. If the administrators of high schools and universities allow these problems to exist, there are no educationally sound reasons for their schools to continue sponsoring varsity sport programs.

Varsity sport programs never will be perfect. There always will be a need for critical evaluation and change, just as there is in any part of the curriculum. This means that the educational relevance of these programs depends on constant evaluation and assessment. A critical approach is the only approach that will enable sports to be meaningful activities in the everyday lives of students and in the social organization of the schools themselves.

SUGGESTED READINGS

Dobie, M. 2000. Race and sports in high school. In *Best newspaper writing 2000* (pp. 319–87), edited by C. Scanlon. St. Petersburg, FL: The Poynter Institute for Media Studies (this five-part series of reports, originally published in *Newsday* received a major national award for newspaper writing about diversity; provides a unique view of racial and ethnic relations in a high school).

Gerdy, J. R. 2000. *Sports in school: The future of an institution.* London/New York: Teachers College Press, Columbia University (thirteen articles dealing with four main topics: the educational benefits of sports, the preparation of coaches and athletes, race and gender in sports, and athletics and education).

Hawkins, B. 2000. *The new plantation: The internal colonialization of black student athletes.* Winterville, GA: Sadiki (analysis using an internal colonial model to focus on the structural inequities and the systemic exploitation that characterize racial relations as they impact black athletes in predominantly white institutions).

King, C. R., and C. F. Springwood. 2001. *Beyond the cheers: Race as a spectacle in college sport.* Albany: State University of New York Press (analyses of the racial dimensions of intercollegiate sports, especially as they are represented in the commercial packaging of those sports, the dynamics of the events themselves, and the media coverage of the events and the athletes involved; shows how traditional racial ideology has become deeply embedded in the taken-for-granted practices of college campuses).

Mahiri, J. 1998. *Shooting for excellence: African American and youth culture in New Century Schools.* New York: Teachers College Press, Columbia University (illustrates how sport experiences can be a source of critical self-reflection and empowerment among students and of effective pedagogical strategies in the classroom).

Rees, C. R., and A. W. Miracle. 2001. Education and sport. In *Handbook of sports studies* (pp. 277–90), edited by J. Coakley and E. Dunning. London: Sage (overview providing a brief history, discussion of important issues, and review of relevant research).

Sack, A. L., and E. J. Staurowsky. 1998. *College athletes for hire: The evolution and legacy of the NCAA's amateur myth.* Westport, CT: Praeger (provides data to show how the NCAA has systematically developed big-time college sports into professional and commercial activities while marketing them as amateur sports and denying the fact that athletes are workers in a professional sport system; suggestions for reform are offered).

Shulman, J. L., and W. G. Bowen. 2001. *The game of life: College sports and educational values.* Princeton, NJ: Princeton University Press (highly influential book based on data gathered from selective colleges and universities; a thoughtful and provocative analysis that raises serious questions about the educational value of intercollegiate sports as they are now organized in many schools).

Sperber, M. 2000. *Beer and circus: How big-time college sports is crippling undergraduate education.* New York: Henry Holt (critique of the state of higher education; emphasis on how intercollegiate sports have been associated with a decline in critical thinking on campuses).

WEBSITE RESOURCES

Note: Websites often change. The following URLs were current when this book was printed. Please check our website (www.mhhe.com/coakley8e) for updates and additions.

www.mhhe.com/coakley8e Additional material on the sport participation–academic achievement relationship; discussions of school-community relations and pay for intercollegiate athletes.

www.aahperd.org/nagws/template.cfm The National Association for Girls and Women in Sports,

a member organization of AAHPERD; site provides information on Title IX issues.

www.ncaa.org National Collegiate Athletic Association; site has information about intercollegiate sports and links to NCAA sport sciences programs and NCAA-sponsored studies, including graduation rate data.

www.knightfdn.org Site of the Knight Foundation; link to the Knight Foundation Commission on Intercollegiate Athletics, where there are summaries of the 1991, 1992, and 1993 reports and a copy of the 2001 report *A Call to Action: Reconnecting College Sports and Higher Education.*

www.nfhs.org National Federation of State High School Associations; information about varsity high school sports in the United States; data on participation, rules, and other topics.

www.naia.org National Association of Intercollegiate Athletics; information about this organization and member organizations.

www.njcaa.org National Junior College Athletic Association; information about intercollegiate sports at two-year community and junior colleges in the United States.

www.thenccaa.org National Christian College Athletic Association; general information and news.

www.sportinsociety.org Center for the Study of Sport in Society collects annual data on the ethnic and gender composition of athletic department employees at major colleges and universities; click on the "Racial and Gender Report Card" to find data on the affirmative action records of Division I institutions in the United States.

(Jay Coakley)

Sports and Religions

Is It a Promising Combination?

I'M NOT PLAYING for the fans or the money, but to honor God. . . . Every night I try to go out there to honor Him and play great.

—David Robinson, NBA
player (1996)

Online Learning Center Resources

Visit *Sports in Society*'s Online Learning Center at **www.mhhe.com/coakley8e** for additional information and study material for this chapter, including

• Self-grading quizzes
• Learning objectives
• Related websites
• Additional readings

A complete outline is available online at
www.mhhe.com/coakley8e.

THE GREATEST FEELING I get playing baseball
right now is knowing that I can go out and be a
warrior for the Lord. I can go out . . . and say my
prayer and then be a very aggressive, warrior-like
pitcher, glorifying Him.

—Randy Johnson, Major League Baseball
player (1996)

The relationships between sports and religions have shifted and changed from one time and place to another. As noted in chapter 3, physical activities and sports in many preindustrial societies were linked to religious rituals. This remains true today in traditional cultures where physical games and challenging activities may be incorporated into cultural rituals that are linked to the supernatural. For example, the histories of many native cultures in North America contain long traditions of games and running races defined as having spiritual significance.

The histories of Jews and Christians in Europe and North America indicate that there have been times and places in which Judeo-Christian religious authorities approved or even sponsored various forms of physical activities, games, and sports. In other cases, all or most forms of physical activities were ignored or even condemned as indulgent and sinful. During the last half of the twentieth century, religious organizations in North America and Europe were more likely to approve sport activities as worthwhile pursuits, and even sponsor sports. Furthermore, individuals, especially in the United States, have been more likely to combine sport participation with their religious beliefs and publicly express what this combination means to them. Today, this is a common practice.

The purpose of this chapter is to explore how religion and religious systems of meaning are combined with sports and sport participation. As you read this chapter, remember that similar religious systems of meaning can be combined with sports in various ways, depending on the experiences, relationships, and interests of individuals and groups. The major questions we will discuss in this chapter are

1. How is *religion* defined and why do sociologists study it?
2. What are the similarities and differences between sports and religions?
3. Why have people combined sports and religions and why are Christians more vocal about this combination than are Jews,

Muslims, Hindus, Buddhists, Sikhs, and other religious people?
4. What are the challenges faced when combining sports with religion in general and Christianity in particular?

In discussing the last question, we will give special attention to whether the combination of religion and sports offers any promise for eliminating racism, sexism, deviance, violence, and other problems in sports and sport organizations.

HOW DO SOCIOLOGISTS DEFINE AND STUDY RELIGION?

Sociological discussions of religion often create controversy in sociology of sport classrooms. This happens when students and teachers use only their own religious beliefs and practices as a point of reference when they think about religion. Therefore, they have strong feelings about how religion *should be* discussed.

Religion is powerful, because it forms a foundation for general systems of meaning that help people come to terms with ultimate issues and questions and help them justify and specify their relationships with God or gods (Stark, 1999). These systems of meaning are a part of cultural ideology. They inform how people think about the world, and they affect social relationships and the organization of social life. They also inform ideas about the body, movement, physical activities, and even sports.

A sociological discussion of religion and sports requires that we view religion as a part of culture. Although there are many definitions of *religion*, the traditional definition used by many sociologists is that a religion is a socially shared set of beliefs and rituals focused on the ultimate concerns of human existence: birth, life, suffering, illness, tragedy, injustice, and death. Religious beliefs and rituals consist of meanings and cultural practices that are special because people connect them with a sacred and supernatural realm and base these connections primarily on faith, which is the foundation for religions and religious beliefs.

Objects, symbols, and ceremonies are defined as *sacred* when people connect them directly with the supernatural or with forces beyond the here-and-now world. Sacred things inspire awe, mystery, and reverence. Some religious belief systems distinguish the realm of the **sacred** from the realm of the **profane.** The profane consists of objects and activities that are not directly connected with the supernatural or the divine.

Many Christians perceive churches as sacred places by connecting them with their God and spiritual Savior. Christian churches have been given symbolic meaning, which can be understood only in terms of their connection with the supernatural. They have been incorporated into the realm of the sacred.

On the other hand, the stadiums in which sport teams play have no connection with the sacred or supernatural within Christian religious belief systems, although they may have important

In secular societies, such as the United States, it is often easy to distinguish between the sacred and the profane. However, in many cultures, it is difficult to make clear distinctions between these two spheres because they are merged almost seamlessly in everyday life. This is especially the case for many Muslims, who merge religion with the rest of their lives. (Marco Di Lauro; AP/Wide World Photos)

meanings for many people in a community. Stadiums are understandable in terms of everyday meanings and experiences; they exist in the realm of the profane. For example, when large billboards advertising Pepsi, Budweiser, and McDonald's are mounted on scoreboards and stadium walls, few people become concerned. However, if those billboards were mounted on the altars, walls, or stained-glass windows of a church, synagogue, or mosque, most people would object; a Pepsi logo on an altar would be seen as degrading the sacred meaning given to the church.

This explanation of religion requires qualification. For many peoples around the world, religion and religious beliefs are simply built into culture and cultural beliefs; they are one and the same (Fowler et al., 1997). Unlike Christianity and Judaism, many religions do not consist of identifiable dogma and are not organized under the authority of what many of us in Europe and North America would call "church authorities." Furthermore, it is not always easy to draw lines between the sacred and the profane in some cultures. However, we often are able to identify objects, beliefs, and rituals that a collection of people has agreed are associated with a sacred and supernatural realm that transcends the everyday world.

The diversity of religions and religious beliefs around the world is great. Human beings have dealt with ultimate questions about life and death and have coped with the inescapable problems of human existence in many ways (Lemert, 1999). In fact, they have developed literally thousands of rich and widely varied religions.

Sociologists are not concerned with the truth or falsity of particular religious belief systems. Instead, they assume that all religions are true in their own way, because they enable believers to define and deal with ultimate questions and issues. This makes religion important sociologically, because it informs how people think about the world, themselves, and their connections with the world and other people.

Religions are studied by sociologists because they have important social meanings, dynamics, and consequences. When people connect power, authority, and wisdom with God, gods, or other supernatural forces[1] or when religious beliefs set believers apart from others and then explain that separation in otherworldly terms, religion becomes socially important. For example, under certain conditions, religions and religious beliefs might lead to the following:

- Powerful forms of group unity and social integration *or* devastating forms of group conflict and violent warfare
- A spirit of love and acceptance *or* forms of moral judgment through which ideas and people are marginalized or condemned
- Commitment to prevailing social norms *or* rejection of those norms and commitment to new norms
- Acceptance of the systems of power that influence social relations among men and women, racial and ethnic groups, social classes, homosexuals and heterosexuals, the able-bodied and the disabled, and other groups *or* opposition to those systems of power combined with visions for new forms of social relations

These examples show that religions influence individuals and groups, and that religious beliefs have an important impact on the cultural ideology that people use to make sense of the world, themselves, and their connections with others.

SIMILARITIES AND DIFFERENCES BETWEEN SPORTS AND RELIGIONS

Discussions about sports and religions are often confusing and sometimes controversial. Some people argue that sports are a new form of religion, or at least "religion-like" in important ways.

---

[1]The word *God* refers to *the* Supreme Being or *the* Creator in monotheistic religions. The words *god(s)* and *godliness* refer to deities across all religions, including polytheistic religions, in which people believe in multiple deities or gods.

Others argue that there are *essential* differences between what they define as the *true nature* of sport and the *true nature* of religion. Still others argue that sports and religions are simply two distinct sets of cultural practices, which sometimes overlap as people devise ways to live with one another and attempt to make their lives satisfying and meaningful. The purpose of this section is to explain and clarify each of these three positions.

Sports as a Form of Religion

When I have attended NFL games or World Cup soccer matches and watched 75,000 or more people yelling, chanting, and moving in unison in the shadow of an alterlike scoreboard, I could not help but think about the religious dimensions of sports. The most extreme position to take when discussing this issue is to say that sports are a new form of religion, because they involve expressions of beliefs and meanings that are stronger and more relevant to people today than the beliefs and meanings associated with "Christianity, Judaism, or any of the traditional religions" (Prebish, 1993). Others stop short of this position and say that sports are simply religion-like because both sports and religions have similar characteristics and produce similar consequences (Hubbard, 1998; Mathisen, 1992; Novak, 1976; Price, 2000). For example, comparisons of religions and sports have highlighted the following similarities between Judeo-Christian religious systems of meaning and modern sports (see Hoffman, 1992):

- Both have places and buildings for communal gatherings and special events. Sports have stadiums and arenas decorated with pictures of athletes and championship trophies, whereas most religions have churches and temples decorated with statues of sacred figures and/or stained-glass windows depicting sacred events and achievements.

- Both have procedures and dramas linked to personal betterment. Sports have playbooks, practices, and time-outs, whereas religions have sacred books, prayers, and retreats.

- Both emerge out of the same quest for perfection in body, mind, and spirit. Sports emphasize body development and performance, whereas religions emphasize physical denial or discipline for the sake of spiritual purification.

- Both are controlled through structured organizations and hierarchical systems of authority. Sports have commissioners, athletic directors, and coaches, whereas religions have bishops, pastors, and priests.

- Both have events scheduled to celebrate values in the context of festivals and festive occasions; both capture considerable attention on the Sabbath and set aside certain times as special. In sports, there are the World Cup, Wimbledon's fortnight, and Super Bowl Sunday, whereas in religions there are Ramadan, Easter Week, and Sunday morning worship.

- Both have rituals before, during, and after major events. Sports have initiations, national anthems, halftime pep talks, hand slapping, band parades, and hand shaking after games. Religions have baptisms, opening hymns, regular sermons, the joining of hands, and ceremonial processions.

- Both have heroes and legends about heroic accomplishments. Sport heroes are elected to "halls of fame," with their stories told repeatedly by sports journalists, coaches, and fans. Religious heroes are elevated to sainthood or sacred status, with their stories told repeatedly by religious writers, ministers, and members of congregations.

- Both are used to celebrate and reproduce the values of particular groups in society. Sports emphasize attitude and achievement, whereas most religions emphasize salvation through some form of valued belief or action.

- Both can evoke intense excitement and emotional commitment from individuals and groups.
- Both can give deep personal meaning to people's lives and many of their activities.
- Both can be sources of existential experiences involving the temporary suspension of boundaries between self and the rest of the world and sites for the transcendence of self and for expressions of emotional euphoria.
- Both can distract attention from important social, political, and economic issues and thereby become an "opiate" of the masses of people in a society.

This list enables us to understand why many people perceive sports as religion-like. After all, sport participation, as a player or spectator, is characterized by many factors and feelings that also characterize religious participation. In fact, the similarities are so apparent that it is easy to ignore the differences between these two spheres of life.

"Essential" Differences Between Sport and Religion

Some people argue that religion and sport each has a unique, separate truth, or "essence": the essence of religion is grounded in divine inspiration, whereas the essence of sport is grounded in human nature.[2] They argue that religion and sport reveal different parts of a basic truth, which is unchanging, regardless of history, culture, or social circumstances. Religion and sport, they say, each have a unique essence that transcends time and space. People "live out" those essences when they participate in religion and in sport.

People who think in these terms are usually called "essentialists." In the humanities and the

Those who use "essentialist" approaches to religion and sport might not like this statue and what it suggests. In sociological terms, the statue can be taken to illustrate that both sports and religions are socially constructed cultural practices, which change over time in connection with larger social forces and contexts (see pages 533–544). How many other religions would create statues that put their prophet or "Savior" in a similar scene—playing a heavy contact sport that sometimes involves violence? (Jay Coakley)

social sciences, including sociology, essentialists are concerned with discovering the "truth" they believe is inherent in "nature" and then outlining that truth in the form of laws about human behavior and social life. When they turn their attention to religion and sport, they argue that the fundamental character and truth of religion are different from the fundamental character and truth of sport. For example, they might highlight the following differences:

- Religious beliefs, meanings, rituals, and events are fundamentally mystical and grounded in *sacred* and supernatural realms, whereas sport beliefs, meanings, rituals, and

---

[2]These people refer to *sport* and *religion* in the singular, because they assume that all sports and all religions express the same essence. I explain the problems associated with this approach in chapter 1, pages 6, 21–29.

events are fundamentally clear-cut and grounded in *profane*, here-and-now realms.

- The purpose of religion is to transcend the circumstances and conditions of material life in the pursuit of spiritual goals and eternal life, whereas the purpose of sport is to focus on material issues, such as victories and the rewards they bring in this life.
- Religion is fundamentally rooted in faith, whereas sport is fundamentally rooted in concrete, factual rules and relationships.
- Religion involves cooperation among believers, whereas sport involves competition between opponents.
- Religion emphasizes a spirit of humility and love of others, whereas sport emphasizes a spirit of personal achievement and defeat of others.
- Religious rituals are essentially expressive and process-oriented, whereas sport rituals are essentially instrumental and goal-oriented.

Most functionalists and some conflict theorists would use an essentialist approach to studying sport, religion, and the relationship between them. They would say that there are natural differences between Super Bowl Sunday and Easter Sunday, even though both are important days in different people's lives. Similarly, they would say that there are fundamental differences between a hockey team's initiation ceremony and a baptism, between a seventh-inning stretch and a scheduled prayer, and between St. Patrick's Cathedral in New York and Yankee Stadium.

Some essentialists may be religious people who claim that religion and sport are fundamentally different because religion is divinely inspired and sport is not. They believe that their religious beliefs are grounded in the realm of the sacred, whereas the rules of sport are grounded in profane concerns. These people often worry that, when religion and sport come together, the essential character of religion becomes secularized and corrupted by the profanity of sport (Hoffman, 1992, 1999).

Essentialists who study sport would admit that the social and psychological consequences of sport are sometimes similar to the consequences of religion, but they would also stick to their position that sport and religion are fundamentally and essentially different from each other.

Religions and Sports as Cultural Practices

Most people who study sports in society see religions and sports as two forms of cultural practices created by groups of people as they devise ways to live with one another and struggle to make their lives satisfying and meaningful. This approach is based on a "social constructionist" approach, because it does not assume that either religions or sports have essential or identical characters grounded in unchanging truths. Instead, it identifies all religions and sports as "social constructions" or "social formations," with social structures, dynamics, and consequences, which overlap or differ, depending on social conditions in particular situations.

Social constructionists generally use critical theories to guide their work. Therefore, they focus on social relations and issues of power when they study religions and sports. For example, they might study how people give meaning to the body in connection with different religious belief systems and how those meanings influence movement, physical activity, sport participation, and even the organization of sports. They might ask why sports and religion are male-dominated spheres of life and then study gender ideology as it is related to religion, the body, and sports. They would be concerned with how people combine religious beliefs with sport participation and how those combinations are formed and expressed in particular cultural and subcultural settings.

Social constructionists using critical theories assume that the systems of meaning and cultural practices connected with both sports and religions *do* undergo change. They assume that religious beliefs and rituals vary from one social and cultural group to another and that beliefs and rituals change with new revelations and visions, new prophets and prophecies, new interpretations of sacred writings, and new teachers and teachings. On the one hand, they see these variations and changes as examples of how religious beliefs reaffirm and reproduce the cultural contexts in which they occur. On the other hand, they see them as potential expressions of opposition and resistance, which could lead to transformations in social relations and social life. Of course, they would see sports in similar terms—as regularly changing cultural practices that sometimes reproduce various cultural forms and practices but sometimes challenge and transform them.

Studying Sports and Religions: An Assessment

A debate about whether sports and religions are the same or different in terms of their nature or social functions does not inspire exciting questions. I am much more concerned with critical questions about how people participate in the formation and transformation of social and cultural life, as well as how sports and religions are used in those processes. This means that I see religions and sports as sets of cultural practices. I try to understand their connections to each other by using a constructionist approach guided by a combination of critical, critical feminist, and interactionist theories—the ones I find most helpful when it comes to this and most other topics. This enables me to ask questions that deal directly with people's experiences and social relations. It also alerts me to the different meanings that religions and sports have for different people, and it helps me understand those meanings in terms of the social and cultural contexts in which they are formed and changed.

Few people who study sports in society have done research on the connection between sports

> Jesus would be aghast at how we use his name to bless our sports contests.
> —Col. F. R. Lewis, retired
> U. S. Army chaplain (1996)

and religions. People who study religions are seldom interested in studying sports, and people who study sports are seldom inclined to study religions. Furthermore, published studies of sports and religion focus almost exclusively on Christian belief systems, especially in North America (see Hoffman, 1992; Overman, 1997). We know little about the connections between sports and religious beliefs other than those based in Christianity, and there is only a handful of studies that look at the connections between different religious beliefs and conceptions of the body, expressions of human movement, the integration of physical activity into everyday life, and participation in organized competitive sports.

There have been historical analyses of Jews in sports, especially Jewish men in the United States (Klein, 1999; Reiss, 1998). A common theme in some biographies of Jewish men is that they have refused to participate in sport events on the Jewish Sabbath or on sacred Jewish holidays.

There also have been a few popular media accounts of African American Muslim men, especially in professional basketball, who fast from dawn to sunset while they practice and play games during the sacred time of Ramadan as it is celebrated in Islamic religion (Hubbard, 1998). In the 1990s, there was extensive coverage of Mahmoud Abdul-Rauf, the NBA player whose interpretation of Islamic beliefs led him to keep his head bowed or to remain in the locker room while the U.S. national anthem was played before a game. By most accounts, the negative popular response to his actions contributed to the decline of his career in the NBA; acting on non-Christian beliefs was defined by many Christians as controversial, even when it involved a secular song.

A few scholars in the sociology of sport have been interested in the idea that religions may influence the opportunities and barriers that women face in sports and other forms of physical activity (Pfister, 2001). Belief systems in many religions often outline, in moral terms, ideas about femininity and masculinity. These ideas serve as a basis for defining what is moral and immoral when it comes to the body and what people do with their bodies. For those who study sports and gender, this makes religion a potentially important topic for study (Chandler, 2002; Randels and Beal, 2002).

Most people who study this topic focus on Hindu and Muslim beliefs and practices, rather than those of Christians and Jews. They note that many Hindus and Muslims believe that women's bodies are inherently sexual. This leads, they explain, to the creation of various "modesty policies" regulating the clothing worn by girls and women. Related norms also regulate the movements of women and the circumstances in which they may or may not be seen by or come into contact with males. These norms, in turn, influence the conditions and patterns of sport participation among girls and women (Hargreaves, 2000; Maguire et al., 2002; Pfister, 2001). Although such norms may not prevent sport participation, they influence and often limit the ways that girls and women integrate sports into their lives.

Such norms are certainly not limited to cultures where Hindu and Muslim beliefs predominate. They have existed in cultures connected with other religious beliefs, including various forms of Christianity, through history. The diversity in how people express their religious beliefs makes this a complex topic to study. But, as more people from various religious backgrounds migrate to new locations around the world, such studies will become increasingly important.

Despite the shortage of information about sports and religions other than Christianity and Judaism, issues related to this topic will be discussed later in the section "Sports and Religions Around the World." First, it is important to explain why certain forms of Christianity have become closely associated with organized competitive sports.

MODERN SPORTS AND RELIGIOUS BELIEFS AND ORGANIZATIONS

Despite important differences between the organization and stated goals of modern sports and those of religions, these two spheres of life have been combined in mutually supportive ways over the past 150 years. People with certain religious beliefs have used sports to achieve religious goals, and people in sports have used various forms of religion to achieve goals in sports. This has occurred frequently enough in recent years to make the combination of sports and religious organizations and beliefs very popular in some Western nations, especially the United States and Canada (Ladd and Mathisen, 1999).

The growing popularity of these combinations raises interesting questions. Why have Christian organizations and beliefs, in particular, been combined directly and explicitly with sports? Why have these combinations not occurred in connection with most other religions? How have Christian organizations used sports and how have athletes and sport organizations used Christianity and Christian beliefs? What are the dynamics and social significance of these combinations? These are the major issues discussed in sections, "The Protestant Ethic and the Spirit of Sports" and "How have Christians and Christian Organizations Used Sports?"

The Protestant Ethic and the Spirit of Sports

To understand the links between modern sports and contemporary Christian beliefs, it is necessary to review some history.

In the late nineteenth century, German sociologist/economist Max Weber did a classic study titled *The Protestant Ethic and the Spirit of Capitalism* (1904, reprinted, 1958). His research focused on the connection between the ideas embodied in the Protestant Reformation and the growth of capitalist economic systems. His conclusion was that Protestant religious beliefs, especially those promoted by John Calvin, were

Organized competitive sports emphasize work and achievement. These values are compatible with traditional Protestant religious beliefs. (Kristie Ebert)

supportive of changes that served as a basis for the development and growth of capitalism. Weber provided examples of how Protestantism promoted a "code of ethics" and a general approach to life that created in people deep moral suspicions about erotic pleasure, physical desire, and all forms of idleness. "Idle hands are the devil's workshop" was a popular Protestant slogan.

Weber used historical data to show that this "Protestant ethic," as he referred to it, emphasized a rationally controlled lifestyle in which emotions and moods were suppressed in a quest for worldly success and eternal salvation. This orientation involved defining work as a "calling" from God and using one's job as a means for displaying and proving one's spiritual worth. This was a socially significant idea because it linked material success with spiritual goodness.

Of course, Protestant beliefs have been defined and integrated into cultural ideology and everyday behaviors differently over time and from one group to another. However, most expressions of those beliefs have emphasized values supportive of the spirit that underlies high-performance sports as they have developed since the middle of the nineteenth century, especially in Europe and North America.

In his book *The Influence of the Protestant Ethic on Sport and Recreation*, Steven Overman (1997) explains that various expressions of the

Protestant ethic have emphasized a combination of the following seven key values or virtues:

1. *Worldly asceticism.* This refers to the idea that suffering and the endurance of pain has a spiritual purpose. Goodness is expressed through self-denial and disdain for self-indulgence; spiritual redemption is gained through self-control and self-discipline.

2. *Rationalization.* This refers to the idea that the world is rationally organized and that religious truth can be discovered through human reason. Virtue is expressed through efficiency measured in terms of concrete achievements.

3. *Goal directedness.* This refers to the importance of focusing on salvation. The spiritual worth of human action is demonstrated through its results. If actions lead to measurable achievements and success, they are good; if they do not, they are worthless or evil.

4. *Individualism.* This refers to the belief that salvation is personal, that it is tied to individual responsibility, initiative, and choice. Virtue is tied to an individual's conscience and his or her personal relationship with God/Christ.

5. *Achieved status.* This refers to the idea that success is associated with goodness and salvation, whereas failure is associated with sin and damnation. Taken to the extreme, this idea emphasizes that worldly success is a means of earning salvation, not simply a sign that a person is predestined to be saved.

6. *The work ethic.* This refers to the notion that work is a calling from God. People demonstrate their virtue by honoring this calling through working hard, developing their "God-given potential," and avoiding idleness.

7. *The time ethic.* This refers to the idea that time has a moral quality. Time is not to be wasted, because people are judged in moral terms on how prudent and efficient they are in using their time.

How are sports related to these seven key virtues of the Protestant ethic? Overman argues that these virtues are closely matched with the general orientation or spirit that informs the organization, meaning, and purpose of modern sports in general and power and performance sports in particular. I would agree, although I also would emphasize that expressions of the Protestant ethic have been integrated into people's lives in various ways, depending on historical and cultural factors. Overman's analysis focuses specifically on the United States. Furthermore, some of these virtues are not exclusive to Protestantism. Other religions, such as Catholicism, may emphasize one or more of these virtues, although no other religion has a similar overall belief system.

I also would hypothesize that Protestant beliefs have been associated with important changes in the way people in Europe and North America view the body. Traditional Catholic beliefs, for example, have emphasized that the body is a divine vessel, a "temple of the Holy Spirit." Before the twentieth century, Catholics were taught to keep the body pure, rather than to develop it through physical activities. Most Protestant believers, on the other hand, emphasized that the body was a divine tool to be used in establishing mastery over the world. The perfect body was a mark of a righteous soul (Overman, 1997, p. 201).

Protestant beliefs have also supported the idea that individual competition is a legitimate means of demonstrating individual achievement and moral worth. Overall, organized competitive sports, because they are oriented around work and achievement, are logical sites for merging various aspects of Protestant beliefs. Unlike free and expressive play, these sports are worklike and require sacrifice and the endurance of pain. Therefore, Protestant/Christian athletes can define sport participation as their calling (from God) and make the claim that God wants them to be the best they can be in sports, even if it involves the physical domination of others.

Furthermore, Christian athletes can define sport participation as a valuable form of religious witness and then link it with the Christian goal of individual salvation.

Research supports these hypotheses (see Overman, 1997, pp. 150–57). West German data collected by Günther Lüschen (1967) in the 1950s showed that Protestants, as opposed to Catholics and others, were overrepresented in German sport clubs. The same is true for national team membership in religiously mixed countries and for winners of Olympic gold medals: athletes from Protestant backgrounds disproportionately outnumber athletes from Catholic backgrounds and far outnumber athletes from Islamic, Buddhist, Shinto, or Jewish backgrounds. Even the international success of athletes from non-Protestant nations can be traced in some cases to the influence of cultures where Protestant beliefs are dominant.

Sports and Religions Around the World

Most of what is known about sports and religions focuses on various forms of Christianity, especially evangelical fundamentalism. Little has been written about sports and Buddhism, Confucianism, Hinduism, Islam, Judaism, Sikhism, Shinto, Taoism, or the hundreds of variations of these and other religions. The systems of meaning associated with each of these religions have implications for how people perceive their bodies, view physical activities, and relate to each other through human movement (see figure 15.1). However, these systems of meaning do not seem to support participation in organized competitive sports in the same way that various forms of Christianity do.

I have found in no other religions an equivalent of the self-proclaimed "Christian athlete," which is an increasingly visible character in competitive sports in North America and parts of Australia, New Zealand, and Europe. This may be due in part to the Christian notion of individual salvation and how it has been defined among

"Well, sports fans, let's hope you've placed your bet on the right competitor here!"

FIGURE 15.1 Those who study religions and sports are not interested in the truth or falsity of religious beliefs, but they are interested in the athletes who bring their religious beliefs to the playing field and why they do so.

certain believers. Apart from Christianity and Islam, most other religions focus on a transcendence of self. The goal of believers is to merge the self with spiritual forces. Developing and highlighting the self through a quest for success in competitive sports generally is not consistent with this goal. In fact, it generally violates the very spirit of these religions.

Unfortunately, our knowledge of these issues in the sociology of sport is very limited. We know more about how some North American athletes and coaches have converted Zen Buddhist beliefs into strategies for improving golf scores and marathon times than we do about how Buddhism is related to sports and sport participation among the nearly 400 million Buddhists around the world. This is a classic example of how our knowledge is grounded in a combination of Eurocentric science and limited personal experiences.

Buddhism and Hinduism: Transcending Self

It is interesting that Buddhism and philosophical Hinduism, two systems of religious meaning that emphasize physical and spiritual discipline, do *not* seem to inspire believers to strive for Olympic medals or to physically outperform or dominate other human beings in organized competitive sports. Instead, most current expressions of Buddhism and Hinduism focus on transcending the self and the material world. This focus does *not* support a person's interest in becoming an elite athlete. In fact, the major beliefs emphasized by many Hindus and Buddhists are incompatible with seeking competitive success in physical activities. The idea of expressing self-development through a quest for competitive victories would make little sense within most Hindu and Buddhist traditions as they are practiced today.

It is primarily elite athletes from Christian, capitalist countries who want to know how the meditation practices and rituals from these religions can be used to improve sport performances and give meaning to lives that revolve around competitive sports. However, there is a segment of a growing Hindu nationalist movement in India that uses exercises, games, and sports combined with yoga and prayers to develop loyalty and affection for Hindu culture and the Hindu nationhood (McDonald, 1999). Of course, sports have been used in many cultures as sites for training minds and bodies for military service and "defending the culture." However, when this training is tied to religion and religious practices, it takes on additional dimensions, because the sacred and the secular become mixed in ways that have strong social relevance.

Some traditional Hindus in India may enforce policies of secluding and veiling women. These cultural practices are linked with the legacy of the caste system in India. The caste system consisted of a complex set of social norms that regulated activities and relationships throughout Indian society. Every person was born into a particular caste, and his or her caste position

This youth league game in Japan is played with a massive statue of Buddha in the background. However, athletes in Japan do not connect sport participation with religion, as do some athletes in North America, where sport participation is linked regularly with Christian beliefs. (Jay Coakley)

marked his or her social status in society as a whole. On an official, political level, the caste system is no longer recognized as legal, but its impact on cultural life continues to exist. For example, women from previously middle and upper castes have considerable freedom, but women and many men from previously lower castes face problems of poverty, unemployment, and illiteracy. Patterns of sport participation are influenced by these factors. Although the caste system was never grounded exclusively in Hindu religious beliefs, Hinduism often reaffirmed and perpetuated the caste system. This has yet to be studied in terms of its connection with sports and other physical activities.

REFLECT ON SPORTS

Allah's Will
Dilemmas for Islamic Women Athletes?

Imagine winning an Olympic gold medal in an event for which you've trained many years. Imagine coming home, receiving death threats from those who brand you as an immoral and decadent women, and then being forced to live in exile. At the same time, imagine that you are a heroine to many young women, who see you as inspirational in their quest for equal rights and opportunities to play sports at all levels of participation.

These are the circumstances faced by Hassiba Boulmerka, the gold medalist in the 1,500 meters at the 1992 Olympic Games in Barcelona, Spain. As an Algerian Muslim woman, Boulmerka believed that it was possible to participate in the modern world without violating her religious beliefs. She felt that being a world-class athlete and participating in international sports did not require her to abandon her faith and commitment to Islam. Under the social and political conditions in many Muslim nations, this has made Boulmerka a radical Muslim woman—a feminist feared and rejected by some, a feminist embraced and followed by others.

Those who have feared and rejected Boulmerka are primarily fundamentalist Muslims. It is permissible, they say, for women to participate in sports—but *not* in shorts or T-shirts, *not* while men are watching, *not* when men and women train together, *not* when facilities do not permit total privacy, and *not*, if you are married, without the permission of their husbands (Beiruty, 2002). To complicate matters, Boulmerka has also been rejected by some Islamic feminists, who see her as a woman co-opted and used by a system of sports grounded in secular ideas and fueled by the interests of powerful corporations whose goal is to promote a soulless consumer culture around the globe. To participate in such a system, they say, is to endorse global forces that are dangerously oppressive.

Those who have embraced and followed Boulmerka are primarily those who want to revise the restrictive norms governing many Muslim women. They promote women's rights and the transformation of societies and communities in which women live without a voice, without public legitimacy, and without power (Hargreaves, 2000). However, Boulmerka

Sources: Hargreaves, 2000; Morgan, 1998.

Islam: Submission to Allah's Will Studying the connections between Islam and sports also is a challenge, because Muslims, like many Buddhists and Hindus, make no distinction between the religious and the secular. Every action is done to please Allah (God) and is therefore a form of worship. Religion and culture are merged in a single ideology, with an emphasis on peace through submission to Allah's will. Using the body to participate in physical activities or sports may occur, but it is tightly regulated by dominant beliefs about how such actions may or may not please Allah. Muslim men and women have participated in sports, even at the international level, but the connection between sport participation and the religious mandate to submit to Allah's will has not been studied. Research

by historian John Nauright (1997; Nauright and Magdalinski, 2002) refers to "muscular Islam," which existed in one area of South Africa during the apartheid era. Nauright notes that Muslim rugby players between 1930 and 1970 used a highly aggressive style of play to symbolize their struggle against apartheid. However, Nauright does not discuss whether the players, or the women and families who supported them, connected rugby or their use of intimidation and violence on the field to Allah's will.

There are noteworthy examples in the United States of black Muslims who have excelled at sports. Boxer Cassius Clay's conversion to Islam in the 1960s created global publicity. When he changed his name to Muhammad Ali and articulated his Muslim beliefs, most people in the has also been embraced by those who do not know or understand Islam and reject Muslim beliefs because of their own ethnocentrism and religious beliefs.

This complicated, real-life scenario illustrates that the bodies of Muslim women today are "contested terrain." They are at the center of deep political, cultural, and religious struggles about what is important, what is right and wrong, and how social life should be organized. Women athletes embody and personify these struggles. On the one hand, women athletes are subjects that assert new ideas about what it means to be a Muslim woman. On the other hand, they are the objects about which people debate matters of character and morality in society at large.

Is there social and cultural space in Islamic nations for Hassiba Boulmerka and others like her? Is it possible to merge Islamic beliefs with ideas about equal rights and sport participation among women? Can the Qur'an (Koran) be interpreted in ways that give women the power to make choices in their lives? Can people live peacefully together as they interpret the Qur'an in different ways?

Sociologist Jennifer Hargreaves (2000) explains that intervening in the struggles over these questions is challenging and must be done with sensitivity and cultural awareness. Efforts to promote change from the outside are risky because they are easily linked with ethnocentric beliefs about the superiority of Western values and the need to reform cultural practices that don't fit with them. This means that intervention must be done carefully through and with Muslim organizations that will make changes in their ways and on their terms. Hargreaves notes that these changes may not take the forms envisioned by Western observers, but if they free women from oppressive forms of social control they will represent progress.

Many Muslims, including Muslim women, continue to disagree with each other about whether changes should occur and how they should occur. This means that struggles over these issues will continue long into the future. Understanding and coming to terms with "Allah's will" is not easy and creates dilemmas for Islamic women athletes. *What do you think?*

· ·

United States did not understand Islam or why some African Americans embraced it. Since then, other black male athletes who have grown up as Muslims or have converted to Islam have participated successfully in sports, even in power and performance sports. However, the traditions of sport participation and the quest for excellence in sports have not been as strong in Muslim countries as they have been in secularized, Christian-Protestant countries.

It is important to note that some Muslims continue to use their religious beliefs to legitimize patriarchal[3] structures and maintain definitions of male and female bodies that discourage

girls and women from sport participation or restrict their access to many forms of sport participation. For example, physical activities among Muslims are nearly always sex segregated. Men are not allowed to look at women in many public settings, and women must cover their bodies in certain ways, even when they exercise. Norms such as these are especially strong among fundamentalist Muslims. This is why national Olympic teams from some Muslim nations may not include women athletes or women's teams. This issue is discussed further in the box "Allah's Will."

The popularity of sports among men in Islamic countries is often tied to expressions of political and cultural nationalism, rather than to expressions of religious beliefs (Stokes, 1996). Similarly, when Muslims migrate from Islamic countries to Europe or North America, they may

---

[3]Patriarchy is a form of gender relations in which men are privileged relative to women, especially in regard to legal status and access to political power and economic resources.

Sumo wrestling in Japan occurs in connection with centuries-old Shinto beliefs. "Purity and purification rituals are central to the practice of Shinto and many have been incorporated into the contemporary practice of sumo" (Light and Kinnaird, 2002, p. 142). (Katsumi Kasullara; AP/Wide World Photos)

participate in sports, but their participation is tied more to learning about life and gaining acceptance in their new cultures than to expressing Muslim beliefs through sports. Muslim girls and women in non-Islamic countries have very low sport participation rates (Verma and Darby, 1994), and Muslim organizations are unlikely to sponsor sports for their members.

Shinto: Sumo in Japan   Sumo, or traditional Japanese wrestling, has strong historical ties to Shinto, a traditional Japanese religion (Light and Kinnaird, 2002). *Shinto* means "the way of the gods," and it consists of a system of rituals and ceremonies designed to worship nature rather than to express an established theology. Modern sumo is a nonreligious activity, although it remains steeped in Shinto ritual and ceremony. The dohyo (rings) in which the bouts take place are defined as sacred sites. Religious symbols are integrated into their design and construction, and

the rings are consecrated through purification ceremonies, during which referees dressed as priests ask the gods to bless the scheduled bouts. Only the wrestlers and recognized sumo officials are allowed in the dohyo. Shoes must not be worn, and women are never allowed to stand on or near the ring.

The wrestlers take great care to preserve the purity of the dohyo. Prior to their bouts, they ritualistically throw salt into the ring to symbolize their respect for its sacredness and purity; they even wipe the sweat off their bodies and rinse their mouths with water presented to them by fellow wrestlers. If a wrestler sheds blood during a bout, the stains are cleaned and purified before the bouts continue.

Shinto motifs are included in the architecture and decorations on and around the dohyo. However, wrestlers do not personally express their commitment to Shinto, nor do Shinto organizations sponsor or promote sumo or other sports.

Religion and Life Philosophies in China   Anthropologist Susan Brownell (1995) discusses very briefly the connections between physical culture and various forms of Taoist, Confucian, and Buddhist ideas and practices in her comprehensive study of the body and sport in China. She notes that each of these life philosophies is actually a general theory of the nature and principles of the universe. As with Islam, this makes it difficult to separate "religious beliefs" from cultural ideology as a whole. Each of these life philosophies emphasizes the notion that all human beings should strive to live in line with the energy and forces of nature. The body and physical exercise often are seen as important parts of nature, but the major goal of movement is to seek harmony with nature rather than to overcome or dominate nature or other human beings.

Tai chi is one of the forms of exercise grounded in this cultural approach to life and living. Some versions of the martial arts are practiced in this spirit, but other versions, including the practices outside of China, are grounded clearly in a practical commitment to self-defense and military training. China's success in many international competitions raises other questions about the possible connections between religious beliefs and sport participation, but these questions have not been explored in studies of sports or religion.

Native Americans: Merging the Spiritual and Physical   Through history, many Native Americans have often included physical games and even running races in some of their religious rituals (Nabokov, 1981). However, the purpose of these games and races has been to reaffirm social connections within specific native cultural groups and to gain the skills needed for group survival. Outside of these rituals, sport participation has had no specific religious meaning.

Making general statements about religions and sports among Native Americans is impossible because there have been many variations in their religious beliefs. However, many Native American cultures are based in part on animistic religious beliefs. They emphasize that material things, such as the earth, wind, sun, moon, plants, and animals, contain elements directly linked to the sacred and supernatural. Many native games reflect these beliefs, and, when Native Americans participate in sports constructed by people from European or other backgrounds, they often define what they do in connection with animistic beliefs. After Peter Navokov studied running among Native Americans, he noted that

> Before the coming of the white man Indians ran to communicate, fight, and hunt. But, as I discovered, they also ran to enact their myths and to create a bridge between themselves and the forces of the universe. (1981, p. 9)

Native American athletes whose identities have been firmly grounded in native cultures often have defined their sport participation in connection with cultural traditions and beliefs. However, little is known about how they have incorporated specific religious beliefs and traditions into sport participation that occurs outside of their native cultures.

Sports and Religions Around the World: Research Is Scarce   We need more information about the connections among various religious beliefs around the world, ideas about the body, and participation in physical activities and sports. Research could help us understand the lives of billions of people who participate in various forms of physical activities and sports but do not connect them directly with religious organizations or use them as sites for religious witness.

At this time, I can find no equivalent of the "Christian athlete" in any religion. Apart from Christianity, the combination of religion and sport has occurred in connection with religious rituals in which the purpose of the occasion is primarily religious. Physical activities and sports are designed to fit with and satisfy the purpose of the religious ritual. This is different from the tendency of some Christians to attach their religion

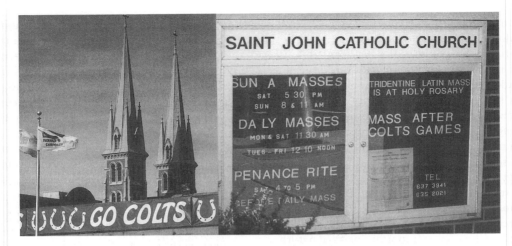

Stadiums and arenas have replaced churches as the dominant structures in many urban landscapes. Sport teams now attract more publicity than religious services. In this cultural context, religious services are scheduled around big games. This is true in Indianapolis, where the local cathedral is dwarfed by the RCA Dome and Conseco Fieldhouse and where mass is scheduled after the Colts' NFL games. (Jay Coakley)

to institutionalized, competitive sports that already exist for nonreligious purposes.

How Have Christians and Christian Organizations Used Sports?

To Promote Spiritual Growth   At the middle of the nineteenth century, influential Christian men, described as "muscular Christians" in England and New England, promoted the idea that the physical condition of one's body had religious significance. They believed that the body was an instrument of good works and that meeting the physical demands of godly behavior required good health and physical conditioning. Although most religious people at the time did not agree with this approach, many began to consider the possibility that there might be a connection between the physical and spiritual dimensions of human beings and that there might be important links between body and spirit (Guttmann, 1978, 1988).

These new ideas, that the body had moral significance and that moral character was associated with physical conditioning, encouraged many religious organizations to use sports in their membership activities and programs. For example, the YMCA and the YWCA grew rapidly between 1880 and 1920; these organizations built athletic facilities in many communities, and they sponsored teams in numerous sports. In fact, Canadian James Naismith invented basketball in 1891 while he was a student at the Springfield, Massachusetts, YMCA, and William Morgan invented volleyball in 1895 while he was the physical activities director at a YMCA in Holyoke, Massachusetts.

Although mainline Protestants endorsed sports through the end of the nineteenth century, the changes that occurred in many sports during the first half of the twentieth century made many of them skeptical about sports' religious relevance. The publicity given to scandals, violence, and other problems in sports caused evangelicals, in particular, to question the value of sports.

It was not until after World War II that evangelical Christians again used sports in connection with their religious beliefs (Ladd and Mathisen,

1999). It is important to note that the evangelicals were not alone in establishing ties to sports in the postwar period. Numerous Protestant churches and congregations, Catholic dioceses and parishes, Mormon wards, the B'nai B'rith, and a few Jewish synagogues also embraced sports as worthwhile activities, especially for young people, boys in particular. These organizations sponsored sports and sport programs because their members and leaders believed that sport participation developed moral character.

For example, as World War II was ending, Pope Pius XII gave a worldwide address in which he talked about the moral value of sports:

> Those who accuse the Church of not caring for the body and physical culture . . . are far from the truth. . . . In the final analysis, what is sport if not a form of education for the body? This education is closely related to morality. . . . If a sporting activity is for you a recreation and stimulus which aids you in better fulfilling your duties of work and study, then it can be said that it is being used in its true sense, and is attaining its true end. (in Feeney, 1995, p. 27)

Other religious leaders of the twentieth century gave similar messages about sports. In 1971, evangelist Billy Graham, a longtime outspoken promoter of sports as a builder of moral character, summarized the spirit in which many religious organizations have made use of sports over the past hundred years:

> The Bible says leisure and lying around are morally dangerous for us. Sports keep us busy; athletes, you notice, don't take drugs. There are probably more committed Christians in sports, both collegiate and professional, than in any other occupation in America. (*Newsweek*, 1971, p. 51)

In light of publicized cases of drug use by many athletes, part of Graham's statement sounds naïve today. However, he accurately noted the commitment among many Christians to use sports as activities that symbolized and promoted moral development—especially among boys and young men. This commitment is as strong today as it ever was (Ladd and Mathisen, 1999).

To Recruit New Members and Promote Religious Beliefs and Organizations Using sports to attract and recruit boys and men to churches and religious groups has occurred since the late nineteenth century. This practice became so common after World War II that sociologist Charles Page referred to it as "the basketballization of American religion" (in Demerath and Hammond, 1969, p. 182).

Starting in the early 1990s, Bill McCartney, the former football coach at the University of Colorado, used sport images as he formed and attracted men to his religious organization, The Promise Keepers. McCartney and others in the evangelical men's organization emphasized the idea that a "manly man is a Godly man." Other Christian fundamentalist groups and organizations have recently used images of tough athletes to represent ideal "Christian men." Through this strategy, they tried to attract men into their churches and organizations and create a masculinized Christianity, which they felt would allow them to "rescue the Bible from women and overly refined preachers" (Flake, 1992, p. 165).

In a similar manner, church-affiliated colleges and universities in the United States have used sports as an organizational recruiting and public relations tool. They know that seventeen-year-olds today are more likely to listen to college recruiting advertisements if the ads use terminology, images, and spokespeople from sports (Ladd and Mathisen, 1999). Of course, this is not a new strategy. When the famous preacher Oral Roberts founded his university in Tulsa, Oklahoma, in 1965, he highlighted the importance of its sport programs with this explanation:

> Athletics is part of our Christian witness. . . . Nearly every man in America reads the sports pages, and a Christian school cannot ignore these people. . . . Sports are becoming the No. 1 interest of people in America. For us to be relevant, we had to gain the attention of millions of people in a way that they could understand. (in Boyle, 1970, p. 64)

Jerry Falwell, noted television evangelist, initiated the sport program at his Liberty University in the 1970s with a similar statement:

> To me, athletics are a way of making a statement. And I believe you have a better Christian witness to the youth of the world when you competitively, head-to-head, prove yourself their equal on the playing field. (in Capouya, 1986, p. 75)

Then, in his opening prayer, Falwell declared,

> Father, we don't want to be mediocre, we don't want to fail. We want to honor You by winning. (in Capouya, 1986, p. 72)

Other church-affiliated colleges and universities have used sports in similar but less overt ways to attract students. Catholic schools—including the University of Notre Dame, Boston College, and Georgetown University—traditionally have used their football and/or basketball programs to build their prestige as church-affiliated institutions. Brigham Young University, affiliated with the Mormon Church, also has done this. Smaller Christian colleges around the United States formed the National Christian Collegiate Athletic Association (NCCAA) in the mid-1960s to sponsor championships and recruit Christian

The connections between sports and religions in general, and Christian religious organizations in particular, have changed throughout history. Today, for example, the public profiles of some universities are connected with both sports and religion. This is the football stadium at the University of Notre Dame. In the background is the library. The south wall of the library has a mural image of Christ. The image has come to be known affectionately among ND football fans as "Touchdown Jesus." (Jay Coakley)

student-athletes to their academic programs (Ladd and Mathisen, 1999).

Some religious organizations have developed solely around sports to attract more people to Christian beliefs and to provide support for athletes who already hold Christian beliefs. Examples include Sports Ambassadors, the Fellowship of Christian Athletes (FCA), Athletes in Action (AIA), Pro Athletes Outreach (PAO), Sports Outreach America (SOA), and dozens of smaller groups associated with particular sports. There are Christian Surfers Australia, Cowboys for Christ, Golfers for Christ, Wheel Power Christian Cyclists, and the Christian Wrestling Federation, among hundreds of others. These organizations often have a strong evangelical emphasis, and members are usually eager to share their beliefs in the hope that others will embrace Christian fundamentalism as they do.

Christian organizations and groups also have used sports as sites for evangelizing. For example, thousands of volunteers at the Barcelona Olympics in 1992 distributed *Winning for Life*, a short book published by the International Bible Society. Thousands were given to athletes and Olympic officials, and volunteers also contacted hundreds of thousands of households and spectators in Barcelona. A spokesperson for the Bible Society explained:

> The Olympics serve as an opportunity to piggy-back on the respect athletes have and communicate Christianity to those who would not normally be interested. (in Rabey, 1992, p. B1)

During the Atlanta Games in 1996, Sports Outreach America and RBC Ministries teamed up to produce a catalog, so that churches, organizations, and individuals could order materials for creating an "evangelistic ministry through sports." Materials included videos, audiotapes, CDs, magazines, books and pamphlets, pins,

> **Our youth basketball team is back in action Wednesday at 8 PM in the school recreation hall. Come out and watch us kill Christ the King.**
>
> —Poster announcing an elementary school basketball game (2002)

sport ministry kits, and sport planning and clinic guides. Most of these featured athletes giving witness to the importance of Bible-based religious beliefs in their lives. One of the books, *A Path to Victory*, published by the International Bible Society, contained 350 pages of Bible chapters and athlete testimonies. A 32-page book, *More Than Gold*, used Olympic terminology and images to promote religious beliefs. Hundreds of groups and thousands of volunteers used these materials in Atlanta and other places in the United States and around the world to deliver their messages. Attempts were even made to bring Christian messages to athletes and spectators from Islamic countries. These organizations also evangelized at the 2000 Games in Sydney, Australia, and the 2002 Winter Games in Salt Lake City, Utah.

Efforts to evangelize are not new, but they are becoming increasingly organized and coordinated. Major sport ministries have been linked together through Sports Outreach America, an umbrella organization whose goal is to "create a greater evangelistic ministry through sports." RBC Ministries, another fundamentalist Christian organization, publishes *SportsSpectrum*, a widely circulated magazine that uses a biblically informed perspective to report on sports and athletes. Articles in the magazine highlight Christian athletes and their religious testimonies. Most athlete profiles emphasize that life "without a commitment to Christ" is superficial and meaningless, even if one is successful in sports. Accepting Christ, they explain, gives life meaning and enables them to put sports into a "proper" perspective in their lives, and they often encourage others to do the same.

The forms of Christian witness published in *SportsSpectrum* are clearly designed to promote religious beliefs among readers who look up to the athletes. This method of using elite athletes to promote religious conversions has become a basic strategy in most of these organizations. As John Dodderidge, a representative of the Fellowship of Christian Athletes says, "If athletes can sell razor blades and soft drinks, why can't they sell the Gospel?" This approach has given the FCA and other organizations national and global visibility, and it has been used effectively to create audiences ready to listen to the messages of muscular Christianity.

To Promote Conservative Fundamentalist Beliefs

Most of the religious groups and organizations previously mentioned promote a specific form of Christianity—one based on a loosely articulated conservative ideology and a fundamentalist orientation toward life.

Religious fundamentalism is a complex social phenomenon (Hadden, 2000; Marty and Appleby, 1995). Even though it may not appeal to most people in a particular society or religious population, it can capture the interest and involvement of a wide array of people from different social and economic backgrounds. This is true of Islamic fundamentalism in Iran and Christian fundamentalism in North America and Europe.

Fundamentalists in all religions believe there is a need for people to return to what they define as the basic moral and religious roots of their cultures. They emphasize that this return can occur only if individuals develop personal relationships with the supernatural source of truth (God, Allah, Christ, Mohammed, "the universe," the spirit world, etc.). Fundamentalists see the supernatural realm as the source of absolute, unchanging truths, offering clear answers to personal and social problems. These answers are revealed through sacred writings, the verbal teachings of divinely inspired leaders and prophets, and personal revelations.

Fundamentalist movements arise when people perceive moral threats to or crises in an entire way of life that was once ideal because it was based on pure religious principles. Therefore, fundamentalists emphasize the "moral decline of society" and a need to return to past ways of doing things—ways that were shaped by what they believe is a "one-and-only truth." Their beliefs may be so deeply held that believers become isolated from other people in the society.

Ladd and Mathisen (1999) have explained that fundamentalist Christians have embraced sports, in part, to reduce their separation from society and increase their legitimacy in it. The tendencies of Christian fundamentalist movements in English-speaking, predominantly Protestant countries to use sports to promote their traditional and conservative beliefs support this explanation, although there certainly are important variations among countries.

How Have Athletes and Coaches Used Religion?

Athletes and coaches have used religion, religious beliefs, prayers, and rituals in many ways. Research on this topic is scarce, but there is much anecdotal information in statements by athletes and coaches. In general, they indicate that athletes and coaches use religion for one or more of the following reasons:

1. To cope with uncertainty
2. To stay out of trouble
3. To give meaning to sport participation
4. To put sport participation into a balanced perspective
5. To establish team solidarity and unity
6. To reaffirm expectations, rules, and social control on teams
7. To assert autonomy in the face of power
8. To achieve personal and competitive success

To Cope with Uncertainty

Through history, people have used prayers and rituals based in religion, magic, and/or superstition to cope with uncertainties in their lives (Ciborowski, 1997; Womack, 1992). Because sport competition involves a high degree of uncertainty, it is not surprising that many athletes use rituals, some based in religion, to make them feel as if they have a degree of control over what happens to them on the playing field.

Wrestler Kurt Angle, the winner of a gold medal in the 1996 Olympic Games used religion in this way. He explained that, when he had a serious neck injury before his qualifying matches, he prayed to God for guidance. His doctor advised him not to wrestle because he would risk paralysis if he injured his neck again. However, in answer to his prayers, "God said to do it." Thus, before each match, his doctor shot Novocaine into his neck, so that he could endure the pain. After he won the gold medal, he explained:

> I knew my neck was hurt, God was there, watching over me. I knew when I was wrestling in the Olympic Games that He was watching over me. I knew when I won the gold medal that He intended me to win. He wanted someone like me to spread the Word and be a role model for kids. (in Hubbard, 1998, p. 147)

Willye White, a former gold medalist in the women's long jump, explained her use of religion to cope with the uncertainties of competition in the Olympics in this way:

> I was nervous, so I read the New Testament. I read the verse about have no fear, and I felt relaxed. Then I jumped farther than I ever jumped before in my life. (*Life*, 1984, p. 31)

Of course, the use of prayers and rituals is not limited to Christian athletes. Former NBA player Hakeem Olajuwon engaged in a regular Islamic prayer ritual as he faced challenges in his life as a professional athlete. He said,

> My religion gives me direction, inner strength. I feel more comfortable. You can take life head on. (*USA Today*, 1994, p. 6C)

Not all religious athletes use prayer and religious rituals in this manner, but many call on their religion to help them face challenges and uncertainty. Therefore, many athletes who pray before or during games may not pray before or during practices; uncertainty is lower at practice than in a game. Few athletes make the sign of the cross during batting practice in baseball or when they practice free throws in basketball: it is the actual competition that produces the uncertainty that evokes the prayer or religious ritual.

North American athletes have sometimes used Christian beliefs to give special meaning to their sport participation. (Jay Coakley)

Sometimes it is difficult to separate the use of religion from the use of **magic** and superstition among athletes. Magic consists of recipe-like rituals designed to produce immediate and practical results in the material world. **Superstitions** consist of regularized, ritualistic actions performed to give a person or group a sense of control and predictability in the face of challenges. Thus, when athletes pray, it may be difficult to say whether they are using religion or magic and superstition. However, regardless of the basis of a ritual, its primary goal is to control uncertainty.

To Stay out of Trouble   Reggie White, an ordained minister and a retired defensive lineman in the NFL (he was called the "minister of defense"), explains how religion kept him out of trouble during the time he played football:

> Studying God's Word helped keep my life on track, even though there were bad influences like drugs and crime all around me. To continue to be the man God wants me to be, I have to stay in his word. (IBS, 1996b, Section A)

Other athletes have said similar things about how religion helps them avoid the risky lifestyles that often exist in the social worlds that develop around certain sports. NFL player Sean Gilbert has said, "Before I found the Lord, I drank! I whoremongered! I cussed! I cheated! I manipulated! I deceived!" (in Corsello, 1999, p. 435).

The fact that religious beliefs may separate athletes from risky off-the-field lifestyles and keep them focused on training in their sports has not been lost on coaches (Plotz, 2000). Journalist Andrew Corsello explains that, "regardless of their own beliefs, coaches are attracted to the self-control that Christian convictions instill in a man" (1999, p. 435). Futhermore, team owners may see "born-again athletes" as better long-term investments, because they believe that religious athletes "are less likely to get arrested" (Smith, 1997). Finally, religious beliefs also may keep athletes out of trouble by encouraging them to become involved in church-related and community-based service programs. This involvement can separate them from risky off-the-field lifestyles.

To Give Meaning to Sport Participation   Sport participation emphasizes personal achievement and self-promotion, and it involves playing games that do not produce any essential goods or services, even though people may create important social occasions around sport events. In many ways, sport participation is a self-focused, self-indulgent activity. Although training often involves personal sacrifices and pain, it focuses on self-development and the individual use of physical skills in meets, matches, and games. Realizing this can create a *crisis of meaning* for athletes who have dedicated their lives to personal achievements in sports.

Ironically, some athletes who make millions of dollars and are idolized by millions of people are among those who experience this crisis of meaning. They want to know, "Why me?"

How do these athletes give meaning to the focus on self required by their training and competition? How do they justify the expenditure of so much time and energy on sports? How do they explain why they have allowed sport participation to disrupt their families, or why so many family resources have been used to support their sport participation? How do they deal with the need to outperform and even dominate others as they strive to continue playing or to move to higher levels of competition? How do they rationalize their tendencies to overconform to the sport ethic to the point of jeopardizing the health and well-being of themselves and others? How do they answer, "Why me?"

One way to answer this question is to define sport participation and achievements in sports as acts of worship, avenues for giving witness, or manifestations of God's overall plan for their lives (Hoffman, 1992). This enables athletes to "sanctify" their commitment to sport. Through their religious beliefs, they convert sport participation into an activity done for the glory of God, to bring God's word to others, or to follow God's will. This gives sport participation ultimate meaning and makes it part of a person's spiritual destiny. At the same time, this way of defining sports keeps athletes motivated. As volleyball player Kim Oden says,

> Learning what Jesus knowingly went through for me gave me a lot of self-confidence. It also gave me a lot more reason to do what I do. (IBS, 1996b, Section D)

An increasing number of athletes today have turned to religion for this reason: to give special meaning to their sport participation (Stevenson, 1997). When Glyn Milburn played in the NFL, he said that he kept Jesus on his mind so much during games that, "for me, it's almost a form of worship when I'm on the field" (in Briggs, 1994). NBA player David Robinson says that playing basketball is a way "to honor God" as well as "a great opportunity to model Christ in front of a lot of people by the way I play and the way I conduct myself" (in Bentz, 1996, p. 14). Olympic swimmer Josh Davis, winner of four gold medals in the 1995 World University Games, explains that swimming is part of God's plan for him:

> I've been given a gift to swim fast, and I think God expects me to use that gift to the best of my ability to reach my potential. . . . What Christ did on the cross supplies me with an everlasting motivation. (in Robbins, 1996, p. 21)

Many Christian athletes and coaches also refer to Colossians 3:23 in the Bible: "Whatever you do, work at it with all your heart, working for the Lord, not for men." Of course, when athletes follow the advice in this Bible verse, their sport participation is elevated in their minds from the realm of the profane to the realm of the sacred. In the process, athletes define their sport participation as having *ultimate* meaning. Thus, they have fewer doubts about the worthiness of what they do as athletes, and they define sport participation as part of their spiritual life, as a calling from God.

To Put Sport Participation into a Balanced Perspective   The issue of meaning is related to the need for some athletes to feel that they will not be swallowed up by sports or become overwhelmed by the drama, challenges, and regular failures that occur in sports. Some athletes feel that religious beliefs are vehicles for transcending their lives in sports. Elana Meyer, an Olympic silver medalist in the 1992 10,000-meter run, explains this use of religion:

> Running is a way God can use me for His glory. Athletics is not my life. . . . Every competition is a challenge for me, but I don't make a separation between Elana the runner and Elana the Christian. God's love for me is unconditional— it doesn't depend on my winning a gold medal. (IBS, 1996c, Section G)

With beliefs such as this, playing sports becomes part of God's plan in athletes' minds, and it becomes easier for them to face challenges and deal with the inevitable losses experienced in sports. In the process, they keep sports in perspective.

To Establish Team Solidarity and Unity   Religious beliefs and rituals can be powerful tools in creating bonds of attachment between people. When religious beliefs and rituals are combined with sport participation, they can link athletes together as spiritual teammates. This, of course, is an effective strategy for building team solidarity and unity (see figure 15.2). Many coaches know this, and some have used their own Christian beliefs as rallying points for their teams. Because of the desire to promote their Christian beliefs and create a collective focus for team members, they bring religion into sports. George Allen, a widely respected former NFL coach, once said that he supported religious worship and team prayers among his athletes because they "foster togetherness and mutual respect like nothing I have found in 21 years of coaching" (in Hoffman, 1982, p. 18).

Objections to this practice, especially when it involves the use of pregame prayers in public

"She says this is 'voluntary.' Who is she trying to fool?!?"

FIGURE 15.2   Religious beliefs and rituals often create team solidarity, but they can also create dissent and subvert team unity. When coaches promote prayers and say that team prayers are voluntary, players may feel pressure to go along with the coaches' beliefs, even when they do not match their own.

schools, has led some U.S. students and their parents to file lawsuits to ban religious expression in connection with sport events. However, some coaches and athletes continue to insist that prayers bring team members together in positive ways. Despite lawsuits, most people in the United States agree that it is appropriate for sporting events at public high schools to begin with a public prayer (Lieblich and Ostling, 2000). This controversial issue is discussed in the box "Public Prayers at Sport Events."

To Reaffirm Expectations, Rules, and Social Control on Teams   Religion also can sanctify norms and rules by connecting them with the sacred and supernatural. Therefore, it can be used to connect the moral worth of athletes with the quality of their play and their conformity to team rules and the commands of coaches.

Wes Neal, founder of the Institute for Athletic Perfection, a Christian sport organization, explained that a person's performance in sport reveals his or her love for God (Neal, 1981). This means that performances in sports are indications of the moral worth of athletes. This inferred connection between performance and moral worth encourages athletes to be committed to improvement and excellence and to be willing followers of their coaches and trainers. Neal noted, "You may not agree with [your coach] on every point, but your role [as a Christian athlete] is to carry out his assignments. The attitude you have as you carry out each assignment will determine if you are a winner in God's sight" (1981, p. 193).

This combination of religion and sport is very powerful: when the rules and assignments of coaches are tied to religious beliefs, the athletes

Do problems emerge when people associate athletic performance with an athlete's moral worth? When coaches do this, the stakes for athletes become very high. Should coaches use this connection to motivate athletes and demand their obedience? Of course, there are many ways to "read" this shirt. (Jay Coakley)

are much more likely to obey coaches without question. In this way, coaches may use religion, either intentionally or unintentionally, as a means of controlling the behavior of athletes.

From a sociological perspective, this connection between religion and social control is important, because many coaches are very concerned with issues of authority and control on their teams. They see obedience from players as necessary for team success, and religious beliefs can promote obedience. If athletes also use religious beliefs to stay out of trouble, coaches are even more pleased.

According to Lee Corder, a chaplain for one of the teams in the NFL, many team owners and coaches feel that "a player has to be capable spiritually, as well as mentally and physically, to play the game" (in Corsello, 1999, p. 435). In baseball, the team president of the Texas Rangers notes that the Rangers don't have a religion test for prospective players, but "there is a value test" (in Smith, 1997). The inference here is that people with power in sports see a possible connection between a player's religious beliefs and social control on their teams. Of course, they assume a form of Christian belief that does not interfere with performance. If the player is a Christian Scientist, whose beliefs lead to the refusal of medical treatment needed to get back on the field, many owners and coaches would think differently about religion among their players.

To Assert Autonomy in the Face of Power

This reason for using religion in sports is relatively new. Journalist Andrew Corsello (1999) discussed it in an article based on interviews with NFL players. He noted, "It should come as no surprise that the assertion of individuality through religious testimony in the NFL comes at a time when the game has never been more corporatized, more dehumanized" (p. 439). Thus, when a player thanks God and infers that there is something more important in his life than football, he is resisting the impact of football's organized structure on his identity.

Corsello thinks that this is especially important for black athletes, who may have more reason to seek out a vehicle for asserting their individuality and identity in the face of the white-dominated governance structures in sports, especially in college and professional football in the United States. Corsello's analysis raises a hypothesis worth investigating.

To Achieve Personal and Competitive Success

People often debate whether it is appropriate to pray for victories or personal athletic success. Some people feel that using prayer in this way trivializes religion and turns it into just another training technique, such as weightlifting or the use of muscle-building substances. However, Howard Griffith, a former NFL running back, says,

> It's not that we're trivializing anything. The question was posed to [the Christians on our team], 'Does He control wins and losses?' Yes, He does. . . . It is not anti-Christian to pray for wins. (in Nack, 1998, p. 47)

Another player explains that he prays for victories "so I have even a bigger platform to use for [God]" (in Nack, 1998, p. 48).

Some athletes have believed that their God or gods actually intervene in the events that occur during sport contests. Isaac Bruce, a wide receiver in the NFL, said that prayers "work" for him, "Like when we played Minnesota last year. I had a pretty good first half, but God really manifested in the third quarter—I had eighty-nine yards!" (in Corsello, 1999, p. 435). When Bruce and other athletes are questioned about this issue, they often respond that they believe that prayer makes a difference in what happens in the world and that sports are part of that world. Of course, many people debate whether sports, especially sports such as boxing and football, are "worthy" of divine intervention and whether God would actually take sides in a competitive event.

An extreme case of using prayer and religion to achieve success occurred in 1996, when Evander Holyfield faced Mike Tyson in a

REFLECT ON SPORTS

Public Prayers at Sport Events
What's Legal and What's Not?

Prayers before sport events are common in the United States. They often are said silently by individuals, aloud by small groups of players or entire teams in their pregame huddles, and over public address systems by students or local spokespeople.

Public prayers are allowed at private events, and all people in the United States have the right to say silent, private prayers for any purpose at any time. Some people have questioned the appropriateness of prayers said at events such as professional wrestling and extreme fighting, but, as long as an event is sponsored by private organizations, or as long as people pray privately and silently, prayers are legal.

According to a 1962 U.S. Supreme Court decision, which banned organized prayers in public schools, there *are* legal problems when prayers are said publicly and collectively at sport events sponsored by state organizations, such as public schools. The histories of these legal problems vary from state to state in the United States, but Texas has received much attention when it comes to this issue.

Controversy in Texas began in 1992, when two families near Houston filed a lawsuit requesting a ban on prayers in public schools. They appealed to the First Amendment of the U.S. Constitution, which says, "Congress shall make no law respecting an establishment of religion." After thinking about what "an establishment of religion" actually means, the federal district judge in the case ruled that public prayers are okay as long as they are nonsectarian and general in content, initiated by students, and not said in connection with attempts to convert anyone to a particular religion. This decision was qualified during an appeal, when the appellate judges ruled that school prayers can be said at graduation ceremonies, but *not* at football games and other sport events. Sports, they said, are not serious enough occasions to require the solemnity of public prayer. Apparently, they knew little about the seriousness of high school football in Texas!

Despite this decision and two similar decisions in 1995 and 1999, people in many Texas towns and other towns around the United States continue to say public prayers before public school sport events. References to "Jesus," "Lord," and "Heavenly Father" often are included by student "prayer leaders" when they recited prayers over the public address system and by student-athletes when they pray with their teams. Many of these prayers have long traditions, and local people object when federal government judges tell them that they

· ·

heavyweight boxing title bout. Tyson, a "born-again Muslim," prayed while he trained. Holyfield, a "born-again Christian," called on God to bless the fight and intercede on his behalf. Holyfield said, "I will beat Mike Tyson. There is no way I cannot, if I just trust in God. God is that good" (in Hoffer, 1996, p. 34). Holyfield had "Phil 4:13" stitched on his boxing trunks. This referred to Saint Paul's statement in the Bible: "I can do all things in Him who strengthens me." Holyfield won and thanked God for his victory; Tyson lost and said nothing about Allah. After the fight, Holyfield bought a full-page ad in *USA Today* (25 November, 1996, p. 5C). In the text of the ad, he thanked his supporters and proclaimed

that it was prayer and God that made him a three-time heavyweight champion.

The Use of Sport in Christianity   The sport-Christianity connection seems to be stronger than ever, especially in the United States. According to one journalist,

> Christianity is sweeping the locker rooms of big-time professional and college teams. . . . [M]ore and more players are turning to God for direction, inspiration and the will to win. Never before, it seems, has the tie between religion and big-time sports been tighter. (Briggs, 1994, p. 12)

As this occurs, some sociologists have been interested in the challenges faced by Christian must not publicly express their religious beliefs before football games and other sport events at public schools. They argue that it violates their "freedom of speech," which is guaranteed in the U.S. Constitution.

What's the harm in public prayer? According to those who have filed lawsuits, public prayers at state-sponsored athletic events violate the constitutional separation of church and state. Those who have filed lawsuits have usually held beliefs that did not fit with the particular Christian beliefs of the majority of students and community members. These plaintiffs have objected to the particular "Christian tone" of the prayers as well as the informal pressures for religious conformity that often accompany the public prayers. They have expressed fears of being ridiculed or socially rejected if they do not join in and pray, even though participation may contradict their own beliefs.

The Christians who support public prayers say they do not put pressure on anyone. They also note that, in many cases, the teams and crowds that say the prayers are *all* Christians. Of course, these people generally assume that the public prayers will *not* be Jewish, Islamic, Hindu, Buddhist, Baha'i, or Sikh prayers. Similarly, they assume that the prayers will

not contradict their Christian beliefs about the sacred and supernatural. When these people pray to "Jesus," they generally do not consider what the prayer might mean to a Jew or Muslim in the crowd or on the team (see figure 15.2). When they pray to a single "Lord" or "God," they usually do not think about what the prayer would mean to those who believe in no single God or who believe in multiple gods. Would these supporters of public school prayers remain supportive if the prayers represented beliefs other than their beliefs? Would *they* file suits to stop prayers if they were said in praise of Allah or the Goddess? Would there be religious conflict in public schools if Muslim students said their daily prayers over the public address system during an afternoon basketball game?

In light of these issues, there seem to be good reasons to maintain the ban on public prayer at sport events sponsored by state organizations, such as public schools. The U.S. Supreme Court agreed in July 2000, when it ruled that student-led prayers in public schools violate the constitutionally mandated separation of church and state. Therefore, officially sanctioned public prayers before sport events sponsored by public schools are illegal. *What do you think?*

athletes and organizations and whether they deal with these challenges in ways that change the organization of sports and how sports are played.

THE CHALLENGES OF COMBINING SPORTS AND RELIGIOUS BELIEFS

Organized competitive sports and religion are cultural practices with different histories, traditions, and goals. Each has been socially constructed in different ways, around different issues, and through different types of relationships. This means that combining religious beliefs with sport participation may require

adjustments—either in a person's religious beliefs *or* in the way a person plays sports.

Although a growing number of black athletes around the world, especially African Americans, have combined their Islamic beliefs with their sport lives, this section will focus specifically on the challenges faced by Christian athletes.

Challenges for Christian Athletes

Physical educator Shirl Hoffman (1992, 1999) has made the case that there are built-in conflicts between some Christian religious beliefs and participation in elite power and performance sports. Christianity, he explains, is based on an ethic that emphasizes the importance of means over ends, process over product, quality over quantity, and caring for others over caring for self. Today's sports, however, especially those based on a power and performance model, emphasize an ethic focused on winning, final scores, season records, personal performance statistics, and self-display.

Do these differences present a challenge to Christian athletes? If so, how do they deal with it? For example, do Christian athletes wonder if their behaviors in highly competitive power and performance sports are proper spiritual offerings and acts of worship?

Does a Christian boxer have any doubts about using performance in the ring as a spiritual offering, even though the goal is to punch another human being into senseless submission? (see figure 15.3). Do Christian football players see any

"I just want to thank my Lord and Savior, who made this all possible."

FIGURE 15.3   This statement has become a standard part of postgame interviews with some athletes from victorious teams. Is overpowering other human beings an acceptable way to express religious beliefs?

problems associated with using intimidation and "taking out" opponents with potentially injurious hits and then saying that such behaviors are "acts of worship"? Can athletes turn these actions into Christian acts simply by saying they are motivated by Christian love? Does this help heal the concussions and broken bones of those injured by the "loving hits"? What about Christian pitchers who throw high and inside as part of their pitching strategy? Does a strategy that deliberately risks hitting a batter's head with a ball thrown at 90 mph qualify as an act of worship? Is it part of God's plan for Christian base runners to slide into second base with spikes aimed at the opposing infielders in attempts to break up double plays? Do Christian athletes ask such questions, and, if so, how do they answer them?

Research suggests that Christian athletes combine their religious beliefs with sport participation in many ways. A study by Kelley et al. (1990) found that, at small liberal arts colleges, Christian varsity athletes who valued religion as a tool for achieving secular goals tended to emphasize the importance of winning in sports. Those who valued religion for its own sake were more likely to emphasize personal goals and the enjoyment of competition. Overall, the Christian athletes asked no critical questions about the "fit" between their religious beliefs and their actions in sports. Of course, these were athletes in small colleges, where there may have been little encouragement to emphasize a power and performance orientation in sports.

A study by Dunn and Stevenson (1998) at the University of New Brunswick in Canada reported that the members of a local church-sponsored hockey league were successful in their attempt to play hockey in a way that reflected Christian values. There was a stated commitment in the league to fair play. There was to be no body contact, fights, or swearing on the ice, nor beer in the locker rooms. There was a public prayer before each game, and official league standings were not kept, although scores were kept in the games. Interviews with twenty players indicated that the league generally was a success. Most players played within the spirit of the established rules, although some had difficulty applying Christian principles in all game situations, especially when they were caught up in the action. A few others seemed to be only nominally committed to Christian principles, and they wanted to be "good hockey players" rather than "Christian hockey players." The authors concluded that, in a recreational league, it is possible to have a good fit between Christian values and sport participation.

Chris Stevenson's (1991a, b, 1997) research on elite athletes associated with the Christian organization Athletes in Action (AIA) indicated slightly different patterns. Stevenson found that some of the elite athletes avoided conflicts by compartmentalizing their religious beliefs and sport participation. They simply ignored the possibility that Christian values did not fit with how they played sports. They raised no questions, and they had no problems playing sports as everyone else did. However, most of the elite Christian athletes in Stevenson's sample experienced a "crisis of meaning" as they recognized conflicts between their religious beliefs and what they were expected to do on the playing field.

Most of the athletes in the Stevenson study dealt with this crisis through one or both of two strategies: (1) they defined their sport participation as a means of giving glory to God, and (2) they defined sport participation as a platform for spreading the Gospel. In other words, the athletes emphasized that it was their duty to perfect their skills as much as they could, or they emphasized that they could use their success and visibility to increase the effectiveness of their evangelizing. This enabled them to redefine on-the-field actions to fit their definitions of what a Christian is supposed to do. Finally, a small number of Christian athletes recognized conflict between their religious beliefs and their sport participation and eliminated the conflict by dropping out of elite sports to do other things more consistent with their beliefs.

We should remember that Stevenson's research focused on young adults who were members of Athletes in Action. Of course, most Christian athletes are not members of such organizations, and there have been no studies of these athletes. Anecdotal data in magazines and newspapers suggest that elite athletes who identify themselves as Christians do not play sports differently than others. In fact, some Christian athletes actually make the point that their religious beliefs make them more intense, if not more aggressive, on the playing field.

Danny Scheaffer, a former Major League Baseball player, said that his religious beliefs made him more intense but not less aggressive during practices and games. While he was still playing, he proudly noted, "I'll be the first person to knock a Christian shortstop into left field on a play at second. I've been hit before by Christian pitchers. I've charged Christian pitchers [who have thrown pitches at me]" (in Briggs, 1994, p. 14).

When NFL player Reggie White was asked about the toughness of Christians on the football field, he said, "It's really an insult when people accuse Christians of being weak. If you think Christians are weak, put on some pads and line up across from me. We'll see [who is tough]" (in Lee, 1996, p. 22).

Other statements from Christian athletes and stories about their lives (as described in Christian publications) suggest that some of them try to combine their religious beliefs and sport participation by becoming especially dedicated to the ascetic aspects of sport. *Asceticism* emphasizes discipline, self-denial, and avoidance of bodily pleasures. Focusing on these aspects of sport experiences enhances the moral worth of their lives and of the sports they play. For these athletes, "Jesus the teacher" becomes "Christ the competitor," and, "if Jesus were alive today, He would play sports like everyone else, only better."

Using Stevenson's research as a starting point, I hypothesize that most Christian athletes in elite sports avoid conflicts by assigning moral significance to their sport participation, or they use their visibility as athletes to do "Christian" things off the field. For example, some Christian athletes publicly thank God for their achievements and use their visibility to express their religious beliefs to others. Others use their resources and reputations to support worthy projects sponsored by community or church organizations.

A proposed model of what may occur when a person with strong Christian beliefs plays power and performance sports is depicted in figure 15.4. The model identifies the aspects of playing sports that can create doubt about the intrinsic worth of sport participation as an act of worship. Then it identifies the strategies that Christian athletes may use to minimize or eliminate these doubts.

Challenges for Christian Sport Organizations

One might think that the combination of Christianity and sports would lead Christian organizations to focus on issues and problems in sports, especially power and performance sports, and inspire them to call for reforms. However, these organizations seldom do this, at least in the United States (Hoffman, 1999; Ladd and Mathisen, 1999). Instead of calling for changes in sports, most U.S. Christian sport organizations have consistently focused on using sports to recruit new members and promote fundamentalist religious beliefs. They give primary emphasis to building faith, not changing sports. Consequently, they have not tried to identify problems or initiate reforms in how sports are defined, organized, and played.

According to Shirl Hoffman, this seems surprising, given the content of Christian beliefs. He says,

> The extent to which people are willing to overlook the moral crisis in sports to have a vehicle of mass evangelism is astounding. As soon as you apply the tenets of the [Christian] message to the medium [of sports, you would

expect these organizations] to become staunch critics of sport. (in Blum, 1996, p. A36)

However, this has not happened.

The policy position in many Christian sport organizations is that sports will be reformed only when everyone associated with them accepts Christ into their lives. Therefore, the racism, sexism, deviance, violence, recruiting violations, exploitation, greed, and other problems that now exist will not disappear until all athletes, coaches, administrators, and spectators have developed a personal faith in Christ.

When journalist Frank Deford did a special story on sports and Christianity in 1976, he observed,

> No one in the movement—much less in any organization—speaks out against dirty play, no one attacks the evils of recruiting, racism or any of the many other well-known excesses and abuses. Sport owns Sunday now, and religion is content to lease a few minutes before the big games. (p. 100)

Although some Christian organizations have condemned drug use and commercial values in sports (Ladd and Mathisen, 1999), Deford's comments still describe the major policy orientation of most Christian organizations with sport ministries.

This orientation is not very popular among people interested in more progressive goals, regardless of their religious beliefs. For example, there are people in Christian organizations who have recognized the need for changes in sports and who wish that the organizations would support and promote reforms in sports. However, they have had little influence on policies and programs in these organizations.

Others accuse Christian sport organizations of being hypocritical when they ignore ethical and social problems. This accusation often is grounded in a response to organizational philosophies and policies that are based on what is called the "primacy of faith." This means that faith is given priority over charity in the organizations and that salvation is linked with accepting Christ

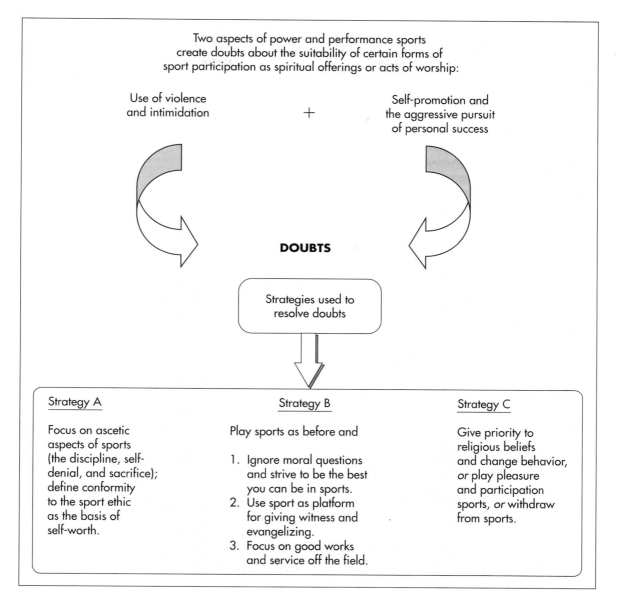

Two aspects of power and performance sports
create doubts about the suitability of certain forms of
sport participation as spiritual offerings or acts of worship:

Use of violence
and intimidation

+

Self-promotion and
the aggressive pursuit
of personal success

DOUBTS

Strategies used to
resolve doubts

Strategy A

Focus on ascetic
aspects of sports
(the discipline, self-
denial, and sacrifice);
define conformity
to the sport ethic
as the basis of
self-worth.

Strategy B

Play sports as before and

1. Ignore moral questions
   and strive to be the best
   you can be in sports.
2. Use sport as platform
   for giving witness and
   evangelizing.
3. Focus on good works
   and service off the field.

Strategy C

Give priority to
religious beliefs
and change behavior,
or play pleasure
and participation
sports, *or* withdraw
from sports.

FIGURE 15.4   Christian religious beliefs and power and performance sports: a proposed model of conflict, doubt, and resolution.

into one's life rather than with doing good works alone. The critics claim that faith should be combined with good works and that good works should not be enacted on the conditions that oth- ers accept Christ. Evangelical organizations, however, rarely accept such an approach. For them, faith is primary and good works are the means for promoting faith.

Adapting Religious Beliefs to Fit Sports

History shows that both religion and sports undergo changes as people's values and interests change, and as power is gained or lost by various groups in communities and societies. In light of this, it is interesting that, when Christian religious beliefs are combined with the most visible forms of competitive sports, sports change very little. Instead, it seems that religious beliefs and rituals are called into the service of sports or modified to fit with the ways that dominant sports are defined, organized, and played.

Robert Higgs makes this point in his book *God in the Stadium: Sports and Religion in America* (1995). Higgs argues that the combination of sports and Christian beliefs has led religion to become "muscularized." A muscularized religion, he explains, emphasizes a gospel of discipline, duty, and self-righteousness, rather than a gospel of stewardship, social responsibility, and

When religious beliefs are combined with power and performance sports, some people construct religious images and beliefs to fit their ideas about sports. This image of a muscular Christ on a T-shirt, found in a Christian gift shop, clearly shows how some athletes conceptualize their religion. In fact, images of deities in a culture or group tend to reflect idealized concepts of dominant values in that culture or group. (Jay Coakley)

humility. Muscularized religion gives priority to the image of the knight and the sword over the image of the shepherd and the staff (Higgs, 1995). This, of course, fits the power and performance model in today's sports.

As Higgs points out, it seems that Christian religious beliefs have been used more often to transform winning, obedience to coaches, and commitment to improving sport skills into moral virtues than to call attention to problems in the social worlds created around sports. In other words, the use of Christian beliefs and rituals generally has reaffirmed and intensified current dominant characteristics of sports, sport experiences, and sport organizations in North America. The only exceptions to this seem to exist when sports are played in recreational settings where all the participants have the same religious beliefs.

SUMMARY

IS IT A PROMISING COMBINATION?

Religion is focused on a connection with the sacred and supernatural. This makes the systems of meaning associated with religion a unique part of cultural life. Because these systems of meaning affect how believers think about the world, themselves, and their connections with others, religion can exert powerful influence on social life in groups, communities, and society as a whole. This makes religion and religious practices important phenomena to study.

Discussions about sports and religions often focus on how these two spheres of cultural life are similar or different. Certainly, they are socially similar, because both create strong collective emotions and celebrate certain group values through rituals and public events. Furthermore, both have heroes, legends, special buildings for communal gatherings, and institutionalized organizational structures.

On the other hand, those who assume that sport and religion each have unique fundamental essences fixed in nature argue that the inherent differences between these spheres of life are more important than any similarities. Some have even argued that sports corrupt religious beliefs.

Most of those who study sports in society, however, recognize that sports and religions consist of socially constructed sets of cultural practices and meanings. These practices and meanings sometimes overlap and sometimes differ, depending on the social relations among fans and believers within communities and society as a whole. Therefore, they see the beliefs and rituals of sports and religions as subject to change as people struggle over how to live with one another and what their lives mean.

Little is known about the relationships between sports and major world religions other than particular forms of Christianity. It seems that certain dimensions of Christian beliefs and meanings can be constructed in ways that fit well with the beliefs and meanings underlying participation and success in organized competitive sports. In fact, it may be that organized competitive sports offer a combination of experiences and meanings that are uniquely compatible with the major characteristics of what sociologists describe as the Protestant ethic.

Sports and certain forms of religion have been combined for a number of reasons. Some Christians have promoted sports because they believe that sport participation naturally fosters spiritual growth, along with the development of strong character. Christian groups and organizations have used sports to promote their belief systems and attract new members, especially young males who wish to see themselves as having "manly virtues." They also have used athletes, especially those who are visible and popular, as spokespersons for their messages about conservative fundamentalist beliefs.

People in sports, especially athletes and coaches, have used religious beliefs and rituals for many reasons: to cope with the uncertainty of competition; to stay out of trouble; to give meaning to sport participation; to put sport participation into a balanced perspective; to establish team solidarity and unity; to reaffirm expectations, rules, and social control on teams; to assert autonomy in the face of power; and to achieve personal and competitive success.

Although the differences between the dominant ethos of Christianity and the dominant ethos of competitive sports would seem to create problems for Christian athletes and sport organizations, this has not occurred to a significant degree. With the exception of sports played at the recreational level and sponsored by Christian organizations, data suggest that many athletes define their religious beliefs in ways that generally reaffirm and intensify the orientations that lead to success in competitive sports.

Neither Christian athletes nor Christian organizations have paid much attention to what might be identified as moral and ethical problems in sports. Instead, they have focused their resources on spreading religious beliefs in connection with sport events and sport involvement. Their emphasis has been on playing as hard and as well as possible for the glory of God, using athletic performances as a platform for giving Christian witness, and working in worthwhile off-the-field church and community programs.

In conclusion, the combination of sports and religious beliefs offers little promise for changing dominant forms of sport in North America, and especially in the United States. Of course, individual athletes may alter their sport-related behaviors when they combine sports and religion in their own lives, but at this time such changes have had no observable effect on what occurs in elite, competitive sports.

SUGGESTED READINGS

Baker, W. J., and C. Alexander. 2001. *If Christ came to the Olympics*. Seattle: University of Washington Press (using a historical approach, the authors take a brief and entertaining look at the connection between religion and sports).

Hargreaves, J. 2000. *Heroines of sport: The politics of difference and identity*. London/New York: Routledge (chapters 1, 2, 3, and 7 all contain materials related to religion and the participation of women in sports; chapter 3 is devoted to women in Muslim countries).

Higgs, R. J. 1995. *God in the stadium: Sports and religion in America*. Lexington: The University of Kentucky Press (historical analysis of connections between sports and religion as cultural formations in the United States).

Hoffman, S. J. 1992. *Sport and religion*. Champaign, IL: Human Kinetics (twenty-five papers organized into four sets devoted to sport as religion, sport as religious experience, religion in sport, and sport, religion, and ethics; section introductions are informative).

Hubbard, S. 1998. *Faith in sports: Athletes and their religion on and off the field*. New York: Doubleday (a journalist looks at how religion has permeated U.S. sports; presents views and voices of athletes and how they have incorporated religious beliefs into their lives and their sports).

Ladd, T., and J. A. Mathisen. 1999. *Muscular Christianity: Evangelistic Protestants and the development of American sport*. Grand Rapids, MI: Baker Books (social historical study of "muscular Christianity" in the United States; presents hypotheses about the future of Christian evangelical fundamentalism and its connections with sports).

Magdalinski, T., and T. J. L. Chandler, eds. 2002. *With God on their side: Sport in the service of religion*. London/New York: Routledge (ten articles, including case studies of sport and Catholicism in Northern Ireland, Muhammad Ali and Islam, sumo and religious traditions in Japan, sports and Islam in South Africa, and sports and Christian fundamentalism in the United States).

Overman, S. J. 1997. *The influence of the Protestant ethic on sport and recreation*. Aldershot, England: Avebury (grounded in a functionalist approach, this discussion of the Protestant ethic and the ethos of sports in the United States contains historical information and analyses of leisure, child rearing, the transformation of amateur sports, and the rise of professional sports).

Pfister, G. 2001. Religion. In *International encyclopedia of women and sports* (pp. 923–28), edited by K. Christensen, A. Guttmann, and G. Pfister. New York: Macmillan Reference USA (short article provides a general overview of how religion is related to the sport participation of girls and women around the world).

WEBSITE RESOURCES

Note: Websites often change. The following URLs were current when this book was printed. Please check our website (www.mhhe.com/coakley8e) for updates and additions.

www.mhhe.com/coakley8e List of Christian sport organizations; discussion of "Total Release Performance," a concept developed by a Christian sport organization; discussion of the uses of rituals and magic in sports.

www.christianitytoday.com/sports Contains links, including one to *SportsSpectrum* magazine.

www.crosssearch.com/Recreation/Sports Forty-five links to Christian sport groups and organizations, such as Anglers for Christ, Christian Surfers, Christian Skateboards and Skate Gear, Christian Deer Hunters, Rodeoministries.

www.mauiinc.org Site for Muslim Athletes United International, Inc., a new organization striving to become a global organization to promote Islam in and through sports.

www.islamzine.com/women/women-sports.html Article written from a conservative point of view; author Hikmat Beiruty outlines fundamentalist Islamic moral guidelines for girls and women in sports.

www.christiancoaching.com Site for Christian Coaching Network, an organization dedicated to training and supporting Christian coaches as they build their lives around the "foundational truths of the Bible."

www.nccaa.org 118-member National Christian College Athletic Association; general information and news.

www.fca.org Fellowship of Christian Athletes; information about mission, organization, and programs.

www.athletesinaction.org Athletes in Action; information about mission, organization, and programs.

chapter 16

Sports in the Future

What Can We Expect?

THE PRIMARY GOAL of futurists is not to predict the future but to uncover images of possible, probable, and preferable futures that enable people to make informed decisions about their lives.

—**W. Bell, futurist (1997)**

OLC **Online Learning Center Resources**

Visit *Sports in Society's* Online Learning Center at **www.mhhe.com/coakley8e** for additional information and study material for this chapter, including

- Self-grading quizzes
- Learning objectives
- Related websites
- Additional readings

A complete outline is available online at
www.mhhe.com/coakley8e.

SPORT IS THE MOST DYNAMIC activity in the world today, with the potential to contribute powerfully to a better world. . . . The power and influence of sport is only just being understood.

—Robert Davies, chief executive, International
    Business Leader Forum (2002)

Discussions of the future are often full of exaggerations, especially at the beginning of a new century. Predicting dramatic changes is always more exciting than predicting that tomorrow will look much like today. Therefore, people often describe the future in science-fiction terms and emphasize extreme hopes and fears. These predictions spark our interest and sometimes leave us temporarily awestruck. However, in most cases, they are neither accurate nor realistic accounts of what is likely to happen.

For better or worse, the future seldom unfolds as rapidly or dramatically as some forecasters would have us believe. Instead, changes usually are tied to a combination of existing social conditions and the efforts of people to shape those conditions to fit their visions of what life should be like. Of course, some people have more power and resources to promote their visions, and those people seldom want revolutionary changes, because their privileged positions depend on stability and controlled change. This tends to slow the rate of deep structural change in societies, although it may speed up changes in technology and the availability and range of consumer products.

As you read this chapter, it is important to remember two things: (1) sports are contested activities, and (2) the future is not determined by fate, computer forecasts, supernatural forces, or sociologists. This means that the future of sports will not unfold according to what is written in this chapter. Much more important are the visions we all have for the future and the choices we make in connection with sports in our lives.

Sports will take many forms in the future, and each form will be produced through the collective actions of human beings. Therefore, the primary goal of this chapter is to describe and evaluate the various models of sports that we might use as we envision the future and make choices in our lives.

MAJOR SPORT FORMS IN THE FUTURE

The major theme running through this book is that sports are social constructions: they are cultural practices invented and played by people as they interact with one another and shape social life to fit their ideas of what it should be. Therefore, the dominant sports in any culture are strongly related to the interests and ideas of those who have power in that culture, and they usually celebrate the values and experiences of powerful people. However, not everyone in society accepts dominant sport forms. In fact, it is possible for people to modify dominant sports or develop alternative sport forms that challenge the current systems of power relations and promote interests and ideas related to their own lives.

History shows that the dominant sports in most societies have been grounded in the values and experiences of men concerned with military conquest, political control, and economic expansion. As noted in previous chapters and explained

The descriptions of power and performance sports and pleasure and participation sports are intended as starting points for an examination of sports in our everyday experiences. Many sport experiences include elements from both these types. Ultimate (Frisbee) is a good example of this. (Bob Byrne, Ultimate Players Association)

in chapter 4, these sports are based on a **power and performance model.**

Although many people have used the power and performance model as the standard for determining the meaning, organization, and purpose of sports, not everyone has accepted it. In fact, some people have maintained or developed other sports, grounded in values and experiences related to their connections with one another and their desire to express those connections through playful and enjoyable physical activities. As noted in chapter 4, these sports are based on a **pleasure and participation model.**

These two models do not encompass all the ways that sports might be defined and played. However, they represent two popular conceptions of sports in people's lives, so they are a practical starting point for thinking about what sports might be like in the future.

Power and Performance Sports

Power and performance sports will continue to be the most visible and publicized sport forms in the near future. These sports, based on key aspects of cultural ideology in many postindustrial societies, emphasize the use of strength, power, and speed to push human limits and aggressively dominate opponents in a competitive quest for victories and championships.

Although power and performance sports take many forms, they are based on the idea that excellence is proved through competitive success and achieved through intense dedication and hard work, combined with making sacrifices and taking risks. They also encourage people to stress setting records, pushing human limits, using the body as a machine, and viewing technology as a performance aid. According to many athletes in power and performance sports, the body is to be trained, controlled, and constantly monitored, so that it will respond to the challenges and demands of sports efficiently and forcefully; sports are defined as battles in which the opposition is to be intimidated, punished, and defeated.

Power and performance sports also tend to be exclusive. Participants are selected for their physical skills and abilities to achieve competitive success. Those who lack skills and abilities are cut or put in "developmental" programs. Organizations and teams in power and performance sports feature hierarchical authority structures, in which athletes are subordinate to coaches and coaches are subordinate to owners and administrators. In coach-athlete relationships, it is generally accepted that coaches can humiliate, shame, and derogate athletes as they try to push them to excel. Athletes are expected to respond to humiliation and shame with toughness and a willingness to give all of themselves in the quest for excellence.

The sponsors of power and performance sports know that it is good for them to be associated with people and activities that stress efficiency, organization, competition, hard work, and the endurance of pain for the sake of progress (Hoberman, 1994). Being associated with athletes and teams popularly identified as winners is also important. Sponsors use these associations to promote products while establishing favorable public relations profiles. Sponsors assume that their association with winning athletes and teams makes them special in the eyes of consumers and in the lives of people throughout a culture.

Of course, as long as the rewards of sponsorship go to those who are successful in power and performance sports, these sports will continue to thrive, and the athletes who play them will continue to be cultural celebrities who are paid to endorse the values of the sponsors. Power and performance sports will remain dominant in most cultures for many years to come; people who possess power and influence want it to be so.

Pleasure and Participation Sports

Even as power and performance sports have become increasingly visible forms of popular culture, many people have continued to realize two important things: (1) there are many ways to do sports, and (2) power and performance sports may not be consistent with their personal values and experiences. In the past, this dual realization gave rise to sport forms that differed from the sports usually covered in the mainstream media. This will continue to occur in the future.

A trend that will grow more in the future is the creation of alternative sports emphasizing a combination of *pleasure and participation.* These sports will involve physical activities in which participants are committed to a combination of challenge, freedom, authenticity, and personal connections—connections between people, mind and body, and physical activity and the environment.

Although pleasure and participation sports take many forms, they generally emphasize an ethic of personal expression, enjoyment, growth, good health, and mutual concern and support for teammates and opponents. They focus on personal empowerment rather than the domination of others, as well as on the notion that the body is to be experienced and enjoyed rather than trained and used as a tool. People who play pleasure and participation sports tend to see their bodies as gardens, which must be cultivated and cared for to promote growth, rather than as machines to be used as tools or weapons and then repaired when they break down.

Pleasure and participation sports are characterized by inclusiveness. Playing, not winning, is the most important thing. Differences in physical skills among participants are accommodated informally, or formally through the use of handicap systems, so that players can enjoy competition *with* each other even when they have unequal skills. Sport organizations and sport teams based on this model have democratic decision-making structures characterized by cooperation, the sharing of power, and give-and-take relationships between coaches and athletes. Humiliation, shame, and derogation are inconsistent with the spirit underlying these sports.

The sponsorship of pleasure and participation sports generally is grounded in two ideas: (1) it is socially useful to promote widespread participation in a wide range of physical activities and

"*I love the XGames . . . because they're all about . . . freedom and individual expression.*"

FIGURE 16.1   Some athletes in alternative sports are uneasy about what happens when their sports become commercialized.

sports, and (2) it is important to emphasize participation, health, and enjoyment over trying to set records and record wins.

Unfortunately, many people and corporations with power and money are more interested in sponsoring sports that emphasize power and performance than pleasure and participation (see figure 16.1). However, not everyone thinks that way, so there will be support for the latter type of sports in the future. Support will grow only as increasing numbers of people choose to include pleasure and participation sports in their lives, and even then it will grow slowly.

FUTURE TRENDS IN SPORTS

The Growth of Power and Performance Sports

Power and performance sports will continue to be the most visible and publicized sport forms in the foreseeable future. Vested interests in these sports are very strong, and those who benefit from them have considerable power and influence. For example, the popularity of power and performance sports is tied to dominant forms of gender relations. When attention is focused on pushing physical limits, men are the center of that attention, especially when the limits are related to strength, power, and speed. Women athletes are attracting more attention, but efforts to push human limits usually celebrate differences between men and women and the superiority of men over women. This preserves the dominance of sports based on the power and performance model for many years to come.

Power and performance sports will remain dominant for another reason: they attract corporate sponsors. American football, the classic embodiment of these sports, continues to attract billions of dollars in television rights fees and other revenues, and games are televised in an increasing number of countries around the world, even though few people play heavy contact football.

In the United States, the NFL proudly markets its games under the slogan "Feel the Power." Athletes in the NFL and in other power and performance sports are portrayed in the media as heroic figures and exemplars of corporate images emphasizing productivity, efficiency, and dedication to performance despite pain and injury. Spectators are encouraged to identify with these athletes and their teams and to express their identification through the consumption of licensed merchandise and other products. As long as people identify with athletes and teams in power and performance sports, and as long as their identification can be used to promote consumption, these sports will receive the sponsorships and media coverage they need to maintain their dominance.

Because power and performance sports often involve pushing human and normative limits, they are especially alluring to many people. Attempts to break barriers or do what no one else

> In 1899, no one could foresee sports becoming such a national obsession.
> —Tom Weir, *USA Today* (1999)

has done before can be seductive. Sports emphasizing these things are relatively easy to market and sell if they are combined with storylines that resonate with the experience of consumers. This is epitomized in the performance spectacles of professional wrestling, in which promoters and participants push limits as a form of entertainment. Drug-enhanced bodies, carefully constructed entertainment personas, impressive physical skills, and shocking antics that push moral limits are combined in a format that was the highest-rated cable television content in the United States at the beginning of the twenty-first century.

Bob Rinehart (1998) suggests that pro wrestling is a caricature of the main themes that have long been a part of power and performance sports. I agree and add that there are many cases in mainstream sports in which people use technology to push limits for the purpose of competitive success:

- Parents give synthetic human growth hormone to their children in the hope of "creating" world-class athletes.
- Athletes are in a constant quest to find substances and technological aids to help them become bigger, stronger, and faster.
- People of all ages seek sports equipment made with new, lightweight, strong materials, such as kevlar, titanium, and carbon fibre, so that they can develop new challenges and experiences.
- Some people dream of the day when the Human Genome Project provides information that permits the creation of genetically engineered "designer athletes."
- Those people also dream of the day when the brain and central nervous system can be regulated to facilitate training and enhance performance.

The limits pushed by pro wrestling were minor, compared with the limits that might be pushed by genetic engineering and its application to power and performance sports.

These changes will raise many bioethical issues, but the people who use power and performance sports to form standards for judging what sports should be in the future may find it easy to ignore those issues. For example, many young people today are growing up with rapidly changing media images that blur the boundaries between human and nonhuman, and they expect that science will provide artificial organs as well as synthetic bones, tendons, and ligaments to those who need them in the future. Therefore, it won't be shocking when superstrong synthetic ligaments, bones, and joints are used to repair bodies injured in power and performance sports. It may not even be shocking when mechanical body parts are used to replace injured limbs and improve performance in sports. In fact, those who watch athletes in power and performance sports will increasingly accept the injuries and the abuse of athletes' bodies as the medical and physical costs of pushing limits, and they will expect science to repair the damage.

However, this acceptance will *not* come without resistance. Questions *will* be raised about using technology and pushing limits in sports. Dominant sports in the future will not simply be the result of what is technologically possible. Using technology could eliminate the human element in contests and games, so that athletes reach their potential only when they become machinelike.

This approach to sports ultimately subverts creativity, freedom, spontaneity, and expression among athletes, and it turns sports into programmed spectacles involving dramatically presented physical actions—such as professional wrestling. As this occurs, some athletes and spectators will resist it. There will be athletes who will not accept becoming pawns in such spectacles, and there will be spectators who will not watch them regularly, because it will be difficult to identify with programmed athletes playing prepackaged games lacking human spontaneity and

expression. Unless athletes *feel pressure, emotionally respond* to victory and defeat, *make mistakes, work hard* for success, and *have their good and bad days,* spectators may have trouble identifying with them. If this happens, the prevailing power and performance sports will lose much of their commercial value. The success of these sports depends on fan identification with athletes, and, if technology makes athletes too unlike the spectators who pay to watch them, fan identification could fade. After all, why watch cyborg athletes when you can buy a video game that enables you to control the images of the same athletes in your media room at home? The video game costs less than buying a ticket to a game, and it gives you more control than watching a game on television and listening to announcers tell you what you're supposed to see and think.

The use of technology in power and performance sports also raises questions about fairness and access to sport participation. When the cost of technology is so high that only wealthy individuals, corporations, and nations can use it to their benefit, many people will question the meaning of athletic success. Will new definitions of *success* emerge? Who will benefit from these definitions? These and many other questions will beg for answers as new forms of pushing limits enter the realm of power and performance sports.

The Growth of Pleasure and Participation Sports

The future will bring diverse sport forms, and many of these forms will embody at least some characteristics of the pleasure and participation model. The reasons for this include growing concerns about health and fitness, participation preferences among older people, values and experiences brought to sports by women, and groups seeking alternative sports.

Growing Concerns About Health and Fitness
As health-care policies and programs around the world increasingly emphasize the prevention of

Young people seeking alternatives to organized competitive sports will increase the diversity of pleasure and participation sports in the future. Mountain boarding is a good example. (Jason Lee, Mountain Board Sports)

and performance sports and toward teaching them a range of alternative sports involving lifetime skills, noncompetitive challenges, inclusive participation philosophies, respect and support for other participants, responsible attitudes toward the environment, and concerns for health—all of which are characteristics of pleasure and participation sports.

When people realize that healthy exercise can promote personal health, family fun, and a sense of community, there are powerful incentives for involvement in a wide array of pleasure and participation sports. This will be an important trend in the future.

Participation Preferences Among Older People
As the median age of the population in many societies increases, as people live longer, and as older people represent an increasingly larger segment of the world's population, there will be a growing interest in sports that do not involve intimidation, the use of physical force, the domination of opponents, and the risk of serious injuries.

As people age, they are less likely to risk their physical well-being to establish a reputation in sports. Older people are more likely to see sports as social activities and are more interested in making sports inclusive rather than exclusive. Older people also realize that they have but one body, and it can be enjoyed only if it is cultivated as though it were a garden, rather than driven as if it were a machine.

Older people generally are not attracted to power and performance sports. Instead, they prefer noncompetitive physical activities and modified versions of competitive activities. Thus, the future will see more "senior" sport leagues, in which rules are changed to emphasize the pleasure of movement, connections between people, and the challenge of controlled competition. But there also will be an increased emphasis on walking, hiking, strength training, yoga, tai chi, and similar activities, which will be taken seriously but done in settings in which the focus is

illness and injury, people will become more sensitive to health and fitness issues. In North America, for example, health-care and insurance programs in the future will give higher priority to staying well as a strategy for cutting costs and maximizing their profits. In connection with this, people may be encouraged to avoid participation in certain power and performance sports and to increase their participation in pleasure and participation sports for which health benefits are much higher (Waddington, 2000b).

Health and fitness concerns also will be promoted through changes in physical education curricula. Physical educators will continue to move away from teaching students to play power on health, fitness, and social connections, rather than on setting records or using the body to dominate opponents.

The rising popularity of golf is indicative of general trends we will see in this century. Golf involves healthy exercise, it's nonviolent, it doesn't involve "punishing" the opposition, and it has a handicap system, so that people with different skills can play as equals in competitive events. An important feature is that men and women, and parents and children, can play golf together. Although golf has traditions of exclusiveness and is too expensive for many people to play, older people will develop similar but less expensive pleasure and participation sports as they seek healthy physical activities with aerobic and anaerobic benefits. Bowling has served this purpose for many years, and it remains one of the most popular sports in the United States.

Pleasure and participation sports also could be sites for challenging dominant ideas about aging. In the past, aging has been seen as a process that involves increasing dependency and incapacity, but the achievements of older athletes support the notion that getting old doesn't automatically mean becoming weak and incapacitated. "Seniors" and "masters" sport programs will become increasingly popular, and they will provide many images of older people who are fit, healthy, and accomplished athletes.

Values and Experiences Brought to Sports by Women

As women continue to gain more power and resources, many of them will reject traditional power and performance sports. Others will continue to seek equity in those sports and, in the process, challenge the very gender ideology on which they are organized.

Today, there is a growing number of cases in which women have transformed the rules and spirit of a sport to moderate the emphasis on power and performance and increase the emphasis on pleasure and participation (Fasting, 1996; Griffin, 1998; Hargreaves, 1994, 2000; Nelson, 1998; Porterfield, 1999; Theberge, 2000b;

Zipter, 1988). Even when women play sports such as rugby, soccer, and hockey, there are indications that they often emphasize inclusiveness and support for teammates and opponents in explicit ways that are seldom present in the men's versions of these sports. The "in-your-face" power and performance orientation is replaced by an orientation that is expressive of the joy of participation.

Women sometimes encounter difficulties when trying to enlist sponsors for sports that differ from men's power and performance sports. Without an emphasis on physical domination, the women's sports often are seen as second-rate or not serious enough to attract the attention sponsors seek. However, if women choose such sports in greater numbers, sponsors will respond. As they do, various versions of pleasure and participation sports will receive increased support.

Groups Seeking Alternative Sports

Sport participants who reject power and performance sports also will fuel the formation of alternative sports. For example, high school students will continue to form their own sport groups and play games on their own, rather than put up with the constraints of playing on varsity teams, on which coaches often try to control their lives and on which the emphasis on competition and win-loss records is given priority over enjoyment and the experience of participation. Whether more students will look outside the school for alternatives to dominant sports largely depends on how schools organize their sport programs in the future.

Unique sport subcultures have developed around many alternative sports. For example, studies of skateboarders and snowboarders have found that many young people have resisted attempts to turn their sports into commercialized, competitive forms (Beal, 1995; Crissey, 1999). Even in official, formally sponsored contests, many skaters, for example, have deliberately subverted the power and performance dimensions of events. Unregistered skaters have crashed the events. Registered skaters have pinned competition numbers on their shirts, so that they were upside down or difficult to read. "Competitors" have focused on expressing themselves rather than outdoing opponents, and they have deviated from the prearranged patterns for warming up and competing. In some cases, mass protest has stopped events after nonconforming athletes were disqualified for their actions.

There are segments of many sport subcultures that resist attempts to dilute the pleasure and participation emphasis in their activities. They don't want competition and the domination of opponents to replace the expression and support of fellow participants. For example, when a twelve-year-old snowboarder was asked in 1996 what he thought about the possibility of adding his sport to the Olympics, he said, "Don't kill the ride, dude. Let us be free." Even at age twelve, he knew that the ideology of power and performance would subvert the elements of pleasure and participation in his sport. After snowboarding was added to the Olympics in 1996, Terje Haakonsen, reputedly the best boarder in the world, refused to compete in Nagano. He said, "Snowboarding is about fresh tracks and carving powder and being yourself and not being judged by others; it's not about nationalism and politics and money" (in Perman, 1998, p. 61).

People who are disabled or physically challenged have sought to develop alternative sports, as well as to adapt dominant sports to fit their needs and physical characteristics. Although some sports for athletes with disabilities clearly emphasize power and performance, others emphasize pleasure and participation. Concern and support for teammates and opponents, as well as inclusiveness related to physical abilities, characterize these latter sports.

When children with disabilities are more frequently mainstreamed into organized sports, able-bodied children will have more opportunities to integrate the characteristics of pleasure

In the future, people with disabilities not only will participate in sports in greater numbers but also will influence how sports are played and what new sports are developed. Creatively designed equipment now permits new forms of sports involvement for both the able-bodied and the disabled, as shown in this photo of trail riders. (Rob Schoenbaum)

and participation sports into their experiences as they interact and play with peers with disabilities. As my granddaughter with cerebral palsy grows up, I suspect she will favor pleasure and participation sports. But, if she chooses to play in other sports, I suspect she will encourage her peers to qualify their emphasis on power and performance and to remember that connections between people always involve accommodating difference and uniqueness.

The Gay Games and gay athletic clubs and teams also are an example of an alternative sport form emphasizing participation, support, inclusiveness, and the enjoyment of physical movement (Pronger, 1999). The sixth quadrennial Gay Games in Sydney, Australia, in 2002 involved more than 13,000 competitors from 82 nations. Although the Gay Games resemble dominant sports in some ways, they explicitly challenge the gender ideology that underlies dominant sports, and they are free of the homophobia that permeates them. The organizers of the 2006 Gay Games in Montreal, a more accessible location than Sydney, expect up to 25,000 participants, which would make the 2006 Gay Games the largest international sport event in history.

Gay and lesbian athletes will continue to form sport groups and teams to provide enjoyable experiences in their social lives. One lesbian explains:

> I use sports . . . to meet people. . . . Team sports are the main social outlets in my life. I depend on them for emotional support, physical activity, a sense of belonging, a comfortable atmosphere, and an outlet for my competitive nature. (in Zipter, 1988, p. 82)

A gay man in Brian Pronger's study of sports and homosexuality expressed similar feelings:

> The nice thing about playing gay sports is . . . to interact with gay people . . . [so you] don't have to be on guard. You can joke around, you can play. That's a good feeling. It's also the sense of community that comes from it. . . . It's not that I didn't fit in [when I played volleyball at work, but it] is probably more relaxed in gay sports. (in Pronger, 1990, p. 238)

In summary, we will continue to see alternatives to power and performance sports in the future. Most will embody at least some aspects of pleasure and participation sports. One of the challenges we will face in the future is how to maintain alternative sports as sport participation rates increase.

SPECIFIC FORECASTS

Professional Sports

In the future, professional sports will become increasingly global in a number of ways. Leagues will have more teams and more athletes from different countries, and more games will be televised around the world. Sport organizations from wealthier nations will push for international expansion. The political implications of this expansion will be significant, because a North American model of professional and commercial sports will be taken all over the world and presented as the "right" (i.e., most profitable) way to organize, play, and sponsor sports; there also will be a "McDonaldization" of sports, with an emphasis on standardization and service provision (Ritzer, 2000).

Soccer, basketball, and volleyball will be the most widely played team sports; baseball and hockey will grow in popularity, and football will attract spectator attention but little on-the-field participation in countries outside North America. The number of pro teams and leagues will increase, but many will fail, especially in connection with the sports that are not already established in a society.

New stadiums for professional teams will be built as "sport malls," where the focus will be on shopping, eating, and drinking, as well as watching sport events. Pro teams will organize events as total entertainment experiences for spectators. *Entertainment* will be defined in terms of shopping, eating, drinking, and any other form of consumption from which revenue streams can be generated. The goal of team owners will be to induce spectators to spend as many of their entertainment dollars as possible inside the stadium. Public money will continue to be used to subsidize many wealthy owners and their players, although this practice will be challenged more frequently and with more success than during the recent past.

If academic requirements for participation in intercollegiate sports continue to become more strict, new professional "junior," or "rookie," leagues in basketball and football will be established in the United States. These leagues will attract young athletes who are more interested in playing professional sports than going to college. These leagues will have age limits (under

Gender equity in intercollegiate sports will continue to be an issue, although women will continue to participate in record numbers. The focus of future issues will be on women gaining power and changing the culture of athletic departments. At present, men make nearly all the important decisions at that level, and the culture of athletic departments reflects the values and experiences of men. (NCAA Photos)

twenty-one or under twenty-four), and athletes will earn salaries much lower than those of their NBA and NFL counterparts; they will be modeled, partly, on minor league baseball and hockey.

As this happens, more communities will make bids for league franchises, and more voters will be asked to pass bond issues and tax increases to fund the building of arenas and stadiums. As new teams come into midsized cities, attendance at local high school games will be jeopardized, and revenues for high school and college sports will decline, except for a few big-time college teams. In addition, the talent pool for revenue-producing intercollegiate sports will decrease; this will jeopardize gate receipts and television rights contracts for all but 50 to 100 universities.

Top pro athletes will continue to be global celebrities, and their lives will more closely resemble film and rock music stars. The dynamics of celebrity will enable athletes to capitalize on new publicity and revenue streams, such as money that might be made in connection with fans visiting athletes' websites. The athletes will take their public images more seriously and manage them more assertively.

Professional athletes will gain more autonomy and power in the future, but they will not use their power to make any major changes in the structure of commercial sports or in society as a whole; their primary goal will be to increase control over their careers and enhance their wealth.

Intercollegiate Sports

Intercollegiate sports in the United States will continue to exist, despite all the investigations, exposés, and doomsday predictions. Gender equity will remain the central issue in many intercollegiate programs, and court decisions will put new pressures on athletic departments to achieve equity in terms of participation opportunities and resource allocation. The gender equity issue will cause discussions about the place of football in intercollegiate programs. However, most big-time football programs will continue to exist.

In the face of budget crises, colleges and universities will continue to cut the number of varsity sports they offer. Intercollegiate programs will become increasingly polarized in terms of size and emphasis. The programs with revenue-producing teams will maintain a big-time emphasis; other programs will abandon the hope of becoming big-time and will maintain fewer teams at lower levels of competition. Student-organized club teams will replace varsity teams in certain so-called minor sports. There also will be a continuation of efforts to make intercollegiate sport programs academically accountable. In some cases, athletic programs will be evaluated in connection with academic accreditation processes.

The NCAA will change its rules so that college athletes in revenue-producing sports can receive some form of financial support in addition to their athletic grants. Student-athletes will continue to lack autonomy and power, although there will be token efforts to include them in discussions about college sports. Some student-athletes will try to organize teammates to protest the unfair and coercive tactics used by coaches, but the success of these groups and organizational efforts will be mixed.

High School Sports

Playoffs, league championships, and state titles will continue to be important in high school sports, although funding shortages will force many schools to question the necessity of elitist sport programs in the schools. Despite these questions, some U.S. high school teams will strive to be included in new national ranking systems, and high school games around the country will be available to spectators through Internet broadcasts; grandparents in Ohio will be able to use the Internet to see their granddaughter's basketball game in Oregon.

These developments will continue to encourage high schools to maintain sport programs along the lines of big-time college programs, if they can afford to do so. Standout athletes in elementary schools will be recruited heavily by high schools seeking national reputations. Private high schools will recruit most heavily, because they can use sport programs to recruit tuition-paying students and market their academic programs. This trend will lead to national tournaments and national championships in certain high school sports.

> *The use of drugs, and, perhaps more startling, the engineering of genes to enhance performance, raises questions about the notion of what an athlete is.*
>
> —Richard Sandomir, journalist,
> *The New York Times* (2002)

Along with a trend toward sports elitism in some high schools, an increasing number of schools will experience financial problems forcing them to cut back or eliminate varsity sports. As this happens, some schools and coaches will seek corporate sponsors for programs and teams or will develop new alliances with local agencies and groups to maintain certain programs. Even if outside funding and support are acquired, some high schools will cut most of their varsity sports. The sports least likely to be cut will be boys' football and basketball and girls' basketball and volleyball. Outside of these sports, high school students increasingly will play in programs sponsored by community clubs. In the varsity sports that continue to exist, the participation of girls will be encouraged, but their programs and teams will be modeled after boys' programs and teams. A function of varsity programs will continue to be the development of players who have superior abilities, so that they can be "fed into" programs at higher levels of competition.

Youth Sports

Organized youth sports will become increasingly privatized in most American communities. Publicly funded programs will be cut back or eliminated, and parks and recreation departments increasingly will become brokers of public spaces and facilities. Youth programs in middle-income and wealthy communities will be organized and funded through participation fees, and children in these communities will be encouraged by parents to join teams.

Coaching education programs, such as those that have been flourishing in Canada and Europe will become more popular in the United States. This change will occur to satisfy parents' demands for more professional approaches to youth sports, to certify coaches as experts, and to minimize legal liability in private sport programs.

Youth programs will emphasize sports development rather than recreation, and parents will become increasingly concerned about how their children's participation may pay off in the future—in scholarships and in social acceptance. In response to the structured character of youth programs, many young people will seek out alternative sports, such as skateboarding, rollerblading, BMX biking, and various informal games in which they can make up their own rules and develop skills without being under the control of adults. Nine-year-olds, after playing organized sports twelve months a year since they were four years old, will seek to retire from adult-controlled sports, and their parents will force them to continue or sign them up for other organized activities.

Spectators and Spectator Sports

People will continue to watch sports, and obesity rates will increase as people watch more and more and play less and less. There will be shifts and increasing variation in the sports that people watch. For example, more people may watch soccer, whereas fewer may watch basketball, and

people will watch a greater range of sports than ever before, including everything from bass fishing that attracts retired people to alternative sports that attract young people. Most people will continue to watch at escalating rates. The media, including the Internet, will encourage this trend with increased sports content (see figure 16.2). At the same time, more pay-per-view sports, from Little League games to pro games around the world, will be available on cable and satellite television and the Internet.

Spectators and athletes will "connect" via websites for athletes. Fans will be able to ask athletes questions, and athletes will be able to create and present personas that can be converted into valuable commodities and sold back to fans in various forms. Athletes (and their agents) will manage these connections with fans to maximize

"Pu-leaze, Mom! Who wants to play soccer with a bunch of kids when I can play on the virtual World Cup Team with Mia Hamm and Brandi Chastain?!?"

FIGURE 16.2 The future of sports is difficult to predict. Will children prefer videogame and virtual sports over the dominant sport forms of today?

their commodity value. Athletes' presentations of themselves on websites will be consistent with the self-presentations "staged" by film and television celebrities.

Some spectators will form ad hoc organizations to represent their interests when it comes to setting prices for tickets and concessions, controlling the location of team franchises, and guaranteeing fan safety at events. However, most ad hoc spectator organizations will not be influential. This is because they will not attract those fans who already accept commercialized sports, expensive ticket prices, and high salaries for athletes.

Spectator betting on sports will become more common. Local and regional governments will continue to legalize sport gambling. Lotteries, which already have been used extensively in Canada to fund sport activities, will be used increasingly in U.S. states to pay for sports and sport teams in their cities or schools. An issue will be betting on the Internet, and people will debate whether betting laws should apply to wagering on the Internet, to fantasy leagues with entry fees and cash prizes for winners, and to betting clubs in which wagers involve only individual bettors without a third-party bookie taking a "cut."

Technology

Issues related to technology in sports are not new. However, the rapid developments of new technologies during the latter half of the twentieth century alerted us to changes and issues that we can expect in the future.[1]

We will continue to see new developments in the equipment used in sports. From race cars to skateboards, there will be new technologies to make athletes go faster and maintain control, sometimes, in the process. When this creates

risks deemed to be too great, there will be regulations limiting certain technologies during official competitions. However, the tendency will be to use new technologies even when they do add risk to sport participation, especially when the norms in sport cultures emphasize taking risks as important in establishing and reaffirming identity as an athlete.

Other technologies will enable athletes, from recreational to elite levels, to alter the experiences they have as they do their sports. Skis have been designed to increase speed, carve sharper turns, perform free-style tricks, extend the length of jumps, and allow recreational skiers greater control of their experiences on snow. These changes will continue, fueled by the quest for financial profits as well as curiosity and the search for new experiences.

Tennis rackets will enable players to hit balls with more accuracy and speed while absorbing impact and reducing injuries to shoulders, elbows, and wrists. Golf clubs and golf balls will be redesigned for greater accuracy and distance. New materials will be developed to improve performance and alter experiences in a wide range of sports. In some cases, these changes will be regulated by the official governing bodies of sports; in other cases, they will be embraced by athletes and sports officials as improvements to their sports.

Some technologies will make sport participation safer; others will increase risks, along with the frequency and seriousness of injuries. Regulating these technologies will present constant challenges to athletes and sports officials. Scientists will be called on, as they have been in the past, to do research that enables athletes and officials to anticipate the outcomes of their equipment choices and their regulatory decisions.

By far, the most contentious new technologies in the future will be those that alter the human body to maximize performance. Up to this point, drugs and other performance-enhancing substances were the focus of athletes and regulatory organizations in sports. However, some people

---

[1] See "Building the Elite Athlete: The Science and Technology of Sport," a special issue of *Scientific American*, Fall 2000, Volume II, Number 3.

anticipate that, before 2010, athletes will be using genetic-enhancement technologies to improve their performances and treat their injuries.

Of course, genetic manipulation technologies will present challenges that go far beyond sports. The scientific, medical, and moral implications of these technologies are so complex and fuzzy that we face major dilemmas related to how gene-related technologies will be used in the future. We will need to create new norms to guide our use of those technologies, and it will not be easy to produce consensus in this process of creating norms.

Injured athletes should be able to use medical technologies that are available to others. But what about repairing an injured knee by genetically altering ligament tissues, which would make an athlete's knee nearly indestructible?

What about changing an athlete's genetic makeup to improve performance? Or, even more controversial, what about altering the genetic structure of a fetus, so that a child will have physical characteristics that create performance potential beyond the potential of anyone who has not been genetically altered? Will the use of such technologies increase or limit the choices that a human being has during his or her life? How will we know? How will we deal with issues of fairness if this occurs?

The drug testing that sports officials are now putting into place will be irrelevant in the face of such changes. If athletes use genetic vaccines that enhance muscle development or endurance, how will testers distinguish DNA created through genetic manipulation from natural DNA (Begley, 2002; Entine, 2002; Sandomir, 2002;

Technology has long been a part of sports. Issues related to the impact of technology on the environment and the conflicts created between trail bikers and hikers and between snowmobile riders and cross-country skiers have not been studied much by sociologists in North America. As more young people incorporate technology into their sports and leisure, what issues will they raise?

Zorpette, 2000)? How will bodies that are genetically enhanced be distinguished from those enhanced through training or other means? What will *natural* mean? What will it mean to be an athlete or set a record? Today's "chemical games" played by some athletes will soon become tomorrow's "genetic games," and they will raise new questions and issues.

Genetic technologies are not the only ones that will present us with difficult challenges in the future. Scientists will develop new forms of surveillance to enable athletes to monitor their own bodies. At the same time, these technologies will enable coaches and other training personnel to monitor the bodies and actions of athletes. This will have interesting implications for power relations in sports (Johns and Johns, 2000). Athletes may need unions to resist the power of coercive coaches and trainers, and they may need advisors who can help them make decisions about how they will use technologies in their own lives. These advisors will need backgrounds in history, philosophy (ethics), sociology, and psychology. Technology offers challenges to sport scientists as well as athletes and coaches.

Electronic Media

Television and the Internet will provide the visual images and narratives that will influence how sports are imagined, created, and played in many societies around the world. People may not mimic what they see in those images or hear in those narratives, but they will use them as a standard against which they will assess their activities and experiences. Those who control the world's media will have a great influence on discourse about sports and what sports should be like in the future.

Major private business conglomerates will continue to connect sport teams, sport events, the media, the entertainment industry, and the Internet. The impact of these connections on sports is difficult to predict. However, sports increasingly will become online content and a

valuable form of programming for major media corporations. As this occurs, media sports will become more interactive. They will be presented in new ways, and spectators will experience and connect with teams, coaches, and players on the field, in the locker room, and even at home.

Internet rights will be tied contractually to broadcast rights in general, as when CBS purchased from the NCAA in 1999 the rights to broadcast intercollegiate men's basketball games through 2013. This means that, although spectators will gain more choices about how they will experience sports, the control of sports will become consolidated increasingly in the hands of powerful executives and stockholders, whose interests in sports are peripheral to their interests in expanding their presence and control in the realm of the economy and popular culture. Of course, when spectators participate in interactive ways, they will require detailed knowledge about players, teams, tactics, and strategies—all of which will be available for fees or in a commercial format. The goal of media sports will not change: it will continue to be to sell audiences to sponsors and products or information to audiences.

The Internet will continue to recruit new fans in various fantasy leagues, which allow fans to choose players, construct teams, and qualify for prizes if their teams do well. Improved video games will enable people of all ages to create and coach their own simulated video teams made up of the players they select. Video games will also provide sophisticated new simulated and virtual sport experiences. For example, for a few dollars, a person will be able to ski at Aspen, select from actual ski runs, face virtual challenges, and fall and break bones—virtual bones, that is.

Video and virtual games will play a more central role in the mix of sport images and narratives experienced by people of all ages, especially children. These games will have a greater impact than television presentations of sports on how people integrate sports into their lives. This is because the games are interactive and engage players in a more personal and emotional way than watching televised games.

Organization and Rationalization

At elite levels of competitive sports, athletes and teams will continue to enlist specialists to help them improve their performances. Therapists and sport psychologists, fitness consultants and drug/substance consultants, aerobics instructors, nutritionists, chefs, biomechanists, and exercise physiologists will make up an expanding corps of "sports consultants" expected to help athletes hit their performance peaks when they compete in important events. Even couples who are pregnant will hire these experts because they want their future children to have the benefit of prenatal training and an optimal sports environment in the womb.

An expanding emphasis on the "constructive" use of leisure time will lead to an increasing number of highly organized leisure and sport programs. People will link sport participation with rationally chosen "participation goals" and with the consumption of clothing and equipment that will facilitate the achievement of these goals. "Sport experts" will be hired in greater numbers to assist children and adults to play correctly. Wealthier people will join exclusive athletic clubs in increasing numbers, and their social lives and friendships will be more heavily connected with their patterns of participation in sport activities. Their children will learn how to swim, skate, kick soccer balls, hit backhands, ski,

Commercialism and consumerism will prevail in the future. Sportainment, such as professional wrestling and other forms of dramatic spectacle, will come and go as marketing schemes resonate with segments of people eager to be consumers. (Jay Coakley)

sail, and do a variety of other things under trained sport consultants, who will teach them that fun depends on playing sports the right way, by the right rules, with the right equipment, clothes, and shoes.

Like sport fans and athletes of today, people will continue to be interested in scores, statistics, and records. They will continue to value rationality, hard work, the pursuit of excellence, and the achievement of goals through well-planned efforts and specialized skills. Corporate sponsors will promote these themes in connection with sports media coverage. Sport participation will continue to be linked to character building, success, and science.

In general, if physical activity is not organized and controlled by experts, if it doesn't have winners and losers, if fun is more important than measurable achievement, it will not be considered a sport by many people.

Commercialism and Consumerism

Entertainment and consumption will be the major organizing principles for sports in the future. Financial profits and economic expansion will be the goals of most sports. The ideology and organization of sports will continue to reflect the distribution of resources in society. People with economic and political power will have the most influence on who watches and participates in sports and under what circumstances they will do so. As they have in the past, these people will have much to say about how sports are presented to and defined by the masses of people in societies around the world.

The emphasis on entertainment will fuel the success of sport spectacles. Forms of "sportainment" will be developed and presented to capture gate receipts and media revenues. The competition for market share will be so great that sportainment events will emphasize the spectacular to whatever degree sponsors and fans will allow them. Market forces will set the parameters for these spectacles; some people will love

them, whereas others will complain that they push the boundaries of decency and safety.

We will see large media and entertainment companies continue to enter sports as team owners. Corporate conglomerates will buy teams and link them to their media, entertainment, and Internet divisions. The model of Disney owning ESPN and ESPN owning the XGames will become more popular as corporations use sports to make money and sell interconnected products, from cartoon videos and toys to shoes and drugs, to people around the world.

The images of athletes and teams will be used to sell action figures to four-year-olds and drugs to sixty-year-olds, both of whom will want to act as athletes act on television. Disney has already partnered with massive media conglomerates News Corporation, Ltd., and Comcast-Spectacor to the point that they collectively control many teams and much media coverage of sports on every continent.

On the local level, voters will be pushed into publicly funding new stadiums, and, if they refuse, large corporations will build the stadiums themselves and turn them into monuments celebrating their corporate logos and products. A $400 million investment in a stadium is certainly not out of the question for a multibillion-dollar corporation seeking legitimacy and acceptance in global culture.

Sports equipment manufacturers will continue to sell the idea that involvement in sports requires highly specialized and expensive equipment and clothing. Wealthy people will use sports as contexts for announcing their status and identities through appearance and visual display as much as through their physical abilities; they will buy luxury suites at games and ski at Vail, Colorado, and top resorts in Switzerland, with personal instructors and thousands of dollars worth of high-tech gear.

Finally, we will see sport science language increasingly used in the marketing programs of large corporations. This tactic already helps sell everything from athletic shoes to candy.

Pharmaceutical companies will be new players in this realm, and they will use sport science to sell drugs and nutritional supplements to anyone and everyone, regardless of their health. These companies will use sports and athletes in their marketing programs.

Gender Equity and Ethnic Diversity

Gender equity will remain an important issue in postindustrial nations, and it will become more important in the rest of the world. Excluding or limiting the participation of half the population in traditional and developing nations will no longer be accepted. The women's movement has become global, and women from around the world are working with each other to raise consciousness and to make changes in their lives. Many of those changes are related to everyday issues of sustenance, but, when standards of living begin to rise, gender equity in sports will emerge as an important social issue, especially in countries that have strong sport programs for men.

Sociologist Harry Edwards has predicted that "the challenge in sports in the twenty-first century is going to be diversity" (2000, p. 24). His prediction is grounded in the fact that ethnic diversity is increasing in nearly all nations around the globe. Geographical mobility, labor migration, and political turmoil will push and pull people from diverse backgrounds into new social and political contexts. This will create challenges as governments, communities, and individuals try to come to terms with cultural differences among people.

Ethnic diversity will increase in sports at all levels, and it will create challenges for players, coaches, spectators, and sport organizations. The number of teams on which players speak two or more languages will grow in many sports, coaches will require translators, agents will need courses in cultural issues, diversity training will become common for players, teams will hire language teachers and anthropologists to assist new players making adaptations as they enter and live in new cultures, and family members will need support as they do the same.

Increasing diversity goes hand in hand with globalization. Teams in U.S. universities and in professional leagues in every nation will recruit more widely on a global basis. Citizenship will become less important than height, weight, and speed in the 40-meter dash. Corporations will scout the world for young athletes who can endorse their products in emerging markets. Issues will be raised about regulating global recruiting. "Age of consent" for signing contracts varies from culture to culture, and different cultures have different norms about what is legal. The political importance of international governing bodies will become more important as these issues are faced in more sports. Conflicts will occur as leagues and teams in wealthy nations recruit star athletes out of other nations. Bidding wars for athletes will become international in scope, and they will raise new political issues, which will involve nation-states, transnational corporations, and international governing bodies for sports.

Overall, we will face diversity issues that we have not even dreamed of yet as we begin this century. The question will be whether these issues will create reactionary, jingoistic, and isolationist backlash or new forms of openness and acceptance of cultural differences. To the extent that the former response prevails, conflict will increase. If the latter response prevails, positive new experiences will emerge in sports and in social life generally.

THE CHALLENGE OF MAKING THE FUTURE

The predictions in this chapter are meant to be a challenge for us. We are not locked into the predictions offered in this chapter or anywhere else. The meaning, organization, and purpose of sports can be transformed. It is possible to create goals and organizations so that sports are more democratic and more compatible with a wider range of values and experiences: *we can make the future*.

The growing importance of sports in society makes it more necessary for us to take a closer and more critical look at how sports are defined, organized, and played. As we do this, some of us will call for changes in dominant sport forms or even reject those forms and call for new and alternative sports. However, we should not expect widespread, revolutionary changes to occur overnight. Social transformation is always a challenging and tedious process. It requires long-term efforts and carefully planned strategies, but it does not occur without a clear vision of possible futures and strategic efforts to turn visions into realities.

As we think about changing sports, we should also think about using sports to change other parts of the world. Robert Davies, chief executive of the International Business Leaders Forum, an organization dedicated to promoting global social responsibility, has noted that the visibility and popularity of sports on both the global and local levels gives them a great "potential to contribute powerfully to a better world." He told a large audience at the 2002 World Sports Forum in Lausanne, Switzerland, that "the power and influence of sport is only just being understood" by people concerned with

Social transformation does not occur without a struggle. Producing transformation is always a challenging and tedious process. It requires dedication and long-term commitment, just as some sports require dedication and commitment. Never ever ever ever cease to be a critical citizen. (Jay Coakley)

social responsibility (Davies, 2002a). He also told an international assembly of journalists and media representatives that "high profile global sporting events are seen as a frontier for raising issues of injustice and social responsibility" and that the media have a responsibility to explore that frontier (Davies, 2002b). These are crucial issues to keep in mind as we form visions and strategies for change.

Theories Used to Inspire Visions and Strategies to Change Sports

Playing an active role in transforming the world in which we live is part of being a citizen in a democracy. As noted in chapter 2, theories are useful in constructing our visions and taking actions to promote them. The following are some examples of how theories can be used in making the future.

Functionalist Theory Despite its limitations, this theory is widely used to construct visions of sports in the future. Those with power and influence like functionalism, because it takes the existing social system for granted and focuses on how sports contribute to maintaining that system. Functionalism usually inspires efforts to improve and expand existing sports and to use *conservative* and *reformist* strategies for making changes.

A *conservative strategy* is based on the assumption that changes in sports, like changes in the rest of society, involve raising more money, developing more effective marketing strategies, and generally strengthening traditional values, definitions, experiences, and organizational structures. A functionalist using a conservative strategy focuses on growth through strengthening what already exists, rather than transforming existing social relations or social structures.

A *reformist strategy* focuses on eliminating problems and making sports more socially useful by making them bigger parts of people's lives. A functionalist reformist strategy emphasizes social control more than cultural transformation.

The focus is on such things as encouraging girls and women to play sports, eliminating cheating and drug use in sports, making athletes into role models, expanding opportunities to play sports, and tying sports to economic and community development processes. The Women's Sports Foundation in the United States is an example of an organization that often uses reformist strategies based on a functionalist approach, although it occasionally uses additional strategies grounded in critical and critical feminist theories as well.

Conflict Theory Conflict theorists envision a society in which sports are expressive, humane activities through which people are free to explore a full range of democratically organized physical challenges. This vision cannot become reality in a society in which the profit motive, economic exploitation, and oppressive forms of class relations destroy the possibility of freedom in and through sports. Therefore, conflict theory emphasizes a *radical strategy* of change in which the goal is the complete transformation of society itself. Unless there are revolutionary changes in the structure of social relations in society as a whole, playing sports will never involve true freedom, liberation, and pleasure.

A radical strategy for bringing about change is to create class awareness in sports and society, thereby enabling people to transform the economic system and the political system that supports it. This involves creating organizations and political action groups through which players and fans could take the control of sports away from those with power and wealth.

Few people have used conflict theory in this way. It was popular during the 1960s and 1970s, but the monumental challenges that it presented to its proponents generally discouraged them and kept them from becoming effective agents of broad social change. However, conflict theorists did inspire important efforts to challenge racism, sexism, nationalism, and militarism in connection with sports, and they have inspired athletes to push for representation in sport organizations. This has kept the spirit and visions of conflict theory alive among some people around the world.

Interactionist Theory   Interactionists envision sports created from "the bottom up" by the participants themselves. These sports would take many forms, each representing the unique perspectives and definitions of the world formed by participants as they interact with each other. *Conservative, reformist,* or *radical* strategies would be used, but interactionists would emphasize the importance of participants themselves creating the meaning, organization, and purpose of sports in their lives. Interactionists using a *reformist* or *radical* approach would work to make sports and sport organizations more democratic and to inspire the creation of alternatives to existing organized sports. As they do this, they would also borrow ideas from other theories, especially critical and critical feminist theories.

Critical Theories   Critical theorists envision a future in which people resist exclusive, exploitive, and oppressive ideologies and social relations in sports and create new sport forms that represent the interests and experiences of people from many backgrounds. They would use *reformist* and *radical strategies* focused on changing how people think about sports and changing how sports are defined, organized, and played. These strategies would also use sports to change the structure and dynamics of social relations related to gender, race, class, sexuality, and (dis)ability. A primary radical strategy would be to disrupt structures, relationships, and discourses that reproduce forms of power relations that systematically marginalize or erase the identities and voices of particular groups of people in society. The ultimate goal would be to establish processes through which underrepresented voices might be heard and through which opportunities are distributed in a fair and representative manner in sports and society.

Critical Feminist Theories   Critical feminist theorists envision sports in which the values and experiences of women are used as central organizing principles and envision a society in which these sports would be funded and supported. They advocate reformist strategies designed to promote equity, and they advocate radical strategies designed to resist and transform the dominant gender ideology, which privileges men and all sports based on men's values and experiences.

Feminists also advocate pushing the boundaries of gender, so there would be many accepted ways to "do" gender in everyday life. Another feminist strategy is to critique and transform traditional definitions of *masculinity* and create spaces in sports for men who view masculinity in terms of nurturance and support for others, rather than in terms of toughness and dominance over others.

The International Working Group on Women and Sport is grounded in feminist consciousness. Its members around the world use many strategies, including radical strategies aimed at changing ideologies and institutions that systematically exclude women from sports and disadvantage women when they do play sports. Strategies vary from nation to nation, because the problems faced by women are different in different cultures (Hargreaves, 2000). Conservative strategies are used to increase opportunities for girls and women to play established sports in a group or society. Reformist strategies are used to advance women into positions of power in society and in sport organizations. Radical strategies are used to transform the gender ideology on which male privilege is based and female disadvantage is guaranteed.

Figurational Theory   Figurational theorists envision sports free of oppressive power, exploitation, and violence. Their primary strategy is to engage in rigorous programs of research that eventually inspire socially responsible and effective efforts to bring about change and social transformation.

Figurational theorists realize that being an effective agent of social change is very difficult in a world where the interconnections between sports and other spheres of life are becoming increasingly complex. However, their hope is that, if research accurately identifies interconnections between collections of people and the processes of power used in social relations, it will be possible to design strategies for challenging and transforming social figurations that are exploitive and oppressive.

Change Means Different Things to Different People

When most people discuss changes in sports, they think in terms of *conservative strategies* grounded in a form of functionalist theory. They see change in terms of expansion and growth, not cultural and social transformation. They focus on *management* issues and strategies for keeping things organized and profitable. They do not advocate deep changes in how sports are organized and played or changes in the structures and ideologies that underlie those sports. Conservative strategies usually emphasize an underlying concern with using sports as tools for social control and teaching people how to conform to traditional values and expectations.

Reformist strategies also emphasize expanding participation opportunities, but they stress that those opportunities must be fair and free of social practices that systematically privilege some groups over others. *Radical strategies* also are concerned with inequities and democratic participation, but they emphasize deep structural and ideological changes; they advocate a combination of the redistribution of power in society, the transformation of social relations, and new ideologies that give voice to the experiences of previously disenfranchised groups of people.

Radical strategies make many people nervous, because they advocate the interests of socially marginalized groups and challenge the structures and ideologies that have privileged certain groups

Major professional sport teams have their own foundations and community service organizations. Players, especially those with radical ideas about change, may be encouraged to funnel their community involvement through these team-controlled programs. These programs, such as the Pacers Academy in downtown Indianapolis, are valuable assets in communities, but they usually take a conservative approach to change. They emphasize supporting youth sports, educational programs and scholarships, disaster relief, and health-related charities.

of people. This threatens those who live comfortably within the context of those structures and ideologies. Privileged people don't like radicals.

Each of these strategies for change is found in sports today. *Conservative strategies* remain dominant. Those with power tend to be conservative and use their resources to convince others to agree with them. They see power and performance sports as excellent vehicles for promoting values consistent with their interests. For them, sports are a means for making money, increasing influence, and promoting consumption and economic expansion. *Reformist strategies* are relatively common, especially among women and others who have lived on the margins of mainstream sports and wish to be included in those sports or in revised versions of them. *Radical approaches* are rare in sports, because most radicals are concerned with issues of poverty, homelessness, universal health care, quality education

REFLECT ON SPORTS

Athletes as Change Agents
Does It Ever Happen?

Athletes are among the most visible and popular people in many cultures today. Some have the highest name and face recognition of any human beings in history. Such recognition puts them in good positions to act as change agents in society—or does it?

To explore this issue, we must understand that the visibility and popularity of athletes are tied to the public display of physical skills and media images out of which their public personas are formed. Athletes control their sport skills, but their images are controlled by others, including team publicity departments, the media, agents, and advertisers who create and use the athletes' images to promote and sell products. Celebrity athletes have valuable market status, but not much real power, in society.

This "context of celebrity" limits the extent to which athletes can be effective agents of change; if their words and actions don't fit the interests of those who control their images, they risk losing the coverage and support on which their celebrity depends. Team owners and corporate sponsors shy away from players who speak out on social issues. Athletes know this, even if fans do not.

Speaking out can even create problems for college athletes. For example, a former basketball player at the University of North Carolina explained that he never addressed the need for social change while he played because he knew that "athletes are loved by everybody until their consciousness is raised and they start to speak out on social issues" (Hayes, 1993, p. 18). This is especially the case in communities and societies where conservative political ideologies are dominant.

When athletes become involved in community affairs, they usually take a conservative approach. They make speeches and do charity work that reaffirm dominant societal values and strengthen the status quo. They may form foundations or programs to help poor children learn to read, but they won't form organizations to reform or radically alter how resources are allocated to schools. They may make public service announcements supportive of charitable organizations, but they won't identify poverty as a social issue and then call for policy changes related to employment, public

transportation, and child care. Even when athletes enter politics, they most often represent conservative political positions aligned with preserving the status quo in society.

Athletes identified as role models are usually those who strengthen the status quo. As spokespersons, they generally represent those who have an interest in keeping things as they are or in selling products to make profits. They do promotions in which they urge children to stay in school, and they do radio and television commercials to sell cars for local dealers. However, they do not advocate deep *reforms* or *radical changes* in the community processes and structures that intensify poverty, despair, and other social problems.

Starting or working with a foundation to help children from low-income neighborhoods is great, but it does not necessarily call attention to the need for changes in the social system that is failing the children from those neighborhoods.

When athletes do become agents of change, they usually do so in connection with established organizations. For example, the Center for the Study of Sport in Society is a reformist organization that has programs through which current and former athletes work to improve social conditions. The center's Athletes in Service to America, funded by AmeriCorps, uses college athletes to assist high schools as they institutionalize networks of students to eliminate fighting and violence, promote racial and ethnic respect, and intervene when boys threaten or take violent action against girls. Its efforts have been effective, and it demonstrates that athletes can be agents of change if an organization provides the training and support they need to become involved.

Without backup in the form of organized support, athletes seldom speak out on social issues or initiate political actions. On minor issues such as what shoes or soft drinks to buy, people listen to athletes. However, when athletes talk about racism, sexism, economic exploitation, or violence, many people do not take them seriously, or they reject them outright. Look at what happened to Cassius Clay (Muhammad Ali) in the 1970s, when he spoke out on racism and the war in Vietnam. Look at what happened to Tommy Smith and John Carlos when they protested racial relations on the victory stand during the 1968 Olympics. Where was the backup for these athletes? Is this why so many athletes now decide to be corporate shills instead of speaking out on broader issues of social injustice and change? *What do you think?*

Athletes often encounter difficulties when they speak out or demonstrate for certain social issues. Tommy Smith and John Carlos discovered this when they used the victory stand during the 1968 Olympics in Mexico City to protest racial relations in the United States and around the world. They were expelled from the Olympic village, were sent back to the United States amid widespread criticism and condemnation, and then faced social rejection among many people in the United States. (AP/Wide World Photos)

for children, accessible public transportation, full employment, and guaranteed minimum standards of living. It is difficult to work on these issues in connection with sports. However, some radicals concerned with ideological issues have used sports as sites for challenging dominant definitions of *masculinity* and *femininity*, raising questions about the meaning of race, and encouraging people to think critically about the antidemocratic features of hierarchical relationships.

Four Vantage Points for Making Changes

Making the world a better place is a never-ending task. Participating in this process as a change agent is always challenging, regularly frustrating, and sometimes rewarding. For those interested in making changes related to sports and social life, there are four vantage points from which changes might be initiated (Hall et al., 1991):

1. *Work within the system of sports.* You can become involved in sports and sport organizations and then use your position or power to influence and initiate changes. Having an "insider" vantage point can be very effective; sometimes, you can use it even to promote changes in society as a whole. However, becoming an insider often involves adopting the existing values of the organization where you work. This means that, even though you have ideas about reforms or radical changes, your commitment to making those changes may decrease as you move up the organization into positions of increasing power. Once you are in a position to make changes, you may have vested interests in keeping things as they are or taking a conservative approach to change. This is not inevitable, but it happens often. Although an insider vantage point can be a good place from which to make changes, it is important to be realistic about what insiders can do. This is important to remember when we think of athletes as

possible change agents. This issue is discussed in the box "Athletes as Change Agents," pages 588–589.

2. *Join "opposition" groups.* You can become a change agent by forming or joining political groups that challenge problematic or unjust sport policies and put pressure on sport organizations that have antidemocratic policies and programs. For example, such groups might lobby for the building of a community sport center in a low-income neighborhood or lobby against using public funds to build a stadium that would serve primarily the interests of already privileged people in your community. Such groups might apply pressure, so that hosting a major sport event, such as the Olympics, would involve building low-cost housing for low-income community residents, in addition to using public money to enhance economic expansion benefiting certain segments of the business community. The possibilities are endless.

3. *Create alternative sports.* You can reject or ignore dominant power and performance sports, and the organizations that sponsor them, and develop new sports grounded in the values and experiences of a wide array of different groups of people. This is often difficult, because resources are seldom available when you choose this vantage point for making change. However, this vantage point can be effective even when it doesn't lead to concrete institutionalized changes, because it provides clear-cut examples of new ways to look at and play sports, as well as new ways to look at and interact with other people. These examples then may inspire others to envision how they can create alternative sports in their own lives and communities. Former Olympian and current health and physical educator Bruce Kidd reminds us, "The effort to create alternatives to the commercial sport culture will continue to be an uphill fight. But such

alternatives do exist. They have a long, rich, and proud history" (1996, p. 270).

4. *Focus on culture and social relations.* You can ignore sports and work to produce changes in social relations that indirectly raise questions about the organization and structure of sports in society. For example, as people question dominant ideas about masculinity and femininity and the cultural practices associated with these ideas, they may push for changes in the sports that reproduce ideas and practices that are destructive in the lives of many people. This strategy has been used by some groups working to lower sexual assault rates in the United States: they have pressured the NFL, the NCAA, and other sport organizations to support policies that increase awareness of the problem and encourage behavioral changes in connection with gender relations.

Regardless of the vantage point used to make change, any significant social transformation requires a combination of the following three things:

1. Visions of what sports and social life *could* and *should* be like
2. Willingness to work hard to put visions into actions
3. Political abilities to rally the resources needed to produce results

The future of sports and the impact of sports on the social world will be created out of this combination of visions, hard work, and politically effective actions. How we participate in making the future is up to each of us.

SUMMARY

WHAT CAN WE EXPECT IN THE FUTURE?

Sports are social constructions; they change as ideas and relationships change in sports and in society. Although the meaning, organization, and purpose of sports will become increasingly diverse in the future, power and performance sports will remain dominant. They will receive continued funding and sponsorship from those with resources and power in society. Pleasure and participation sports will grow in connection with demographic trends and ideological changes, but they will not receive the funding and support enjoyed by sports organized around the power and performance model.

Sports at all levels will be sites for struggles over who should play and how sports should be organized. The major trends at all levels of sports will be increases in the use of technology, increased coverage through an expanding range of media, a continuing emphasis on organization and rationalization, and a growth of commercialization and consumerism.

Changing sports remains a difficult challenge. Changes reflect the visions that people have about what they want sports to be in the future. Theories about sports are important because they inform and extend our visions of what is possible. Most people, especially those who are advantaged by the status quo, do not want to change sports as much as they want to expand them in their current forms. This conservative strategy fits with the assumptions and goals of functionalist theory. Strategies emphasizing reform and radical changes are more apt to be inspired by conflict theory and combinations of interactionist, critical, and critical feminist theories. Figurational theory emphasizes research that builds the knowledge needed to make effective and progressive interventions in the future.

Changes in sports can be made from any one of four vantage points: within sport itself, in connection with opposition groups, through efforts to create new and alternative sport forms, and indirectly by making changes in the social worlds in which sports exist.

Regardless of the vantage point, change and transformation depend on clear visions of what sports could be, a willingness to work hard to turn those visions into reality, and the political abilities to produce lasting results. Unless we work to create the sports we want in the future, sports will represent the interests of those who would like us all to play on their terms and for their purposes.

This leaves us with an interesting choice: we can be consumers who accept sports as they are, or we can be citizens who use sports as contexts for actively making the world a better place. The goal of this book has been to prepare you to make this choice.

SUGGESTED READINGS

Hellison, D., ed. 2000. *Youth development and physical activity: Linking universities and communities.* Champaign, IL: Human Kinetics (articles written by scholars who have used physical activities as a means of connecting with young people and the neighborhoods where they live; many examples of applied sociology and how an insider perspective can be used to make changes in children's lives through physical activities and sports).

Note: Those who study sports in society usually believe that the best way to understand the future is to critically assess sports today and then promote changes that will make sports more democratic and more open to those who can benefit from participation. Ideas about the future can be gained by creating your own versions of sports to fit the needs and experiences of people who are not often included in dominant forms of sports. Therefore, instead of looking for readings about the future, watch and talk to children as they play sports and develop new sport forms with their friends. They will give you ideas about what is possible in the future. Your visions will inspire a range of strategies for making change.

WEBSITE RESOURCES

Note: Websites often change. The following URLs were current when this book was printed.

Please check our website (www.mhhe.com/coakley8e) for updates and additions.

www.mhhe.com/coakley8e Predictions on what happens to the control and organization of sports when more people play them; information on the impact of technology on sports and athletes.

www.sportinsociety.org Official site of the Center for the Study of Sport in Society; click on all the center's programs—Athletes in Service to America, Mentors in Violence Prevention Program, Project TEAMWORK, Urban Youth Sports, SportsCAP, and Additional Outreach Programs—to see examples of how sports can be changed and changes can occur through sports and the work of athletes using their skills to have a positive impact on the social world.

www.abcsports.go.com This site plus www.espn.com have links to Enhanced TV, an interactive television experience that enables TV viewers to access game-related data and to play along with televised sport events; the future of spectator experiences is being developed in connection with these and related sites.

www.paralympic.org Official website of the International Paralympic Committee, an international nonprofit organization formed and run by 160 National Paralympic Committees and 5 disability-specific international sports federations.

www.gaygames.com Site of the Federation of Gay Games; links to the history of the games, what occurred in Sydney at the 2002 Gay Games, and what happens in Montreal at the 2006 Gay Games.

www.AforBW.org Site of Athletes for a Better World, a group that encourages athletes to use what they learn in sports to make a difference in their communities and the world as a whole; however, there are no specific statements about the types of "difference" athletes can or should make, other than just making things better.

www.adventuretime.com Online magazine for many outdoor adventure sports; shows alternatives to traditional organized sports; there are literally thousands of sites like this for alternative sports.

www.bmxweb.com/list.cfm Links to more than 500 sites used by BMX bikers; illustrates that athletes in the future will be able to form networks with fellow athletes around the world.

www.hotrails.com The key site for aggressive in-line skaters; provides a "feel" for the sport, who participates, and the norms underlying participation; note gender, racial/ethnic, and social class patterns among participants, because they provide information about the social dynamics of certain alternative sports as they develop.

www.gravitygames.com Is this the site of the future, with its heavily commercialized profile and ties to the major media and corporations?

Selected References*

Acosta, R. V., and L. J. Carpenter. 1996. *Women in intercollegiate sport: A longitudinal study—Twenty-five year update, 1977–2002.* www.northreadingsoftball.com/25YearsInWomens Sports.pdf

Adelson, E. 2002. Hot to trot. *ESPN The Magazine* 5 (13), 24 June, 74–76.

American Academy of Pediatrics. 2000. Intensive training and sports specialization in young athletes. (RE9906). Pediatrics 106 (1): 154–57 (or www.aap.org/policy/RE9906.html).

Anderson, E. 2002. Openly gay athletes: Contesting hegemonic masculinity in a homophobic environment. *Gender and Society* 16 (6): 860–877.

Anderson, S., and J. Cavanagh. 2002. *Report on the top 200 corporations.* Washington, DC: Institute for Policy Studies.

Andrews, D. L. 2001. Sport. In *Culture works: The political economy of culture* (pp. 131–62), edited by R. Maxwell. Minneapolis: University of Minnesota Press.

Andrews, D. L., and S. J. Jackson. 2001. *Sport stars: The cultural politics of sporting celebrity.* London/New York: Routledge.

AP—Associated Press. 2000. Fox relishes his role as Lakers' enforcer. *The Denver Post*, 20 June, C10.

Araton, H. 2002. Playing with pain has no gender. *The New York Times*, 22 December, Section 8.7, online (www.nytimes.com/2002/12/22/sports/ soccer/22ARAT.html).

Armstrong, G. 1998. *Football hooligans: Knowing the score.* Oxford, England: Berg.

Atkinson, M. 2002. Fifty-million viewers can't be wrong: Professional wrestling, sports-entertainment, and mimesis. *Sociology of Sport Journal* 19 (1): 47–66.

Axthelm, P. 1970. *The city game.* New York: Harper and Row.

Bairner, A. 2001. *Sport, nationalism, and globalization: European and North American perspectives.* Albany: State University of New York Press.

Baker, W. J., and C. Alexander. 2001. *If Christ came to the Olympics.* Seattle: University of Washington Press.

Bale, J. 2002. Lassitude and latitude: Observations on sport and environmental determinism. *International Review for the Sociology of Sport* 37 (2): 147–58.

Bale, J., and M. Cronin. 2002. *Sport and postcolonialism.* New York: Berg.

Bass, A. 2002. *Not the triumph but the struggle: The 1968 Olympics and the making of the black athlete.* Minneapolis: University of Minnesota Press.

Beals, K. A. 2000. Subclinical eating disorders in female athletes. *Journal of Physical Education, Recreation & Dance* 71 (7): 3–29.

Begley, S. 2002. Science of speed. *Newsweek*, 18 February, 56–57.

Berger, J. 2002. Pain game. *Rocky Mountain News*, 23 February, 6S.

Blair, D. 2002. Odds are against recruits. *Fort Collins Coloradoan*, 5 February, D1, D3.

Bloom, J. 2000. *To show what an Indian can do: Sports at Native American boarding schools.* Minneapolis: University of Minnesota Press.

Booth, D., and J. Loy. 1999. Sport, status and style. *Sport History Review* 30 (1): 1–26.

Borish, L. 2002. Women, sport and American Jewish identity in the late nineteenth and early twentieth centuries. In *With God on their side: Sport in the service of religion* (pp. 71–98), edited by T. Magdalinski and T. J. L. Chandler. London/ New York: Routledge.

Bradley, J. 2002. IX to watch. *ESPN The Magazine* 5 (13), 24 June, 80–84.

---

*There are over 880 sources cited in this edition of *Sports in Society*. This list of "Selected References" contains only the 271 new sources cited in this edition. For the complete references, including more than 615 sources carried over from the seventh edition (2001), go to www.mhhe.com/coakley8e, or see pages 513–537 in the seventh edition for the references that were not carried over to this list.

Bradley, J. M. 2002. The patriot game: Football's famous "Tartan Army." *International Review for the Sociology of Sport* 37 (2): 177–97.

Brennan, C. 2002. Augusta sticks with boyish act. *USA Today*, 11 July, 3C.

Brewer, B. D. 2002. Commercialization in professional cycling 1950–2001: Institutional transformations and the rationalization of "doping." *Sociology of Sport Journal* 19 (3): 276–301.

Brookes, R. 2002. *Representing sport*. New York: Oxford University Press.

Brown, G. T. 2000. Beating the odds. *The NCAA News*, 18 December, Extra section, A1, A4.

Bruening, J. E., D. L. Pastore, and K. L. Armstrong. 2002. *Society's message and the individual's response: The socialization process of African American female student-athletes*. Paper presented at the annual conference of the North American Society for the Sociology of Sport, Indianapolis (November).

Bunker, Linda, et al. 2000. *Check it out: Is the playing field level for women and girls at your school?* Washington, DC: National Women's Law Center.

Chandler, T. J. L. 2002. Manly Catholicism: Making men in Catholic public schools, 1945–80. In *With God on their side: Sport in the service of religion* (pp. 99–119), edited by T. Magdalinski and T. J. L. Chandler. London/New York: Routledge.

Christopherson, N., M. Janning, and E. D. McConnell. 2002. Two kicks forward, one kick back: A content analysis of media discourses on the 1999 Women's World Cup Soccer Championship. *Sociology of Sport Journal* 19 (2): 170–88.

Clayton, J. 2002. Lack of minority coaches not addressed. 8 February, www.espn.com.

Coakley, J. 2001a. Observing youth sports. Unpublished paper.

Coakley, J. 2001b. Youth sports. In *International Encyclopedia of Women & Sport* (pp. 1298–1302) edited by K. Christensen, A. Guttmann, and G. Pfister. New York: Macmillan Reference.

Coakley, J. 2002. Using sports to control deviance and violence among youths: Let's be critical and cautious. In *Paradoxes of youth and sport* (pp. 225–240), edited by M. Gatz, M. A. Messner, and S. J. Ball-Rokeach. Albany: State University of New York Press.

Coakley, J., and J. Lever. 2001. Sports. In *Encyclopedia of sociology* (Rev. ed., pp. 2985–91), edited by E. F. Borgatta and J. V. Montgomery. New York: Macmillan Reference.

Cochran, J. L., and C. Mehri. 2002. *Black coaches in the National Football League: Superior performance, inferior opportunities*. Report presented to the National Football League (October).

Colton, L. 2000. *Counting coup: A true story of basketball and honor on the Little Big Horn*. New York: Warner Books.

Crist, S. 1998. All bets are off. *Sports Illustrated* 88 (3), 26 January, 88–92.

Cronin, M. 2002. Catholics and sport in Northern Ireland: Exclusiveness or inclusiveness? In *With God on their side: Sport in the service of religion* (pp. 20–36), edited by T. Magdalinski and T. J. L. Chandler. London/New York: Routledge.

Danish, S. 2002. Teaching life skills through sports. In *Paradoxes of youth and sport* (pp. 49–60), edited by M. Gatz, M. A. Messner, and S. J. Ball-Rokeach. Albany: State University of New York Press.

Davies, R. 2002a. Media power and responsibility in sport and globalisation. Presentation made to the 3rd International Conference for Media Professionals in a Globalised Sport World, Copenhagen (November). www.iblf.org

Davies, R. 2002b. Sports, citizenship and development: Challenges and opportunities for sport sponsors. Presentation at the World Sports Forum Lausanne (September). www.iblf.org

Davis, L. R. 2002. The problems with Native American mascots. *Multicultural Education* 1: 11–15.

Deford, F. 2002. Black coaches still can't make headway in football. 31 January, www.sportsillustrated.cnn.com/inside_game/frank_deford/news/2002/01/03/deford

Denham, B., A. C. Billings, and K. K. Halone. 2002. Differential accounts of race in broadcast commentary of the 2000 NCAA men's and women's Final Four. *Sociology of Sport Journal* 19 (3): 315–32.

Dillon, D. 2001. TSN's Power 100: Guiding might. *The Sporting News*, 31 December, 12–17.

Dobie, M. 2000. Race and sports in high school. In *Best newspaper writing 2000* (pp. 319–87), edited by C. Scanlon. St. Petersburg, FL: The Poynter Institute for Media Studies.

Dodd, M. 2002. Tiger: Membership up to Muirfield. *USA Today*, 17 July, 1C.

Duberstein, M. J. 2002a. *NFL 2002: Franchise history and values—Stadium data*. New York: National Football League Players Association.

Duberstein, M. J. 2002b. *2002 off-season signing averages and 2002 club and position salaries*. New York: National Football League Players Association.

Dyck, N., ed. 2000. *Games, sports, and cultures*. New York: New York University Press.

Early, G. 1991. Delusions of grandeur: Young blacks must be taught that sports are not the only avenue of opportunity. *Sports Illustrated*, 19 August, 78.

Edwards, J., and J. Hargreaves. 2001. Feminism. In *International encyclopedia of women and sports* (pp. 395–402), edited by K. Christensen, A. Guttmann, and G. Pfister. New York: Macmillan Reference USA.

Eitzen, D. S. 2003. *Fair and foul: Beyond the myths and paradoxes of sport*. 2nd ed. Lanham, MD: Rowman & Littlefield Publishers, Inc.

Eley, D., and D. Kirk. 2002. Developing citizenship through sport: The impact of a sport-based volunteer programme on young sport leaders. *Sport, Education and Society* 2 (October): 151–66.

Elling, A., A. Knoppers, and P. deKnop. 2001. The social integrative meaning of sport: A critical and comparative analysis of policy and practice in the Netherlands. *Sociology of Sport Journal* 18 (4): 414–34.

Entine, J. 2002. The coming of the über-athlete. www.solon.com/news/sports/2002/03/21/genes/index.html

Ewing, M. E., et al. 2002. The role of sports in youth development. In *Paradoxes of youth and sport* (pp. 31–48), edited by M. Gatz, M. A. Messner, and S. J. Ball-Rokeach. Albany: State University of New York Press.

Farber, M. 2002. Clubhouse confidential. *Sports Illustrated* 96 (2), 14 January, 62–69.

Farhood, S. 2000. Typical girls. *Boxing Monthly* 12 (1): www.boxing-monthly.co.uk/content/0005/three.htm

Fatsis, S. 2002. On sports: The good fight. *The Wall Street Journal*, 24 May, W6.

Fejgin, N., and R. Hanegby. 2001. Gender and cultural bias in perceptions of sexual harassment in sport. *International Review for the Sociology of Sport* 36 (4): 459–78.

Freeman, M. 2002. Painkillers a quiet fact of life in the NFL. *The New York Times*, 31 January, C17, C19.

Friend, T. 2001. Higher power. *ESPN The Magazine* 4 (10), 14 May, 46–52.

Fulks, D. L. 2002. *Revenues and expenses of Division I and II intercollegiate athletics programs: Financial trends and relationships*. Indianapolis, IN: National Collegiate Athletic Association.

GAO—Government Accounting Office. 2000. *Gender equity: Men's and women's participation in higher education*. Report number GAO-01-128 (15 December); online www.gao.gov—go to "GAO Reports" and then to "Find GAO Reports."

GAO—Government Accounting Office. 2001. *Intercollegiate athletics: Four-year colleges' experiences adding and discontinuing teams*. Report number GAO-01-297 (8 March); online www.gao.gov—go to "GAO Reports" and to "Find GAO Reports."

Gerdy, J. R. 2000. *Sports in school: The future of an institution*. London/New York: Teachers College Press (Columbia University).

Glasser, J. 2002. King of the hill. *U.S. News & World Report* 132 (8), 18 March, 52–60.

Grant, A. 2002a. Body shop. *ESPN The Magazine* 5 (03), 4 February, 50–54.

Grant, A. 2002b. A painful reality. *ESPN Mag.com*. 30 January, http://espn.go.com/magazine/grant20020130.html

Greenfield, P. M., et al. 2002. Understanding intercultural relations on multiethnic high school sport teams. In *Paradoxes of youth and sport* (pp. 13–30), edited by M. Gatz, M. A. Messner, and S. J. Ball-Rokeach. Albany: State University of New York Press.

Hadden, J. K. 2000. Religious movements. In *Encyclopedia of sociology* (pp. 2364–76), edited by E. F. Borgotta and R. J. V. Montgomery. New York: Macmillan Reference USA.

Harrison, L. 2001. Understanding the influence of stereotypes: Implications for the African American in sport and physical activity. *Quest* 53 (1): 97–114.

Harrison, C. K. 2002. Scholar or baller in American higher education? A visual elicitation and qualitative assessment of the student-athlete mindset. *NASAP Journal* 5 (1): 66–81.

Harrison, L., C. K. Harrison, and L. N. Moore. 2002. African American racial identity and sport. *Sport, Education and Society* 2 (October): 121–33.

Hassan, R. 2000. Sociology of Islam. In *Encyclopedia of sociology* (pp. 2937–53), edited by E. F. Borgotta and R. J. V. Montgomery. New York: Macmillan Reference USA.

Hawes, K. 2001a. Honor or affront? *The Chronicle of Higher Education* 38 (9), 23 April, 1, 20–22.

Hawes, K. 2001b. Mirror, mirror. *The NCAA News, Special Report*, 24 September, A1–A4.

Hawkins, B. 2000. *The new plantation: The internal colonialization of black student athletes*. Winterville, GA: Sadiki.

Hellison, D., ed. 2000. Youth development and physical activity: Linking universities and communities. Champaign, IL: Human Kinetics.

Hellison, D., and D. Walsh. 2002. Responsibility-based youth programs evaluation: Investigating the investigations. *Quest* 54 (4): 292–307.

Henry, I., and C. Gratton, eds. 2001. *Sport in the city*. London: Routledge.

Hiestand, M. 2002. Security tighter, more costly for teams, venues. *USA Today*, 11 September, 3C.

Holland, T. 2002. Financial missions at odds with NCAA goal. *The NCAA News* 39 (10), 13 May: 4–5.

Hoover, N. C., and N. J. Pollard. 2000. *Initiation rites in American high schools: A national survey*. Alfred, NY: Alfred University.

Houlihan, B. 1997. *Sport, policy, and politics: A comparative analysis*. London: Routledge.

Houlihan. B., and A. White. 2002. *The politics of sports development: Development of sport or development through sport?* London/New York: Routledge.

Hudson, I. 2001. The use and misuse of economic impact analysis: The case of professional sports. *Journal of Sport and Social Issues* 25 (1): 20–39.

Ingham, A. G., M. A. Chase, and J. Butt. 2002. From the performance principle to the developmental principle: Every kid a winner? *Quest* 54 (4): 308–31.

Jackson, D. Z. 2001. The growing graduation gap. *The Boston Globe*, 28 December, A27.

Jackson, S. J., and B. Hokowhitu. 2002. Sport, tribes, and technology: The New Zealand all blacks *Haka* and the politics of identity. *Journal of Sport and Social Issues* 26 (2): 125–39.

Jackson, S. J., and J. Scherer. 2002. *Screening the nation's past: Adidas, advertising and corporate nationalism in New Zealand*. Paper presented at the annual conference of the North American Society for the Sociology of Sport, Indianapolis (November).

Jenkins, C. 2000. Caught in gambling's web. *USA Today*, 13 March, 1C–2C.

Jenkins, C. 2002a. The new face of NASCAR. *USA Today*, 24 May, 1A–2A.

Jenkins, C. 2002b. Prize plan participation can make big difference. *USA Today*, 17 July, 3C.

Jenkins, C. 2002c. Rich want to keep getting richer. *USA Today*, 17 July, 3C.

Jenkins, C. 2002d. Teams: Track owners should share TV cut. *USA Today*, 17 July, 11C.

Jenkins, C. 2002e. Wanted: Salesman must drive. *USA Today*, 12 July, 1A–2A.

Johns, D. P., and J. S. Johns. 2000. Surveillance, subjectivism and technologies of power. *International Review for the Sociology of Sport* 35 (2): 219–34.

Jutel, A. 2002. Olympic road cycling and national identity: Where is Germany? *Journal of Sport & Social Issues* 26 (2): 195–208.

Kamiya, G. 2000. The black edge: Are athletes of African descent genetically superior? Salon, 28 January (http://dir.salon.com/books/feature/2000/01/28/taboo/index.html).

Kaplan, D. A. 2002. The end of baseball again. *Newsweek* 140 (9), 26 August, 46–47.

Keating, P. 2002a. Artful dodging. *ESPN The Magazine* 5 (01), 7 January, 93.

Keating, P. 2002b. Boys, don't cry. *ESPN The Magazine* 5 (13), 24 June, 78.

Kidd, B., and P. Donnelly. 2000. Human rights in sports. *International Review for the Sociology of Sport* 35 (2): 131–48.

Kilvert, G. 2002. Missing the X chromosome. *Sports Illustrated Women* 4 (4), July, 21–22.

King, K. 2002. The ultimate jock school. *Sports Illustrated* 97 (21), 25 November, 48–54.

King, C. R., and C. F. Springwood. 2001a. *Beyond the cheers: Race as a spectacle in college sport*. Albany: State University of New York Press.

King, C. R., and C. F. Springwood, eds. 2001b. *Team spirits: The Native American mascots controversy*. Lincoln: Bison Books and University of Nebraska Press.

King, C. R., E. J. Staurowsky, L. Baca, L. R. Davis, and C. Pewewardy. 2002. Of polls and race prejudice: *Sports Illustrated*'s errant "Indian Wars." *Journal of Sport & Social Issues* 26 (4): 381–402.

Kirby, S., L. Greaves, and O. Hankivsky. 2000. *The dome of silence: Sexual harassment and abuse in sport*. New York: Zed Books.

Kizla, M. 2001. Denver 'D' short for 'dark side'. *The Denver Post*, 20 March, 1D, 3D.

Klein, N. 2002. *No logo*. New York: Picador USA.

Knight Foundation. 1991. *Keeping faith with the student-athlete*. Miami, FL: Knight Foundation.

Knight Foundation. 1992. *A solid start: A report on reform of intercollegiate athletics*. Miami, FL: Knight Foundation.

Knight Foundation. 1993. *A new beginning for a new century: Intercollegiate athletics in the United States*. Miami, FL: Knight Foundation.

Knight Foundation. 2001. *A call to action: Reconnecting college sports and higher education*. Miami, FL: Knight Foundation. www.knightfdn.org/

Kozol, J. 2002. Malign neglect. *The Nation* 274 (22): 20–23.

Krane, V., J. Waldron, J. Michalenok, and J. Stiles-Shipley. 2001. Body image concerns in female exercisers and athletes: A feminist cultural studies perspective. *Women in Sport and Physical Activity Journal* 10 (1): 17–54.

Lafeber, W. 2000. *Michael Jordan and the new global capitalism*. New York: W. W. Norton.

Lapchick, R. 2002. *Keeping score when it counts: Graduation rates for 2002–03 bowl-bound college football teams*. Report by The Institute for Diversity and Ethics in Sport, University of Central Florida, Orlando.

Latimer, C. 1999. NBA springs from humble roots. *Rocky Mountain News*, 24 October, 31C.

Lavalee, D., and P. Wylleman, eds. 2000. *Career transitions in sport: International perspectives*. Morgantown, WV: Fitness Information Technology.

Layden, T. 2001. Does anyone remember the Titans? *Sports Illustrated* 95 (15), 15 October, 72–83.

Layden, T. 2002. The loneliest losers. *Sports Illustrated* 97 (20), 18 November, 69–72.

Lenskyj, H. J. 2000. *Inside the Olympic industry: Power, politics, and activism*. Albany: State University of New York Press.

Lewin, T. 2002. Ruling fuels drug-test debate in schools. *The Denver Post*, 29 September, 12A.

Lieber, J. 2003. Playing dirty, playing mean. *USA Today*, 3 January, 1C–2C.

Light, R., and L. Kinnaird. 2002. Appeasing the gods: Shinto, sumo and "true" Japanese spirit. In *With God on their side: Sport in the service of religion* (pp. 139–59), edited by T. Magdalinski and T. J. L. Chandler. London/New York: Routledge.

Lipsher, S. 2001. Alive and kicking. *The Denver Post*, 26 December, 1A, 18A.

Lipsyte, R. 1999. The jock culture: Time to debate questions. *The New York Times*, 9 May: 11 (Section 8).

Lipsyte, R. 2001a. In purest form, basketball is a playground game. *The New York Times*, 28 October, S13.

Lipsyte, R. 2001b. Questions line the road as NASCAR steers into a new year. *The New York Times*, 30 December, S9.

Longman, J. 2001a. Getting the athletic edge may mean altering genes. *The New York Times*, 11 May. www.nytimes.com/2001/05/11/sports/11GENE.html

Longman, J. 2001b. A town where football is the glue and the hope. *The New York Times*, 23 November, A27–A28.

Lord, M. 2002. Athletics for all. *U.S. News & World Report*, 18 March, 68–69.

Loveless, T. 2002. *The 2002 Brown Center report on American education: How well are American students learning?* Washington, DC: Brookings Institution.

Lyon, B. 2002. Fallen legends were beset by life's frailties. *The Denver Post*, 29 September, 4C.

MacNeill, M., P. Donnelly, and G. Knight. 2001. Corporate training: Identity construction, preparation for the Sydney Olympic Games and relationships between Canadian media, swimmers and sponsors. *Olympika* 10: 1–32.

Magdalinski, T., and T. J. L. Chandler, eds. 2002. *With God on their side: Sport in the service of religion*. London/New York: Routledge.

Magee, J., and J. Sugden. 2002. "The world at their feet": Professional football and international labor migration. *Journal of Sport & Social Issues* 26 (4): 421–37.

Magnusson, G. K. 2001. The internationalization of sports: The case of Iceland. *International Review for the Sociology of Sport* 36 (1): 59–69.

Maguire, J. S. 2001. Fit and flexible: The fitness industry, personal trainers and emotional service labor. *Sociology of Sport Journal* 18 (4): 379–402.

Maguire, J., G. Jarvie, L. Mansfield, and J. Bradley. 2002. *Sport worlds: A sociological perspective.* Champaign, IL: Human Kinetics.

Malcolm, C., and K. Sheard. 2002. "Pain in the assets": The effects of commercialization and professionalization on the management of injury in English Rugby Union. *Sociology of Sport Journal* 19 (2): 149–69.

Malloy, D. C., and D. H. Zakus. 2002. Ethics of drug testing in sport: An invasion of privacy justified? *Sport, Education and Society* 2 (October): 203–18.

Marvez, A. 2002. Steroid abuse grips wrestling, too. *Rocky Mountain News*, 19 July, C8.

Mason, D. S. 2002. "Get the puck outta here!" Media transnationalism and Canadian identity. *Journal of Sport & Social Issues* 26 (2): 140–67.

McCallum, J. 2002. Citizen Barkley. *Sports Illustrated*, 11 March, 34–38.

Merrill, D. 2002. Skateboarding grinds out urban revival. *USA Today*, 30 July, 6C–7C.

Messner, M. A. 2002. *Taking the field: Women, men, and sports.* Minneapolis: University of Minnesota Press.

Messner, M. A., and M. A. Stevens. 2002. Scoring without consent: Confronting male athletes' violence against women. In *Paradoxes of youth and sport* (pp. 225–40), edited by M. Gatz, M. A. Messner, and S. J. Ball-Rokeach. Albany: State University of New York Press.

Meyer, J. 2002a. Added danger. *The Denver Post*, 15 September, 1C, 8C.

Meyer, J. 2002b. Ward's fire within. *The Denver Post*, 14 July, 1C, 12C.

Michaelis, V. 2002. Weathering Olympic crises. *USA Today*, 26 August, C3.

Mihoces. G. 2002. Football is king—Now more than ever. *USA Today*, 30 August, 6A.

Miller, S. 2003. The power 100: Win-win situation. *The Sporting News*, 13 January, 4–11.

Miller, T., ed. 2001. *Globalization and sport: Playing the world.* London: Sage.

Moore, D. L. 2002. Parents pay dearly to coach kids for stardom. *USA Today*, 26 July, 1A–2A.

Moran, M. 2002a. Numbers speak volumes about blacks as head coaches. *USA Today*, 11 October, 6D.

Moran, M. 2002b. Success fails to open college doors for black football coaches. *USA Today*, 11 October, 1A–2A.

Moye, J., and C. K. Harrison. 2002. Don't believe the hype: Do the automatic suspensions of student-athletes for alleged misconduct withstand constitutional scrutiny? *Texas Entertainment and Sports Law Journal* 11 (1): 5–15.

Nack, W., and L. Munson. 2000. Out of control. *Sports Illustrated* 93 (4), 24 July, 86–95.

Nance, R. 2001. Long shots step into spotlight. *USA Today*, 26 October, 3C.

Nauright, J. 1998. *Sport, cultures and identities in South Africa.* London: Cassell Academic.

Nauright, J., and Magdalinski, T. 2002. Religion, race and rugby in "Coloured" Cape Town. In *With God on their side: Sport in the service of religion* (pp. 120–38), edited by T. Magdalinski and T. J. L. Chandler. London/New York: Routledge.

Newfield, J. 2001. The shame of boxing. *The Nation* 273 (15): 13–22.

Neyer, R. 2000. A matter of size. *Scientific American* 11 (3): 14–15.

NHANES—National Health and Nutrition Examination Survey. 2002. *Prevalence of overweight and obesity among adults: United States, 1999–2000.* Hyattsville, MD: National Center for Health Statistics.

Oriard, M. 2001. Football and education are a team no more. *The New York Times*, 23 December, S8.

Parrish, P. 2002. The height of gaining an edge. *Rocky Mountain News*, 21 September, 1B, 12B–13B.

Pascall, B., with S. White. 2000. *Eliminating violence in hockey in British Columbia.* Vancouver: BC Amateur Hockey Association.

Patrick, D. 2002a. Let the kids play. *USA Today*, 26 July, 1C–2C.

Patrick, D. 2002b. U.S. Anti-Doping Agency willing to administer testing for baseball. *USA Today*, 14 June, 6C.

Pearson, D. W. 1999. The rodeo cowboy: Cultural icon, athlete, or entrepreneur? *Journal of Sport and Social Issues* 23 (3): 308–27.

Pearson, D. W., and C. A. Haney. 2000. The rodeo cowboy as an American icon: The perceived social and cultural significance. *Journal of American Culture* 22 (4): 17–21.

Perrucci, R., & E. Wysong. 2002. *The new class society: Goodbye American dream?* Lanham, MD: Rowman & Littlefield Publishers, Inc.

Pettavino, P., and P. Brenner. 1999. More than just a game. *Peace Review* 11 (4): 523–30.

Pollitt, K. 2001. Summer follies. *The Nation* 273 (8): 10.

Potter, J. 2002. Thorpe looks at old ways to bring blacks to game. *USA Today*, 26 June, 12C.

Price, S. L. 2002a. The Ichiro paradox. *Sports Illustrated* 97 (2), 8 July, 50–56.

Price, S. L. 2002b. Indian wars: The campaign against Indian nicknames and mascots presumes that they offend Native Americans—But do they? *Sports Illustrated* 96 (10), 4 March, 66–70.

Price, S. L. 2002c. The savior of South Bend. *Sports Illustrated* 97 (13), 30 September, 38–44.

Pringle, R. 2001. Competing discourses: Narratives of a fragmented self, manliness and Rugby Union. *International Review for the Sociology of Sport* 36 (4): 425–40.

Randels, G. D., Jr., and B. Beal. 2002. What makes a man? Religion, sport, and negotiating masculine identity in the Promise Keepers. In *With God on their side: Sport in the service of religion* (pp. 160–76), edited by T. Magdalinski and T. J. L. Chandler. London/New York: Routledge.

Renck, T. E. 2002. For richer or poorer. *The Denver Post*, 10 March, 1C.

Rinehart, R. 2000. Arriving sport: Alternatives to formal sports. In *Handbook of sports studies* (pp. 504–19), edited by J. Coakley and E. Dunning. London: Sage.

Rinehart, R., and C. Grenfell. 2002. BMX spaces: Children's grass roots' courses and corporate-sponsored tracks. *Sociology of Sport Journal* 19 (3): 302–14.

Rinehart, R., and S. Syndor, eds. 2003. *To the extreme: Alternative sports inside and out.* Albany: State University of New York Press.

Riordan, J. 1996. Introduction. In *The story of worker sport* (pp. vii–x), edited by A. Krüger and J. Riordan. Champaign, IL: Human Kinetics.

Risman, B., and P. Schwartz. 2002. After the sexual revolution: Gender politics in teen dating. *Contexts* 1 (1): 16–24.

Ritzer, G. 1999. *Enchanting a disenchanted world: Revolutionizing the means of consumption.* Thousand Oaks, CA: Pine Forge Press.

Roadburg, A. 1980. Factors Precipitating Fan Violence: A Comparison of Professional Soccer in Britain and North America. *British Journal of Sociology* 31 (2): 265–276.

Romano, L. 1995. The reliable source. *The Washington Post*, 11 January, C3.

Ruibal, S. 2002. Super 25 a private domain. *USA Today*, 19 November, 1C, 10C.

SAMHSA—Substance Abuse and Mental Health Administration. 2002. *The 2000 National Household Survey on Drug Abuse: Team sports participation and substance use among youths.* Rockville, MD: SAMHSA. www.DrugAbuseStatistics.samhsa.gov

Sandomir, R. 2002. Athletes may next seek genetic enhancement. *The New York Times*, 21 March. http://nytimes.com/2002/03/21/sports/othersports/21DRUG.html

Scheerder, J., B. Vanreusel, M. Taks, and R. Renson. 2002. Social sports stratification in Flanders, 1969–1999: Intergenerational reproduction of social inequalities? *International Review for the Sociology of Sport* 37 (2): 219–46.

Schefter, A. 2002. Players facing ban of ephedra. *The Denver Post*, 14 June, 1D, 7D.

Scher, J. 1993. Mr. Dirty. *Sports Illustrated* 78 (8): 40–42.

Schimmel, K. S. 2000. Take me out to the ball game: The transformation of production-consumption relations in professional team sport. In *Cultural production and consumption: Readings in popular culture* (pp. 36–52), edited by C. L. Harrington and D. D. Bielby. Oxford, England: Blackwell.

Schimmel, K. S. 2002. The political economy of place: Urban and sport studies perspectives. In *Theory, sport and society* (pp. 335–53), edited by J. Maguire and K. Young. Oxford, England: JAI (Elsevier Science).

Schneider, J. 2002. The fairness factor. *U.S. News & World Report* 132 (8), 18 March, 63–65.

Sellers, R. M., T. M. Chavous, and T. N. Brown. 2002. Uneven playing field: The impact of structural barriers on the initial eligibility of African American student-athletes. In *Paradoxes of youth and sport* (pp. 173–86), edited by M. Gatz, M. A. Messner, and S. J. Ball-Rokeach. Albany: State University of New York Press.

Shaw, M. 2002. *Board with sports*. Paper written in introductory sociology course, University of Colorado, Colorado Springs, spring semester.

Shropshire, K. 2002. Race, youth, athletes, and role models. In *Paradoxes of youth and sport* (pp. 135–40), edited by M. Gatz, M. A. Messner, and S. J. Ball-Rokeach. Albany: State University of New York Press.

Shulman, J. L., and W. G. Bowen. 2001. *The game of life: College sports and educational values*. Princeton, NJ: Princeton University Press.

Simon, S. 2002. New stadiums becoming tough sell. *The Denver Post*, 30 May, 4A.

Slack, T. 2002. *The commercialization of sport*. London: Frank Cass.

Sokolove, M. 2002. Football is a sucker's game. *The New York Times Magazine*, Section 6, 22 December, 36–41, 64, 68–70.

Sperber, M. 2000. *Beer and circus: How big-time college sports is crippling undergraduate education*. New York: Henry Holt.

Spielvogel, L. G. 2002. The discipline of space in a Japanese fitness club. *Sociology of Sport Journal* 19 (2): 189–205.

Staurowsky, E. J. 2000. The Cleveland "Indians": A case study in American Indian cultural dispossession. *Sociology of Sport Journal* 17 (4): 307–30.

Staurowsky, E. J., A. Sack, R. Southall, and J. Reese. 2002. *Through the narrow gate: Reframing the college sport reform movement as a reform movement of the professoriate and students*. Presentation made at the annual conference of the North American Society for the Sociology of Sport, Indianapolis (November).

Stevenson, C. L. 2002. Seeking identities: Towards an understanding of the athletic careers of masters swimmers. *International Review for the Sociology of Sport* 37 (2): 131–46.

Stevenson, D. 2002. Women, sport, and globalization: Competing discourses of sexuality and nation. *Journal of Sport & Social Issues* 26 (2): 209–25.

Stoll, S. K., and J. M. Beller. 2000. Do sports build character? In *Sports in school: The future of an institution* (pp. 18–30), edited by J. R. Gerdy. New York: Teachers College Press.

Suggs, W. 2001. Left behind. *The Chronicle of Higher Education* 48 (14), 30 November, A35–A37.

Suggs, W. 2002a. How gears turn at a sports factory. *The Chronicle of Higher Education* 49 (14), A32–A37.

Suggs, W. 2002b. Title IX at 30: In the arena of women's college sports, the 1972 law created a legacy of debate. *The Chronicle of Higher Education* 48 (14), 21 June, A38–A42, or http://chronicle.com/weekly/v48/i41/41a03801.htm

Sundgot-Borgen, J. 2001. Eating disorders. In *International encyclopedia of women and sports* (pp. 352–58), edited by K. Christensen, A. Guttmann, and G. Pfister. New York: Macmillan Reference USA.

Swift, E. M., and D. Yaeger. 2001. Unnatural selection. *Sports Illustrated* 94 (20), 14 May, 87–93.

Swift, E. M. 2000. Hey fans: Sit on it! *Sports Illustrated* 92 (20), 15 May, 70–85.

Theberge, N. 2000. Gender and sport. In *Handbook of sport studies* (pp. 322–33), edited by J. Coakley and E. Dunning. London: Sage Publications.

Toohey, K., and A. J. Veal. 2000. *The Olympic Games: A social science perspective*. New York: CABI.

Trivett, S. 1999. Rampart goes back to smash-mouth in win over Mitchell. *Rocky Mountain News*, 31 October, 30C.

Tuaolo, E., with L. Cyphers. 2002. Free and clear. *ESPN The Magazine* (13): 11 November, 72–77.

Tucker, L. W., and J. B. Parks. 2001. Effects of gender and sport types on intercollegiate athletes' perceptions of the legitimacy of aggressive behaviors in sport. *Sociology of Sport Journal* 18 (4): 403–13.

USADA—United States Anti-Doping Agency. 2001. *USADA guide to prohibited classes of substances and prohibited methods of doping*. Colorado Springs, CO: U.S. Anti-Doping Agency.

Van Bottenburg, M. 2001. *Global games* (translated by B. Jackson). Urbana: University of Illinois Press.

Verducci, T. 2001. Learning curve. *Sports Illustrated* 95 (13), 14 October, 74–87.

Verducci, T. 2002. Totally juiced. *Sports Illustrated* 96 (23), 3 June, 34–48.

Waddington, I. 2000a. Sport and health: A sociological perspective. In *Handbook of sport studies* (pp. 408–21), edited by J. Coakley and E. Dunning. London: Sage Publications.

Waddington, I. 2000b. *Sport, health and drugs: A critical sociological perspective*. London: Routledge.

Wann, S. ed. 2000. Sport fans: *The psychology and social impact of spectators*. New York and London: Routledge.

Wechsler, H., and B. Wuethrich. 2002. *Dying to drink: Confronting binge drinking on college campuses*. Emmaus, PA: Rodale.

Weed, M. 2001. Ing-ger-land at Euro 2000: How "handbags at 20 paces" was portrayed as a full-scale riot. *International Review for the Sociology of Sport* 36 (4): 407–24.

Weisman, L. 2000. Why the NFL rules. *USA Today*, 22 December, 1A–2A.

Weiss, O. 2001. Identity reinforcement in sport: Revisiting the symbolic interactionist legacy. *International Review for the Sociology of Sport* 36 (4): 393–406.

Wertheim, L. J. 2002. The big score. *Sports Illustrated* 97 (18), 4 November, Scorecard Extra.

Whannel, G. 2002. *Media sport stars: Masculinities and moralities*. London/New York: Routledge.

Wharton, D. 2002a. Future of pro sports: Common touch (part two). *The Los Angeles Times*, 6 May, http://www.latimes.com/business/la-000031990may06.story

Wharton, D. 2002b. Future of pro sports: Generation gap (part three). *The Los Angeles Times*, 7 May, www.latimes.com/business/la-000031990may07.story

Wharton, D. 2002c. Future of pro sports: Turbulance in the air (part one). *The Los Angeles Times*, 5 May, www.latimes.com/business/la-000031990may05.story

Wideman, J. E. 2001. *Hoop roots*. New York: Houghton Mifflin.

Wildavsky, B. 2002. Graduation blues. *U.S. News & World Report* 132 (8), 18 March, 69–70.

Wilson, B. 2002. The "anti-jock" movement: Reconsidering youth resistance, masculinity, and sport culture in the age of the Internet. *Sociology of Sport Journal* 19 (2): 206–33.

Wilson, B., and P. White. 2002. Revive the pride: Social process, political economy, and a fan-based grassroots movement. *Sociology of Sport Journal* 19 (2): 119–48.

Wines, M. 2002. When Putin says "Exercise!" Russia treads a beaten path. *The New York Times*, 10 February, 1, 8.

Wolff, A. 2000. Crying foul. *Sports Illustrated* 93 (24), 11 December, 42–47.

Wolff, A. 2002a. The high school athlete. *Sports Illustrated* 97 (20), 18 November, 74–78.

Wolff, A. 2002b. Scorecard: Invisible men. *Sports Illustrated* 97 (20), 18 November, 29.

Wolff, A. 2002c. The vanishing three-sport star. *Sports Illustrated* 97 (20), 18 November, 80–92.

Women's Sports Weekly. 2002. People are talking. 26 September. Women's Sports Foundation Newsletter online.

Wong, E. 2001. Athletes take entitlement out of bounds. *The New York Times*, 23 December, S1, S9.

Wong, L. L., and R. Trumper. 2002. Global celebrity athletes and nationalism: Fútbol, hockey, and the representation of nation. *Journal of Sport & Social Issues* 26 (2): 168–94.

Yaeger, D. 2002. Prisoner of conscience. *Sports Illustrated* 96 (16), 15 April, 54–57.

Yiannakis, A., and M. J. Melnick, eds. 2001. *Contemporary issues in sociology of sport*. Champaign, IL: Human Kinetics.

Young, K. 2002a. From "sports violence" to "sports crime": Aspects of violence, law, and gender in the sports process. In *Paradoxes of youth and sport* (pp. 207–24), edited by M. Gatz, M. A. Messner, and S. J. Ball-Rokeach. Albany: State University of New York Press.

Young, K. 2002b. Standard deviations: An update on North American crowd disorder. *Sociology of Sport Journal* 19 (3): 237–75.

Zengerle, J. 2002. Driving the company car. *New York Times Magazine*, 10 February, 40–43.

Zimmer, M. H., and M. Zimmer. 2001. Athletes as entertainers. *Journal of Sport and Social Issues* 25 (2): 202–15.

Zorpette, G. 2000. The chemical games. *Scientific American* 11 (3): 16–23.

Name Index

Subject Index

Page numbers followed by f indicate figures; those followed by t indicate tables.